W9-AHR-824

Property of the SAAC

ABOUT WINE

SECOND EDITION

J. Patrick Henderson and Dellie Rex

ABOUT WINE

SECOND EDITION

J. PATRICK HENDERSON AND DELLIE REX

DELMAR
CENGAGE Learning™

Australia • Brazil • Japan • Korea • Mexico • Singapore • Spain • United Kingdom • United States

About Wine, Second Edition
Authors: J. Patrick Henderson and Dellie Rex

Vice President, Career and Professional Editorial: Dave Garza

Director of Learning Solutions: Sandy Clark

Senior Acquisitions Editor: Jim Gish

Managing Editor: Larry Main

Product Manager: Nicole Calisi

Product Manager: Anne Orgren

Editorial Assistant: Sarah Timm

Vice President, Career and Professional Marketing: Jennifer Baker

Marketing Director: Wendy Mapstone

Senior Marketing Manager: Kristin McNary

Associate Marketing Coordinator: Jonathan Sheehan

Production Director: Wendy Troeger

Senior Content Project Manager: Glenn Castle

Senior Art Director: Casey Kirchmayer

Cover and layout Illustrator: Lisa Kuhn and Aaron Maurer/ Curio Press, LLC

© 2012, 2007 Delmar, Cengage Learning

ALL RIGHTS RESERVED. No part of this work covered by the copyright herein may be reproduced, transmitted, stored, or used in any form or by any means graphic, electronic, or mechanical, including but not limited to photocopying, recording, scanning, digitizing, taping, Web distribution, information networks, or information storage and retrieval systems, except as permitted under Section 107 or 108 of the 1976 United States Copyright Act, without the prior written permission of the publisher.

For product information and technology assistance, contact us at
Cengage Learning Customer & Sales Support, 1-800-354-9706

For permission to use material from this text or product,
submit all requests online at **www.cengage.com/permissions.**
Further permissions questions can be e-mailed to
permissionrequest@cengage.com

Library of Congress Control Number: 2010939814

ISBN-13: 978-1-4390-5650-9

ISBN-10: 1-4390-5650-1

Delmar
5 Maxwell Drive
Clifton Park, NY 12065-2919
USA

Cengage Learning is a leading provider of customized learning solutions with office locations around the globe, including Singapore, the United Kingdom, Australia, Mexico, Brazil, and Japan. Locate your local office at: **international.cengage.com/region**

Cengage Learning products are represented in Canada by Nelson Education, Ltd.

To learn more about Delmar, visit **www.cengage.com/delmar**

Purchase any of our products at your local college store or at our preferred online store **www.CengageBrain.com**

Notice to the Reader

Publisher does not warrant or guarantee any of the products described herein or perform any independent analysis in connection with any of the product information contained herein. Publisher does not assume, and expressly disclaims, any obligation to obtain and include information other than that provided to it by the manufacturer. The reader is expressly warned to consider and adopt all safety precautions that might be indicated by the activities described herein and to avoid all potential hazards. By following the instructions contained herein, the reader willingly assumes all risks in connection with such instructions. The publisher makes no representations or warranties of any kind, including but not limited to, the warranties of fitness for particular purpose or merchantability, nor are any such representations implied with respect to the material set forth herein, and the publisher takes no responsibility with respect to such material. The publisher shall not be liable for any special, consequential, or exemplary damages resulting, in whole or part, from the readers' use of, or reliance upon, this material.

Printed in the United States of America
1 2 3 4 5 6 7 13 14 12 11

ABOUT WINE
SECOND EDITION

J. Patrick Henderson and Dellie Rex

COMPREHENSIVE TEACHING

INSTRUCTOR RESOURCES

Please visit login.cengage.com and log in to access instructor-specific resources:

CourseMate

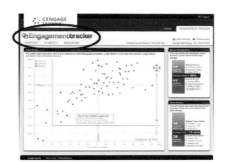

CourseMate to accompany *About Wine*, second edition, includes Engagement Tracker, a first-of-its-kind tool that monitors student engagement in the course. See also Student Resources on CourseMate listed below.

Instructor Website

The instructor website is designed as a complete teaching tool for *About Wine*. It assists instructors in creating lectures, developing presentations, constructing quizzes and tests, and offers additional lesson plans. This valuable resource simplifies the planning and implementation of the instructional program. This complimentary resource package is available upon adoption of the text and consists of the following components:

- The **Instructor's Manual** provides chapter outlines, answers to end-of-chapter review questions, and additional assessment questions and answers. The Instructor's Manual is available at no charge to adopters of the text.
- **Electronic Support Slides** are designed as a visually-appealing way to extract key points from the textbook to enhance class lectures.
- **Computerized Test Bank,** which consists of a variety of test questions including multiple choice and true/false.
- **Lesson Plans** and **Activities** are available as additional resources to aid the instructor in preparing lessons.

STUDENT RESOURCES

Log into www.cengagebrain.com to access student resources, including:

CourseMate

CourseMate to accompany About Wine, second edition, includes:
- an interactive eBook
- interactive teaching and learning tools including:
  - Quizzes
  - Flashcards
  - Food and wine pairing exercises
  - and more

AND LEARNING PACKAGE

KEY FEATURES

EXERCISES AND REVIEW QUESTIONS: Chapter-end exercises and review questions reinforce important chapter topics.

EXERCISES

1. Define the term *gran reserva* in Spanish wine law.
2. List some of the responsibilities of the two government agencies, Spain's INDO and Portugal's IVV.
3. What is the winemaking process that is used to make Cava? Describe how Cava differs from Champagne.
4. How has membership in the European Union affected the quality and marketing of wines produced in Portugal and Spain?

REVIEW QUESTIONS

1. What is the principal red grape of Rioja?
3. What is the most widely planted grape in Navarra?
4. What is the highest level of classification within Portugal's quality control laws?
5. Sherry is produced in what region of Spain?
6. Name the 11 vinho regional areas in Portugal.
7. Why is ruby Port still red while tawny Port is a golden color?

KEY TERMS: Key terms are listed in the beginning of each chapter enforcing the importance of new terminology presented in each chapter.

Key terms are bolded at first use within the chapters for easy identification.

Flights are usually composed of similar wines of the same variety or style; however, there are some variations. A **vertical flight** is a series of consecutive vintages of the same grape variety or type of wine from a single winery. Vertical flights can be very instructive about how a particular wine will age, or how a winery changes its style over time. Tastings also can be set up with a number of different wines from a single producer. While these tastings are not always done blind, they can still be very informative.

KEY TERMS

astringency
blind tasting
Brettanomyces
brilliant
depth
descriptive analysis
dull
enologist
flight
hue
mouthfeel
olfactory bulb
sensory evaluation
spritz
tannin buildup
texture
threshold
vertical flight
volatile
Wine Aroma Wheel

{ GLOSSARY }

A

aeration (air-AY-shun) The process of incorporating oxygen into a wine.

Aglianico (ah-LYAH-nee-koh) Widely planted red grape of southern Italy.

Airén (ahr-yehn) The most widely planted grape in Spain, accounting for about one-third of total acreage. Especially prevalent in the dry central parts of the country, the grape is used in the production of brandy. It is also increasingly vinified into nondescript, but fresh, dry white wines.

Albariño (ahl-bah-REE-n'yoh) A white grape grown in Galicia, Spain (also called Alvarinho, grown in the Vinho Verde region of Portugal). It produces complex, aromatic wines with bracing acidity.

alembic still A type of copper "pot" still used for making Cognac Brandy, as well as Pisco.

alluvial Soils created by the flooding along rivers and streams.

Alvarinho (ahl-vah-REEN-yoh) See *Albariño*.

amabile (ah-MAH-bee-lay) Italian. Off-dry or semisweet.

American Viticultural Area (AVA) A particular area of grape growing with specific boundaries sanctioned by the government.

amphora (AM-fuhr-uh) A jar with an oval body, narrow neck, and two handles used by the ancient

Appellation d'Origin Contrôlée (AOC) (ah-pehl-lah-SYAWN daw-ree-JEEN kawn-traw-LAY) French. "Controlled Place of Origin." In the French system, the highest level of classification for wine regions. The designation applies to all wines made from grapes grown in that region if the wine is made according to all guidelines for that appellation, as outlined in the AOC laws.

astringency The drying or "puckery" tactile sensation that is produced by tannins in wine.

Auslese (OWS-lay-zuh) German. Selected. Describes grapes picked at a high level of ripeness, thus with considerable sugars.

Australian Wine and Brandy Corporation (AWBC) A governmental organization responsible for the regulation and promotion of the Australian wine industry.

autolysis (aw-TAHL-uh-sihss) The breakdown of yeast cells.

AVA See *American Viticultural Area*.

B

Bacchus (BAK-uhs) The Roman god of wine.

Beerenauslese (BAY-ruhn-OWSlay-zuh) German. Literally "selected berries," the term refers to grapes that are picked one-by-one depending on the level to which they have been affected by *botrytis*. The wine

GLOSSARY: Key terms with phonetic spelling and definitions are provided at the back of the book.

VISUALLY APPEALING DESIGN

SPECIAL FEATURES

NEW TO THIS EDITION: FOOD AND WINE PAIRING MENUS at the end of each regional chapter suggest pairings of regional wines with foods. An entire **new chapter on food and wine pairing** delves more deeply into this topic.

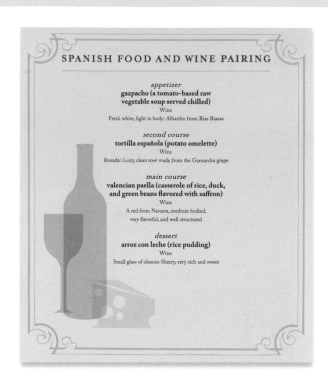

© Pat Henderson

PHOTOGRAPHS: This beautifully illustrated textbook contains over 300 full-color photos.

WINE LABELS: A special feature on how to read a wine label is integrated throughout the chapters. This allows students to understand the sophisticated nature of the world's wine labels and interpret the abundance of available information.

Reading a United States Wine Label

As the wine industry has advanced in recent decades, wine labels have become much more elaborate. While in the 196 's wine was usually bottled with relatively plain labels with a minimum of information, today they are designed to be more eye-catching with multiple colors, embossing, gold leaf, and distinctive shapes. This is to try to get potential customers to notice the wine on the shelf; also, expensive labels are used to try to convey an impression of quality for the wine in the bottle. The importance of packaging to wineries is evidenced by the industry saying, "you sell your first bottle of wine to a customer with the outside of the bottle, and the second bottle of wine to the customer with what is inside." In addition to their importance in selling wine, labels must also provide information to the consumer. Some of the information on wine labels is provided by the winery to describe what the wine tastes like and how it was made. The federal government also mandates what information must be placed on a bottle of wine to accurately describe what the wine is, including standards of composition that must be met before certain claims can be made on the label. In recent years the amount of information required by law has expanded to include warnings about health and whether there are sulfites present in the wine.

The next three pages outline the basic requirements for wine labels in the United States. Different countries have different standards and terms that they use to describe their wines. Information on the labels of imported wines is outlined in their respective chapters of this book.

Front Label

Winery Name: Most names are acceptable as long as they are not offensive or misleading.

Vintage Date: 85 percent of the grapes used to make the wine must be harvested in the year listed as the vintage. If an AVA is listed as the appellation, then a minimum of 95 percent of the grapes must be from the vintage stated. If a vintage date is used, the appellation must be stated as well.

Appellation: The district the grapes were grown in. If listed as a political region such as county or state, at least 75 percent must be from the region listed. Some states have laws requiring that for a state to be listed appellation, 100 percent of the grapes must be grown in that state.

Alcohol Content: The percentage of alcohol by volume must be listed; if it is 7 to 14 percent, the label may also state "Table Wine" or "Light Wine."

KENWOOD VINEYARDS

2009

SONOMA COUNTY

SAUVIGNON BLANC

13.8% ALCOHOL BY VOLUME

F. Korbel & Bros.

Variety: The varietal of the grapes used to make the wine. The variety listed must be at least 75 percent of the grapes used to make the wine. Some states have higher percentage requirements and *Vitis labrusca* varieties like Concord need to have only 51 percent. If a varietal is designated on the label, an appellation must also be listed.

SPANISH FOOD AND WINE PAIRING

appetizer
gazpacho (a tomato-based raw vegetable soup served chilled)
Wine
Fresh white, light in body: Albariño from Rías Biaxas

second course
tortilla española (potato omelette)
Wine
Rosada: fruity, clean rosé made from the Garnacha grape

main course
valencian paella (casserole of rice, duck, and green beans flavored with saffron)
Wine
A red from Navarra, medium bodied, very flavorful, and well structured

dessert
arroz con leche (rice pudding)
Wine
Small glass of oloroso Sherry, very rich and sweet

TO ILLUSTRATE KEY CONCEPTS

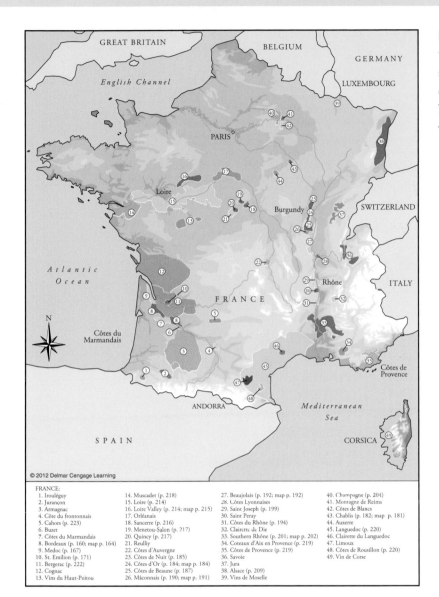

MAPS OF WINE REGIONS: Presented at the beginning of each regional section and chapter, and throughout the regional chapters, maps highlight specific regions being discussed and feature some top wine producers of that region.

FRANCE:
1. Irouléguy
2. Jurançon
3. Armagnac
4. Côte du frontonnais
5. Cahors (p. 223)
6. Buzet
7. Côtes du Marmandais
8. Bordeaux (p. 160; map p. 164)
9. Medoc (p. 167)
10. St. Emilion (p. 171)
11. Bergerac (p. 222)
12. Cognac
13. Vins du Haut-Poitou

14. Muscadet (p. 218)
15. Loire (p. 214)
16. Loire Valley (p. 214; map p. 215)
17. Orléanais
18. Sancerre (p. 216)
19. Menetou-Salon (p. 217)
20. Quincy (p. 217)
21. Reulliy
22. Côtes d'Auvergne
23. Côtes de Nuit (p. 185)
24. Côtes d'Or (p. 184; map p. 184)
25. Côtes de Beaune (p. 187)
26. Mâconnais (p. 190; map p. 191)

27. Beaujolais (p. 192; map p. 192)
28. Côtes Lyonnaises
29. Saint Joseph (p. 199)
30. Saint Peray
31. Côtes du Rhône (p. 194)
32. Clairette de Die
33. Southern Rhône (p. 201; map p. 202)
34. Coteaux d'Aix en Provence (p. 219)
35. Côtes de Provence (p. 219)
36. Savoie
37. Jura
38. Alsace (p. 209)
39. Vins de Moselle

40. Champagne (p. 204)
41. Montagne de Reims
42. Côtes de Blancs
43. Chablis (p. 182; map p. 181)
44. Auxerre
45. Languedoc (p. 220)
46. Clairette du Languedoc
47. Limoux
48. Côtes de Rousillon (p. 220)
49. Vin de Corse

DETAILED ILLUSTRATIONS: Colorful line art is displayed throughout the text emphasizing and simplifying different processes with ease.

FIGURE 3.6

Diagram of a grape stemmer-crusher.

© 2012 Delmar Cengage Learning

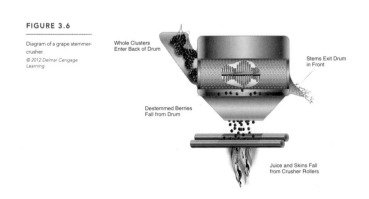

Whole Clusters Enter Back of Drum

Stems Exit Drum in Front

Destemmed Berries Fall from Drum

Juice and Skins Fall from Crusher Rollers

TABLES AND CHARTS offer visual representation of important information for easy comprehension.

TABLE 14.3 Wine Regions of New Zealand

Appellation	Best-Known Varieties
Auckland/Northern	Chardonnay, Merlot
Canterbury	Pinot Noir, Chardonnay, Riesling
Central Otago	Pinot Noir
Gisborne	Chardonnay
Hawke's Bay	Chardonnay, Merlot, Cabernet Sauvignon
Marlborough	Sauvignon Blanc, Pinot Noir, Chardonnay
Nelson	Sauvignon Blanc, Pinot Noir, Chardonnay
Waikato/Bay of Plenty	Produces a number of varieties
Waipara	Pinot Noir, Riesling

ix

{BRIEF CONTENTS}

{ CONTENTS }

Going out for the evening and enjoying a delicious meal in a restaurant is one of the most popular leisure activities. Wine has been a part of civilization for thousands of years and over time has become closely associated with food and fine dining. The selection, presentation, and ultimate enjoyment of a wine accompanying a meal is an integral part of the dining experience. Beyond the importance of wine to those who consume it, it is also an important source of a restaurant's income. There is a saying in the food industry that a restaurant breaks even with the kitchen and makes a profit off the wine list. While this may not be the case for every establishment, wine nonetheless is a vital attraction to customers deciding whether to frequent a particular restaurant. Therefore, it is essential for restaurant managers and chefs to have knowledge of wine, how to taste and evaluate it, and have an understanding of how wine is made and the region it comes from. This knowledge coupled with the ability to manage wine inventory allows restaurateurs to fully meet their diners' needs and maximize the returns on their investment in wine.

The second edition of *About Wine* provides the essential information that serves as the foundation for both a successful career in either the wine or culinary trades as well as an increased enjoyment of wine on a personal level. Chefs, restaurant managers, and retailers are just a few of the professionals in the culinary and hospitality industries who sell and serve wine on a daily basis. These professionals require a fundamental understanding of wine and how to both manage and sell it. *About Wine* second edition is a valuable resource for culinary students and professionals, as well as amateur wine enthusiasts.

The Purpose of This Textbook

Wine is a diverse field of study that can be intimidating to the novice learner, yet extensive knowledge about wine is not necessary to enjoy its qualities. The purpose of this book is to provide a solid base in the subject that can be built upon with further practice. Once the foundation in wine knowledge is established, new experiences with wine will be easier to comprehend and to incorporate into your work. This book is a reference that can aid in the understanding of new wines you encounter long after the coursework has been finished. To those who already have a familiarity with wine, the book will offer a deeper grasp of areas in wine studies and winemaking regions you may be less acquainted with. *About Wine* interprets the comprehensive subject of wine in a way that can be easily understood and applied.

New for the Second Edition

The second edition of *About Wine* builds upon the success of the prior edition with revised, expanded, and updated content in every chapter. The clearly written text is enhanced with an eye-catching layout that features new artwork and photos as well as updated maps and label diagrams. The chapters on wine regions have been updated to reflect the latest information on appellations and labeling regulations. There is a special emphasis on the interaction of food and wine in the second edition, with a **new chapter** devoted to the fundamentals of food and wine pairing. Additionally, the chapters on wine regions feature menu examples of successful combinations of the local wines with food.

The educational features of the book have been greatly expanded and improved for this new edition. There are more review questions and self-study exercises that allow readers to work independently and augment the assignments given in the classroom. Phonetic spellings of key terms and foreign wine names are given in the text to allow readers to learn to correctly pronounce new vocabulary as they learn the definition. The final section of the book, "The Business of Wine," has been completely reorganized and features an entirely **new chapter** on the marketing and distribution of wine.

ORGANIZATION OF THE TEXT

The chapters are organized into five sections that deal with specific areas of wine studies, along with appendices, a glossary, and an index.

Section I: The Fundamentals of Wine
Section II: Wine Regions of Europe
Section III: Wine Regions of North America
Section IV: Wine Regions of the Southern Hemisphere
Section V: The Business of Wine
Appendices, Glossary, and Index

Section I

"The Fundamentals of Wine" begins with a chapter that covers the history of wine and its place in society over the centuries. The next chapter focuses on the vineyard and discusses grape growing and the importance of the vineyard in winemaking with an expanded section on organic grape growing. The third chapter on winemaking explains how table wines, dessert wines, and sparkling wines are produced. Next is an extensive chapter on tasting and evaluating wines, which is valuable to anyone who deals with wine in a professional or amateur basis. The first section concludes with a new chapter on the fundamentals of food and wine pairing.

Section II

"Wine Regions of Europe" covers in five chapters France; Italy; Spain and Portugal; Germany; and other European Regions and the Mediterranean, which may be less familiar to readers. Knowledge of these regions is important to all students of wine because Europe is the birthplace of modern winemaking and most of the styles of wine and grape varieties grown throughout the world have their origins on this continent. The individual chapters cover the regions within the country, their history of winemaking, and the wines that they produce. Full-color, detailed maps of the wine-producing areas help readers familiarize themselves with each region. Information on appellations and labeling laws has also been updated for the second edition. The chapters conclude with menu examples showing winning combinations of the region's wines with food.

Section III

"Wine Regions of North America" covers in three chapters California; the Pacific Northwest; and New York, Canada, and other North American Regions. Domestic wines come in as many forms as their European counterparts and make up the majority of wine consumed in the United States. The wine regions of North America are covered in much the same way as the European countries, with sections on local grape-growing and winemaking techniques as well as updated and detailed maps of grape-growing appellations. As was the case in the European chapters, menus featuring regional wines are included in every chapter.

Section IV

"Wine Regions of the Southern Hemisphere" consists of three chapters discussing the wine regions of the Southern Hemisphere. This is one of the fastest-growing and most innovative regions of winemaking in the world today. Chapters devoted to Australia and New Zealand; Chile and Argentina; and South Africa include their winemaking history, grape-growing and wine-production methods, and maps of their wine regions and diagrams that explain how to read their labels. The second edition features the most current information on export trade for these countries and like the other chapters incorporates food and wine pairing to the regions' wines.

Section V

"The Business of Wine" covers in depth in three chapters how wine is presented and managed in food service. Beginning with a new chapter on the marketing and distribution of wine, the section then describes how to develop and manage a wine list before concluding with a detailed chapter on the proper service techniques for selling wine in a restaurant. The chapters clearly illustrate how to develop a successful and profitable wine program. Important subjects include staff training and working with distributors as well as a new section on how to serve wine in a responsible and safe manner. This edition of *About Wine* differentiates itself from many other wine books with this detailed section containing practical knowledge for those in the restaurant and hospitality trade.

Appendices

The book concludes with four appendices that provide useful information as a reference to readers. Appendix A outlines the laws that govern wine in the United States. Appendix B lists the appellations of the American Viticultural Area system. Appendix C lists the classifications of Bordeaux producers. Appendix D is a list of wine organizations and publications that are useful sources of further information to students of wine. *About Wine* concludes with a detailed glossary of the key terms presented in the text and a comprehensive index that allows readers to quickly find the information that they are looking for.

SUPPLEMENTS

Instructor Resources CD

The Instructor Resources CD includes an instructor's manual; chapter-by-chapter PowerPoint lecture slides; image library; and a computerized test bank in ExamView format.

Instructor Companion Site

Instructors, please visit login.cengage.com and log in to access instructor-specific resources.

CourseMate to Accompany *About Wine*, Second Edition

To access additional course materials including CourseMate, please visit www.cengagebrain.com. At the CengageBrain.com home page, search for the ISBN of your title (1439056501) using the search box at the top of the page. This will take you to the product page where these resources can be found.

CourseMate to accompany *About Wine*, second edition, includes:
- Engagement Tracker, a first-of-its-kind tool that monitors student engagement in the course
- an interactive eBook
- interactive teaching and learning tools including:
  - Quizzes
  - Flashcards
  - Food and wine pairing exercises
  - and more

{ ACKNOWLEDGMENTS }

I would like to thank my friends, family, and coworkers at Kenwood Vineyards and Santa Rosa Junior College for their assistance and cooperation during the writing of this book. Most of all, I give special thanks to my wife, Stephanie, whose daily support and encouragement as well as her exceptional skill in editing helped me write a much better book than I ever could have on my own.

PAT HENDERSON

First, I want to thank my son, Dan Rex, for his unquestioning support over the years, both of me and of my work. Special thanks to my wine-tasting buddies, Ralph Protsik, Liz Weiner, Bob Farrar, and Ernie and Robin Krieger who, over the 26 years we have tasted together, have kept my mind open to all types of wine and my palate attuned to all levels of quality. I also want to acknowledge my students, at Boston University's School of Hospitality Administration and later at New England Culinary Institute; they are still a source of inspiration.

DELLIE REX

The authors wish to thank the following individuals and organizations for their many contributions to the writing of *About Wine:* Australian Wine and Brandy Corporation, Marc Beyer, Jeff Brooks, Jennifer Burns, Emily Bush, Jerry Comfort, Adam Dial, Patrick Fallon, Ed Flaherty, German Wine Information Bureau, Italian Trade Commission, Kenwood Vineyards, Kobrand Corporation, F. Korbel & Brothers, Byron Kosuge, Deidre Magnello, Donald Murie, New York Wine and Grape Foundation, Ann C. Noble, Oregon Wine Board, Mel Sanchietti, Steve Schukler, Rhonda Smith, Sopexa-USA, Mark Stupich, Valley of the Moon Winery, Washington Wine Commission, Nik Weis, Wine Institute, Wines of Argentina, Wines of Chile, Wines from Spain Program, and Zonin Corporation, among many others listed in the photography credits.

The authors also wish to thank all of the people at Delmar Cengage Learning, especially our product managers Nicole Calisi and Anne Orgren for their constant encouragement and hard work, as well as senior acquisitions editor Jim Gish, content project manager Glenn Castle, editorial assistant Sarah Timm, and senior marketing manager Kristin McNary. Their skill and patience combined with an incredible enthusiasm for the project made this book possible.

Delmar Learning and the authors would like to give a special thanks to the contributing authors of *About Wine,* David Garaventa and Angela Lloyd, for their dedication to this project.

The authors and Delmar Cenage Learning would like to thank the following reviewers for their invaluable feedback and suggestions for improvement:

ROBERT B. BANSBERG
General Manager/Wine Director, Gabriel's Restaurant
Wine Instructor, Kendall College
Chicago, Illinois

MAXINE BORCHERDING
Lead Chef Instructor
Oregon Culinary Institute
Portland, Oregon

JOHN B. ELIASSEN
Instructor—Beverages
Western Culinary Institute
Portland, Oregon

MARTHA FRANKLIN
Chef Instructor
New England Culinary Institute
Montpelier, Vermont

PHILIPPE GARMY
Clinical Instructor
Hotel and Restaurant Administration
Oklahoma State University
Stillwater, Oklahoma

COLIN JOHNSON, PhD
Professor
Department of Hospitality, Recreation and Tourism
San Jose University
San Jose, California

FRANK E. JUGE
Professor, Hospitality Management
Sommelier
Rosen College
University of Central Florida
Orlando, Florida

ALEXANDER G. MURRAY
(TECHNICAL REVIEWER)
Assistant Director of Beverage Strategy
Legal Sea Foods, Inc.
Boston, Massachusetts

JENNIFER D. PEREIRA
Instructor of Wines and Spirits
Johnson & Wales University College of Culinary Arts
Providence, Rhode Island

LACHLAN W. SANDS, MEd
Department Chair—Faculty Development
The California School of Culinary Arts
Pasadena, California

STEVE SITNICK, FMP, MBA
Chef Instructor, Associate Dean
Florida Culinary Institute
West Palm Beach, Florida

ANTHONY (TOBY) J. STRIANESE, CCE
Chairperson and Professor
Department of Hotel, Culinary Arts and Tourism
Schenectady County Community College
Schenectady, New York

JAMES R. TAYLOR, MBA, CEC, AAC
Associate Professor
Hospitality Management
Columbus State Community College

DAVID W. TINER, CEC, CCA, FMP
Director/Chef Instructor
Louisiana Culinary Institute
Baton Route, Louisiana

MICHAEL L. WRAY, PhD
Sommelier Diploma, International Sommelier Guild
Professor, Restaurant Management
Certified Culinary Instructor
Metropolitan State College of Denver
Denver, Colorado

{ ABOUT THE AUTHORS }

J. Patrick Henderson
Senior Winemaker for Kenwood Vineyards,
Winemaking Instructor at Santa Rosa Junior College

A graduate of the winemaking program at the University of California at Davis, Pat began his pursuit of a life in wine when he was still a teenager by helping neighbors make wine at home. While at school learning the technical aspects of winemaking, Pat interned at a number of wineries during harvest to supplement his formal education. The winemakers at the different wineries he worked for gave him broad exposure to many different styles of winemaking. After graduating, he returned to the site of one of his internships and was hired as enologist for Kenwood Vineyards in California's Sonoma Valley and worked there for nine vintages. In 1995 Pat became Winemaker at Hedges Cellars in Washington State where he established a new winery being built at the estate vineyard in the Columbia Valley. In his first year at Hedges, wines he produced won both a best of show and ratings of more than 90 points.

After two vintages in the Northwest, Pat returned to the Sonoma Valley to become Winemaker/General Manager at Valley of the Moon Winery. Here he worked to rebuild the historic winery and introduce a new line of wines featuring less-common varietals such as Syrah, Sangiovese, and Pinot Blanc. After seven vintages as winemaker at Valley of the Moon he returned to Kenwood Vineyards as Senior Winemaker, 20 years after his first vintage at Kenwood. Pat strives to combine both the artistic and scientific aspects of winemaking to produce unique wines that are multidimensional in character. His philosophy of winemaking is one that relies heavily on the quality of a wine's flavors and balance.

Beyond his role as a winemaker, Pat has also shared his interest in wine with others as an instructor for a semester-long course in winemaking at Santa Rosa Junior College. Since 1991 Pat has taught hundreds of students the fine points of wine and the craft of winemaking. Using the knowledge gained by decades of making wine as well as teaching about winemaking, he has judged numerous professional wine competitions and has written many articles for winemaking publications. He is a member of both the American Society of Enologists and Viticulturists and the Society of Wine Educators. Pat and his wife Stephanie currently reside in the Sonoma Valley.

Dellie Rex, MBA
Wine Consultant and Educator,
President of Wine Experiences, Inc.

Dellie Rex has been in the wine business for almost 30 years. She has taught as adjunct professor at Boston University's School of Hospitality Administration, and at the New England Culinary Institute. Currently she is teaching through her wine education service, Wine Experiences, Inc., as well as advising several clients on the marketing of their wines.

Dellie is a member of the Society of Wine Educators and of La Commanderie de Bordeaux, an honorary society of wine connoisseurs. She serves on the board of the Elizabeth Bishop Wine Resource Center in Boston. In 1999 *Boston Magazine* listed Dellie as one of the 50 most intriguing women in New England, dubbing her "the wine expert's wine expert."

SECTION I

THE FUNDAMENTALS OF WINE

THIS SECTION begins with a chapter that covers the history of wine and its place in society over the centuries. Subsequent chapters discuss grape growing; the importance of the vineyard in winemaking; how table, dessert, fortified, and sparkling wines are produced; and how to taste and evaluate wines. The section concludes with a chapter that discusses food and wine pairing, how wines age, and the connections between wine and alcohol consumption and health.

{WHAT IS WINE?}

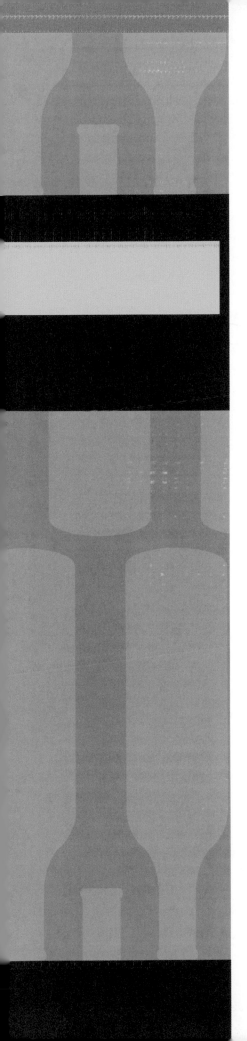

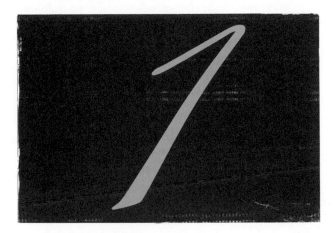

This chapter defines what wine is, and discusses its historical origins and its role in society from ancient times up through the twenty-first century. The chapter also explores the economic cycles of grape growing and winemaking, and looks at the status of wine in today's world and its prospects for the future.

KEY TERMS

amphorae

Bacchus

boom and bust

Champagne

coopers

Dionysus

enology

international
varietals

phylloxera

Prohibition

vintage

viticulture

Volstead Act

FIGURE 1.1

Tasting and enjoying a glass
of wine with a meal has been
a part of civilization for many
centuries.

© Ignacio Gaffuri/Wines of
Argentina

INTRODUCTION

Wine has been an integral part of the human experience for nearly 70 centuries. Though its origins are somewhat uncertain, it has been made and consumed wherever grapes or, for that matter, a variety of fruits are grown. Although people still make wine from tree fruits, berries, grains such as rice, and even flowers, for the purpose of our study, we will hold to a narrower definition. Wine, as is commonly understood around the world today, is the result of processing and subsequent fermentation of the juice from grapes. Fermentation is a natural process that acts to stabilize grape juice and protect it from spoilage, allowing it to be stored as wine for later consumption. The alcohol in wine that is produced by fermentation also prevents the growth of pathogenic microorganisms. This means that wine was always safe to drink even when the local water supply was contaminated.

In addition to preserving the wine, alcohol affects both the body and mind when it is consumed. Over the centuries different cultures have had contrasting opinions on alcohol and wine. While many societies have regarded it as an essential and healthful beverage, often incorporating it into religious rites, others have shunned its use and considered it sinful. Simply put, wine is a beverage available in a number of styles and that is often consumed with food. However, there is more to wine than this simple description implies. The wide variety of wines available and the complexity of their flavors allow it to mean many things to many people. For some people wine is a simple, inexpensive drink that comes in a jug and is consumed with the daily meal; to others it is an expensive and mysterious beverage that is enjoyed only a few times a year on special occasions. These contrasting ideas have influenced the development of wine during the course of history, and continue to affect its place in the world today.

THE HISTORY OF WINE

Because civilization itself began in the Middle East, it is not surprising that the origins of wine lie in the same region. Popular belief is that wine was first consumed in the areas of Persia (modern-day Iran) around 5000 to 6000 BC. Although the exact nature of the wine is uncertain, it may have been made from dates or other tree fruits native to the region rather than grapes and was undoubtedly rudimentary in nature. *Vitis vinifera* (VEE-tihs vihn-IHF-uh-ruh), the species of grape that is most often used for the production of wine, is native to the region between the Black and Caspian Seas just to the northwest of Iran—where the Republic of Georgia is today. Some scholars speculate that winemaking using grapes may have begun in this region and moved south from there (McGovern, 2003).

Egypt and Greece

The exact origin of when and where the first wine was made remains unclear; however, we can be certain that by 3000 BC winemaking from grapes had begun. During this period both the Egyptians and the Phoenicians produced wines from grapevines that were cultivated specifically for that purpose. Ancient Egyptian artwork and sculptures

FIGURE 1.2

Egyptian wall painting of winemaking showing vines of ripe grapes and crushing and amphorae for storage, circa 1400 BC.

© Gianni Dagli Orti/Corbis

provide a great deal of information about the winemaking practices of the time. Paintings and reliefs on the walls of tombs document how grapes were grown, picked, crushed, and fermented and how the resulting wine was stored (Figure 1.2). It is clear from these paintings that wine production had evolved into an elaborate procedure. The paintings also show that wine was an essential part of meals and celebrations of the Egyptian aristocracy. Containers of wine have been found in royal burial chambers for the dead to enjoy in the afterlife. Much like the practice today, the vessels were marked with information on the origin of the grapes that produced the wine and the year, or **vintage**, they were harvested. It is also believed that wines were made in China during the same period, although it is not clear whether they were made from grapes or rice (Johnson, 1989).

By 2000 BC, wine had become an important part of Greek culture, its praises lavishly sung by the poets of the day. Beginning around 1000 BC, the expansion of the Greek Empire brought vineyards and winemaking to regions throughout the Mediterranean basin, including parts of North Africa, southern Spain, southwestern France, Sicily, and much of the Italian mainland. Apart from the fact that it was made from fermented grape juice, the wine of ancient Greece bore little resemblance to modern wine. It was most likely made from dried grapes or raisins, as are some wines still made today. The result would have been a heavy, sweet, almost syrupy liquid, perhaps even concentrated by cooking. Barrels and bottles were not yet invented so the Greeks stored their wines in containers called **amphorae** (AM-fuhr-uh). These were cylindrical pottery jars with narrow necks and two handles similar to those used by the Egyptians.

There was little understanding of the microbiology of winemaking so contamination and early spoilage was undoubtedly a frequent problem. Wine was often served with jugs of warm water (sometimes seawater) to dilute it. Like the Egyptians before them, wine occupied a large place in Greek society. The Greeks created a deity, **Dionysus** (di-uh-NI-suhs), in honor of wine, and no festival or banquet was complete without it. They used the term *symposium* to describe a gathering of people that featured intelligent conversation and the drinking of wine.

The Roman Era

The Romans took grape growing, or **viticulture** (VIHT-ih-kuhl-cher), and winemaking to a new height. Though the growing of wine grapes in Italy predated the rise of the Roman Empire by many centuries, it was the Romans who began the practice of trellising vines off the ground by training them to grow up trees, a practice that is still followed in parts of Italy and Portugal.

The Romans' technological advances in viticulture and **enology** (ee-NAHL-uh-jee), the study of winemaking, were thoroughly documented in literature and art (Figure 1.3). Even the great poet Virgil offered advice to grape farmers ("Vines love an open hill . . ."). Unlike the Greeks, the Romans were first-rate barrel makers or coopers, and storage in wooden barrels, similar to the barrels used by winemakers today, as well as in clay amphorae, was common.

Although no one can say for certain what the wines of the Roman era tasted like, we do know that some wines from the best vintages were stored and drunk for up to a century or longer. In its most common form, Roman wine was possibly similar to the inexpensive table wines of today that one finds throughout the Mediterranean growing region—young, light, and somewhat rough. Its best examples were probably somewhat more robust and flavorful and could age for many years.

As it had with the Greeks, Roman viticulture and winemaking followed closely on the heels of the Roman legions as they pushed the boundaries of their empire north and westward. The Romans grew grapes throughout Italy, expanded the vineyards of Spain north to the Pyrenees, and planted vines throughout what is now modern Portugal. Around the first century, they also began a steady expansion north from Provence through a wild and savage territory that would later become France and into parts of what is now modern Germany. By AD 250, the Romans had expanded the growing of grapevines into the regions of Languedoc, Auvergne, the Rhône and Loire Valleys, Burgundy, Bordeaux, Paris, Champagne, and along the Rhine and Moselle Rivers.

This great expansion of vineyards laid the foundation for modern viticulture, as it included all the principal regions that would come to make up the wine map of modern Europe. Not to be outdone by their Greek predecessors, the Romans adopted their own god of wine, **Bacchus** (BAK-uhs) (Figure 1.4). Moreover, like the Greeks, no holiday was complete without its Bacchanalia, or drunken feast.

In addition to the Greeks and Romans, wine was also significant to Jewish and early Christian cultures. Wine is mentioned more than 150 times in the Old Testament and is an important part of Jewish religious celebrations such as weddings and

FIGURE 1.3

First-century Roman stone carving depicting a man drawing wine from a barrel. The Roman civilization brought much advancement to the practice of winemaking and extended vineyards throughout the empire.

© Museo Nationale de Arte Romano, Merida, Spain/ SuperStock

Passover. In fact, during the Exodus, several Israelis expressed their regret at leaving the Egyptian vineyards behind. As Christianity grew in popularity, the religious significance of wine also grew, spreading throughout the Roman Empire. In the New Testament, the first miracle that Christ performed was the conversion of water to wine at the wedding feast of Canaan. Christians also consume wine as a sacrament during Mass in a reenactment of the Last Supper, referring to the consecrated wine as "the blood of Christ."

The medicinal qualities of wine were also highly regarded by the Romans. The physician Galen, doctor to Emperor Marcus Aurelius, freely prescribed wine in moderated daily doses as a cure for most illness. Galen, who had free access to the imperial cellars, believed that the older the wine, provided it had not spoiled in storage, the better was the cure.

By the first century AD, the Roman understanding of viticulture and winemaking had reached new heights. Although they lacked the knowledge and technology to perform even rudimentary chemical analysis, they were keen observers of the agricultural process. Several texts, dating from as early as the third century BC, describe grape growing and winemaking in considerable detail. Columella, a second-century naturalist, dedicated his life's work to the study and improvement of wine. Another naturalist, Pliny the elder, writing in the first century AD, provided instructions on planting and

FIGURE 1.4

Renaissance statue of the Roman deity of wine Bacchus, called Dionysus by the Greeks. The deity was also portrayed as a child.

© Bacchus (Michelangelo Buonarotti—photo © The Bridgeman Art Library/ Getty Images

tending more than 90 varieties of wine grapes. The Roman devotion to the physical, intellectual, and spiritual attributes of wine remains unique in history. Their knowledge of matching grape varieties to soils and climates, trellising, and other growing techniques form the foundation of many contemporary practices.

When Romulus Augustus was overthrown in AD 476, it marked the end of the Roman Empire. By this time the Roman Empire had been declining in size and influence since the third century. Rome had been fighting a war of attrition with the Gothic tribes of northern Europe. Having battled them for nearly 200 years, Rome eventually proved unable and unwilling to raise the armies necessary to keep them subdued.

The Middle Ages

The fall of Rome ushered in a long period of great strife throughout the civilized world. Competing groups battled for control of territory and commerce. France and Spain, both of which eventually would evolve into great nation-states, provided the landscape for much of the turmoil. Wars between the Franks, Teutons, and Goths brought widespread destruction. In the seventh century AD, the Moors of North Africa crossed the Straits of Gibraltar and invaded Spain. Their occupation, reaching as far north as the Pyrenees and lasting until 1492, would eventually unite Christian Europe against them. Although the Moors' Islamic faith prevented them from consuming alcohol, they were tolerant of others living in the region, allowing viticulture and winemaking to continue in Spain, albeit at a more limited scale than during the Roman period.

During the Middle Ages, the 1,000-year period between the fall of Rome and the beginning of the Renaissance, the practice of agricultural activity on any meaningful scale fell to the Catholic Church. Monasteries were established by the various religious orders throughout Europe. The goal was both to expand Christian teaching and beliefs and to broaden the political power of the Church. Some of the monasteries became great centers of study and knowledge, the forerunners of Europe's finest universities, while others fostered the learning of trades and still others became important commercial outposts.

No matter what their primary focus, the monasteries of Europe engaged in all aspects of agriculture, from growing food and feed crops to raising animals for milk and meat. Given the already lengthy history of winemaking in Europe, it is little wonder that the Church took over stewardship of the continent's vineyards (Figure 1.5). In fact, in exchange for accepting the teaching of the Church, the peasants of Europe soon came to expect the much-needed assistance by the monastic orders in meeting their daily needs.

Pope Gregory the Great instructed the monastic orders to expand wine production, and the planting of wine grapes again began to spread. As was true with much of its activities, the Church kept strict control of winemaking. All grapes were required to be pressed in monasteries, for which a "donation" of 10 percent of production was taken. The Church also controlled the commerce in wine, ensuring that the monasteries' stocks were fully sold before others were allowed to market their wines.

FIGURE 1.5

A sixteenth-century French tapestry depicting grapes being crushed and then pressed into barrels.
© Bettmann/Corbis

The wealth created by wine allowed the monks to continue viticulture (grape growing) and the study of enology (winemaking) begun by their Roman predecessors. Matching grape varieties to soil conditions and climate, propagation and planting, trellising, crushing, fermenting, fining, and storage were all meticulously studied and improved, resulting in great advancements in the quality of their wines. Meanwhile, the peasants were often left to make inferior wines from lesser grapes for their own consumption.

Despite the inherent inequities, the relationship between peasants and monks was a fruitful one for both sides. As the Church grew in wealth and power, the countryside prospered with the flourishing of trades and crafts that monasteries had helped promote, not the least of which were farming and winemaking. Villages formed around monasteries, many growing into bustling towns and some into cities of 20,000 or more. Farmers began using the skills learned from the monks to improve and expand their own vineyards, and viticulture quickly became a major form of agricultural activity.

During the reign of Charlemagne (768–814), medieval viticulture and enology reached a peak. A great scholar as well as king, Charlemagne nurtured the monasteries, bestowing great gifts of land and other wealth to the Church. In exchange, he required that vines be planted and well maintained throughout Europe. Consequently, viticulture and winemaking reached new heights.

Twelfth Century to Modern Times

By the twelfth century, the political landscape of Europe had undergone great changes. The Crusades, or holy wars against the Moslem world, were well under way. With the cooperation of a grateful Church, the European monarchies were rapidly consolidating their power. City-states were developing into nation-states. The wine world of the time profited greatly from the involvement of a rising aristocracy. Like Charlemagne, the nobles of the day bequeathed large tracks of land to the Church, much already planted to vineyards. The monastic orders made good use of their increasing endowment. Some of the finest vineyards in France, Germany, Italy, and Spain trace their origins to monastery plantings of the period.

A major event in wine history took place during this period when in 1152 Henry II, King of England and Duke of Normandy, married Eleanor of Aquitaine, the divorced wife of Louis VII of France. The Norman Conquest in 1066 had created a situation where English kings were also French nobility with the right to own lands on both sides of the English Channel. Eleanor's dowry included the entire winemaking region of what is now Bordeaux in southwestern France. These vast vineyards were combined with those of Henry's Anjou estates in the Loire Valley, and represented perhaps the single largest holding of vineyards of its time.

During the reigns of Henry II and his son, Richard the Lion Hearted, the English developed an enormous thirst for the wines of France. A huge fleet, the forerunner of the British Navy, was developed to accommodate the demand on shipping. Wines from Languedoc, Loire, and Bordeaux poured across the channel in a seemingly never-ending flow.

It took nearly three centuries, including a continuing series of wars between 1337 and 1453 (known collectively as the Hundred Years' War) for the French to dislodge the English from their precious vineyards. In 1429, led by Joan of Arc, the French drove the English out of the Loire Valley, and in 1453, they succeeded in expelling them from Bordeaux. With the loss of their French territories, the British turned to other regions such as Germany, Italy, Portugal, and Spain to satisfy their thirst for wine. This trade stimulated the developing wine industry all over Europe and introduced wine drinkers to regional wine styles that were made in foreign lands.

By the end of the fifteenth century, the great European Renaissance was well under way. Literally a "rebirth" in creative thinking, the Renaissance was to have a profound and lasting effect on religion, philosophy, science, and art. The Church, though a leader in many areas of the Renaissance, soon found its authority shaken by such free thinkers as Martin Luther. The monastic orders became easy targets for religious reformers, and it was not long before their economic and political hold on the populace began to fade. By the end of the seventeenth century, much of the Church's vineyard holdings throughout Europe had been broken up and passed back into private hands.

The early eighteenth century saw improvements in glass manufacturing which led to stronger bottles along with the widespread use of cork as a bottle stopper. This same period also saw the development of sparkling wine or **Champagne**. This is more than a coincidence because sparkling wine requires a strong bottle as well as a good seal to hold in the pressure. Although the Benedictine monk Dom Pérignon is often credited with the discovery of sparkling wine, he probably produced it by accident and others developed the techniques of production (Kolpan, Smith, & Weiss, 2002). Champagne soon became fashionable, not only in Europe, but also throughout the extensive colonies and settlements in Africa, Asia, and the New World (North and South America) which France traded with at the time. Cork, with its unique sealing properties, revolutionized the storing and aging of wines, making it possible to age wines for long periods and to ship them in bottles to distant markets for sale and consumption.

Golden Age of Wine

It was in the nineteenth century, however, that wine enjoyed its greatest advances and suffered one of its most devastating blows. The advent of modern studies of chemistry and microbiology brought a deeper understanding of the winemaking process, and the laboratory soon began playing a major role in winemaking. Louis Pasteur, perhaps the most famous microbiologist of all time, used wine in many of his experiments and determined that the fermentation of grape juice into wine was the result of action by microorganisms. This better understanding of technology, combined with the knowledge gained by centuries of trial and error in European vineyards, resulted in huge advances in the quality of wine. As the science and caliber of wine took a leap forward, wine appreciation in the modern sense was born. Attracted to the glamour of winemaking, the wealthy soon began acquiring vineyards throughout Europe. These new wine "lords" showed off their holdings by labeling their products with both their family and estate names (bottles were typically unlabeled before). The French established a system to classify their vineyards. Great vintage followed great vintage throughout the first half of the century, creating what some have called a "golden age of wine."

In the second half of the century, disaster struck in the form of a root louse, **phylloxera** (fihl-LOX-er-uh), which is native to the eastern United States. Similar to an aphid, phylloxera is a small, sap-sucking insect that feeds on roots and leaves. The pest was brought to France on a merchant ship carrying grapevines that were native to North America. By 1868, phylloxera had been identified in the vineyards of southern France. Within 20 years, it spread throughout the country, destroying most of the vineyards. By 1874, it had also infected Germany. Some French producers migrated to Spain, taking their grape varieties with them. However, eventually the pest followed, and soon all the wine regions of Europe were infected. It was not until growers began replanting their vineyards with rootstocks from North America that Europe's winemaking industry was revived. These rootstocks, being native to the region phylloxera was from, had evolved to be resistant to the pest.

The phylloxera epidemic, coupled with economic and political turmoil, sent many winemakers, both wealthy and of modest means, in search of new vineyard land. It was during the late nineteenth and early twentieth centuries that the wine industry in the New World became commercially important. Vineyards in North and South America, Australia, and South Africa flourished with the influx of emigrants from Europe. Though some areas, especially California, had an already established wine industry, many of today's New World wine regions grew rapidly in the years between 1880 and 1910. The New World producers took their cue from their European predecessors, in many cases borrowing grape varieties, techniques, and technologies (Figure 1.6). However, when winemakers from different growing regions of Europe came to the New World they adapted Old World methods to the particular conditions in their new homes. This combination of winemaking techniques from around Europe helped create many innovations.

The first half of the twentieth century, with its two devastating world wars, again saw setbacks in winemaking worldwide. In America, this was compounded by **Prohibition**, which outlawed the sale or consumption of alcoholic beverages from

FIGURE 1.6

Pressing grapes and pumping juice into fermentation tanks at a California winery in 1911.

© Wine Institute

1919 until 1933. The temperance movement had been gaining ground in the United States for 100 years and at the end of World War I, the **Volstead Act** was passed implementing Prohibition as the Eighteenth Amendment. During this time most wineries went out of business save for a few that were allowed to make sacramental wine or medicinal "wine tonics." Prohibition did little to control alcohol consumption, and Americans continued to drink "bootleg" alcohol obtained illegally or primitive wines made at home. Organized crime flourished distributing alcohol, and the government lost the alcohol sales tax revenues it had received before Prohibition. The Eighteenth Amendment was repealed in 1933 when it became obvious that it was not working. During Prohibition, Americans' tastes changed because wine drinkers became used to drinking substandard homemade wines that were often sweetened and fortified with distilled alcohol to cover up the flaws. As part of repeal, each state was allowed to make its own regulations concerning the commerce of alcohol that led to a confusing patchwork of state laws that survive to this day.

Following the Second World War, both the Old and New World wine industries saw a resurgence as reconstruction monies flowed to Europe and returning U.S. service members came home with a newly acquired interest in wine. By the 1950s, wine, as a beverage and as a business, was again on the rise. Throughout the 1960s and 1970s, wine production and consumption grew at an increasing pace. In America, some producers took the revolutionary step of naming their wines after the grape varieties they were made from (i.e., Cabernet, Sauvignon, or Chardonnay) instead of following the common practice of using European geographic names, such as Bordeaux or Chablis, to identify their wines. The public's taste also changed from preferring sweet, fortified wines to dry table wines.

Wine Today

Since the early 1970s, the wine world has been undergoing another huge transformation. Where before, in both the Old and New Worlds, there were only a handful of producers making high-quality, premium wines, today there are thousands of producers throughout the world making excellent wines (Figure 1.7). Behind this explosion of quality producers lies a greater consumer interest in fine wines and the broader availability of state-of-the-art technology and winemaking expertise. There are now excellent viticulture and enology schools in Europe, North and South America, Australia, and South Africa. Modern technology in both the vineyard and winery is widespread.

In Europe, the lesser-known regions of southern France, Italy, Spain, Greece, Hungary, and even the former countries of the Eastern Bloc are now making wines that can compete with those of some of the more famous European wine-growing regions. In addition to California, states such as New York, Washington, Oregon, Virginia, and Texas are now recognized wine producers. In fact, North America's reputation as a winemaking region today rivals that of Europe, and many consumers continue to discover the moderate price and excellent value of the wines of Australia, New Zealand, Chile, Argentina, Hungary, and South Africa. This global competition from new wine regions has put pressure on producers in traditional regions, such as California and Europe, to keep their prices competitive, and it has given consumers access to a multitude of quality wines at attractive prices.

FIGURE 1.7

Spurred on by an expanding and more knowledgeable consumer base, winemaking regions throughout the world have modernized their operations and improved their products. This has given consumers a broad range of high-quality wines that are available at reasonable prices.

© Pat Henderson

Over the past 30 years, the world's wine industry has become vastly more consistent in quality. Countries that once produced inexpensive wine of mediocre quality for their domestic market found that if they improved their winemaking practices to make better wine, they could get a better price selling it for export. The worldwide focus on quality improvement has led to the increasing standardization of taste and styles. This is particularly evident in the growing vineyard acreage dedicated to the so-called **international varietals** (also called classic varietals) such as Chardonnay, Sauvignon Blanc, Pinot Noir, Cabernet Sauvignon, Merlot, and Syrah. In France, Italy, Spain, and even California, growers are removing lesser-known traditional varieties to compete in the international varietal market. This allows consumers to purchase a recognizable variety from an obscure region with which they may be unfamiliar. There has also been a movement toward making softer, less tannic wines that require little bottle aging before they are consumed. This global market and increased competition has resulted in consolidation of many winemaking companies. Frequently smaller family-owned wineries are purchased by large multinational corporations that also import and export wine as well as produce it. While this globalization of the industry has led to better prices and a more consistently high-quality product, some wine enthusiasts feel it has also made wines from around the world more homogeneous and uninteresting.

ECONOMIC CYCLES IN THE WINE BUSINESS

Wine, because it is made from grapes, is considered an agricultural product, and like many other agricultural products, exhibits a **boom and bust** economic pattern. Because of the time it takes to establish a new vineyard, get a crop from its vines, and then produce a wine from its grapes, it is very difficult for growers and vintners to respond quickly to changing market conditions. For example, the popularity of a certain variety of wine will lead to scarcity of the grapes used to produce it, resulting in high prices. When this happens, many growers will plant the variety to take advantage of the higher prices; however, the return on their investment is delayed for several years while the young vines grow old enough to produce grapes. By the time the vineyard comes into production, many other grape growers have planted the variety, resulting in overproduction and ultimately lower prices for their crop.

The globalization of the wine market has allowed wine anywhere in the world to be shipped anyplace in the world. While it is common for wine consumers to drink what is made locally, many countries do not have a significant wine industry and there is always demand for high-quality wine at a good price regardless of its origin. Moreover, when wine crosses international borders its price is affected by changes in the exchange rate, leading to dramatic fluctuations in the price of a given bottle of wine that the producer has little control over. Another factor influencing the economics of winemaking is the fact that many wine consumers consider wine a "luxury item" and not a food. In difficult economic times, fine wines are one of the things consumers cut back on to save money.

LOOKING TO THE FUTURE

Over the next decades, grape growing and winemaking will likely continue the course it has been on since the 1970s. Technological advancement in both the vineyard and the winery should continue at its current or at an even greater pace, with much of the effort being put into not only growing better grapes and making better wine but also doing it in a more environmentally responsible way. New technology will continue to be integrated with traditional winemaking techniques, especially in the more established wine regions of the world. Emerging countries, like Argentina and South Africa, have invested heavily in new vineyards and wineries to take advantage of the export market. This reflects the continued growth in consumer wine knowledge and interest.

After years of steady growth, the consumption of wine has begun to slow down, due in part to the economic slowdown that began in 2008. There are also two important milestones that took place in 2008 that reflect the changes in the international wine market. First, the United States surpassed Italy in terms of total wine consumption, and second, for the first time the vineyards of the New World produced more wine than those of Europe. In the United States, demand for California wines has been tempered by inexpensive imports from South America and Australia, putting pressure on California vintners to keep their prices low and quality high. In California at the end of the first decade of the new century, the cost of grapes has remained high while economic conditions and competition keep wineries from raising their prices on the wines that they produce. Despite the uncertain, cyclical nature of the wine business, it will undoubtedly remain an integral part of fine dining, as it has for thousands of years.

FIGURE 1.8

A young vineyard being established in California.
© Pat Henderson

Summary

While the exact time and place that the first wine was ever made remains unknown, we do know that wine has been a part of civilization since its very origin. Over the millennia, each society that has made wine has increased the understanding of viticulture and enology. From the Greeks and Romans, through the European golden age of wine, to today's progress in the New World wine regions, all have strived to make great wine that can stand next to the best in the world. Like many internationally traded agricultural products, the business of wine is subject to periods of boom and bust brought on by economic cycles and currency fluctuation. Notwithstanding this instability, the future of wine looks bright as more and more consumers are introduced to this natural and delicious beverage.

EXERCISES

1. When did winemaking begin and what fruits were used to make the first wines?

2. When did winemaking come to Europe, and what culture brought it?

3. What were the causes of Prohibition, and what factors influenced its repeal?

4. How has globalization of the world's economy affected the wine business?

REVIEW QUESTIONS

1. Where did the phylloxera-resistant grapevines used for rootstock originate?
   A. Europe
   B. Eastern United States
   C. Australia
   D. Northern Africa

2. The economic cycles that affect grape growing and winemaking are called _____.
   A. Bubble economy
   B. Depression/recession
   C. Boom and bust
   D. Consistent growth

3. Sparkling wine was first produced ____.
   A. In the second century AD
   B. In the 1700s
   C. During Prohibition
   D. In the golden age of wine of the nineteenth century

4. Who proved that fermentation was the result of action by microorganisms?
   A. Louis Pasteur
   B. Charlemagne
   C. Marcus Aurelius
   D. Dom Pérignon

REFERENCES

Johnson, H. (1989). *Vintage: The story of wine*. New York: Simon & Schuster.

Kolpan, S., Smith, B. H., & Weiss, M. A. (2002). *Exploring wine*. New York: Wiley.

McGovern, P. E. (2003). *Ancient wine*. Princeton, NJ: Princeton University Press.

{ THE VINEYARD—FROM SOIL TO HARVEST }

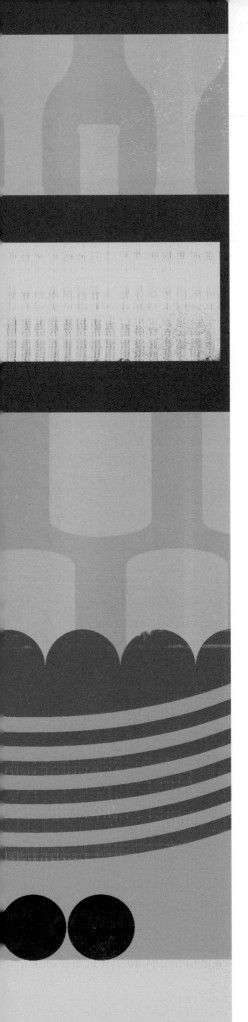

This chapter discusses vineyards and describes how grapevines are grown for wine production. It also explains how a vineyard's location and environmental conditions influence the flavor of its crop, as well as the annual growth cycle of vines and farming practices that grape growers employ. The chapter concludes with a discussion on the most common grape varieties used for winemaking.

KEY TERMS

alluvial soil

biodynamic

bloom

canes

clone

cordon

fighting varietal

grafting

heavy soil

light soil

loam

macroclimate

mesoclimate

microclimate

organic

rootstock

scion

shatter

sustainable viticulture

terroir

trellis

véraison

Vitis vinifera

winterkill

INTRODUCTION

Superior wines are made from superior grapes, and the ultimate quality of a wine is determined in the vineyard as much as it is at the winery (Figure 2.1). Most fruit crops are grown with an emphasis on appearance, and picked before ripeness so they can survive the trip to the market without deterioration. Additionally, many agricultural crops are grown as a commodity, where the quality of the product and prices are uniform among growers. In contrast, premium wine grapes are one of the few crops that are still grown primarily for their flavor, and there is greater variation in prices that growers receive based on quality of their fruit. There are two factors that influence the character of grapes from a given vineyard, environmental and cultural. Environmental factors are all of the natural attributes of the vineyard site, including climate, soil, and drainage, while cultural practices are all of the actions performed by the grower, such as pruning, trellising, and selection of grape variety.

GRAPES USED FOR WINEMAKING

Before covering the types of grapes that are used for winemaking, it is important to consider why grapes are the preferred fruit for wine production. While it is possible to make "wine" out of many fruits and berries, it cannot be done without adding amendments to the juice before it can ferment. For example, when making a wine out of a fruit such as blackberries you must first add sugar, water, and yeast nutrients for a successful fermentation to occur. Grape juice by contrast already has all of these attributes. Most importantly, the high concentration of sugar in grape juice allows the yeast to ferment wine to a sufficient alcohol content to inhibit microbial spoilage. The chance of spoilage is also reduced by the natural acidity that grapes possess. Moreover, there is also an inherent association between grapes and yeast. The outside of the grape berry is covered with a waxy layer that contains naturally occurring yeast. Therefore, it is possible to make a rudimentary wine by simply crushing grapes into a vessel and letting the natural yeast ferment the juice. The great majority of wine produced in the world is from grapes, so much so that the term *wine* has become synonymous with wine made from grapes.

There are many indigenous species of grapes worldwide but the overwhelming majority of wine produced is from the species **Vitis vinifera** (VEE-tihs vihn-IHF-uh-ruh). Native to Asia Minor it has been spread by humankind throughout the Old and New Worlds. Within the species *Vitis vinifera,* also called *V. vinifera,* estimates for the number of named cultivars, or cultivated varieties, vary from 10,000 to 14,000; of these only a small fraction are grown commercially. The reason for the wide range of numbers is that there is no standardized method of naming and categorizing grapevines. These cultivars, such as Cabernet Sauvignon and Chardonnay, exhibit great latitude in growing characteristics, appearance, and flavors. The difference in grape varieties is analogous to those in other fruits, where a single species like *Malus domestica,* or the common apple tree, has a number of varieties that look and taste very different from one another, such as Red Delicious and Pippin.

FIGURE 2.1

Pinot Noir grapes. The dark purple color of the skins is one indication that they are ready for harvest.

© Oregon Wine Board/Patrick Prothe Photography

Clone = cutting from parent plant to form another

There is also variation within a single grape variety. Grapevines can be propagated by taking cuttings off the parent plant and grafting them onto another grapevine—or, if the cuttings are planted, they will form roots to become a separate vine that is a **clone** (genetically identical) of the original vine. Different clones have different growing and flavor characteristics. In the Burgundy region of France viticulturists have developed more than 50 certified clones of Pinot Noir (Entav, Inra, Ensam, & Onivins, in Cowham & Hurn, 2001), each with its own unique properties (Table 2.1) These clones range from large-clustered, heavy-producing vines that are suited to sparkling wine production to small-clustered "Burgundy" clones with dark skins that are better for table wine production.

Although the *vinifera* grape is very versatile, it is not well suited to cold or humid climates. In the eastern United States, native grape varieties such as Concord *(Vitis labrusca)* and Scuppernong *(Muscadinia rotundifolia*, also known as *Vitis rotundifolia)* are grown for winemaking. Since these species are indigenous to the east coast of North America, they evolved to thrive in the climate as well as being naturally resistant to pests of the region. In an effort to combine the hardiness of native American varieties with the flavors of European *(vinifera)* varieties, the two were crossbred to produce hybrids. Examples of these European–American hybrids are Seyval Blanc and Maréchal Foch. These native and hybrid varieties are planted throughout the eastern United States but have exotic flavors and have not found wide acceptance with most wine consumers.

In the second half of the 1800s European interest in developing new grape varieties for winemaking led to the importation of native American grapes. When native American grapevines were transported to Europe, they inadvertently brought with them several grape pests and diseases that had not been known in the Old World. Downy mildew, powdery mildew (also called oidium), black rot, and phylloxera quickly spread throughout the wine-growing regions of Europe in part because the *vinifera* grape has little natural resistance to these maladies. The root louse phylloxera was by far the most

TABLE 2.1 Some Examples of the Multiple Clones Available of Pinot Noir

Clone	Origin	Clone	Origin
Pinot Noir 01A	Sel B111, Wadenswil, Switzerland	Pinot Noir 31	Roederer, France 236
Pinot Noir 02A	Sel Bl 10/16, Wadenswil, Switzerland	Pinot Noir 32	Roederer clone, France 386
Pinot Noir 09	Jackson, CA	Pinot Noir 37	Mt. Eden, CA
Pinot Noir 13	Martini 58, CA	Pinot Noir 38	France 459
Pinot Noir 15	Martini clone 45, CA	Pinot Noir 39	France 386
Pinot Noir 16	Jackson, CA	Pinot Noir 40	France 236
Pinot Noir 18	VEN, UC Davis, GB type	Pinot Noir 44	France 113
Pinot Noir 19	VEN, UC Davis, GB type	Pinot Noir 46	France 114
Pinot Noir 22	VEN, UC Davis, GB type	Pinot Noir 47	France 114
Pinot Noir 23	Clevner Mariafeld, Switzerland	Pinot Noir 48	France 162

devastating of these, destroying nearly all the vineyards of France by 1900 (Figure 2.2). After European vineyards were infested, vines exported from France spread phylloxera to California and other parts of the world.

To combat the problem of phylloxera, viticulturists developed the technique of **grafting**. Grafting is the process of taking a cutting, or **scion** (SI-uhn), from a *vinifera* variety and affixing it to a **rootstock** that is bred from native American grapes that are phylloxera resistant (Figure 2.3). The result is a vine that has roots that are resistant to phylloxera and produces *vinifera* fruit for winemaking. This is still the

FIGURE 2.2

The root louse phylloxera feeding on a grapevine root.

Photograph courtesy Jeffrey Granett

FIGURE 2.3

A young bench-grafted grapevine showing the union between the rootstock and the scion covered with wax to protect it while the graft becomes established.

© Oregon Wine Board, Frank Barret Photography

universal method for growing grapes where the root louse is present or likely to come. There are many different rootstocks available to vineyard managers that are adapted to a variety of soil types, or that have resistance to certain pests and diseases. Which rootstock a grower selects depends on the conditions at the vineyard that is being established.

SOIL AND SITE

The most fundamental aspect of any vineyard is the ground in which it is planted, and the qualities of the soil affect the character of the wine that the vineyard produces. Grapevines are not demanding when it comes to the types of soil that they will grow in; and the vineyards of Europe were originally planted in areas where soils were not fertile enough to grow other foodstuffs. In fact, there is a belief that vineyards that are stressed by environmental conditions produce more flavorful grapes. This is illustrated by a saying they have in Bordeaux, "If these were not the best soils in the world they would be the worst." Soils that are shallow or low in nutrients put pressure on the grapevines, resulting in smaller berries and lower crop load with less vegetative growth. Here *vegetative growth* refers to the vines' production of leaves and shoots; it is not to be confused with *vegetative aroma*, a green bean/bell pepper–like aroma that is sometimes found in wines. For example, Cabernet Sauvignon with small berries has a higher skin-to-juice ratio and will produce a wine with deeper color and more tannin. If there is less vegetative growth, the grape clusters will not be as shaded by the leaves; sun exposure on Cabernet Sauvignon clusters will give them fruitier aromas and less of a vegetative aroma. Grapes grown in fertile soils can also produce high-quality fruit, but they must be managed in such a way as to permit the proper amount of sunlight and air on the grape clusters and leaves and not be overcropped.

The composition of the soil is important to the grapevine's health as well as the quality of the fruit that it produces. A number of parameters go into a soil's makeup:

- The parent material or rock that the soil is composed of
- The size of the particles the soil is made of: clay has very fine particles, silt has larger particles than clay, and sand has larger particles than silt
- The chemical composition and pH (acidity) present in the soil
- The organic matter and nutrients that are present in the soil
- The depth of the soil

Soils are characterized by the ratio of sand, silt, and clay that are present in them. Soils that have a high proportion of clay are said to be **heavy** and have a great capacity to hold water and generally contain more nutrients. Sandy soils are called **light**; they hold less water and usually are lower in nutrients. **Loam** is a mixture of clay, silt, sand, and organic matter that is fertile and drains well. Grapevines generally prefer light or rocky soils that drain well, keeping the roots from being waterlogged. Rocky soils also warm up more quickly in the spring, allowing grapes to be grown in cooler climates with shorter growing seasons. **Alluvial** soils lie in the floodplains that flank rivers and streams; they are usually a mix of silt, sand, loam, and gravel.

Grapevines need adequate, but not excessive, nutrients from their soil to sustain healthy growth. The minerals and nutrients that are present in the soil, such as nitrogen, potassium, phosphorus, and magnesium, have a limited direct effect on the flavor of the grapes unless they are present in quantities that are too low or too high to support healthy vines. If the level of a nutrient or mineral present in the soil falls below the ideal range the soil is said to be deficient; if the level is too high the soil is called toxic.

A vineyard's topography—its elevation, slope, and orientation—is as important as its soil. In the Northern Hemisphere, a vineyard on a south-facing hillside will absorb more sunlight and be warmer than its counterpart on the north side of a hill. Furthermore, hillside vineyards will have better drainage but will be more susceptible to erosion and wind damage. Cold air will settle into valleys and low-lying areas on still mornings without wind, making these locations more susceptible to spring frost and **winterkill,** the death of vine tissue from excessive cold. The Rheingau region of Germany lies at a latitude of 50° north and is at the northern limit of where grapes can be grown, yet by planting in the rocky soils of the south-facing river valleys where the vines receive full sun exposure, the grapes do not have difficulty getting ripe (Figure 2.4).

FIGURE 2.4

Vineyards grown on south-facing hillsides, such as these in Germany's Rhine River Valley, absorb more energy from the sun, allowing them to obtain full ripeness in the cool northern climate.

© www.germanwines.de, German Wine Institute

CLIMATE

A vineyard's climate can have an even greater influence on the quality of the wine it produces than its soil does. Grape varieties not only have a wide range of color and flavors, they are also suited to a diversity of climates. As an example, Pinot Noir tastes more flavorful when grown under cooler conditions, while Cabernet Sauvignon needs a slightly warmer climate to get the best results. Grapevines do best in temperate zones between 30° and 50° latitude north or south. In this zone, winters are sufficiently cold to allow the vines to drop their leaves and go dormant, but do not often get below 0°F (−18°C) and cause winterkill. Grapes also require adequate rainfall to support growth and crop development, but this can be augmented by irrigation. Vines grown in dry areas with drip irrigation have an advantage because rain and humid conditions promote mildew and rot as well as other problems. These broad weather conditions of a particular wine-growing region are defined as the **macroclimate**. Local conditions that influence the weather in a particular vineyard or portion of a vineyard are referred to as the **mesoclimate,** and the climatic conditions around a particular vine are the

TERROIR

Terroir (tehr-WAHR) is the French term to describe all of the environmental factors that nature imparts to a given vineyard. It is a common misconception that when grape growers and winemakers speak of terroir they are referring only to the soil. While the proper soil is very important to growing wine grapes, the climatic conditions of a given vineyard often have an even greater effect on the flavor of a wine that it produces. Terroir is a holistic philosophy that relates not only to the soil properties including its composition, drainage, mineral content, topography, and slope direction but also to the vineyard's climatic conditions such as rainfall, temperature, prevailing wind, and humidity.

Vintners and wine writers sometimes elevate terroir to almost magical proportions, and make comments like "a truly great Pinot Noir can only be grown in the Côte de Nuits" (Figure 2.5). The Côte de Nuits district of Burgundy does grow excellent Pinot Noir, but there are many other grape-growing regions of the world that have a terroir similar to the Côte de Nuits and that also produce excellent wines from Pinot Noir (Figure 2.6). Part of the concept of terroir is not only having the proper environmental conditions but also matching the choice of variety and vineyard management to suit the terroir. A vineyard that grows great Cabernet Sauvignon would be unlikely to produce great Chardonnay; and even if the terroir and variety are perfectly suited to each other, if the vineyard is poorly managed, the crop will be of inferior quality. In Europe, where cultivation of grapevines has been carried on for over 1,000 years, there is a great deal of tradition of which appellations are appropriate for certain varieties. These selections have been worked out by trial and error over hundreds of vintages, and in many of the best grape-growing regions the choice of variety has been codified into law. In the New World there is much less regulation, which allows more innovation and flexibility, but it also means that sometimes varieties are planted in inappropriate terroirs with less than ideal results.

microclimate. The term *microclimate*, however, is often misused in place of *mesoclimate* to describe the meteorological conditions at a given vineyard.

Grapevines are often grown in coastal areas where the ocean has a moderating influence on the climate, keeping it from getting too warm in the summer or too cold in the winter. Warm nights will increase the metabolism of malic acid in ripening grapes so inland areas that do not have the benefit of evening sea breezes will have a lower

FIGURE 2.5

Vineyards in the Burgundy region of France.
© lynnlin/Shutterstock

FIGURE 2.6

Vineyards in the Russian River Appellation of California.
© Pat Henderson

acid level than those that are grown near the coast. This is evident in California where grapes that are grown in the coastal appellations have much higher acid at harvest than those grown in the more inland Central Valley.

TECHNIQUES OF GRAPE GROWING

Vineyard managers rarely get the amount of recognition that winemakers do; however, their contribution to making good wine is every bit as important. If they are not managed properly, even the best vineyards will produce inferior grapes. Growers must always be aware of the status of their grapevines and monitor them throughout the growing season. Water stress, pests, diseases, nutrient deficiencies, and extremes of temperature can all be moderated if the grower is observant and reacts to the problem as soon as it develops. The modern viticulturist has many tools that he or she can use to influence the development of the crop and correct small problems before they get out of hand.

The most important decisions that a grape grower will make all take place before the vineyard is planted. First, the site must be chosen and prepared for planting the grapes. The soil can be tested for its composition and amendments to the soil can be tilled into the ground to get the content of mineral nutrients to the necessary level. If the vineyard site has been used to grow grapes before, grape pests and diseases may be present in the soil (Figure 2.7). There are a number of soil pests such as nematodes (a microscopic worm that can spread grapevine disease) and fungi that will grow on the roots of grapevines and diminish their productivity. These factors can be controlled by

FIGURE 2.7

This old-vine Zinfandel vineyard in the Sonoma Valley has red leaves in the fall, caused by the presence of leaf-roll virus infecting the vines. Vineyards infected with this virus will have diminished vigor and lower yield, but still can produce quality fruit.
© Pat Henderson

FIGURE 2.8

A head-trained Zinfandel vine. Head training and spur pruning was the most popular method of growing grapes in California until the 1970s when more elaborate trellis systems were introduced.
© Pat Henderson

using a rootstock that is resistant to them or by applying pesticides to the soil before planting. Growers looking for a more natural alternative to pesticides may let their land lie fallow for several years before replanting it.

After the vines are planted and begin to grow, there are a number of options for trellising the vines. Young grapevines cannot support themselves and if left on their own will grow spread out along the ground, or in the wild will grow using nearby trees for support. Both of these options are impractical, so growers use an artificial support called a **trellis**. There are many different types of trellis systems from the simple to the complex, and they are used according to varying viticultural situations (Figure 2.8). High-vigor vines with lots of vegetative growth will benefit from a complex trellis that spreads out the shoots and canes in an orderly fashion, providing a maximum of sun exposure to the leaves and adequate ventilation to the grape clusters (Figure 2.9). The proper amount of sunlight will improve the flavor of the grapes and ample ventilation helps prevent mildew and rot. A low-vigor vine will not have an enough growth to fill a large trellis so a simpler system is more appropriate.

Grapevines can be thought of as a type of solar collector that uses water, carbon dioxide, and sunlight to produce sugar for the ripening grapes. The more efficiently the leaves collect the sunlight, the more easily they will ripen the fruit. A vineyard's vigor is also directly related to its yield. While nonirrigated Chardonnay, planted in a cool area with poor soils, may be able to produce only 2 tons per acre, the same vines planted in a warm area with deep fertile soils and plenty of irrigation may produce more than

FIGURE 2.9

A Sauvignon Blanc vineyard trained in a two-curtain trellis called a U-system. How light penetrates the divided canopy is evidenced by the double shadow cast by the row of vines on the right side.

© Pat Henderson

10 tons per acre. It is worth noting that in many countries, particularly in Europe, yields are expressed in terms of the quantity of wine the vineyard produces per hectare, or hectoliters/hectare (hl/ha). Although the amount varies depending on the variety and how the grapes are processed, 1 ton of grapes yields approximately 175 gallons (662 liters or 6.62 hectoliters) of wine, so 1 ton per acre is roughly equivalent to 16 hectoliters per hectare.

THE GROWING SEASON

Grapevines are deciduous, meaning that they lose their leaves in the fall and go dormant during the winter months (Figure 2.10). In the fall when the vine is going dormant, the shoots harden and become woody in texture; and with the leaves gone there is no green tissue on the vine, so photosynthesis does not take place. Because there is no green tissue on the vine, it is more tolerant of cold temperatures than at other times of the year. This dormancy creates an annual cycle of the growing season that begins in the spring and ends in the fall after harvest.

Budbreak

The growing season begins in the early spring—usually between February and April in the Northern Hemisphere depending on latitude. In the Southern Hemisphere the beginning of the growing season occurs six months later, in August to October. When the average temperature reaches 50°F (10°C), the vines end their winter dormancy and the buds formed during the previous year's growing season begin to swell. High soil

FIGURE 2.10

A vineyard of dormant head-trained, spur-pruned vines in the winter.

Photo Courtesy Jennifer Burns

moisture will keep the root zone cool, so in a wet year budbreak will be delayed more than in a dry year. Soon tender green shoots sprout from the buds and begin to grow quickly (Figure 2.11). At this point, the new shoots are very delicate and sensitive to subfreezing temperatures.

Spring frosts are common in low-lying vineyards where the cold air can settle in the early morning hours. Growers pay attention to frost warnings and sleep with a temperature alarm on their nightstand to wake them when a frost is approaching. Once awakened they go to their vineyard and start large wind machines to stir up the cold layer of air along the ground and mix it with the warmer air off the surface to keep the shoots from freezing (Figure 2.12). Sometimes oil heaters are used to help raise the temperature a few degrees more. Another method is to put overhead sprinklers in the vineyard and begin watering as soon as the temperature falls close to freezing (Figure 2.13). It is counterintuitive, but as water freezes it actually liberates heat, and as long as there is constantly a new layer of ice forming on the vines they will not fall below 32°F (0°C).

Once the shoots begin to grow they are also susceptible to rot and other diseases. To control this, growers keep a close watch on their young vines and spray with sulfur or other synthetic fungicides to prevent damage. Later in the year, bunch rot can also grow on ripening fruit and lower its quality, so it is important that it be not established early in the season. Weed control is also done in the form of mowing, tilling, or herbicide application. After the shoots reach

FIGURE 2.11

A young shoot about 10 days after budbreak. As the season progresses this shoot will grow to become a cane with developing grape clusters.

© *Pat Henderson*

FIGURE 2.12

A wind machine in a Chardonnay vineyard in the Carneros region of Sonoma County. On frosty spring nights these large fans stir up cold air on the surface of the ground, mixing it with warmer upper air to keep the tender young shoots from freezing.

© Pat Henderson

FIGURE 2.13

On a frosty spring morning, the hillside vineyard in the foreground has good air drainage and therefore does not need frost protection. In the vineyards in the background located on the valley floor, overhead sprinklers are being used to protect tender shoots from freezing.

© Pat Henderson

about 18 inches (45 centimeters) in length, field workers go through the vineyard and tie the shoots to the trellis to keep them growing in the proper direction.

Bloom

Flower clusters look like miniature clusters of grapes and are located at the base of the young shoots (Figure 2.14). About eight weeks after budbreak, they begin to **bloom**. Grapes are self-pollinating and do not require the action of bees to become fertilized. Once fertilized, a grape flower will begin to develop into a berry. If a flower is not fertilized, it will drop off the cluster in a process called **shatter**. By this time, the danger of frost is usually past, but growers are still very concerned about the weather. For optimum pollination, warm, even temperatures are desired, without too much wind or wet weather. Hot weather or rain will increase the incidence of shatter and if the weather is too cold, bloom will be prolonged, making the ripening of the crop uneven. Some years it is necessary for the grower to go through the vineyard and thin the fruit clusters so there will be less cropload. This is done when flowering clusters set too heavy and the vine has more cropload than the grower thinks will ripen.

FIGURE 2.14

A grape flower cluster. After they are fertilized, these individual flowers will develop into berries, forming a cluster or bunch of grapes.
© Pat Henderson

After bloom, the shoots will continue to grow but the fruit clusters enter a lag phase and grape berries remain green and hard. If tasted at this stage they are very sour with no perceptible sugar. As the summer progresses, vineyard workers continue to spray sulfur and tie up the growing shoots as needed. In vigorous vineyards, some of the leaves that are at the base of the shoots are removed in a process called leaf pulling to allow more sunlight and air to the fruit clusters. In growing regions that do not have adequate summer rainfall, irrigation can be used to keep the vines from becoming water stressed. Grapevines have deep root systems and can survive on very little water once they are mature. Dry-farmed vineyards are known for having low yield and intensely flavored fruit. This being said, a vine that is limited by its water supply would not be able to produce as much fruit as one that is not water stressed. The key is for the grower to balance properly the water demand of the vines so they get just the right amount of water for healthy, but not excessive, vine growth.

Véraison

Véraison (vay-ray-ZON) is the beginning of ripeness and starts in mid to late summer about 8 to 10 weeks after bloom. At this time, the vines have begun to slow their vegetative growth and the shoots are approaching their maximum length. This is also the point where dramatic changes begin to take place in the fruit clusters. Up until now the berries have remained hard and green but at véraison they swell and start to change color (Figure 2.15). The sugar that the leaves are producing through photosynthesis is now going into fruit development instead of producing more leaves and shoots. Irrigation is diminished to help the fruit ripen by slowing vine growth. Spraying is also discontinued because after véraison, rot is less likely and because no residual sulfur or vineyard chemicals should remain on the grapes when they are harvested.

As grape berries begin to sweeten, they become attractive to birds. The damage caused by avian feeding on fruit can range from a mild nuisance to very severe depending on the number of birds that live in and around the vineyard. Growers often use devices such as noisemakers that use loud booms or mimic avian distress calls combined with reflective ribbons to act as a visual deterrent. Vineyards with more serious problems will cover their vines with netting to prevent birds from getting to the fruit, as illustrated in Figure 14.7 on page 469.

Six to 10 weeks after véraison, the grapes will be ready for harvest. The amount of time depends on the variety, the weather conditions, and the degree of ripeness that the winemaker desires. Both growers and vintners keep a close watch on the vineyard, taking samples often and analyzing them for acid and sugar content. In addition to measuring the chemical parameters, the berries are tasted for flavor and observed for signs of ripeness such as the seeds and stems turning from green to brown. The decision to harvest is based on the maturity of the fruit as well as operational concerns. Sometimes crops must

FIGURE 2.15

A Zinfandel grape cluster at véraison, the beginning of ripening.
© Pat Henderson

be brought in before they are ripe to beat an approaching storm, or may become too sweet before a crew of pickers is available during hot weather. When logistics and the weather allow the vineyard to be picked at the optimum sugar and acid levels at the same time that it is at its peak of flavor, it is considered a "vintage year." *Vintage year* means an exceptionally good harvest, not to be confused with the term *vintage*, which refers to the particular year a grape crop is produced.

Harvest

In the traditional method of harvest, grapes are picked by hand into boxes or baskets that are then carried to the end of vineyard rows to be loaded into trailers or trucks for transport to the winery (Figure 2.16). This method is still popular today because it is very gentle to both the fruit and the vines. It also has the benefit of being selective because only the healthy ripe fruit is picked. In some vineyards on steep slopes or with limited access, it is the only way to bring in the crop. Because of these advantages, picking by hand is generally regarded as the best way to harvest premium wine grapes. However, as is the case with many other agricultural products, labor shortages and the high costs of hand picking are causing mechanization to play an increasingly larger role. Mechanical harvesters are designed to straddle a row of vines and shake them vigorously to dislodge their fruit (Figure 2.17). The grape clusters are collected below and

FIGURE 2.16

Pickers hand harvesting grapes in California's Napa Valley. After the boxes of fruit have been filled, the grapes are placed in bins that are loaded onto trucks to be carried to the winery.
© WineCountry.com

FIGURE 2.17

A mechanical grape harvester. These machines straddle a row of vines and shake them, dislodging the clusters of fruit, which are collected at the base of the machine. An example of a mechanical harvester in action is shown in Figure 12.4 on page 413.

© Pat Henderson

carried to a bin on the back of the harvester. Vineyards that are to be mechanically harvested must be trellised with sturdy wires and stakes to keep the machine from damaging the vines during harvest. Mechanical harvesters can also be operated at night so they will bring in cooler fruit. This is particularly an advantage with white grapes in warm climates, because the cooler the fruit is, the less it will degrade on the trip from the vineyard to the winery. Both methods have their advantages and disadvantages, and if done properly they each can provide the winery with high-quality fruit.

After picking, the grapes are weighed and brought to the winery for processing into wine. If there is mild weather after the harvest, some photosynthesis will occur and the sugar that is produced is stored in the trunk and root system of the vine for use when it comes out of dormancy the next spring. At the first frost, the leaves will turn brown and fall off the vine, marking the beginning of the winter dormancy period. At this time in the season, the shoots that grew out in the spring are mature, are woodlike in appearance, and are referred to as **canes**.

Dormancy

While the vine is dormant, no new growth occurs, and as previously stated it is much less sensitive to cold weather. However, vineyard operations do not stop in the cold weather; fertilizers and soil adjustments are made to prepare the plant for the upcoming year. A cover crop of grass or clover may be planted to control erosion. However, the most labor-intensive and important task to be completed is pruning. After a vine is established, the process of pruning removes almost all of the new growth from the previous year. Each bud left on the vine will produce a new shoot in the spring that will have one to three clusters on it, and the amount of the next season's crop is determined by the number of buds. The vineyard manager evaluates the previous year's growing season and cropload and makes adjustments to have more or less in the upcoming season.

ENVIRONMENTALLY-FRIENDLY VITICULTURE

Organic viticulture is the practice of growing grapes without the use of any human-made substances. While simple in concept, it requires a great deal of skill and concentration by the vineyard manager. In an organic vineyard, weed control is done by tilling or planting cover crops. Elemental sulfur can still be used to combat rot, but synthetic chemicals cannot be used. An organic grower must keep alert for any developing problems in the vineyard and react to them quickly because the natural alternatives are often less powerful and slower acting than synthetic pesticides. A small but increasing number of growers in both Europe and the United States are raising their grapes organically. In California, it is currently about 2 percent (California Certified Organic Farmers, 2009). Some growers do this out of a belief that it produces healthier, better tasting fruit; others grow organically out of a commitment to protect the environment. A number of organizations exist to help promote organic agriculture and certify vineyards that have not used synthetic pesticides. Excellent grapes can be grown organically, but the extra handwork required makes them more expensive to produce.

Wine grapes do well organically because they are grown for flavor and not for appearance. Blemishes and marks from insects significantly devalue a fresh fruit crop such as peaches. However, with wine grapes minor cosmetic imperfections do not matter as much since the fruit is crushed when it arrives at the winery. Some vineyards are more suitable than others for going organic, and a vineyard's terroir plays a huge part in determining if it will be a success. A vineyard located in a dry area with low humidity will have less pressure from rot and mildew as well as needing less weed control. Above all, an organic grower who is not attentive to the vineyard will have a great deal of difficulty producing high-quality fruit.

Sustainable Viticulture

More growers use a technique called **sustainable viticulture**. The primary goal of sustainable farming is to ensure that the agricultural practices in the vineyard do not degrade the fertility of land or the surrounding environment. This concept promotes agricultural practices that allow the minimal use of pesticides in the vineyard, use natural mulch, and reduce tilling to preserve the soil. This encourages the development of a natural vineyard ecosystem with predatory insects to help combat grape pests. Since the most expensive aspect of organic farming is hoeing at the base of the vine to control weed growth, in a sustainable vineyard a small amount of herbicide is often sprayed at the base of the vine. If a problem develops that the grower cannot control through natural means, he or she has the option to use synthetic chemicals. Sustainable grape growing is a popular option because it provides much of the benefits of organic farming, with less risk to the crop and at a lower cost of labor.

Biodynamic Viticulture

Biodynamic viticulture is a growing and somewhat controversial method of agriculture that is practiced throughout the world but is most popular in Europe and North America. Used for grapes as well as many other crops, its origins are in a series of lectures that the philosopher Rudolf Steiner set forth in 1924. Proposed as a way to combat the degradation of the soil and the environment caused by the standard agricultural practices of the time, the biodynamic approach sees the farm as a holistic entity that must be managed in a sustainable manner that is in harmony with the natural world. It uses many of the practices found in sustainable and organic farming, but it also incorporates spiritual and homeopathic elements.

The terms *biodynamic* and *organic* are often confused with each other and used interchangeably. Although they share many techniques, there is a distinct difference. Like organic viticulture, biodynamic practices eschew human-made pesticides and embrace sustainable techniques such as promoting natural pest control and leaving a portion of the land fallow for biodiversity. Grazing sheep can be used for natural weed control in the winter leaving their dung as fertilizer. Additionally, there are organizations around the world that certify that a particular vineyard is biodynamic in much the same way as organizations certify that a vineyard is organic. Where they differ is that biodynamic management enters the spiritual realm and involves more esoteric and unscientific practices.

In biodynamic farming, factors such as the phase of the moon and position of the planets are thought to affect vine growth and so the timing of vineyard operations is set by the astronomical cal-

(Continues)

(Continued)

endar. In place of synthetic chemicals, a number of homeopathic compounds are made for applying to the vineyard or incorporating into compost to promote the health of the vine and the quality of the fruit. For example, to promote soil fertility and plant growth a preparation is made by filling a cow horn with manure from a pregnant cow and then burying it in the ground on the autumn equinox. On the spring equinox, it is dug up and the manure is mixed in water and stirred for one hour before being applied to the soil (Waldin, 2004). Although there has been little research done to determine whether wines made from biodynamic vineyards are superior to those that are from sustainable farmed organic vineyards, it is gaining in popularity and is practiced by a number of prominent wineries. Often when biodynamic viticulture is promoted by vintners, its more unusual practices are left unmentioned.

Organic Winemaking

Organic practices can also be adopted by wineries as well as vineyards. If a wine is produced and bottled from organically grown grapes without the use of any synthetic additives in the cellar it can be called organic wine. The use of added sulfur dioxide as a preservative in organic wine is allowed in most of the world; however, in the United States its use is prohibited in organic wines. Sulfur dioxide, not to be confused with vineyard use of elemental sulfur, inhibits oxidation and the growth of microbes that can spoil wine. The lack of sulfur dioxide is most notable in white table wines; if they are bottled without it they will quickly turn darker in color and lose some of their fruity aromas. For this reason there is more wine bottled with the phrase "made from organically grown grapes" than labeled as "organic."

No matter what trellis system is used, vines are either cane pruned or spur pruned. In cane pruning, healthy canes are selected from the past season's growth and trained along wires; each bud on the cane will grow a new cane of its own in the spring (Figure 2.18). With spur pruning, the grapevine is grown with permanent arms or **cordons** that have spurs located about every 6 to 8 inches (15 to 20 centimeters) along their length. Each spur will have one to several buds on them for the next year's growth (Figure 2.19). Cane

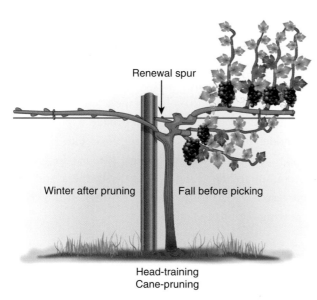

FIGURE 2.18

A dormant head-trained, cane-pruned vine. The left side depicts what the vine looks like in the wintertime after pruning. The right side displays what the vine looks like in the fall just prior to picking.
© Delmar Cengage Learning

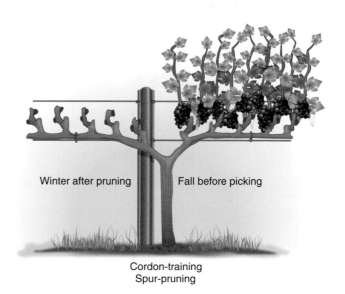

FIGURE 2.19

A dormant cordon-trained, spur-pruned vine. The left side depicts what the vine looks like in the wintertime after pruning. The right side displays what the vine looks like in the fall just prior to picking.
© Delmar Cengage Learning

pruning is more difficult to perform but it is preferred for varieties that have small clusters like Chardonnay. Cane pruning generally leaves more buds and clusters than spur pruning on cordons, and this allows grape varieties with small clusters that do not weigh very much to achieve an adequate crop.

The most important concept in pruning is balance. The vine must be left with the appropriate amount of buds to produce the correct cropload. If a vine is overcropped, having too many clusters, it will have a difficult time producing enough sugar to get the grapes ripe. Overcropping will also stress the vine, leaving it with fewer reserves stored up for the following year. Undercropping also has undesirable consequences because if there is not enough crop, the vine will put too much energy into vegetative growth, making a large canopy of leaves that are hard to manage and shade the fruit clusters. The idea of balanced pruning is to leave the maximum amount of fruit that can achieve the proper level of maturity without weakening the vine. This depends on the vine's vigor, which results from the combination of terroir, variety, rootstock, and management. Grapevines that are grown on fertile soils with good weather can support larger croploads than those grown on less fertile soils in cool climates.

MAJOR GRAPE VARIETIES

Although there are thousands of varieties of *V. vinifera* that are grown for winemaking, only a few make up the vast majority of production. Many obscure varieties are grown around the world that make excellent wine but are not well known outside of their local region. In this section we examine 21 of the most widely planted varieties.

FIGURE 2.20

Barbera.
© Pat Henderson

Barbera

Known for producing intensely colored, tart wines with moderate tannins, the vigorous Barbera (bahr-BEH-rah) grapevine is native to the Piedmont region of Italy (Figure 2.20). The grape's tendency to hold on to its acid in warm climates made it popular as a "blender" in jug wines in warm areas like Argentina and California's Central Valley. Interest in growing premium Italian varietals such as Barbera and Sangiovese have led to increased plantings in the coastal growing regions in California.

Cabernet Franc

Cabernet Franc (kah-behr-NAY frahn) is from the Bordeaux and Loire regions of France and has small berries and loose, compact clusters (Figure 2.21). Related to Cabernet Sauvignon, it ripens somewhat earlier and typically produces wines with less complexity and lighter body than its relative does. Although some wineries, particularly in the Loire, produce excellent varietal Cabernet Francs, it is most often used for blending with Cabernet Sauvignon and Merlot in a Bordeaux-style blend. Its soft qualities make it useful in toning down the sometimes harsh tannins in Cabernet Sauvignon and adding fruity character.

Cabernet Sauvignon

The classic variety of Bordeaux, Cabernet Sauvignon (kah-behr-NAY soh-vihn-YOHN) is one of the most popular varieties grown worldwide. It is a late-season ripener with loose clusters and thick-skinned berries that make it resistant to rot (Figure 2.22). It is known for its excellent color and good tannins combined with complex flavors. At its best Cabernet Sauvignon exhibits a strong cassis (black currant) aroma combined with interesting aromatic notes such as cedar, pipe tobacco, and mint. When grown in cool areas, or on vines with too much canopy so the fruit clusters are shaded, it can have a distinct vegetative or green bean character.

In 1997 researchers studying the DNA of grapevines determined that Cabernet Sauvignon is a cross between Cabernet Franc and Sauvignon Blanc (Bowers & Meredith, 1997). While wines made with 100 percent Cabernet Sauvignon often have great success, blending with other Bordeaux varieties such as Merlot, Cabernet Franc, Malbec, and Petite Verdot can make a wine that is even more balanced and complex. In the New World, Cabernet has gained wide popularity. In California it is one of the most commonly produced varieties by wineries, and there are also extensive plantings in the Southern Hemisphere. The combination of plentiful tannins and fruit flavors allows many well-made Cabernet Sauvignons to improve for up to 10 to 20 years in the bottle.

FIGURE 2.21

Cabernet Franc.
© Pat Henderson

FIGURE 2.22

Cabernet Sauvignon.
© Pat Henderson

Chardonnay

One of the best-known white varieties, Chardonnay (shahr-dohn-AY) comes from the Burgundy region of France. It budbreaks early in the spring, which makes it susceptible to frost damage, but it is a midseason ripener, allowing it to be grown in cool regions (Figure 2.23). This versatile variety can be made in a number of styles. Its aroma can be described as green apple, pear, or citrus, and depending on its production methods, it can have a body that is anywhere from crisp and tart as it is made in the Chablis region to soft and viscous as it is more commonly produced in California. When it is fermented in small oak barrels and undergoes malolactic fermentation, it takes on toasty vanilla and butter flavors. If a winemaker is not careful, it is easy for the flavor of the oak to easily overwhelm the delicate fruity aromas.

Chardonnay's popularity resulted in extensive planting in California throughout the 1980s and 1990s with great success in the cooler coastal valleys. Previously it was always grown as a premium varietal, but in the 1980s, a surplus of Chardonnay wine led to the introduction of Chardonnay as a **fighting varietal**. This category of wine also included popular varieties such as Cabernet Sauvignon and Merlot and was priced similarly to jug wines, but had a varietal identity and was packaged in a 25.4-oz (750-ml) bottle. As part of this market segment, Chardonnay also replaced many of the more neutral varieties like Chenin Blanc and French Colombard that were grown in warmer regions to produce bulk wines.

FIGURE 2.23

Chardonnay.
© David Kay/Dreamstime/Shutterstock

Chenin Blanc

Chenin Blanc (shehn-IHN BLAHN) is native to the Loire Valley of France where it is called Pineau de la Loire (Figure 2.24). It is a prodigious producer adapting well to a number of different soils and climates. For these reasons, it is popular throughout the world, although in most areas outside of France it is considered a simple grape and used for making inexpensive wines. Until the late 1980s, it was the most widely planted white grape in California with most of the vineyards located in the Central Valley. Since that time it has lost more than half of its acreage, much of it to Chardonnay for fighting varietal wines. It is very popular in South Africa where it makes up nearly a fifth of the vineyard acreage. Usually made into a clean, crisp wine with a minimum of oak aging, it can be made in either sweet or dry styles and is known for being easy to process in the wine cellar.

Gewürztraminer

Gewürztraminer (geh-VUHRT-strah-mee-nuhr) is a white grape, but unlike most other white varieties, it turns a deep russet color at ripeness instead of staying green or yellow (Figure 2.25). It has thick, bushy vines and does best in cooler growing areas; it is one of the most popular grapes grown in the Alsace district of France. Gewürztraminer is also grown in New Zealand, the northwestern United States, and the cool coastal regions of Northern California such as Mendocino's Anderson Valley. Cool growing conditions help bring out the distinct floral/spicy aroma for which the variety is famous. Gewürztraminer makes a delicious dry wine; however, it is best known for its sweeter styles including late harvest dessert wines made from clusters infected with *Botrytis cinerea* or "noble rot."

Grenache

Grenache (greh-NAH'SH) is the most popular grape in the southern Rhône Valley, where it is the mainstay of the popular Rhône blend Châteauneuf-du-Pape (Figure 2.26). It has ripe, fruity, plumlike flavors with moderate tannins—qualities that make it useful for blending with Syrah, which can be more tannic. It thrives under warm growing conditions and can support a large cropload on fertile soils. In California, it is often grown in the Central Valley where it makes

FIGURE 2.24

Chenin Blanc.

Photo Courtesy Steve Schukler

FIGURE 2.25

Gewürztraminer.

© *Pat Henderson*

FIGURE 2.26

Grenache.
© *Pat Henderson*

FIGURE 2.27

Malbec.
© *Pat Henderson*

soft, early-maturing red wines that are used mainly in generic blends. In cooler areas with a lighter crop it produces much better wine, but its acreage is limited in California's coastal valleys.

Malbec

One of the classic Bordeaux varieties, Malbec (MAHL-behk) is also grown throughout western France where it is called Côt (Figure 2.27). It is often used as a blender to add complexity and color to Cabernet Sauvignon–based blends. It makes deeply colored wines with rich tannins that have a fruity character reminiscent of plums. In recent years Malbec's acreage has been declining in Bordeaux, but the variety has been gaining in popularity in California and South America. Argentina in particular is known for its extensive plantings of Malbec, which is usually bottled as a varietal wine.

Merlot

Merlot (MEHR-loh) is from the Bordeaux region of France, where it is sometimes made into a wine by itself but more often is used as a blender with Cabernet Sauvignon

(Figure 2.28). It has similar flavors to Cabernet but with a softer mouthfeel, and it ripens earlier in the season. The latter quality makes it even more useful in cooler vintages where Cabernet may not be able to attain full ripeness. In the United States, varietal Merlot is very popular because its good flavor and lighter body make it an approachable wine for consumers who are making the move from white to red wines. Its consumer acceptance has made it one of the most widely planted grapes in California and Washington. However, in recent years Merlot's popularity has diminished somewhat; this combined with overplanting in some areas has resulted in lower grape prices.

Muscat Blanc

Also called Muscat Canelli, Muscat Blanc (MUHS-kat BLAHN) is a member of the Muscat family of grapes (Figure 2.29). There are more than 200 different varieties of Muscat with varying skin color and flavor (Robinson, 1986). They have in common a distinct "Muscat aroma" that is described as intensely fruity and floral. It can be made in a variety of styles from a light-bodied and dry table wine to a sweet dessert wine that is fortified with alcohol in the style of a white port. It can also be made into sparkling wine as in the style of Asti (previously known as Asti Spumante). Muscat does well in a diversity of conditions, with cooler areas producing the best dry styles and warmer areas making the best dessert wines.

FIGURE 2.28

Merlot.
© Pat Henderson

FIGURE 2.29

Muscat Blanc.
© Pat Henderson

Petite Sirah

Called Durif in France, Petite Sirah (puh-TEET sih-RAH) is descended from a cross between the Rhône varieties of Syrah and Peloursin (Figure 2.30). Although native to the Rhône, Petite Sirah has found a great deal of popularity in the coastal valleys and Sierra Foothills of Northern California. It makes a deeply colored, full-bodied wine with lots of fruity aromas such as raspberries and plums. While it makes an excellent varietal wine, it is often blended with other reds, particularly Zinfandel, to provide additional color and body.

Pinot Blanc

Known as Pinot Bianco (PEE-noh B'YAHN-koh) in Italy and Weissburgunder in Germany and Austria, Pinot Blanc (PEE-noh BLAHN) is a mutated clone of the grape variety Pinot Gris. It does best in cooler areas and has small, pale green clusters that have flavors similar to Chardonnay but are more delicate in nature (Figure 2.31). In Europe, it is generally used to make crisp, light-bodied wines with a minimum of oak aging. In California, a riper style is produced with more body and often more oak. In addition to its uses as a table wine, Pinot Blanc can be used along with Chardonnay and Pinot Noir in sparkling wines.

Pinot Gris/Pinot Grigio

The parent of the variety Pinot Blanc, Pinot Gris (PEE-noh GREE) itself is mutated from the red variety Pinot Noir. Although it produces a white wine, the clusters have a

FIGURE 2.30

Petite Sirah.
© Pat Henderson

FIGURE 2.31

Pinot Blanc.
© Pat Henderson

light pinkish brown color (Figure 2.32). It is widely grown in Alsace and northern Italy, where it is called Pinot Grigio (PEE-noh GREE-zjoh). Pino Gris is an early-season ripener and is popular in cool regions with short growing seasons such as Oregon. It makes a mid- to full-bodied wine with a delicate fruity aroma and is currently one of the fastest growing varieties in America in terms of consumption, due to imports as well as new plantings.

Pinot Noir

The primary grape of Burgundy, Pinot Noir (PEE-noh N'WAHR) has a reputation for producing excellent wines surpassed only by Cabernet Sauvignon (Figure 2.33). Although it makes long-aging, complex fruity wines, it has a well-deserved reputation for being both difficult to grow and troublesome in the winery. As previously mentioned, there are a large number of clones of Pinot Noir available to grape growers for both sparkling and table wine production. It is an early-ripening variety that does best when grown under cool conditions such as those found in Oregon. In California, it does well in the Carneros and Russian River appellations as well as the cooler regions of the Central Coast appellation. However, even grown under the best conditions there can be problems with obtaining good color and flavor from the fruit. It is a very delicate wine and must be treated very gently while processing at the winery so that the balance and flavor is not lost.

FIGURE 2.32

Pinot Gris.

© chiyacat/Shutterstock

FIGURE 2.33

Pinot Noir.

© Pat Henderson

Riesling

Called White Riesling or Johannisberg Riesling by some producers in the United States, Riesling (REEZ-leeng) is the most famous variety grown in Germany and is planted throughout its steep river valleys (Figure 2.34). It is similar in character to Gewürztraminer with strong floral and fruity notes but is less spicy. When it is grown in cool areas, the fruity qualities and tart acid that the grape is known for are preserved. Riesling can be made in a number of styles from a dry, tart wine that is low in alcohol to the famous German dessert wine Trockenbeerenauslese, or TBA, that is very concentrated with flavor and sugar. In the 1970s it was the most expensive grape grown in California, and usually made in a sweet style. However, it fell out of favor as the public started to drink drier wines.

Sangiovese

Sangiovese (san-JEE-yoh-VAY-say) is the classic grape of the Tuscany region of Italy, and is the major variety used in Chianti wines. The variety's thin-skinned berries leave it vulnerable to rain and high temperatures at ripeness, and depending on the clone, it can sometimes have light color (Figure 2.35). It produces tart wines with medium body and cherry flavors. Sangioveses do well on their own or blended with other red varieties such as Merlot or Cabernet Sauvignon. It is also planted in California and Australia where the climate is similar to that in Tuscany.

FIGURE 2.34

Riesling.
© Pat Henderson

FIGURE 2.35

Sangiovese.
© Pat Henderson

Sauvignon Blanc

Sauvignon Blanc (soh-vihn-YOHN BLAHN), the classic white variety of the Graves district in France, has also found acclaim in New Zealand and California. Also known as Fumé Blanc (foo-MAY BLAHN), Sauvignon Blanc grows bushy, vigorous vines that produce tight clusters of thin-skinned pale green berries (Figure 2.36). However, these thin skins and tight bunches also make it very susceptible to rot. It has a distinct varietal aroma that runs a spectrum, including vegetative, grassy, gooseberry, and melon. When grown under cool conditions, the varietal character can become very intense. Because of the vigorous nature of the vines when grown in fertile soils, it is necessary to carefully trellis the vine and practice leaf pulling to expose the clusters to the sun to get optimal flavors.

Syrah/Shiraz

From the northern Rhône Valley, Syrah (sih-RAH) produces a meaty wine with lots of tannins and good acid (Figure 2.37). It has a complex aroma that includes fruity flavors of blackberry and plum balanced out with spicy-peppery and earthy-leathery notes. The powerful tannins combined with plentiful fruit allow Syrah wines to age for a very long time. In the southern Rhône, it is often blended with other Rhône varieties such

FIGURE 2.36

Sauvignon Blanc.
© Pat Henderson

FIGURE 2.37

Syrah.
© Pat Henderson

as Grenache and Mourvèdre to balance the tannins and add more complexity. It has great popularity in Australia where it is called Shiraz (shee-RAZ); this name is also used at some wineries in California. In the New World it is sometimes blended with Cabernet Sauvignon and generally is made in a more fruit-forward style (a wine with a predominately fruity character).

Tempranillo

The dominant grape used in Rioja, Tempranillo (tehm-prah-NEE-yoh) is also widely planted throughout the rest of Spain as well as being popular in Argentina. It has vigorous vines that ripen early in the season and produce thick-skinned berries (Figure 2.38). It makes an intense wine with excellent color and tannins, and its aroma typically has notes of strawberries and plums with earthy overtones. It is also grown in Portugal where it is known as Tinta Roriz.

Viognier

Viognier (vee-yoh-N'YAY), a distinctive white grape from the Rhône region, is difficult to grow and has low-yielding vines (Figure 2.39). It makes a relatively low-acid wine with very intense tropical and floral fragrances. Sometimes other varieties such as Chardonnay are blended with it to add structure to its body and tone down its strong aromas. It is becoming increasingly popular in California, but is still not widely planted.

Zinfandel

Like all *vinifera* grapes, Zinfandel (ZIHN-fahn-dehl) is native to Europe; however, it is best known in its adopted home of California where it is widely planted throughout

FIGURE 2.38

Tempranillo.
© Jonas Backman/iStockphoto

FIGURE 2.39

Viognier.
© Pat Henderson

FIGURE 2.40

Zinfandel.
© Pat Henderson

the state. For years it was not known what country Zinfandel came from or what its original name was. This lack of a provenance was cause for a great deal of speculation. It was noticed in the 1970s that it was similar to the variety Primitivo that is grown in southern Italy. Its exact origins remained uncertain until recent DNA analysis determined that Zinfandel and Primitivo are indeed the same variety and native to Croatia where it is called Crljenak Kastelanski (tsurl-yen-ahk kahstel-AHN-ski) (Smith, 2002). Not surprisingly, it did not keep its Croatian name and became known as Zinfandel when it was brought to the New World. Zinfandel has large, tight, thin-skinned clusters that have a tendency to become overripe in hot weather, which can result in a high alcohol wine that has a "raisiny" character (Figure 2.40). It makes a full-bodied wine with blackberry and pepper flavors and light tannins.

Zinfandel is also made into a rosé-style wine called White Zinfandel or White Zin. Although the term *white* is a bit of a misnomer because of the pink color of the wine, it is descriptive of how the wine is made. Grapes for White Zinfandel are usually picked at a lower sugar level than those that are used to make red Zinfandel, and after they arrive at the winery they are processed like a white wine, being fermented at a cool temperature after the juice has been pressed off the skins. White Zinfandels are almost always bottled with some residual sugar, and the wine has been popular with novice wine drinkers since it was first introduced in the late 1970s.

SUMMARY

Growing premium wine grapes is a collaboration between the winemaker and grower where the vintner lets the grower know what qualities are wanted in the fruit and the grower manages the vineyard in a manner that will deliver them. To ensure production of the best wine grapes, the grower should be rewarded with higher prices for producing the best fruit and paid less for fruit of lower quality. Market conditions in the wine business also affect prices where popular varieties in high demand are worth more than varieties that have fallen out of favor with consumers. The best grapes are usually produced from vineyards that have a long and mutually beneficial relationship with the winery. In these situations, a trust between the grower and the winemaker develops and the grower knows exactly what kind of fruit the winemaker wants.

EXERCISES

1. What attributes of grapes make them the ideal fruit for wine production?

2. What species of grape is used for most wine production and where did it originate?

3. Explain the relationship among grape species, variety, and clone.

4. What are the reasons that grape growers prune their grapevines?

5. Outline the stages of the annual growing cycle of a grapevine.

REVIEW QUESTIONS

1. What is the beginning of ripening called?
   A. Véraison
   B. Budbreak
   C. Alluvial
   D. Scion

(Continues)

(Continued)

2. Vineyards located on hillsides are less likely to experience
   _____ than vineyards located on the valley floor.
   A. Erosion
   B. Shatter
   C. Spring frost
   D. Nematodes

3. The concept that refers to all of the environmental conditions that
   influence a vineyard is called _____.
   A. Macroclimate
   B. Biodynamic
   C. Ecosphere
   D. Terroir

4. Which of the following is a descendent of Pinot Noir?
   A. Pinot Chardonnay
   B. Pinot Gris
   C. Sauvignon Blanc
   D. Cabernet Sauvignon

5. In organic vineyards, growers are not able to use _____.
   A. Elemental sulfur
   B. Human-made compounds
   C. Mechanized farm equipment
   D. Trellis systems

REFERENCES

Bowers, J. E., & Meredith, C. P. (1997, May). The parentage of a classic wine grape, Cabernet Sauvignon. *Nature Genetics, 16*(1), 84–87.

California Certified Organic Farmers. (2009, October). *Statistics at a glance.* Santa Cruz, CA: Author.

Cowham, S., & Hurn, A. (2001, April). French Pinot Noir clones—an Australian perspective. *The Australian Grapegrower & Winemaker, 447,* 93–95.

Robinson, J. (1986). *Vines, grapes and wines.* New York: Knopf.

Smith, R. (2002, July 24). *Zin puzzle solved, says researcher.* Santa Rosa, CA: Press Democrat.

Waldin, M. (2004). *Biodynamic wines.* London: Octopus.

{ THE WINERY – FROM GRAPES TO BOTTLE }

This chapter discusses winemaking practices and how grape juice becomes wine. It explains the fermentation and aging of wines, and describes red and white wine production techniques. Also covered in this chapter is how sparkling, dessert, and fortified wines are made.

INTRODUCTION

Great wines begin in the vineyard, but they are finished at the winery. Much like a chef preparing a fine meal, the vintner, or winemaker, takes the produce of farmers and converts it into a beverage that is both nourishing and delicious. Similar to a chef, the winemaker works with flavors and aromas to create a wine that will give the consumer the maximum amount of sensory pleasure. To the untrained observer the choices and decisions the winemaker makes may appear arbitrary in nature, but in reality they are based on a scientific understanding of the ingredients and techniques used to produce wine. In this way, winemaking is a craft that is a combination of art and science. Complicating the winemaker's quest to create great wine is the fact that people have different tastes and preferences, and there is no one "ideal" style of wine. This, of course, is why there are so many different types of wines in various styles. It is also what makes wine such a diverse and interesting subject of study.

As mentioned in the previous chapter, wine is merely grape juice that has been fermented by yeast. Although this definition is quite simple, in the more than 6,000-year history of winemaking, wine production has evolved into a number of complex procedures that produce a wide variety of wines. In the United States the term **table wine** is used to describe a wine designed to accompany food. It is produced in numerous forms, from both red and white grapes, and is the most common type of wine consumed in the United States, making up over 90 percent of the market (Beverage Information Group, 2008). A table wine is a **still wine** (a wine without effervescence) and is a relatively **dry wine** (without sweetness) that has a moderate alcohol content typically about 9 to 15 percent.

In Europe *table wine* has a slightly different meaning. Instead of making a statement about style, the term *table* is used to designate an inexpensive, lower-quality wine. For regulatory purposes the U.S. government has yet another definition of what a "table wine" is, and defines it as a wine that has between 7 and 14 percent alcohol. This is an arbitrary range that was chosen by the U.S. government for reasons of tax collection; wines with higher alcohol content are taxed at a higher rate. The exact alcohol content has little to do with the definition of a table wine being a wine made to complement food, and there are many table-style wines that are bottled at over 14 percent alcohol. Some table wines are also made with a small amount of residual sugar in an "off-dry" style.

TABLE 3.1 Major Types of Wine

Grape Wine	Table	Red
		Rosé
		White
	Sparkling	Méthode champenoise
		Charmat process
	Dessert & Fortified	Late harvest
		Port style wines
		Sherry style wines
	Flavored	Vermouth

The Process of Fermentation

Fermentation is the process of yeast (unicellular or one-celled fungi) (Figure 3.1) converting the sugar in grape juice to alcohol and carbon dioxide, releasing some heat during the process. Yeast ferments sugar to produce energy to sustain life and reproduce. Other microorganisms can do this, but yeast ferment with the most efficiency and can survive in the higher alcohol at the end of fermentation. The species of yeast that is best suited for winemaking is called ***Saccharomyces cerevisiae*** (sack-a-roe-MY-seas sair-a-VIS-e-eye). The name *Saccharomyces* is derived from the Latin "sugar fungus," while cerevisiae refers to grain. This is not surprising because the most common use of *S. cerevisiae* is in bread making. When yeast are added to bread dough, they begin to ferment producing bubbles of carbon dioxide that cause the loaf to rise. Alcohol is also produced during bread making but it is baked off while the loaf is in the oven. This is what gives freshly baked bread its distinctive smell. While the yeast used for winemaking and bread making is the same species, different strains are used that are adapted for their individual roles.

To achieve the desired alcohol content for a table wine (9 to 15 percent), grapes are picked between 16 and 25 **degrees Brix (°Brix)**—the percentage of sugar by weight, also called Balling. Degrees Brix is the most common way to measure sugar content in North America; however, in Europe as well as some parts of the New World, the Baumé (bo-MAY) is more common. Baumé measures sugar content on a different scale than Brix where 1°Brix is equal to 0.55 Baumé. Additionally, the Baumé reading at harvest will approximate the alcohol level of the wine after fermentation. For example, Chardonnay picked at 13 Baumé (23.6°Brix) will have a final alcohol of about 13 percent.

FIGURE 3.1

Microscopic image of cells of the wine yeast *Saccharomyces cerevisiae.*
© Stephanie Burns

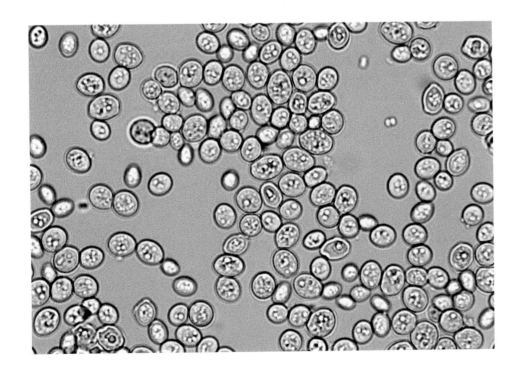

FIGURE 3.2

Stainless steel wine tanks in a fermentation cellar.
© Pat Henderson

Although this formula looks simple, it is actually a biochemical pathway with 12 separate reactions that are controlled by different enzymes in the yeast (Figure 3.2). The rate of fermentation is affected by a number of factors, including:

- **Temperature.** The warmer the juice, the faster it will ferment; however, at temperatures above 100°F (38°C) yeast will die off.
- **Acidity.** The higher the concentration of acid (lower the pH), the slower the rate of fermentation.
- **Nutrients.** If the juice is low in nutrients, such as vitamins and nitrogen, the yeast may not be able to ferment to dryness.
- **Alcohol.** At higher alcohol concentrations, 13 to 16 percent depending on strain, yeast begin to die.
- **Sugar.** Although sugar is required for yeast growth, if the sugar concentration is greater than 30 percent, it starts to inhibit yeast growth.

Alcoholic Fermentation

$$C_6H_{12}O_6 \rightarrow 2\,C_2H_5OH + 2\,CO_2 + Energy$$

(Sugar)   Alcohol   Carbon Dioxide

FIGURE 3.3

The chemical equation for alcoholic fermentation in which one molecule of sugar is converted to two molecules each of ethanol (wine alcohol) and carbon dioxide. By-products of this fermentation include heat and energy for the yeast cell.

Winemakers use these factors to control the fermentation and make different styles of wine. As an example, Port-style wine is made by adding brandy to fermenting wine to kill the yeast before it can ferment to dryness. This way a stable, sweet wine can be bottled without further risk of fermentation (Figure 3.3).

A stuck fermentation is when the yeast begin to die off before all of the sugar is converted to alcohol. This can be due to inadequate nutrients, excessive temperature, or, if the grapes were picked at high sugar, high alcohol at the end of fermentation. This can pose a problem for winemakers because it is difficult to restart the fermentation with new yeast and the leftover sugar can encourage the growth of spoilage microbes during aging. Sometimes if the winemaker wishes to make a slightly sweet off-dry style of wine, he or she will stop the fermentation by chilling the tank or filtering out the yeast so a small amount of residual sugar is left in the wine.

Wine was made for thousands of years before anyone knew how fermentation worked or that there were such things as microscopic organisms called yeast. The conversion of grape juice into wine was considered a miracle of nature. Although early winemakers did not understand the mechanism, they knew how to use the process of fermentation to create good wine. There are still a few wineries that use this method of fermentation with natural or "wild" yeast to make wine. The winemakers at these wineries feel this method can give their wine more complexity, but there also is a higher risk of off-flavors or an incomplete fermentation. Fermentation by wild yeast is often employed by winemakers who use organic grapes in an effort to make a more natural product. Today, most winemakers use commercially available strains of yeast that have been isolated from different wineries and manufactured for sale. These yeasts are usually sold in an "active dry" form that has a similar appearance to baker's yeast, and they give the winemaker a clean, efficient fermentation with no off-aromas.

Red Wine Crush and Fermentation

The harvest is the busiest time of year at the winery because the grapes must be harvested and processed as soon as they reach their peak of ripeness. As discussed in the previous chapter, the vintner is looking for grapes that have the optimum balance of acid and sugar as well as excellent flavor. The weather conditions set the pace of harvest and it is not uncommon for winery workers to be on the job 12 hours a day for 7 days a week when the harvest is at its busiest. Once the grower and the winemaker have determined that the grapes have reached their optimum ripeness and flavor, they are picked and brought to the winery. When the crop arrives at the winery it is weighed, inspected, and analyzed before being processed (Figure 3.4). If the grapes are being purchased and are not grown on the winery's estate, the results of inspection are very important. This is because grape contracts between growers and vintners often include bonuses and penalties that depend on the analysis at harvest and the overall quality of the fruit. Particularly at larger wineries, this inspection and analysis is performed by an independent third party to avoid conflicts of interest.

After the grapes are weighed and inspected, they are brought to the receiving hopper and unloaded. At the bottom of the hopper, there is either a screw or a belt conveyor that is used to transport the fruit to the stemmer-crusher. Some wineries use sorting tables as the fruit leaves the hopper to examine the fruit and cull out clusters that are underripe or have rot. The stemmer-crusher has two functions: first it takes the berries off the stems, and second it breaks open the berries to release the juice.

FIGURE 3.4

Flowchart of operations in making red wine.

© 2012 Delmar Cengage Learning

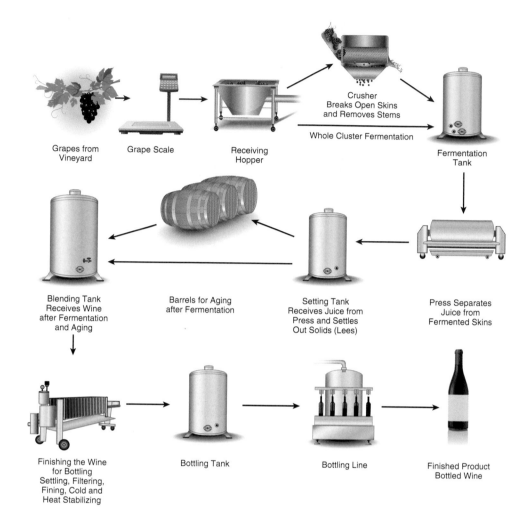

Grapes from Vineyard

Grape Scale

Receiving Hopper

Crusher
Breaks Open Skins
and Removes Stems

Whole Cluster Fermentation

Fermentation Tank

Blending Tank
Receives Wine
after Fermentation
and Aging

Barrels for Aging
after Fermentation

Setting Tank
Receives Juice from
Press and Settles
Out Solids (Lees)

Press Separates
Juice from
Fermented Skins

Finishing the Wine
for Bottling
Settling, Filtering,
Fining, Cold and
Heat Stabilizing

Bottling Tank

Bottling Line

Finished Product
Bottled Wine

Stemmer-crushers (Figure 3.5) are made up of a perforated stainless steel cylinder or drum that is 1 to 4 feet (0.3 to 1.2 meters) across. The perforations are holes that are large enough to let the individual grapes through, but not whole clusters or stems. Inside the cage is a set of bars that are arranged in a helix pattern. When the crusher is started, the bars begin to rotate at several hundred revolutions per minute (rpm), while the cage rotates at a much slower rate. The clusters of grapes enter through the back of the cage and, when they come in contact with the bars, the berries are knocked loose and fall through the holes in the cage. The stems, once they have lost their grapes, are pushed out the front of the machine by the helix pattern of the bars (Figure 3.6).

After the berries are destemmed, they fall to the second part of the machine—the crusher. The crusher is a set of rollers designed to break open the berries and release the juice. In modern crushers, the gap between the rollers can be adjusted to provide a greater or lesser degree of crushing. On some models, the rollers can be removed entirely to allow whole berries to pass through and destem the berries without crushing. The mixture of approximately 80 percent juice, 16 percent skins, and 4 percent seeds produced by the crusher is called **must**. At this point, the must is liquid enough to be pumped to a tank for fermentation.

FIGURE 3.5

A grape stemmer-crusher
with side panels removed to
show the perforated stainless steel drum and bars.

© Pat Henderson

In modern wineries fermentation tanks are most often made of stainless steel (Figure 3.7), although vats made of wood, concrete, or plastic are also used. The tank is filled to three-quarters capacity to allow room for expansion during fermentation and the must is analyzed and adjusted, if necessary. Usually, with the exception of the preservative sulfur dioxide, the compounds that are added to adjust the must, such as sugar, acid, nutrients, and yeast, are natural and already present in the must to some degree.

FIGURE 3.6

Diagram of a grape stemmer-
crusher.

*© 2012 Delmar Cengage
Learning*

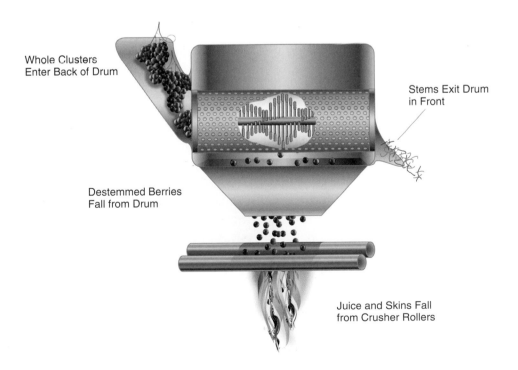

Whole Clusters
Enter Back of Drum

Stems Exit Drum
in Front

Destemmed Berries
Fall from Drum

Juice and Skins Fall
from Crusher Rollers

Top Manway

Double Layer
Cooling Jacket

Racking Valve

Racking Door

Bottom Door

Bottom Valve

FIGURE 3.7

Diagram of a stainless steel fermentation tank showing doors, or man ways, for access to the inside of the tank, valves for the transfer of wine into and out of the tank, and a cooling jacket, a section of double-walled stainless steel that cooling fluid is circulated through to maintain temperature during fermentation.

© 2012 Delmar Cengage Learning

Additives to wine are regulated and vary from region to region. For example, it is legal to add sugar to must in France but not acid, while in California the opposite is true. This is not a hindrance, however, because grapes grown in California seldom need additional sugar and French musts seldom require additional acid.

Sulfur dioxide, also called sulfites, is the most commonly used additive in wine. It is the combination of the element sulfur with oxygen and has the chemical formula SO_2. Sulfur dioxide was first used by the Romans, who noticed if you burned a small amount of sulfur in an empty wine barrel it would prevent the barrel from a taking on a vinegar smell. Sulfur dioxide is added to wine either before or after fermentation and has several important roles: It prevents enzymatic degradation of the juice, it acts as an antioxidant to preserve fresh fruit flavors, and it has antimicrobial properties that prevent spoilage. While sulfur dioxide kills spoilage yeast, wine yeast such as *S. cerevisiae* are resistant to sulfites at the levels typically found in wine of 25 to 75 parts per million (ppm). In fact, yeast produce several ppm of sulfur dioxide during fermentation so even wines that do not have any added SO_2 will have a trace amount present.

When the yeast is first added the must is homogeneous, having a uniform composition throughout the tank; however, once fermentation begins, the carbon dioxide that evolves causes the skins to float to the top of the tank and form a **cap** (Figure 3.8). In large tanks, the cap is several feet thick and very firm. After it is crushed, the juice from most red wine varieties is clear; therefore, to produce a red wine it is necessary to extract the red color out of the skins. If the skins are in a cap that is floating above the

FIGURE 3.8

At the beginning of fermentation the must is homogeneous and the skins and juice are distributed evenly throughout the tank. When fermentation begins, the carbon dioxide gas that is produced causes the skins to separate from the juice and float to the top of the tank forming a cap of skins.

© 2012 Delmar Cengage Learning

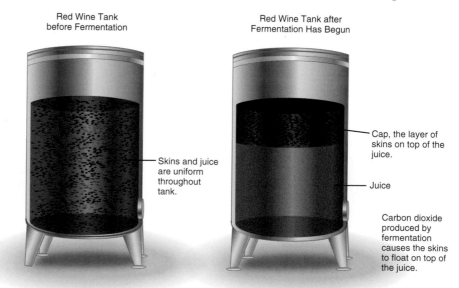

Red Wine Tank
before Fermentation

Red Wine Tank after
Fermentation Has Begun

Cap, the layer of skins on top of the juice.

Skins and juice are uniform throughout tank.

Juice

Carbon dioxide produced by fermentation causes the skins to float on top of the juice.

juice, very little extraction will take place. To combat this, the cap is mixed into the juice several times a day. There are many ways to do this, and the manner and frequency in which it is done have a major effect on the overall style of the wine being made. If a cap is mixed in vigorously and frequently, the result will be a wine with more color, body, and astringency than one with a more gentle treatment.

To increase the extraction of color and tannins from the skins, winemakers sometimes employ either a cold soak or saignée before fermentation. A cold soak is when the must is chilled after crushing and allowed to soak on the skins for several days before it is warmed and yeast is added and fermentation starts. This is a popular technique particularly with Pinot Noir. Saignée (SEN-yay) is a French term that refers to the "bleeding" or draining a portion of the juice, usually about 10 percent, prior to fermentation. This increases the ratio of skins to juice resulting in a more full-bodied and deeply colored wine. The juice that is taken off the skins has a light pink color and can be used to make a rosé wine.

Methods of Cap Management

Punching down (Figure 3.9) is the oldest, simplest, and gentlest method of mixing the cap of skins and the juice. A punch-down device is used to press down the cap into the juice. Done by hand, it works well on smaller tanks with an open top. In larger tanks, pneumatically powered plungers are used.

Pumping over (Figure 3.10) is the method by which the juice is taken from beneath the cap and irrigated over its top. As the juice percolates through the skins it

FIGURE 3.9

Breaking up the cap by hand or punching down.
© 2012 Delmar Cengage Learning

FIGURE 3.10

Pumping over or irrigating the cap.
© 2012 Delmar Cengage Learning

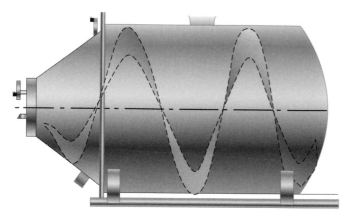

FIGURE 3.11

A rotary fermentation tank for red wines. The dotted lines show the location of the helix-shaped stainless steel vane that mixes the cap and must during fermentation. The vane also removes the skins after fermentation is complete and the wine has been drained off.

© 2012 Delmar Cengage Learning

extracts the color and flavor, similar to the way a drip coffeemaker uses hot water to extract flavor from ground coffee.

Rotary fermenters (Figure 3.11) are the most modern and least labor-intensive way of dealing with the cap. They are large horizontal tanks that have fins along the inside, similar to a cement mixer, and when they are rotated, the cap is rolled over into the juice. The main advantage of rotary fermenters is that they make it very easy to extract the skins from the tank after fermentation by opening the door at the end of the tank and rotating it. The disadvantage is their high cost.

From the time the yeast is added, the fermentation usually takes about one to three weeks. This depends on several factors: the amount and type of yeast added, the nutrients in the must, and the temperature. Most red wine fermentations will peak at about 80 to 85°F (26.6 to 30°C); at this temperature there is good color extraction without the yeast becoming too hot. When the yeast has fermented all of the sugar in the must to alcohol or, in the case of sweet wines, as much sugar as the winemaker wants to be fermented, then the must is considered wine. At this point, the juice is drained off the skins and the skins are removed from the tank for pressing.

CARBONIC MACERATION AND EXTENDED MACERATION

In red wine production, the most important stylistic decision a winemaker has to make is the manner in which the skins are handled during fermentation. How this is done will determine most of the flavor components in the finished wine. There are many ways to influence extraction from the skins beyond how the cap is punched down or pumped over. Two of the most common procedures are carbonic maceration and extended maceration.

Carbonic maceration (kar-BAHN-ihk mas-uh-RAY-shun) is the process whereby either a portion or all of the grapes are not crushed but loaded into the tank as whole clusters. The weight of the fruit crushes some of the berries at the bottom of the tank and releases juice. A small amount of fermenting must is added to begin fermentation and to fill the tank with carbon dioxide. As the fermentation in the juice progresses, it also begins to take place within the cells of the intact grape berries. This intercellular fermentation produces soft tannins and a unique strawberry or bubble-gum aroma. This technique works well with both Pinot Noir and Gamay and is the trademark characteristic of Beaujolais Nouveau (boh-zjuh-LAY noo-VOH).

Another method of production, extended maceration, is more suited to big-bodied red wines such as Cabernet Sauvignon. With this technique the fruit is crushed and fermented with typical cap management; at the end of fermentation, however, the must is not pressed. Instead, the tank is topped off (filled to the brim) with a similar wine from another tank, and the skins are left in contact with the young wine for one to eight weeks. At first, the young wine becomes more bitter and astringent from the increased skin contact, but after several weeks, the tannins begin to polymerize. This is the process whereby small, harsh tannins join together and become so large that they are no longer soluble and begin to drop out, leaving the finished wine softer and more drinkable.

FIGURE 3.12

Removing skins from a tank into a portable must pump that transfers the fermented must to the press for separation of the juice from the skins.

© Pat Henderson

Pressing the Skins

In red wines, when fermentation is complete and the winemaker is satisfied with the flavor extraction, it is time to separate the wine from the skins. The majority of the wine is simply drained out of the tank by gravity. The remaining wine, 10 to 20 percent, is held within the skins still inside of the tank. The skins are then removed and loaded into a press, which squeezes out their remaining liquid. The removal of the skins from the fermentation tank is one of the most labor-intensive aspects of winemaking (Figure 3.12). Great care must be taken when entering a tank that has just finished fermentation due to the danger of asphyxiation from the residual carbon dioxide. Before the tank can be entered, it must be properly ventilated and its atmosphere tested to make sure it is safe.

There are a number of types of presses, but they all work in the same manner. Force is applied to a layer of skins against a screened or slatted surface that allows the juice or wine to drip through, but holds back the skins and seeds. After pressing, the compressed layer of skins is called a cake. To extract the maximum amount of liquid from the skins it is necessary to break up the cake and re-press it a number of times at progressively higher pressures. The first wine to come off is usually combined with that which was dejuiced from the tank and is called the **free run**. As the cycles of pressing continue, the quality of the juice diminishes and becomes more astringent and bitter. Often, the wine that is removed at the end of the press cycles is kept separate from the free run and is called the **press fraction**. The young wine is then collected in a sump at the base of the press before being pumped into a receiving tank. After the skins dry they are called **pomace** (PAH-muss) or marc (MAHR) (the French term for "pomace"), and are removed from the press and used for compost in the vineyard.

The basket press is the oldest and simplest design (Figure 3.13). It is a vertical cylinder made of a stainless steel screen, or more traditionally, by slats of wood arranged with small gaps in between. The fruit is loaded into the top and a plate is pushed down by mechanical means, which causes the juice to drip out through the openings on its side. Basket presses are gentle but require the cake to be broken up by hand in-between press cycles. More modern basket presses are made of fiberglass and mounted horizontally; the cake can then be both broken up and unloaded by simply rotating the press.

Another type of press uses air pressure, or pneumatics, to squeeze the juice out of the skins. There are a number of designs for pneumatic presses; one of the most common is the tank press. Tank presses, also referred to as membrane presses, are cylindrical steel tanks that are 3 to 8 feet (1 to 2.4 meters) in diameter and are mounted horizontally.

FIGURE 3.13

Diagram of a basket press.
© 2012 Delmar Cengage Learning

On one side of the interior there is an inflatable bag or membrane, and on the other side is a series of perforated screens or channels. Once the press is loaded with grapes and the door is closed, it rotates so that the screens are down and the bag is above. The bag then inflates, squeezing the skins against the screens and removing the juice (Figure 3.14). There is less chance for contamination or oxidation with tank presses because they extract the juice inside the press. Their efficiency and gentleness toward the grapes make them the workhorses of most modern wineries. Yield after fermentation is typically about 170 to 180 gallons of wine per ton (700 to 740 liters per metric ton) of grapes.

After pressing, the wine is pumped to a tank in the winery cellar for storage. At this point the new wine is very turbid and full of suspended solids that are primarily yeast cells and particles of grape skins and pulp. After several days, the suspended solids begin to settle to the bottom of the tank, forming a layer of thick, mudlike material or dregs called **lees** (LEEZ). After a week or two, the clean wine is decanted off the layer of lees in a process called **racking**. This process of settling and racking can be done once, or repeated several times, to clarify the wine before it is transferred to the aging cellar and placed into barrels.

Rosé (Pink) Wines

You can think of rosé wines as being kind of a hybrid between red and white wine. They are made in a number of styles that have a great range of both color and sweetness. Rosés are made from red grapes but are pressed before fermentation occurs so the juice does not pick up too much color from the skins. Sometimes the grapes are loaded directly into the press and the juice is a very light pink or "blush" in color; if the fruit is crushed and then soaked on the skins for a few days the resulting wine will take on a much more intense red hue. After the juice is removed from the skins the wine is fermented and processed in much the same manner as a white wine, giving the resulting product a light body and a fruity character. For many years, the rosé wine market was dominated by inexpensive, sweet wines that were popular with beginning wine drinkers, but recently more finely crafted dry rosés are starting to become popular.

White Wine Crush and Fermentation

It is no surprise that white wines are made from white grape varieties. However, since the juice of most red grapes is colorless it is also possible to make a white wine from red grapes, as is done with Blanc de Noir sparkling wine. Therefore, white winemaking is defined not only by the color of the grapes that are used but also by how they are processed. The major difference between white and red wines is that reds receive most

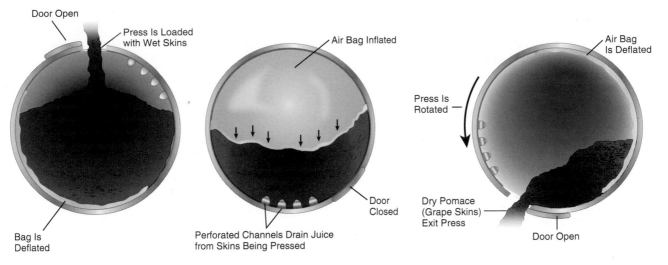

Door Open

Press Is Loaded
with Wet Skins

Bag Is
Deflated

Air Bag Inflated

Door
Closed

Perforated Channels Drain Juice
from Skins Being Pressed

Air Bag
Is Deflated

Press Is
Rotated

Dry Pomace
(Grape Skins)
Exit Press

Door Open

FIGURE 3.14

Diagram of the operation of a tank press.

© 2012 Delmar Cengage Learning

of their flavor from the skins and whites get their flavor from the juice. Therefore, in processing, the most important difference is that red wines are pressed *after* fermentation and white wines are pressed *before*. Because the flavor of white wines is not as dependent on what is extracted from the skins, the grapes are usually picked early in the morning and brought to the winery while they are still cool in order to preserve the fresh fruit flavor of the juice.

White winemaking begins in much the same way that red winemaking does: The grapes are picked, weighed, inspected, and delivered to the receiving hopper in much the same way they are for red wine production (Figure 3.15). However, because of the delicate character of white grapes and the desire to avoid excess contact between the juice and the skins, a special effort is made to handle the grapes gently and transport them quickly to the winery. Once the grapes are unloaded, red and white winemaking techniques diverge and for white wine production the juice is separated from the grape skins before fermentation. The winemaker has several options on how to accomplish this. The fruit can be (1) crushed and pressed; (2) crushed, dejuiced, and pressed; or (3) whole-cluster pressed.

In the first option, the grapes are destemmed and crushed and the must is pumped into the press for the juice to be separated. In the second option, the must is dejuiced before being loaded into the press. This is done by having a slotted screen to drain the juice inline on the way to the press. A dejuicing tank is a gentler method of draining the juice. These tanks are mounted above the press, and the must is pumped into them directly from the crusher. A screen is located on the inside of the tank and the force of gravity helps the grape juice drain through it. The third option of processing white grapes, whole-cluster pressing, is the gentlest method. The stemmer-crusher is bypassed entirely and the whole clusters are loaded directly into the press. This minimizes the amount of skin contact the juice receives, and since the grapes are not macerated by the crusher, it produces a juice with lower solids and a more delicate flavor. Whole-cluster pressing, however, is more difficult and expensive because it requires a

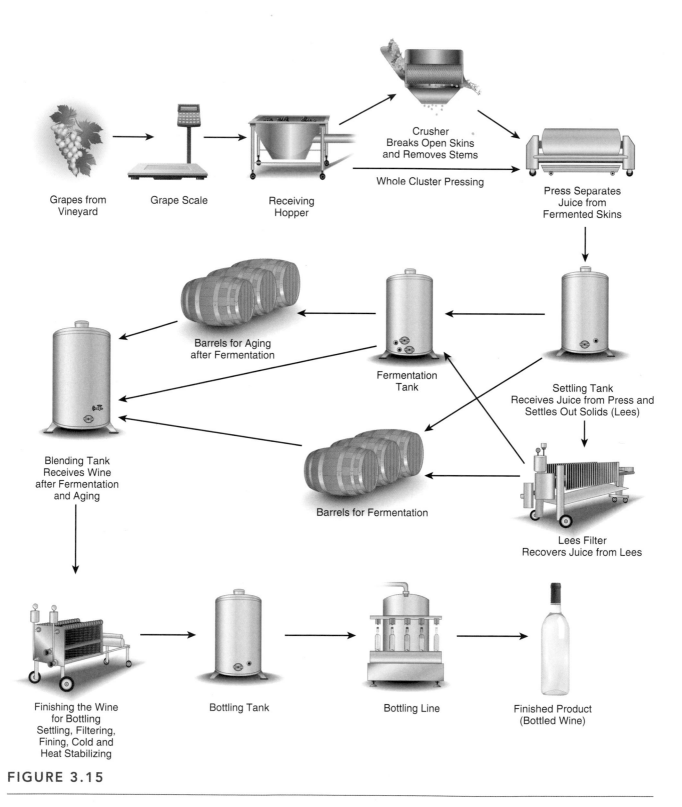

Grapes from Vineyard

Grape Scale

Receiving Hopper

Crusher
Breaks Open Skins
and Removes Stems

Whole Cluster Pressing

Press Separates
Juice from
Fermented Skins

Barrels for Aging
after Fermentation

Fermentation
Tank

Settling Tank
Receives Juice from Press and
Settles Out Solids (Lees)

Blending Tank
Receives Wine
after Fermentation
and Aging

Barrels for Fermentation

Lees Filter
Recovers Juice from Lees

Finishing the Wine
for Bottling
Settling, Filtering,
Fining, Cold and
Heat Stabilizing

Bottling Tank

Bottling Line

Finished Product
(Bottled Wine)

FIGURE 3.15

Flowchart of operations in making white wine.

© 2012 Delmar Cengage Learning

larger press and takes more time to load than crushed fruit. Additionally, whole clusters do not dejuice as readily as crushed fruit.

After pressing, the juice is pumped to a settling tank in the fermentation cellar. In white grape pressing, the difference in quality between free run and press juice is even greater than it is with red wines, so the press juice is usually kept separate from the free run. The juice is kept cool, at around 50°F (10°C), and held in the settling tank for 12 to 72 hours to allow the lees to form. The lees that form in the tank directly after pressing a white wine are called the primary or gross lees. It is necessary to separate the juice from these lees that are made up by grape solids to avoid the production of undesirable flavors during fermentation. After settling is complete, the clean juice is racked off into the fermentation tank (Figure 3.16) where yeast is added and it is adjusted with fermentation additives, if needed. Similar to red winemaking, the tank is not filled to capacity to allow room for the foam that forms during fermentation. Since there are no skins present in the fermentation tank, there is no need for punching down the cap as there is in red wines. White wine fermentations take place at a cooler temperature, 45 to 60°F (7 to 15°C), because there is no need to extract color from the skins as in red wine fermentations. The cooler temperature helps the juice retain its fruity aromas. Because it takes place at a cooler temperature, white fermentations take two to three times longer than red fermentations, about three to six weeks. After fermentation, the new wine is racked off the yeast lees into a holding tank in preparation for aging and processing.

Some white wines are transferred to barrels just as they are starting to ferment. Barrel fermentation of white wine gives it a distinctly toasty aroma and is very popular with Chardonnay. After the fermentation is finished, some of the barrels are used to top off the rest of the lot and the wine is left in contact with the yeast lees at the bottom of the barrel. This technique of aging is called **sur lie** (soor LEE), French for "on the lees," and it gives the wine more of a yeasty, freshly baked bread aroma and more viscosity. It should be noted that postfermentation lees are made up primarily of dead

FIGURE 3.16

Diagram of racking a tank of clean wine off the lees that have settled to the bottom of the tank.

© 2012 Delmar Cengage Learning

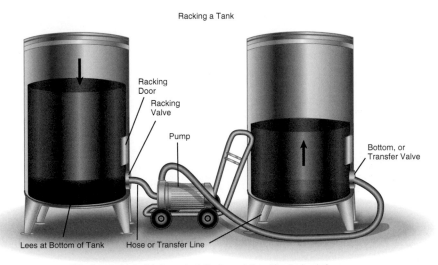

Racking a Tank

Racking Door

Racking Valve

Pump

Bottom, or Transfer Valve

Lees at Bottom of Tank

Hose or Transfer Line

Side view of wine tank being racked after fermentation. After the level of wine in the tank being emptied comes to the level of the racking valve, the racking door can be opened and the hose can be placed through the door to suction off the remaining wine on the top of the lees.

MALOLACTIC FERMENTATION

In addition to being very sweet, grape juice is also quite tart. This natural acidity primarily comes from the presence of two types of acid: tartaric and malic. Malic acid is found in many fruits, whereas tartaric acid is unique to grapes (Yair, 1997). A group of microorganisms, called **malolactic bacteria** (ma-loh-LAK-tihk) that can use malic acid as an energy source for growth. They do this by converting malic acid in wine or grape juice into lactic acid, the type of acid found in milk (Figure 3.17). Malolactic fermentation usually takes place after the primary fermentation, or alcoholic fermentation, and occurs at a much slower pace. Often malolactic fermentation takes place in barrels, sometimes not completing until the spring following the harvest.

Malolactic fermentation has several effects on the wine, the primary effect being deacidification. Since malic acid is stronger than lactic acid, a wine will taste less tart and have a higher pH (lower acidity) after malolactic fermentation. Malolactic fermentation also makes wine more microbiologically stable. If malolactic fermentation finishes during aging, it will not be able to spoil the wine by taking place after the wine is bottled and the wine will not have to be filtered as tightly as a nonmalolactic wine.

Finally, malolactic fermentation produces a compound called diacetyl that has a distinct buttery character. The presence of diacetyl is more noticeable in white wines than reds; Chardonnays often go through malolactic fermentation to get this aroma. Winemakers can encourage malolactic fermentation by adding cultures of the bacteria after primary fermentation or by placing the wine into barrels that have previously been used for wines undergoing malolactic fermentation. Malolactic fermentation is usually encouraged in red wines for reasons of stability, and because it is difficult to prevent it from spontaneously occurring during the long barrel-aging process. With white wines, it is a stylistic concern; in a light-bodied, fruity wine like Riesling, it is usually avoided, while in a rich, oak-aged Chardonnay it would be more appropriate. Malolactic bacteria are much more sensitive to sulfur dioxide than wine yeast are and winemakers should avoid adding too much sulfur dioxide until malolactic fermentation is complete.

FIGURE 3.17

The chemical equation for malolactic fermentation in which one molecule of malic acid is converted to one molecule each of lactic acid and carbon dioxide.

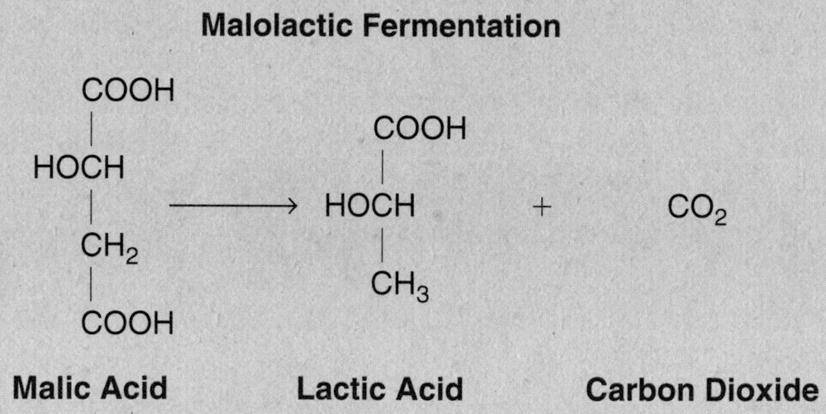

Malolactic Fermentation

$$
\begin{array}{ccc}
\text{COOH} & & \text{COOH} \\
| & & | \\
\text{HOCH} & \longrightarrow \quad \text{HOCH} \quad + & \text{CO}_2 \\
| & | \\
\text{CH}_2 & \text{CH}_3 \\
| & \\
\text{COOH} &
\end{array}
$$

Malic Acid   **Lactic Acid**   **Carbon Dioxide**

yeast cells, and do not cause off-aromas the way primary or gross lees prior to fermentation do. The young wine can be left sur lie for many months; sometimes the yeast in the barrel is stirred periodically to intensify the character.

BARRELS AND AGING

In Europe, barrels have been used in winemaking for more than 2,000 years (Jackson, 2008). The Romans were excellent coopers (barrel makers) and used barrels for storing and transporting wine as well as many other goods. Winemakers of the time

FIGURE 3.18

Barrels of red wine aging in a winery cellar.
© Pat Henderson

soon discovered that storing wine in barrels had positive effects on the wine's flavor and body. The qualities that barrel aging gives to a wine are so positive that barrels are still used for winemaking today, long after their other uses have been discontinued. Although there has been some mechanization, coopers still construct barrels by hand in the method they have used for hundreds of years. There are two types of reactions that take place during aging: The wine undergoes a slow oxidation and it absorbs flavor components from the wood. Both of these reactions make significant contributions to a wine's flavor. Aging a wine in small, 60-gallon (225-liter) barrels is both expensive and labor intensive, but the positive effect that barrel aging has on wine makes it worthwhile (Figure 3.18).

Barrels can be made out of many types of wood; however, oak is the chosen wood for wine-barrel production. In addition to being strong and durable, it is also nonporous so the barrels will not leak. Most important, it has excellent flavor and aroma compounds that are extracted into the wine during storage. Although oak is the wood of choice for winemaking, there are many different types of oak from which to choose. The two major categories of oak are European and American. Two species of European oak are used for making wine barrels: *Quercus sessilis* and *Quercus robar*, and they are grown throughout France and central Europe. European oak is known for giving wine a rich, toasty vanilla aroma. In the United States *Quercus alba*, or white oak, is used for barrel making and has a stronger, woodier flavor than European oak. Beyond the type of oak used, a barrel's flavor varies depending on the forest the wood is from, how the wood is seasoned, and the various methods of production that different coopers use. The inside of the barrel is toasted during production and the amount of time and temperature of the toasting has a large effect on the flavors that it will impart to the wine (Figure 3.19). This variety in styles gives winemakers a wide selection of flavors that they can choose to put into their wine by aging.

Much of the flavor obtained from aging wine in barrels comes from what is extracted out of the oak; however, the softening of the wine's texture that comes with aging is due to the process of slow oxidation. But oxidation can also be a vintner's enemy, spoiling the wine's aroma and color as well as promoting the growth of bacteria that produce vinegar. Oak has the quality of being semipermeable to oxygen, allowing it to be incorporated into the wine at just the right rate. A small amount of oxygen in an aging wine helps tannin molecules polymerize (join together) and settle, softening a wine's body and making it less bitter. Furthermore, a small amount of alcohol and water in the wine can evaporate through the oak of the barrel. This evaporation causes the remaining wine in the barrel to become more concentrated with acid and flavor. From time to time, the ullage (UHL-ihj) (headspace in the barrel) that is produced by this evaporation must be displaced by topping up the barrel with some wine from the same lot.

The period of time that a wine spends in oak depends on the tastes of the winemaker and the body of the wine being made. A big-bodied red such as Cabernet Sauvignon or Syrah may need two or more years in oak before it has sufficiently mellowed for bottling. A fruity, light-bodied wine like a Beaujolais Nouveau or Gewürztraminer may be bottled with little or no oak aging. Wine can also be aged in stainless steel tanks or after it has been bottled. Under these conditions there is much less exposure of the wine to oxygen than there is in barrels, so the aging process is slower and has less of an effect on the flavor of the wine than barrel aging. In addition, during tank or bottle aging no flavor compounds are being extracted into the wine from oak.

In moderately priced wines, the cost of aging in barrels can be prohibitive. In this case, a less expensive option for vintners is to place staves (planks) or chips of toasted oak in stainless steel tanks. While the wine is being aged in the tank, it absorbs the flavor compounds that are in the oak. If the winemaker wants to more fully replicate the conditions that are found in barrels, a small amount of air can be bubbled into the tank periodically in a process called micro-oxygenation or micro-ox. This method comes very close to the flavor of barrel aging but uses less wood and requires much less labor.

FIGURE 3.19

Toasting the inside of wine barrels during production at a cooperage, or barrel-making facility. Toasting helps give the wood the proper flavor for aging wine. Heating during toasting also softens the wood, making the staves more flexible so they can be bent into the characteristic barrel shape without breaking.

© Pat Henderson

FINISHING A WINE

After aging is complete, the wine is pumped out of the barrel and sent to the tank cellar for preparation for bottling. Wines can be bottled from a single vineyard or fermentation batch, but more often different lots are blended together (Figure 3.20). Blending can combine lots from different vineyards, even different regions and varieties, each with its own attributes. For example, an older wine can be given a more youthful, fruitier quality by adding a small amount of a younger vintage wine. Another option is to add a small amount of Chardonnay fermented in stainless steel tanks to a barrel-fermented lot of Chardonnay; this can reduce the oak profile in the wine and give it more varietal character. The art of blending lies in putting different combinations of these lots together in trial blends to find the combination that has the most balance and complexity. After the favorite trial blend is selected, its proportions are used to assemble a bottling blend in the cellar.

Having a wide selection of wine lots with different flavors gives a winemaker many options to fine-tune the blend and achieve the desired style. Sometimes winemakers will blend before or in the middle of the aging process to give the blend time to harmonize in the barrel. After the blend is selected, two more steps must be completed before wine is ready to be bottled: clarification and stability. Clarification produces a wine that is brilliant and free of suspended solids, while stability operations are performed to ensure that a brilliant wine remains so. These operations are closely linked, and often one will complement the other.

The simplest and gentlest form of clarification is settling and racking. As wines age in barrels, particles that are suspended fall out and accumulate at the bottom of the barrel. If the wine is carefully pumped out, the solids remain behind, sending a clean wine to the tank. Two more active methods of clarification are fining and filtering. **Fining** (FI-ning) is the process of adding a substance called a fining agent to the wine that will react with compounds in the wine, causing the two materials to combine and become insoluble. After the wine settles, the fining agent and the wine components that are removed are left behind in the lees when the wine is racked. Most fining agents are proteins, although some, such as bentonite (a type of clay) and carbon, are inorganic. Fining not only helps clarify and stabilize a wine, it can also be used to affect its flavor. A classic example is egg white fining whereby egg whites, which contain the protein albumin, are added to a red wine. The albumin reacts with tannin molecules, causing them to drop out and make the wine softer in character.

The most common fining agent used by vintners is bentonite, which acts to both clarify and stabilize white wines

FIGURE 3.20

An enologist, or wine chemist, making a laboratory trial blend at Kenwood Vineyards in Sonoma County, California. When the favorite trial blend is selected, the same proportions of different lots of wine will be used to make the final blend in the wine cellar.

© Pat Henderson

making them protein or "heat" stable. All wines contain some residual grape protein; this protein can denature (lose its shape) over time and become insoluble. If this happens after the wine is bottled, it will form a milky haze on the bottom of the bottle. To combat this, bentonite is added to white wines to remove excess protein, and in the process it also helps clarify the wine. Red wines have a much higher tannin level than white wines. Since tannins react with proteins in a manner similar to bentonite, it is not necessary to fine with bentonite to make red wines protein-stable.

In addition to protein or heat stability, a wine is also "cold" stabilized to remove excess potassium bitartrate before bottling. Potassium bitartrate, or cream of tartar, is a salt comprised of two natural constituents of wine: potassium and tartaric acid (Figure 3.21). Potassium bitartrate is semisoluble and forms crystals over time, especially under cold conditions. These crystals will form in bottles or in tanks and although they have an appearance similar to ground glass, they are completely harmless. To avoid an excess of tartrates crystallizing in the bottle, wines are chilled in the cellar to just above the freezing point (Figure 3.22). The crystals then settle to the bottom and to the walls of the tank. It is not uncommon for older wines to have a small amount of potassium bitartrate or **tartrates** on the bottom of the cork after aging.

Filtering is another way to obtain clarity in a wine prior to bottling. There are many types of filters designed for different winemaking applications (Figure 3.23). They all work by using pressure to force the wine through a porous substance that allows the

FIGURE 3.21

Crystals of potassium bitartrate formed on the cork of a bottle of Syrah during aging.

© Pat Henderson

FIGURE 3.22

A stainless steel wine tank with its cooling jacket covered with ice during cold stabilization.

© Pat Henderson

FIGURE 3.23

A plate and frame filter filtering a red wine before bottling.
© Pat Henderson

FIGURE 3.24

Bottles of Cabernet Sauvignon on a filling machine.
© Pat Henderson

liquid to go through but holds back solid particles. Filters are available in many grades of "tightness" that retain larger or smaller particles. Filtration is very important when making a wine that has the presence of residual sugar or malic acid. In such cases, if all of the microbes are not removed before bottling, they can begin to ferment in the bottle and spoil the wine. In any case, there are no human pathogens that can tolerate the alcohol in wine, so it is important to keep out microbes only because of their effect on wine stability and quality. Most winemakers use some form of fining or filtration to ensure the quality of their wine; however, others prefer a wine that is unfined and unfiltered. The philosophy here is that although a wine that is not fined or filtered may be less brilliant and less stable, it retains more of its natural flavor. While there is some truth to this argument, if fining and filtering are properly handled, they will have little effect on a wine's flavor.

Bottling

Bottling, the final step in winemaking, must be done with great care because it is not easy to rectify mistakes after the wine is in the bottle. Before bottling, the wine is analyzed and checked for stability one final time and any necessary adjustments are made. The wine is then sent to the bottling room where a filler machine distributes it to the bottles (Figure 3.24). Immediately after being filled, the bottles are sealed with a closure to protect the wine from contamination.

Traditionally wine bottles were sealed with a cork made from the bark of a cork oak tree, *Quercus suber*. Today there a number of options available to winemakers including natural and synthetic corks as well as a number of types of screw caps (also called twist tops). Each closure has advantages and disadvantages and they are discussed more fully in the section on corks and cork taint in Chapter 19 on page 603.

If the bottles are sealed with a cork, they are sent to a capsule machine to have a capsule applied to cover the neck and the cork. The final steps of applying the label and packing the bottles into cases then take place. Bottling is some of the roughest treatment a wine will receive and can leave a wine with less fruity aromas and body for a period of time. This condition is called bottle shock, and will go away if the wine is allowed to have some bottle age before consumption. While this is a real condition, bottle shock is often used as a scapegoat for any character a winemaker dislikes about a new wine.

FIGURE 3.25

The glassware that is used for sparkling wine is called a flute. It is tall and narrow to prolong the evolution of bubbles.
© *Pat Henderson*

SPARKLING WINE

Sparkling wine is defined as wine with bubbles or effervescence (Figure 3.25) and makes up just under 5 percent of the U.S. wine market (Beverage Information Group, 2008). It was first developed in the Champagne region of France in the 1700s, and was the result of two seventeenth-century winemaking inventions: the cork and the wine bottle. These innovations provided, for the first time, an airtight and sturdy package for wine. Inadvertently, young wines were bottled before they had finished primary fermentation. Because of the tight seal, when the wines finished their fermentation in the bottle, the carbon dioxide was trapped inside, giving them effervescence. Over the next 100 years, this accident was developed into the elaborate procedure used to make sparkling wine called **méthode champenoise** (may-TOHD shahm-peh-NWAHZ), or the Champagne method (Figure 3.26). There are other processes used to make sparkling wine; however, the original méthode champenoise is still considered to yield the highest quality product. The term *Champagne* refers to sparkling wine made in the Champagne region of France. In the United States, *champagne* is often used as a generic term to mean any sparkling wine, and it is legal to use the term on the label as long as the region of origin is listed (e.g., California champagne).

Since the Champagne region is very cool, the grapes used for making sparkling wines are early ripeners. Pinot Noir, Chardonnay, and Pinot Meunier are three of the most common grapes used for sparkling wine. In California, the grapes are primarily Pinot Noir and Chardonnay with Pinot

MÉTHODE CHAMPENOISE FLOWCHART

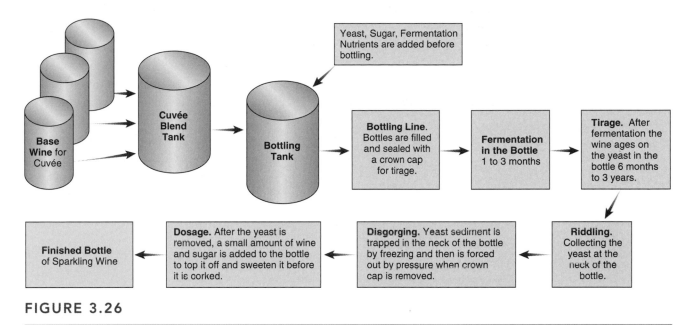

FIGURE 3.26

Flowchart of operations in making méthode champenoise sparkling wine, the traditional method used for making French Champagne.

© 2012 Delmar Cengage Learning

WHAT'S IN A NAME?

Since most types of wine were first produced in Europe, much of the nomenclature of wines and winemaking has French, Italian, and German roots. This is not controversial when the European term describes a winemaking technique, for example, sur lie or méthode champenoise. However, it is much more contentious when the name of a European region is used to describe or label a product that was made elsewhere such as "American champagne" or "California port." Up until the 1960s, it was common to see domestic Pinot Noir being labeled as "Burgundy" or Riesling labeled as "Rhine wine." However, as consumers became more knowledgeable about wine, American wineries started labeling their wines with varietal names of the grape used to produce them. In Europe, wineries are still more likely to emphasize terroir by naming their wines by place of origin rather than grape variety.

In spite of the acceptance of varietal wine names, it is still common to see terms such as *champagne, Sherry,* and *port* on American wines. This has bothered European winemakers for years who often point out that if the tables were turned, American winemakers would be very upset if, for example, a Spanish winery started to label its Cabernet Sauvignon "napa." American vintners counter that most consumers in the United States are less knowledgeable about wine and think that *champagne* is simply a synonym for sparkling wine and are not aware that it is a region in France.

After many years of arguing about the situation, in 2006 the U.S. government and the European Union came to an agreement in which American wineries that have a history of using European place-names could be grandfathered in and continue to use them in domestic (U.S.) markets. However, wineries that did not use the terms prior to 2006 are not allowed to use European names to describe the types of wine they are making.

Meunier and Pinot Blanc as well as other varieties being used less frequently. The grapes used for sparkling wine are picked earlier than those used for still wines for several reasons. The base wine used for sparkling wine should be low in alcohol and should not have a lot of varietal character. This is because the secondary fermentation will increase the alcohol content, and the finished wine should exhibit the flavors produced from the méthode champenoise process. Furthermore, the grapes are usually picked by hand and treated very gently during pressing to avoid extracting too much flavor or color from the skins. Press cycles for sparkling wine are longer and more press fractions are taken to ensure the best juice is kept separate. After fermentation, the wine is racked and stored until blending.

In the winter following harvest, the winemaker tastes the various lots of wine produced and puts together the base blend called the cuvée. **Cuvée** (koo-VAY) is a French word that translates literally to "tub full" or "vat full." The cuvée is low in color and alcohol, but high in acid, and it takes considerable talent as a taster to be able to know how the flavors in the cuvée will ultimately translate into the finished wine. After the blend is made, it is bottled with a small amount of sugar and actively fermenting yeast, and sealed with a crown cap. The wine is then stored in a cool, dark place during the fermentation in the bottle. As the yeast ferment, they produce about 1.5 percent more alcohol and about 90 pounds per square inch (6 atmospheres) of carbon dioxide. The bottles used are much heavier than those for still wine in order to hold back the pressure; they are also dark green because sparkling wine will develop off-flavors if exposed to excessive light. After fermentation, the bottles undergo tirage (tee-RAHZH), whereby they are aged on the yeast cells for a period of several months to many years depending on the style of sparkling wine being made. During this time, the yeast cells begin to break down in a process called autolysis (aw-TAHL-uh-sihss), which is what gives méthode champenoise sparkling wines their unique flavor.

After tirage, it is necessary to remove the yeast from the bottle before the wine can be finished. The bottle is taken from storage, mixed to loosen the yeast from the sides of the bottle, and placed in a riddling rack. Riddling is a process used to accumulate the yeast at the end of the neck of the bottle. The bottle is placed horizontally in the riddling rack (Figure 3.27) and every day it is twisted and pushed back into the rack at a slightly steeper angle. After several weeks, the yeast has settled at the end of the neck and the bottle is upside down, or sur pointe (soor PWANT). Hand riddling is still practiced at some producers but at most wineries the process is now done by machines. There is a photo of an automatic riddling machine in Figure 8.7 on page 287.

Following the riddling process, the yeast is ready to be removed by disgorging (Figure 3.28). The bottles are chilled to just above the freezing point and placed upside down in a brine bath to freeze the wine in the neck of the bottle. This traps the yeast, and when the crown cap is removed, the pressure of the wine expels the plug of frozen wine, taking the yeast with it. The bottle is then topped off with a small amount of base wine called dosage. Since sparkling wine is quite sour, the dosage often has a small amount of sugar to balance out the acid. The bottle is then finished with a wide-diameter agglomerate cork that is inserted only halfway to give it its mushroom shape. Sparkling wine produced by méthode champenoise is labeled as such or alternatively as "traditional method" or "fermented in this bottle."

FIGURE 3.27

Riddling sparkling wine bottles by hand. The bottles are twisted and pushed back in the rack at a slightly steeper angle every day until the bottles are vertical and all of the residual yeast from fermentation has accumulated in the neck of the bottle.

© www.germanwines .de,German wine Institute

Other Methods of Sparkling Wine Production

Although the finest sparkling wines are made by méthode champenoise, this accounts for only 10 percent of production. The majority of sparkling wine is made by the **Charmat** (shar-MAHT) **process** or "bulk" process developed by the French winemaker Eugène Charmat in 1907 (Figure 3.29). In the Charmat process, instead of having the secondary alcoholic fermentation take place in the bottle, it takes place in large steel tanks that are specially designed to withstand the pressure produced by fermentation. After fermentation, the wine is racked off and the yeast is filtered out under pressure. Once the dosage is added, the wine is bottled and usually sealed with a plastic, mushroom-shaped cork. The ability to filter out the yeast saves the effort of riddling and disgorging, making these bulk-processed sparkling wines much less expensive to produce. Without the extended time on the yeast during tirage, however, these wines do not have the same character as those produced by méthode champenoise. The grapes that are used for the Charmat process are typically less expensive varieties such as Chenin Blanc and French Colombard.

There are two other little used methods to make sparkling wine: the transfer method and artificial carbonation. In the transfer method, the cuvée is fermented in bottles and aged in tirage for a time. At the end of tirage, the wine is transferred from one bottle to another, being filtered in the process. Sparkling wine made this way is labeled "fermented in the bottle" instead of "fermented in this bottle." The transfer method, because it incurs extra expense

FIGURE 3.28

Bottles of sparkling wine entering a disgorging machine. The plug of ice visible in the neck of the bottle contains the residual yeast from fermentation in the bottle. When the crown cap that seals the bottle during tirage is removed, the pressure of the sparkling wine in the bottle will eject the ice plug leaving behind the clean wine.

© Pat Henderson

CHARMAT (BULK) PROCESS FLOWCHART

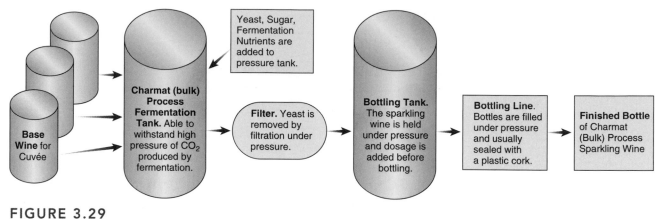

FIGURE 3.29

Flowchart of operations in making Charmat or "bulk" process sparkling wine, the method used for the majority of sparkling wine produced in the United States.

© 2012 Delmar Cengage Learning

without adding significantly to the quality, is not as popular as the méthode champenoise or the Charmat process. In artificial carbonation, a still base wine is injected with carbon dioxide, carbonating it before serving, much the same way a soda pop dispenser works. These wines are usually served at large banquets and have little of the qualities of natural fermented sparkling wine.

DESSERT AND FORTIFIED WINES

There are multitudes of unique dessert wines that are produced throughout the world's winemaking regions. **Dessert wines** are made with appreciable sugar and often have higher alcohol content to stabilize the wine and prevent it from fermenting in the bottle. Dessert wines make an excellent dessert in themselves, and can be offered as a digestive after a meal, or can be a complement to a sweet dessert course. **Fortified wines** have had the addition of brandy during processing and can be either sweet or dry. Brandy is made by distilling wine to concentrate the alcohol resulting in an alcohol content of between 40 and 70 percent. Proof is a measurement of alcohol content used for distilled spirits where 1 percent alcohol is equal to 2° proof, so 100° proof is equal to 50 percent alcohol.

Although the classic definition of a dessert wine is a wine that is sweet, for purposes of taxation the U.S. government classifies all wines that are fortified with additional alcohol as "dessert wines" whether they are sweet or not, and they are taxed at a higher rate than table wines. Next, we examine the production methods used in some of the most common types of these wines: late harvest, Port, and Sherry.

Late Harvest Wines

Late harvest wines are made from grapes picked at a much higher sugar level than grapes used for table wines. Through photosynthesis, grapevines can ripen the crop up to about 26°Brix, while late harvest wine grapes are frequently picked at 35°Brix or more. Late-harvest wines achieve this higher level of sugar concentration due to the fruit partially dehydrating on the vine. Under the right conditions, water will evaporate through the skin of the berry, concentrating the sugar that is left behind. This high sugar means that the yeast will have a difficult time fermenting due to the combined inhibitory effects of alcohol and sugar concentration. Late harvest fermentations progress at a very slow rate and are unable to ferment to dryness. Eventually during the fermentation the inhibitory influences of sugar and alcohol combine in a synergistic effect to arrest the fermentation. In this manner a microbial stable, sweet wine is produced without sterile filtration or the addition of fortifying spirits.

This dehydration is increased by an infection of a mold that is usually considered a vineyard nuisance, *Botrytis cinerea* (boh-TRI-tis sihn-EH-ee-uh) or noble rot (Figure 3.30). This mold is a common problem in vineyards and is normally discouraged by applying sulfur dust; however, under the right conditions with the right varieties, it has the ability to make some of the world's best wines. *B. cinerea* infects ripe grapes that are exposed to high humidity; the growth of the mold perforates the skin of the grape, opening a path for the water to leave. When wet weather is followed by dry, warm weather, the berries then dehydrate to reach the high sugar levels needed for late harvest. Two excellent examples of wines made under these circumstances are the Trockenbeerenauslese (TROH-kehn-BEE-ehr-ehn-OWS-lay-zuh), or TBA, of Germany and the Sauternes (soh-TUHRN) wines of France.

FIGURE 3.30

Growth of *Botrytis cinerea* on a cluster of Chardonnay. In most cases it is considered a spoilage organism by grape growers. However, under the proper conditions with the right variety its growth can produce excellent dessert wines.

© Pat Henderson

In the United States, the growth of *Botrytis* is sometimes encouraged by artificial means, such as watering the grapes with overhead sprinklers, to get the needed humidity to start growth. In addition to the concentration of sugar, *Botrytis* produces a number of compounds that affect the flavor of the wine. One of these, botrycine, has a distinctly apricot aroma. Thin-skinned grape varieties like Zinfandel will shrivel up in hot weather during the harvest season and significantly concentrate the sugar without the presence of mold. However, these late harvest wines have a different, more "raisiny" character than *Botrytis*-affected wines. Late harvest grapes, because of their high solids and sugar, are notoriously difficult to press, and fermenting and clarifying the wine is no easier. The unique weather conditions that are required, combined with the difficulty of their production, make botrytized late harvest wines both rare and expensive.

Late harvest wines can also be made without the growth of *B. cinerea*. In Germany and other cold-climate growing regions, the grapes can be left on the vine until freezing weather sets in at the end of the fall. Wines that are made from frozen grapes are called Eiswein (ICE-vyn), or ice wine. As the water in the berries freezes the remaining juice is concentrated, increasing the sugar level to about 35°Brix. The grape clusters are then picked, transported, and pressed while they are still frozen. The pressing is done very slowly and, as the juice is removed from the grapes, some of the water in the berries remains behind as ice. Like botrytized wines, the fermentation proceeds slowly and stops before it can complete, resulting in a sweet dessert wine.

Port-Style Wines

Port wines are full-bodied red wines that have about 10 percent sugar and 20 percent alcohol, and are native to the Douro River wine region in northern Portugal. **Port-style wines** are wines made in the style of Port, but produced outside the Port region. Port-style wines are made around the world and, like *champagne*, *port* has become a generic term for the style of sweet, red, fortified wine produced in the Douro region of Portugal. A number of styles of Port made in Portugal are outlined in the section on Port in Chapter 8.

To obtain their high level of sugar, Port wines have their fermentation stopped halfway through while the must is still very sweet. Yeast are sensitive to alcohol and have difficulty surviving at levels above 16 percent. By adding brandy, or fortifying, the must to a level greater than this the yeast are killed arresting the fermentation with residual sugar. In Port production harvesting and fermentation begins in a similar method to table wine production, but when the must ferments down to about 13°Brix, the juice is pressed off the skins and brandy with 70 percent (140° proof) alcohol is added at a ratio of about three parts juice to one part brandy. This results in the desired levels of about 10 percent sugar and 20 percent alcohol in the final wine.

Because a deep-red wine with lots of tannins is desired for Port, and the time of the fermentation is limited, intensely colored red grape varieties are used for winemaking and winemaking practices are designed to maximize extraction from the skins. Traditionally the skins were mixed with the juice by treading by foot continuously throughout the brief fermentation. Today, while foot treading is still practiced by a few wineries, it is much more common to mix the juice and skins during fermentation by mechanical means. When it has fermented to the desired level of sugar, the must is pressed and the brandy is added. After fortification, the wine is then settled and racked before it is blended and aged. Port is made in a wide diversity of styles and is aged in barrels anywhere from 2 to 40 years before bottling.

In California, sweet dessert wines are often made from the Zinfandel grapes. Called "Zinfandel Port" the winemaking is a hybrid of the late harvest and Port wine-making methods. The Zinfandel grape has thin skins and, when allowed to hang on the vine during warm fall weather, it can achieve sugar levels of about 30°Brix through dehydration. The grapes are then harvested and fermented on the skins and when the must reaches the desired sugar level it is pressed and the juice is fortified with alcohol to arrest the fermentation.

Sherry

Sherry originated in Spain and, like Port it is produced in a variety of styles. The Spanish have a saying that "there is a Sherry for every occasion." This reflects the wide range of Sherries from light and dry wines suitable for accompanying a meal, to the more common rich and sweet dessert wines. This is also an indication that Sherry was so important to the region that different styles have been designed to complement many types of food. The defining characteristic of Sherry is that it is pur-posely oxidized, making it high in acetaldehyde, which is the result of the reaction of **ethanol** (wine alcohol) and oxygen. This gives Sherry wines their distinctive roasted nut aroma. Wine drinkers who are not accustomed to Sherry can sometimes find this aroma unsettling because it is the same compound found in a table wine that has been spoiled by oxidation. Fifty years ago Sherry-style wines were the most popular wine sold in the United States; however, in recent decades its consumption has declined dramatically.

The flavor of Sherry is produced during the aging process so, like sparkling wines, a fairly neutral wine is desired as a base for Sherry. For this reason, neutral grape varieties like Palomino (pah-loh-MEE-noh) and Pedro Ximénez (PEH-droh hee-MEE-nihs) are used for its production. Sherry production starts by fermenting the base wine to dryness and then fortifying to achieve an alcohol content of about 15.5 percent. The high alcohol level inhibits the growth of the bacteria that produce vinegar. To reach this level, the grapes must be very sweet and sometimes they are dried on mats after picking to reach the appropriate sugar concentration. After the base wines are made, they are graded by color, taste, and body to determine which type of Sherry they will be used to make. The lighter wines are inoculated with flor (FLAWR) yeast and called fino; the more full-bodied wines are fortified with brandy to 18 to 20 percent alcohol and called oloroso (oh-loh-ROH-soh). The wines are then placed in partially full bar-rels to expose the wine to oxygen.

In the fino Sherries, the flor yeast begins to grow, using the alcohol that is present as an energy source. As it grows it forms a thick film on the surface of the aging wine because it can grow only in the presence of oxygen. Sherries made in this style are light and dry and are an excellent table wine to accompany savory foods. In the United

States, however, the more popular style Sherry is the full-bodied oloroso. After it is fortified, oloroso Sherries are aged in partially full barrels but without flor yeast. Oloroso Sherries are often sweetened before bottling to make a dessert wine. The traditional method of aging Sherry is also unique; it is done in a fractional barrel system called a solera which is described in more detail in Chapter 8 on page 290.

In California, methods of production differ significantly from those in Spain. Flor yeast is often grown in a submerged culture made possible by bubbling oxygen through the tank until it has reached the desired flavor. California Sherry is often finished by aging in barrels at an elevated temperature, more similar to the production of Madeira than of Spanish Sherry.

Flavored Wines

A flavored wine is simply a wine made from grapes that has been augmented with natural flavorings such as herbs, spices, honey, and fruit juice. Flavored wines are made around the world in a wide number of styles both sweet and dry, as well as fortified and unfortified, yet despite their variety they make up only a small fraction of wine consumed. Their origin goes back to ancient times when herbs and spices were added to wine to augment its flavor or cover up imperfections. Vermouth (ver-MOOTH), probably the best-known flavored wine, consists of a fortified wine that is flavored with aromatic herbs and is consumed by itself or used as a mixer in alcoholic drinks. Another example is retsina (reht-SEE-nah), which is a nonfortified wine seasoned with pine resin. Not all flavored wines have historic roots; more modern examples include wine coolers and fruit-flavored jug wines.

THE ATTRIBUTES OF WINE

Wine is a complex mixture of nearly 1,000 different, naturally occurring chemical compounds. These constituents come from three sources: (1) the compounds that are present in grape juice, (2) the compounds that are produced by microorganisms fermenting the grape juice, and (3) the compounds that are added by processing and aging the wine. In addition to the natural chemicals in wine, a small amount of human-made materials are added to wine, usually in the form of sulfites used as a preservative (Figure 3.31).

The major component of wine is water, making up 80 to 90 percent of the solution. Water content affects the chemical and sensory qualities of wine, but its most important role is as the solvent in which all other wine constituents are dissolved. After water, alcohol, or more specifically ethyl alcohol (ethanol) is the next most prevalent compound. It plays a significant role in the sensory and stability aspects of wine, as well as having many physiological effects. Glycerol is another type of alcohol that is produced by yeast. Unlike ethanol, it is nonintoxicating but it does make sensory contributions to the viscosity, or body, of the wine. Organic acids are present in about the same quantity as glycerol but have much more of a sensory effect. A wine's natural tartness is one of the qualities that make it an excellent accompaniment to

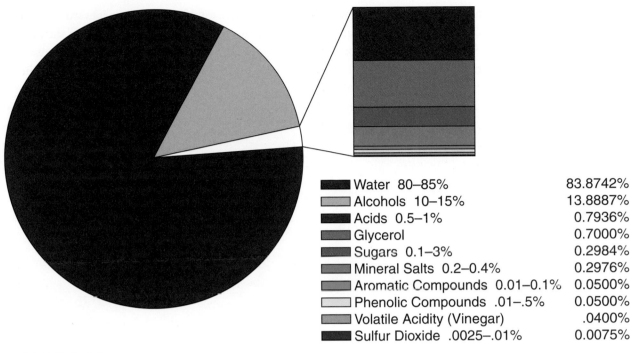

Water 80–85%	83.8742%
Alcohols 10–15%	13.8887%
Acids 0.5–1%	0.7936%
Glycerol	0.7000%
Sugars 0.1–3%	0.2984%
Mineral Salts 0.2–0.4%	0.2976%
Aromatic Compounds 0.01–0.1%	0.0500%
Phenolic Compounds .01–.5%	0.0500%
Volatile Acidity (Vinegar)	.0400%
Sulfur Dioxide .0025–.01%	0.0075%

FIGURE 3.31

Table wine composition.

© 2012 Delmar Cengage Learning

food. The acids in wine also contribute to its microbial stability by inhibiting the growth of bacteria.

Some of the most important flavor compounds in wine are present in very small amounts. Trace constituents such as phenols, esters, and sugars each represent groups of complex chemical compounds with similar structures. Each of these groups has many members; for example, there are 10 different alcohols found in wine besides ethanol and glycerol. Each individual wine has a unique combination of these chemicals that gives it a distinctive character. The various amounts of these compounds present are determined by factors such as grape variety, the vineyard's terroir (total environment, including soil, climate, and location), and the production decisions that the winemaker and the grower make.

SUMMARY

A wine's sensory qualities are determined by its chemical makeup, and the chemical makeup of a wine is influenced by a vineyard's terroir and the actions of the grape grower and the winemaker. As described in the previous chapter, the grower sets the stage for a wine's flavor by controlling factors such as selection of a clone and how the vineyard is pruned. Once the fruit is delivered to the winery, the winemaker takes over. Winemaking decisions including when to press, and what type of barrels to age in, build upon the flavors that the grape grower established in the vineyard. The great complexity of a wine is ultimately shaped by numerous choices available to the people who produce it. This is why there are so many different types of wines made around the world and also why they are made in such a variety of styles. The interpretation of what a Cabernet Sauvignon should taste like varies from region to region, winery to winery, and vintage to vintage. In the end, the consumers of the wine make the ultimate decision on which interpretation is the proper one by choosing the wines they enjoy the most.

EXERCISES

1. Discuss the three major products of alcoholic fermentation and explain their significance in the winemaking process.

2. What are the definitions of a table wine?

3. Describe the various methods of sparkling wine production.

4. Why is sulfur dioxide used by winemakers?

5. Discuss the various methods of cap management used by vintners during red wine fermentation.

REVIEW QUESTIONS

1. When is a white wine pressed?
   A. Before fermentation
   B. During fermentation
   C. After fermentation
   D. White wines are usually not pressed

2. Which of the following is not an effect of aging a wine in oak?
   A. The amount of oxygen in the wine is reduced.
   B. It picks up the flavor of oak from the barrel.
   C. It concentrates due to evaporation.
   D. The level of tannins in the wine is reduced.

(Continues)

(Continued)

3. What is the primary effect of malolactic fermentation?
   A. The level of acidity in the wine is reduced.
   B. The alcohol level of the wine is increased.
   C. The wine acquires an oxidized "nutty" aroma.
   D. The fruity aroma of the wine is increased.

4. When is alcohol added to Port-style wines during their production?
   A. Before fermentation
   B. Midway through fermentation
   C. After the wine has fermented dry
   D. Just prior to bottling

5. The process of removing clean juice or wine off settled lees is called _____.
   A. Maceration
   B. Filtration
   C. Fining
   D. Racking

REFERENCES

Beverage Information Group. (2008). *Adams wine handbook*. Norwalk, CT: Author.
Jackson, R. S. (2008). *Wine science* (3rd ed.). San Diego, CA: Academic Press.
Yair, M. (1997). *Wine chemistry*. San Francisco: The Wine Appreciation Guild.

{ TASTING WINES }

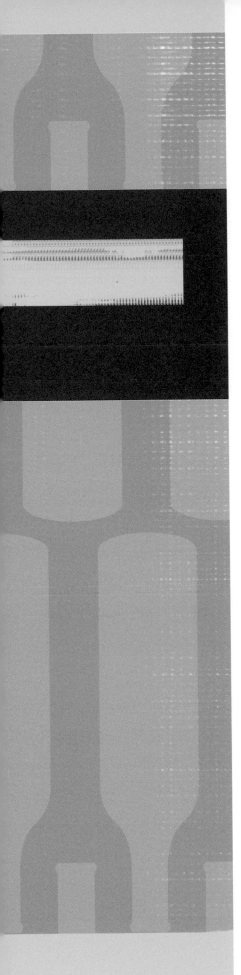

This chapter covers the

fundamentals of tasting and evaluating wines. It begins with the physiological responses that make up our senses of taste and smell. It then discusses how to set up a tasting and explains how to use our perceptions for wine assessment as well as how to critically evaluate and describe a wine's taste. The chapter finishes with a section on understanding wine reviews and rankings.

INTRODUCTION

Learning how to taste wine is similar in many ways to learning music appreciation. In both areas one can enjoy the experience of listening to a piece of music or drinking a glass of wine without fully understanding what in particular about it is enjoyable. In other words, what is it about this individual song or glass of wine that "speaks to you". However, with experience and training the novice can develop the critical faculties that give a greater understanding of wine or music and learn how to describe it to others. Tasting, or **sensory evaluation**, is the process of using the effect a wine makes on one's senses to review and describe a wine. Giving pleasure to the senses is the primary purpose of tasting wine and it is important not to lose sight of this when reviewing or critically evaluating a wine. Even though one is concentrating and taking the task seriously, sensory evaluation should ideally be an enjoyable and enlightening process.

The interaction of wine and food is also of primary importance to the sensory experience of wine. Making the proper match of a wine for the meal it will be served with greatly enhances the flavors of both. Wine also has both positive and negative physiological effects on the body that should always be taken into consideration when serving or consuming wine. Both of these subjects are more fully explored in Chapter 5.

SENSORY EVALUATION: HOW THE SENSES RESPOND TO WINE

Wine is a natural beverage with a very complex chemical structure. The complexity of its composition is what is responsible for the multitude of flavors that are present in wine. For an **enologist**, someone who studies wine, there are many laboratory methods for analyzing the chemical makeup of a wine. Using analytical chemistry, the basic constituents of wine flavor such as acids and tannins can be measured. In recent years there have been great advancements in the science of flavor chemistry. Trace flavor compounds present at levels as low as a few parts per trillion can now be detected and quantified by using sophisticated instruments such as gas and liquid chromatographs and mass spectrometers. Despite this level of precision, there is still no laboratory procedure that can give an accurate overall picture of what a wine will taste like.

When winemakers are producing wine they take into consideration both laboratory analysis and sensory analysis by taste in making their decisions. Laboratory analysis is useful in determining the physical parameters that are important in wine stability, while sensory analysis is used to guide winemakers when making choices that affect taste.

Of the five senses, sight, smell, taste, touch, and hearing, only the first four are significant to evaluating a wine. One can hear the pop of a cork, or the fizz of a glass of champagne, but to assess a wine's flavor, hearing is not required. Of the four senses that are used the flavor of a wine is defined by the impression it makes on one's sense of smell (aroma), sense of taste, and sense of touch (texture). Sight is important to evaluate the aesthetic visual aspects of a wine, such as color or turbidity, which are part of the sensory evaluation but does not directly play a role in a wine's taste.

The Sense of Sight: Appearance

Although sight does not play a direct role in determining flavor, the visual appearance of a wine is a very important part of sensory evaluation. The color of the wine is observed for the **hue** (shade) along with its **depth** (intensity) and how appropriate these are for the type of wine being tasted (Figures 4.1 and 4.2). The clarity of the wine is also observed and noted whether it is **brilliant**, clear of any defects, or **dull**, turbid and cloudy. Looking at a glass can give the taster clues on what to expect when the wine is consumed. If a wine is an inappropriate color, or is cloudy or turbid, it will have a negative effect on its visual appreciation. The positive or negative aspects of appearance play a role in how the taster will perceive the wine when it is consumed. We are all familiar with how a food can look appetizing and stimulate hunger or look unappetizing and have the opposite effect. While a wine's appearance gives us clues on what it might taste like before it is consumed, it is important not to let the expectation of how a wine will taste prejudice your judgment. We have all had the experience of sampling a food that looks tempting but tastes terrible.

The Sense of Smell: Aroma

The sense of smell is the oldest and one of the most highly developed senses. The sense of smell is also much more acute than the sense of taste, being able to distinguish many more compounds and detect them at much lower concentrations. The human nose can identify thousands of different types of aromas, some at levels as low as several parts per trillion. For a compound to have an aroma it first must be **volatile**, or able to evaporate and be carried by air. Inhaling through the nose carries the air with any volatile compounds present into the upper sinus where there are two membranes called the olfactory epithelium; each is about the size of a postage stamp and is located to either

FIGURE 4.1

One-year-old Sauvignon Blanc (left) and 10-year-old Sauvignon Blanc (right). As a white wine ages, the phenolic compounds present in the wine oxidize and turn brown, giving it an amber color.

© Pat Henderson

FIGURE 4.2A

Six-month-old Cabernet Sauvignon. Young red wines have a bluish purple tint to their red color.

© Pat Henderson

FIGURE 4.2B

Five-year-old Cabernet Sauvignon. After a few years, the wine becomes more red as the bluish purple tint is lost.

© Pat Henderson

FIGURE 4.2C

Twenty-year-old Cabernet Sauvignon. After many years, the oxidation of phenolic compounds gives red wines an amber/tawny color.

© Pat Henderson

side of the nasal septum (Figure 4.3). Volatile chemicals in the air react with receptor neurons located in these membranes. There are more than 200 different types of receptor neurons, and the degree to which a certain compound reacts with different types of receptors is what is responsible for a particular smell. Neurons in the olfactory epithelium transmit signals from the receptors to the **olfactory bulb** above the nasal cavities before these signals are sent on to the brain where the information is processed. Smell is one of the most evocative senses, and how we describe an aroma is usually based on comparisons to aromas we remember having smelled before. There is a great deal of variation in sensitivity to smell in the general population; however, with training it is possible to increase one's ability to distinguish different aromas.

Wine has a very complex chemical composition with volatile compounds that originate from the grapes as well as from processing activities such as fermentation and aging. Wine has as many as 800 volatile compounds, some present in very low quantities; this high number is what is responsible for the great complexity of a wine's aroma. When describing a wine's aroma it is common to isolate and identify the different aromas present and describe what they smell like; this is called **descriptive analysis**. A taster might mention detecting the aroma of black pepper, raspberries, and vanilla in a wine. This does not mean that these flavors are from ingredients added to the wine by artificial means, but rather that some of the same or similar compounds that are responsible for these aromas in other products are also present in wine. Descriptive analysis works particularly well because of the evocative nature of the sense of smell.

FIGURE 4.3

Diagram of sinuses, retronasal pathway, and olfactory organs.

© Delmar Cengage Learning

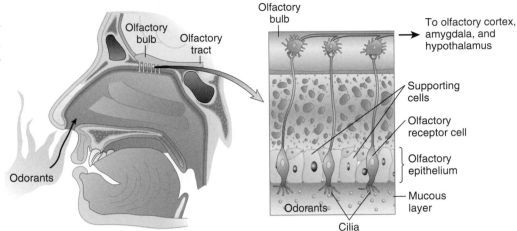

Whenever we encounter a new aroma we naturally try to categorize it by what other smells it is reminiscent of.

The Sense of Taste: Flavor

The sense of taste is very simple when compared to the sense of smell. Most people identify only four flavors that can be discerned by taste alone: bitter, salty, sweet, and sour. Some flavor chemists also include the tastes of both metallic and umami, neither of which has much of a role in wine. Most people are familiar with the concept of a metallic taste but umami is less well known. Umami was first described in Japan and is the savory character that is found in broths and meat as well as monosodium glutamate, or MSG (Jackson, 2009). The sense of taste comes from receptor cells located within the taste buds. Taste buds lie within small, fleshy protuberances called papillae that are located throughout the soft tissue of the mouth and upper esophagus but are concentrated primarily on the tongue.

For many years it was thought that different areas of the tongue were sensitive to different tastes resulting in "tongue taste maps" (Figure 4.4) being published in many texts. Recently this theory was discredited; the different tastes can be identified on all parts of the tongue (Smith & Margolskee, 2001). In spite of the limitations of the sense of taste it is possible to experience more than the four basic flavors when tasting a food or beverage. This comes from the interaction of the senses of taste and smell working together. Much of the flavor you perceive when tasting something comes from the aroma that enters the sinuses through the retronasal pathway at the back of the mouth. These aromas stimulate the olfactory nerves at the same time the taste is being perceived. This is evidenced by how bland food tastes if the sinuses are congested and the sense of smell is blocked.

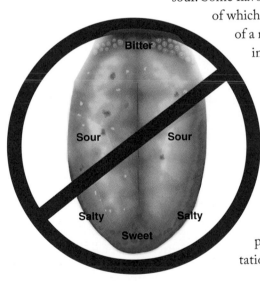

FIGURE 4.4

Tongue taste map—popular, but incorrect. While it is still found in a number of texts, researchers have found that the concept of different parts of the tongue being specialized to perceive certain tastes is incorrect.

© Delmar Cengage Learning

The Sense of Touch: Texture

Called **mouthfeel** or **texture**, the tactile sensations that are produced when one drinks a glass of wine are integral to describing its flavor. The nerve endings of the mouth and tongue detect parameters such as the following:

- **Temperature**: The temperature a wine is served at has a great effect on how the wine is perceived. At warmer temperatures, the aroma will become more intense because of the greater volatility of the aromatic compounds in the wine. Cooler temperatures will give a wine a more refreshing quality, but will diminish its aroma. On the palate, lower temperatures will diminish the perception of acidity and sweetness, making the wine's bitterness and astringency more pronounced. Red wines are traditionally served at room temperature, 59 to 65°F (15 to 18°C); while white wines are usually served at a lower temperature, 50 to 59°F (10 to 15°C). Sparkling wines are served at the coolest temperature, around 41°F (5°C), which helps slow the evolution of bubbles, prolonging the effervescence in the glass. Serving temperatures are more fully discussed in Chapter 19.

- **Viscosity**: The body or "thickness" of a wine is influenced by its temperature and composition. Alcohols, acids, tannins, and sugar all play a role in a wine's body.

- **Effervescence**: This is the prickly sensation from the carbonation or dissolved carbon dioxide (CO_2) present in the wine that is residual from fermentation. Its qualities are readily apparent in sparkling wines as well as young white wines where CO_2 contributes to the tartness and "fresh" taste.

- **Alcohol**: Wines with higher alcohol have a burning or "hot" character that is reminiscent of distilled spirits (Figure 4.5).

- **Astringency**: Of these sensations **astringency** is the most poorly understood. It is the drying or "puckery" sensation that is often confused with bitterness. Astringency is a tactile drying sensation, whereas bitterness is a flavor. It is produced by the reaction between phenolic compounds, such as tannins, with proteins in the saliva. Astringency is perceived more slowly than the other mouthfeel sensations and is important to the aftertaste of a wine as well as how it will complement food.

FIGURE 4.5

Tears, also called "legs," on a wine glass are formed by the interaction between alcohol and water in the wine as it evaporates from the side of the wine glass. Tears are often incorrectly thought to be an indication of viscosity but actually are a function of the wine's alcoholic strength.

© Pat Henderson

The physical sensations that are perceived when drinking a glass of wine interact with its aroma and taste to make up a wine's overall impression of flavor. The perception of a wine's flavor can also be influenced by its appearance. Among wine tasters there is a great deal of variation in their natural ability of sensory perception. This can be compensated for by using proper tasting techniques combined with training and experience.

Organizing a Tasting

There are many different ways to taste wine, from formal and analytical to relaxed and social. Less structured tastings often offer a number of wines from a variety of different regions and producers. Tasters usually walk around the room sampling the wines they wish to try as well as any food offered as an accompaniment (Figure 4.6). While informal tastings of wine with pleasant conversation and good food can be a very enjoyable experience, it is difficult to evaluate wine carefully under these circumstances. For purposes of serious sensory evaluation, there is a certain procedure for setting up a tasting that minimizes distractions and allows tasters, also called wine judges in this context, to concentrate on the wine. While social tastings are common and very popular with the public, more analytical tastings are used by students, enologists, and judges of wine for

FIGURE 4.6

The Zinfandel Advocates and Producers (ZAP) tasting in San Francisco features more than 250 wineries and draws nearly 10,000 wine enthusiasts each year. Large public tastings offer an enjoyable opportunity to taste a number of wines. However, the fact that the wines are usually not tasted blind, combined with the distracting atmosphere, makes them difficult places to perform careful sensory evaluation.
© Pat Henderson

FIGURE 4.7

Judges tasting at a wine competition. Wine competitions are usually judged by industry professionals working in small groups in a quiet setting so they are not distracted and can concentrate on the task at hand. Additionally, the wines are always tasted blind to remove any prejudice.
© Pat Henderson

more careful evaluation (Figure 4.7). Next, we focus on the proper protocol for setting up an analytical tasting.

The Proper Setting for a Tasting

Like any task that requires concentration, sensory analysis should take place in an environment that has a minimum of distractions. The location in which the tasting is to take place should be quiet and free of any distracting activities taking place nearby. The room should be at a comfortable temperature and without drafts. Since part of sensory evaluation is to appraise the color and clarity of a wine, good lighting is also important. Natural light from the sun is best, but since sunlight is not always available, care must be taken when selecting indoor light sources. It should be bright enough to illuminate deeply colored red wines as well as have a neutral white hue. Some fluorescent lights can have a blue tint to them and incandescent lights have a yellowish character, while wide-spectrum bulbs provide a more natural color.

Most importantly, the tasting area should have no distracting smells that would interfere with the sometimes delicate aromas of the wines to be evaluated. Cleaning products, fresh paint, and smoke from fireplaces or tobacco all affect a taster's ability to discern aromas in wine. Even pleasant aromas such as those from food preparation, flower arrangements, or scented candles can interfere with the tasting process.

The importance of limiting distractions applies not only to the setting of the wine tasting, but to the tasters themselves as well. Tasting etiquette requires that people who attend the tasting be conscious of personal deportment and any odors that might be coming from them or their clothes. It goes without saying that one should be clean and free of body odor; however, care must also be taken that they do not use any strongly scented soap or shampoo that could distract fellow tasters. Perfumes, colognes, and aftershave must also be avoided. Additionally, some types of lipstick can be difficult to remove from fine glassware and considerate tasters should not use them. Sensory evaluation requires concentration; therefore, participants should arrive at the tasting well rested and fresh so they can remain focused on the task at hand. Tasters should also be punctual because the commotion caused by setting up and serving the wines for a late arrival is very distracting to the other judges.

If food is consumed right before evaluating wines, its aftertaste can interfere with the wine's flavor. Research also shows that if you are hungry when you are tasting a wine, your sense of smell and taste become more acute. However, tasting on an empty stomach allows the alcohol in the wine to be absorbed more quickly by the body. This does not present a problem if you limit what you ingest by spitting after tasting. In a social situation where spitting is not an option, having a meal an hour or two before the tasting begins will help moderate the effect of the alcohol.

Tasting protocol also dictates what the proper behavior is during formal tastings. In most wine judgings and critical tastings one group, also called a **flight**, of similar wines is evaluated at a time. When the flight is presented, the wines are first assessed by the tasters, and afterward they are discussed. During the first phase, individual tasters carefully appraise each wine's attributes and take note on their impressions. While this is going on, conversations and talking should be kept to a minimum so that fellow tasters are not distracted. To avoid influencing fellow judges, opinions should also be kept to oneself and not shared at this time. After all judges have finished their own evaluations and recorded their impressions of the wine, then a lively discussion of each wine's qualities can proceed.

Presenting the Wines

The table setting for a formal tasting should be simple, yet provide everything that the taster needs (Figure 4.8). It begins with a basic white linen tablecloth that will absorb spills as well as provide a good backdrop for evaluating a wine's color. Place settings should also include a napkin, water glass, and a small cup or bucket to be used as a spittoon. Tasters may bring their own notebooks for recording observations, but it is always a good idea to have pen and paper available in case they are needed.

One of the most important aspects of setting up for a tasting is selecting the proper glassware. Wine glasses come in a diverse array of sizes and styles. Some glasses incorporate elaborate colors and patterns into their designs that are attractive to the eye, but interfere with the evaluation of the wine and should be avoided. There are also a number of wine glasses available that are designed for use with a particular type of wine such as Cabernet Sauvignon or Chardonnay. With these types of glasses the shape and size of the bowl is designed to emphasize the positive aspects of the wine they are

FIGURE 4.8

A proper place setting for an analytical wine tasting, featuring glasses that are clearly marked with letters representing the different wines, notepaper and pen for writing down impressions, and water with unflavored crackers to refresh the palate. Although it is not pictured, a spittoon should be made available to tasters as well.

© Pat Henderson

FIGURE 4.9

A wine-tasting glass suitable for the evaluation of table wines. The curved-in rim at the top of the glass helps hold in the wine's aroma and prevent spills as the glass is being swirled.

Courtesy Riedel Glassware

made for. Matching the glass to the wine being poured is an important part of serving fine wine and is discussed in Chapter 19; however, for critical evaluation of wine, a more basic tasting glass is all that is needed.

A glass for general tasting should have a capacity of about 8 to 12 ounces (235 to 350 milliliters), and when the wine is served, it should be filled about one-quarter to one-third full. This allows the taster to swirl the glass without spilling and provides enough wine for several tastes. The glass should be wider near the base of the bowl and narrower at the top, forming the shape of a tulip (Figure 4.9). This curved-in shape at the top makes swirling easier and helps concentrate aromas and keep them in the glass. Most wine glasses have their bowls connected to their base with a glass stem. This provides a convenient place to hold onto the glass without your hands warming up the wine. There are also several styles of glasses designed specifically for wine evaluation that do not have stems (Figure 4.10). On these models, the bottom of the bowl on the glass is flattened to form the base. For sparkling wines a narrow "Champagne flute" should be used, as illustrated in Figure 3.25 on page 74.

Another factor to consider when selecting a wine-tasting glass is whether to use one made out of crystal or glass. Crystal stemware is usually handmade and considered a finer product. The stem and sides of the bowl are thinner on fine crystal, and this both gives the glass an elegant appearance and allows the taster to clearly view the wine in the bowl. Additionally, the slender surface at the rim of the glass makes it more pleasant to drink from. The thin construction, however, makes crystal stemware much more fragile than glass stemware. This, coupled with the more expensive price tag, means that many wine tasters prefer to use glass stemware because of its durable and inexpensive nature. Whatever the wine glass is made of it should be very clean before it is used for tasting and great care should be taken that it has been well rinsed so that no residual soap remains to alter the taste of the wine. Most, but not all, crystal stemware uses the toxic compound lead in its manufacture. When using "lead crystal," the amount of exposure is not significant if the wine is served only in the crystal. However, wine should never be stored in lead-crystal containers for more than a short period of time.

FIGURE 4.10

A stemless wine glass. The bowl of a stemless glass is similar to that of a traditional wine glass. Some tasters prefer stemless glasses because they are easy to handle and less likely to break during cleaning.

Courtesy Riedel Glassware

Water should always be available to wine tasters for rinsing out their mouths as well as for drinking. Occasional sips of water will help prevent tasters from becoming fatigued or getting dehydrated while consuming alcohol. Food is also a useful tool while tasting wine; a small bite of French bread or plain crackers between sips of wine will help keep the taster's palate fresh. For more tannic red wines, a small bite of rare roast beef can help cleanse the palate between sips. While good food complements the taste of wine, it can also distract from the qualities of the wine itself. Spicy foods with strong aromas and flavors will interfere with the taste of a wine, making it more difficult to evaluate. Aromatic foods such as soft cheeses and smoked meats, while popular at social tastings, should be avoided when performing serious sensory evaluation. The interaction between food and wine is more thoroughly examined in the next chapter.

Other Considerations

It is human nature to have preferences and prejudices; however, they should not be allowed to influence a taster's judgment when evaluating a wine. If a wine judge is biased toward a particular wine region or producer, it can either consciously or subconsciously affect his or her opinion of that wine. It is important to always judge a wine based on its attributes and not by its reputation or price. The simplest and best way to eliminate any potential bias is to taste the wines blind. A **blind tasting** is set up with the tasters not knowing specific information about the wines that they evaluate. They may be informed of the variety or vintage of the flight of wines they are tasting, but the appellation and producers should remain anonymous. For example, if a Napa Valley Cabernet is compared in a flight with a Cabernet from a less renowned region, the taster might subconsciously favor the Napa wine based on the appellation's reputation and not the quality of the wine. There is one difficulty in this approach, however; without knowing the appellation, a taster cannot determine if the wine is a good example of the region's terroir. If all of the wines being evaluated are from the same region or vintage, it is acceptable to let the tasters know because the information does not bias one wine over another. After the evaluation of the wines is completed and ranking or scoring is done, then they can be unveiled while they are being discussed. To hide a wine's identity, the bottles can be covered with paper bags and labeled with numbers or letters before serving (Figure 4.11). If a bottle has a distinctive shape that might give clues to its identity, it can be decanted into a standard bottle or a carafe.

The number of wines in a flight can vary anywhere from 4 to 12, with 6 being a good average number. This allows the judges to easily compare the different wines to one another and rank them in order of preference. Giving wines an absolute score on a scale of 1 to 20 or 1 to 100 is another way of reviewing a wine. This method is simple to understand and popular with consumers, but often is arbitrary and difficult to standardize among judges. After the judges complete their evaluations, their scores or rankings can be compiled to find the overall group ranking of the wines. Using statistics to evaluate the data from tastings is essential for making accurate conclusions about the wines being tasted. Because statistics are difficult to perform, this important step is often neglected, except by enologists doing research on wine.

FIGURE 4.11

To hide the identity of wines being tasted, they can be placed in bags marked with letters or numbers.

© Pat Henderson

No matter how one ranks or scores a wine, it is essential to be able to describe the wine's particular attributes and explain why the wine received the score that it did. If a taster carefully describes the impressions of the flavors and aromas perceived in a wine, it will help others in the group understand the judge's viewpoint, regardless of whether or not they agree with the taster's opinions. Novices at wine tastings are often intimidated by the serious setting and by other tasters with more experience. Beginners should remember that because taste is subjective there are no wrong answers when it comes to which wine they prefer. It is important to be honest when expressing your opinions and not change them to fit in with the rest of the group.

Flights are usually composed of similar wines of the same variety or style; however, there are some variations. A **vertical flight** is a series of consecutive vintages of the same grape variety or type of wine from a single winery. Vertical flights can be very instructive about how a particular wine will age, or how a winery changes its style over time. Tastings also can be set up with a number of different wines from a single producer. While these tastings are not always done blind, they can still be very informative. When tasting multiple flights of wine, or different types of wine within a single flight, there are several basic rules in how to set up the order of the tasting:

- White wines should be evaluated before red wines.
- Dry wines should be evaluated before sweet wines.
- Light-bodied wines should be evaluated before full-bodied wines.
- Young wines should be evaluated before older wines.
- Table wines should be evaluated before dessert or fortified wines.

This method of tasting wines with more delicate flavors before those with stronger flavors prevents the flavors of the first wines from overwhelming those that come later. This helps prevent tasters from becoming fatigued and allows them to have impressions that are more accurate. The order of tasting previously outlined is not only used for serious sensory evaluation, it is also appropriate when enjoying multiple styles of wine in a more relaxed and informal setting.

Proper Tasting Techniques

Tasters use a systematic procedure for the sensory evaluation of a group of wines. This method is designed so that the taster is less likely to become fatigued while tasting, and to make sure each wine in the flight gets an equal treatment. All the wines are first appraised by their appearance, then by their aroma, and then by their taste and mouthfeel. By using the senses in order of sight, smell, and then taste, the taster's senses will not tire as quickly. This is because the sense of sight seldom becomes fatigued and the sense of smell remains more acute than the sense of taste as multiple wines are sampled. Additionally, by evaluating the wines by sight, then smell, before moving on to taste, it gives each of the wines in the group more equal treatment. If each wine were completely evaluated by sight, smell, and taste before moving on to the next wine, the last wine in the flight would not have equal treatment. This is because the taster could become less focused as the tasting goes on and the aroma of the wine can change as the wine sits in the glass. While the wines are being tasted, it is important to keep track of your impressions by taking notes on the sensory attributes of the wines. These will be useful later in the tasting when the judge is ranking the wines and discussing them with others in the tasting group.

Evaluation by Sight

When a taster approaches a group of wines the first attribute that is obvious is their appearance. To begin the assessment, the taster selects one and observes it for its clarity and color. The easiest way to view the clarity is to hold the glass up to a light source and see how clear the image of the light passing through the wine is. This step can be difficult to perform with a tasting area that is not well lit or with deeply colored red wines. In these cases, the wine glass can be held at an angle to reduce the layer of wine the light has to pass through. The wine is studied to see if there is any turbidity or haze present, or if the wine is free of any particulate matter and is brilliant. Most modern commercial wines are brilliant; exceptions are wines that are bottled unfined or unfiltered, as well as older wines that have dropped sediment as they aged. In older wines the sediment can be removed before tasting by decanting as outlined in Chapter 19.

To observe color the glass should be held at a 45° angle and viewed against a white surface such as the tablecloth or a napkin (Figure 4.12). The hue and depth of the wine's color should be observed, compared to the other wines in the flight, and recorded. In red wines, looking at the edge of the wine in the glass can show subtle differences in color that are otherwise not as obvious. Young red wines have a bluish /purple tint to them that changes to a brick red/orange tone as the wine ages. White wines can have a light-yellow/greenish tint when they are young that becomes more golden as they age. Dessert wines have their own color standards, with late harvest whites tending to have a golden hue and tawny ports an amber color.

FIGURE 4.12

Evaluation by sight.

Courtesy NECI Photography:
Paul O. Boisvert

In sparkling wines, note the color as well as the size and quantity of the bubbles. Sometimes still wines will have small bubbles of CO_2 that form at the bottom of the glass after the wine is poured. This slight degree of effervescence is caused by residual CO_2 left over from fermentation. Called **spritz**, it is usually found in white wines that were bottled soon after harvest. It can also be caused by microbial spoilage in the bottle, but this is exceedingly rare in commercially bottled wines. All of the wines in the group should be judged for appearance and observations noted before moving on to the next step.

Evaluation by Aroma

The second step in wine tasting, appraising a wine's aroma, is the most important part of the sensory evaluation of a wine. An experienced wine judge can tell much about a wine's identity by simply smelling it. To begin, the glass is selected and then, while held by the stem, briefly swirled to concentrate the wine's aroma (Figure 4.13). After this is done, place your nose inside the glass and inhale deeply (Figure 4.14). First, note the aromas that are present, what types of smells are detected, and whether they are pleasant or unpleasant. Assess the intensity of these aromas, making note of which are more obvious and which are more subtle. The Wine Aroma Wheel can be a useful tool when looking for descriptors, especially for novices (see Figure 4.19 on page 107). For sparkling wines, there is no need to swirl the glass. First impressions tend to be the most accurate, but remember a wine's aroma can change over time. Some unpleasant aromas, such as the rotten egg aroma from hydrogen sulfide, can dissipate quickly and "blow off," so the wine's aroma will improve later in the tasting. While resting for 15 to 30 seconds write down your observations on the aroma of the wine. After this, repeat the swirling and sniffing, then record any changes in the aroma or qualities that you may not have observed when smelling the wine the first time.

FIGURE 4.13

Swirling the glass.
Courtesy NECI Photography:
Paul O. Boisvert

FIGURE 4.14

Evaluation of aroma.
Courtesy NECI Photography:
Paul O. Boisvert

It is important to resist sharing your observations, good or bad, with the other judges at this time so they are not prejudiced by your opinion. One exception to this rule is if the wine smells as if it has cork taint, a musty, mildew smell from a bad natural cork. If a wine has this character and a second bottle is available, a new glass can be poured. If a second bottle is not available, the wine can be withdrawn from the flight.

Cork taint is described in more detail in Chapter 19 on page 603. The aroma will be reduced if the wine is too cool; in incidences such as these the wine glass can be warmed with the hands to increase the aroma. After all of the wines in the group have been judged for aroma, then the tasting or evaluation by mouth can begin.

Evaluation by Mouth

Before the wine is tasted, it is once again swirled and smelled but instead of stopping at this point, a small sip of wine is taken immediately after inhaling the wine's aroma (Figure 4.15). Hold the wine in your mouth for a few seconds examining its acidity, sweetness, bitterness, and astringency as well as any flavors or new aromas that are perceived. While the wine is in your mouth, appreciate the tactile sensations it makes such as viscosity, alcohol content, and astringency. Observe how the sensory qualities of the wine develop over time, swallow or spit out the wine, and then note the aftertaste. As in the previous steps, record your thoughts on the wine for later discussion. Some tasters like to swish the wine around in their mouth, coating all of the taste buds to intensify the flavors and the texture that is experienced. Another technique that tasters use is to draw a small amount of air through the wine in their mouth or "gurgle" the wine. This increases the concentration of volatile aromatic compounds and intensifies the aroma that is perceived. Both of these practices are popular, but by no means universal, and individual tasters can try them and determine what works best for them.

After the wine is tasted and the observations recorded, this step is repeated by taking a second sip. This gives the wine judge another chance to confirm his or her impressions and look for flavors or aromas they may not have noticed the previous time. One of the most important aspects of evaluation of a wine by mouth it to appraise its overall balance. Does the acid, bitterness, or astringency seem insufficient or too

FIGURE 4.15

Evaluation by mouth.
Courtesy NECI Photography:
Paul O. Boisvert

FIGURE 4.16

	Sight	Evaluation by sight
	Swirl	Swirling by glass
	Smell	Evaluation of aroma
	Sip	Evaluation by mouth
	Spit (or Swallow)	Spitting or swallowing the wine and evaluating the finish

strong? It is important to remember that many wines that taste out of balance when consumed alone taste much better when consumed with food. A red wine that seems to be too astringent may taste much better when accompanied with roasted meat; likewise a white that tastes too sour may be the perfect complement to seafood. If you noticed some spritz in the glass, do you detect a prickling sensation from the bubbles on your tongue? If so, it may not necessarily be considered a fault if the sensation is not objectionable and a small degree of sprtiz can make a young white wine seem more refreshing.

To appreciate fully the aftertaste it is a good idea to swallow a small amount of the wine. This is usually not a problem if there are only a few wines being tasted but can be more troublesome with large or multiple flights. Professional judges at competitive tastings often are required to sample several hundred wines a day. Through limiting what they ingest by spitting out tastes, they can do this without their judgment or senses becoming impaired. Students of wine need to learn to ignore any personal inhibitions they may have to spitting in public. In fact, at a professional tasting *not* spitting after tasting will raise more eyebrows among your colleagues than swallowing will. For this reason, it is important to always provide a spit cup or spittoon when setting up for a tasting.

FIGURE 4.17

Sheet for tasting notes. Here, five Sauvignon Blancs from a single vintage were evaluated. The judge records his comments, including the personal and group rankings. A blank version of this sheet is at the end of the chapter for copying (Figure 4.22).

© Delmar Cengage Learning

Wines: 2010 California Sauvignon Blanc

Wine #		Comments			Personal Rank	Group Rank
A	Sight: Slight haze	Aroma: Not much fruit or grass aroma—rotten egg smell	Taste: Low acid Short finish	General Comments: Worst of the group	5	5
B	Sight: Brilliant pale straw color	Aroma: Fresh cut grass	Taste: Tart and a little thin	General Comments: Average quality	3	2
C	Sight: Brilliant	Aroma: Lots of grassy varietal character guava & pineapple	Taste: Crisp, tart finish	General Comments: Most intense flavor of group	1	1
D	Sight: Brilliant	Aroma: Fresh melon & gooseberry	Taste: Nice acid balance Touch of sweetness	General Comments: Almost as good as wine C	2	3
E	Sight: Brilliant	Aroma: Bellpepper–Herbaceous aroma Oak aged smell	Taste: Thick body A little bitter	General Comments: Too vegetative for my taste	4	4
	Sight	Aroma	Taste	General Comments		
	Sight	Aroma	Taste	General Comments		
	Sight	Aroma	Taste	General Comments		

Tabulation of Judge's Scores					
Judge	Wine A	Wine B	Wine C	Wine D	Wine E
Mark	5	3	2	1	4
Kryss	4	2	1	3	5
Joe	3	4	1	5	2
Nick	5	2	3	4	1
Pat	5	3	1	2	4
	22	14	8	15	16

FIGURE 4.18

Tabulation of judges' scores. Here five judges taste the five Sauvignon Blancs that were described on the tasting sheet in Figure 4.17. By summarizing the judges' ranks for each wine, the overall preferences for the group can be determined. Since the lower the number the more preferred the wine, wine C was the favorite with 8 points and wine A was the least favorite with 22 points. Wines B, D, and E with 14, 15, and 16 points, respectively, were not statistically very different from one another in preference.
© Delmar Cengage Learning

Group Discussion of the Wines

After all of the wines in the flight have been evaluated for appearance, aroma, and taste you can go over your notes to see if you would like to taste any of the wines again. Since aromas change over time, it is a good idea to re-smell any of the wines that had an off-character to see if it persists. If the wine has improved, note it but do not discount the fact that it was originally flawed when first tasted. This is also the time to select which were your most and least favorite wines in the group and assign them scores or rank them. If you are finished before the others, wait quietly until everyone else is done. After everyone has completed tasting and the scores or ranks are compiled, discussion of the wines can begin.

When discussing the wines do not be shy about sharing your observations and opinions with the others in the group; your opinion is as valid as theirs is. This being said, be sure to give others the chance to share their thoughts as well. Often a fellow taster may point out an attribute about the wine that you failed to notice, but seems obvious to you once it is mentioned. Novice wine tasters *must not* give in to the temptation to change their scores or reviews to match the more experienced members of the group; just be prepared to explain the reasons you arrived at your decisions. If the wines were tasted blind, they can be unveiled as they are being discussed or after the discussion is completed.

Many tasters will have a notebook to record their observations so that they can refer to it at a later date. Tasting notebooks are useful to keep all of the taster's notes and the results of tastings they have attended in the same place, as well as to refer to when shopping for the wines that they liked. Tasting sheets (Figure 4.17) are also a useful method of taking notes and can be copied and handed out before the tasting. The steps to evaluate a wine are useful in formal settings, as previously outlined, in addition to situations that are more informal. Whether one is tasting wines in a class or at the table while enjoying a meal at a fine restaurant, the procedure for evaluating a wine is the same. If the basic steps for tasting a wine are followed, it does not detract from the enjoyment of wine, and it allows tasters to turn every wine they sample into a learning experience.

Practicing Your Wine Evaluation Skills

When studying any subject it is crucial to be able to describe and categorize it. Moreover, while tasting and evaluating a wine is initially a solitary undertaking, after your observations are recorded it is always beneficial to discuss them with others. By expressing your point of view and listening to others' opinions, you can gain a better understanding of wine. The best method of improving your sensory evaluation ability is practice. Therefore, one of the best ways to develop your skill in evaluating wine is to taste frequently with a group. This way a larger sampling of different wines can be obtained at a lower per-person cost, and a great deal of knowledge comes from discussing the wines that you taste.

Although sensory evaluation is the definitive method to evaluate what a wine will taste like, it is not without its complications. In laboratory analysis of wine it is important that the data be reproducible by others as well as quantifiable. By contrast, in sensory analysis of wine these objectives are much harder to obtain. The sensory evaluation of wine is by its very nature a personal experience, and because the experience of tasting wine relies on the interpretation of individual tasters, the results can be as varied as the wine tasters themselves can. Furthermore, when evaluating a wine for its quality, the results are dependent on the preferences of those doing the judging.

Difficulties in Evaluating Wine

Evaluating wine does have challenges, including the following:

- **Individual sensitivities**: Among wine tasters there is variation in ability to differentiate aromas and tastes. The level at which a taster can detect a given flavor is called the **threshold**. For example, a level of 0.5 percent residual sugar in a wine may taste sweet to some, while other judges may not be able to identify the character as sweet. Because sugar level also affects viscosity, to them the wine might taste more "full bodied." Through tasting experience and training, it is possible to hone one's skills of identification and to lower the threshold level for identifying wine aromas and tastes.
- **Definitions**: The lexicon of wine terms is often obscure and full of jargon. It is not uncommon to find terms being used that are unfamiliar to most people such as *hazelnut* and *cassis* to describe a wine's aroma. In addition to this problem, different judges may use different terms to describe the same flavor or aroma. What one person calls fruity another might identify as floral. Another example is the aroma of vanilla and French oak. French oak barrels impart a vanilla quality to a wine that is aged in them. An inexperienced judge will describe the aroma as vanilla and a judge that is familiar with the effect of barrel age will describe it as "oaky." Like thresholds, this problem can be overcome by training and tasting experience, making standards of unfamiliar smells. Use of the *Wine Aroma Wheel* outlined in Figure 4.19 is particularly helpful.

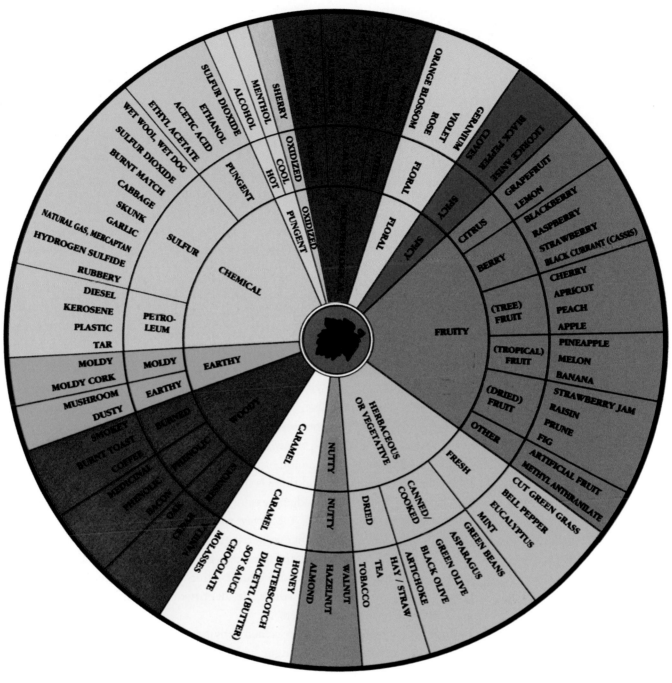

FIGURE 4.19

The Wine Aroma Wheel organizes smells commonly found in wines into groups that have similar qualities, and is a useful tool for experts and novices alike.

Copyright 1990 A. C. Noble. Colored laminated plastic wine aroma wheels may be obtained from www.winearomawheel.com.

THE WINE AROMA WHEEL

Beginning wine tasters often have a difficult time coming up with terms to describe the aromas that they find in wine. Furthermore, experienced tasters often use obscure terminology to describe wine aromas, or individual tasters may use different terms to describe the same aroma. In an effort to combat these difficulties Dr. Ann Noble at the University of California at Davis developed the Wine Aroma Wheel. The **Wine Aroma Wheel** categorizes the most common aromas that are found in wine, organizing similar aromas together on the different tiers, or rings, on the wheel. For example, the first-tier term of fruity is divided into six different categories of fruity aroma on the second tier. These second-tier terms are further divided into 19 individual types of fruity aromas on the third tier.

In addition to categorizing the aromas that are commonly found in wine, the Wine Aroma Wheel also provides procedures for preparing aroma standards for the smell of third-tier terms in wine. The third-tier term of eucalyptus aroma is found under the first- and second-tier terms of vegetative and fresh. The aroma of eucalyptus is unfamiliar to many wine tasters who live in areas where eucalyptus trees do not grow. A standard for this term can be made to train tasters by placing one crushed eucalyptus leaf in a glass of base wine (Noble et al., 1987). Tasters can then use the eucalyptus standard to become familiar with what the character smells like in wine. Procedures for preparing the Wine Aroma Wheel standards are available at the Web site www.winearomawheel.com, or in the article cited previously (Noble et al., 1987).

- **Preferences/Prejudices**: This is perhaps the most difficult problem to overcome when evaluating a wine. When performing sensory evaluation it is important to be able to describe objectively the characteristics of what the wine smells and tastes like without letting your opinion of their quality affect your results. After fully evaluating the wine's sensory characteristics, you can then complete a review on your opinion of the flavors. Different judges will always have different preferences, and there is "no accounting for taste." However, if the flavor of a wine and the judge's reasons for liking or disliking it are accurately portrayed, people reading the review will be able to determine how they might like the wine and whether or not they would agree with the reviewer. A taster's prejudices are not limited to certain flavors; they might also include certain wine varieties, regions, and producers. This can easily be overcome by always reviewing wines "blind," where the identity of the wine is not known until after the review is completed.

- **Fatigue**: Wine tasting, like any reasoned activity, requires concentration, and it is easy to become fatigued. Fatigue can also be compounded with the ingestion of alcohol. When tasting red wines, repeated sips of the same wine will taste increasingly astringent; this is called **tannin buildup**. To combat these effects it is important to taste in an area free of distractions and taste a reasonable number of wines, 4 to 10, per flight. Aroma is less likely to become fatigued than taste and gives you more information, so it can be relied on more readily when tasting large numbers of wines. Having water available with neutral-flavored crackers or plain French bread will help keep the palate fresh in-between wines. Particularly when tasting a large number of wines, spitting out the wine rather than swallowing will prevent the taster from becoming intoxicated.

UNDERSTANDING WINE DESCRIPTORS

As previously mentioned the sense of smell is a particularly evocative experience. This attribute allows even the inexperienced wine tasters to describe a wine's aroma by how it reminds them of other things they have tasted before. Wine often has a very complex aroma made up of many different types of aromas without one smell dominating the others. Familiar aromas that are reminiscent of pear, green apple, melon, and bell pepper are all commonly found in wine. When smelling a wine, examine the qualities that remind you of items you have smelled before. As the taster gains experience, he or she will learn how to identify some of the aromas and be able recognize and identify the source of those aromas. For example, the aroma produced by the growth of the **Brettanomyces** yeast has a smell reminiscent of a barnyard, leather, or horse sweat. When the taster learns to identify these particular smells, he or she may just refer to them as being *Brettanomyces* or "*Brett.*"

TABLE 4.1 Fifty Common Wine Descriptors

Acetaldehyde	A component of wine that gives off a nutty smell, found in sherry and oxidized wines.
Acetic	Vinegar smell, referring to the chemical name for vinegar, acetic acid. See Volatile acidity.
Aftertaste	The flavor of a wine that lingers after it is swallowed. See Finish.
Astringent	The drying or "puckery" sensation that is produced by tannins, most obvious in red wines.
Attack	The first impression a wine's flavor makes.
Backbone	The tannin structure of a red wine.
Balanced	A wine that has a harmonious balance of flavors, such as acid and sweet, or tannins and fruitiness.
Barnyard	A slightly earthy smell that is reminiscent of manure, sometimes found in wines that have had the growth of *Brettanomyces*. See Horse sweat.
Black currants	A berry fruit popular in Europe that has a flavor often found in Cabernet Sauvignon, also called cassis.
Botrytized	The apricot-like aroma that is produced from the growth of *Botrytis* mold on grapes.
Bouquet	An old term for aromas that are produced by wine processing, such as fermentation bouquet or bottle-aged bouquet.
Burnt match	The smell of sulfur dioxide, a preservative that is used in wine.
Cloying	Overly sweet taste.
Complex	A wine that has a number of different aromas and tastes.
Corked	The musty-wet newspaper smell of compounds that are produced by mold growth, most often caused by bad corks. See Musty.
Crisp	A wine that has a high level of acid and a light body.
Diacetyl	A compound that has a buttery smell produced by malolactic fermentation.
Distinctive	A wine that has a strong aroma, the opposite of Vinous or Dull.
Dry	A wine that has no perceptible sugar.
Dull	A wine that has little aroma or flavor. See Vinous.
Earthy	The smell of freshly turned earth, similar to barnyard.

(Continues)

TABLE 4.1 Fifty Common Wine Descriptors *(Continued)*

Finish	The flavor of a wine that develops after it has been sipped and as it is being swallowed. See Aftertaste.
Flat	A low-acid wine that is out of balance.
Foxy	The distinctive varietal aroma of native American grape varieties such as Concord.
Herbaceous	The herbal/vegetable-like aroma that is often found in Cabernet Sauvignon as well as Sauvignon Blanc and Merlot.
Horse sweat	The distinctive aroma of the growth of *Brettanomyces*, usually reserved for wines that have a very strong "barnyard character."
Hot	The tactile sensation that is produced by wines with high alcohol content.
Hydrogen sulfide	A compound that has a strong rotten egg smell.
Jammy	A cooked fruit smell that usually results from very ripe grapes.
Legs	The small rivers of wine that roll down the sides of a glass after it has been swirled. See Tears.
Linalool	A type of monoterpene that has a floral aroma often found in Gewürztraminer and Muscat wines.
Mercaptan	A strong, unpleasant aroma that can have a variety of characteristics such as the smell of onion, garlic, or rubber.
Methoxypyrazines	A group of compounds that produce herbaceous and vegetal aromas.
Monoterpenes	A group of compounds responsible for the spicy character in Gewürztraminers, Muscats, and Rieslings.
Mousse	A French term for the bubbles in sparkling wine.
Musty	A moldy smell associated with cork taint. See Corked.
Nutty	The smell produced by acetaldehyde. See Oxidized.
Oaky	The woody smell produced by aging in oak barrels.
Oxidized	The nutty smell produced by acetaldehyde, often accompanied by a yellowish (in whites) or brownish (in reds) color change in the wine.
Raisiny	The raisin like smell produced by making wines from grapes that have been partially dehydrated, often found in Zinfandels.
Sec	A French term for "dry" in regard to sparkling wine it refers to a wine with a low level of residual sugar.
Spicy	A distinct aroma found in Gewürztraminers, Muscats, and Rieslings. See Monoturpenes.
Spritzy	A wine with a detectable amount of dissolved CO_2, usually found in young white wines.
Tears	The small rivers of wine that roll down the sides of a glass after it has been swirled. See Legs.
Thin	A wine that has a light body, not very viscous.
Vegetal	A wine with an aroma of fresh vegetables. See Herbaceous.
Vinous	A term that literally means "smells like wine," sometimes used to describe a wine that has little identifiable character. See Dull.
Volatile acidity	A term used to describe vinegar or acetic acid. See Acetic.
Woody	The smell of a wine produced by aging in oak barrels. See Oaky.
Yeasty	A freshly baked bread smell produced by the breakdown or autolysis of yeast, found in méthode champenoise and sur lie aged wines.

What Makes a Good Wine "Good"?

Using sensory analysis, tasters can determine the overall flavor profile of a wine, accurately describing its aroma, flavor, and mouthfeel. However, a perfect description of a wine's flavor does not necessarily make a distinction of the wine's quality. To do this you must determine what the judge's preferences are for the wines being examined. Adjectives such as *bad, good,* and *great* are poor terms to use to describe a wine. This is because they do not describe the wine itself; they describe your *opinion* of the wine. By its very nature, wine tasting is subjective and a wine that one person enjoys immensely, another may find awful. That being said, and opinions aside, there are certain qualities that are typically found in wine that most tasters find enjoyable.

- **Distinctive flavor**: The wine should have discernable flavors and aromas that are characteristic of the varietal or the type of wine being tasted. Ideally the sensory qualities of the wine should be true to the region or terroir that the wine is from.
- **Complexity**: Wines with many types of flavors are more interesting than one-dimensional wines that have a single sensory trait that dominates all others.
- **Balance**: The different attributes of a wine's flavor should be in harmony with one another. This is particularly true during the examination by mouth when the bitter, sweet, and tart qualities all interact.
- **Intensity of flavor**: Strong flavors make more of an impression than subtle wines. This is more apparent when wines are tasted as a group rather than as individual wines paired with food. A wine with a lot of flavor will stand out against a backdrop of more delicate wines; however, a strongly flavored wine may be harder to match with a meal.
- **Quality of flavors**: The flavors that make up a wine's sensory profile should be pleasing to experience with no unpleasant or "off" characteristics.

There is almost an infinite variety of wines available to consumers and their flavor profiles are determined by a number of factors. These factors include the variety of grape used for production, the terroir of the vineyard that produced the grapes, the cultural practices used by the grape grower, and the cellar practices used by the winery that made the wine. Every step of the way from vineyard to bottle, grape growers and winemakers are making decisions that influence the sensory profile of the final product. The multitude of options available to growers and winemakers means there is a multitude of styles for even a single variety of wine. For example, from a single vineyard a winemaker can create either a Chardonnay that is light bodied, tart, dry, with no discernable oak aroma and a delicate scent of green apple, or a Chardonnay that is full bodied, high alcohol, sweet, with a lot of oak character and an aroma that has a strong smell of butter but little fruit.

In spite of this diversity, there are certain flavors that grape varieties usually exhibit no matter in which style the wine is being made. In Table 4.2 lists some of the most popular wine varieties along with the aromas and flavor profiles that a taster would likely find in them. It is by no means a list of the *only* attributes one would expect to find, nor is it a list of what should *always* be found. Simply think of it as a list of what to keep any eye out for when you taste. Table 4.2 is expanded in Chapter 5 to include a list of foods that would complement the wines. Chapter 2 provides additional information on these as well as other varieties.

TABLE 4.2 Flavor Profiles of Common Wine Varieties

Wine	Flavor Profile
Sparkling wine (méthode champenoise)	Bubbles should be small and evolve slowly so the effervescence lasts. For méthode champenoise (traditional) sparkling wine, aroma is more derived from the fermentation in the bottle giving it a yeasty, freshly baked bread character with a slight nutty scent. Fruit aroma is usually subtle with notes of apple or pear, citrus and berry aromas can also be found. Sparkling wine usually has a lot of acid and can be quite tart depending on how much sugar is added at dosage.
Riesling	Made in a wide varieties of styles from light-bodied, dry, crisp wines to late harvest rich and sweet versions. Riesling has a distinctive floral/spicy aroma, and typical descriptors include clove, peach, apple, and orange zest. As Rieslings age they can take on notes of honey and diesel (which is not considered a fault). When done in a late harvest style the wines are rich and very sweet with an apricot aroma.
Pinot Gris (Pinot Grigio)	Pinot Gris is usually produced as a light-bodied refreshing wine with little to no oak aging. It can have varying degrees of sweetness. Typical aroma descriptors include apple, pear, tropical fruit, almond, lemon, lychee, and honeysuckle. By mouth, Pinot Gris should have good acidity and often has what is described as a "mineral" or "stony" character.
Sauvignon Blanc (Fume Blanc)	Usually bottled in a light-bodied dry to slightly off-dry style, Sauvignon Blanc expresses a wide range of flavors depending on the terroir where it is grown. Cooler climates produce aromas of green pepper, gooseberry, boxwood, grapefruit, and lemongrass; more temperate vineyards have notes of guava, passion fruit, melon, and kiwi. In either case, vegetative and grassy aromas are common. Usually there is little oak aging or malolactic fermentation, so Sauvignon Blancs typically have good acidity and a fresh taste. The variety can also be made into a late harvest-style dessert wine.
Chardonnay	This popular variety has a broad range of styles from the lean-bodied and crisp Chardonnays of Chablis, to the big-bodied oaky versions popular in California. The sugar level varies from dry to slightly sweet, with the less expensive offering usually being a little sweeter. The smell is subtle but complex featuring fruity aromas of green apple, pear, white peach, and citrus. Depending on how it was made in the cellar, it may have a buttery aroma from malolactic fermentation and a vanilla/toasty character from barrel aging. If the wine was aged sur lie, it will exhibit a yeasty, freshly baked bread aroma along with a more viscous body.
Pinot Noir	Pinot Noir is a medium-bodied red with delicate and complex flavors. When grown in cooler regions the acidity is more pronounced and when in a warmer area there is less acid and more of a ripe fruit scent. The wine features fruity aromas such as strawberry, plum, cherry, and rhubarb as well as notes of leather, mushroom, and tar. Like most red wines if aged in barrels a vanilla/woody/toasty fragrance will be added to the mix. Pinot Noirs are typically a little lighter in color than other red wines; if one is encountered that has a deeply red hue another variety such as Syrah may have been blended with it to add body and color.
Zinfandel	Red Zinfandels characteristically are medium- to big-bodied wines but since they are often picked at a greater degree of ripeness they have relatively high alcohol, which makes them taste fuller bodied than their tannins alone would. Fruity/jammy aromas predominate such as blackberry, raspberry, black currant, and raisin, which are usually accompanied by spicy notes of black pepper. Also found is a vanilla/woody/toasty aroma from barrel aging. If picked at a very high sugar level at harvest, they may exhibit a touch of sweetness or vinegar character from a sluggish fermentation. White Zinfandels have a very different flavor profile than their red wine siblings do. "White Zins" are pink in color with fresh and fruity aroma, low alcohol, and a sweet finish.

(Continues)

TABLE 4.2 Flavor Profiles of Common Wine Varieties *(Continued)*

Wine	Flavor Profile
Syrah (Shiraz)	One of the most big-bodied of wines, Syrahs usually have firm tannins that allow them to age well. The aroma profile includes fruity notes of plum, blackberry, black current, and cherry as well as aromatic notes of rosemary, leather, white pepper, and licorice. In general, New World examples tend to be on the fruity side with more of an oak profile, while French Syrahs tend to be less dominated by fruit and oak.
Merlot	Medium to full bodied, Merlot has flavors that are reminiscent of Cabernet Sauvignon but it usually has softer tannins and is not quite as complex. Common aroma descriptors include plum, cherry, fig, mint, sage, cinnamon, smoky, and herbaceous along with oaky/woody notes. Merlots from warmer climates tend to be fruitier in nature and cooler climate Merlots have a more herbaceous scent.
Cabernet Sauvignon	Full bodied with well-structured tannins, Cabernet Sauvignon is made in styles that range from wines that are tannic with good acidity and can age for many years, to wines that are very ripe with a lot of fruit character that do not age well. It has one of the most complex aroma profiles of any wine. Descriptors include mint, bell pepper, black current, tobacco, chocolate, fig, green bean, leather, eucalyptus, olive, and violet. It is often blended with other Bordeaux varieties such as Merlot and Cabernet Franc that provide it with even more balance and complexity. Cabernet Sauvignon is almost always aged in oak that give the wine either a light or heavy oak profile depending on the type of barrel and how long it is aged.

INTERPRETING WINE RATINGS AND REVIEWS

As previously stated, the experience of tasting wine is very subjective and whether someone likes a wine or not is a matter of personal taste. However, as is the case with many other "matter of taste" decisions, wine consumers look to the professionals who rank and rate wine to help them make sense of the literally thousands of options that are available to them when they are choosing a wine. Recommendations can come in personal ways in the form of suggestions from the sommelier at the restaurant or a wine shop manager. Advice on which wine to purchase is also available from a multitude of publications, Web sites, and competitions that review wines.

Methods of Ranking

The system for rating wines that consumers are most familiar with is the 100-point scale introduced by Robert Parker in 1978. It quickly became popular with American wine drinkers who at the time were less sophisticated than their European counterparts and desired a system that was simple and easy to understand. Its success helped Parker's newsletter, *The Wine Advocate*, to gain notoriety and today he remains one of the world's most influential wine critics. Later in the 1980s, the 100-point system was picked up by another leading periodical, *The Wine Spectator*, and many more publications were to follow. Despite the popularity of the 100-point scale, it is not without its limitations. Since very few wines score below 70, only about a third of the scale is actually used. Furthermore, the assignment of scores can be somewhat arbitrary and, if pressed, a reviewer may have a difficult time explaining why a particular wine deserves a score of 88 instead of 87 or 89. Scoring can be nonnumerical as well;

FIGURE 4.20

Wine publications and medals. Publications that review wines and wine competitions both have their strengths and weaknesses. Magazines and newsletters offer good descriptions of a wine's flavor profile, while competitions provide an unbiased viewpoint from a team of wine industry professionals.
© Pat Henderson

some publications use ratings like "5 stars" or "highly recommended" to designate their favorite wines.

No matter how they score wine, nearly all reviewers include a written description of the wine that is being appraised. Often overlooked, this is perhaps the most important part of a wine review. If the description is well written, readers can get an clear impression of what the wine being reviewed tastes like and get a better understanding of how the reviewer arrived at his or her opinion. The consumers then can decide for themselves if the wine sounds appealing to them. For example, a critic may give a Chardonnay a low score for having an oak character and slight sweetness if he or she does not like those flavors in a Chardonnay. However, if you prefer a Chardonnay with lots of oak in it and a little sugar, the wine would be a good choice.

Wine Competitions

The results of wine competitions are another source of information that wine drinkers can use to help them choose a wine. Usually sponsored by trade organizations, fairs, and publications such as magazines and newspapers, in these contests, wineries submit their products to be judged against those of other wineries by panels of impartial judges. The wines are grouped into categories by type and variety, and in some competitions they are also organized by price so expensive wines do not compete against inexpensive ones. The criteria for winning and the type of award or medal vary from contest to contest but most divide wines into four classifications: gold, silver, bronze, and no award. Some competitions also give out a "double gold" medal for a wine that receives a gold medal ranking unanimously by the all of the tasters on the panel. Best of show rankings, also called "sweepstakes" awards, are usually given to the favorite white and red wines of the competition.

Wine competitions have several advantages and disadvantages when compared to published wine reviews. On the plus side, the wines are always tasted blind to remove any favoritism and it is not uncommon for the judges never to know the identity of the wines that they have reviewed. Additionally, tasting panels are typically made up by three to five wine experts from diverse backgrounds. When tasters with this broad range of experience reach a consensus, their opinion has more validity than that of a single reviewer. On the down side, many of the best wines often are not submitted to competitions because if the wine already has a good reputation its status may be diminished if it does not bring home the gold. A panel of judges faces the same inherent difficulties in evaluating wine that individual reviewers do. A recent study showed that in one prestigious competition only about half of the panels were consistent in their awards when tasting the same wine more than once (Hodgson, 2008).

What to Look for in a Review

There are literally hundreds of individuals from blogs, organizations, and publications that offer opinions on the many thousands of commercial wines that are available to consumers. When deciding which source to trust there are several attributes that you should be looking for. The most important of these is that the critic or publication is unbiased. Does the critic receive gifts or travel from the wineries whose products he or she reviews? If the publication reviewing the wine takes advertising from wineries, how removed are the reviewers from the department that sells ads? Are the wines *always* tasted and reviewed blind? This means that the scores and descriptions are finalized before the identity of the wine is revealed and there are no after-the-fact adjustments made to the score. Look for reviewers with a reputation of honesty and consistency, and whose tastes in wine match your own. A team of several well-trained reviewers working together is less likely to be biased toward a particular style of wine than an individual critic. Last, the description should be well written and accurate so that it allows you to envision what the wine tastes like just by reading it.

Although wine reviews are created for consumers, the people who sell and produce wine probably have the most interest in them. The primary reason that wineries submit their wines to competitions and reviewers is to help them sell their wine. A good review from a prominent wine writer can literally make or break a winery. This is because the people who sell wine know that their customers will be much more likely to buy a wine that they are unfamiliar with

FIGURE 4.21

© Bob Johnson

if it has a high score than if it does not. The difference between a "good" score and a "bad" one is very small; a gold medal or a score of 91 points is a great deal more helpful to sales than a silver or a score of 89. In recent years, the critics themselves have acquired their own critics. Some complain that the most famous reviewers wield too much power and wineries shape their wines to suit the critics' tastes, leading to homogeneity of wine styles around the world (Rivlin, 2006).

Ultimately, it is the wine drinkers who decide what wines they will buy and their criteria for selection is fairly straightforward. They should ask themselves these questions when selecting wines: Do I like it? If it is being served to guests or customers, do I think they will enjoy it? Is the quality a good value for the price? How well does it go with the food that is being served? While these four questions are the most important factors, the importance of reviews and ratings cannot be denied. Consumers not only use the judgment of critics to help them decide which bottle to buy, the views of the critics also shape their own opinions.

SUMMARY

The ability to taste a wine and enjoy its flavor requires very little skill and can be done by almost anyone. However, tasting a wine and being able to evaluate it critically is a talent that can take many years to master. It is by gaining this knowledge of how to taste and understanding the sensory qualities of a wine that we are able to fully appreciate and share with others how the many components present in wine combine to make up a wine's flavor. The protocol for setting up a tasting to evaluate wines is designed to help minimize distractions so the tasters can concentrate on the qualities of the wines. Whenever possible, wines should be evaluated blind so that preconceived notions do not affect the taster's opinions. Like any creative industry, the wine trade has critics and reviewers to help consumers make the best selections from the multitude of wines that are available. Understanding how these reviewers work, and the terminology that they use, helps wine drinkers decide which reviewers they should pay attention to.

The sensory evaluation of wine usually involves some degree of ingestion. Whenever wine or any other alcoholic beverage is consumed, one must consider issues concerning health and safety. Both of these subjects are covered in detail in later chapters. How to serve wines responsibly is discussed in Chapter 19, and the topic of wine and health is explored in Chapter 5.

EXERCISES

1. What considerations are important to take into account when setting up a formal tasting?

2. How do the different senses respond to wine?

(Continues)

(Continued)

3. Explain how the Wine Aroma Wheel can be used to train wine tasters.

4. What are some of the qualities that most wine drinkers would find enjoyable in a wine?

5. Describe the differences between the perception of bitterness and astringency.

REVIEW QUESTIONS

1. The most important sense one uses when evaluating a wine is your sense of _____.
   A. Sight
   B. Touch
   C. Smell
   D. Taste

2. When taking part in a professional wine judging, which of the following should always be true?
   A. The wines are at room temperature.
   B. The wines are served "blind."
   C. All of the wines in the tasting are from the same appellation.
   D. The wines are served in crystal stemware.

3. The proper order for sensory evaluation of wine is _____.
   A. First by sight, then by nose, finally by mouth
   B. First by mouth, then by nose, finally by sight
   C. First by nose, then by mouth, finally by sight
   D. It makes no difference what order the wine is evaluated in

4. A substance must _____ for it to be perceived by smell.
   A. Be warm
   B. Contain water
   C. Contain alcohol
   D. Be volatile

5. Astringency in red wines is caused by _____.
   A. Alcohol
   B. Tannins
   C. Sugar
   D. None of the above

Wines: _____

Wine #	Comments				Personal Rank	Group Rank
	Sight	Aroma	Taste	General Comments		
	Sight	Aroma	Taste	General Comments		
	Sight	Aroma	Taste	General Comments		
	Sight	Aroma	Taste	General Comments		
	Sight	Aroma	Taste	General Comments		
	Sight	Aroma	Taste	General Comments		
	Sight	Aroma	Taste	General Comments		
	Sight	Aroma	Taste	General Comments		

FIGURE 4.22

Blank tasting sheet for photocopying.

Tasting Exercise

Table 4.3 shows an outline for a 12-week wine-tasting lab designed to provide a survey of major wine types and varietals. It can be done as part of class or as self-directed study with a group of fellow wine students. It works best when led by a knowledgeable instructor, but it can also be used by students independent of a wine class to provide supplemental experience in tasting wine. The program begins with multiple types of wine in one tasting to provide an overview of table wine styles before moving on to more specific tastings that showcase varieties or regions.

This outline provides an example of how to organize a tasting group and it can be modified by changing the number or types of wines to be tasted per gathering. Additionally the number of meetings can be reduced or expanded depending on the interests of the group. If there is no formal leader of the class, students can rotate buying the wines and hosting the event. It is also a good idea for whoever is leading the tasting that day to do some research on the wines being tasted and spend a few minutes before the tasting discussing the variety or region being presented. Four to six wines are selected per tasting and a good group size is anywhere from 6 to 12 tasters. Except for those poured in the first meeting, all wines should be tasted blind and their identities not revealed until the wines have been discussed. For the varietal focus classes only the type of grape should be known to the tasters, and for the regional focus classes only the appellation should be divulged. If desired, the wines can be ranked in terms of preference by the participants and the overall group score for each wine can de determined.

TABLE 4.3 Outline for Tasting Lab

Meeting	Wines to Taste	Examples	Instructional Goals
1 Introduction	Off-dry fruity white Dry, oak-aged white Light-bodied red Full-bodied red	Gewürztraminer California Chardonnay Pinot Noir Cabernet Sauvignon	To introduce sensory evaluation, and to practice tasting procedures both individually and with a group
2 Varietal Focus I	4 to 6 Sauvignon Blancs, including at least 1 from California, the Southern Hemisphere, and Europe	Sonoma County, California; Marlborough, New Zealand; Sancerre, France; Stellenbosch, South Africa	To practice tasting skills and to taste and discuss different styles of Sauvignon Blanc
3 Varietal Focus II	4 to 6 Pinot Noirs, including at least 1 from California, Oregon, the Southern Hemisphere, and Europe	Carneros, California; Willamette Valley, Oregon; Burgundy, France; Casablanca Valley, Chile	To practice tasting skills and to taste and discuss different styles of Pinot Noir
4 Wine Component Tasting I	Component tasting of acid and sugar, wines adjusted with varying levels of acid and sugar	A white and red wine each adjusted with 3 levels of acid and sugar and then compared to the unadulterated base wine (recipes follow)	To focus on the flavors of different levels of acidity and sweetness in the same wine
5 Wine Component Tasting II	Component tasting of alcohol and oak, wines adjusted with varying levels of alcohol and types of oak	A white and red wine each adjusted with 3 levels of alcohol and both French and American oak; then it is compared to the unadulterated base wine (recipes follow)	To focus on the flavors of different levels of alcohol and types of oak in the same wine

(Continues)

TABLE 4.3 Outline for Tasting Lab (Continued)

6 Varietal Focus III	4 to 6 Chardonnays, including at least 1 from California, the Southern Hemisphere, and Europe	Monterey and Russian River, California; Burgundy, France; Hunter Valley, Australia	To practice tasting skills and to taste and discuss different styles of Chardonnay
7 Varietal Focus IV	4 to 6 Cabernet Sauvignons, including at least 1 from California, Washington, the Southern Hemisphere, and Europe	Napa Valley, California; Columbia Valley, Washington; Bordeaux, France; Mendoza, Argentina	To practice tasting skills and to taste and discuss different styles of Cabernet Sauvignon
8 How Wines Age	The same wine from three different vintages, tasting both red and white wines	A 1-, 2-, and 3-year-old Sauvignon Blanc from the same winery, and a 2-, 4-, and 8-year-old Cabernet Sauvignon from the same winery	To examine how a wine changes over time
9 Regional Focus I	4 to 6 white wines, all from the same vintage and appellation	5 different German Rieslings from the Rhine region	To examine the style of a particular appellation
10 Regional Focus II	4 to 6 red wines, all from the same vintage and appellation	5 different Italian reds from the Tuscany region	To examine the style of a particular appellation
11 Sparkling Wine	3 to 5 méthode champenoise sparkling wines, one Charmat process	2 sparkling wines from California (1 Charmat), 2 from Champagne, 1 Spanish cava	To examine different appellations and production methods of sparkling wine
12 Wine and Food	The 5 wines and types of food listed in the Chapter 5 tasting experiments	See the tasting experiments in Chapter 5	To examine how the flavors of wine and food interact

Recipes for Component Wines

To make the wines for component tasting, the first ingredient required is the base wine that will be altered to highlight a particular attribute found in the flavor of wine. By tasting a wine that has been adjusted with different levels of sugar, acid, alcohol, and oak the contribution of each can be observed. For either the white or the red, the base wine should be fairly neutral in character without noticeable oak aroma and should also be dry (without sugar). Most of the ingredients required can be obtained at a home winemaking or beer making supply store. The solid ingredients should be measured with a small lab scale and liquid ingredients can be measured with a volumetric pipette. To adjust the base wine for alcohol, use a neutral beverage alcohol such as 190-proof Everclear. In some states the 190-proof Everclear is not available and 151 proof can be used instead. Be certain to use nothing but food grade ingredients for all of the component tasting wines.

It should be noted that the flavors produced by adding these components will only approximate the taste they will have when they occur naturally in an unadulterated wine.

Ingredients Needed

Granulated sugar

Tartaric acid

Grain alcohol (Everclear 190 or 151 proof)

French oak granules (small diameter—toasted)

American granules (small diameter—toasted)

Red base wine, nonvarietal, dry (no sugar), low/no oak profile, between 12 and 13 percent alcohol

White base wine, nonvarietal, dry (no sugar), low/no oak profile, between 12 and 13 percent alcohol

Sugar	Take 3 bottles of base white wine (750 ml each) and add 1.5 grams of sugar to one, 3 grams to the second, and 6 grams to the third. This will elevate the sugar level of the wines by 2, 4, and 8 grams per liter, respectively. Mix thoroughly and repeat with the base red wine.
Acid	Take 3 bottles of base white wine (750 ml each) and add 0.75 gram of tartaric acid to one, 1.5 grams to the second, and 2.25 grams to the third. This will elevate the acid level of the wines by 1, 2, and 3 grams per liter, respectively. Mix thoroughly and repeat with the base red wine.
Alcohol	Take 3 bottles of base white wine (750 ml each) and add 9 milliliters of 190-proof Everclear to one, 18 milliliters to the second, and 27 milliliters to the third. This will elevate the alcohol level of the wines by approximately 1, 2, and 3 percent, respectively. If 151-proof Everclear is used the amounts to add are 11.5, 23.0, and 34.5 milliliters, respectively. In either case, the volume of the wine will be greater than the capacity of the bottle so the wine and alcohol will need to be combined in a carafe and mixed thoroughly before returning the wine to the bottle. Repeat with the base red wine.
Oak	Take 2 bottles of base white wine (750 ml each) and add 1.5 grams of toasted French oak granules to one bottle and 1.5 grams of toasted American oak granules to the second bottle. Repeat with the base red wine. This should be done one week prior to the tasting to allow enough time for the wine to extract the flavor from the oak and the granules to settle.

REFERENCES

Hodgson, R. T. (2008). An examination of judge reliability at a major U.S. wine competition. *Journal of Wine Economics, 3*(2), 105–113.

Jackson, R. S. (2009). *Wine tasting: A professional handbook.* London: Academic Press.

Noble, A. C., Arnold, R. A., Buechsenstein, J., Leach, E. J., Schmidt, J. O., & Stern, P. M. (1987). Modification of a standardized system of wine aroma terminology. *American Journal of Enology and Viticulture, 38*(2), 143–146.

Rivlin, G. (2006, August 13). Wine ratings might not pass the sobriety test. *New York Times.*

Smith, D. V., & Margolskee, R. F. (2001, March). Making sense of taste. *Scientific American, 284*(3), 32–39.

{FOOD AND WINE}

This chapter first examines

the historical and cultural origins of pairing food and wine. It explores the basic principles of food and wine pairing and how these principles can be used to find the appropriate wine for almost any dish. Next, the chapter explains how a wine's flavor profile changes as it ages. Finally, it discusses the health effects of alcohol and wine consumption, both positive and negative.

KEY TERMS

anthocyanins

bottle bouquet

esters

French paradox

fusion cuisine

haute cuisine

quercetin

resveratrol

sediment

INTRODUCTION

When done properly, the marriage of wine and food is a mutually beneficial relationship, with the qualities of each partner benefiting the other (Figure 5.1). Water, being neutral in flavor, does not affect the taste of food; it merely serves to moisten the mouth during ingestion. Wine, in contrast, can have a profound effect on the flavors of the food with which it is consumed. In the previous chapter we discussed the role of analytical tasting where wines are tasted by themselves, or with food that is bland such as soda crackers or plain bread, so one can concentrate on their flavors and aromas. In the study of food and wine pairing the opposite is true, where individual foods and wines are matched so their flavors complement each other. While this makes it more difficult to evaluate the wine on its own merits, it usually makes for a more enjoyable experience. Most people are familiar with the overused and oversimplified rule of "white wine with fish and red wine with meat" but not surprisingly, the subject is a little more complex than this simple rule implies. However, by understanding a few straightfor-

FIGURE 5.1

Serving wine with food improves the taste of both items. While there are many books written on the subject of wine and food pairings, there are no absolute rules of which wine must be served with a certain dish. Wine drinkers should feel free to experiment with different combinations and come up with matches that they themselves enjoy.

© Bureau Interprofessionnel des Vins de Bourgogne (BIVB)/Image & Associes

ward principles about the interaction of food and wine it is possible to find a delicious accompaniment to almost any dish.

Historically many classic food and wine pairings began simply by putting together the best matches from what limited food and wine choices were available. Today these classic combinations remain popular, but many chefs have found success joining exotic foods and wines from around the world in untraditional combinations. One can think of the job of the vintner as being to produce a quality wine, while the role of the sommelier and the chef is to match the wine with the proper food.

As a wine ages, it undergoes a number of chemical changes that alter the color, aroma, and flavor of a wine and how it interacts with food. Whether a wine benefits from these developments depends on the style of the wine as well as the preferences of the consumer who will ultimately be drinking it. Also covered in this chapter is the role of wine and alcohol on human health. Anyone who consumes or serves alcohol should know what happens to the body physiologically when alcohol is consumed. Although excess consumption of wine can certainly have negative consequences to one's health, moderate wine consumption has been shown to have positive health effects.

HISTORICAL AND CULTURAL INFLUENCES ON FOOD AND WINE PAIRING

Throughout history, people have produced beverages from whatever fruit or grain their region could produce, such as sake from rice, beer from barley, cider from apples, as well as wine from regions where grapes were grown. These beverages were usually consumed with food, but little thought was given to choosing a specific beverage to accompany a specific dish. People simply consumed what was available. As was observed in Chapter 1, wine has been a factor in human history for close to 7,000 years, and since its very beginnings it has been consumed with food as part of a meal. Wine-making spread quickly throughout the ancient world and became an integral part of the culture of Greece and, later, the Roman Empire. The Romans, as they expanded their empire, brought winemaking to the Iberian Peninsula (present-day Spain and Portugal) and later to France and then Germany. In more recent times, colonists from Europe brought grape growing and wine production to the New World. By the middle of the 1800s, wine was being made in the United States, on both the East and the West Coasts, as well as in Australia, New Zealand, and South Africa.

Each of the cultures mentioned here—Italy, Greece, Spain, Portugal, France, and later the New World—evolved their own cuisines over the centuries. Each individual country developed its cuisine based on the foodstuffs available in its region. The beverage to accompany meals in European countries and their colonies was naturally wine from their respective countries. This was in part due to the great difficulties involved in importing wine from other countries hundreds of years ago. Even though various foods and cooking techniques began to intermingle as early as the sixteenth century in Europe, each country's wines and cuisine evolved separately, with specific recorded culinary traditions, involving unique practices and combinations. Moreover, the wines of each region were made with grape varietals indigenous to that region, and reflected

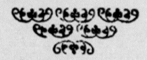

FIGURE 5.2

The seventeenth-century book *Le Cuisinier François* was one of the most influential texts in establishing the concept of French national cuisine.

Source: Library of Congress

the terroir of the region. Thus, not too much effort was put into the matching of wines to food. As far as most people of that time were concerned, Mother Nature had taken care of that detail.

Wine Pairing Develops

Coming into the late seventeenth century, regional cuisines became more clearly defined. Specific cuisines, especially that of France, became easily identifiable. The French were certainly leaders in defining a national cuisine. As early as 1652, a book titled *Le Cuisinier François* was published. It was written, not surprisingly, by a French chef, La Varenne (Figure 5.2). By the mid-1800s France's national cuisine came to be called la **haute cuisine** (OAT kwee-ZEEN), which translates to "high cuisine" and was considered the quintessential expression of fine dining. As it was further developed and improved, especially under Escoffier in the late nineteenth and early twentieth centuries, and as the concept of restaurants—where people could congregate and socialize over a great meal—evolved, more attention was given to wine as an integral part of cuisine.

As Europeans and Americans became more sophisticated, and cosmopolitan in their tastes in food, they also began to become more and more aware of the role wine can play in complementing fine food to make a meal even more enjoyable. People in Europe tended to choose wines from their own country to accompany domestic food. In countries where fine wines were made, such as France and Italy, such chauvinism made good sense. However, in countries where wine could not be produced due to climate, for instance, England, Scandinavia, and Russia, choices had to be made. In these countries, and increasingly in the New World, more often than not French wines were chosen to accompany local cuisine. As the international wine trade developed, choices could be made as to what wines would be imported and sold, the concept of matching specific wines to specific dishes fully developed.

In modern times, roughly from the beginning of the twentieth century to the present, gastronomy has become an ever-more international science. There is a noticeable increase in the intermingling of various cuisines. Even though pride in one's local cuisine remained strong in most countries, people became more interested in experimenting with other countries' top dishes,

FIGURE 5.3

The Austrian-born chef Wolfgang Puck popularized the notion of fusion cuisine that combined New and Old World cooking techniques into exciting new dishes.

© AP Photo/Reed Saxon

and perhaps finding ways to incorporate into those dishes some locally produced ingredients. This type of culinary synthesis came to be known as **fusion cuisine**. The term refers to a blending of the culinary traditions of two or more nations to create innovative and sometimes quite fascinating dishes. It tends to be more common in culturally diverse and metropolitan areas, where there is a wider audience for such food.

Fusion cuisine got its start in the 1970s. The chef most often credited with furthering the emerging trend of taking ingredients or dishes or cooking practices from more than one country and mixing them together into a truly creative dish was Wolfgang Puck. Born in Austria in 1949, he worked in France as a chef before coming to the United States in 1973. After his arrival he quickly became one of the most prolific and successful chefs in this country (Figure 5.3). Perhaps due to his eclectic background, Puck had an early interest in blending various diverse traditions and components into new dishes. He was especially fascinated with the possibility of synthesizing the old traditional European styles, such as France's haute cuisine, with the equally old and equally traditional, but very different, Asian cuisines. Puck called his new creation "Eurasian cuisine," a creative blending of European with Asian cuisines. An example may be a traditional French tournedos of beef with a wassabi reduction sauce.

Many restaurants throughout the United States now feature fusion cuisine, with some of them featuring the cuisines of several different Asian countries, and others being creative enough to feature perhaps Italian cuisine with a touch of American Southwest mixed in. In this country, over the past 25 years people have become very sophisticated in their tastes for food, and more knowledgeable about food preparation. As Americans become more adventuresome with food, they are free to become more adventuresome in their choices of wines as well. Recently Americans have become much more wine knowledgeable. No longer does one feel obligated to buy a French wine just because the dish it will go with is of French origin. With an appetizer of rich pâté de foie gras, why not try a rich Chardonnay from California? With the assistance of a trustworthy retailer or sommelier, consumers are now quite comfortable ordering a German Riesling with a spicy, chili-laden Tex-Mex dish, or a lovely white Burgundy to accompany Maine lobster in lemon-butter sauce. Once a wine consumer has grasped the basic guidelines for matching wine to food, and is comfortable with his or her understanding of how a wine's components, flavor, and texture will affect different foods, he or she will find that matching a good and exciting wine to each dish will greatly enhance any meal.

AN EXERCISE IN MATCHING WINES TO FOOD

To demonstrate how an adventuresome approach to matching wine to food can lead to different experiences based on the wines chosen, we have devised a full menu and matched it to two different sets of wines. Our hypothetical meal is served in a fine American restaurant that features Italian cuisine.

THE MENU

Appetizer
Pesto and walnuts on rigatoni

First Course
Shrimp scampi sautéed with garlic

Main Course
Lamb osso buco with risotto Milanese

Dessert
Classic Ricotta Cheesecake

Since this menu consists entirely of Italian dishes, the traditional approach would be to match each course to a suitable Italian wine. The result may be as follows:

Appetizer
Pesto and walnuts on rigatoni
Wine
Soave Classico (light dry white from Veneto)

First Course
Shrimp scampi sautéed with garlic
Wine
Gavi di Gavi (a dry, complex white from Piedmont)

Main Course
Lamb osso buco with risotto Milanese
Wine
Barbaresco (full-bodied but refined red from Piedmont)

Dessert
Classic Ricotta Cheesecake
Wine
Passito di Pantelleria (a very sweet wine made from Moscato grapes that have been dried out before fermentation)

These combinations are certainly appropriate, and will help make the meal enjoyable. However, a person who chooses to be more adventuresome might decide to match these Italian dishes with wines from around the world.

Appetizer
Pesto and walnuts on rigatoni
Wine
Sauvignon Blanc from Lake County in California

First Course
Shrimp scampi sautéed with garlic
Wine
Unoaked Chardonnay from Hunter Valley, Australia

Main Course
Lamb osso buco with risotto Milanese
Wine
Cabernet Sauvignon from Napa Valley; or Shiraz from Australia's Yarra Valley

Dessert
Classic Ricotta Cheesecake
Wine
Sauternes from France with some age on it; or a late-harvest Riesling from New York State.

In class, discuss which matches you prefer, and why you think those pairings will best complement the dish with which it will be served.

The goal of combining a wine together with a particular dish is to provide an arrangement where the flavors of the wine both complement and elevate the flavors of the food and vice versa. If the arrangement works well it is a classic case of the whole being greater than the sum of the parts. However, as with any good marriage, the pairing is usually more successful if one partner does not dominate over the other. Intensely flavored wines should be matched with rich, flavorful foods because they would overwhelm lighter fare. It is not uncommon that highly rated wines that are much sought after by collectors do not necessarily make good food wines. An award-winning big-bodied Cabernet Sauvignon with a lot of alcohol may be delicious by itself but would overpower all but the richest dishes.

When deciding on which wine to select with a meal the best way to think about it is to consider the wine as you would a condiment or a seasoning to the dish. In this role, a wine can provide two functions. First, it can act as a seasoning that adds a new flavor and extra dimension to the food. Second, a wine's flavor can complement the dish so that the flavor of the food is emphasized. This enhancement of flavors does not apply only to the food, if the match is well done, the wine will taste better as well. This is illustrated by an old saying among wine merchants, "Buy with bread, sell with cheese." When wine and bread are consumed together, the combination does not improve the flavor of the wine, allowing the merchant to critically evaluate the wine on its own merits. If a merchant wants to improve the flavor of his or her wines, they can be offered for tasting paired with cheese. The cheese will soften the tannins and make the wine taste more balanced and appealing, consequently increasing the merchant's sales.

The qualities of the wine and food being paired can complement or clash with one another. Although there are some exceptions to the rule, usually the most successful combinations are between foods and wines that have similar characteristics that complement one another: light wines with lighter fare, and big, more full-bodied wines with rich foods, and so on. Thinking of wine as it were a seasoning or condiment to food allows us to illustrate this principle in terms of how spices are used to enhance a food flavor. For example, cayenne pepper is an excellent seasoning when used with a hot, spicy dish such as chili, but would be completely out of place and clash with the flavors of a food that was milder and sweeter, such as a vanilla crème brulée. The lessons that a chef learns about how to properly season a particular entrée can also be applied to the kind of flavors you should look for in a wine to be a good match for a food.

Food and Wine in a Restaurant Setting

Choosing the right wine to accompany a meal in a restaurant can be particularly challenging. This is not because the food and wine served is somehow inferior to what would be served at home. In fact, in a fine dining establishment the food is usually better and the wine selection more varied than in the typical home kitchen. The problem lies in the variety of food the diners are eating. When cooking at home for friends and family most often everyone is enjoying the same dish that would be complemented by a particular wine. However, in a restaurant setting with all of the guests ordering different items off the menu, you may need to find a wine that would go well with steak, salmon, chicken, and pasta that are all being consumed at the same table. This is a tall order and, in such cases, it might be best if everyone chooses the particular wine they would like off the wine by the glass list. Another option would be to select a versatile medium-bodied wine such as Pinot Noir that would go with all of the dishes at least to some degree.

The principles used when pairing wine and food can also be applied to other beverages such as beer, coffee, or tea when selecting proper drink for a meal. As you would with a wine, look at the flavor and richness of the food you would like to match, and then select a beverage that has complementary qualities. For example, in the case of beer a light dish such as vegetables or salad may be best with a refreshing lighter-bodied beer like a Pilsner or Hefeweizen while rich food such as a roast beef dish would do well with a more full-bodied amber ale.

FIGURE 5.4

The concept of joining the cuisine of different regions into interesting new combinations is not limited to food alone but also applies to food and wine pairing. The savory nature of sushi makes it an excellent match with French Champagne.

© Pat Henderson

BASIC CONCEPTS OF MATCHING WINE TO FOOD

The topic of food and wine pairing is an extensive one and there are many articles and books devoted to the subject. Many of these references provide long lists of different types of food opposite the particular, and often obscure, wine that they are best served with. This information is not particularly helpful to most people because it is difficult, if not impossible, to memorize the hundreds of food and wine combinations and often there are interesting pairings that might be overlooked on these lists. By understating the fundamentals of how the flavors of wine and food harmonize together, consumers and wine servers alike should be able to determine several types of wine that would complement particular dishes without having to consult a reference. Table 5.1 summarizes the basic guidelines for pairing wine and food.

When eating food, wine serves not only to moisten the mouth but also to freshen the palate between bites. A sip of wine will help to cleanse your mouth of the foods' aftertaste and make your senses ready to fully appreciate another mouthful. The first bite you take of a food always seems more flavorful than your last. By cleansing your palate with wine between bites, each mouthful you take will be as flavorful as your first (Figure 5.4). An example of this principle is the interaction of the astringency of red wine with the rich "fatty" taste of red meat or cheese. The internal fat and marbling of beef is responsible for much of the flavor and juiciness of the meat when it is cooked. This rich flavor and fatty character makes red meat a great match for big-bodied astringent reds such as Cabernet Sauvignon and Syrah. Lighter meat dishes such as chicken and pork generally go better with more medium-bodied red wines like Pinot Noir or Merlot.

The method of preparation can greatly affect how the dish will pair with the wine. A chicken or pork dish that is served with a rich, creamy sauce would be able to stand up to the tannic flavor of a Cabernet Sauvignon. Additionally the same cut of meat prepared with a spicy dry rub may be perfect with a light and crisp white wine. This is an example of how the seasoning, sauce, or a glaze of a dish can be used to bridge the gap between the food's flavors and those of the wine. Once again, this principle can go both ways and how a wine is made can affect how it will go with food. For example, Merlot is usually considered a medium-bodied red wine; however, if it is produced from grapes grown on a hillside vineyard with low yields, and gets a lot of skin contact during fermentation, it will be a very full-bodied wine.

TABLE 5.1 Ten Simple Guidelines for Successful Food and Wine Pairing

Pairing Guideline	Example
Rich foods are complemented by full-bodied wines (tannic wines complement fatty foods).	Beef tenderloin in béarnaise sauce, paired with a Cabernet Sauvignon made in a rich ripe style.
Light-bodied foods are complemented by light-bodied wines.	Butter-poached fillet of sole, paired with a dry unoaked Pinot Gris.
Sour foods decrease the perception of acid in wine and are best paired with tart wines.	A tangy tomato-based pasta sauce, paired with a tart Sangiovese.
Sweet foods accentuate the perception of acid and are best paired with wines that are slightly sweeter than the food.	Apricot tart paired with a late harvest Gewürztraminer.
Foods with fruity flavors go best with wines that also have a fruity character.	Appetizers of melon wrapped in prosciutto, paired with rosé of Pinot Noir.
Complex foods with intricate flavors go best with simple wines; conversely, wines with complex flavors go best with simple foods.	Molasses roasted pork tenderloin with sweet potatoes, apples, and walnuts with medium-bodied Merlot. Conversely, grilled steak paired with a Bordeaux-style blend of Cabernet Sauvignon, Malbec, Petit Verdot, and Merlot.
Spicy foods bring out the bitterness and astringency in wine and are best paired with tart, light-bodied, off-dry wines. They also do well with aromatic spicy wines with a little sugar.	Szechuan kung pao chicken, paired with an off-dry Riesling.
Salt in food decreases the perception of bitterness and astringency in wine.	Grilled, brined pork chops, paired with a Syrah from the Rhône region.
Salty foods pair well with sparkling wine.	Caviar or potato chips with Champagne.
A sauce or glaze can be used to bridge the gap between flavors to allow a particular food to go with a certain wine.	Roast turkey breasts with blackberry glaze paired with a Zinfandel that has ripe, jammy flavors and a little bit of residual sugar.

Young, crisp wines also do well with spicier dishes where their acidity stands up to the food's strong flavors. Since a spicy food will emphasize a wine's bitterness, an off-dry wine with a small amount of residual sugar will counteract this effect and help balance out the heat of a spicy dish. The sweetness of the wine will refresh the palate between bites so your sense of taste is not overpowered by the food's spicy flavors.

Another basic principle of food and wine pairings is that the textures and body of the food and wine should complement each other. Ideally the flavors and textures of the two should be somewhat evenly matched and not overwhelm each other. For example, light-bodied foods such as fish and chicken are better paired with light-bodied wines. Alternatively, full-bodied "big" wines do better with rich foods and red meats. Tart wines generally do not do well with sweet foods because the sugar content of the food brings out the acidity in the wine, making it appear too sour. A dry wine paired with a dessert course will make the dessert seem too sweet, therefore a wine with higher sugar content would be more appropriate.

Sparkling wines such as Champagne are an excellent accompaniment to a number of dishes and can usually be paired as a light-bodied white wine would be. The older and more complex a sparkling wine is, the better it goes with heavy foods. Foods with a salty flavor like caviar do especially well served with a sparkling wine. In fact, in two much less traditional matches, the salty/savory qualities found in both sushi and potato chips make them an excellent combination with sparkling wines.

How a Wine's Flavor Affects Food

A wine's chemical and physical attributes determine not only what the flavor of the wine will be but also how the wine will relate to food. The individual components that make up a wine's flavor profile each have an effect on how wine and food go together.

- **Alcohol level**: Alcohol also greatly affects a wine's body and viscosity and higher levels of alcohol are often found in full-bodied wines that are made from very ripe grapes. The intense flavors found in these wines make them popular, but they must be matched with rich, full-bodied foods or they will seem out of balance and detract from the meal. Wines with lower alcohol content usually go best with light-bodied dishes. Another way to think of this is that the amount of alcohol in a wine affects the wine's body and richness much in the same way that the fat content in a food affects the food's body and richness.
- **Acidity:** Acid makes a wine taste fresh and crisp and contributes to the quality of its finish. To properly match a food, a wine should always be a little tarter than the dish with which it is being served. This will keep the wine from tasting too tart.
- **Sweetness:** Wines have a wide range of sweetness from dry, as is the case with most table wines, to very sweet, as is found in dessert wines. A rule of thumb is that the wine should be as sweet as or sweeter than the food it is being served with. Dry and off-dry wines are a good match for savory foods, and desserts are best paired with sweet wines. A bit of sweetness in a wine also helps moderate the hot flavors found in spicy foods.

- **Astringency/Bitterness:** As mentioned in Chapter 4, astringency is a drying sensation in the mouth and bitterness is a flavor. Tannins, found particularly in red wines, are responsible for astringency and bitterness and contribute to the impression of body that a wine has. A red wine's tannic flavors allow it to complement rich, fatty foods like beef and cheese and freshen the palate between bites. A general rule is the more tannic a wine is, the richer the food it should be served with.
- **Oak level:** Most red wines and many Chardonnays are aged in oak during the winemaking process. A wine with a high degree of oak character will have a more full-bodied flavor and go best with heavier foods.
- **Body/Viscosity:** All of the wine components listed previously come together to some degree in the perception of a wine's overall body. The richer and more full-bodied a wine is the better it will be able to stand up to a pairing with rich and flavorful foods. Conversely, wines with light and fresh flavors do best with lighter dishes.

How a Food's Flavor Affects Wine

Just as a wine's qualities influence how the wine will go with a particular dish, how a food is prepared affects how it will match up with wine. Method of cooking, as well as how it is seasoned or what type of sauce is used, should always be taken into consideration when selecting a wine (Figure 5.5). These variables can cause what otherwise

(A)

(B)

FIGURE 5.5

(A) Cedar plank salmon. (B) Poached salmon. The method of preparation can influence how a wine and food go together as much as the selection of the food itself. The more robust flavor of the cedar plank salmon makes it a better match for a medium-bodied red wine, while the delicate character of the poached salmon makes white wine a better choice.

a: © Olga Lyubkina/Shutterstock. b: © Monkey Business Images/Shutterstock.

would have been a good combination to be unpalatable as well as bridge the gap between unlikely matches of food and wine to make them successful.

- **Method of cooking:** The method by which a food is cooked, as well as to what degree it is cooked, both influence the flavor and richness of a food. More delicate techniques, such as poaching or steaming, are lighter in nature and preserve the foods' subtle flavors making them more suited to medium- and light-bodied wines. More robust methods of cooking such as broiling and grilling over an open flame, and food that is well done, do better with fuller-bodied wines.

- **Richness:** The primary contributor to a food's richness is its fat content and a wine with significant astringency will balance out the fatty qualities of the food and help keep the palate fresh. Foods that are rich and filling do best with a full-bodied wine that is not overpowered by their flavor. Lighter dishes with low fat content do better with wines that are low in tannins and have a more delicate mouthfeel.

- **Spiciness:** Spicy foods are delicious but their fiery character can easily overwhelm a wine. Wines paired with hot and spicy food need to be refreshing in nature to provide a contrast to the palate. White wines with a tart flavor fill this role nicely, and since spicy foods enhance the perception of bitterness, the wine should have a small amount of residual sugar to keep it from tasting too harsh.

- **Saltiness:** Salt is one of the most common ingredients used in the kitchen and has been used to both preserve and season food for millennia. Salty flavor in foods interacts with red and white wine in different ways. The acid found in a crisp, light-bodied white wine will diminish the salty flavor of food and provide a good match. Salt in food also lowers the perception of bitterness and astringency of wine so a salty dish can also pair with a tannic red wine.

- **Acidity:** Acid flavors are of course found in food as well as wine. As previously mentioned, the acidity of a food should always be a little less than the wine that it is being served with, otherwise the wine will taste flat and not very refreshing. High-acid foods, particularly those that are vinegar based such as salad dressing, can be difficult to match. In addition to using a high-acid wine, it may be necessary to lower the acid level of the food as well.

- **Sweetness**: Sweetness in food enhances the taste of acid and bitterness in wine. To taste in balance with a wine, the food should be a little less sweet than the wine it is served with. If it is not, the wine will taste flat compared to the food. If a red wine is not as sweet as the food, it will taste harsh and bitter. The perceived sweetness of a food can be diminished if the food is also tart or spicy, and this will lower the degree of sweetness needed in the wine being served with the food. The high sugar level in desserts will make dry red wines taste bitter and astringent unless the wine also has a lot of sugar as in the case of Port-style red dessert wines. This principle is illustrated in the tasting experiment "Finding the Right Wine for Chocolate" on pages 136–137.

A SIMPLE EXPERIMENT IN PAIRING WINE AND FOOD

Chefs and wine researchers at Beringer Vineyards in California have developed a simple experiment that demonstrates how the basic flavors found in wine and food interact. This experiment is easy to perform and can be done by individuals in a home setting, but is even more instructive when done with a tasting group so the wine tasters can discuss how the flavors of the foods and wines interact. To conduct the experiment assemble the following materials.

Ingredients Needed for Each Tester

1 glass of a light-bodied off-dry white wine (such as an early-harvest Gewürztraminer)
1 glass of a dry, full-bodied, oaky white wine (such as Chardonnay)
1 glass of a medium-bodied red wine (such as Merlot)
2 wedges of apple
2 wedges of lemon
2 slices of cheese (mild flavor with firm texture such as Monterey Jack or Colby)
Several black olives (unpitted)
Saltshaker

FIGURE 5.6

© Pat Henderson

Step One

Assemble the materials and then taste each of the wines by itself, starting with the light-bodied white wine, then the full-bodied white wine, then the medium-bodied red. With each wine, write down your impression of its flavors, particularly how the qualities of sweet, sour, and bitterness/astringency taste.

Step Two

Taste an apple wedge followed by the off-dry white wine; then taste the apple again followed by the full-bodied white wine; and finally, taste the apple once again before sampling the red wine. Record how the sensory qualities of the wine change from food to food. Repeat these steps for the lemon wedges, the cheese slices, and the olives. Each time you taste the wine, be sure to write down how the taste is affected by the food that it is sampled with.

Results

Apple: Notice how the sweet, fruity taste of the apple goes best with the off-dry white wine, while it makes the dry white wine taste tart and the red wine taste bitter and astringent.
Lemon: The acidic taste of the lemon makes the off-dry white wine taste sweet and the dry white wine taste more balanced. The tart character of the lemon also makes the red wine taste less bitter.

Cheese: The rich flavor of the cheese has a subtle effect on the flavor of the off-dry white wine. However, notice how the cheese lowers the perceived astringency and bitterness in the dry white and red wines.
Olives: The bitter and slightly tart nature of the olives makes the off-dry wine taste sweeter and the dry white taste less acidic. In the red wine, notice how the taste of the olives makes the flavors appear less bitter and astringent.

Step Three

To show how flavors can be used to bridge the gap between food and wine, start by tasting an apple wedge again followed by a sip of the red wine. Notice how the wine tastes bitter and astringent after sampling the apple. Now take another slice of the apple and squeeze a bit of lemon juice over it followed by a sprinkle of salt. Taste the apple with the lemon and salt again following it with a sip of the red wine. This time notice how the tart flavor of the lemon juice combined with the savory character of the salt makes the red wine taste more balanced and less harsh than when the apple is tasted by itself. This effect can easily be demonstrated at the dining room table where a squeeze of lemon and a pinch of salt can help many light-bodied foods stand up to the tannins that are found in red wine.

FINDING THE RIGHT WINE FOR CHOCOLATE

A popular wine and food pairing for many people is the combination of Cabernet Sauvignon and chocolate. Despite this popularity, it is a match that often does not work particularly well. The sweetness in food accentuates the bitterness in wine; therefore, the sweet flavors in chocolate make a dry Cabernet Sauvignon seem overly bitter and astringent.

To demonstrate how the sweetness level of both wine and food interact with each other we will taste both wine and chocolate with varying degrees of sweetness. High-quality chocolate bars are often categorized by the percentage of their makeup that is derived from coco beans; other ingredients include sugar, milk solids, and flavorings. A chocolate bar with a higher coco percentage will have less sugar and more of a bittersweet flavor. Chocolate with high coco content is called dark or bittersweet chocolate. Chocolate with less coco is called milk chocolate and will have a much sweeter taste.

Ingredients Needed for Each Tester

1 glass of a medium- to full-bodied Cabernet Sauvignon
1 glass of "Vintage-character" Port
1 glass of water

1 ounce (28 g) of milk chocolate of about 40 percent coco
1 ounce (28 g) of dark chocolate of at least 70 percent coco

Step One

Assemble the materials and, starting with the Cabernet Sauvignon, taste the two wines by themselves. Write down your impressions of the flavor profiles of the two wines paying particular attention to their levels of sweetness and astringency. After you have finished tasting the wine rinse your mouth with water several times and wait for 60 seconds before proceeding.

Step Two

Next, try the two chocolate samples starting with the milk chocolate first. As you did with the wines, write down your impressions of the flavor profiles of the two chocolates, paying particular attention to their levels of sweetness and bitterness. After you have finished tasting, rinse your mouth with water several times and wait for 60 seconds before proceeding.

Vegetarian Cuisine

Wine can be an excellent accompaniment to vegetarian cuisine but there are a few special considerations that should be taken into account. Being meatless by nature, most vegetarian dishes are not as rich and fatty as meat-based entrees usually are. This means that big-bodied tannic wines may not make a good match and a light- to medium-bodied wine would do better. The term *vegetarian* can also mean different things to different people. Lacto/ovo vegetarians consume milk and egg-based foods while vegans eschew the consumption of any animal-based products. As with any type of cuisine, it is desirable to present a variety of flavors and textures in the meal. So using a rich sauce—or, if it is possible, adding some butter or cheese to the recipe—will allow a more full-bodied wine to be served with a vegetarian dish. If a vegan meal is being served, you must be certain not only that there are no animal-based products in the food but also that no animal-based products were used in the wine production. Some, but by no means all, wineries use animal-based fining agents such as egg whites or gelatin to soften the tannins in their red wines. Whether a wine is vegan or not is usually not listed on the label; however, most wineries are happy to answer the question if contacted via their Web site.

FIGURE 5.7

© Pat Henderson

Step Three

Now take a small taste of the milk chocolate and then a sip of the Cabernet Sauvignon without rinsing your mouth in between. After you have noted your impressions of the flavor of the wine, take a small taste of the milk chocolate again, but this time have a sip of the Port wine afterward. Repeat step three a second time replacing the milk chocolate with the dark chocolate, being sure to record your impressions of the flavor of the wine after each type of chocolate.

Results

After tasting the chocolate, the flavor of the Cabernet Sauvignon should seem much more bitter than it did when it was tasted alone. This effect should be less pronounced with the dark chocolate sample because it is not as sweet. As for the Port wine, its sweetness may have seemed overwhelming when it was tasted alone. However, the Port's sweetness provides less of a contrast between the sugar levels of the food and the wine. Since the dark chocolate does not taste as sweet as the Port, it should have been the best partner to accompany the Port.

Putting It All Together

If they are followed, the guidelines outlined in this chapter will allow the chef or sommelier to provide an appetizing combination of food and wine. That being said, they should not be thought of as absolute laws; cooks and wine drinkers alike should always be encouraged to experiment and think outside the box. Much like wine itself, pairing a food and a wine is a matter of taste and everyone has their own opinions and preferences. While some combinations tend to be more successful than others, there is nothing wrong with you or your guests enjoying an unconventional match of food and wine. Additionally, experimentation with different food and wine combinations leads to a greater understanding of how the flavors of the two come together and enhance each other.

AGING WINES

Many people who are not familiar with wine believe that all wines get better as they get older. While some wines improve with aging, the vast majority of wines made and consumed around the world are designed to be enjoyed when they are released and have relatively little to gain from further aging. Furthermore, if the storage conditions are

FIGURE 5.9

Wines such as Sauvignon Blanc that have primarily fruity/floral flavor profiles usually have little to gain from long-term bottle aging. Red wines that have plenty of tannins and acid, such as this Bordeaux, can be matured in the bottle for many years.

© Pat Henderson

those tannins bind together and settle out of solution. For tableside wine service, this sediment is removed during the process of decanting which is discussed in Chapter 19.

Which Wines Should Be Aged?

As previously mentioned, most wines sold do not benefit from extensive aging. If a wine is out of balance, or is lacking in taste or aroma, aging will do little if anything to make it taste better. Wines that depend on fruity qualities for the majority of their flavor do not age well. These include crisp and fruity whites such as Pinot Gris, Gewürztraminer, and Sauvignon Blanc as well as light and fruity reds (Figure 5.9). Wines that are made from very ripe grapes often have high alcohol and low acid. Since acid is needed to preserve a wine during aging as well as contribute to the development of bottle bouquet, low-acid wines age poorly.

The additional alcohol and big body of fortified dessert wines will help preserve them for many years. This being said, except for Vintage Port, most Port-style wines are made to be enjoyed shortly after bottling. Bottle size also influences how a wine ages. Natural cork allows a small degree of oxygen into the bottle during aging. Since large-format bottles, those that are larger than 750 ml in size, have more volume of wine the effect of the oxygen is diminished. Consequently, large bottles age more slowly than small bottles.

For a wine to age well, it should have a high level of tannins and acid yet still be in balance. Additionally, because every wine is unique in how it responds to aging, the best method is to evaluate the wine by taste when it is young to make an estimate of when you think it will be ready, and then taste a bottle of it from time to time to see how it is developing. This of course requires a number of bottles for each wine being aged and a lot of storage space. Reds that meet all of these criteria can usually age for 5 to 25 years. As for whether these wines are better or worse after being aged is a matter of opinion and taste, and up to the individual wine drinker.

Matching Older Wines with Food

As a wine ages, it goes through a number of changes that affect how it will pair with food. Since the wine is becoming softer and less tannic in nature, it will be less likely to go with rich and fatty dishes. An older wine's flavors are also more delicate and less likely to be able to match strongly flavored or heavily seasoned foods. Older wines have more subtle and complex flavors that develop over time and do better with foods that possess more subtle flavors as well. This illustrates one of the most fundamental principles of matching a wine and food, which is to pair foods and wines that have similar qualities.

Wine and Health

Like any food, when wine is consumed it has effects on the human body. Moreover, whether you are a consumer or a purveyor of alcohol you should never lose sight of the responsibilities that this entails. The role of wine on human health is influenced by two contradictory concepts. First, wine is a beverage that should be considered a food. Second, alcohol is a drug and should be regulated and controlled. Society's attempts to come to terms with these competing philosophies have resulted in a wide variety of customs and laws that affect wine consumption. In some parts of the world consuming wine is not only prohibited but is considered sinful; in other areas wine is thought of as an essential part of a healthy diet and incorporated into religious rites. The era of Prohibition began in the United States as a popular movement by those who saw the damage that was caused by alcohol abuse and thought that outlawing alcoholic beverages would eliminate the problem. However, during Prohibition, alcohol abuse did not diminish, and many more problems were created because it was illegal and its production and distribution were unregulated. Today scientific studies show that moderate consumption of wine can have positive health effects, and moderate drinkers outlive those who abstain. Whenever producing or serving alcoholic beverages, it is important to be cognizant of their role in human health.

Negative Effects from Excessive Alcohol Consumption

Alcohol in its many forms is involved to some degree in the deaths of nearly 80,000 Americans a year (Centers for Disease Control and Prevention, 2009). The majority of these deaths are due to driving under the influence and cirrhosis of the liver from alcoholism, but this figure also includes accidents and homicides in which at least one of the parties involved had been consuming alcohol. The harmful effects of excessive consumption can occur chronically over many years, or acutely in a single "binge drinking" episode. The long-term consequences of overconsumption include liver damage, as well as an increased risk of cancer and heart disease.

Those who chronically overconsume are usually referred to as alcoholics or problem drinkers; however, the term *problem drinker* can also apply to someone who rarely drinks but when they do, they drink in excess. Becoming intoxicated affects one's judgment and behavior. Although it is possible to drink so much that the level of alcohol in the body becomes toxic, many of the deaths from binge drinking are associated with risky behavior. Drunk driving, or driving under the influence, is by far the most common form of accidental death while intoxicated. Despite more awareness of the problem it continues to kill almost 12,000 Americans a year (National Center for Statistics and Analysis, 2009), many of them innocent bystanders.

Positive Effects from Moderate Wine Consumption

While excessive consumption of alcohol results in higher mortality rates, epidemiologists have known for many years that people who consume wine in moderation have a longer life span than both alcoholics and those who abstain completely from alcohol

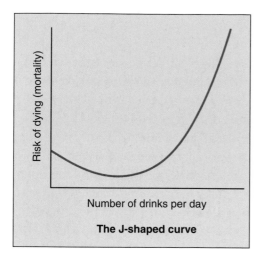

FIGURE 5.10

The J-shaped curve illustrates how mortality rates decrease for moderate wine drinkers and increase for excessive wine drinkers.

© Delmar Cengage Learning

(Figure 5.10). In recent years, numerous scientific studies have shown a direct link between modest wine drinking, particularly red wine, and increased cardiovascular health. This research shows that people who consume an average of one to two glasses of wine per day have a 30 to 50 percent reduction in mortality from heart disease (Goldfinger, 2003). This substantial figure is surprising to many people, and health officials are reticent to recommend alcohol consumption for fear that citizens would use it as a license for excess. This effect is not due to the alcohol in wine because laboratory studies show that mice given a solution of alcohol and water did not have the same lower rate of heart disease as was seen in mice that were given wine. The exact mechanism for these results is still unknown, but it is believed to be a product of naturally occurring antioxidant phenolic compounds present in wine such as **quercetin** (KWER-si-tin) and **resveratrol** (rez-VEHR-ah-trawl).

There are many opinions of what is considered a "moderate" amount of wine to consume, but most researchers consider one to two 6-oz (175 ml) glasses per day with meals to be moderate, depending on one's circumstances. The positive effect on cardiovascular health is often referred to as the **French paradox.** This is because, despite the fact that French citizens smoked more and had a much higher intake of saturated fat than Americans, studies showed they enjoyed a much lower level of heart disease. This positive effect of wine on health gained wide recognition in 1991 when the television series *60 Minutes* broadcast a program on the French paradox featuring Boston University epidemiologist Dr. Curtis Ellison, who pioneered research in the role of wine and longevity. Immediately after the broadcast, many wineries noticed a spike in sales of red wine. This increase was particularly noticed in the Midwest region of the United States, which was singled out in the program for having both the lowest per capita consumption of red wine in the country, as well as the highest rate of stroke and heart attack.

Special Considerations for Women

The health benefits of moderate wine drinking are more clear-cut for men than they are for women. This is primarily due to the relationship between alcohol consumption and breast cancer. Although women receive the same benefit that men do in cardiovascular health, studies show a correlation between moderate consumption of wine and an increased risk of certain types of breast cancer. Alcohol consumption affects estrogen levels in the body and may encourage estrogen receptor-positive tumors. Women also have to take into account the effects of alcohol consumption on pregnancy. About 1 in 20 women who are heavy drinkers during pregnancy give birth to babies with a form of mental retardation called fetal alcohol syndrome, or FAS (Abel, 1995). While there is little evidence suggesting that moderate wine drinking plays a role in FAS, to be absolutely safe most obstetricians recommend that their patients abstain during pregnancy (Figure 5.11).

It is important for both men and women to evaluate honestly their personal health and family history when deciding what a healthful level of consumption is for them.

FIGURE 5.11

While there is little evidence that a single glass of wine with dinner contributes to birth defects, most women abstain from drinking during pregnancy to be absolutely safe.
© Nicole Calisi

Additionally, if serving alcohol, whether professionally or to guests in your home, it is important to make sure it is enjoyed in a responsible manner. The subject of encouraging healthy and safe consumption of alcohol is called responsible hospitality, and is explored more fully in Chapter 19. The role of wine and health can be summarized by the statement that the majority of scientific studies show that moderate consumption of wine increases the life span for most individuals, with the possible exception of premenopausal women with a family history of breast cancer.

SUMMARY

Finding the proper match of a wine with a food has the effect of making both products taste more pleasing. The practice of combining wine and food historically began by people simply eating and drinking the products that were available to them. Over time, as regional culinary and winemaking practices became more advanced, chefs and vintners found combinations that worked well for the kinds of food and wine they were producing. Today, what were originally considered regional cuisine and winemaking styles are found all over the world and are being combined in innovative and exciting ways. Although there is an infinite number of combinations possible between wine and food, by following a few simple guidelines on how to combine flavors it is possible to find the proper wine for almost any dish.

As a wine ages its sensory profile changes, becoming softer in body and less tannic. The aroma is influenced by aging as well, losing some of its fruity character and developing a bouquet that is more complex. These changes affect not only the wine itself but also how it pairs with food. When one has a better understanding of the sensory characteristics of different wines it is easier to match them with food in a way that enhances the qualities of both. This knowledge, combined with an awareness of how wine has an effect on the body, allows the consumer to enjoy fully its consumption in a healthful manner.

FIGURE 5.12

Analytical tasting methods are useful for understanding the qualities of a wine that make it appealing to the senses, but it is important not to forget that a wine is best enjoyed as part of a delicious meal with friends.

© A. Inden/Corbis

EXERCISES

1. Discuss the various positive and negative health effects of wine consumption.

2. Prepare a list of different types of foods and wines that would accompany them.

3. Discuss what happens to a wine as it ages. Select two types of wine that would benefit from long-term aging and two that would not.

4. How would a light-bodied food such as chicken or fish be prepared to match well with a tannic red wine?

5. What types of foods would go best with a light, crisp Chardonnay such as Chablis? Which foods would go best with a Chardonnay made in a very rich, ripe style with less acidity and a lot of oak aging?

REVIEW QUESTIONS

1. Which of the following does not affect how a food would pair with a wine?
   A. How it is cooked
   B. How salty it is
   C. The fat content of the food
   D. Whether it is steamed or grilled
   E. None of the above

(Continues)

(Continued)

2. When serving a wine with dessert, it should always be a little
_____ than the dish.
   A. Sweeter
   B. Tarter
   C. More bitter
   D. It does not matter; wine should not be served with dessert

3. Which of the following American chefs has been most influential
in developing fusion cuisine?
   A. Emiril Lagasse
   B. Wolfgang Puck
   C. Alice Waters
   D. Ming Tsai

4. The positive effect that wine has on cardiovascular health is
thought to be primarily due to _____.
   A. Alcohol
   B. Phenolic compounds
   C. Tartaric acid
   D. Glycerol

5. Which of the following wine attributes is not significantly affected
by long-term bottle aging?
   A. Tannin level
   B. Color
   C. Acidity
   D. Alcohol

REFERENCES

Abel, E. L. (1995). An update on incidence of FAS: FAS is not an equal opportunity birth defect. *Neurotoxicology and Teratology, 17*(4), 437–443.

Centers for Disease Control and Prevention. (2009). *Alcohol attributable deaths report, average for United States 2001–2005.* Atlanta, GA: Author.

Goldfinger, T. M. (2003, August). Beyond the French paradox: The impact of moderate beverage alcohol and the consumption in the prevention of cardiovascular disease. *Cardiology Clinics, 21,* 3.

MacNeil, K. (2001). *The wine bible.* New York: Workman.

National Center for Statistics and Analysis. (2009). *Fatalities and fatality rates in alcohol-impaired-driving crashes by state, 2007–2008.* Washington, DC: Author.

Robinson, J. (Ed.). (2006). *The Oxford companion to wine* (3rd ed.). New York: Oxford University.

SECTION II
WINE REGIONS
OF EUROPE

THIS SECTION COVERS THE WINE regions of Europe in five chapters: France; Italy; Spain and Portugal; Germany; and Other European Regions and the Mediterranean. Europe is the birthplace of modern winemaking, and most of the styles of wine and grape growing throughout the world have their origins on this continent. Burgundy, Champagne, and Chianti are specific wines made in Europe, while Chardonnay, Cabernet Sauvignon, and Pinot Grigio are wine grapes originally grown in Europe. The chapters of this section cover individual regions within the country, their history of winemaking, and the wines they produce.

{ FRANCE }

This chapter discusses the grapes,

regulations, and wine styles of the six major wine regions of France, lists the subdistricts (the appellations) of each major region, and describes the climate and topographic differences among regions. The chapter also defines the concept of terroir and explains why it is crucial to understanding and appreciating French wines. Additionally, the chapter covers the French system of Appellation Contrôléc laws, as well as the heritage, history, and philosophy behind the evolution of this system, what it accomplishes, and how it may affect the future of French wines in the international marketplace.

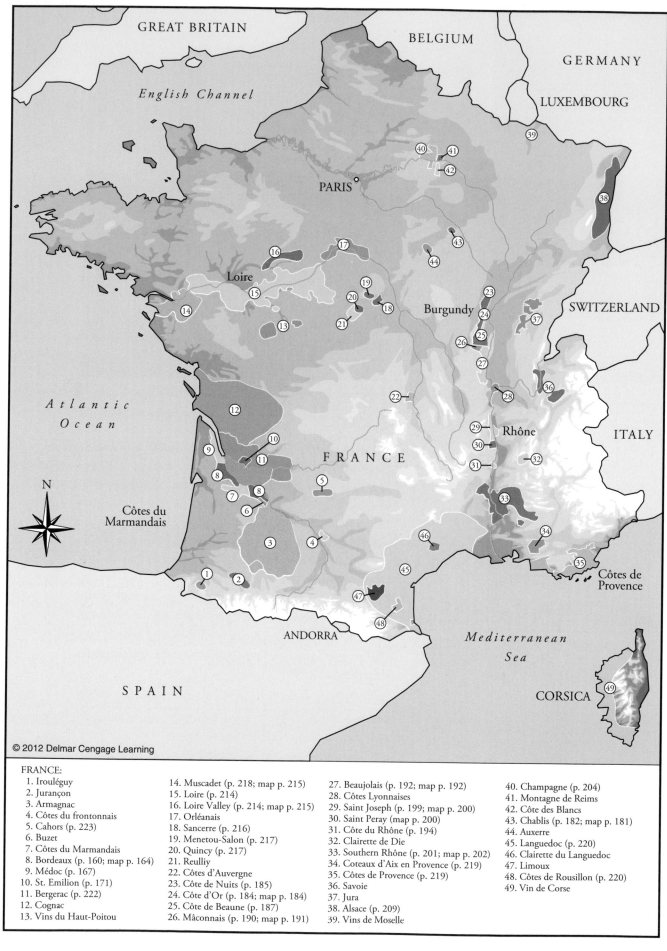

FRANCE:
1. Irouléguy
2. Jurançon
3. Armagnac
4. Côtes du frontonnais
5. Cahors (p. 223)
6. Buzet
7. Côtes du Marmandais
8. Bordeaux (p. 160; map p. 164)
9. Médoc (p. 167)
10. St. Emilion (p. 171)
11. Bergerac (p. 222)
12. Cognac
13. Vins du Haut-Poitou

14. Muscadet (p. 218; map p. 215)
15. Loire (p. 214)
16. Loire Valley (p. 214; map p. 215)
17. Orléanais
18. Sancerre (p. 216)
19. Menetou-Salon (p. 217)
20. Quincy (p. 217)
21. Reulliy
22. Côtes d'Auvergne
23. Côte de Nuits (p. 185)
24. Côte d'Or (p. 184; map p. 184)
25. Côte de Beaune (p. 187)
26. Mâconnais (p. 190; map p. 191)

27. Beaujolais (p. 192; map p. 192)
28. Côtes Lyonnaises
29. Saint Joseph (p. 199; map p. 200)
30. Saint Peray (map p. 200)
31. Côte du Rhône (p. 194)
32. Clairette de Die
33. Southern Rhône (p. 201; map p. 202)
34. Coteaux d'Aix en Provence (p. 219)
35. Côtes de Provence (p. 219)
36. Savoie
37. Jura
38. Alsace (p. 209)
39. Vins de Moselle

40. Champagne (p. 204)
41. Montagne de Reims
42. Côte des Blancs
43. Chablis (p. 182; map p. 181)
44. Auxerre
45. Languedoc (p. 220)
46. Clairette du Languedoc
47. Limoux
48. Côtes de Rousillon (p. 220)
49. Vin de Corse

KEY TERMS

appellation

Appellation
d'Origine
Contrôlée (AOC)

blanc de blancs

blanc de noirs

brut

clos

cru

demi-sec

doux

extra brut

extra dry

moelleux

mousseux

négociant

propriétaire

sec

tête de cuvée

tirage

vin délimité de
qualité supérieure
(VDQS)

vin de pays

vin de table

vin doux naturel

INTRODUCTION

In addition to producing great wines in nearly every category, France is also the original home to most of the "noble varietals," the grapes from which the best wines are made. Of the 12 most important noble varietals, 8 are indigenous to France: Chardonnay, Riesling, Sauvignon Blanc, and Chenin Blanc for whites, and Cabernet Sauvignon, Merlot, Pinot Noir, and Syrah for reds. Although Riesling is also indigenous to Germany, and the Sangiovese and Nebbiolo of Italy and the Tempranillo of Spain are also counted among the noble varietals, the majority of important grape varietals originated in France.

The French also demonstrated important initiative in the creation of a countrywide system of laws to control viticultural practices and the production of wines, along with a federal-level government agency to oversee the wine trade and enforce the regulations. One of the primary purposes of these laws is to protect the geographic names of the places of origin of specific wines. This protection is very important as French wines (like most European wines) are named for the region where the grapes were grown. This geographic designation of origin is called the **appellation** (ap-puh-LAY-shuhn) of the wine.

The French are passionate about wine, and are understandably proud of the wines they produce. As proof that the French believe in the quality of their wines, one need look at just one statistic: Only 3 percent of all wine consumed in France is imported (Osborne, 2004). Although great wine is being produced elsewhere in the world, to truly understand wine, one must understand French wines.

FRENCH WINE—HISTORICAL PERSPECTIVE

The history of wine production in France is inextricably intertwined with the politics and sociological development of the country. The first wine grapes were planted in the southern part of what is now France by Greek traders as far back as 600 BC. As the Romans spread into Gaul (as France was then called) and colonized the country, the planting of grapes and the production of wine increased. By the time of the birth of Christ the exporting of wine from Gaul to Rome was well established. When the Roman Empire began to crumble in the second century AD, the expansion of viticulture ceased, although wine continued to be produced, often by the monasteries and abbeys of the Christian Church that had been established in Gaul by the Romans. Barbarians from the north invaded Gaul and caused the collapse of the Roman Empire by AD 400. During the Middle Ages, the period from the fall of the Roman Empire to the Renaissance in AD 1450, it was the Christian Church that kept viticulture and enology alive in Gaul and elsewhere in Europe.

Charlemagne brought stability to Gaul during his reign which began in AD 768. He introduced the first laws on wine production. Although he was based in the north of Gaul, in the Champagne region, his influence was felt as far south as the Mediterranean. Charlemagne and his successors encouraged the export of wine (Figure 6.1).

FIGURE 6.2

red wine and for its memorable name with a quaint story behind it. The name came about when Bertrand the Goth was elected Pope Clement V in 1305. At the time, the relationship between the king of France and the papacy in Rome was badly strained, and Italy was in political turmoil. Clement chose to stay in France, and established his papal court in Avignon, an ancient city on the Rhône River. His successor, Pope John XXII, improved the papal finances sufficiently to build himself a summer palace outside the city, on the foundations of an old castle (Figure 6.2). This palace became known as Châteauneuf-du-Pape, "the new castle of the Pope." Of course, the old castle's vineyards came with the property and Pope John made sure these vines were well tended so that he could produce his own wines. Thus began the Châteauneuf-du-Pape wine-producing region.

By the 1920s the demand for the red wines of this historic region was very high. Fraud in the form of inflated production numbers had been going on for years, and now became widespread throughout the region. A group of producers, under the expert guidance of Baron LeRoy of Château Fortia, set out to define their own boundaries and to set prescriptions on which grapes could be used in wine to be labeled as Châteauneuf-du-Pape. They decreed what viticultural practices were to be allowed and spelled out specific techniques that were banned. The vintners also set out strict standards for minimum ripeness of grapes at harvest, minimum alcohol level in wines, and other factors that are critical to quality and authenticity. The system devised by this dedicated group of Châteauneuf-du-Pape vintners eventually became the model for the national system of quality control laws.

In other regions, especially Burgundy, trouble in the form of fraud and blackballing of recalcitrant growers continued for many more years. Most of the wrongdoing was at the hands of négociants. A **négociant** (nay-goh-SYAHN), is a merchant who acts as a middleman between grape growers, producers, and shippers of wine. Due to the Great Depression, demand for wine was down severely, and many growers could not afford to protest against négociants who bought cheaper grapes from outside areas and then sold the wine as something far more expensive than its quality merited. Authenticity and quality took a serious step backward in Burgundy and other premier wine regions of France.

Finally, in 1935, the French government passed legislation creating the Institut National des Appellations d'Origine des Vins et Eaux-de-Vie (INAO) under the Ministry of Agriculture. The charge given to the INAO was to work with local growers, to establish legally defined appellation boundaries, along with a codification of grape-growing and winemaking practices appropriate to each area. The system has continued to evolve and is continually under review.

All wine regions of France are classified into one of four levels of quality. Wine coming from each region also carries that classification. The four levels are, in descending order of quality, **Appellation d'Origine Contrôlée (AOC)** (ah-pehl-lah-SYAWN daw-ree-JEEN kawn-traw-LAY), higher-quality wines from one of the better limited areas of production; **vin délimité de qualité supérieure (VDQS)** (van deh-lee-mee-TAY duh kah-lee-TAY soo-pehr-YUR), quality wines from a limited area; **vin de pays** (van doo pay-YEE), country wine; and **vin de table** (van deu TAH-bl), table wine.

Appellation d'Origine Contrôlée (AOC)

To carry the name of an AOC region, a wine must meet very specific criteria:

- The wine must be made 100 percent from grapes approved for that appellation.
- The grapes must have all been grown within a limited zone or area of production. In general, the smaller that geographic designation, the better and more distinctive the wine. Some AOC wines attain even higher recognition of quality if the vineyard or estate where the grapes were grown is further rated by the authorities as being a particularly impressive location. Rated vineyards are usually designated as grand cru or premier cru or some comparable term indicating high quality.
- The grapes must have been picked at the minimal level of sugar, and reach the minimal alcohol level, specified for that appellation.
- The amount of grapes harvested must not exceed a certain amount per hectare. In general, the smaller or more specific the area, the smaller the yield allowed. If all the vigor of the vine goes into fewer bunches, those bunches will have more concentrated flavors.
- The methods used in the vineyard and in the winery must conform to the regulations of the region.
- The wine must be bottled in the same region as the appellation.
- The wine must pass a tasting test by the local branch of the INAO. What the tasters are judging is not the quality of the wine so much as its terroir, that is, they are determining if the wine reflects the character of the appellation.

Presently almost one-half of the wine produced in France is designated as AOC. According to many members of the wine trade in France, 48 percent is too large a percentage to label as the country's "greatest wines." They also say that the fact that there are 472 regions now carrying the AOC designation reduces the impact of being so designated. However, it is unlikely that the number of AOCs will be reduced as there is no mechanism that would allow a region to be declassified.

Vin Délimité de Qualité Supérieure (VDQS)

The VDQS designation was begun in 1949. These wines are also produced according to INAO guidelines, and producers are supervised by the local bureau. However, standards are not as strict nor as numerous as at the AOC level. Growers and producers in these regions often aspire to have their area elevated to AOC status. At this time, less than 1 percent of French wines are designated VDQS.

Vin de Pays

Higher yields and a higher percentage of nonindigenous grapes are allowed at this level. Since 1979, wines at this level have been permitted to be labeled by varietal (although region of production must also be listed). Vins de pays, most of which come from the south of France, differ considerably in quality, style, and price.

Vin de pays regions can fall within three different types.

1. *Regional.* There are six of these. They are very large, covering wide swaths of land with many different soil types and microclimates.
2. *Departmental.* This covers an entire *département,* the French equivalent of an American state or Canadian province.
3. *Zonal.* This is the smallest type of region, often just one district or even one town. There are over 100 zonal vin de pays regions.

The number of vin de pays regions continues to increase as producers realize these wines are easier to sell in the New World due to inclusion of varietal on the label. As of 2006, 34 percent of all French wine was designated vin de pays. With the success of marketing these wines into the United States, that percentage may well increase.

Vin de Table or Vin Ordinaire

This type of wine can be made from grapes grown anywhere in France. There are no limits on yield and no specifications on varietals. The European Commission is putting pressure on France to decrease the amount of acreage dedicated to this level of wine, as the glut of bulk wine and wine grapes causes prices to fall. In the last few years there has been a reduction in the amount of vin de table produced. It now accounts for only 17 percent of French wine production.

Recent Changes

In an effort to make their system of classifying and naming wines more uniform with other European countries, and easier for all consumers to comprehend, French lawmakers recently made some changes in terminology within their wine regulations. Passed in 2009, the new laws changed Appellation d'Origine Contrôlée (controlled place of origin) or AOC to Appellation d'Origin Protégée (protected place of origin) or AOP. The next level of quality, VDQS, will continue to be labeled as such. Both these levels of quality will also carry the European Union designation of Quality Wine Produced in a Specific Region (QWPSR).

The two uncontrolled and unclassified levels of wine in France were also changed somewhat. Vin de pays, or country wine, will now be labeled as Indication Géographique Protégée or IGP. At this level, producers can continue to show varietal, vintage, and the specified growing region. The lowest level of everyday wine, that is, the wine that can be produced from grapes grown anywhere in France, will continue to be labeled as vin de table. However, there is a strong movement to change that term to vin de France. At this level the producer is still forbidden to show a geographic designation, but will now be allowed to show a vintage and a grape varietal.

All changes in terminology must be implemented by the 2010 vintage.

Weaknesses of the System

The French system of wine laws is one of the most comprehensive and strictest in the world. These laws have done a great deal to guarantee the authenticity of wine names, and thus, to protect the prestige of the finest wine appellations. The purpose of the laws is *not* to guarantee quality. The government feels that that is up to individual producers, and that the open market will determine a wine's success or failure. Rather, what the wine laws are intended to do is to ensure that each wine carrying a region's name will be typical of that region. This way the consumer will know the essential style and character of the wine when purchasing it. In meeting this objective the wine control laws of France are successful. Moreover, the system does rate regions (the highest rating being AOP, formerly AOC), and also rates some of the highest-quality locations within AOC regions. These ratings also assist the consumer in making purchasing decisions.

However, despite its successes and strengths, the system does have its weaknesses, the worst being that in some of its applications the system of laws protects the grower and producer more than it does the consumer. Changes advocated by experts, including Clive Coates, a leading authority on French wines, include adding consumer representation to the local INAO commissions. In other words, each tasting panel and regulatory body should have an objective observer, with a vote, who has no direct involvement with any facet of the wine trade, but will speak simply as a consumer, for consumers.

The tasting and analysis of AOC and VDQS wines should be done with an eye to quality, not just to typicality. True, the open market will eventually eliminate low-quality wines that are not worth the price being asked, but it seems the authorities should step in before consumers have wasted money on a low-quality wine.

Labeling laws could also be improved. The changes of 2009 were intended to make French labels less confusing, especially for non-French consumers. However, the changes do not seem likely to accomplish that objective. Moreover, from a marketing viewpoint, the French authorities and wine producers should expand the use of explanatory back labels. U.S. consumers like to have helpful information on the style of the wine in the bottle, how to serve that wine, what grapes it was made from, and so forth. Explanatory labels have greatly helped in the sales of Australian and Californian wines. The French should follow suit.

Wine Regions of France

The major wine regions covered in this chapter are Bordeaux, Burgundy, Côtes du Rhône, Champagne, Alsace, and the Loire Valley. These six AOC regions account for less than 20 percent of France's total wine production, but their wines are the country's most famous and most impressive wines. We will also look at some of the promising regions in the South of France.

Bordeaux

Bordeaux is quite possibly the world's most famous wine region, and with good reason. Some of the world's best wines hail from this corner of southwestern France. Bordeaux is the second largest wine region in France, and one of the largest in the world, with 290,000 acres (116,160 hectares) under vine, producing nearly one-quarter of the country's AOC production and approximately 2 percent of the total world wine production.

Not only is Bordeaux one of the world's largest wine-producing regions, it is also one of the most diverse. Annual production is over 700 million bottles of wine. Bordeaux produces fine wine in three major categories—red table wine, dry white table wine, and excellent dessert wine.

The city of Bordeaux, eighth largest in France and for centuries an important port, is the capital of the département of Gironde, the largest of France's 95 départements. Bordeaux is a region of large, self-sufficient estates in which the vineyards, the winemaking facilities, and often the owner's house are all under one ownership and located in close proximity. Many of these estates have been under the same ownership for centuries. This uninterrupted proprietorship has allowed development of high-quality vineyards, confident winemaking skills, and a pride in name, heritage, and product. There is a distinguishable style for each major estate that stays the same year after year.

History

Although wine has been made in Bordeaux for centuries, it was not until the late seventeenth and early eighteenth centuries that many of the great estates developed. Prior to that time, a large quantity of wine was exported, but much of it was not of high quality. After the marriage in 1152 of Eleanor of Aquitaine the planting of vineyards in Bordeaux expanded. The extent of trade with England also expanded enormously when Eleanor's husband ascended the throne of England. However, most of the vineyards were not in the Médoc, which was much too swampy to be useful for growing grapes. The grapes were grown further inland, in the Dordogne region.

After the English were expelled from Gascony in 1453, the French kings were wise enough not to disrupt the Bordeaux wine trade. The privileges and favors granted under the English monarchy to Bordeaux wine producers and merchants remained in place. Trade with England continued, and business with the Dutch expanded.

The quality of wine from this area took a major step forward in the seventeenth century due to the ingenuity of Dutch entrepreneurs who had become increasingly involved in the exporting of wine from Bordeaux. Long familiar with marshy lowlands, the Dutch businessmen brought in engineers from their homeland who were able to drain the marshes of the Médoc peninsula. This process exposed gentle hills of very gravelly soil, perfect for *vinifera* vines. Many of Bordeaux's great estates are now located in the Médoc.

As the wine trade grew, a new social class emerged and became the new aristocracy. The merchants who attained success in trading and exporting wine began to purchase land and build châteaux. This moneyed class replaced the old nobility. The merchant families invested resources into improving their vineyards. After the French Revolution, the top properties remained largely intact. These estates became the great, highly rated estates of modern Bordeaux.

As in other regions of France and Europe, production of wine in Bordeaux was set back by the infestation of phylloxera in the late nineteenth century. By 1869, land under viticulture in Bordeaux had decreased by over a third, with many more hectares dying each year. At a conference called in the city of Bordeaux in 1881 to study the problem of phylloxera, the Bordelais vintners agreed to accept the proposed solution of grafting their vines onto American rootstock.

The process of replanting vineyards proceeded slowly, partly due to a fear on the part of Bordeaux landowners that American rootstock would adversely affect the flavor of their wines, and partly due to an infection of the vineyards by downy mildew, a disease that primarily affects the leaves of the plant. This scourge was quickly controlled by the spraying of copper sulfate solution. By the early twentieth century, the vineyards of Bordeaux were well on their way to recovery.

In the first half of the twentieth century, the tribulations of the Bordeaux wine region, as was true throughout France, were not at the hands of Mother Nature, as in the previous half-century. Rather, the ensuing years saw an unprecedented string of human-caused disasters: The First World War, the Great Depression, Prohibition in the United States, and, of course, the Second World War. The production of wine fell drastically during World War II and the German occupation, partly due to lack of workers, and partly due to German forces seizing supplies of wine. Many Bordeaux producers used ingenious methods to hide their wine from the Nazis. Fortunately, most of the German occupying forces had the foresight to realize it was in the long-term best interest of Germany to allow the Bordeaux trade to remain as undisturbed as possible. When the war ended, they wanted there to be Bordeaux wine to import into Germany (Kladstrup & Kladstrup, 2001).

In the second half of the twentieth century and on into the twenty-first century, the Bordeaux wine trade grew and strengthened. A rising standard of living throughout the Western world, an increasing appreciation for fine wine as an inherent part of cuisine, and the emergence of the United States as a particularly important and sophisticated market for wine have all worked to widen the consumer base for Bordeaux's wines.

Soil and Climate—Terroir of Bordeaux

The département of Gironde is located on the west coast of France, on the Atlantic Ocean. Exactly halfway between the North Pole and the equator, extending about

65 miles (105 km) from north to south and 80 miles (129 km) from east to west, the Gironde is spared any temperature extremes. A thick pine forest along the coast protects the vineyards from cold ocean breezes. The region contains many different soil variations that can nourish a wide variety of grape types. The soil composition is a major factor in deciding which vine shoots will be planted. The style of wine produced within each appellation of Bordeaux is a direct reflection of the proportion of each varietal planted there.

In Bordeaux, the grape varietals allowed by AOC laws are:

Red	*White*
Cabernet Sauvignon	Sauvignon Blanc
Merlot	Semillon
Cabernet Franc	Muscadelle
Malbec	
Petit Verdot	
Carmenère	

From this lineup of varietals, one can easily surmise that Bordeaux wines are not single-varietal wines. Rather, winemakers are free to blend the allowed varietals together to obtain the most complex and interesting combination possible. French wines made in Mediterranean-influenced zones tend to be blends, whereas wines from cooler, continentally influenced regions tend to be single varietal.

In Bordeaux, red varietals take up 88 percent of total acreage, and Merlot is the most widely planted red varietal (Figure 6.3). Next is Cabernet Sauvignon, followed by the third most important grape, Cabernet Franc.

For the high-quality, dry white grapes, Sauvignon Blanc is the most important. However, the most widely planted white grape is Semillon (Figure 6.4).

Within a region as large as Bordeaux, there are many different terroirs, each favorable to different varietals. In general, Merlot and Cabernet Franc are dominant on the right bank of the Gironde River, in St. Émilion and Pomerol, and Cabernet Sauvignon is dominant on the left bank of the river, in Médoc and Graves.

Classifications of Bordeaux Estates

The tendency to rank wine-producing estates has become quite prevalent in recent times. During the late nineteenth and on through the twentieth century, as the market for wine became less regional and eventually international in nature, the need arose for a simple and understandable rating for the many diverse wines available. The most famous rating, and the most enduring, was the Classification of 1855 for the wine-producing estates of the Médoc. In that year, the Exposition

FIGURE 6.3

Merlot grapes ripening in the sun. Merlot is the most widely planted varietal in Bordeaux.
© Sherri Camp/iStock Photo

FIGURE 6.4

Semillon bunch almost ready to be picked. In Bordeaux, 55 percent of acreage devoted to white grapes is planted to Semillon.

© Cephas Picture Library/Alamy

Universelle (the World's Fair) was to be held in Paris. To be sure that only the very best of France's great wines would be shown to visiting dignitaries, Napoleon III asked the wine merchants of Bordeaux to judge the recognized wine-producing estates of that region in a formal, quantified ranking.

The merchants (also called brokers or négociants) took their task very seriously and proceeded to formalize the ranking that they, and the open market, had been using for Bordeaux's wines. Referring back to prices fetched over the previous century, the brokers were able to divide the top Médoc estates into five tiers of quality. Their final classification remains the official ranking to this day, with only one change. In the top tier, called first growth or premier **cru** (KROO), there were only three Médoc estates, Lafite, Latour, and Margaux, as well as one estate, Château Haut-Brion, located in the Graves region. This estate was of such a high caliber and its wines were so highly regarded that it could not be omitted from this ranking of the Médoc. In 1973, Château Mouton-Rothschild was elevated from second growth to first growth. An additional 56 estates from the Médoc were rated at deuxième cru or second growth, and on down to cinquième cru, or fifth growth. Since there were thousands of properties producing wine at the time, it is indeed impressive to be included in the Classification of 1855. These 61 châteaux continue to be regarded as among the world's very best wine-producing estates. Even today the classification done so many years ago affects the pricing for Bordeaux wines in the highly competitive international marketplace.

In 1855, the wine brokers of Bordeaux also classified the estates of Bordeaux that produced sweet white wines. They ranked these estates into two classes, again based on market demand, price, and quality of the wines. These estates are all within the appellations of Sauternes and Barsac.

The wine-producing estates of the Graves region were not officially classified until 1953 for the red wines and 1959 for the white wines. Both lists consist of one class.

The estates of St. Émilion on the right bank of the Gironde River were first classified officially in 1955. To ensure that their ranking is always current, the vintners of St. Émilion arranged for periodic reassessments of the classification, supposedly every 10 years. This plan makes sense because, although the vineyards themselves may be immutable, there are often changes in ownership or other human influences that need to be factored in. The system allows poorly managed vineyards to be demoted, while promising, well-cared-for estates can be promoted. The first modification took place in 1969 and was followed by further modifications in 1986 and again in 1996. (The update of 2006 has been nullified due to a lawsuit brought against the INAO by the owners of several estates that were downgraded in that rating.)

Bordeaux

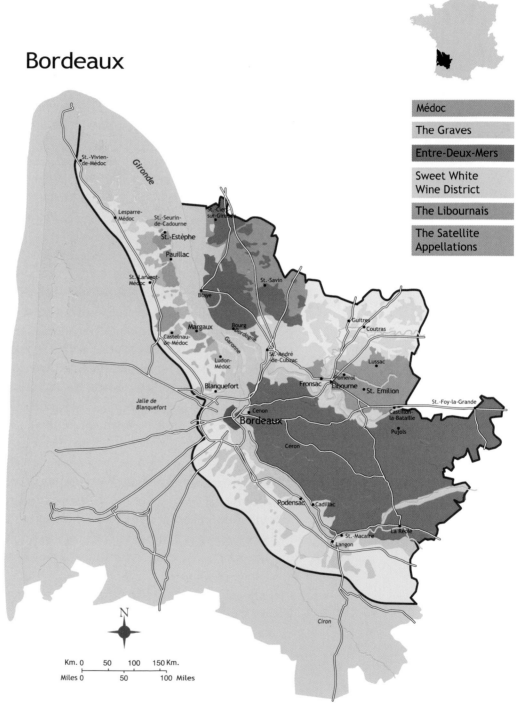

Médoc

The Graves

Entre-Deux-Mers

Sweet White Wine District

The Libournais

The Satellite Appellations

Map courtesy of Kobrand Corporation (www.kobrandwine.com)

The estates of the other famous appellation on the right bank, Pomerol, have never been officially classified. It is widely accepted, however, that the best wines from this region rank among the world's very best red wines.

The classifications of Bordeaux estates can be found in Appendix C.

Wine Regions of Bordeaux

The Médoc peninsula lies between the Atlantic Ocean and the muddy estuary of the Gironde River. For any wine lover, driving along the D2 highway, the Route du Vin, that wends its way up the peninsula from the city of Bordeaux is a magical experience. The landscape is not particularly spectacular. It is a bit flat, and in the southern portions there are signs of urban sprawl. What is magical are the names one sees on the signs at the entranceways to the various wine-producing estates along the way. Château Margaux, Château Brane-Cantenac, Château Gruaud-LaRose, Château Lafite-Rothschild, Château Mouton-Rothschild, Cos d'Estournel—these are words any wine connoisseur has seen on bottles of extraordinary wines. Some of the châteaux are simple country homes. Some are large, beautiful mansions (Gruard-LaRose). Some have an unexpectedly exotic look to them (Cos d'Estournel resembles a Chinese pagoda). There are even former priories (Château Meyney). What ties these diverse estates together is the quality of the great red wines made here, in Bordeaux's Médoc region (Table 6.1).

The Haut-Médoc

Most of the very best of Bordeaux's wines come from famous estates in the lower two-thirds of the Médoc peninsula. This subregion, known as the Haut-Médoc, begins in the suburbs just north of the city of Bordeaux, and continues on up the peninsula for just over 30 miles (48 km) as the crow flies. There are 29 communes (towns or villages) and a total of 25,000 acres (10,121 hectares) of vineyards within the Haut-Médoc. The greatest estates have been classified, that is, officially rated as superior. Most of these classified estates are located within the boundaries of four villages. These villages, listed from south to north, are Margaux, St. Julien, Pauillac, and St. Estèphe. Each of these towns is a separate appellation.

Margaux   The appellation Margaux actually encompasses five villages: Labarde, Arsac, Cantenac, Margaux, and Soussans. The soil varies considerably throughout the Margaux appellation, but it is essentially sandy gravel, quite thin and light in color.

TABLE 6.1 Appellations of France: Bordeaux

Region	Subregion	Principal Varietal*
Haut-Médoc	Margaux	Cabernet Sauvignon, Merlot
	St. Julien	Cabernet Sauvignon, Merlot
	Pauillac	Cabernet Sauvignon, Merlot
	St. Estèphe	Cabernet Sauvignon, Merlot
Libournais	St. Émilion	Merlot, Cabernet Sauvignon
(The "Right Bank")	Pomerol	Merlot, Cabernet Sauvignon
Graves		Sauvignon Blanc, Semillon
	Pessac-Léognan	Cabernet Sauvignon, Merlot
Sauternes/Barsac		Semillon (botrytized)
Entre-Deux-Mers		Semillon, Sauvignon Blanc
Médoc		Cabernet Sauvignon, Merlot

*The varietal mentioned first is the prevalent one for that region. Remember, all Bordeaux wines are blends.

FIGURE 6.5

Picking Cabernet Sauvignon grapes at Château Finegrave in St. Julien.

© Cephas Picture Library/Alamy

In the town of Margaux, the gravel lies atop a base of clay and marl. (*Marl* is a geological term for the conglomerate of magnesium and calcium from the shells left behind when the seawater drained out of this part of the peninsula.) In the surrounding villages, the base is sometimes gravel, sometimes iron-rich sandstone, and in some places even sand and grit. The percentage of plantings to Merlot is higher in Margaux than in the communes farther north in the Haut-Médoc.

The wines of Margaux tend to be raspberry scented, smooth and medium-bodied on the palate, and redolent of rich, ripe berry flavors. The Margaux appellation is home to 20 classified estates, more than any other appellation in Bordeaux.

St. Julien North of Margaux there is a wide stretch of land unsuitable for grapevines because the land is too marshy and flat. The next great vineyards appear as one comes into the commune of St. Julien. This is the smallest and most compact of the Haut-Médoc appellations, with only about 2,200 acres (891 hectares) under vine. The average quality of wine in this commune is very high. Eleven estates in St. Julien are classified (rated).

The soil is gravelly with some clay; the subsoil has more limestone than Margaux's. Drainage is good. The vineyards are planted primarily to Cabernet Sauvignon such as these being picked in Figure 6.5. The wines of St. Julien have more tannic backbone and are fuller bodied than those of Margaux, but still elegant.

Pauillac This is perhaps the most famous of the communes in the Haut-Médoc. Virtually all of its 2,916 acres (1,180 hectares) of vines belong to or are controlled by its 18 classified estates. The soil throughout has the gravelly composition that permits excellent drainage, and retains the sun's heat and reflects it back on the vines in the cool evening, thus assisting ripening. Despite the relative uniformity of the top levels of soil, the subsoils differ from vineyard to vineyard, thus allowing for noticeable differences in style. In general, however, one can say that the wines of Pauillac tend toward full bodied, smooth texture, exhibit a distinctive lead pencil/cedar aroma, and are very long lived.

Three of the very top-rated estates are in Pauillac—Lafite-Rothschild, Mouton-Rothschild, and Latour (Figure 6.6). Each of these estates has a recognizable style. For instance, Lafite-Rothschild's vineyards, in the northern part of the appellation, have a limestone base, resulting in a particularly complex bouquet and subtle flavors of currants. Mouton-Rothschild sits on a gravelly ridge looking down on the small town of Pauillac. Its vineyards have more sandstone in their base soil than Lafite, and its wines are more opulent and complex, as well as very structured. Latour, a grand old estate located in the southern reaches of Pauillac next to St. Julien, produces wines that are more supple and open. Latour's vineyards are entirely on loose, fine gravel, affording excellent drainage and heat retention. Latour's style is unmistakable, complex and full of fruit yet very elegant.

The famous trio of top-rated estates (first growths) are just the beginning of great Pauillac wines. There are many distinctive second growths also.

FIGURE 6.6

Château Latour, a "first growth" in Pauillac. On the left is the tower *(la tour)* from which the estate derives its name.

© Cephas Picture Library/Alamy

St. Estèphe   When one goes past Latour and over a small human-made drainage ditch, the land suddenly rises to the commune of St. Estèphe, perhaps the least lauded of the Haut-Médoc's appellations. There is not as high a percentage of rated estates here, but there are many fine properties that, although unrated, produce attractive, balanced, and affordable wines. The style of these wines, as well as those coming from the five rated estates located here, is more tannic than that of other communes. The vintners in St. Estèphe have made an effort to produce more approachable wines by increasing percentages of the less-tannic Merlot and by allowing longer ripening and less maceration. Their endeavors are made more difficult by the presence in most of St. Estèphe of a thick, dense claylike soil with inferior drainage and lower heat retention results in wines that are more acidic, and a bit awkward when compared to wines that come from finer, gravelly soils.

This is not to imply that there are no world-class wines in St. Estèphe. Wine experts and consumers agree that Cos d'Estournel is indeed one of the world's great red wines. It is also the first estate one sees after crossing over into the commune from Pauillac. The strange pagoda-style chai (winemaking facility) sits on a slight ridge, overlooking Pauillac's famous Lafite-Rothschild. Because of the high percentage of Merlot (40 percent), extensive use of new oak, and very careful attention to quality, the wines of Cos are fleshy, full bodied, and complex (Figure 6.7).

The Médoc

North of Calon-Ségur, the land dips down and becomes too marshy for quality vineyards. This is the beginning of the Bas-Médoc, a low-lying area viticulturally inferior to its famous neighbor, the Haut-Médoc. Much of the land is dedicated to pasture rather than grapes. The soil here is sandy and has poor drainage. There are 14 wine-producing

commenced within the Bas-Médoc (often called simply the Médoc) and a total of 11,600
acres (4,696 hectares) of vines, mostly planted to Cabernet Sauvignon and Cabernet
Franc. Some very decent and affordable red wines are made in the Médoc, and the adventuresome buyer can be rewarded with some exciting finds from this region.

Graves

Unlike the appellations Médoc and Haut-Médoc, which can be applied only to red
wine, the appellation Graves applies to both reds and whites. A large area that runs
about 34 miles (55 km) along the southern edge of the Garonne River (one of the
two tributaries to the Gironde), Graves' 8,255 acres (3,342 hectares) of vineyards are
planted 4,540 acres (1,838 hectares) to red wine grapes and 3,715 acres (1,504 hectares) to white wine grapes. Just over 45 percent of Graves' production is white wine.
The dry whites of Graves can be among the most complex and food-friendly wines
based on the Sauvignon Blanc grape. The Semillon that is blended in softens the acidic
edge and makes the wines rounder and smoother, as well as adding complexity through
complementary flavors. The wines are fragrant with appealing citrus, gooseberry, and
fresh grassy aromas.

The best red wines of the Graves region are velvety smooth, full of ripe berry flavors. They are not as full as some Haut-Médoc reds and mature more quickly, primarily
because of the good dose of Merlot in most Graves reds. The leading estates are planted
anywhere from 25 to 40 percent Merlot and 50 to 65 percent Cabernet Sauvignon,
with the balance being the three lesser varietals (Cabernet Franc, Malbec, and Petit
Verdot).

The soil of the Graves region is different than in other parts of Bordeaux. The
region actually gets its name from the gravelly, pebble-strewn soil (Figure 6.8),
the vestige of ancient Ice Age glaciers. This top level of gravel allows for excellent

FIGURE 6.8

This pebble-strewn soil in a Graves vineyard is typical of the region. Graves takes its name from the gravelly nature of its soil.

© Cephas Picture Library/Alamy

FIGURE 6.9

Château Haut-Brion in the commune of Pessac was included in the 1855 Classification of the Haut-Médoc. When Graves was classified in the 1950s, Haut-Brion was classified for its red wine. Although it is widely accepted that Haut-Brion makes one of the best white wines from Graves, the estate was not included in that classification at the request of the owners.

© Cephas Picture Library/Alamy

drainage and heat retention that helps the grapes ripen fully. The gravel sits on base soils of sand and clay. Pine forests to the west afford considerable protection from the ocean's cool winds, just as in the Médoc.

The finest vineyards in Graves are in the communes of Pessac and Léognan (Figure 6.9) in the northern section. The soil here is more alluvial where sediment has been deposited by the river over the millennia. In recognition of the fact that the best reds and the best whites of Graves come from these two towns, they were granted a separate appellation in 1986, Pessac-Léognan. The appellation covers 10 communes and essentially divides Graves in two, with all the classified estates being in Pessac-Léognan. The reds from this appellation have complex bouquets of berries, earth, chocolate, and minerals. They feel full and firm, yet supple, on the palate and exhibit delicious flavors of ripe berries.

South of the busy towns of Pessac and Léognan, the region of Graves becomes more rural and even bucolic. Although not classified-growth territory, many lovely wines are produced in this part of Graves. It is possible to find some attractive, well-made reds, most of them primarily Cabernet Sauvignon, which certainly rival the bourgeois-level Médoc reds. Some of the estates in this part of the Graves make very good (and affordable) red wines.

Many properties also produce clean, fresh white wines. In this southern part of Graves, as is typical in the entire region, almost 45 percent of the wine produced is white. The

FIGURE 6.11

The caves (aging cellars) of St. Émilion's famous Château Ausone are carved directly into the stone hillside. This same limestone is found throughout the vineyards of the estate and contributes to Ausone's unique terroir.

© Per Karlsson-BKWine.com/Alamy

town. Here the vineyards look down on the valley of the Dordogne below. The soil is a thin layer of limestone debris on top of a solid limestone rock base (Figure 6.11). The vineyards receive bountiful sunshine tempered by cooling breezes. Of the 13 estates presently included in St. Émilion's classification, 8 have at least part of their vineyards on this plateau and its slopes.

The range of styles among the great classified St. Émilion estates is impressive. There are also many very fine, up and coming estates, as yet unclassified, that may well be included in future revisions. (A list of St. Émilion's classified growths is found in Appendix C.)

Pomerol   Pomerol is a much smaller grape-growing region than its neighbor St. Émilion, having only 1,900 acres (769 hectares) of vines versus St. Émilion's 12,800 acres (5,182 hectares). Fully three-quarters of the vineyards in Pomerol are planted to Merlot with Cabernet Franc playing a supporting role. The soils vary throughout Pomerol, with a mixture of sand, clay, and gravel over a base of either sedimentary rock or iron. The presence of iron is one reason the wines of Pomerol are rich and concentrated, with a distinctive aroma of minerals and pencil lead. Pomerol may be the smallest of Bordeaux's important wine regions, but its wines are among the most impressive in the world. They are also among the most expensive because of the combination of superb quality and very limited production. Even though the wines of Pomerol have never been officially rated, their reputation is such that demand will always outpace supply.

The undisputed star of Pomerol is Château Pétrus. Some experts will state unequivocally that Pétrus is the best Merlot-based wine made anywhere. (Vineyards are planted 95 percent to Merlot.) A very small estate, just 28.4 acres (11.5 hectares), Pétrus year after year turns out wonderfully rich, smooth, complex wines that spend more than two years in barrels. Demand for Pétrus always exceeds supply.

Lesser Appellations   Beyond the five regions of Bordeaux that produce its undisputed champion wines—the Haut-Médoc, Graves, Sauternes/Barsac, St. Émilion, and Pomerol—several other Appellation d'Origine Contrôlée districts produce admirable wines.

Entre-Deux-Mers   This fairly large appellation, whose name means "between two seas," lies between the two tributaries of the Gironde, the Dordogne, and the Garonne. The appellation is restricted to dry white wine. Any red wine made from grapes grown here can be labeled only as Bordeaux Rouge. Although small quantities of lesser grapes, such as Ugni Blanc and Colombard, are allowed in Entre-Deux-Mers wines, most producers use high proportions of Sauvignon Blanc, which imparts racy citrusy flavors. This region produces large quantities of very affordable, clean, crisp white wine, light in body and straightforward in flavor. Entre-Deux-Mers whites are very food-compatible, particularly good with seafood.

Premières Côtes de Bordeaux   Stretching along the northern bank of the Garonne for 37 miles (60 km), the Premières Côtes de Bordeaux produces mostly red wine. Due in part to the high amount of gravel in the soil, some of these reds are quite distinctive.

Lalande de Pomerol   This small satellite appellation lies just north of Pomerol. The wines, understandably, are like lesser Pomerols—full of Merlot, soft, fruity, and approachable even when young. They often represent excellent value.

Bordeaux   The most general appellation, Bordeaux, can be used for white or red wines made from grapes grown anywhere within the boundaries of this large region. This is also the appellation used if grapes from two or more subdistricts of Bordeaux are blended together and for wines that do not conform to the restrictions of the appellation in which the grapes were grown (e.g., red wine from Entre-Deux-Mers). Even at this regional level, the law spells out specific requirements such as minimum alcohol content and yield per acre.

Bordeaux Supérieur   Bordeaux Supérieur has 0.5 percent higher minimum alcohol requirement than wines labeled as Bordeaux, and must have lower yields. Moreover, lesser grape varietals are excluded whereas in Bordeaux appellation whites, up to 30 percent can be from these subsidiary grapes.

The region of Bordeaux is an immensely complex and varied wine region, with a long history of wine production and a stellar reputation in the international marketplace. The producers of Bordeaux have become fiercely competitive with each other, and with wine producers the world over. However, younger Americans are not buying Bordeaux wines at the rates their forbears did. There is a movement under way now in Bordeaux to regain ground lost over the past 20 years in the United States. Consumption of Bordeaux wines have fallen from being 1.7 percent of all still wine consumed in this country to being only one-half of 1 percent of still wine (Asimov, 2010). The vintners of Bordeaux are astute enough to realize that they must maintain high levels of quality if they are to continue to hold their prominent position in the eyes of wine consumers.

Reading a French Wine Label

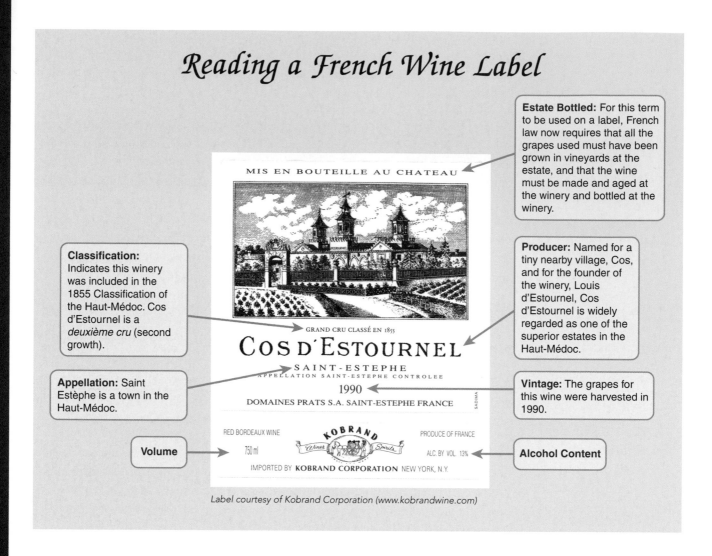

Estate Bottled: For this term to be used on a label, French law now requires that all the grapes used must have been grown in vineyards at the estate, and that the wine must be made and aged at the winery and bottled at the winery.

Producer: Named for a tiny nearby village, Cos, and for the founder of the winery, Louis d'Estournel, Cos d'Estournel is widely regarded as one of the superior estates in the Haut-Médoc.

Classification: Indicates this winery was included in the 1855 Classification of the Haut-Médoc. Cos d'Estournel is a *deuxième cru* (second growth).

Appellation: Saint Estèphe is a town in the Haut-Médoc.

Vintage: The grapes for this wine were harvested in 1990.

Volume

Alcohol Content

MIS EN BOUTEILLE AU CHATEAU

GRAND CRU CLASSÉ EN 1855

COS D'ESTOURNEL

SAINT-ESTEPHE
APPELLATION SAINT-ESTEPHE CONTROLEE

1990

DOMAINES PRATS S.A. SAINT-ESTEPHE FRANCE

RED BORDEAUX WINE   PRODUCE OF FRANCE

750 ml   ALC. BY VOL. 13%

IMPORTED BY **KOBRAND CORPORATION** NEW YORK, N.Y.

Label courtesy of Kobrand Corporation (www.kobrandwine.com)

Burgundy

Burgundy is much smaller than Bordeaux, produces only half as much wine, but is far more complicated. Burgundy is difficult to comprehend because of the plethora of appellations, maze of ownership patterns, and prevalence of négociant labels. The main complicating factor is the pattern of land ownership. In Bordeaux, the wine-producing estates are self-sufficient entities in that they grow their own grapes, have the winemaking facility and aging caves on the property (and in many cases, the proprietor's dwelling also), and market the wines under the name of the estate. This is not the case in Burgundy. Each village here has its own appellation, and the vineyards within that village may each have their own individual appellations. Those vineyards may have several owners. For instance, Clos Vougeot, a single 123-acre vineyard of high quality, is subdivided into 100 parcels and has 80 owners (Figure 6.12). Moreover, the winemaking facilities are located in the towns, away from the vineyards. The name under which a wine is marketed may be that of a merchant or négociant, who is in no way connected to the owner of the vineyards where the grapes were grown. The négociant buys grapes or juice

FIGURE 6.12

Clos Vougeot is one of the most famous wineries in Burgundy. Its vineyards produce some of the best Pinot Noir grapes in the world.

© Lazar Mihai-Bogdan/ Shutterstock

from several different growers and blends them together, often to the detriment of distinctive character due to terroir.

The effort to learn about Burgundy's wines is well worth it. This region produces elegant and complex whites based on Chardonnay and beautifully refined reds made entirely of Pinot Noir. Sadly, one must shop for Burgundies carefully for despite high prices, due to limited supply and considerable demand, the quality is not consistent. Part of the problem is the northern location of the region, where continental weather patterns can make grape growing problematic. Another important factor, at least for the reds, is that Pinot Noir is a notoriously finicky and difficult varietal to grow. There is real variation from vintage to vintage and from producer to producer. The wise consumer does his or her homework and buys Burgundies from good vintages and only from reputable producers. Fortunately, in the past few decades, more moderately priced wines of good quality are being produced in Burgundy. The trend is away from selling to négociants and toward **propriétaire** (proh-pree-ay-TEHR) labels, that is, wines for which the winemaking, bottling, and marketing are all done by the growers themselves.

History

The history of wine production in Burgundy precedes the Roman Empire. There is clear evidence that viticulture was well established here by the second century AD. The region survived the collapse of the Roman Empire and the invasion of barbarian tribes with little disruption to wine production. In fact, the name of the region evolved from one of those tribes. The Burgondes were a little-known people who migrated from Germany in the second half of the fifth century and stayed in the area well into the next century. At that time (approximately AD 530), they were absorbed into the Frankish kingdom after being defeated in battle (Coates, 2000).

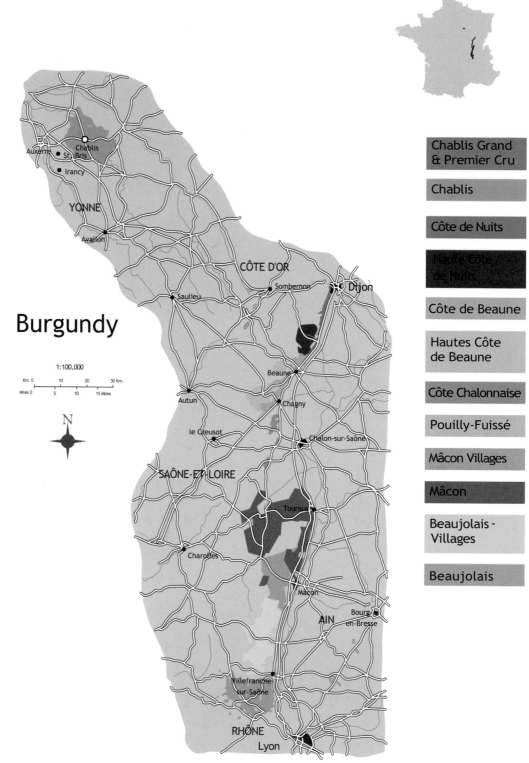

Burgundy

1:100,000

Km. 0   10   20   30 Km.
Miles 0   5   10   15 Miles

N

YONNE

CÔTE D'OR

SAÔNE-ET-LOIRE

AIN

RHÔNE

Auxerre
Chablis
St. Bris
Irancy
Avallon
Saulieu
Sombernon
Dijon
Autun
Beaune
Chagny
le Creusot
Chalon-sur-Saône
Tournus
Charolles
Mâcon
Bourg-en-Bresse
Villefranche-sur-Saône
Lyon

Chablis Grand & Premier Cru

Chablis

Côte de Nuits

Haute Côte de Nuits

Côte de Beaune

Hautes Côte de Beaune

Côte Chalonnaise

Pouilly-Fuissé

Mâcon Villages

Mâcon

Beaujolais - Villages

Beaujolais

Map courtesy of Kobrand Corporation (www.kobrandwine.com)

Over the next thousand years, Burgundy evolved first into an independent kingdom, which lasted until the early eighth century, and then an autonomous duchy, enlarging its boundaries and its power into the Middle Ages through carefully negotiated dynastic marriages. The most important single factor in the development of the region was the ever-increasing influence of the Catholic Church. In no other region of France did the Church play such an important role vis-à-vis wine production. The church's vineyard holdings in Burgundy were enormous. Much of the land owned by monasteries and parishes was acquired as gifts from knights of the aristocracy as they left to fight in the Crusades. The knights' hope was that the monks and priests would pray for their souls should they die in battle far from home.

During the Middle Ages, as its landholdings increased, the Church played a crucial role in perfecting techniques of viticulture and winemaking. The Cistercian order, for instance, which by 1336 owned over 123 acres (50 hectares) of prime vineyards in the northern part of Burgundy, did extensive systematic research into the relationship among grape varietal, soil and climate conditions, and the wine that resulted. These monks were among the very first to investigate and define the concept of terroir. From their meticulous work evolved the idea of crus (growths), the dividing of vineyards into sections each with its own distinct character. Many of the viticultural steps now practiced in Burgundy, such as pruning, grafting, and soil preparation, were developed by the Cistercians, as were important winemaking techniques (Phillips, 2000).

The invaluable contributions of the Catholic Church continued, as did the expansion of its landholdings, up to the time of the French Revolution and the abolition of the monarchy, at which time the pattern of land ownership in Burgundy changed. After the Revolution, the new government confiscated the lands of the Church and aristocracy, and sold them to the bourgeois families and to the peasants. Shortly thereafter, in 1790, the Napoleonic Code contributed even further to the fragmentation of landholdings by abolishing primogeniture, the age-old custom of leaving all one's holdings to one's oldest son. All children, including daughters, were to receive equal portions of an inheritance. It did not take many generations for a family's landholdings to become very small indeed. In modern-day France, one individual's holding can be as small as a few rows of vines.

After the Napoleonic Wars ended in 1815, and the new patterns of land ownership were firmly established, and economic and political conditions stabilized throughout France, wine production in Burgundy expanded. With the rise of the bourgeoisie, France's middle class, a new market for Burgundy's wines opened up. Unfortunately, attention to quality and authenticity was not always maintained. It was not unusual for a vintner to expand production by blending in juice from grapes grown in inferior vineyards, or even grown outside of Burgundy. This type of fraud became even more prevalent as increasing numbers of négociants emerged.

Before Burgundy could correct the problem of fraud, the region was hit hard by phylloxera. Many of Burgundy's vineyards were wiped out. The one benefit of the phylloxera epidemic was that, when replanting was undertaken on American rootstock, only the most suitable locations were planted, thus eliminating inferior vineyards. Most vineyards are now on slopes leading up from the river valley. The upper reaches of the hills are too exposed and cold for vines, and the low-lying sites along the valley floor are too alluvial and marshy.

FIGURE 6.13

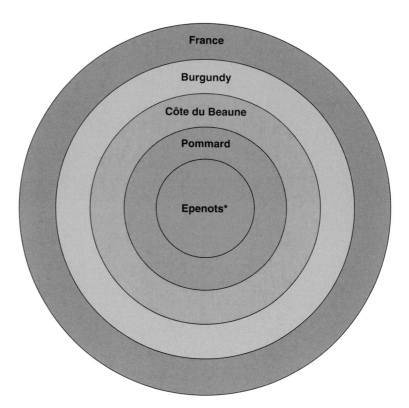

The analogy of concentric circles illustrates how French appellations fit one inside the other as the geographic designation gets smaller. Generally, the smaller the appellation, the better and more distinctive the wine.

© *Delmar Cengage Learning*

*Epenot is a 1st cru vineyard in the town of Pommard.

FIGURE 6.14

An example of a general appellation. These Chardonnay grapes could have been grown anywhere within the boundaries of the Burgundy region. (*Burgundy* is the English spelling for the Bourgogne region.)

© *Vineyard Brands*

The passage of the Appellation d'Origine Contrôlée laws in 1935 eliminated the worst of the fraud and gave protection to place names within Burgundy. The AOC laws also established standards of viticulture and winemaking. Since the 1990s, there has been a trend away from small growers selling their grapes to négociants, and instead the number of propriétaire labels has increased.

Classification System of Burgundy

When learning to decipher Burgundy's classification system, it is helpful to think in terms of concentric circles (Figure 6.13), while bearing in mind our maxim about European appellations: "The smaller and more specific the geographic designation, in general, the better and more distinctive the wine." In the case of Burgundy, the outermost concentric circle is the general appellation, Burgundy. The label will say simply "Bourgogne Rouge" or "Bourgogne Blanc" (Figure 6.14). Grapes for this level of wine may be grown anywhere within the region of Burgundy. Burgundy is a small region, with only 98,000 acres (39,676 hectares) under vines, and the grapes used must be the approved varietals of Pinot Noir (for reds) or

TABLE 6.2 Appellations of France: Burgundy

Region	Subregion	Principal Varietal*
Chablis	Petit Chablis	Chardonnay
Côte de Nuits	Fixin	Pinot Noir
	Gevrey	Pinot Noir
	Morey-St.-Denis	Pinot Noir
	Chambolle-Musigny	Pinot Noir
	Vougeot	Pinot Noir
	Vosne-Romanée	Pinot Noir
	Nuits-St.-Georges	Pinot Noir, Chardonnay
Côte de Beaune	Aloxe-Corton	Pinot Noir, Chardonnay
	Pommard	Pinot Noir
	Savigny-lès-Beaune	Pinot Noir
	Volnay	Pinot Noir
	Beaune	Chardonnay, Pinot Noir
	Meursault	Chardonnay
	Puligny-Montrachet	Chardonnay
	Chassagne-Montrachet	Chardonnay
Côte Chalonnaise	Rully	Chardonnay, Pinot Noir
	Mercurey	Pinot Noir, Chardonnay
	Givry	Pinot Noir
	Montagny	Chardonnay
Mâconnais	Pouilly-Fuissé	Chardonnay
	St. Véran	Chardonnay
	Mâcon-Villages	Chardonnay
Beaujolais	Morgon, St. Amour, Fleurie	
	Moulin-à-Vent, Brouilly, Côte de Brouilly	Gamay
	Julienas, Chenas, Regnie, Chiroubles	
	Beaujolais-Villages	Gamay

*Burgundy wines are *not* blended. The grape mentioned for each village indicates whether that village produces red wine or white. When both varietals are mentioned, the one shown first indicates which type of wine the village is more famous for.

Chardonnay (for whites). Therefore, a wine labeled as generic Burgundy can still be quite distinctive as it will be made from noble varietals (Table 6.2).

The next circle in our hypothetical "target" is that of the regional appellation. For these wines, the grapes must all be grown within a specific subregion of Burgundy. An example would be Côte de Beaune or Côte de Nuits-Villages. Sometimes a regional appellation signifies that grapes from vineyards located in two or more villages have been blended together.

The next smaller circle is the commune appellation. A commune is a village or town. All the grapes used in a wine labeled with the name of a specific commune must come from vineyards located within the boundaries of that village or town (Figure 6.15).

FIGURE 6.15

An example of a commune label. Chassagne-Montrachet is a village in the Côte de Beaune, famous for the quality of its white wines. *Vieilles Vignes* means "old vines." This is not an official designation, but is used by vintners to indicate the grapes come from older vines that usually impart more intense flavor to wine.

© *Vineyard Brands*

FIGURE 6.16

A premier cru (first growth) label will show both the specific rated vineyard (in this case Boucherottes) and the commune (Beaune). Note the full official appellation reads "Appellation Beaune 1er Cru Contrôlée."

Label courtesy of Kobrand Corporation (www.kobrandwine.com)

The next two levels are for specific single vineyards, often very small indeed. The vineyards that carry their own individual appellation are those that have been officially rated by the authorities. Only in the best regions of Burgundy are there any rated vineyards. Single vineyard appellations are found only in Chablis and the Côte d'Or. The first level of rated vineyards is the premier cru appellation (first growth designation) (Figure 6.16). The label for premier cru wines will show both the name of the vineyard and the name of the commune in which it is located. For instance, "Pommard (the commune) Epenots (the rated vineyard)" or "Beaune (the town) Clos de la Mousse (the rated vineyard)."

The final level of quality for Burgundy, the "bull's eye" of our concentric circles analogy, is the grand cru appellation, or "great growth designation" (Figure 6.17). The grand cru vineyards have been rated by the authorities as the very best sites for growing Pinot Noir or Chardonnay. Due to immutable physical factors such as hours of sunshine, protection from cold winds, drainage, and unique makeup of the soil these vineyards are capable of producing, year after year, grapes that are superior to those harvested from other vineyards. Wines from grand cru vineyards carry just the name of that vineyard. An example would be "Grands Échezeaux" or "Le Corton." The

FIGURE 6.17

A grand cru label shows only the name of the specific rated vineyard, in this case, Grands Échezeaux, one of Burgundy's most acclaimed sites for the Pinot Noir grape.

© *Vineyard Brands*

Chablis

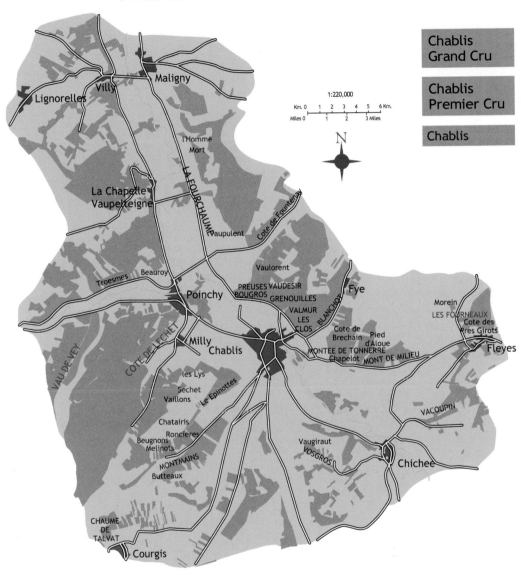

Map courtesy of Kobrand Corporation (www.kobrandwine.com)

commune name is not mentioned. There are only 7 grand cru vineyards in Chablis, and 30 in the Côte d'Or. These vineyards are small in area and their production limited. Needless to say, grand cru wines are very expensive.

Wine Regions of Burgundy

Burgundy is divided into six main regions: Chablis, Côte de Nuits, Côte de Beaune (which together are often referred to as the Côte d'Or), Côte Chalonnaise, Mâconnais,

THE CLASSIFICATION SYSTEM OF BURGUNDY

Burgundy has five different levels of classification, the top two of which are relevant only to Chablis and the Côte d'Or. These quality levels are:

1. Non-specific general appellation with no geographic definition, i.e., Bourgogne.
2. Regional appellation. Usually a blend of one or more commune wines made by a merchant, or *négociant*. Example: Côte de Nuits-Villages.
3. Commune appellation. All the grapes used in the bottle were grown within the boundaries of one town, or commune, but not from vineyards that are rated as superior by the authorities. Example: Vosne-Romanée.
4. First growths (*premier cru*). The label shows the name of the commune *and* the name of the rated vineyard. Example: Vosne-Romanée "Les Malconsorts."
5. Great growths (*grands crus*). These are the very finest vineyards. The label will show the name of the vineyard *only*. Example: La Tâche.

In Chablis the label will say Chablis Grand Cru, followed by the name of the rated vineyard, e.g., "Blanchots."

These are the 14 most important communes of the Côte d'Or, moving from north to south. The best-known *grand cru* vineyard of each commune are also shown.

Côte de Nuits:

1. Fixin. Red wine only.
2. Gevrey. Red. Eight *grand crus*, two of which are extraordinary:
   Chambertin, Clos de Beze
3. Morey-St.-Denis. Red.
   Bonnes Mares (a small portion)
4. Chambolle-Musigny. Mostly red.
   Bonnes Mares Musigny
5. Vougeot. Mostly red.
   Clos de Vougeot
6. Vosne Romanée. Red only.
   Échezeaux Grand Échezeaux
   La Tâche Richebourg
   Romanée-Conti La Romanée
7. Nuits-St.-George. Mostly red.

Côte de Beaune:

8. Aloxe-Corton. Some white; mostly red.
   Le Corton (red) Corton (white)
   Corton-Charlemagne (white)
9. Pommard. Red only. No *grand crus*. Six *premier crus*.
10. Volnay. Red. No *grand crus*. Thirteen *premier crus*.
11. Beaune. Red and white. No *grand crus*. 34 *premier crus*.
12. Meursault. White only. No *grand crus*. 17 *premier crus*.
13. Puligny-Montrachet. Mostly white; some red.
    Bâtard-Montrachet Bienvenues-Bâtard-Montrachet
    Chevalier-Montrachet Le Montrachet
14. Chassagne-Montrachet. Mostly white; some red.
    Bâtard-Montrachet Criots-Bâtard-Montrachet

and Beaujolais. Chablis lies geographically separate from the rest of Burgundy, some 81 miles (131 km) to the northwest. The remaining regions are spread in a contiguous line along the Saône River valley, from the city of Dijon in the north to the city of Lyon in the south. The vineyards are not contiguous, however. Burgundy is not a tightly planted region, as vineyards are planted only on the slopes where vines can receive enough sunlight to flourish.

Chablis

Chablis is an appellation restricted to dry white wine. These are among the most crisp and elegant wines made from the Chardonnay grape. The climate here is cool enough that the grapes maintain an excellent crisp acidity. The flavors fully evolve because the

FIGURE 6.18

The soil of Chablis' best vineyards is white because of the high concentration of chalk and limestone. Stretching over the gently rolling hills in this photograph are portions of four of the seven grand cru vineyards.

© Cephas Picture Library/Alamy

grapes enjoy a lengthy ripening period as they hang on the vines into fall. However, the vintners must be constantly alert to the danger of frost.

Chablis is a fairly small region, with fewer than 7,000 acres (2,834 hectares) under vines. The soil throughout Chablis is uniform, a unique mix of chalky limestone and clay. This mixture imparts distinctive aromas (hay, apple, and wet slate) and flavors unlike those found in Chardonnay grapes grown even a few miles away. There is a minerally, almost flinty, edge to Chablis that perfectly sets off its subtle flavors and crisp acidity. Visually, Chablis whites have a vibrant yellow color with a touch of green at the edge. These wines are superb companions to a wide variety of foods, especially seafood, poultry or pasta in creamy sauces, and certain veal dishes.

Classification within Chablis   In 1936, the French authorities began the process of rating the vineyards of Chablis. The very best vineyard sites, on a slope above the town of Chablis, face southwest, thus benefiting from more sun exposure than other locations. On this slope the soil also has a higher level of fossilized oyster shells, which add a subtle but highly desirable extra dimension of complexity to the wines. In 1938, seven vineyards on this slope were awarded the grand cru rating (Figure 6.18). These seven vineyards are very small, averaging less than 40 acres (16 hectares) each. Wines made from grapes grown in these vineyards are labeled Chablis grand cru, with the specific vineyard also listed (Table 6.3).

Next in quality are those vineyard sites designated premier cru. The original group of 11 premier cru vineyards was classified in 1967. Some of these vineyards actually encompass several subsidiary vineyards, but the authorities streamlined the original list of 26 vineyard sites down to the more comprehensible eleven. In 1986, an additional 7 sites were designated premier cru, while 1 of the original 11 was absorbed into its neighbor. Consequently, there are now a total of 17 premier cru vineyards. The wines from these sites are labeled Chablis premier cru, with the specific vineyard also listed (Table 6.4).

TABLE 6.3 Grand Cru Vineyards of Chablis

Bougros	Vaudésir
Preuses	Grenouilles
Valmur	Les Clos
Blanchot	

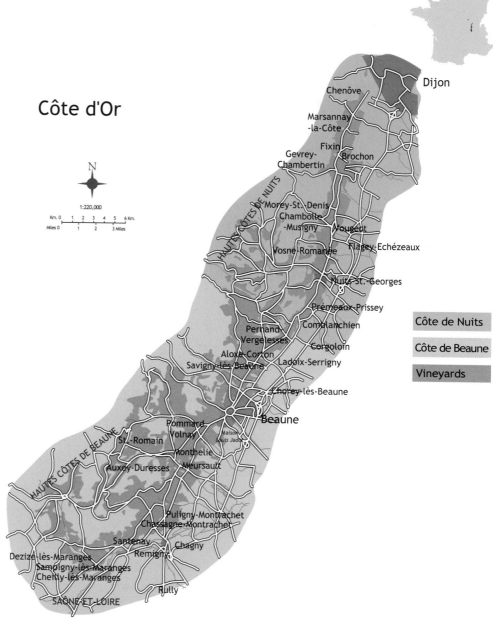

Côte d'Or

N

1:220,000

Km. 0 1 2 3 4 5 6 Km.
Miles 0 1 2 3 Miles

Dijon

Chenôve

Marsannay
-la-Côte

Fixin

Gevrey-
Chambertin

Brochon

HAUTES-CÔTES DE NUITS

Morey-St.-Denis

Chambolle
-Musigny

Vougeot

Vosne-Romanée

Flagey-Echézeaux

Nuits-St.-Georges

Prémeaux-Prissey

Comblanchien

Pernand-
Vergelesses

Corgoloin

Aloxe-Corton

Ladoix-Serrigny

Savigny-lès-Beaune

Chorey-lès-Beaune

Beaune

Maison
Louis Jadot

Pommard

Volnay

St.-Romain

Monthelie

Auxey-Duresses

Meursault

HAUTES CÔTES DE BEAUNE

Puligny-Montrachet

Chassagne-Montrachet

Santenay

Chagny

Remigny

Dezize-lès-Maranges

Sampigny-lès-Maranges

Cheilly-lès-Maranges

Rully

SAÔNE-ET-LOIRE

Côte de Nuits

Côte de Beaune

Vineyards

Map courtesy of Kobrand Corporation (www.kobrandwine.com)

Wine made from Chardonnay grapes grown anywhere else within the official boundaries of the Chablis appellation is simply labeled Chablis. A step below that is the appellation of Petit Chablis, which encompasses vineyards on the hills and plateaus at the outskirts of the region. Approximately 85 percent of the wine produced in the region is classified as generic Chablis or Petit Chablis.

Côte d'Or

Burgundy's Côte d'Or, or Golden Slope, is widely regarded as one of the world's best areas for growing cool-climate grapes. It is only about 30 miles (48 km) long and less

TABLE 6.4 Premier Cru Vineyards of Chablis

Classified in 1967	
Fourchaume	Montée de Tonnerre
Monts de Milieu	Vaucoupin
Les Fourneaux	Beauroy
Côte de Léchet	Vaillons
Montmains	Vosgros
Mélinots (absorbed into Vaillons)	
Classified in 1986	
Vaudevey	Vau Ligneau
Côte de Vaubarousse	Chaume de Talvat
Les Landes	Les Beauregards
Berdiot	

than 2.5 miles (4 km) at its widest. Elevation is between 720 and 1,000 feet (219 and 305 meters). The hills protect the vineyards from excessive rain and provide south and east facing slopes that catch more sunlight.

The Cote d'Or is divided into two subregions. The northern portion is the Côte de Nuits (named for the town of Nuits-St.-George). The southern portion is the Côte de Beaune (named for the city of Beaune). In general, the Côte de Nuits is famous for its red wines and the Côte de Beaune for its whites. The reds of the Côte de Nuits are big but not tannic, elegant with solid structure, and incredibly complex. The complex mélange of aromas and flavors is all the more surprising when one realizes that the wines are made from only one grape, the Pinot Noir. The bouquet is earthy, displaying enticing aromas of mushrooms, root vegetables like beets, or even the typical barnyard aroma of old manure. The fruit is reminiscent of cherries or strawberries. These wines can be consumed as early as 2 to 6 years after the vintage year, but can age very well, often not reaching maturity until 15 or 20 years old.

The whites of the Côte de Beaune are made entirely from Chardonnay grapes. Côte de Beaune whites are noted for their complex bouquets of hazelnut or blanched almond, apple, appealing vegetable tones of fresh cabbage, and a hint of toast. The flavors are of ripe fruit and toasty oak, perfectly balanced by fresh acidity. The lesser whites of Burgundy are fermented in stainless steel and bottled young, never spending any time in barrels. But the great whites of the Côte de Beaune are both fermented and aged in oak, which adds to their nutty/buttery richness.

The Côte de Nuits   The Côte de Nuits starts in the north with the village of Marsannay, just south of the city of Dijon and continues for 14 miles (22.6 km). There are small quantities of rosé and white wines made here, but the Côte de Nuits is famous for its world-class reds. The important communes of the Côte de Nuits, from north to south, are Marsannay, Gevrey-Chambertin, Morey-St.-Denis, Chambolle-Musigny, Vougeot, Vosne-Romanée, and Nuits-St.-George.

Marsannay   This small village just south of Dijon is famous for its rosé, a dry wine made from Pinot Noir grapes. The bouquet is of strawberries, and the flavors are clean

FIGURE 6.19

The historic village of Gevrey-Chambertin in the Côte de Nuits. The old wooden wine press stands in front of a castle that was built in the tenth century.

© Stockfolio®/Alamy

and fresh. These wines are best served young. Like all rosés, Marsannay rosés are very good with salty foods, such as ham or anchovies.

Gevrey-Chambertin The name of this commune reflects a common practice in the Côte d'Or: Hyphenating the name of the commune's most famous grand cru vineyard (in this case, Chambertin) to the original name of the commune (Figure 6.19). Gevrey-Chambertin is an appellation for red wine only. There are eight grand cru vineyards in the commune. Besides Chambertin, the most famous vineyard is Clos de Beze. (A **clos** (KLOH) is a small, walled-in vineyard. It is a common way of naming vineyards in Burgundy.) The soil of the grand crus vineyards varies depending on how high up the hillside the vineyard is located. The primary component is limestone, mixed with some clay and flint. The amount of clay decreases in sites higher up the hills. Gevrey-Chambertin also has 24 premier cru vineyards. The wines from Gevrey-Chambertin are among the best of Burgundy's reds. They are full bodied, smooth, and very complex. They can age extremely well, often not reaching their prime until 15 years after the vintage.

Morey-St.-Denis The commune of Morey-St.-Denis produces primarily red wine. Lying between the more famous villages of Gevrey and Chambolle, Morey-St.-Denis is often overlooked even though its wines can be as concentrated and refined as the best produced in either of its neighbors. There are 4 grand cru vineyards in Morey-St.-Denis. There are also 25 premier cru vineyards.

Chambolle-Musigny A small amount of white wine is made in Chambolle-Musigny, but the commune is renowned for its great reds. The outstanding characteristic of these wines is their aromatic bouquet, reminiscent of strawberries and roses, as well as their finesse and delicacy. Both of Chambolle's grand crus are of very high quality. The soil in both vineyards contains very little clay, a factor that contributes to the delicacy of the wines. There are also 22 premier cru vineyards in Chambolle, covering a total of just over 150 acres (61 hectares).

Vougeot Vougeot is a tiny village with only a couple dozen inhabitants. The village is dominated by its one grand cru vineyard, Clos de Vougeot, which, at 124 acres (50 hectares), is one of Burgundy's largest rated vineyards. Fully four-fifths of Vougeot's wine production is red wine from this one grand cru vineyard. Because it is so large and is owned by many different entities, the wines of Clos de Vougeot can differ considerably in style.

FIGURE 6.20

This stone pillar marks the corner of the world famous La Romanée vineyard outside the town of Vosne-Romanée. The name derives from "Roman" because it is believed the Romans may have first planted grapes on the site.

© Cephas Picture Library/Alamy

A tiny amount of white wine has the commune appellation. The remainder is red wine from the 44 acres (18 hectares) of premier cru vineyards. The reds of Vougeot have a distinctive truffle or mushroom hint to their bouquet, and have concentrated flavors.

Flagy-Échezeaux   No commune wine is made in this village. Production is almost entirely from its two grand cru vineyards, Échezeaux and Grands-Échezeaux, which together cover 113 acres (45.7 hectares). The smaller one, Grands-Échezeaux, is regarded as the superior vineyard. In both vineyards there is more clay than in other important Côte de Nuits villages, a factor that gives more weight and density to the wines.

Vosne-Romanée   This village produces red wine only. According to some wine experts, the Pinot Noir grape achieves its absolute pinnacle of quality in the grand cru wines from Vosne-Romanée. There are six grands cru vineyards, all of them famous and justly celebrated. These wines are among the world's most expensive. In 1650, a vineyard formerly known as Le Cloux was renamed Romanée because Roman artifacts had been found nearby. When the vineyard was purchased in 1760 by the Prince of Conti, it was given the name Romanée-Conti. Lying on the slope right above it is La Romanée (Figure 6.20). In both vineyards, the soil is primarily calcareous with up to 45 percent clay. The resulting wines have a superb balance of concentration and refinement. Fewer than 1,000 cases of wine from these two legendary vineyards are made each year.

Nuits-St.-Georges   In the industrialized town of Nuits-St.-Georges there are no grand cru vineyards, but there are many fine wines made at the premier cru and village levels of quality. There are an impressive 28 premier crus within the boundaries of the town, plus an additional 13 in the adjoining town that are entitled to use the Nuits-St.-Georges appellation. Many of the premier crus lie north of the town, near Vosne. The soil here is primarily iron-rich limestone, like that of the Vosne grand cru vineyards.

Côte de Beaune   Since the Côte de Beaune is so famous for its elegant, complex whites—with one exception, all the grand cru vineyards are white—it is often forgotten that three-quarters of the production here is red wine. These reds are not as full bodied and complex, nor as long-lived, as those of the Côte de Nuits. However, Côte de Beaune reds can be very appealing, with vibrant fruit and silky texture. The Côte de Beaune is a large region, more than twice the size of the Côte de Nuits, stretching some 71 miles (114.5 km) from north to south. The hills here have gentler slopes and face primarily southeast.

Côte de Beaune-Villages   In the French appellation system, the word *villages* affixed to a regional appellation indicates that the vineyards are of higher quality than those in surrounding areas. Thus, Côte de Beaune-Villages is a more distinctive appellation than Côte de Beaune. In fact, only 74 acres (30 hectares) of vineyards are designated Côte de Beaune. Sixteen villages are included in the Côte de Beaune appellation. Many of these villages are of high enough quality that they also have their own appellation, but when grapes from two or more villages are blended together, the only appellation allowed is Côte de Beaune-Villages. Many of these wines, both red and white, represent very good value.

Aloxe-Corton   This commune produces primarily reds, but some superb whites are made here. It is home to Burgundy's largest grand cru vineyard, Corton. This famous vineyard, which is spread over three communes, is close to 400 acres (162 hectares) in size. This vineyard produces both grand cru red, usually labeled as Le Corton, and grand cru white, which is labeled as Corton.

The Pinot Noir in the Corton vineyard is planted on heavier soil with a preponderance of clay. The resulting red wines seem to have the heft of Côte de Nuits reds combined with the grace and vibrancy of Côte de Beaune reds. The Chardonnay grapes are planted in higher sections of the Corton vineyard and its adjacent grand cru, Corton-Charlemagne, where the soil is lighter and finer, full of chalk and pebbles.

Savigny-lès-Beaune   The commune of Savigny is one of the larger villages in the Côte de Beaune. It has 19 premier cru vineyards and produces mostly reds that are fruity and charming.

Beaune   The city of Beaune is the center of the Burgundy wine trade. It is an ancient walled city with the distinct feel of medieval times, but it is bustling with commerce and wine-oriented activities. The appellation to which the city lends its name is a large one, with 13,300 acres (5,263 hectares) of vines. Over 90 percent of production is red wines and there are 42 premier cru vineyards, covering almost 800 acres (324 hectares), but there are no grand crus.

The soil content among these many premier crus is complicated and varied. The soil structure is based on limestone, but to the north, near Savigny, the soil is very thin and the vine roots have to reach deep for nutrients. The result is wines that are intensely flavored and concentrated, with good structure. As one moves into the middle section of premier crus, to the west of the city, the soil becomes more gravelly and less thin. The wines from these vineyards are riper, rounder, and more succulent. To the south of the city, the soil has less gravel and more clay. The wines are fuller bodied, softer and fruitier, and quicker to mature.

Pommard   Pommard and its neighbor to the south, Volnay, are home to some of the best reds in the Côte de Beaune. The name *Pommard* comes from the French word for apple, but there are almost no apple orchards left. All available agricultural land has long been planted to wine grapes. There are 832 acres (337 hectares) of vines, of which 275 acres (111 hectares), or about one-third, are rated as premier cru. The reds of Pommard are among Burgundy's most popular.

Volnay The reds of Volnay are justly famous for their charm and seductive fruit. A perfect illustration of the overall quality of Volnay's vineyards is that, of its 527 acres (213 hectares), over half are rated at the premier cru level. Like Pommard, Volnay is well balanced and approachable when young, full of vibrant, berrylike fruit. There are 34 premier crus in Volnay.

Meursault Just south of Volnay is Meursault, a tiny village that produces some of the region's most popular white wines. The wines of Meursault are round and smooth with considerable complexity and often a subtle touch of oak. There are no grand cru vineyards here, but 15 are classified as premier crus. The best of these are Perrière and Genevrières.

Puligny-Montrachet and Chassagne-Montrachet These two adjoining villages are famous for the quality of their wines. Many experts say that the wines from these villages, especially from the grand cru vineyard Montrachet that straddles the boundary between them, produce the world's very best white wine.

Santenay Santenay is the southernmost village of importance in the Côte de Beaune. It is a fairly large commune with 975 acres (395 hectares) under vine. There are 11 premier cru vineyards. Santenay's production is 85 percent red. Santenay reds are charming: medium bodied, fruity, and very pleasant, albeit a little more rustic than Volnay.

Côte Chalonnaise

The southern edge of the Côte de Beaune marks the end of Burgundy's prestigious appellations, with its world-class wines. That does not mean, however, that there are no more wines worth seeking out. Many excellent wines are produced in the southern regions of Burgundy. Immediately south of the Côte de Beaune, the region of Côte Chalonnaise begins. The region is named for the town of Châlone on the Saône River. The vineyards are planted on hillsides a little east of where the vineyards of the Côte de Beaune end. The soil on these hills is similar to the soils of the southern communes of the Côte de Beaune—a mixture of gravel and marl on limestone. The wines of the Chalonnaise lack the elegance, depth, and longevity of those from the Côte d'Or, but they can be charming, balanced, and appealing. These wines are also excellent values.

In the Côte Chalonnaise, there are four commune appellations of particular importance. Moving from north to south these villages are Rully, Mercurey, Givry, and Montagny.

Rully The village of Rully produces approximately equal quantities of red and white wines. Its vineyards are also a good source for the sparkling wine of the Burgundy region, Crémant de Bourgogne. There are 19 vineyards rated as premier cru. The whites of Rully are fresh and clean with apple flavors, and can be drunk young. Several négociants are using oak aging to round out their Rully whites.

Mercurey The vineyards of Mercurey begin just south of Rully. There is more clay and iron in the soil here, and the resulting Pinot Noirs are fuller, rounder, and have more cherry/berry nuances than Rully reds. Mercurey was granted AOC status in 1936 and has maintained its reputation for affordable, attractive reds.

Givry   This small village, which produces mostly red wine, lies a few miles west of the town of Châlone. The soil here begins to shift away from the clay and marl that sits atop the limestone base of the Cote d'Or. At Givry a sandy, lighter limestone is evident. The Pinot Noirs are simpler than those of Mercurey, but have more depth than the reds of Rully.

Montagny   All wines from Montagny are white. The wines are light to medium bodied, have crisp acidity, and are made to be drunk young. The designation premier cru on a Montagny does not indicate a superior vineyard site, but rather is assurance that the wine has attained an alcohol level of at least 11.5 percent.

Mâconnais

The Mâconnais region, surrounding the small town of Mâcon, marks the transition, climatically and geologically, from northern to southern France. Although winters can be very cold and spring chilly enough that frost can be a concern, the summers are sunny and balmy. The limestone base of farther north is still present, but the topsoil is more sandy and less chalky, with patches of granite. The majority of Mâconnais wines are white. They are primarily Chardonnay, but another grape, Aligoté, is also allowed. Red wines, which represent only about 15 percent of production, are made from Pinot Noir or Gamay. Gamay-based red wines are fruitier, softer, and lighter bodied than Pinot Noirs.

Mâcon-Villages   Grapes grown in any of 43 villages can be blended together to make Mâcon-Villages. If a wine is made exclusively from grapes grown in one village, the label can show that village's name (e.g., Mâcon-Viré or Mâcon-Lugny). Mâcon-Villages is a pleasant, light wine, perfect for everyday consumption.

Pouilly-Fuissé   In the United States, Pouilly-Fuissé is perhaps the most recognized of any Burgundy wine (Figure 6.21). It is now ubiquitous on wine lists and in liquor stores, probably because it is made in large quantities, is affordable, and can be

FIGURE 6.21

A Chardonnay vineyard looks down on the town of Fuissé in the Mâconnais. The wines produced here are among the best-known French wines in the United States.

Pixfolio/Alamy

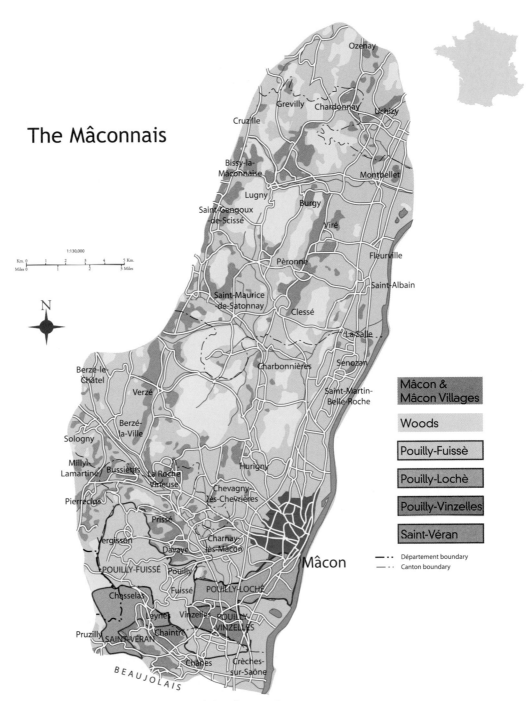

The Mâconnais

1:130,000

Km. 0   1   2   3   4   5 Km.
Miles 0   1   2   3 Miles

N

Ozenay

Grevilly   Chardonnay   Uchizy

Cruzille

Bissy-la-
Mâconnaise

Montbellet

Lugny

Saint-Gengoux-
de-Scissé

Burgy

Viré

Pèronne

Fleurville

Saint-Albain

Saint-Maurice-
de-Satonnay

Clessé

La Salle

Charbonnières

Senozan

Berzé-le-
Châtel

Verzé

Saint-Martin-
Belle-Roche

Berzé-
la-Ville

Sologny

Hurigny

Millyl
Lamartine

Bussières

La Roche
Vineuse

Chevagny-
lès-Chevrières

Pierreclos

Prissé

Charnay-
lès-Mâcon

Mâcon

Vergisson

Davayé

POUILLY-FUISSÉ   Pouilly

POUILLY-LOCHÉ

Chasselas

Fuissé

Léynes   Vinzelles   POUILLY-
VINZELLES

Pruzilly   SAINT-VÉRAN   Chaintré

Chânes   Crèches-
sur-Saône

B E A U J O L A I S

**Mâcon &
Mâcon Villages**

Woods

Pouilly-Fuissè

Pouilly-Lochè

Pouilly-Vinzelles

Saint-Véran

– · · – Département boundary
– · – Canton boundary

Map courtesy of Kobrand Corporation (www.kobrandwine.com)

quite distinctive with its nutty aromas, fresh apple/lemon flavors, and good acidity. There are no officially rated premier cru vineyards, although a producer can list a specific vineyard on the label if desired.

St. Véran The appellation St. Véran was approved in 1971. It was carved out of areas that previously made Mâcon-Villages or Beaujolais Blanc. The soil is chalky and the wine, all white, is light and crisp and best consumed young. St. Véran is very affordable.

The Beaujolais

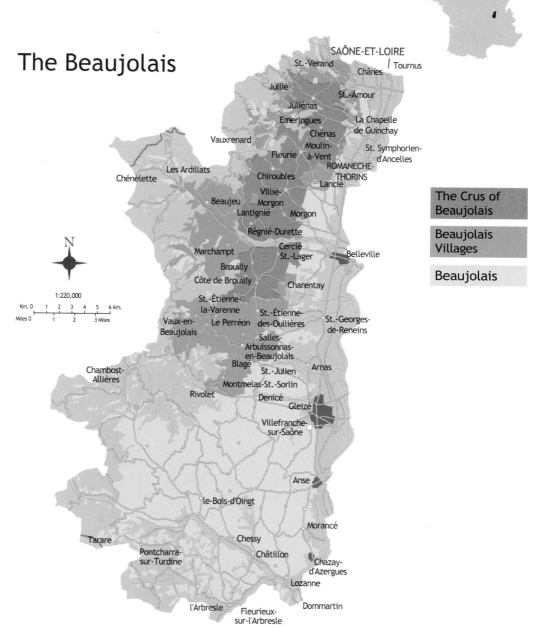

Map courtesy of Kobrand Corporation (www.kobrandwine.com)

Beaujolais

Beaujolais is classified as part of Burgundy, although the climate and soil are different, it is in a different département than the rest of Burgundy, and the primary grape is Gamay, not Pinot Noir. The style of the wine is entirely different. Nonetheless, this large region is treated as a subdistrict of Burgundy. (There is a very small amount of white wine produced as Beaujolais Blanc. It comprises less than 1 percent of total production.)

FIGURE 6.22

The release of Beaujolais Nouveau wine is eagerly antici-
pated each fall.

© Charles O'Rear/Corbis

FIGURE 6.23

A Cru Beaujolais label from the commune of Moulin-à-
Vent. Notice that the label mentions only the town.

Label courtesy of Kobrand Corporation (www.kobrandwine.com)

Beaujolais is one of the most popular red wines in many countries around the world. One reason, of course, is that Gamay makes easy-to-drink reds with cherry/raspberry fruitiness, soft tannins, and light body. Another is that it is widely available—10.5 million cases of Beaujolais are produced annually from 49,540 acres (20,057 hectares) of vines. Also helpful is the annual widely publicized release of Beaujolais Nouveau (Figure 6.22), a very light, simple wine that, by tradition, is released by mid-November. Since the wine is only a few weeks old at the time of release, it is termed *nouveau*, or new. As much as one-third of a Beaujolais producer's wine is released as Beaujolais Nouveau, which is helpful to the producer from a cash-flow viewpoint. Most producers export as much as one-half of their nouveau.

The portion of any vintage year's wine that is not sold as nouveau is released starting the next spring. In ascending order of quality, Beaujolais is classified as AOC Beaujolais, Beaujolais Supérieur (higher minimum alcohol content; rarely exported), Beaujolais-Villages, and Cru Beaujolais (from specific villages whose vineyards have been judged to be better than those in surrounding areas).

The Winemaking Process in Beaujolais As stated earlier, Gamay grapes make soft, easy-to-drink wines with lots of fresh fruit flavors. However, Beaujolais is even softer and fruitier than Gamay-based wines made elsewhere because of a unique wine-making process employed in this region, carbonic maceration (see Chapter 3). With this method, whole bunches of uncrushed grapes are placed in a container from which oxygen has been removed by pumping in carbon dioxide. A mini-fermentation takes place inside each berry, producing very small quantities of alcohol and releasing aromatic flavorful compounds. The portion that went through carbonic maceration allows the whole batch to be softer and more vividly fruity than would have otherwise been the case. The Beaujolais (other than nouveau) is then allowed to age in oak barrels for anywhere from a few weeks to several months before being released for sale.

Cru Beaujolais In the Beaujolais region there are 10 villages where conditions are judged to be ideal for Gamay grapes. The wine from these towns is deeper in color, has more weight and substance, and is longer-lived than wine at the other levels of Beaujolais. The soil in these 10 towns is granite-schist based with topsoil containing varying amounts of sand, clay, and chalk. The wines from these top vineyards are fuller bodied and deeper in flavor than other Beaujolais, but still much lighter than Pinot Noir–based wines. A Cru Beaujolais shows the name of the village on the label (Figure 6.23).

TABLE 6.5 Comparison of Bordeaux and Burgundy

	Bordeaux	Burgundy
Size	Very large; 209,000 acres (84,500 hectares)	Small; 98,000 acres (39,600 hectares)
Climate	Warm and dry, good for early-ripening grapes	Cool and moist, perfect for late-maturing grapes
Viticulture	Red: Cabernet Sauvignon, Merlot, plus three others	Pinot Noir
	White: Sauvignon Blanc, Semillon	Chardonnay
Winemaking	All wines are blends	No blending
Landownership	Large, discrete, self-sufficient properties	Many small holdings; few proprietary bottlings
Classification	General appellation	General appellation
	Regional (e.g., Graves)	Regional (e.g., Côte de Beaune)
	Commune (e.g., Margaux)	Commune (e.g., Volnay)
	Single estates, nonrated	Rated vineyards: *premier cru*
	Classified estates	*Grand cru*
Styles	Whites: Very dry, crisp, herbaceous bouquet	Whites: elegant, complex, dry, nose of nuts/butterscotch/fruit
	Reds: Full bodied, tannic, very complex; nose of cedar/coffee/blackberry	Reds: Medium bodied, elegant, earthy nose, strawberry/cherry flavors
Bottle shape	Shoulders	Sloping sides

A comparison of the wines of Bordeaux and Burgundy can be seen in Table 6.5.

Côtes du Rhône

The region along the Rhône River in southern France is an ancient wine-producing area (Figure 6.24). It is believed that vines were planted here as early as 600 BC by the Greeks. The valley of the Rhône extends from the city of Lyon in the north where it is joined by the River Saône, and extends south for approximately 120 miles (194 km) to the city of Avignon. For much of the length of the river the valley is bursting with commercial activity and is heavily industrialized. The lowlands near the river are not promising for growing quality grapes. However, if one climbs up the slopes (the côtes) on either side of the river, the topography changes drastically and is better suited to growing grapes, especially along the southern section.

History of the Rhône Valley

Although introduced by the Greeks, viticulture did not take hold in the valley along the Rhône until many centuries later, in the early Christian period, when wine was exported to Rome. After the decline of the Roman Empire, winemaking essentially disappeared until the popes moved to Avignon, as discussed earlier in this chapter.

FIGURE 6.24

The Rhône River flows for 120 miles (194 km) through countryside and small towns. The côtes (slopes) along its length are often covered with grapevines.
© PHB.cz (Richard Semik)/ Shutterstock

Historically, perhaps the most significant contribution to French wine production to emerge from the Côtes du Rhône is the work done by Baron LeRoy of Château Fortia on quality control laws. It was the baron who, after the First World War, led an orderly revolt against the desecration of the appellation Châteauneuf-du-Pape. The region was famous for its big, robust red wines, and the name, with its quaint history of popes and summer castles, was well known and memorable. The temptation to falsely label inferior wine as Châteauneuf-du-Pape to receive a higher price was hard to resist. This type of fraud was widespread when the baron assembled his fellow vintners. Under his expert guidance, the group set out to define their own boundaries and to set prescriptions on which grapes could be planted in Châteauneuf-du-Pape. They also decreed certain viticultural practices that they knew worked well in their region. They outlined minimum ripeness at harvest and many other factors that were critical to quality and authenticity. The system of laws and regulations devised by Baron LeRoy's group eventually became the model for the national system of quality control laws adopted in 1936.

Terroir of the Côtes du Rhône

Geographically and climatically it makes sense to separate the Rhône into two regions, the Northern Rhône and the Southern Rhône. The entire region is a warm, dry region whose climate is influenced by the Mediterranean Sea. However, the north is definitely cooler, and the vineyards there cling to the stony soil of steep hillsides. The narrow northern section extends from Lyon to the village of Valence, a distance of about 45 miles (72.6 km). For the next several miles, there are no vineyards. The soil is not suited for wine grapes. The southern section begins south of the town of Montélimar and continues on south of Avignon, into the delta of the river. The climate is definitely Mediterranean, very warm, sunny, and dry. The soil is more alluvial with a complex mixture of gravel, sand, clay, and limestone left as glaciers receded millions of years ago, and then moved and ground up and redeposited as the river changed course repeatedly over the centuries.

There is considerable variation among soil types and climatic patterns in the northern section of the Rhône Valley. In the northernmost sites, vineyards are protected from drying hot winds by tall ridges on the west side of the river. Cooler temperatures make for higher acidity and lower alcohol in the wines. The soil on these sheltering ridges is mostly granite. Farther south, the prevailing winds are a little warmer, and the soil less stony, and more calcareous. There are varying amounts of sand, clay, and chalk, and the differences in terroir come through in the widely varying character of the fine wines made here. In the Southern Rhône, there is even more variation among soil types from commune to commune.

The principal grape varietals of the Northern Rhône are Syrah for reds and Viognier for whites. The Syrah grape is one of the noble varietals, producing full-bodied wines famous for their deep color, tannic structure, and glorious aromas of blackberry, spice, and tar. Tight and austere when young, Syrah-based reds will open up to show warm, accessible flavors when mature. Viognier is considered by some to be one of the noble white varietals. The grapes are a deep yellow color, and the resulting wines are vivid in color and high in alcohol, possessing an intriguing bouquet of peach, almond, and spring flowers. The wines are usually very dry and show excellent acidity.

The southern section of the Rhône valley is much larger than the northern one. The total acreage for the entire Rhône appellation is almost 207,000 acres (83,800 hectares). Of that, only 5,900 acres (2,389 hectares) are in the nine communes and crus of the Northern Rhône. The rest is in the very large, highly varied region of the Southern

Rhône. The variation in soil among the many communes and individual vineyard sites of the Southern Rhône is tremendous.

The vineyards of the Southern Rhône support a much more complex array of grape varietals. Whereas the wines of the Northern Rhône, both reds and whites, are mostly single-varietal, those of the Southern Rhône are blends of several varietals. In Châteauneuf-du-Pape, for instance, 13 different grapes are authorized. The principle red grape of the southern appellations is the Grenache, a noble varietal that thrives in warm, sunny climates. It produces soft, mellow, round reds with succulent ripe plum flavors and a distinct aroma of fresh-ground black pepper. Other varietals used for blending in the Southern Rhône are Mourvèdre and Cinsault, both red grapes, and Marsanne and Roussanne, white grapes. Syrah is also often blended into Southern Rhône reds.

Appellations of the Côtes du Rhône

The appellations of the Rhône fall into three quality levels.

Côtes du Rhône

Almost 100,000 acres (40,000 hectares), scattered in peripheral sections of the Southern Rhône, are classified simply as Côtes du Rhône. With 7 million cases of generic Côtes du Rhône produced annually (the vast majority of it red), quality can vary widely. Producers, most of whom are either négociants or local cooperatives of growers, have greatly improved their winemaking equipment and techniques and are using lower percentages of the coarser local grapes in favor of higher quantities of noble varietals. The result is that the region is turning out softer, smoother, classier wines of medium body, good balance, and nice black fruit. The newer style of wine labeled as plain Côtes du Rhône can be an excellent value.

Côtes du Rhône-Villages

The standards at this level are higher, and certain requirements must be met. Most important, the yield of grapes per acre must be lower, and the minimum alcohol content is higher. There are 25 villages included within this appellation, 16 of which are authorized to add their village name to the label.

Commune

The best wines from throughout the Rhône valley carry the name of the commune or village where the vineyards are located. Twenty-one percent of the Rhône's wines are labeled by commune. In some cases, a specific vineyard will also be included. Although there is no system for rating vineyards as premier or grand cru, the very best vineyard sites, especially in the Northern Rhône, are well known, and can be shown on the label, thus adding considerably to the value of the bottles so labeled.

The Northern Rhône

Moving from north to south, the important communes of the Northern Rhône are Côte Rôtie, Condrieu, Château-Grillet, St. Joseph, Crozes-Hermitage, Hermitage and Cornas (Table 6.6).

TABLE 6.6 Appellations of France: Côtes du Rhône

Region	Subregion	Principal Varietal
Northern Rhône	Côte Rôtie	Syrah
	Condrieu	Viognier
	Hermitage	Syrah
	Crozes-Hermitage	Syrah
	St. Joseph	Syrah, Viognier
	Cornas	Syrah
	St. Péray	Marsanne and Roussanne
Southern Rhône	Coteaux du Tricastin	Grenache, Syrah, Mourvèdre
	Châteauneuf-du-Pape	Grenache, Syrah, Cinsault, Mourvèdre, Marsanne, 5 others
	Vacqueyras	Grenache, Cinsault
	Gigondas	Grenache (red and rosé)
	Tavel	Grenache, Cinsault (rosé only)
	Beaumes-de-Venise	Muscat (sweet only)
	Côtes du Ventoux	Grenache, Syrah, Mourvèdre
	Côtes du Lubéron	Grenache, Syrah (reds), Ugni Blanc, Marsanne (whites), Grenache (rosé)

Côte Rôtie

This commune's name translates as "the roasted slope," an apt name as the vineyards here receive excellent sunshine from their southeastern exposure on the steep ridges (Figure 6.25). The combination of hours a day of sun, stony minerally soil, and moderate temperatures results in the great red wines of unusual power and finesse for which the Côte Rôtie is justly famous. The world has discovered these wines, and they are not as affordable as they were 15 or 20 years ago.

The 470 acres (180 hectares) of vineyards in the Côte Rôtie are planted primarily to Syrah, with some Viognier also showing up. As much as 20 percent Viognier is allowed to be added to the red wines for aromatics and delicacy. However, most producers add less than that. The wines are typically medium to full bodied, deep in color, redolent of blackberries and currants, and incredibly long-lived. The best of these big red wines will hold their own for 20 years or more.

Condrieu

The elegant, flinty, and highly aromatic Condrieu whites have become some of the world's most expensive dry white wines. This is as much because of scarcity as quality. The Condrieu appellation is small, only 230 acres (95 hectares) of Viognier

FIGURE 6.25

Harvesting grapes in one of the vineyards in the Côte Rôtie owned by the famed Guigal family. The workers need a winch to haul boxes full of grapes up the steep hill.

© Cephas Picture Library/Alamy

vineyards clinging to the west bank of the Rhône River. The ripe peach, melon, and honey flavors are held together by good acidity.

Château-Grillet

Château-Grillet is France's smallest appellation (fewer than 10 acres [4 hectares]) and one of the very few single-owner appellations. Château-Grillet is an enclave within the Condrieu appellation.

St. Joseph

This is a fairly large appellation, stretching 40 miles (64.5 km) along the west bank of the Rhône. The production of St. Joseph is 80 percent red wines. These reds, made from Syrah grapes, are medium bodied and full of berry and red currant flavors. Their acid and tannic structure is not adequate to allow long-term aging; the wines are at their best within three to six years of vintage.

Crozes-Hermitage

This is the largest appellation in the Northern Rhône, with just over 3,000 acres (1,300 hectares) of vines. Annual production is over 600,000 cases of wine, 90 percent of which is red. These wines are made from Syrah grapes to which two white varietals, Marsanne and Roussanne, are added to make the wine more delicate. There are 11 communes within this appellation. (The name is from one of these villages, Crozes.) Crozes-Hermitage could be called the poor man's Hermitage, for it is more affordable than its prestigious neighbor is. Although lighter than many Syrahs, Crozes-Hermitage can be quite good, with ripe berry fruit mingled with peppery spiciness.

Hermitage

The story behind the name Hermitage is another example of a predilection for folklore, or at best, a tendency to embellish history. Apparently, a French knight who went to fight in the Middle East during the Crusades came home to the south of France in 1220 feeling so guilty about the ravages imposed on the conquered people and their countries that he vowed to spend the rest of his life as a hermit, praying for redemption. He bought some land on the east slopes of the Rhône, built a small chapel (Figure 6.26), and prayed devoutly. Eventually, the hermit wanted wine to drink, so he planted grapevines and began to make very good wine. The peasant families nearby followed suit, and the region around this hermit's chapel eventually became known as Hermitage.

Regardless of the truth of the legend, it is an indisputable fact that the wine from Hermitage is superb. The hermit chose his site well, for the hill on which he planted is solid granite covered with a thin but complex layer of chalk and decomposed flint. To some connoisseurs, Hermitage is as elegant and complex as the best reds from Bordeaux or Burgundy. In the small town of Hermitage, which only has 345 acres (140 hectares) of vineyards, Syrah reaches its pinnacle of quality. Hermitage is deeply colored, beautifully structured, and full bodied. The nose is redolent of blackberries and raspberries, and on the palate the multiple layers of flavor open. Able to age incredibly well, the best Hermitage is not really mature and fully accessible for 20 years or more.

Northern Rhône

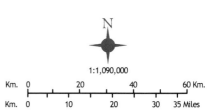

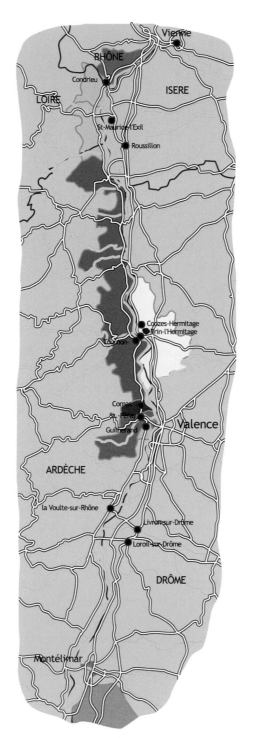

Côte Rôtie

Château Grillet

Condrieu

Condrieu / St. Joseph

St. Joseph

Hermitage

Crozes-Hermitage

Cornas

St. Péray

Coteaux du Tricastin

Map courtesy of Kobrand Corporation (www.kobrandwine.com)

FIGURE 6.26

La Chapelle Vineyard in the Hermitage appellation is named for the small stone chapel built by the hermit who lived here after returning from the Crusades. This site is now famous for the quality of its Syrah grapes.
© Chiya Li/iStockphoto

Cornas

Located south of St. Joseph on the west banks of the Rhône, Cornas has 173 acres (70 hectares) of Syrah planted on steep granite slopes. The hills give shelter from the cold north winds while affording the vines plenty of sun from the southeastern exposure. The terraced vineyards have a top layer of limestone. The best Cornas is deeply flavored, full bodied, and harmonious. It can hold its own against the wines from the more illustrious commune across the river, Hermitage, and is far more affordable.

The Southern Côtes du Rhône

Whereas the communes and crus of the Northern Rhône are compact and dense, the Southern Rhône's appellations spread out in a huge lopsided circle from the town of Montélimar in the north along the Rhône and its tributaries all the way south to the city of Avignon, with a long bulging arm reaching east and south along the Durance River. In this enormous appellation of over 100,000 acres (40,485 hectares) of vineyards, there is tremendous variation in terroir and styles of wine. Approximately 85 percent of the wine made here is red. About 5 percent is dry white. There is also some very good rosé made, and very small quantities of fortified dessert wine. From north to south, the most important appellations of the Southern Rhône are Coteaux du Tricastan, Gigondas, Muscat Beaumes-de-Venise, Vacqueyras, Châteauneuf-du-Pape, Tavel, Côtes du Ventoux, and Côtes du Lubéron.

Coteaux de Tricastan

This region on the eastern fringe of the Rhône valley produces pleasant reds and dry rosés. The reds are blended from the traditional grapes of Grenache, Syrah, Mourvèdre, and two lesser varietals. Several white varietals are also allowed to be added. The rosé is primarily Grenache with white grapes blended in. The climate is decidedly Mediterranean, but because of altitude and exposed terrain, the grapes do not ripen as much as in surrounding areas.

Gigondas

Located at the foot of the limestone-rich Dentelle Mountains, Gigondas produces primarily red wines from its red clay soils. Despite having adopted some of the same stringent requirements as Châteauneuf-du-Pape, Gigondas spent several decades as part of the general Côtes du Rhône appellation, much to the commercial disadvantage of the district. In 1966, it was elevated to the Côtes du Rhône-Villages classification. Not until 1971 did Gigondas receive its own AOC designation. The regulations stipulate that Gigondas reds can be no more than 80 percent Grenache. The balance is Mourvèdre and/or Syrah. Rarely as distinguished a Châteauneuf-du-Pape, Gigondas can represent good value.

Muscat Beaumes-de-Venise

The **vin doux naturel** (van doo nah-tew-REHL) Beaumes-de-Venise is one of France's prettiest dessert wines. It is made by arresting the fermentation of the Muscat grapes with neutral alcohol, which kills the yeast cells. The residual, or unfermented, sugars give the wine a delightful natural sweetness. The wine is medium bodied, honeyed, and fairly high in alcohol (15 percent minimum).

The Southern Rhône

Map courtesy of Kobrand Corporation (www.kobrandwine.com)

Vacqueyras

Elevated to AOC status only in 1990, Vacqueyras makes reds, whites, and rosé. Only a tiny portion of the 1,700 acres (688 hectares) is planted to white varietals. The reds are medium-bodied blends with pleasant berry, spice, and floral tones. At least half the blend must be Grenache. Vacqueyras resembles concentrated Côtes du Rhône-Villages.

Châteauneuf-du-Pape

The most celebrated of the Southern Rhône appellations, Châteauneuf-du-Pape has become increasingly popular in the past two decades. Although this is a large appellation—over a million cases each year—the standards are high. The vintners of Châteauneuf imposed on themselves stringent requirements including a very low yield per hectare, a high minimum alcohol content (12.5 percent), and the practice during harvest of the grape-sorting technique known as **tirage** (tee-RAHZH), by which at least 5 percent of the grapes must be rejected before fermentation begins. This way the substandard grapes, whether underripe, overripe, or diseased, never find their way into the final batch. Tirage is an expensive and labor-intensive process, but it is helpful in maintaining the highest quality.

The vineyards of Châteauneuf-du-Pape are on gently sloping hillsides that provide good drainage and exposure to the sun. The soil of reddish clay is covered with large pebbles that retain the day's heat (Figure 6.27) and reflect it back onto the grapes in the cool evenings, thus helping them fully ripen. Only 3 percent of Châteauneuf-du-Pape

FIGURE 6.27

The Châteauneuf-du-Pape region has unique soil: red clay under large stone pebbles.
© David Mixa/Shutterstock

is white, made from white Grenache, Roussanne, and several lesser grapes. The reds are immensely complex wines blended typically from 50 to 70 percent Grenache, 10 to 30 percent Syrah, up to 20 percent Mourvèdre and other reds, and up to 10 percent white varietals. These are deeply colored, full-bodied wines with incredible bouquets reminiscent of everything from blackberry, fig, cinnamon, and clove to tar, coffee, and cedar. Many of the better wines can age for decades.

The producers of Châteauneuf-du-Pape are usually self-sufficient estates similar to Bordeaux's, in which the vineyards, winemaking facilities, and aging cave are all at one location and under one ownership. Each of the famous estates has its own recognizable style, some more fruit-driven, some austere and ageworthy. Among the best producers are Château Fortia, Château de Beaucastel, Chante-Perdrix, Château la Nerthe, and Domaine de Mont Redon.

Tavel

The appellation Tavel is restricted to rosé made from Grenache (no more than 60 percent) and Cinsault (at least 15 percent) and several local grapes. The clay-based soil and warm climate produce medium-bodied, flavorful rosés. The wine is surprisingly dry and fruity, and a versatile food wine.

Côtes du Ventoux

The large sprawling region of Côtes du Ventoux takes its name from the 6,500-foot (1,981-meter) high Mount Ventoux that towers over the area. The appellation contains over 18,000 acres (7,287 hectares) of vines, the best of which are on the flanks of the mountain. Elevated to AOC status in 1973, Côtes du Ventoux produces mostly red, plus some rosé, wines made from Grenache, Syrah, Mourvèdre, and Cinsault. A typical Côtes du Ventoux is a pleasant lighter wine intended for early consumption.

Côtes du Lubéron

Stretching from the southern boundary of the Côtes du Ventoux to the banks of the Durance River in the south, the Côtes du Lubéron appellation was created in 1988 and contains 7,410 acres (3,000 hectares) of vines. The wines are of all three colors. The reds, light and juicy, must contain some Syrah, blended with Grenache, Mourvèdre, and other traditional varietals. The whites, dry and clean, cannot contain more than 50 percent of Ugni Blanc (a lesser grape used to make brandy) and can have five other grapes blended in. The rosés are mostly Grenache and are soft, fruity, and pretty. Stylistically, the Côtes du Lubéron creates a bridge between the wines of the Rhône and those of Provence.

Champagne

No appellation in the history of wine has been more misused than the term *Champagne*. Champagne is not merely a type of wine. It is a geographic region in France, and only wine made in a specific method from specified grape varietals grown inside the boundaries of that region is technically Champagne. In referring to the world's sparkling wines, the essential point to remember is that Champagne is from Champagne.

Sparkling wine made elsewhere is not Champagne. As winemakers well know, geographic factors, unique to specific locations, do affect the character of the products raised or captured there. In the case of the Champagne region, the differentiating characteristic are its unique soil, a mixture of clay and chalk, and its climate as one of the northernmost fine wine regions in the world. There is no terroir quite like Champagne's. So although very fine sparkling wines are made elsewhere in the world, they will not be quite like Champagne.

History

Champagne was not always famous for its sparkling wine. Rather, it started out in the time of the Roman Empire as a producer of still white wines most of which were consumed by Roman legions. After the decline of the empire, communications with other regions deteriorated, commerce was interrupted, vineyards were destroyed, and winemaking disappeared. As Christianity moved into northern Europe, winemaking reemerged, receiving a huge boost when Clovis, king of the Franks, was converted to Christianity by the bishop of Rheims, the major city of Champagne. The baptism of Clovis in AD 460 is said to have taken place where the magnificent Cathedral of Rheims now stands. With the support of the church, the vineyards of Champagne flourished, winemaking techniques were perfected, and markets for the wine were expanded (Paris is only 90 miles, 145 km away).

It was monks who rescued the vineyards of Champagne, and it was a monk who developed the style of wine for which the region has become famous (Figure 6.28). Dom Pérignon did not invent Champagne. What he did do was lend his viticultural genius to sorting out which grapes to plant and how best to tend them, and he perfected numerous winemaking procedures.

Pierre Pérignon was born in 1638 and, at a young age, entered a monastery near Épernay in Champagne, where he stayed until his death in 1715. During his long tenure as cellar master, Dom Pérignon greatly improved the quality of the wine made at the monastery. His greatest discovery was a process for capturing effervescence in the glass bottles by allowing a second sugar-to-alcohol fermentation to proceed. The by-product of fermentation is carbon dioxide, which remained trapped in the bottle. It cannot be proven that Dom Pérignon was the very first to bottle an effervescent wine, but there is no doubt that he greatly improved the quality of wines from the Champagne region.

The sparkling wine of Champagne did not find immediate favor, but once it was discovered by the fun-loving aristocracy surrounding the royal court in the late eighteenth century, Champagne soon became the wine of celebration. New markets opened in continental Europe, the British

FIGURE 6.28

The monk Dom Pérignon is often cited as the inventor of Champagne. Although he did not actually invent this style of wine, he made crucial contributions to the viticulture of the Champagne region, and perfected the methods of producing the famous sparkling wine.

© Per Karlsson-BKWine.com/Alamy

Isles, and even as far away as Russia. Over the next 150 years, demand for Champagne increased at such a rate that supply could not keep up. Some producers started expanding production with inferior grapes brought in from other growing areas. Fraud became so widespread that the legitimate growers of the Champagne region revolted in 1911, demanding protection of their place-name.

In 1927 the French government did implement laws spelling out the exact boundaries of the Champagne region. With the passage in 1935 of the national Appellation d'Origin Contrôlée laws, the Champagne name received full protection, as did the quality of the product. In 1941, even with the Second World War raging, the vintners of Champagne formed a trade association, the Comité Interprofessionnel du Vin de Champagne (CIVC), to give further protection to the authenticity and prestige of the appellation. The CIVC remains active today, both in the Champagne region overseeing production and pricing, and in markets around the world, assisting with marketing and promotion.

Viticulture in Champagne

Three grapes are allowed in Champagne: Chardonnay, Pinot Meunier, and Pinot Noir, all of which are early ripeners and therefore well suited to the cool climate and short growing season of this northerly region. The two Pinots are red grapes, but the juice of these grapes is white. There are more than 72,000 acres (29,150 hectares) of vineyards, owned by 19,000 individual growers. Physical conditions determine which varietal to plant in each location. Legislation, based on centuries of close observation of weather and soil patterns by vignerons (grape growers), now dictates what is to be planted in each site. For instance, in the Vallée de la Marne, the hardy Pinot Meunier is widely planted. Throughout the Champagne region, more acres are dedicated to this relatively easy-to-grow varietal than to Chardonnay or Pinot Noir.

As stated earlier, the terroir of the Champagne region is truly unique. The most distinguishing characteristic of this environment is the high concentration of chalk in the soil (Figure 6.29). Essentially two types of chalk (which is a form of limestone) can be found in soil. One of these types, belemnite chalk, is found only in Champagne. The topsoil is a thin layer of clay with some chalk. The underlayer of chalk reaches as deep as 800 feet (244 meters).

The roots of the vines can push through the soft crumbling chalk to great depths in order to reach water. Chalk does an effective job of draining rainwater so that it does not pool near the surface, risking rotting of the vines. Moreover, as the water drains downward, the chalk forms natural storage chambers for it, where the deeper roots can reach. A further advantage of heavily chalky soil is heat retention. The warmth of the sun is absorbed by chalk, and radiated back onto the vines in the cooler evenings. Also, the poor nutritional content

FIGURE 6.29

This vineyard in the Côtes des Blancs is typical for the depth and density of the chalk soil that is unique to the Champagne region.
© Cephas Picture Library/Alamy

of chalk discourages the growth of leaves on the grapevines, thus allowing more sunlight to hit the grape bunches, which assists ripening. A meager canopy also allows better circulation by the breezes, which reduces the likelihood of mildew forming on the bunches.

Soil is only one part of terroir (albeit a critical one). The other determinant is, of course, climate. The climate of Champagne holds many perils for grape growers. Most obvious is cold. Champagne is farther north than any other important wine region, and the damp cold weather patterns of the North Atlantic (only 110 miles, 77 km away) are not blocked by any mountain range or other natural barrier. The average temperatures in Champagne are barely enough to allow grapes to ripen. Acidity levels stay high in such a cool climate, which is desirable in any sparkling wine. However, a minimum sugar level (set by law) must be reached, and if the temperatures stay too cool, the grapes have a difficult time reaching the necessary ripeness. Another constant concern for the vignerons is frost, either in the spring when the vines are budding or in the fall before the grapes are harvested. Growers in Champagne use the method called *aspersion* to protect their vines. This method, also used in other very cool wine regions, consists of spraying the vines with a fine mist of water that freezes on the buds or the grape bunches, forming a protective shield from the cold.

The weather in Champagne presents still another danger for wine grapes, and that is moisture. Grapes are susceptible to mildew if they remain damp for extended periods. With a high average annual rainfall of 25.6 inches (65 cm), Champagne is often very damp indeed. Fungicides are sometimes employed to decrease this danger. Other potential problems in years of heavy rainfall are swelling of the grapes with too much water and a reduced rate of pollination.

Champagne Producers and the Style of Wine

There are approximately 110 companies, called houses (or, in French, *marques*), that make Champagne. Because these companies own only 10 percent of the vineyards in Champagne, they buy the vast majority of their grapes from growers. The oldest, most established houses are called grands marques. They are required by law to maintain a presence in export markets. Exports of Champagne play a vital role in the French economy, accounting for 20 percent of wine and spirits exports.

The various vineyards of Champagne have been officially rated, but these ratings do not show on a label. Rather, the rating of a vineyard was used to determine what price the houses would be required to pay for grapes from that vineyard. The most highly rated sites would act as benchmarks, and once their prices were set, other vineyards' grapes would be priced accordingly. The law was changed in 1990 so that even though prices are still officially determined according to the quality rating of a vineyard, the houses are not required to pay that amount.

Each of the major Champagne houses has a distinct style that it maintains year after year. Champagne is made from still wine that has been fermented dry (see Chapter 3 for the winemaking process). Some producers use malolactic fermentation to reduce the acidity and add complexity to their wines. After fermentation is complete, the wine is racked, and a careful blending of different batches and varietals (assemblage) is undertaken. The wine is put into thick glass bottles and a second sugar-to-alcohol

FIGURE 6.30

A cellar worker riddles bottles in preparation for the disgorging, which will remove all dead yeast cells from each bottle.

© Cephas Picture Library/Alamy

fermentation is induced by adding the liquer de tirage, a mixture of reserve wine, sugar, and cultured yeasts. As the second fermentation occurs, the secondary by-product of carbon dioxide is trapped in the bottle, giving the wine its effervescence. After the wine is aged, the yeast cells are removed from the bottle by a careful disgorging (Figure 6.30). The dosage of sugar and water is then quickly added to give the finished product the amount of sweetness its classification requires.

Other important terms show up on Champagne labels. Most of these types will be made in a brut style, even if that word does not show on the label.

- **Nonvintage:** A nonvintage wine is not made exclusively from grapes grown in one vintage year. Grapes from several different years are blended together to get consistency of quality, even in years when weather patterns are less than ideal. A portion of each year's wine is held back for this purpose (Figure 6.31).
- **Vintage:** When conditions are favorable, the winemaker can choose not to blend in wine reserved from lesser vintages. To be declared a vintage Champagne, the wine must contain at least 80 percent grapes from the declared year. Not every year is a vintage year. The winemaker at each house decides whether to declare a vintage.

CLASSIFICATION OF CHAMPAGNE STYLES

Extra Brut: Bone dry. Residual sugar is less than 0.6 percent per liter. At this level there is usually no dosage.
Brut: (BROOT) This is the most common classification, and forms the backbone of any house's line. Residual sugar is 0.5–1.5 percent per liter (Figure 6.31).
Extra Dry: These Champagnes are off-dry, with residual sugar 1.0–2 percent.
Sec: Although sec means "dry," these Champagnes have noticeable sugar—between 2 and 3.5 percent. They are rarely seen in the United States.
Demi-Sec: (DEHM-ee-sehk) The literal translation is "off-dry" but these Champagnes are quite sweet. The dosage causes residual sugar to be between 3.5 and 5 percent. These Champagnes are meant to be served with dessert.
Doux: (DOO) The sweetest form of Champagne has a minimum of 5.5 percent sugar, and in some cases contains as much as 8 percent.

FIGURE 6.31

Label for nonvintage Brut from the house of Taittinger.

Label courtesy of Kobrand Corporation (www.kobrandwine.com)

- **Blanc de Blancs:** Blanc de blancs (BLAHN du BLAHN) literally means "white from whites" and is a Champagne made exclusively from Chardonnay grapes. Since only 25 percent of the vineyards in the region are planted to Chardonnay, the grapes are expensive and therefore so is this type of wine. These are the most delicate and lightest of Champagnes.
- **Blanc de Noirs:** Literally "white from blacks," **blanc de noirs** (blahn duh NWAHR) wine is made exclusively from the two allowed red varietals. These are the fullest of Champagnes, with considerable fruits and complexity.
- **Rosé:** If some red wine is added to a cuvée of white wine, or if the juice of the red grapes is given some skin contact, the resulting Champagne will be a rosé. Most rosés are in the brut style and are full flavored and elegant.
- **Tête de cuvée:** Most marques have a prestige label, the top of the line. These bottlings are almost always made from vintage brut. Each marque has a name for its **tête de cuvée** (TEHT duh koo-VAY), which means literally "top batch." For instance, Veuve Clicquot names its prestige label La Grande Dame to honor the Veuve ("widow") Clicquot.

Each marque's distinct house style guarantees consistency of quality and recognizable character in every release. The factors that influence the distinct style of a Champagne house are numerous. Among them are the proportion of Chardonnay to the red grapes; the vineyard sites from which grapes are purchased; the blending; the amount of time the wine spends aging on the lees.

Some of the major Champagne houses are listed as follows, with the name of their tête de cuvée to the right.

Champagne House	*Tête de Cuvée*
Billecart-Salmon	Cuvée Columbus
Bollinger	Année Rare R.D.
Charles Heidsieck	La Royale
G. H. Mumm	Grand Cordon Rouge
Gosset	Cuvée Grand Millesième
Krug	Grande Cuvée, Clos de Mesnil, Blanc de Blancs
Moët et Chandon	Dom Pérignon
Piper Heidsieck	Cuvée Florens-Louis
Pol Roger	Cuvée Sir Winston Churchill
Taittinger	Comte de Champagne
Veuve Clicquot	La Grande Dame

Alsace

Alsace is a small region only 60 miles (96 km) north to south. On the western edge the Vosges mountains separate Alsace from the rest of France. On the east, the Rhine runs between Alsace and Germany. Forced by conflicts between these two powerful nations to change political affiliation many times over 1,000 years, the people of Alsace have absorbed the best of each culture. The language, the arts, the cuisine, and certainly the wines of Alsace reflect the best of both French and German influences. For instance, the wine produced here (90 percent of which is white) are named for the varietals, mostly of German origin, from which they are made. But the wines are made in a quintessentially French style, dry and elegant, intended to complement food, never overpower it.

Despite, or perhaps because of, the many conflicts and opposing national pressures, the heritage of Alsace is first and foremost Alsatian. These are fiercely independent people, proud of their heritage and history. But winemakers here are thoroughly modern in their approach to grape growing and winemaking. By combining ancient traditions with up-to-date technology, Alsace has emerged as one of the world's premier regions for white wine.

History

Clovis, king of the Franks, established Alsace as a Frankish territory in AD 496, when Christianity was taking hold in northern Europe. As in other parts of France, the Catholic Church played a crucial role in the winemaking of the region. Monasteries came to own and plant many of the sites best suited to grapevines. The monks and priests produced wine for the sacraments, for use as medicine, and for their visitors.

The first change of sovereignty took place in 843 when Charlemagne's kingdom was divided, and Alsace was ceded to Louis the German. In the seventeenth century, Alsace was annexed to France at the end of the Thirty Years' War. During this time several of the leading families of Alsace started their wine companies—Beyer in 1580, Dopff around 1600, Hugel in 1639. In 1870, Alsace was reclaimed by the new German empire. Soon the plight of phylloxera wiped out the vineyards. The Germans replanted only the easier-to-work sites on the flat plains, with inferior but hardy hybrids to use in blending. Most of the more desirable locations on the rocky hillsides were left fallow. Noble varietals essentially disappeared.

In 1918, after the defeat of Germany in the First World War, Alsace was again part of France. Vineyards, even the inaccessible sites on the steep hillsides, were replanted to noble *vinifera* grapes, including Riesling, Pinot Gris, and Gewürztraminer. The quality of the wines increased dramatically. Sadly, Alsace suffered a devastating setback during the Second World War, when the Nazis occupied the region. The oppression of Alsace under the Nazis was far more severe than during the 1870–1918 period. Everything French was forbidden, even the language, and many young men were conscripted into the German army to fight on the Russian front. Exporting was forbidden and all wine produced was shipped to Germany (except the sizable cache that the Alsatians concealed from their occupiers). After the Allied victory in 1945, Alsace returned to France. Again the residents put strong emphasis on quality. The vintners worked with the authorities to forbid inferior grapes, define boundaries, establish regulations, and set quality standards. In 1962, Alsace was granted AOC status.

Geography and Climate: Terroir of Alsace

To understand the unique soil composition of Alsace, it is necessary to go back 60 million years to the period when the mighty Alps were forced up out of surrounding waters by the violent collision of tectonic plates. The Black Mountains and the Vosges chain were formed, but with a large fault between the two chains. This fault flooded and became a huge inland sea, which was further eroded as glaciers came and then

THE HOUSE OF LEON BEYER: FIFTEEN GENERATIONS OF WINE-MAKERS

When it comes to the wines of Alsace, Marc Beyer has many strong opinions. He is entitled to speak out on this topic since his family has been growing grapes and making wine near the village of Equisheim since 1580. Presently Marc is the President of the house of Léon Beyer, and his son, Yann, is also involved with the business. (Marc's father, Léon, was deeply involved with the business right up to his recent death.)

One topic about which Marc Beyer has strong opinions is what he terms the "classic style" of Alsace's wines, that is, dry and elegant. He regrets the recent trend among wine producers in Alsace (and elsewhere in France) to leave residual sugar in the traditionally very dry white wines. In the opinion of Mr. Beyer and his later father, wine's raison d'être is to complement food. As Marc puts it, "We believe that the best way and the most frequent way to enjoy wine is in partnership with food." The Beyers believe that wine complements food best when there is no residual sugar in the wine to fight with the flavors of the dish it accompanies. For this reason, all Beyer wines are fermented entirely through to dryness (except, of course, Vendage Tardive and Selection de Grains Noble).

Another issue on which Marc Beyer has expressed heartfelt opinions is that of the classification of his region's vineyards. The process of officially declaring Alsace's best vineyard sites to be "Grand Cru" vineyards, which began in 1983, is superfluous, according to Marc. His objections are myriad. First, many of the "Grand Cru" vineyards have several noble varietals planted in them, as many as six to eight different grapes. A site that is excellent for one varietal may produce only mediocre specimens of another varietal. Secondly, with 50 vineyards already approved, and another 40 or so under consideration, there will soon be too many vineyards in a relatively small region for the designation to carry much validity. Thirdly, and perhaps most important, the array of soil types within Alsace is extremely varied. Within one vineyard, there could be dozens of different terroirs. As Marc Beyer says, "We would need over 500 'Grand Crus' to demarcate every site in Alsace that has a unique terroir."

Marc Beyer's advice to consumers of Alsace wines is to become familiar with the styles of different houses, as one would when buying Champagne. When you find a style you like, stick with that producer and do not worry about vineyard designations or sugar levels. He advises, "Stick with the producers who allow the varietal character and the natural terroir to speak for themselves."

FIGURE 6.32

In this family picture, winemaker Yann Beyer uncorks a bottle of his Riesling. Yann follows in the footsteps of his father Marc (seated to the left) and his late grandfather Léon. The Beyer family has been making wine in Alsace since 1580.

Photo courtesy of Mr. J.L. Delpal

FIGURE 6.33

The Léon Beyer winery labels its top-level wines as Comtes d'Eguisheim, named for the village located near their vineyards and winemaking facility.

© Léon Beyer

receded. Eons of accumulating rocks being pulverized, of deep erosion, of volcanic eruptions have given Alsace an incredibly complex pattern of soil composition. There are at least 20 different soil formations in this small area. (Total vineyard acreage in Alsace is 37,000 acres [15,000 hectares].)

The upper steep reaches of the Vosges Mountains have thin topsoil on a base of well-worn granite, schist, and volcanic sediments. The gentler slopes further down the hillsides have deeper topsoils derived from the delta of the Rhine, and subsoils of clay, marl, limestone, and sandstone.

Although Alsace lies quite far north (of French wine regions, only Champagne is more northerly), it enjoys a far milder climate than other regions at the same latitude. The warmer temperatures and lower rainfall are due primarily to protection from the prevailing westerly winds by the Vosges Mountains. Winters can be quite cold, but spring is mild, allowing for good bud-set, summers are usually warm and sunny, and very importantly, fall stays sunny, dry, and frost-free on into October.

The noble varietals of Alsace (listed here roughly in order of importance) are Riesling, Gewürztraminer, Pinot Gris, Pinot Noir, Muscat, Pinot Blanc, and Sylvaner. Riesling takes just over 20 percent of vineyard acreage, and that is increasing as Sylvaner, a blending grape, is being removed, and now accounts for only 9 percent of acreage. Pinot Blanc is also widely planted, which, along with the lesser varietal Pinot Auxerrois, is sometimes blended into it, accounts for another 14 percent of acreage. Gewürztraminer can be a difficult grape to work with, being slow to ripen, but it accounts for almost 20 percent of the vineyard space. Pinot Gris currently accounts for 15 percent of acreage, and it continues to increase in plantings as consumers discover its spicy flavors and crisp acidity. More rapidly increasing in plantings is Pinot Noir, Alsace's only red varietal, which now covers almost 10 percent of acreage. The remaining vineyard space is divided among Muscat, Chasselas, and the ubiquitous Chardonnay. Not yet an approved varietal, Chardonnay can be used only in the sparkling wine Crémant d'Alsace.

The great vineyards of Alsace have long been recognized by producers and consumers alike. These vineyards are those with superior terroir. The names of these finer vineyards have traditionally been shown on labels. For two decades after being awarded AOC status, the vignerons of Alsace saw no need for a system of classification of their vineyards. However, in the early 1980s a cooperative effort between the government authorities and landowners to give official recognition to superior properties was begun. Regulations were written requiring that only the four truly noble varietals—Riesling, Gewürztraminer, Pinot Gris, and Muscat—could be planted in classified vineyards; that the yield not exceed 4 tons per acre (64 hectoliters/hectare); and that wine to be labeled with the classification must be made from one varietal only.

The grand cru appellation was created in 1983, and has been creating controversy ever since. Of the 94 sites originally considered for designation as grand cru, 25 were chosen in 1983. However, other sites continued to be added. There are now 51 grand cru vineyards. Even though several producers feel the classification of Alsace vineyards was a superfluous gesture, one must bear in mind that the grand crus vineyards account for only 4 percent of the region's total production (http://www.vinsalsace.com).

While the disagreement over the validity of the classification system goes on, some producers continue to use the traditional name for their reserve-level wines while ignoring the grand cru designation. For example, the Beyer family has always labeled its top wines "Comtes d'Eguisheim." They continue to use that designation, not mentioning the grand cru vineyards they own.

The Wines

Many Americans shy away from Alsace wines in their tall green bottles and Teutonic-looking labels, assuming that the wines are German and will, therefore, be too sweet. People who make that assumption are wrong on two counts: Alsace wines are French in style, and German wines are not all sweet (see Chapter 9). In passing by the Alsace wines, consumers are depriving themselves of an extraordinary experience. The whites of Alsace are fermented dry and are extremely versatile food wines.

- *Riesling:* Usually bone dry, Alsace Rieslings have superb steely acidity to hold up their flavors of green apple and minerals. When young, the wines often have a floral aroma, which with age, evolves into gunflint and wet slate.
- *Gewürztraminer:* With its unique nose of lychee nuts and its racy acidity and pronounced spice flavors overlaying ripe forward fruit, Alsace Gewürztraminer is the ideal accompaniment to highly spiced food.
- *Pinot Gris:* Traditionally known as Tokay d'Alsace or Tokay Pinot Gris, but since an agreement with Hungary in 1993, now called just Pinot Gris, this is perhaps the most underrated of Alsace's noble varietals. Pinot Gris combines some of the spice of Gewürztraminer with the steely acidity of Riesling. The aromas and flavors are reminiscent of peaches or ripe melon and are perfectly balanced by firm acids.
- *Pinot Blanc:* Perhaps the lightest and least complex of Alsace whites, Pinot Blanc can nonetheless be a charming and appealing wine. It is clean and dry, with crisp acidity and can be sipped alone or matched to a variety of light, simple dishes.
- *Pinot Noir:* In vineyards this far north, red grapes have a hard time fully ripening. Rouge d'Alsace has traditionally been light in color and body, full of young strawberry aromas and flavors, and soft on the palate. These are pleasant quaffing wines.

There are other styles of wine produced in Alsace in addition to the dry table wines just described.

- *Crémant d'Alsace:* Based primarily on Pinot Blanc, with Pinot Noir and Riesling sometimes blended in, Alsace's sparkling wine is made in the méthode champenoise. It now accounts for about 10 percent of total production in the region, and that number is increasing as the wine achieves commercial success. The wine is fairly light in body, has excellent mousse (fizziness) and pleasant fruit, and is quite dry.

- *Vendange Tardive:* The French term for these wines means "late picked." Left on the vine to develop additional sugars, these grapes result in delicious wines, usually off-dry in style. The flavors of late-picked wines are very rich and deep. To be labeled as Vendange Tardive, a wine must be from one vintage of the approved varietals—Riesling, Gewürztraminer, Muscat, or Pinot Gris—and cannot be enriched with additional sugar. The grapes have to be picked on a date set by the authorities, when the natural sugars have reached a specified level. They do not have to be botrytized.
- *Sélection de Grains Noble (SGN):* Wines at this level almost always contain some grapes infected with *Botrytis*, or noble rot. This makes them sweeter, richer, and heavier than Vendange Tardive wines. SGN wines are made from the same four permitted varietals as Vendange Tardive. A rich, unctuous SGN with just enough acidity to hold up its complex mélange of apricot, ripe peach, and honey can be an unforgettably ambrosial wine.

The Loire Valley

There is a large, regional appellation of the vin de pays level that encompasses all of the Loire Valley and some of its surrounding areas: *Vin de pays du jardin de France,* "Wine from the Garden of France." This is a beautiful name, and an appropriate one. The region is truly beautiful, like one very large, plentiful, and well-tended garden. The Loire Valley used to be the center of power in France, for it was in this wealthy, bountiful region that the French royal family had its roots. The region reached its pinnacle of power and influence in the late 1400s to early 1500s. In 1589, Henri IV moved the royal court, and the sphere of influence shifted to Paris and its environs. Wine had been produced along the Loire River for centuries but the region's wines sank out of favor when the Court moved. For hundreds of years, Loire Valley wines were not seen outside the area. Only in the past 50 years have the Loire's more important appellations been rediscovered in Europe, and only in the past 20 years have Loire wines been widely available in the American market.

The Loire is a very long river, the longest in France. It starts in the south and flows north for 635 miles (1,024 km) before spilling out into the Atlantic Ocean. The Loire and its tributaries drain a quarter of the landmass of France. The jardin de France is a huge area, where a variety of fruits and vegetables is grown, livestock and dairy cows graze, and a total of almost 440,000 acres (178,138 hectares) of grapevines is planted. However, the fine wines of the Loire AOC appellation are found only in the final third of the area, after the river takes a turn and starts its westward journey to the sea.

History

Viticulture in the Loire Valley has been traced back as far as the eighth century AD. Many of the aristocrats who built their châteaux along the river during the next several hundred years also planted grapevines. By the late eleventh century, the wines of the Loire were highly regarded in France. That fame soon spread outside the country, and exportation to northern markets was simplified by the ease of transport by boat along

The Loire Valley

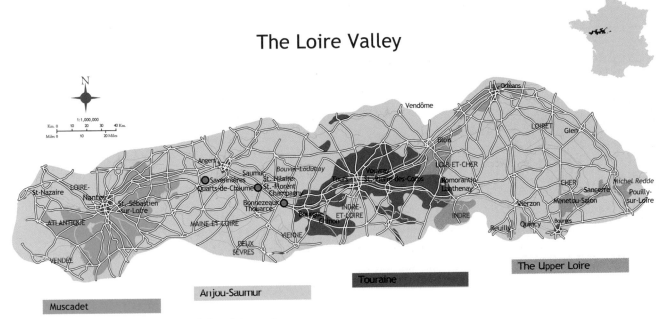

Map courtesy of Kobrand Corporation (www.kobrandwine.com)

the river itself and its tributaries. Demand for Loire wines was particularly strong in the cities of Flanders. Some wine was shipped even farther, to England. Commerce in the fine wines of the Loire continued to grow and its reputation spread until the move by King Henri IV to Paris in 1589. The royal trendsetters turned their attention to other wines, and Loire wine production was cut back. Most wine was consumed locally.

Geography and Soil: Terroir of the Loire

The Loire River stretches for such a long distance that no generalizations can be made about the appellations along its bank (Figure 6.34). Viticulturally it makes sense to divide the Loire into four distinct regions. First is the Upper Loire, where the river makes its jog to the west. The climate is continental, with cold winters and hot dry summers. The primary grape is Sauvignon Blanc. Moving down river into the Central Loire, the climate becomes gradually more temperate, and the soil less rocky. In the two subregions of the Central Loire, Anjou/Saumur and Touraine, the principle white grape is Chenin Blanc. Some red grapes are also planted—most important, Cabernet Franc. Here spring frost can still be a problem, as can drought. In the westernmost reaches of the river valley, the Loire is joined by its tributaries. Here the climate has a maritime influence, warmed by the Gulf Stream and more humid than

FIGURE 6.34

The Loire River flows for over 600 miles (1,000 km) through the French countryside. There are many different terroirs along its banks.
© Cephas Picture Library/Alamy

farther upriver. Occasionally the weather is too damp and overcast, hindering efforts to ripen the grapes.

The Appellations

The appellations of the Loire are not divided into levels, but rather are characterized solely by location (Table 6.7).

The Upper Loire

The majority of wine made here is dry, zesty white made entirely from Sauvignon Blanc grapes. Many culinary experts believe that Sauvignon Blanc is the most food-friendly white because of its excellent clean acidity and restrained citrusy fruit. A little red wine is made from Pinot Noir. Appellations are the names of individual communes.

Pouilly-Fumé   The village of Pouilly-sur-Loire dates from Roman times. Its wine is named Pouilly-Fumé, not because there is a "smoky" component to the bouquet, as some have believed. Rather, *fumé* refers to the grey-green nuances of color on the ripening Sauvignon grapes (Coates, 2000). The area received AOC status in 1937, and today there are close to 1,600 acres (648 hectares) of vines, virtually all Sauvignon Blanc. Most vineyards are owned by farming families. There are few large landholdings. The soil is mostly a clay–limestone mix. The wines are very dry and have forward grassy bouquets with often a whiff of what the French call *pipi du chat*. The acidity is crisp and clean, the flavors of citrus fruit.

Sancerre   Across the river from Pouilly lies the village of Sancerre. In 1936 the white wines were granted AOC status, but it was not until 1959 that the Pinot Noir–based reds and rosés achieved equal status. Most of the 5,800 acres (2,348 hectares) of vineyards are held by small growers. The vineyards, mostly on limestone mixed with some clay, are on gentle slopes facing east, south, and west. The white wines are very similar to those of Pouilly, perhaps a bit more pronounced in their aromas and flavors and showing a little more finesse. The reds are light in body and color, with strawberry aromas and flavors.

TABLE 6.7 Appellations of France: Loire Valley

Region	Subregion	Principal Varietal
The Upper Loire	Sancerre	Sauvignon Blanc
	Quincy	Sauvignon Blanc
	Pouilly-Fumé	Sauvignon Blanc
	Menetou-Salon	Sauvignon Blanc
	Reuilly	Sauvignon Blanc
Touraine	Vouvray	Chenin Blanc (dry, semisweet, and sparkling)
	Chinon	Cabernet Franc
	Bourgueil	Cabernet Franc
Anjou/Saumur	Savennières	Chenin Blanc
	Coteaux du Layon	Chenin Blanc (sweet and semisweet only)
	Quarts de Chaume	Chenin Blanc (sweet and semisweet only)
Nantes	Muscadet	Melon de Bourgogne

Quincy   Twenty-five miles (40.3 km) southwest of Menetou-Salon, across a tributary river, the Cher, is the town of Quincy. Its chief claim to fame is that it was the second appellation in France (after Châteauneuf-du-Pape) to be granted AOC status in 1936. The soil here is a little more calcareous than in other villages, the average temperature is a little cooler, and frost is more of a problem. The wines are very racy and zesty and in some years can taste a bit unripe.

Reuilly   This is a small appellation, only 150 acres (60.7 hectares) of vines, very near to Quincy. The soil and climate are essentially the same. The wines are quite austere and very dry.

Touraine

Named for the city of Tours, this region is home to a variety of wines—white, red, rosé, and sparkling. Wine made from approved varietals grown within the boundaries of the Touraine region, but outside any of the commune appellations, or a blend of grapes from two or more communes, is given the generic appellation of Touraine. This appellation can be applied to both white and red wines, which are produced in almost equal quantities. The name of the varietal can show on a generic Touraine label. There is also a small amount of Touraine Mousseaux made primarily from Chenin Blanc.

Vouvray   In the commune of Vouvray, the Chenin Blanc grape reaches its zenith of quality. There are 5,000 acres (2,024 hectares) of vines in Vouvray, virtually all of them Chenin Blanc. This lovely varietal is often overlooked, but with its delightful aromas of ripe pear, its round mouthfeel, and its smooth but lively acidity and ripe fruit, Chenin Blanc is capable of making delightful wines in a wide variety of styles. In some cases, Vouvray is dry and crisp. Sometimes it is made off-dry (demi-sec) with a hint of residual sugar complementing the ripe pear nuances. Vouvray can also be sweet, in which case it is labeled as Vouvray **moelleux** (mwah-LEUH). Chenin Blanc is also made into a sparkling wine, Vouvray **mousseux**.

Chinon and Bourgueil   The commune of Chinon and its neighbor across the Loire to the north, Bourgueil, are the two major regions for red wine within the Loire. The wine is primarily Cabernet Franc, although Cabernet Sauvignon is also authorized. Loire reds can be described as charming—light, pleasant, fruit-forward, soft, easy to drink, and easy to like.

Anjou/Saumur

The large province of Anjou contains 19 appellations at the AOC level, including generic Anjou and generic Saumur. The vineyards of Anjou cover 35,600 acres (14,412 hectares). A variety of wines is made here, including dry whites, reds, rosés, sparkling wine, and sweet whites. Rosé d'Anjou is made in copious quantities from a lesser grape. Much better are the dry and semisweet rosés, Cabernet d'Anjou and Cabernet de Saumur, which must be made from the Cabernet Franc varietal.

Also prevalent are Saumur Mousseux (also called Saumur d'Origine) and Anjou Mousseux, sparkling wines made in the méthode champenoise. For both the rosé and white styles, red grapes can be used: Cabernet Franc, Cabernet Sauvignon, Gamay, and three others. The white grapes allowed are, naturally, Chenin Blanc, but also small percentages of Sauvignon Blanc and Chardonnay. The wines are usually made in the brut style, although Loire bruts are sweeter than those of Champagne are.

Savennières This elegant Chenin Blanc–based wine is a rarity among Loire whites in that it is made to age. When young, the wine is austere and closed, very dry. Given time, Savennières can evolve into a complex, full, round wine. Savennières is on the north bank of the Loire, where weather is cool enough that keeping the grapes on the vines longer into the fall in order to fully develop that panoply of flavors is sometimes risky due to frost. One of the more important producers of Savennières is Nicolas Joly of Château de la Roche-aux-Moines.

Coteaux du Layon This is an appellation restricted to sweet and semisweet wines based on botrytized Chenin Blanc grapes. The wines are rich and honeyed, but never cloying, thanks to their acidity. These wines can age for many years and gain further complexity and fullness. The dessert wines of Coteaux du Layon are among Europe's best, and are comparatively affordable.

Quarts de Chaume This is a tiny appellation within the Coteaux du Layon. It is essentially a single-vineyard appellation that is rated as one of the best sites for the sweet botrytized wines. The standards, including yield, sugar content, and alcohol level, are more stringent than for Coteaux du Layon.

Nantes

The Nantes, or Atlantic region, of the Loire is home to the bone-dry white wine, Muscadet. There is more Muscadet made each year than the wines of Touraine and Anjou combined. The grape, which has come to be called Muscadet, is actually Melon de Bourgogne. This varietal was brought to the Nantais region of the Loire from its native home of Burgundy in the eighteenth century by Dutch traders. The grape is easy to grow, has high yields, and produces a clean, fresh, uncomplicated wine that perfectly complements the seafood, shellfish, and freshwater fish that are such an integral part of the diet of the Atlantic section of the Loire.

Over three-quarters of Muscadet comes from vineyards in the Sèvre et Maine district, named for the two rivers that flow through it to join the Loire. The soil here has a good amount of clay mixed in with the sand and gravel, so its wines are a tad less tart than wine labeled as Muscadet. Sur lie is a technique widely used in Muscadet. It gives the wine a prickly feel and adds complexity.

Muscadet is now widely distributed around the world, where it has found favor in many markets, including the United States, as a refreshing aperitif and a perfect companion for light seafood dishes.

The South of France

Having covered the six major wine regions of France, where its world-class wines are made, we have covered the most important wines of France, but we have certainly not covered all there is to French wine. There are a great many other regions producing very nice wine. Many of the best of the lesser-known Appellations d'Origine Contrôlée regions are found in the South of France. In the past the south was known for rugged, sometimes coarse wines, mostly red, made from indigenous varietals like Mourvèdre,

FIGURE 6.35

Terraced vineyards in Provence soak up warm sunshine above the Mediterranean Sea.
© lillisphotography/IStock Photo

Cinsault, and Carignan. In the past several decades, however, there have been remarkable improvements in the quality of wines. Part of the reason is a trend to planting more of the noble varietals that can survive the heat and small amount of rainfall, such as Cabernet Sauvignon and Syrah. These are being planted on superior, cooler sites farther up the hillsides. The best of these face north or east so that exposure to sunlight is reduced, thus lessening the chance of overripening. Another important change has been the modernization of winemaking techniques. For instance, many winemakers are now fermenting at cooler temperatures in stainless-steel tanks; this protects the aromas and natural flavors of the grapes. In the South of France, one can now find some impressively elegant and balanced wines.

Provence

In southeastern France, Provence extends from the delta of the Rhône east to the border with Italy (Figure 6.35). This is beautiful, rugged country, extremely hot in the summer and rather desolate in the winter, but fertile and well suited to the vine. For decades, Provence was known for its large quantities of light rosé made from the high-yielding Carignan and some Grenache. Production is still 60 percent rosé, but the percentage of Carignan has decreased, and the wines have more depth. Reds account for 30 percent of production and are made with Mourvèdre, along with increasing percentages of Syrah and Cabernet Sauvignon. White wine is also made in Provence, but native varietals like Ugni Blanc and Clairette are being replaced with Semillon.

There are eight AOC appellations in Provence, two of which, Bellet and Palette, are so small as to be inconsequential. There is also a large section, the Coteaux Varois, which is rated VDQS.

Côtes de Provence

With 44,500 acres (18,016 hectares), most of them in the easternmost section of Provence, this is the largest of the region's three generic AOC appellations. Production is mostly red wine, which typically is a blend of Carignan (no more than 40 percent by law), Cabernet Sauvignon, and Syrah. Several of the better producers are giving their red wine more time in new oak barrels, which allows the wine to mellow out and become smoother than was previously the case.

Coteaux d'Aix-en-Provence and Coteaux d'Aix-en-Provence-les-Baux are the other two generic AOC appellations. They encompass 10,550 acres (4,271 hectares) of vines in the western section of Provence and are named for the city of Aix-en-Provence. The wines, mostly red, are similar to those of Côtes de Provence.

Bandol

The old fishing port of Bandol is right on the coast of the Mediterranean and is now a popular tourist destination. It is also home to the best and most interesting wines of Provence— big, structured, and full reds based on Mourvèdre (by law at least 50 percent) blended with Grenache and Cinsault. The regulations also allow up to 20 percent white varietals to be blended in. Bandol reds have a unique spiciness sprinkled in with the ripe plummy fruit flavors. They can age for at least a decade.

Languedoc-Roussillon

The very sizable region of Languedoc-Roussillon, also known as the Midi, is a popular tourist destination on the Mediterranean. The region produces ever-improving wines as investment in the area and awareness of its wines in foreign markets have increased. This varied region reaches from the western side of the Rhône delta along the coast to the border with Spain at the Pyrenees. There is a total of 700,000 acres under vine, making this the world's largest single wine region. The Midi was long famous for its simple, rustic table wines, and though quality of many of its wines has certainly improved, the Midi is still the source of much of France's vin ordinaire, as well as copious quantities of vin de pays. Eighty percent of the country's vin de pays is from this area.

Throughout the Midi, the climate is Mediterranean with mild winters and warm, sunny, dry summers, perfect for ripening a wide variety of varietals, from Chardonnay to Viognier, from Cabernet Sauvignon to Syrah. The soils are consistently limestone-based, with enough variation in topsoils to allow discernible if subtle differences in terroir among the regions.

The largest vin de pays appellation is the regional Vin de Pays d'Oc, and its subregions. Other important vin de pays appellations include l'Hérault and Aude. The trend in these and other vin de pays regions within the nearby départements of Gard and Pyrenees Orientales is toward varietally named reds and whites. These are produced by large international négociant firms that have invested considerable amounts of capital to replant vineyards with noble varietals, install giant stainless-steel fermentation tanks, and equip their caves with oak barrels for aging the wines. These mass-produced wines can be quite pleasant and very affordable.

AOC Appellations of the Midi

Côtes du Roussillon and Côtes du Roussillon-Villages

Between them, these two appellations cover 15,000 acres (3,700 hectares). The smaller one, Côtes du Roussillon-Villages, is located in the northern portion along the Argly River and its tributaries. The vineyards here are superior, with a complex mix of topsoils (schist, sand) on limestone. Regulations require a lower yield in villages-level wines, and a higher minimal alcohol level. Twenty-five communes are included in this appellation. The wines of both Roussillon and Rousillon-Villages are primarily red, blended from Syrah, Cinsault, and Grenache. They show considerable depth and character.

FIGURE 6.36

Very old vines are gnarled and stubby like those in this vineyard in the picturesque region of Corbières in the Midi.

© Pamela Uyttendaele/Shutterstock

Corbières

Corbières is the largest appellation in the Midi, with over 35,000 acres (14,170 hectares) of AOC-level vineyards (Figure 6.36). This is primarily a red wine appellation, although a small amount of rosé and a minuscule amount of white are also made. The reds are solid, perhaps a bit dense, but with appealing aromas of lavender and plum. They are widely available in the United States, and are affordable everyday wines.

Minervois

Just northwest of St. Chinian, across the valley of the Aude River, lies the Minervois. There are 45,000 acres of wine grapes, but only a small percentage of these vineyards (10,400 acres [4,200 hectares]) are rated at the AOC level. The remainder are vin ordinaire or vin de pays. The AOC vineyards, on terraced slopes in the eastern part of the region, are planted mostly to red varietals.

St. Chinian

Once a commune within the Coteaux du Languedoc appellation, St. Chinian received AOC status in 1982. This appellation can be applied to red and rosé wine only. Noble varietals—Syrah, Grenache, and Mourvèdre—are slowly displacing the rougher Carignan as the maximum amount allowed of this traditional grape is decreased.

Banyuls

Banyuls is one of six appellations for vin doux naturel within the Midi. Vins doux naturel in the Midi can be made from either Muscat, like Beaumes-de-Venise in the Rhône, or for the delicious richly flavored red vin doux naturel, from the Grenache grape. Banyuls is a red vin doux naturel, which by law must be 50 percent Grenache. The wine spends many months in oak barrels. It is aromatic, rich, intensely fruity, and ages very well.

The other Midi vin doux naturel appellations are Muscat de Frontignan, Rivesaltes, Muscat de Lunel, Muscat de Mireval, and Maury.

Coteaux de Languedoc

In May 2007, the appellation Coteaux de Languedoc was officially changed to Languedoc AOC. Within this large regional AOC there are seven sub-regional zones, and 12 communal (one town) zones. The vineyards of this sprawling appellation lie on the hills that run in a line behind the city of Montpellier. From vineyards on the lower levels, where the soil is alluvial and fertile, come vast quantities of vin ordinaire, most of which will be distilled into spirits. Further inland, as elevations increase, the soil becomes rockier. From these better vineyards come the wines, predominately red, that are labeled with the AOC Languedoc.

Large quantities of vin de pays wine is produced in Languedoc, much of it under the regional vin de pays appellation of Vin de Pays d'Oc. Some of these wines are very good indeed, but cannot carry the AOC appellation because they are made from noble varietals not authorized for this region.

The quality of both the vin de pays wines and the AOC wines is increasing steadily in this huge, wild region of small family growers and large cooperatives. As outside investment continues to grow, and better viticulture, more noble varietals and more modern equipment result, the wines of the Coteaux de Languedoc will become substantially more attractive while maintaining, one hopes, their eminently affordable prices.

The Southwest

The catchall term *the Southwest* encompasses a huge part of France, including all viticultural areas south of Bordeaux and east of the Midi. In such a large area, there is obviously a huge variety of terrains, microclimates, soil types, and winemaking preferences. Of the 70,000 acres (28,340 hectares) of vines in the Southwest, only about half produce AOC wines (Table 6.8).

Madiran

In the extreme southwest, the most important appellation is Madiran. The principal grape is Tannat, which is made into big, heavy, complex wines, quite tannic (the name of the grape derives from the same root as the word *tannin*), and, therefore, ageworthy. In many Madiran reds, Tannat makes up 40 to 60 percent of the blend, the balance being Cabernet Sauvignon, Cabernet Franc, and a lesser red grape.

Bergerac

Just east of France's largest fine wine region, Bordeaux, in the département of Dordogne lies Bergerac, with vineyards planted along the banks of the Dordogne River. Source of a variety of wines—dry whites, reds, rosé, sparkling, and sweet whites—Bergerac has long been eclipsed by its more prestigious neighbor, Bordeaux. The varietal mix is the same as in Bordeaux. The reds are of medium-to-full body, fresh, and nicely balanced.

TABLE 6.8 Appellations of France: The South

Region	Subregion	Principal Varietal
Provence		Mourvèdre, Cinsault, Grenache
Languedoc-Roussillon (The Midi)	Corbières	Mourvèdre, Cinsault, Grenache, Carignan
	Minervois	Mourvèdre, Cinsault, Grenache, Carignan
	Banyuls	Grenache (*vin doux naturel* only)
The Southwest	Madiran	Tannat, Cabernet Franc
	Bergerac	Cabernet Sauvignon, Merlot, Cabernet Franc Semillon, Sauvignon Blanc
	Cahors	Malbec

The whites have lively citrus and herbal aromas and flavors and sprightly acidity. Rosés are fruity and pretty.

Within Bergerac are several subdistricts of AOC status:

Monbazillac   Located on the south side of the river, Monbazillac produces a sweet wine, made in the same manner as Sauternes and from the same grapes. It can be delicious, if well made, with just enough acidity to hold up the lush honeyed flavors. Unfortunately, many producers in Monbazillac do not leave the grapes on the vine to become fully botrytized for fear of losing them to a killing frost.

Cahors   South of Bergerac is the old town of Cahors, an important trading center in the late Middle Ages. The town lends its name to the surrounding wine-producing area. The principal wine is a big, deeply colored (almost inky), tannic but balanced red made from the Malbec grape.

Corsica

The island of Corsica, off the coast of southern France, has always produced wines. By some accounts, Corsica is Europe's oldest wine-producing region, dating from 570 BC when Phoenicians first settled there. This mountainous island in the Mediterranean is actually closer to Italy than to France, but has been under French jurisdiction since 1768.

Corsica produces a wide variety of wines—red, white, rosé, still, sparkling, and sweet. Most is vin de pays and vin ordinaire. Very little Corsican wine, even the minuscule amount that is AOC, is exported off the island.

SUMMARY

The incredible variety of wines from France is quite mind-boggling. Although the task of becoming familiar with France's many different wines may seem daunting, it is well worth the effort. The best of French wines will provide a benchmark against which all other wines can be measured. Moreover, an understanding of France's Appellation d'Origine Contrôlée laws is helpful in understanding the quality control laws of other European wine-producing countries, as most of them modeled their systems on the French system. France has long been a major player in the international wine marketplace, and has proven over the past several decades that it can adjust to changes in demand and in tastes, while maintaining pride in heritage and tradition.

FRENCH FOOD AND WINE PAIRING

appetizer
tarte à l'oignon (small pie with caramelized onions)
Wine
A dry, but complex white from Burgundy, such as Rully

main course
**poitrine de veau farcie aux olives
(breast of veal stuffed with olives)
pommes de terre à la français
(new potatoes French style)
haricots vert avec beurre blanc
(green beans with butter)**
Wine
A medium-bodied red with good acidity,
such as Chinon from Loire Valley

salad course
**salade forestière (green salad with
sliced fresh mushrooms)**
Wine
Continue with the Chinon

dessert
**perles de cantaloupe au rhum
(melon balls macerated in rum)**
Wine
Coteaux du Layon, slightly sweet and very fruity late-harvest wine

EXERCISES

1. List the primary purpose of the Appellation d'Origine Contrôlée laws enacted in 1935, and then discuss whether or not the laws have been successful in achieving that purpose.

2. Explain la méthode champenoise, and list the various styles of wine that can be made by changing certain steps in the method. Are all wines made by this process entitled to be called "Champagne"?

3. What was the purpose of the Classification of 1855? In your opinion, should this classification continue to be used, or would periodic updates be desirable? Explain.

REVIEW QUESTIONS

1. What are the varietals allowed in red Bordeaux wines? What varietals are used to make white Bordeaux?

2. Name the six subdistricts of Burgundy.

3. Are dry white wines the only style of wine made in the Loire Valley?

4. What is the most important grape in Alsace? In that region, what does the term *Vendange Tardive* mean?

5. What is the principal red varietal of the Northern Côtes du Rhône?

6. What is Beaujolais Nouveau?

REFERENCES

Asimov, E. (2010, May 18). The pour. *The New York Times*, p. D-1

Buzzeo, L. (2009, November). Deconstructing the Languedoc. *Wine Enthusiast*, 66-68

Coates, C. (2000). *The Wines of France*. San Francisco: The Wine Appreciation Guild.

Kladstrup, D., & Kladstrup, P. (2001). *Wine and War: The French, the Nazis and the Battle for France's Greatest Treasure*. New York: Random House.

Kramer, M. (1989). *Making Sense of Wine*. New York: William Morrow & Co.

Osborne, L. (2004). *The Accidental Connoisseur: An Irreverent Journey through the Wine World*. New York: North Point Press.

Phillips, R. (2000). *A Short History of Wine*. New York: HarperCollins.

{ ITALY }

This chapter focuses on

the important historic role Italy has played in the development of viticulture and winemaking, as well as describing the important wine regions of Italy—their climates, their varietals, and the styles of wine produced in each region. It also discusses the wine laws of Italy, both what they accomplish and how they could be improved. Finally, the chapter describes Italy's role in the international wine trade.

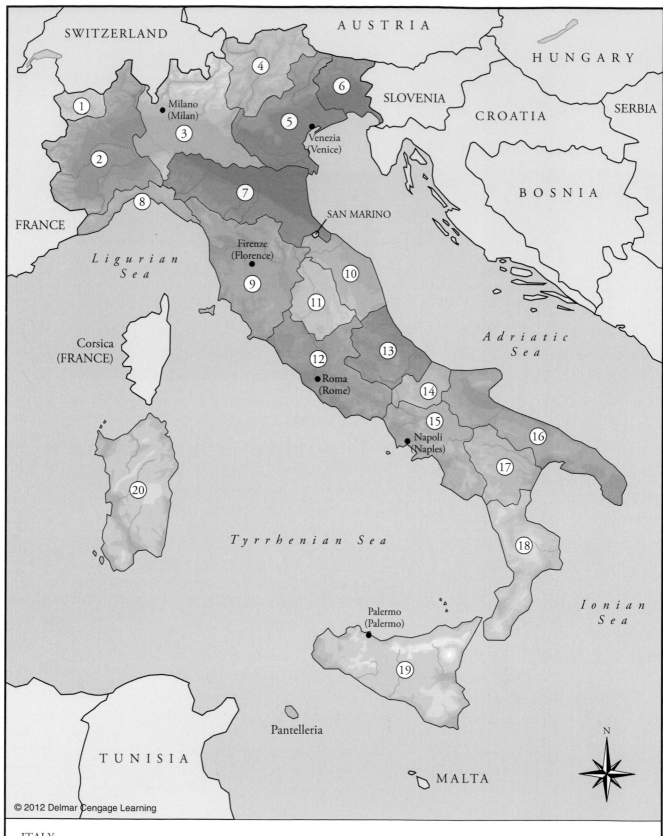

© 2012 Delmar Cengage Learning

KEY TERMS

amabile

classico

Cortese

Denominazione di
Origine Controllata
e Garantita (DOCG)

Denominazione di
Origine Controllata
(DOC)

dolce

frizzante

imbottigliato
dal produttore
all'origine

Indicazione
Geografica Tipica
(IGT)

metodo classico

metodo
tradizionale

Moscato

Nebbiolo

Recioto

riserva

Sangiovese

secco

spumante

superiore

vino da tavola

INTRODUCTION

It would be difficult to overemphasize the significance of Italy as a wine-producing country. It has played a vital role for thousands of years in the development of effective viticultural practices, cultivation of new varietals (there are currently over 400 grape types grown in the country), perfection of winemaking techniques, and the shipping and selling of wines. Modern Italy is the world's largest producer of wine. In all phases of the wine business, Italy's government and its vintners are working hard to increase the country's presence in the global marketplace while maintaining time-honored traditions. This chapter explores Italy's wine heritage, the emergence of the modern wine business (including the development of the wine laws), and the present conditions in its 20 wine regions. Based on the information presented, we make some predictions as to the future of Italy's wine trade.

ITALIAN WINE—HISTORICAL PERSPECTIVE

For almost as long as there have been people in Italy, there has been wine made in Italy. Evidence of grape growing and of wine consumption (earthenware jars with stains and residues of wine) dating from the Neolithic period, or late Stone Age, have been discovered in northern Italy near the city of Venice. This would date winemaking in Italy to as far back as 4000 BC. Central and southern parts of the Italian peninsula were colonized by the Greeks starting in 1000 BC as part of the expanding Greek Empire. With the colonizing forces came increased knowledge of viticulture (along with new varietals) and improved methods of making and storing wine. By the fifth century BC a true wine industry had evolved in Greece, and trading became prevalent throughout the Greek colonies around the Mediterranean Sea (Figure 7.1). It was during the Greek domination of the region that viticulture was perfected and wine became, along with olives and grain, one of the mainstays of Mediterranean agriculture. The Greeks did not colonize northern Italy, for the Etruscans already had a long history of vine cultivation there. The Etruscans (believed to have come originally from Asia Minor) were trading their wine as far north as modern-day Burgundy. The Etruscans did however purchase from the Greeks vessels for the drinking and storage of wine, and like the Greeks, they came to consider consumption of fine wine one of the sure signs of a civilized people.

A new empire began to control southern Italy when the Romans emerged as the dominant force in the region between the third and second centuries BC. The Romans' interest in wine is proven by the many mentions of wine in their writings. The oldest surviving Latin work on wine, Cato's *De Agri Cultura*, dates from 200 BC and suggests that wine was no longer a rare luxury in the Roman world, but a crucial ingredient in the growing commercial activities of the Empire. As the population of the city of Rome grew, reaching 1 million inhabitants by the start of the Christian era, it became the single most important market for the wine made from vines throughout the peninsula and in outlying regions of the empire. As the empire grew, the

FIGURE 7.1

This antique wine vessel is typical of the ones used by the Greeks to transport wine.

© Dejan Sarman/iStockphoto

Romans continued to develop their vineyards, and to trade with wine in all parts of the known world. Evidence of Roman wine vessels have been found as far north as England, as far west as the Iberian Peninsula, and as far south as northern Africa. The Romans also introduced viticulture to any colony where climatic and soil conditions were appropriate. It is under the Romans that vineyards were planted throughout Gaul (modern-day France), reaching into Bordeaux by the first century AD and into Alsace and Burgundy by the third century. It is fair to say that most of the great wine regions of Europe were originally planted by the Romans.

When the Holy Roman Empire fell to the combined invasion of barbarians from the north and the Turks from the east in approximately AD 300, wine production in Italy essentially came to a standstill. Although wine continued to be produced in former colonies, within Italy virtually the only wine produced was for the sacraments of the Christian Church and to fill the daily allocated ration for members of religious orders living in monasteries. Wine's integral role in Christian (and Jewish) religious ceremonies was a strong factor in its survival of Europe's Dark Ages. In Italy, as elsewhere in Europe, monasteries became the owners of large swaths of vineyard land, and monks became proficient winemakers. The sale of their wines became an important source of income for religious orders.

As Europe emerged from the Dark Ages into the later Middle Ages, wine once again became an important commodity for trade. The demand for wine was growing as population increased across the European continent, and vibrant urban centers of commerce grew, especially in northern Italy (Venice, Milan, Genoa, and Florence). As trade increased, a wealthy middle class of merchants developed, with an interest in, and the money for, luxury items like wine. No longer was wine merely for the aristocrats and the Church. The vineyards of France, Iberia, and Germany could not supply enough wine to meet the new demand. Into the breach stepped the vintners of Italy. From the south of Italy, from farmlands in northern Italy, and from the provinces in central Italy, especially Tuscany, came domestic wine to fill the demands of markets in the northern urban centers. Moreover, because wine from Italy's warm climate was hardy, sweet, and high in alcohol, it could travel well. The enterprising merchants and traders of Italy's wine business soon found new markets for their product in Paris, the British Isles, and as far away as Eastern Europe and the Baltic area. As Europe emerged from the Middle Ages at the time of the Renaissance, more people acquired a taste for the beverage, and that taste became more discriminating. Consumers began to differentiate among wines from different regions, and developed preferences. Winemaking techniques were improved during the sixteenth century, and in the seventeenth and early eighteenth centuries, Tuscany became the center of Italy's wine trade. Vintners in Tuscany formulated their first wine laws in the early 1700s. During this time, Italy was still fractured into many small competing provinces, some independent states, some under the control of Austria's Hapsburg Empire. The unified country of France, with the central government lending support to the wine industry, became the leading force in the international wine trade.

By the 1800s, the various provinces of the Italian peninsula began their steady emergence into the modern wine trade. A stronger insistence on quality among wine consumers across Europe and in emerging markets in the New World forced Italian winemakers to be more conscientious in their viticulture and vinification methods. Most Italian wine at this time was of average quality and was marketed locally. However, certain wine regions became recognized as producing wine superior to the everyday wine being made elsewhere in the country. Barolo and Barbaresco in Piedmont, Valpolicella in Veneto, and Chianti and Brunello in Tuscany became known for the quality of their wines, thus opening up foreign markets to Italian wines. When Italy finally united as one country in 1860–1861, progress toward a modern wine trade gathered real momentum.

In the late nineteenth century Italy, like the rest of Europe, suffered a serious setback in the production of quality wine when phylloxera, and later the powdery mildew, decimated vineyards up and down the country. The process of replanting vines on American rootstock was expensive, and many small vintners who could not afford to replant ceased operation. Also lost to phylloxera were many of Italy's indigenous varietals. These traditional varietals were often expensive to replant and to trellis, required labor-intensive care, and were low yielding. Cash-strapped landowners instead replanted with hardy, disease-resistant, high-yielding varietals that produced acceptable wines, lacking in complexity, but plentiful and less expensive to produce. Italy acquired a reputation over the ensuing decades as a producer of large quantities of undistinguished, affordable wines (Figure 7.2). This reputation was to continue into the 1970s. Only recently has the country been able to shake this image. One important factor was the adoption of meaningful quality control laws in 1963. Also significant was the leadership, in various regions, of conscientious, dedicated vintners determined to put the emphasis on quality.

FIGURE 7.2

The Denominazione di Origine Controllata (DOC) Laws

After the Second World War, Italian vintners and government officials agreed that if the country was to continue its progress into the modern commercial world of wine, there would need to be standards set for the production of wine. Regions that had already acquired a reputation for quality wine, like Barolo and Chianti, needed regulations to protect the authenticity of wines bearing their names, and regions that were struggling to improve the quality of their wines needed guidelines and standards to ensure progress. Italian leaders also recognized that it would be wise to work as closely as possible with the French who already had a system of quality control laws in place, and who also had earned, over the previous 100 years, the respect of wine consumers throughout Europe and the rest of the world. Accordingly, the Italian Parliament passed, in 1963, the Denominazione di Origine laws, based on the French Appellation d'Origine Contrôlée laws. The laws, which became effective in 1966, created the **Denominazione di Origine Controllata (DOC)** (day-nohm-ee-nay-t'zee-OH-nay dee oh-ree-GEE-nay kohn-troh-LAH-tah) designation, which guarantees the place of origin of any wine bearing the name of a region that held the DOC designation. The laws also established basic standards of quality for DOC regions. The first DOC designation was granted in 1966 to Tuscany's white Vernaccia di San Gimignano. The wine laws included a top category of classified wines, the **Denominazione di Origine Controllata e Garantita (DOCG)**, (day-nohm-ee-nay-t'zee-OH-nay dee oh-ree-GEE-nay kohn-troh-LAH-tah eh gah-rahn-TEE-tah) that not only regulated the production of wine in regions so

Reading an Italian Wine Label

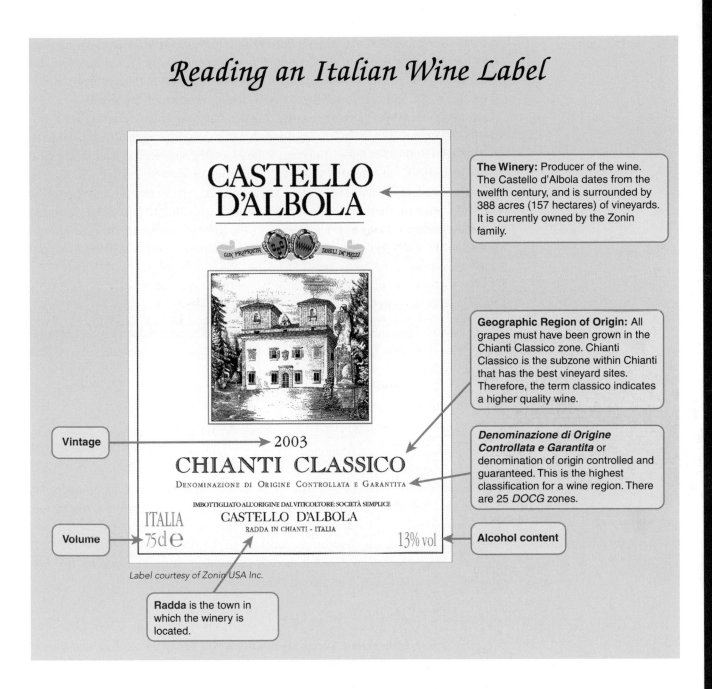

CASTELLO D'ALBOLA

GIR' PROPRIETA   NOBILI DE' PAZZI

2003
CHIANTI CLASSICO
DENOMINAZIONE DI ORIGINE CONTROLLATA E GARANTITA

IMBOTTIGLIATO ALL'ORIGINE DAL VITICOLTORE: SOCIETÀ SEMPLICE
CASTELLO D'ALBOLA
RADDA IN CHIANTI - ITALIA

ITALIA
75cl e

13% vol

The Winery: Producer of the wine. The Castello d'Albola dates from the twelfth century, and is surrounded by 388 acres (157 hectares) of vineyards. It is currently owned by the Zonin family.

Geographic Region of Origin: All grapes must have been grown in the Chianti Classico zone. Chianti Classico is the subzone within Chianti that has the best vineyard sites. Therefore, the term classico indicates a higher quality wine.

Denominazione di Origine Controllata e Garantita or denomination of origin controlled and guaranteed. This is the highest classification for a wine region. There are 25 *DOCG* zones.

Vintage

Volume

Alcohol content

Radda is the town in which the winery is located.

Label courtesy of Zonin USA Inc.

designated but further guaranteed they would be of high quality. These would be Italy's most elite wines, more impressive than even DOC wines. At both levels, the laws specified which varietals could be grown, what the yields could be, minimum alcohol levels, and even acidity levels.

From the time the DOC laws were first enacted, there was resentment on the part of many vintners who did not want the government dictating how they should tend their vineyards or make their wines. As a result, there was minimal immediate effect on the overall quality of Italian wines. Some vintners reverted to cheaper methods, easier-to-cultivate vineyards sites, or higher-yielding varietals to produce wine that met the basic standards for their respective regions, but was really no better than what had been made in the past. Other more adventuresome and innovative producers began to make wine outside the parameters of the new laws, bypassing the DOC designation to make interesting, exciting wines. The legitimacy of the wine laws was further eroded after 1980, when the authorities began elevating to the DOCG level regions whose wine was clearly not among Italy's finest.

In 1992, Italy's wine laws were revised under the leadership of the former Prime Minister, Giovanni Goria. In his new position of minister of agriculture, Goria was determined that the laws set legitimate guidelines and be respected as a reliable indicator of quality. In the overhaul of the laws, new designations were created and existing regulations were tightened. The tougher, fairer laws earned the respect and support of powerful landowners and businesspeople within the wine industry. With government, vintners, and corporations now working together, Italy has improved the quality of its wines considerably in the past 15 years and, as a result, is again recognized as an important producer of a wide variety of fine wine.

Quality Designations

The new DOC laws encompass all of Italy's many wines, even those that do not meet any specific standards. The laws divide all of Italy's numerous wine regions into four levels of quality.

Vino da Tavola

At this level—**vino da tavola** (VEE-noh dah tah-VOH-lah), or "table wine"—no geographic place of origin can be named. There are essentially no regulations imposed on producers except those required for health and safety standards. If the wine is bottled, only the color of the wine (e.g., vino da tavola rosso) and the name of the producer can show on the label. The only other conditions to be met are that the wine be made from grapes recognized by the European Union community, and that alcohol content and volume of wine per bottle show on the label. Even the vintage date is not required. A large percentage of wine produced in Italy is in the vino da tavola category. This category includes wine that will be sold in bulk or distilled into spirits.

Indicazione Geografica Tipica (IGT)

The category of **Indicazione Geografica Tipica (IGT)** (en-dee-KAH-zee-oh-nee gee-oh-GRAF-fee-kah TIP-eh-kah) was newly created under Goria to include wines that were made in a DOC region, but not according to the laws of that region. This way some of the very good wines that had been made in previous decades by imaginative vintners like Piero Antinori in Tuscany, who blended the native **Sangiovese** (San-JEE-yoh-VAY-say) grape with Bordeaux varietals, could have a designation higher than just vino da tavola. This would be allowed as long as they reflected the terroir of the larger region whose name was indicated on the label, hence the name: *Geografica tipica* translates as "typical of the region." In other words, if a wine is typical of 1 of the 20 provinces of Italy, it can show the name of that region. An IGT label cannot however, show a smaller subregion or specific village or an individual vineyard. Since 1996, when some of the first Sangiovese–Cabernet Sauvignon blends from Tuscany, the so-called

Supertuscans, were granted IGT status, the number of IGT wines in Italy has steadily increased. These wines, most of which are made in Tuscany, cover a wide range of styles from solid, good-value Sangiovese-based brands to very fine proprietary wines, usually Sangiovese blended with Cabernet or other French varietals. Some of the wines in this latter category, such as Antinori's Solaia and Tignanello, Ornellaia from the Marchese Lodovico, and Sassicaia from the della Rocchetta family, are among the most expensive wines produced in Italy, but also among its most impressive. Understandably, they have had tremendous success in export markets, and by some estimates, are now 40 percent of Italy's total production.

Denominazione di Origine Controllata (DOC)

As in the original 1963 law, a DOC wine must be made from specified grape varietals grown within a delimited geographic area, according to prescribed methods of viticulture. The major improvement of the 1992 overhaul was to allow the dividing of a large DOC region into more specific subzones, townships, villages, microzones, or even into individual vineyard sites. The recognition of variability of terroir within a DOC gave credibility to the system that it had previously lacked. There is now a hierarchical basis to the geographic delimitations, mandating that the smaller the zone, the more rigid are the standards, especially on production limits. This hierarchy actually allows more flexibility to vintners as they can choose to declassify a wine from a smaller, more restricted DOC to a larger, in a sense "lower" DOC. A consumer can now assume that a wine from a restricted, homogeneous zone with a proven track record for producing fine wine will be more distinctive than one from a larger region that may incorporate the small zone, but will also contain grapes from a variety of other, lesser zones. The "concentric circles" hierarchical concept that holds true for French appellations is now applicable also to Italy's classified wines. There are currently a total of 315 DOC regions in Italy.

Denominazione di Origine Controllata e Garantita (DOCG)

This category was first created in 1963 to designate the most prestigious subregions within the DOC regions. The four subregions that were designated in the next few years, Piedmont's Barolo and Barbaresco, and Tuscany's Chianti and Vernaccia di San Gimignano, are indeed among Italy's best. However, over subsequent years some questionable designations were made. By 1992 there were 11 DOCGs, 7 red and 4 white. Among the revisions of the wine laws that year was a tightening of the requirements for DOCG status. As of 2009, there are 35 DOCGs, 23 red and 12 white. Wines from these DOCG regions are given more stringent taste analysis than wines from the 315 DOC regions. To qualify for DOCG status, a DOC zone must have at least five years' record as a recognized demarcated zone, its wines must have established a reputation for distinctive style and high quality, and the wines must have attained a measurable commercial success domestically and in export markets. The criteria may be difficult to quantify, but there is general consensus that DOCG zones that have been elevated in the past 10 years are indeed worthy of the honor. For a summary of the current DOCGs, refer to Tables 7.1 through 7.4.

At both the controlled levels of Italy's wine laws, very specific requirements are listed and closely regulated. For each DOC and DOCG in Italy the following factors of wine production are spelled out:

- Grape varietals allowed and the percentage of each that must be used, usually listed as a minimum and maximum allowed
- Yield per hectare that can be harvested and allowable pruning methods
- Total amount of wine to be produced
- Vinification methods, for example, chaptalization (the adding of sugar to must) is not allowed in any Italian DOC)
- Aging requirements and methods (the use of the term *riserva* is carefully controlled).

Additionally, these wines undergo taste analysis to confirm that they meet standards for their denomination. The quality analysis of DOCG wines is more stringent than for DOC. Moreover, each bottle of wine within an approved cuvée of DOCG wine is sealed with a numbered government seal over the cap to prevent any further manipulation. Currently, 18 percent of wine produced in Italy is from a controlled denomination, at either the DOC or DOCG level.

FIGURE 7.3

IGT wines can have a brand name like Il Bastardo. The label will also indicate the geographic region of origin, here *Toscana* (Tuscany).

© RS/RG Associates

Naming of Italian Wines

Within Italy's DOC laws there are several ways a wine can be named. At the vino da tavola level a label carries only a brand name (or the producer's name) and the color of the wine. No geographic location, no vintage date, and no grape varietal can be named. For a wine of the indicazione geografica tipica category, a brand or proprietary name is often used. However, at this level the label can provide information on the varietal used and the geographic region. Refer to the IGT label in Figure 7.3. It shows both the varietal (Sangiovese) and the geographic region (*Toscana*, or Tuscany).

At the classified levels, that is, DOC and DOCG, there are two ways a wine can be named. First, the name of the wine could be just the geographic region of origin—for instance, Barolo or Chianti. A second method of naming a classified wine is by region of origin and varietal (Figure 7.4). Barbera d'Asti (red wine made from Barbera grapes grown in the subregion of Asti in Piedmont) and Cortese di Gavi (a white wine made from **Cortese** (kohr-THE-zeh) grapes grown in the subregion of Gavi in Piedmont) are both good examples. If a wine is to be named in the latter method, the varietal must be one approved for use in that region. If the wine is a blend of two or more varietals, the wine can be named for its color. Examples are Bianco di Custoza (a

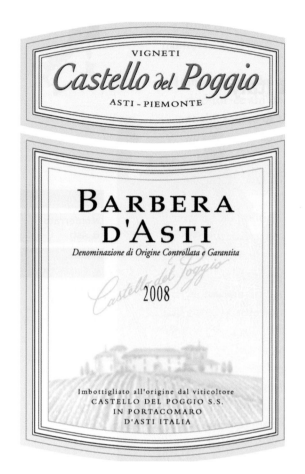

FIGURE 7.4

The wine here is named both for varietal (Barbera) and region (the commune of Asti in Piedmont).

Label courtesy of Zonin USA Inc.

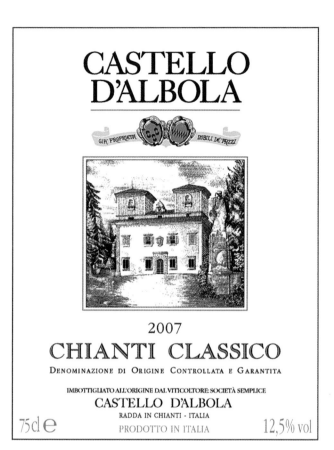

FIGURE 7.5

Wine can be named for the region where the grapes were grown, in this case Chianti Classico.

Label courtesy of Zonin USA Inc.

blended white from the Custoza subregion of Veneto) or Rosso di Montalcino (a blended red from the Montalcino subregion of Tuscany).

Other words that may be part of a wine's name could indicate information about the style of the wine, its vinification methods, or additional information about its place of origin. Some terms that can be incorporated into a wine's name are the following:

Classico (KLA-sih-koh) is a geographic term indicating that the vineyards where the grapes were grown are in the portion of the wine region that traditionally has produced better, more distinctive grapes (Figure 7.5). An example is Chianti Classico.

> **Riserva:** (ray-ZEHR-vah) A winemaking term indicating additional aging. Each classified wine region has its own minimal aging requirements regulating the use of the term riserva. Example: Chianti Classico Riserva.

TABLE 7.1 Wine Regions of Northwest Italy

Region	Subregion	Classification	Varietal	Style
Piedmont	Barolo	DOCG	Nebbiolo	full-bodied red
	Barbaresco	DOCG	Nebbiolo	full-bodied red
	Barbera d'Alba	DOC	Barbera	medium-bodied red
	Gattinara	DOCG	Nebbiolo (Spanna)	medium red
	Ghemme	DOCG	Nebbiolo (Spanna)	medium red
	Roero	DOCG	Nebbiolo	full/medium red
	Dolcetto	DOC	Dolcetto	light red
	Brachetto d'Acqui	DOCG	Brachetto	light, frizzante red
	Cortese di Gavi	DOCG	Cortese	dry white
	Arneis de Roero	DOCG	Arneis	dry white
	Asti	DOCG	Moscato	sparkling
	Barbera d'Asti	DOC	Barbera	medium-bodied red
	Moscato d'Asti	DOC	Moscato	semi-sparkling; off-dry
Emilia-Romagna	Lambrusca	DOC	Lambrusco	frizzante red
	Albana di Romagna	DOCG	Albana	dry white
Lombardy	Valtellina Superiore	DOCG	Nebbiolo	medium reds from 4 subzones
	Sforzato di Valtellina	DOCG	Sforzato	full-bodied red
	Franciacorta Spumante	DOCG	Chardonnay/Pinot Noir	sparkling

[1]Lambrusco is made in four separate DOCs.

here Pinot Gris and Pinot Bianco are also allowed to be blended in). So impressively elegant is this sparkler, with its austere flavors and tight, frothy mousse that it has been elevated to DOCG status. Lombardy also has two other DOCG wines, Valtellina Superiore and Sforzato di Valtellina, both full-bodied reds made from local indigenous grapes in the subzone of Valtellina. For a summary of some of the DOCs of Lombardy and Emilia-Romagna, see Table 7.1.

Piedmont is unquestionably the source of the best wines from the northwest. It is the home of two of Italy's most esteemed wines, Barolo and Barbaresco, the second and third DOC regions, respectively, to be elevated to DOCG status. Both wines are made entirely from the region's famous red grape, the **Nebbiolo** (neh-b'YOH-loh). This grape is site-specific in that it easily reflects the terroir of whatever vineyards in which it is planted. Both Barolo and Barbaresco are big, rich, tannic, concentrated wines with full bouquets but because of the differences in terroir, they are different, even though the two subregions are only a dozen or so miles apart. Connoisseurs claim the aromas of Barolo tend more toward tar, licorice, and truffle while Barbaresco sends forth nuances of rose petal and plum. Both wines are extremely long-lived.

The two big Nebbiolo-based reds of Piedmont are not the everyday wines of the people of Piedmont. They are too expensive for that. Fortunately, there are other more affordable wines available. The most widely planted grape in the region is the Barbera, less tannic, lighter, and more acidic than Nebbiolo, it is made into pleasant, zippy, cherry-flavored wines that accompany tomato-based pasta sauces well. Also prevalent is the Dolcetto grape, naturally fruit-driven and juicy, softer at the edge than Barbera. Piedmont is also home to Italy's most famous sparkling wine, Asti (formerly called Asti Spumante), easy and pleasant to drink, in its soft, off-dry style. There are also attractive dry whites made in Piedmont from the Arneis and Cortese grapes, as well as a delightful sweet wine made from the **Moscato** (mow-SKAT-oh) grape (Italian name for Muscat). Piedmont undoubtedly produces a wider variety of fine wines than any region of Italy.

Barolo

Named for the village at its center, the region of Barolo produces the most impressive and powerful expression of the Nebbiolo grape (Figure 7.6). Planted on hillsides around the village of Barolo and surrounding townships, the Nebbiolo grape takes its name from the Italian word *nebbia*, meaning "the fog," because it ripens late in the autumn when the hills are shrouded in mist. These cool, misty hillsides mean that Barolo is the more austere, restrained, structured, and muscular of Piedmont's two famous

FIGURE 7.6

Vineyards surround the town of Barolo.
© Pietro Basilico/Dreamstime.com

Both of these wines were recently elevated to DOCG status, perhaps in hopes that the increase in stature would encourage local vintners to strive to upgrade the quality of these two historically important wines. In the past decade, progress certainly has been made to correct weaknesses of the past. Through the 1980s, many of the wines from these two DOCs and from their neighboring DOCs were sloppily made, with inadequate or incomplete malolactic fermentation, or excessive time in oak barrels leading to oxidation. Today, many versions of Gattinara and Ghemme are big, sturdy, fragrant wines that show strong Nebbiolo character, even though their blends include two lesser red grapes. This blending is necessary because high elevation vineyards in the hills of these provinces are cool enough that the grapes have a difficult time ripening. Without the addition of the fruitier, less tannic grapes, the wines would be too harsh and thin. Although Gattinara and Ghemme do not attain the nobility and great intensity of Barolo and Barbaresco, it is possible to find well-made, very attractive versions of each.

Dolcetto

Dolcetto translates literally as "sweet little thing." The wine made from this grape is not actually sweet, but rather a soft, fruity pleasure, often compared to Beaujolais. The comparison is apt, although Dolcetto does have more of a bitter bite from tannin. This serves to nicely balance the savory fruit. The better Dolcettos come from DOC zones around the town of Alba. Best consumed young and fresh, they are admirably versatile food wines, matching nicely to roast poultry, lighter veal dishes, many pasta sauces, and risottos.

White Wines of Piedmont

Although renowned for the variety and quality of its red wines, from the light, charming Dolcetto to the massive, multifaceted elegance of Barolo, the region does also produce several whites worth seeking out. The best known of these is Cortese di Gavi, which was awarded DOCG status in 1999. Made entirely from the Cortese grape, the wine is flinty-edged and full of mineral nuances. Very dry and crisp, Cortese di Gavi (which can also be labeled as Gavi di Gavi or simply as Gavi) has been dubbed "this nation's Chablis" by no less an authority than Hugh Johnson. Johnson, who is one of the world's best-selling wine writers, describes Gavi as "Italy's most prestigious white wine."

Of increasing importance are the wines made from the Arneis grape. For many centuries it was used solely as a blending grape for overly tannic Nebbiolo-based reds, but Arneis is now made into pleasant, round, straightforward whites reminiscent of Pinot Blanc from Alsace (see Chapter 6). Arneis exhibits a unique hint of blanched almonds in the finish. The best of these whites is the Arneis di Roero, a DOCG made from grapes grown in the Roero Hills northwest of the town of Alba. It is the perfect match for any elegant fish or pasta dish with a creamy white sauce.

While demand for Gavi and Arneis is increasing, the most famous white wine from Piedmont remains the sparkling wine, Asti (Figure 7.7). This wine was known as Asti Spumante since it was first made in 1850, but after its elevation to DOCG status in 1995, only the word *Asti* shows on the label. Asti is not made in la méthode

FIGURE 7.7

This Asti is in the dolce, or sweet, style. Zonin is the producer of the wine.

Label courtesy of Zonin USA Inc.

champenoise, nor is the Charmat process or the bulk method used. Asti, made from the Moscato (Muscat) grape, often does not go through a second fermentation at all. Instead, after the crush, the must is kept in stainless steel tanks at a temperature low enough to prevent fermentation. Batches of the must is racked to new tanks and put through a cool fermentation during which the carbon dioxide is captured inside the sealed tanks. When the required level of alcohol is reached, the temperature is quickly lowered to allow the proper amount of residual sugar. The wine is bottled only as needed. This way the Asti, with its delicate flavors, is always fresh when bottled. Its light, off-dry style has proven very popular in export markets. In sheer volume, it is now one of Italy's most important wine exports.

Moscato d'Asti is a frizzante wine, made from the same grape grown in the same region as Asti, but produced in a different style. There is less of a mousse, the alcohol content is lower, and there is more residual sugar. With its light effervescence, floral bouquet, and touch of sugar, Moscato d'Asti is a simple charmer that is best enjoyed with informal fruit-based desserts.

Summary

There is little doubt that the wines of Piedmont will continue to be evident in the North American market. The easy-to-like and highly affordable Asti and Moscato d'Asti (Moscato is the Italian name for Muscat) are made primarily by large négociant companies and shipped regularly, and in considerable quantities, into U.S. and Canadian markets. The demand for the increasingly elegant Cortese di Gavi is improving, especially in fine restaurants where alert wine stewards have recognized its food compatibility. The soft, likable, and reasonably priced reds of Piedmont such as Barbera and Dolcetto continue to carve out market niches. Unfortunately, the high prices of the great reds of Piedmont will preclude their becoming any more prevalent in North America. Barolo and Barbaresco are made in small quantities and are expensive to produce, so it is not likely those prices will come down. Nonetheless, most producers of Piedmont's noble reds sell everything they can make every vintage.

Tuscany

The Apennines Mountains descend down the boot that is Italy, effectively dividing the country in half, geographically and culturally. In the central portion of the country, east of the mountains and over to the Adriatic Sea, lie the Marches, Abruzzi, and Molise. On the other side of the mountain range, on the western coast, are Tuscany, Latium, and Umbria. All six of these regions produce great quantities of fine wine (Table 7.2). The people of the Marches are proud of their wines and export a great deal of their

TABLE 7.2 Wine Regions of Central Italy

Region	Subregions	Classification	Varietal	Style
The Marches	Verdicchio di Matelica	DOC	Verdicchio	very dry white
	Verdicchio dei Caselli di Jesu	DOC	Verdocchio	very dry white
	Vernaccia di Serrapetrona	DOCG	Vernaccia	frizzante red
	Conero	DOCG	Montepulciano	medium red
Abruzzi	Montepulciano d'Abruzzi	DOC	Montepulciano	light red
	Colline Teramane	DOCG	Montepulciano	full-bodied red
Latium	Frascati	DOC	Malvasia, Trebbiano	very dry white
Umbria	Orvieto	DOC	Trebbiano, 3 others	secco, amabile, or dolce
	Sagrantino di Montefalco	DOCG	Sagrantino	full-bodied red
	Togiano Rosso Riserva	DOCG	Sangiovese, Trebbiano, Canaiolo	medium red
Tuscany	Chianti	DOCG	Sangiovese, plus 7 others	full-bodied red
	Chianti Rufina	DOC		
	Chianti Colli Senese	DOC		
	There are five other subregions within the Chianti DOC, but these names rarely show on labels.			
	Chianti Classico	DOCG	Sangiovese, plus 7 others	full-bodied red
	Brunello di Montalcino	DOCG	Sangiovese	full-bodied red
	Rosso di Montalcino	DOC	Sangiovese	medium-bodied red
	Vino Nobile di Montepulciano	DOCG	Sangiovese, plus 3 others	full-bodied red
	Carmignano	DOCG	Sangiovese & Cabernet	full-bodied red
	Vernaccia di San Gimignano	DOCG	Vernaccia	dry white
	Bolgheri	DOC	Several are allowed	rosé; some dry white
	Vin Santo	DOC[1]	Trebbiano, Malvasia	sweet white

[1]There are 12 DOC subregions that can produce Vin Santo.

bone-dry white Verdicchio. The frizzante red wine of the Marches, Vernaccia di Serrapetrona, was recently elevated to DOCG status. (Do not be confused by the name of the grape. There are several grape varietals in Italy called Vernaccia. Most are white; this one is red.) Considerable quantities of the blended red Montepulciano d'Abruzzo are also exported to the United States where its lush, smooth, fruity appeal is appreciated. (Molise is a very small, rugged, and sparsely populated region. Most of the tiny amount of wine produced there is consumed locally.)

Latium, despite the fact that the metropolitan area of Rome lies at its center, manages to produce a large percentage of central Italy's white wines, the most popular in this country being the fresh, crisp Frascati. Landlocked Umbria produces several DOC wines with distinct regional character, the best known being the dry white Orvieto. Made in the western section of Umbria, on the border with Tuscany, Orvieto is made in various styles, from secco to amabile and even the truly sweet dolce. Umbria also has two DOCG wines. One, Torgiano Rosso Riserva, is a medium-bodied, spicy wine with snappy acids and good structure. The blend is similar to Chianti's: Sangiovese,

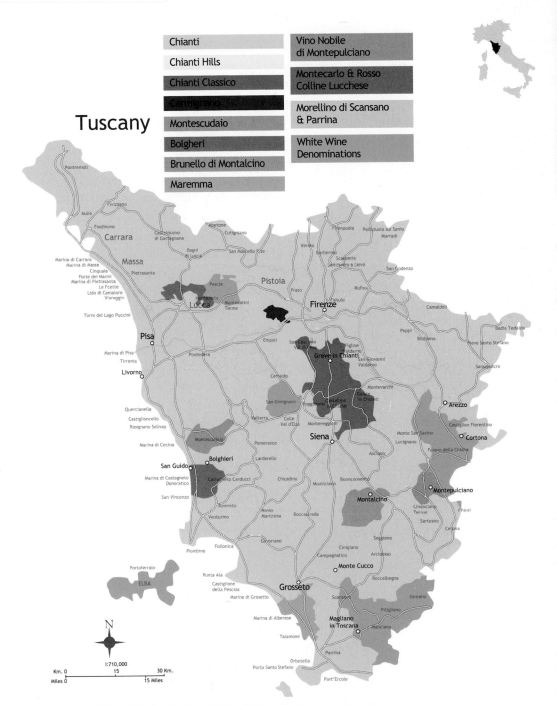

Tuscany

- Chianti
- Chianti Hills
- Chianti Classico
- Carmignano
- Montescudaio
- Bolgheri
- Brunello di Montalcino
- Maremma
- Vino Nobile di Montepulciano
- Montecarlo & Rosso Colline Lucchese
- Morellino di Scansano & Parrina
- White Wine Denominations

Map courtesy of Kobrand Corporation (www.kobrandwine.com)

Canaiolo (a lesser red grape), and small amounts of the simple white grape, Trebbiano. The other DOCG from Umbria is Sagrantino di Montefalco, a tannic, full-bodied red made from the local varietal, Sagrantino, grown only in the small subzone of Montefalco in central Umbria. The wine can sometimes be overly tannic and very tight. However, some producers are starting to make softer, more approachable Sagrantino.

Though many of the wines from the six regions of central Italy may be popular and successful in the global market, the undisputed leader in wine production is Tuscany.

Tuscany, along with Piedmont, is certainly one of Italy's premier wine regions. Its DOCG red wines—Chianti, Brunello di Montalcino, Vino Nobile di Montepulciano, and more recently, Carmignano—are well known and widely appreciated around the world. In addition to these proud reds, Tuscany also produces many appealing whites.

As we saw earlier, Tuscany was one of the first wine regions in Europe. The Etruscan people started making wine in what is now Tuscany shortly after arriving there from Asia Minor. By 1000 BC the Etruscans were trading their wine with the Greeks. The Etruscans (from whom the Etruscan Coast and Tuscany itself got their names) flourished in central Italy until their territories were absorbed into the Roman Empire in the third century AD. Viticulture has been a proud tradition ever since. Some wine-producing estates in Tuscany have been owned by the same families since the Middle Ages. The pattern of landownership in which the majority of land in Tuscany was owned by a few wealthy, noble families and the Roman Catholic Church, while the land was worked by sharecroppers, started to die out in the 1950s and 1960s. The ensuing two decades saw a decrease in investment and thus a deterioration of vineyards and cellars, and a plummeting in the quality of wine. Starting in the 1980s, landowners became more directly involved with the management of their estates or the estates were sold to new owners, either individuals or companies, that had the capital to upgrade vineyards and winemaking facilities, as well as the business acumen to effectively promote their wines in domestic markets and abroad. The new breed of Tuscan vintners are showing an admirable respect for age-old traditions while still engaging in creative and exciting innovations. The improvement in the quality and variety of Tuscan wines in the past 25 years is nothing short of remarkable.

The Tuscan countryside is famously hilly—a mere 8 percent of the land is flat (Figure 7.8). The hillside vineyards, with their elevation and good exposure to sunlight during the day, but chilly and calm evenings, produce very high-quality grapes with

FIGURE 7.8

In northern Italy, vineyards are often on steep, rolling hills, like this panorama in the Barbaresco region.
© Roca/Shutterstock

good aromatics and a solid backbone of acidity. At the core of Tuscan winemaking for centuries has been the Sangiovese grape. The undulating hills of Tuscany and its fertile river valleys contain many different zones where the Sangiovese and several other varietals, including the whites Trebbiano and Malvasia, can thrive in the temperate climate and the calcium-rich clay and loam of the hillside plots.

Chianti

In the United States, the best-known Italian wine is undoubtedly Chianti. It may also be the most misunderstood. Because much of the Chianti imported during the 1960s and 1970s, in those ubiquitous straw-covered flasks (Figure 7.9), was insipid, sharp, and boring, many Americans came to think of this as a mediocre, affordable wine to be served at little cafés or around the kitchen table, with simple pizza or pasta. Actually the Chianti of today is not the Chianti of your parents' era. Elevation to DOCG status in 1984 started the turn-around, with the most important change being the mandated lowering of yields. Vintners, perhaps inspired by the new prestige that the DOCG designation brought to their appellation, invested in improved facilities and new technology. Now Chianti made by reputable producers with grapes from the best vineyard sites can be truly world class, exhibiting bright berry/cherry aromas, complex hints of anise or licorice, solid backbone, and suave elegance.

The Chianti region is divided into seven official subregions, each with its own slightly different terroir. These subregions are Chianti Colli Aretini, Chianti Colli Fiorentini, Chianti Colline Pisane, Chianti Colli Senesi, Chianti Montalbano, Chianti Rufina, and Chianti Montespertoli (the most recent). Not all Chianti labels specify the subregion. Rufina is the one most often seen.

Traditionally Chianti was a blend of Sangiovese, four lesser red grapes, and two whites, Trebbiano and Malvasia. The DOC laws of 1963 mandated that all these grapes

FIGURE 7.9

Italian women making straw flasks the traditional way for wine bottles.

© David Lees/Corbis

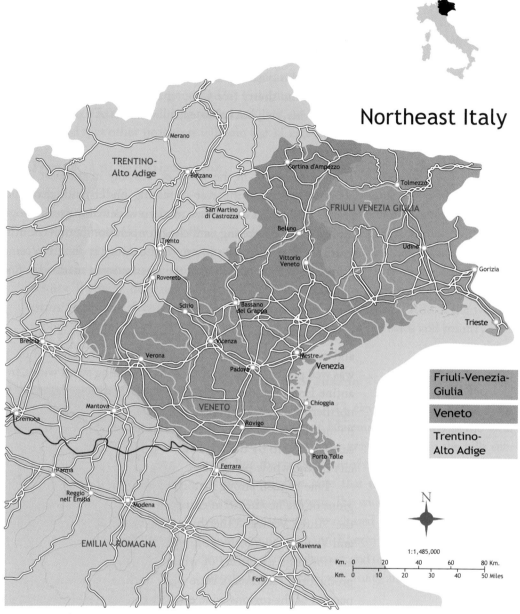

Northeast Italy

Friuli-Venezia-Giulia

Veneto

Trentino-Alto Adige

1:1,485,000

Km. 0   20   40   60   80 Km.

Km. 0   10   20   30   40   50 Miles

Map courtesy of Kobrand Corporation (www.kobrandwine.com)

and a focus to the wines of Friuli that seems far removed from the carefree, sensorial, almost joyful approach to food and wine that we associate with Italy.

Most of Friuli's wines are named for the varietal and the region (Figure 7.15). Because the northern part of the region is right up against the foothills of the massive Alps, it is not suited to viticulture, being too high in elevation, too rocky and rugged to be feasibly cultivated. There are some excellent vineyard sites in the sloping foothills of the Alps, but most of Friuli's vineyards are located on the flat plains extending inland from the Adriatic Sea. The unique combination of mountain air and maritime breezes and humidity make an ideal situation for viticulture: warm sunny days, cool evenings, and adequate precipitation. This mesoclimate explains why

FIGURE 7.15

This Pinot Grigio is named for its varietal (Pinot Grigio) and Region (Friuli).

Label courtesy of Zonin USA Inc.

Friuli's whites are so zippy and flavorful. Grapes get the sun and moisture they need to ripen up and evolve their flavors, while the drop in temperature each evening during the growing season assures that the grapes' acids retain their vibrancy.

The varietals that do particularly well in this sunny but cool region are Pinot Grigio, Pinot Bianco, and Sauvignon Blanc. The white grape that Friulians think of as their own is the Friulano. For centuries the grape was called the Tocai Friulano. *Tocai* is a Slavic word, which is not surprising since Friuli is bordered on the east by Slovenia, Croatia, and farther east, Hungary. Tocai Friulano is not the same grape used in Hungary to make the famous Tokaji Aszú dessert wine. However, vintners of Hungary protested for decades over the use of the word *Tocai* on Italian wine labels. Finally in 2006, the European Union decreed that the Italian grape was henceforth to be identified simply as "Friulano" (Larner, 2009a). Friulano is used on its own to make varietal wines, and it is often blended with other varietals to make some of the many enticing blended whites. Also widely planted and popular for blending, is the indigenous varietal, Ribolla Gialla. Red grapes are also planted in Friuli and make up about 40 percent of total production (http://www.Italianmade.com). Among the more popular red varietals are the local Schioppettino and Refosco, along with the Bordelais varietals that are better suited for export markets. Merlot, Cabernet Sauvignon, and Cabernet Franc are all made into varietally named wines.

Friuli-Venezia Giulia is divided into seven DOC subzones, two of which are in the hilly eastern area near the Alps. These two, Collio (the hills) and Colli Orientali (the eastern hills), have calcareous stony soil. In the flatlands below the foothills the soil is alluvial, with quantities of sand and pebbles having been deposited over the millennia by the numerous rivers that slice through the plains. The five DOCs of the plains are, moving from west to east, Lison-Pramaggiore, Latisana, Grave del Friuli, Aquileia, and Isonzo. Of these seven DOCs, only Collio, Colli Orientali, Grave, and Isonzo are likely to be seen in North America (Table 7.3).

The Wines of Friuli-Venezia Giulia

The wine producers of Friuli-Venezia are committed to protecting their region's reputation for racy, balanced, clean white wines, in which varietal character is allowed to shine through and food compatibility is evident. Friulians, both small private winemakers and larger cooperatives, are resisting the temptation to make the creamy, rich, oaky style of white that seems to have found such acceptance in the U.S. market and in other countries. White wines here are not fermented or aged in oak barrels, so there is no layer of picked in late fall, the bunches of grapes are spread on straw mats for two to three months and allowed to dry out, or raisin, slightly to concentrate the sugars as the water of the grapes evaporates. Fermentation is allowed to continue until all sugars are converted, which leads to a natural alcohol level of between 14 and 16 percent. This is a labor-intensive method, with inherent risks—for instance, a spell of wet weather could cause the grapes to rot as they lie in the drying sheds. Consequently, Amarone is not cheap. It is worth the price, though; big but graceful, intense but elegant, redolent with earthy aromas and mocha/chocolate flavors. This is easily the most impressive wine from the Veneto, and it is probably only a matter of time before Amarone is a DOCG. Some of the best Amarone is made by the Masi winery, and by Zonin.

An interesting recent development is the rapidly increasing interest in the age-old Ripasso method, whereby the pomace (skins, pulp, seeds, and yeast cells left in the tank after fermentation ends) of Amarone is blended into young Valpolicella wine the spring after initial fermentation. (The word *ripasso* is Italian for "passed over twice.") One wine writer has referred to Ripasso as "one of the hottest new wines to emerge in Italy in [recent] years" (Larner, 2009b). Even though this method has been used in the Veneto for centuries, it was only in 2007 that the Italian government authorized the use of the word *ripasso* as part of the DOC Valpolicella. These wines show some of the richness and depth of Amarone, but are less intense and far more affordable. Due to its smoky aromas and spicy flavors, Valpolicella Classico Ripasso is the perfect wine to serve with barbequed meats.

Prosecco

One of the most popular wines in the Veneto is its own frizzante, the delightful Prosecco. Made primarily from the grape of the same name, with some Pinot Grigio and a little Pinot Bianco blended in, Prosecco is frothy, charming, and usually slightly off-dry. The best Prosecco is made from grapes grown in the hills just north of Venice. By law, Prosecco must be made in the **metodo classico** (MEH-toh-doh CLAH-see-coh), la méthode champenoise, and be labeled by its official DOC designations, either Prosecco di Conegliano or Prosecco di Valdobbiadene.

Trentino-Alto Adige

Unlike the other two Tre Venezie regions, Friuli-Venezia Giulia and Veneto, Trentino-Alto Adige is landlocked. Nestled right up against the Alps, it is also the northernmost of Italy's wine regions (Figure 7.17). Politically and culturally, this region is as infiltrated by northern influences as by Italian ones. This is especially true in Trentino, where German is the primary language. In both parts of this region, the approach to winemaking reflects that Teutonic influence. The wines have the precision and focus that is typical of Germany's and Austria's finest whites. While northern climates are usually more conducive to nice white wine, there is more red wine made in Trentino-Alto Adige than white.

Vineyards are planted everywhere that conditions allow—in the south-facing foothills of the Alps, in alpine meadows, in the steep valleys of the river Adige, which flows through the center of the region. The Alps provide enough protection from cool continental weather patterns to allow grapes to ripen well, despite the northern location.

FIGURE 7.17

The Alto Adige region has perfect terroir for Pinot Grigio as well as many red varietals. The soil of volcanic rock and limestone adds unique flavors to the wines made in these beautiful valleys.

© Moreno Soppelsa/Dreamstime.com

Soil content is also close to ideal, with a mixture of well-drained volcanic rock laced with limestone in higher elevations and, in lower meadows and along the valleys, clay and sand left by retreating glaciers in ancient times and by the flowing rivers of more modern times. The white grapes that are prevalent are an interesting mix of varietals including Pinot Grigio, Traminer, Müller-Thurgau from Switzerland and Chardonnay, which was introduced in the nineteenth century. The array of red varietals is similar. There are local grapes, the most prevalent being Schiava and Lagrein, planted alongside imports. Cabernet Sauvignon, Cabernet Franc, and Merlot are all successfully cultivated. The most important of the white varietals is Chardonnay, which is made into crisp attractive still wines and is the basis for the lively **spumante** (spoo-MAHN-tay). The spumantes that are made in the metodo tradizionale, with Chardonnay as the base with some Pinot Bianco blended in, can rival the best sparkling wines made in the world. The ubiquitous Pinot Grigio can be unusually interesting, with nice depth and roundness and pleasant melon tones. The Müller-Thurgau, a rather ordinary grape elsewhere, can be made into nice zippy wines here. Of the reds, the indigenous Schiava produces the most exciting wines, medium to full bodied, well structured, and packed with black fruit overlaid by hints of licorice.

The wines are named for the varietal and for the specific DOC region. Fully two-thirds of wines produced here are DOC. There are 12 DOC zones, but many of them do not show on labels, since varietal differentiation is more relevant than place of origin. There are four DOCs that are likely to show on wines that are exported (fully a third of the region's DOC wines are sold abroad). They are: Alto Adige, Santa Maddalena, Trentino, and Teroldego Rotaliano (A red wine made of the local Teroldego grape in Rotaliano, a subzone of Trentino where gravelly vineyards in the flat plains seem ideal for bringing this somewhat rustic grape to an adequate ripeness level). The wine is considered the best red from the whole region, with its ruby color, full body, and ripe fruit. It ages very well. There is now a lighter style of Teroldego that is released early as a novello. Pinot Noir vineyards were planted in cooler zones in the late 1980s, and many of them show real potential, especially those given oak aging. The Cabernet Francs of the Trentino are also showing increasing promise. As small producers in both Alto Adige in the north and Trentino to the south continue to more carefully match appropriate varietals to the various mesoclimates of their region, the overall quality of the wines is sure to climb.

Southern Italy

The southern part of Italy, much of which is rugged, sparsely populated, and economically disadvantaged, had not been prominent in international wine markets until very recently. Campania, Apulia (Puglia in Italian), Basilicata, Calabria, and the islands of Sicily and Sardinia have made wines, like the rest of the country, for hundreds of years. The amount of wine coming out of these regions is prodigious, especially from Apulia and Sicily. Acreage devoted to vineyards is 406,315 acres (164,500 hectares) on Sicily, which is exceeded only by Apulia where 420,000 acres (170,000 hectares) are devoted to wine grapes. However, quantity does not often equal quality. For instance, only 5 percent of the wine from Sicily and 2 percent from Apulia is classified. Because much of the wine from those regions, as in other parts of southern Italy, is used primarily for blended bulk wine or is distilled into spirits, the entire area accounts for only 10 percent of the country's total DOC production (http://www.Italianmade.com).

In the belief that the flood of mediocre wine from southern Italy has contributed to a worldwide situation in which the supply of wine now exceeds demand, thus leading to a general lowering of prices, the Italian government and the European Union are offering incentives to landowners to reduce production by tearing out vineyards, especially in questionable areas. Some landowners are complying, reducing their acreage, and more carefully managing their crops. Other vintners, whose families have been making quality wine for generations, continue to produce quality wines, never having fallen into the pattern around them of making large quantities of high-alcohol, overly astringent, and highly extracted wine. It appears that the standards of these few pioneers is spreading to other producers around them, with better wines appearing in many sections of the south.

It is certainly possible to make good wine in the south, despite the impression that most of the southern peninsula and the two islands, with abundant sunshine and hot Mediterranean temperatures, would be incapable of producing quality grapes because there would be inadequate hang-time. However, there are numerous sites well suited to

TABLE 7.4 Wine Regions of the South

Region	Wine	Classification	Varietal	Style
Campania	Taurasi	DOCG	Aglianico	full red
	Greco di Tufo	DOCG	Greco	dry white
	Fiano di Avellino	DOCG	Fiano	dry white
Puglia (Apulia)	Locorotondo	DOC	Merdicchio, plus others	dry white
	Salice Salentino	DOC	Negroamaro	full red
Basilicata	Aglianico del Vulture	DOC	Aglianico	full red
Sicily	Bianco d'Alcamo	DOC	Verdello, plus 3 others	very dry white
	Marsala	DOC	Grillo Plus 2 others	fortified
Sardinia (Sardegna)	Cannonau di Sardegna	DOC	Cannonau (90 percent)	medium red
	Vermentino di Sardegna	DOC	Vermentino	dry white
	Vermentino di Galluria	DOCG	Vermentino	dry white

viticulture because of cooling sea breezes and/or elevation. If producers can continue the trend toward reducing acreage in less-suited areas and concentrate on the better vineyard sites, while working to increase the overall quality of their wines, the south will greatly improve its chances of becoming a player in the export market for wines (Table 7.4).

Campania

When thinking of Campania, one is likely to think of the lovely old city of Naples or the stunning beauty of the Amalfi coast more than of wine. Despite the grinding poverty of much of the interior, there is some fine wine produced here, and has been for a very long time. It is well documented that one of the most popular wines in the time of the Roman Empire came from Campania. Named Falernian, this big red wine was made from grapes grown in the foothills of Mount Falernus south of Naples. It is claimed that even Julius Caesar enjoyed this wine (Standage, 2005).

In more modern times, the most famous wine from Campania, indeed one of the most famous from all of southern Italy, has long been Taurasi, a full-bodied red made from the Aglianico grape, which thrives in the volcanic soil of the hillside sites where sunshine is abundant but temperatures are moderated by breezes. Recently awarded DOCG status, Taurasi has unquestionable character. Increasingly evident on wine lists in the United States is another Campanian DOCG wine, this time a white, Greco di Tufo. Greco, as can be seen from the name, was brought to Italy by the Greeks. When grown around the village of Tufo and nearby communes, the grape produces an impressively full-bodied dry wine of considerable depth and rich flavors. Another DOCG white from Campania is also attracting attention. The Fiano di Avellino is full and rich. It perfectly complements the great mozzarella cheeses and pizzas for which Campania is famous.

Puglia

Italy's most prolific wine region, Puglia (Apulia) covers the heel of Italy's "boot." The majority of its wine is distilled into industrial alcohol or is concentrated down into a potent must used to strengthen thinner wines in the north. There are 24 DOC zones in Puglia, but few of them are seen in North America. One standout is widely available, however. Salice Salentino, from the Salento peninsula, is a full, fruit-driven, aggressively flavored red that has found favor in the United States. It is made from the local grape, Negroamaro. The Primitivo grape, known in California as Zinfandel, is also widely planted in Puglia, where it is made into several interesting IGT wines, and into the DOC Primitivo di Manduria. The best white made in Puglia is the DOC Locorotondo, a vivacious wine made primarily from the Verdicchio grape, with four other grapes (including Chardonnay) allowed to be blended in.

Basilicata

From this hardscrabble region comes one wine worth seeking out, Aglianico del Vulture. Aglianico is an ancient grape believed to have been cultivated in this area for over 3,000 years. The grape does especially well in the foothills of Mount Vulture, where volcanic schist imparts a mineral nuance without burying the grape's natural berry aromas. The wine is highly structured and very dry. The riserva must age for five years before release, and two of those years must be in oak. When released, the mature smooth wine is a perfect accompaniment for game meats or pungent cheeses.

The mountainous region of Calabria, south of Basilicata, is more famous for its cheeses, like pecorino and ricotta, than for its wines. There are some respectable red wines made from the native varietals, Primitivo, Aglianico, and Gaglioppo, as well as some pretty whites from Greco and Malvasia.

FIGURE 7.18

Workers at the Speranza family winery press grapes for Sicily's famous fortified wine, Marsala.
© Jonathan Blair/Corbis

Sicily and Sardenia

The two islands off the coast of Italy, Sicily which is right off the "toe" of the boot, and Sardenia to the west of the peninsula in the Tyrrhenian Sea, both have long histories of wine production. The best-known wine from the islands is Sicily's Marsala, a justifiably popular fortified wine, which has been made for over 200 years (Figure 7.18). It can be fortified with both additional alcohol and with concentrated must made from very ripe grapes. For several decades in the mid-twentieth century the quality of Marsala suffered a downturn. It became common practice to sweeten the wine with various syrups, thus hiding its character. That type of degradation has almost disappeared, and several producers are returning to the traditional style of naturally sweetened and well-matured wine. The best Marsala, designated Vergine, is made without the heavy must and, after fortification with pure alcohol, is aged in wooden casks for up to 10 years. Obviously popular with cooks for the delicious sauces made from it, Marsala could regain its status as a delicious beverage if DOC laws governing its production can be streamlined and tightened.

FIGURE 7.19

The climate of this vineyard in Sicily with dry, pebbly soil and baking hot sun is moderated by ocean breezes.
© Zyankarlo/Dreamstime

Another Sicilian wine of a very different style is finding its way into foreign markets. Bianco d'Alcamo, a dry white, is made from the same grapes as Marsala. It is medium bodied and has unique almond aromas. There are several other DOC whites made on the island (95 percent of Sicily's DOC production is white, including Marsala). Sicily's white made from other indigenous grapes make good summer wines—crisp and refreshing. Among red wines from Sicily that are indicative of increasing emphasis on quality the best are those made from the native Nero d'Avola grape. When yields are kept low, and modern winemaking techniques are used, Nero d'Avola can be impressively smooth and balanced. As proof that Nero d'Avola is being made into very good wines, Sicily was granted its first DOCG designation in 2005, when the DOC Cerasuolo di Vittoria was elevated to that status. The wine, by law, must be contain from 50 to 70 percent Nero d'Avola (Figure 7.19).

Sardinia is 150 miles (240 km) off the coast, thus isolated from the rest of Italy. Culturally and viticulturally, the island has been heavily influenced by Spain, its neighbor to the west. Both its most famous red, Cannonau di Sardegna, and its most famous white, the DOCG Vermentino di Gallura, have Spanish roots. The Cannonau grape is the Garnacha of Spain, from whence it was brought to Sardinia centuries ago. (The Garnacha of Spain is originally from France's southern Rhône, where it is called Grenache.) The DOC Cannonau di Sardegna covers the whole island. The wine can be made in a dry style or can be semisweet and fortified. The best is designated riserva. The Vermentino grape of Sardinia's dry white wines was brought from Spain to Corsica in the fourteenth century, and from there to the narrow coastal region of Liguria, just south of Piedmont. It soon became widely planted throughout southern France and parts of coastal Italy, but the grape did not show up on Sardinia until the late nineteenth century when it was brought from Liguria to Gallura, the island's northernmost tip (http://www.Italianmade.com). Although the grape is planted throughout the island, the best Vermintino is still grown in Gallura, where fierce winds from the Alps keep temperatures moderate and the granite-based soil imparts a distinctive mineral character. Vermentino di Gallura, Sardinia's only DOCG, has good body and vibrant acidity well balanced by fruit. Locally it is served with fried calamari, baked cod, and other seafood dishes.

In looking to the future of wine production in the south of Italy, one can only hope that the trend away from quantity and toward quality will continue to gather steam. Many experts are optimistic that the enthusiastic reception in the United States to Campania's Taurasi and Greco di Tufo, Puglia's Salice Salentino, Sicily's Nero d'Avola and Sardinia's Cannonau and Vermentino will encourage producers in the southern peninsula and the islands to become ever more responsive to consumers' tastes and the increasing demand for interesting wines.

SUMMARY

Italian wines have long been popular in the United States, with a real surge in the 1990s, when imports of Italian wines first outpaced those from France. The increase in sales of Italian wines coincided with the wider acceptance of and respect for Italian cuisine during that same period. Perhaps Americans felt the Italian culture was more simpatico with our lifestyle, as French cuisine, wines, art, and even language are perceived as elitist, formal, elegant, and sophisticated, and the Italians represent a more relaxed approach. As one observer, Professor Sean Shesgreen of Northern Illinois University, has put it: "Italy stands for naturalness, informality, accessibility, practicality, spontaneity, optimism, intuitiveness and family feeling" (Shesgreen, 2003). These qualities all reflect the American approach to entertaining and to dining out.

Italy produces and exports more wine than any other country. Italian wineries have also steadily increased their exports to the U.S. market growing by 12 percent in value from 2005 to 2009 (http://www.census.gov), and are the number one imported wine in the United States. Pinot Grigio leads the growth in sales of Italian wines (it is now the fourth most popular varietal in this country), followed closely by Chianti and various spumantes and frizzantes. However, the perennial favorites are being joined more by other, lesser-known Italian wines, such as the top quality wines Barolo and Brunello di Montalcino, and the excellent value, but even lesser-known wines, especially from the south. With the DOC laws of Italy becoming steadily more strict, and with more producers aware of the importance of quality control versus mass production, it is safe to predict that Italian wine will improve its share of the North American market in the years ahead.

ITALIAN FOOD AND WINE PAIRING

appetizer

antipasto of roasted peppers, prosciutto, pepperoncini, and olives

Wine

Fresh sparkling wine, Asti or Proscecco

second course

angel hair pasta with mussels and zucchini

Wine

Lively, aromatic dry white from northern Italy:

Bianca di Custoza

main course

**grilled lamb caponata (traditional sauce
of tomatoes and eggplant)**

Wine

Complex, spicy full-bodied red:

Brunello di Montalcino,

or Montepulciano d'Abruzzi

dessert

gelato and macaroons

Wine

Vin Santo, sweet white

EXERCISES

1. Is there any region in Italy in which white wine plays a more important role than the reds? Which region(s)?

2. List the two methods by which a DOC or DOCG wine may be named. Give an example of each way of naming these classified wines.

3. What is the meaning of the term *Indicazione geografica tipica*?

4. Define the term *Supertuscans*, and explain how these wines first came to be made and by whom.

REVIEW QUESTIONS

1. What is the principal red grape of Piedmont, and what style of wine is made from it?

2. What is the principal red grape of Tuscany? What style of wine does it make?

3. What is the difference between a spumante wine and a frizzante wine? Are they made by the same method?

4. Is Cabernet Sauvignon allowed to be blended into Chianti and Chianti Classico?

5. What people originally brought the Greco grape to southern Italy? What is the most important wine now made from that grape? What region is it from?

6. How many DOCG zones are there presently? How many are red? White?

REFERENCES

Cooke, J. (2002, November). Barolo's New Generation. *The Wine Spectator,* 78–81.

Larner, M. (2009a, August). Friuli's surprising whites. *Wine Enthusiast,* 30.

Larner, M. (2009b, October). Ripasso grows up. *Wine Enthusiast,* 27.

Robinson, J. (Ed.). (2006). *The Oxford companion to wine* (3rd ed.). New York: Oxford University Press.

Shesgreen, S. (2003, March 7). Wet Dogs and Gushing Oranges: Winespeak for a New Millenium. *The Chronicle of Higher Education.*

Sonkin, L. (2009, August). Piedmont's Barbera wines. In Towne Web site.

Standage, T. (2005). *A history of the world in 6 glasses.* New York: Walker & Company.

{SPAIN AND PORTUGAL}

This chapter identifies the

major wine regions of Spain and Portugal and describes the different types of wine produced in each region. It covers the various microclimates and soil types of the Iberian Peninsula, in addition to the importance of the role played by governmental agencies in the production, promotion, and marketing of wine. Finally, the chapter discusses the position of Spanish and Portuguese wines in the U.S. market today and in the future.

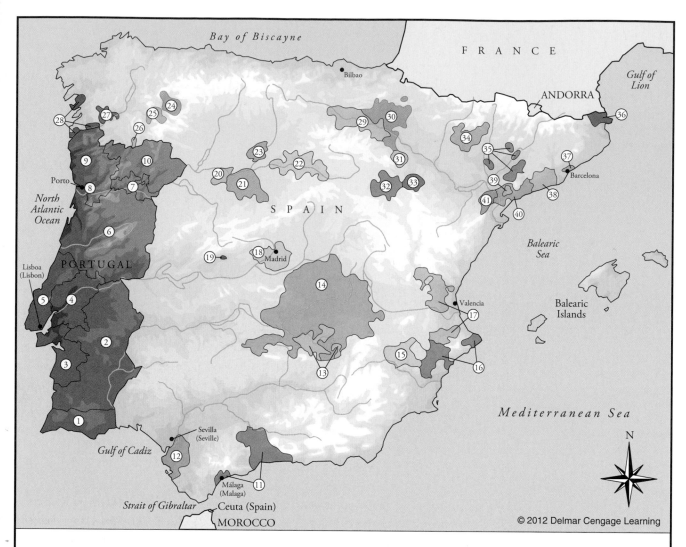

PORTUGAL:
1. Vinho Regional Algarve
2. Vinho Regional Alentejano (p 300)
3. Vinho Regional Terras do Sado (p. 299)
4. Vinho Regional Tejo
5. Vinho Regional Lisboa
6. Vinho Regional Beiras (p. 296)
7. Vinho Regional Duriense
8. Porto (p. 295)
9. Vinho Verde (p. 294)
10. Vinho Regional Transmontano

SPAIN:
11. Málaga and Sierras de Málaga
12. Jerez-Xérès-Sherry (p. 289)
13. Valdepeñas
14. La Mancha (p. 288)
15. Jumilla
16. Alicante
17. Valencia
18. Madrid
19. Dominio de Vadepusa
20. Toro (p. 282)
21. Rueda (p. 282)
22. Ribera del Duero (p. 282)
23. Cigales
24. Bierzo (p. 282)
25. Valdeorras

26. Monterrei
27. Ribeiro (p. 282)
28. Rías Baixas (p. 282)
29. Rioja (p. 284)
30. Navarra (p.284)
31. Campo de Borja
32. Calatayud
33. Cariñena
34. Somontano
35. Costers del Segre
36. Empordà-Costa Brava
37. Alella
38. Penedès (p. 286)
39. Priorato (p. 286)
40. Montsant
41. Terra Alta

INTRODUCTION

Vinifera grapes first reached the region of Spain in Portugal between 4000 and 3000 B.C., and by the time of the Roman Empire wine has been produced and exported from the two countries in what was once known as Iberia. (The Latin word for the Ebro River in the northeast section of the peninsula was *Iberus*.) These countries remain important wine producers to this day, Spain ranking third in the world for total production and Portugal eleventh.

Both countries have suffered through natural disasters and political upheaval, all of which adversely affected wine production. By the 1960s and 1970s, the image of wine from the Iberian Peninsula was not one of quality. Spain was known for overoaked reds and oxidized whites, and the production of its most popular wine, the fortified Sherry, was in turmoil. Outside its own borders, Portugal was known only for sweet rosé, exported in large quantities by Mateus and Lancer's, and at the other end of the price spectrum, the fortified wine, Port. In the past 30 years both countries have made extraordinary progress in modernizing the production of wine, in upgrading the quality of their table wines, and in increasing penetration into foreign markets. In both countries these improvements have been the result of close collaboration between the private sector and government agencies. The close cooperation among property owners, vintners' groups, national and regional governments, and the European Union will continue to reap impressive results. The story of wine from Spain and Portugal, begun so many thousands of years ago, is still unfolding.

HISTORY OF WINE PRODUCTION

The Phoenicians did not introduce grapevines to the Iberian Peninsula; the vines were already growing there when they arrived around 1100 BC. It was the Phoenicians, however, who engaged in the first commercial winemaking on this vast peninsula. The Carthaginians (named for their home city of Carthage in North Africa) invaded Iberia around 250 BC. They ruled for 200 years, coexisting with the Romans, who had possessions east of the Ebro River. The Carthaginians greatly expanded the production of wine. At one point they were shipping wine to all parts of the extensive Roman Empire. The Romans wrested control of Iberia from the Carthaginians and colonized the whole peninsula under Emperor Augustus in the first century BC. Wine production continued, and Iberian wines were sent as far away as Normandy, England, and even the Roman frontier in Germany. The Roman Empire began its fall in the second century AD. Germanic tribes invaded the peninsula. In the fifth century AD, the Visigoth tribe came to control most of what is now western Spain and Portugal, and established a kingdom there. Records are scarce from this period, but enough have survived to offer proof that viticulture continued under the Goths.

In AD 711 the Visigoth kingdom was overthrown by the Moors, an Islamic tribe from North Africa. The Moors ruled peacefully for over 600 years and did not demand the cessation of viticulture. Even though the Prophet Mohammed forbade the consumption of wine (or any alcohol), the Moors did not impose their ways

FIGURE 8.1

This old engraving depicts Queen Isabella and King Ferdinand of Spain as they send Columbus off on his trip that led to the discovery of a whole new world outside Europe for Spanish and Portuguese trade.

© The Art Gallery Collection/Alamy

on the local culture. Wine was taxed, and perhaps the conquerors were wise enough to recognize the need for these revenues. At any rate, Christians and Jews were allowed to continue making and consuming wines under the Moors.

In the early twelfth century, Christians began to rise against the Moors to drive them from the peninsula. During this time, Navarra, Aragon, Castilla y León, and Barcelona in Spain were under Christian rule, and in 1136 Portugal declared itself a Christian kingdom. By 1320, Christians were largely successful in their efforts to reconquer Iberia. Only Granada in southern Spain remained under Moorish rule. Between 1300 and 1500, trade with the rest of Europe increased considerably.

SPANISH WINE— HISTORICAL PERSPECTIVE

In January 1492, Spain became a united Christian country under one crown when the Spanish Army drove the Moors from Granada. In October of that same year, Christopher Columbus discovered the West Indies, opening up a new world for Spanish and Portuguese trade, including wines (Figure 8.1). In 1494, under the arbitration of Pope Alexander VI, the whole of the New World was divided between Portugal and Spain. The entire continent of South America became Spanish, except for Brazil, which became a colony of Portugal.

In 1492 there was yet another historic (albeit very unfortunate) event that affected the wine trade. The Spanish government decreed that all Jews who refused to be baptized as Christians must leave the country. The Spanish Inquisition, although condemned by other Europeans, did open the way for English, Dutch, and French merchants to come into Spain and build up the wine trade. The Spanish wine that attracted the most attention from these foreign traders was Sherry. By the late sixteenth century it was the best selling wine in England. Trade with other parts of Europe also greatly expanded at this time, partly because Spain, through a fortuitous royal marriage, became closely aligned with the Hapsburg Empire. This alignment gave Spanish wine producers access to Holland's exporters and their ships.

Unfortunately, the period of peaceful commercial enterprise did not last. Relations between Spain and England began to deteriorate after Henry VIII divorced Catherine of Aragon in 1533. Tensions escalated into war within a few decades. Trade declined and remained sporadic even after the English defeated the Spanish Navy in 1588. The English imposed heavy excise taxes on Spanish wine, so the

Spaniards concentrated on building their wine business elsewhere in Europe and in the New World, while the Portuguese stepped in as primary supplier of wine to England. Unfortunately for the Spanish, their colonies in South America turned out to be a less lucrative market than hoped. Peru and Chile were so successful at viticulture that they were soon meeting all domestic demand for wine themselves and imported very little from Spain.

Demand for wine did pick up throughout Europe during the seventeenth century as the population increased during a time of relative peace. Gradually wine became an integral part of daily life for many Europeans, especially in cities. The increase in sales of Spanish wines into other parts of Europe continued into the eighteenth century. A small portion of Spanish wine was also exported to the British colonies in the New World. By the late eighteenth and early nineteenth centuries the Spanish wine trade was well established, both to the domestic market and to export markets. By 1825, for instance, two-thirds of wine imported into England was Spanish, most of it Sherry (Phillips, 2000). During the early nineteenth century, vineyard acreage in Spain increased fourfold. By 1850, wine constituted fully one-third of all Spanish exports.

The lucrative expansion of wine production in Spain was dealt a severe blow with the arrival of the devastating phylloxera. The vine-destroying louse made its first appearance on the Iberian Peninsula in 1878, and by 1901 had spread to the vineyards of Rioja. From there the infestation moved across Spain, and the wine business was decimated. The only positive aspect is that after phylloxera was controlled many inferior vineyards were not replanted to grapevines. Moreover, on the advice of French vintners who had come to Spain after French wine regions were destroyed by phylloxera, many vineyards were replanted, not to the lesser grapes that had been there, but to higher quality varietals.

Spain was unable to continue the improvement of its wine production and its expansion into foreign markets because of the political turmoil created by the Spanish Civil War of 1936–1939 and the isolation resulting from the dictatorial regime of General Francisco Franco, who ruled the country from the end of the Civil War until his death in November 1975. In the years since Franco's death, Spain has recovered remarkably and is now a thoroughly modern and prosperous nation. As the nation has progressed into the twenty-first century so has its wine trade. The revitalization of the wine industry was due in part to government controls, which were instigated as early as 1926 with the demarcation of Rioja and continued with a nationwide system of quality control laws in 1972. Another factor in the recovery was the introduction of modern technology such as stainless steel fermentation tanks. Spain is now producing a range of table wines, sparkling wines, and fortified wines for which the demand around the world is steadily growing.

GOVERNMENT INVOLVEMENT

The contemporary governments of both Spain and Portugal have been actively involved with bringing their respective country's wine trade into the increasingly competitive

- *Reserva:* Red wines aged at least three years, with one of those years spent in oak barrels. Most producers of fine reds will exceed the minimum requirements for their **reserva** (reh-SEHR-vah) wines. There are also stipulations for white wines at the reserva level; however, few of these wines are exported because most consumers outside Spain do not like the oxidized character of these aged whites.
- *Gran Reserva:* Produced only in the finest years and only with the approval of the local consejo regulador, **gran reserva** (grahn reh-SEHR-vah) wines must be aged for a minimum of three years in barrels and an additional two years in bottle. Most producers exceed these minimums to give their wines more richness and smoothness. Some Gran Reservas are not released until eight or more years after the vintage year. These reds are wonderfully complex and subtle. Figure 8.3 shows an example of a gran reserva label.

Wine Regions of Spain

The Iberian Peninsula is the westernmost outpost of continental Europe. Its climate is strongly influenced by the Mediterranean Sea to the east and by the Atlantic to the north and west. Four of Iberia's five major rivers, including the Duero/Douro (the Duero is called the Douro once it crosses into Portugal), flow westward and drain into the Atlantic; the fifth, the Ebro, flows southeast to the Mediterranean. Iberia is a large and diverse area, with numerous climatic and cultural differences.

Spain encompasses most of the Iberian Peninsula. This country has 3.5 million acres (1.4 million hectares) of grapevines, more than any other country in the world. Because of a very arid climate in most of the country and a ban on irrigation, yields are very low, averaging 1.4 tons per acre (22 hectoliters/hectare). In the vast central plain and in the southernmost sections, rainfall is minimal and temperatures are high during the long growing season. Only in the north, at the foot of the Pyrenees Mountains that separate Spain from France and in Galicia on the northwestern coast, are temperatures more moderate and rainfall adequate. In these cooler regions, the primary grape varietals for white wines are Viura (also called Macabeo), **Albariño** (ahl-bah-REE-n'yoh), especially prominent in Galicia, and Verdejo. For red wines the most important varietals are **Tempranillo** (tem-prah-NEE-yoh), in some regions called Tinto Fino, which is the most widely planted of the quality wine-producing varietals, and **Garnacha** (gahr-NAH-chah), the Grenache of southern France, the second most planted red varietal. As we move inland and south, conditions are less suited to the early ripening varietals. In the sun-baked Central Plain the drought-resistant white grape, **Airén** (ahr-yehn), is widely planted, covering three times the acreage of any other varietal. Also widely planted in the Central Plain and even further south is the red grape Monestrell (the Mourvèdre of France's Rhône valley). In Spain's warmest and driest section, the southern Andalucía province, most vineyards are planted to the grapes from which Sherry is made—**Palomino** and **Pedro Ximénez**.

Spain is divided into 17 autonomías, or "autonomous communities," analogous to the 50 states in the United States. Most of these regions have demarcated wine zones, or DOs, within their boundaries (see the map of Spain). The majority of DOs are in the cooler, more humid northern regions. Next, we cover in some detail the most important DOs of the north, then touch briefly on the large central plain before moving to the south, where Spain's famous fortified wine, Sherry, is made.

Reading a Spanish Wine Label

This is the name of the winery (**bodega** in Spanish) that made the wine. Montecillo is one of the oldest (founded 1874) and most respected bodegas in Rioja. In Portugal the word for winery or estate is **quinta**.

Vintage Year: The Spanish *DO* laws require that at least 85 percent of the grapes be harvested in that year.

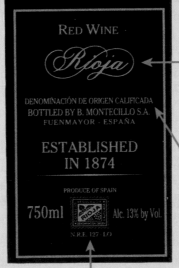

Gran Reserva: Indicates that this wine received additional aging. Each *DO* region has its own requirements for the gran reserva and reserva designations. In Rioja the requirements for gran reserva are 5 additional years of aging, 3 in oak and 2 in bottle.
Portugal has comparable terms: Garrafeira signifies a wine with 2 1/2 years in oak casks and 1 year in bottle. The term reserva on a Portuguese wine shows that the wine is a garrafeira from an exceptional vintage.

Appellation: Designated wine region, in this case, Rioja.

Denominación de Origen (DO): Spanish term for a defined region that produces quality wine. Note that in this case the label says *Denominación de Origen Calificada* (*DOCa*). This is the highest classification for a wine region. Rioja is the only region to be granted this designation thus far.
In Portugal the comparable term for a designated wine region is *Denominação de Origem Controlada* (*DOC*).

Grupo Osborne, permission granted by Janet Kafka and Associates

Seal: The official seal of the local *Consejo Regulador*, the agency that oversees wine production in that region. The presence of such a seal from any *DO* guarantees that the wine conforms to the regulations of that region.

FIGURE 8.3

Gran reserva wines from Bodega Montecillo are made from 95 percent Tempranillo and often receive more than the required three years of aging in oak.

FIGURE 8.8

Freixenet is one of Spain's largest producers of Cava.

Grupo Osborne, permission granted by Janet Kafka and Associates

performs particularly well in higher-altitude vineyards and contributes the earthy aromas connoisseurs now associate with Cava. Some major Cava houses are blending in more of the French transplant, Chardonnay. Total production of Cava is now over 12.5 million cases per year. Major producers include Codorníu, Freixenet (Figure 8.8), Paul Cheneau, and Segura Viudas (owned by Freixenet). Cava is popular in markets around the world for its fresh, fruity flavors, delicate mousse, and very affordable price tag.

Priorato is the second region of Spain to attain DOCa status. It was elevated to this august level only in 2004. Priorato is a small region (only 4,300 acres [1,740 hectares] under vine) surrounded by the large DO of Tarragona. It is in the rugged mountains at the western edge of Tarragona. The soil is volcanic, full of flecks of mica that catch the sun's heat and reflect it onto the ripening grapes. The region has cold winters but long, hot, and very dry summers. The grapes, mostly Garnacha and Cariñena (called Mazuelo elsewhere in Spain), get very ripe in these conditions. The result is a very full-bodied, intense red wine with high alcohol levels (the legal minimum is 13.5 percent but the wine usually goes higher). Winemaking has changed little here since the Carthusian monks began making it at their priory (which gave the region its name) in the twelfth century. However, several producers, among them the Penedès firm of René Barbier and the local vintner Alvaro Palacios, are experimenting with modern technology such as cool fermentation and aging in French oak barrels, and careful blending with French *vinifera* grapes, especially Cabernet Sauvignon and Syrah. Some of the new reds coming out of Priorato are so good that they are putting this DO in contention with Ribera del Duero as the region most likely to topple Rioja from its traditional position as Spain's premier wine region.

La Mancha

The Central Plain of Spain is unimaginably vast and incredibly flat. The DO La Mancha covers most of the autonomía of Castilla-La Mancha. Vineyards stretch as far as the eye can see, broken only occasionally by small groves of olive trees and fields of cereal grains. There are almost a half a million acres (191,700 hectares) of vineyards in this very large DO. La Mancha produces as much as one-third of Spain's total wine production each year. Most of the wine is sold in bulk, distilled into brandy, or used to make vinegar. Over 80 percent of the acreage is devoted to one grape, the white Airén, a varietal of little character and barely adequate acidity. However, it is one of the few varietals able to survive in the barren plain, where winters are long and bleak, and summers are short, arid, and relentlessly sunny and hot. Even with improved modern technology such as cool fermentation in stainless steel tanks, it is impossible, with such a harsh climate and an inferior varietal, to produce much wine that rises above the level of a solid low-alcohol everyday quaffer—light, clean, with a touch of pleasant fruit.

The local Consejo Regulado is encouraging growers to pull out Airén and replace it with the other allowed varietals including Tempranillo, which in this part of Spain is referred to as Cencibel, that can, with carbonic maceration, be made into decent soft red wines. However, most growers are choosing to stay with the tried-and-true, so it appears that for the immediate future, La Mancha will continue to be the source of a seemingly endless supply of bulk white wine.

Andalucía: Jerez (Sherry)

The great fortified wine, **Sherry**, made in the small Jerez section of Andalucía in southern Spain (Figure 8.9), is a wine misunderstood and underappreciated in the American market. (The word "Sherry" is an English corruption of *Jerez*.) Few consumers here realize that Sherry can be a crisp, bone-dry aperitif (**fino** [FEE-noh]) or a luscious, deeply flavored dessert wine (**oloroso** [oh-loh-ROH-soh]), with a range of styles in between. With governmental promotional efforts such as "Wines from Spain," a program organized under the aegis of the Commercial Office of Spain to educate foreign consumers, more Americans are discovering how versatile and delicious Sherry can be.

Sherry-making is a time-honored tradition in Jerez. Today the viticulture and winemaking, although adhering to tradition, are thoroughly modern. The grapes used, Palomino and Pedro Ximénez, are well adapted to the dry, warm climate. Very little rain falls during the long summers, and the porous chalky soils allow vines to push deep to find the retained ground water.

Once harvested, usually in early September, the grapes are brought to the huge wineries owned by the major Sherry houses, where they go through a normal first fermentation until all natural sugars are converted. The new wine is run off into casks that are taken down to the cellars of the bodegas, where they are left as the **flor** (FLAWR), yeast forms on the surface of the wine (Figure 8.10; see also Chapter 3). Wines are normally produced using the yeast *Saccharomyces cerevisiae*, which grows using the sugar in grape juice anaerobically (without oxygen) to produce alcohol and carbon dioxide. Flor yeast will continue to grow after the sugar has been consumed by using the alcohol in

FIGURE 8.9

A view of Andalucía's beautiful sunny coast.
© Mila Petkova/Shutterstock

FIGURE 8.13

For centuries, flat boats like these were used to transport casks of young Port wine from the wineries in the Upper Douro down the Douro River to blending and aging facilities in the city of Oporto. However, since the river was dammed in the 1960s, this method of transport has disappeared in favor of other types of transport such as trailer truck.

© Alan Smillie/Shutterstock

Fortified with clear grape brandy whose high alcohol content (77 percent) kills the yeast cells before fermentation is completed, Port has a natural sweetness from the sugars that were prevented from fermenting. The final product is between 18 and 20 percent alcohol and about 10% sugar.

Since the fermentation is arrested (stopped) with brandy when it is only halfway completed; the amount of time the juice stays in contact with the skins is relatively brief. To extract maximum color and tannins in the short time available the juice and skins are mixed together vigorously and often. Traditionally this was done by treading the skins by foot in shallow stone fermenters called lagares, but today the maceration is done primarily by mechanical means. When it has fermented down to about 13°Brix, the must is pressed, fortified with brandy, and then pumped into barrels where it rests through the winter in the quintas located in the Douro valley near the vineyards. A **quinta** "(KEEN-tah)" is a small winery. The following spring the wine is shipped to the coastal city of Oporto where the Douro River spills into the Atlantic (Figure 8.13). Here the major Port companies, such as Croft, Fonseca, and Dow, have their caves or aging facilities. In these facilities, under the watchful eye of the inspectors from the Instituto do Vinho do Porto, the wine is classified, aged, bottled, and eventually shipped to markets throughout Europe and the New World. Many of these companies have British names as they were founded by British families, originally as export houses. By law no more than one-third of a company's stock can be released for sale in any year.

Bairrada and Dão

The Vinho Regional Beiras is a large region that stretches the width of Portugal, south of Vinho Verde and Douro, from the Atlantic Coast inland to the mountains that separate Portugal and Spain. There are two noteworthy DOCs in Beiras.

Bairrada runs parallel to the Atlantic Ocean, several miles inland from the coast. Bairrada extends from the city of Aveira south to the historic village of Coimbra. Wine had been produced in this region for centuries before the Marquis de Pombal, Portugal's powerful Prime Minister, in 1756 ordered all the vines in Bairrada ripped out as part of his effort to eliminate the fraudulent adulteration of Port. It took Bairrada 200 years to recover, but after strenuous efforts on the part of its many small property owners, it was recognized as an official wine region in 1979, and now carries Denominação de Origem Controlada status.

The soils of Bairrada are primarily heavy but fertile clay. Over 70 percent of the vineyards are planted to one varietal, the hearty Baga (Parode, 2008), which produces the stout, dark, tannic red wine for which the region is famous. When Bairrada was elevated to DOC status, the law required that all red wines must contain at least 50 percent Baga. That law was changed in 2003 to say that only the wines with the "Bairrado Classico" designation need to be 50 percent Baga. There are seven other red grapes also allowed. Some of the more traditionalist vintners reject the "international varietals" like Syrah and Cabernet Sauvignon that have been planted here over the past two decades. They prefer to still adhere to the old method and use a majority of Baga for their big, tannic full-bodied red wines.

STYLES OF PORT

The aging process determines a Port's style, and there are two basic categories. Wood-matured Ports are left for a short time in large wooden casks to age and are ready to be drunk when, after fining, filtering, and bottling, they are released. Bottle-aged Ports, on the other hand, are intended to be aged further upon release. They are aged a short time in wood in the caves, then without filtration, are put into the bottles in which they may take up to 20 to 30 years to fully mature. Within these broad categories there are several different styles.

Ruby

This is the youngest and simplest style of Port (Figure 8.14). Named for the deep red color it retains upon release, **ruby Port** is meant to be consumed early. The berry flavors are robust and aggressive. In the making of ruby, wine from several vintages are blended together and aged briefly in large casks or perhaps steel tanks before being filtered and bottled.

Tawny

This term can be applied loosely to cover a variety of styles. One would assume that the amber color has evolved over years of barrel aging. However, most commercial tawnys are not much older than rubies, but without the fresh fruit flavors. The light color of **tawny Port** is not attained through patient aging in wood barrels thus allowing deliberate oxidation. Rather, the amber color of tawnys is achieved either by fermenting inferior, lighter-colored grapes or by blending in, after fermentation, some white Port. Approximately 80 percent of Port is simple ruby or commercial tawny.

FIGURE 8.14

Ruby Port is rich, smooth, and full of ripe berry flavors. From reliable producers like Osborne, Ruby Port represents very good value.

Grupo Osborne, permission granted by Janet Kafka and Associates

(Continues)

Aged Tawny

This style of tawny Port comes by its color legitimately, as it must be aged in wood casks for six years or more. Aging not only imparts the golden color, but also gives the wine a smooth, soft texture as tannins polymerize. Aged tawny carries an indication of age, either 10, 20, 30, or over 40 years, which is an average of the ages of the various vintages of wines blended together in that bottling. Aged tawnys are made from high-quality grapes, and must pass a taste test by the IVP before being bottled. The best Tawnys have delicate flavors of roasted nuts, honey, and dried fruit. The older the wine, the more subtle and profuse the flavors. Needless to say, as the age increases, so does the price.

Vintage Port

Occasionally an unusually warm and sunny summer will produce grapes of extraordinary character and ripeness. When this occurs, a Port maker will hold the resulting wine apart, rather than blending it in with the wine already aging in his cellars. After a year of careful aging, the winemaker will assess the wine again to determine if it is of a high enough quality to make into a vintage Port. If so, the company will send a sample to the IVP, along with a statement of its intent. If the wine passes the analysis of the IVP, the Port maker can declare a vintage. The single-vintage wine is then aged a further two to three years in wood barrels before being bottled and released. Thereafter the buyer takes over the aging, often holding the vintage Port for an additional 20 to 30 years. During this time the wine will throw considerable sediment, and it will need to be decanted before serving.

Port producers consider their vintage Port to be their

FIGURE 8.15

This 1999 vintage Port was bottled four years after the harvest and is ready to be consumed, although it will improve for many years to come.

Grupo Osborne, permission granted by Janet Kafka and Associates

flagship bottling. These are the rarest and most expensive of Ports. Only 1 percent of Port sold is from this category. Producers use only the best grapes from their finest vineyards. The greatest vintage Ports are velvety smooth and incredibly rich with deep but delicate flavors. Outstanding recent vintages for Port include 1977, 1982, 1985, 1991, 1994, 1997, 2000, 2003, and 2007.

Fine vintage Port, from quality producers such as Delaforce, Croft, Warre, Fonseca, Dow's, Osborne, González-Byass, and Taylor Fladgate & Yeatman, are in high demand in the United States as well as in Great Britain and continental Europe. Vintage Port is usually served as the culmination of a fine meal, accompanied by sharply flavored cheeses such as Stilton or aged cheddar, and walnuts or dried fruits.

LBV Port

Late-bottled vintage (LBV) Port is a single-vintage wine bottled between the fourth and sixth year after harvest. Most of these wines have been filtered and cold stabilized before bottling, so they throw less sediment than vintage Port. Unfortunately, too often the filtration is excessive, stripping the wine of much of its character. Traditional-style LBV is bottled without filtration, and must be decanted before serving. LBV wines are made in good years that were not good enough to be declared a vintage. They need less time to mature than a vintage Port, and can be consumed within five years after bottling (Figure 8.15).

Vintage Character

These are based on ruby Ports that are blended from several vintages and aged 4 to 5 years in oak casks before bottling. Good quality wine but it does not have the intense flavors found in vintage Port. Usually sold under proprietary names by major Port Houses, they are meant to be consumed soon after bottling.

White Port

White Port is made in essentially the same method as red, except that the degree of maceration is much less. Brandy is added to arrest fermentation at the same stage, leaving residual (or unfermented) sugars. White Ports, therefore, are medium-sweet, with fat, grapelike flavors. Alcohol content is between 16.5 and 17 percent as opposed to the 19 to 20 percent common in red Port. White Ports are usually aged no longer than 18 months, primarily in stainless steel tanks. White Port that does spend some time in wood has a golden color and nutty flavor. It is usually served chilled as an aperitif.

Most growers sell their grapes to one of the six cooperatives. However, larger private estates, such as that owned by Luis Pato, are emerging, where efforts are under way to produce Baga-based reds of more refinement. Two large corporations based in Bairrada, Sogrape and Aliança, are also using modern vinification methods to make wines that are less rustic and more approachable.

Dão lies inland to the east of Bairrada. Surrounded on three sides by high, granite-laden hills, Dão is protected from the winds and moisture of the Atlantic. It has the reputation of producing some of Portugal's finest red table wines. Unfortunately, the region was ill served by the Salazar government's efforts to assist wine production by forcing the creation of many cooperatives and then restricting the sale of grapes to private producers. Standards fell as individual involvement was stifled. Such monopolistic practices were deemed inappropriate by the European Union and were discontinued upon Portugal's admission to that group in 1986. Now, with many talented individual vintners, Dão has reemerged as a producer of fine table wines, with a strong adherence to traditional grapes. As one wine writer has said about the Dão, "This is one of the last places where tradition remains simply a way of life" (Voss, 2009).

Red grapes thrive in the granite-based soils, and 80 percent of the region's wine production is red. Many of the vineyards are on steep, terraced vineyards in the hills. There are nine red grapes authorized, the most important being Touriga Nacional. According to a recently passed law, all Dão reds must now be at least 30 percent Touriga Nacional. These reds spend several months in oak barrels, and when released they are mellow, with vanilla tones mingling with natural red-berry and black pepper flavors.

White grapes are planted in the sandier, flatter area at the western edge of Dão. Most prominent of these is the Encruzado, a top grape with nice fruit and good acidity. It is unfortunately a low-yielding varietal. Other white grapes, such as Malvasia Fina (here called Arinto do Dão) and the ominously named Borrado das Moscas ("fly-droppings") are blended in. Dão whites, when not overly oaked or oxidized, can be fresh, crisp, and fragrant.

Setúbal

The Setúbal Peninsula, south of Lisbon, Portugal's capital city, protrudes into the Atlantic between the estuaries of the Sado and Tagus Rivers. The ocean and rivers provide moderating influences on the climate, and the warm temperatures and regular rainfall are excellent for growing grapes. The fishing town of Setúbal lends its name to the peninsula, and Terras do Sado is the regional name for the wide range of table wines made on the peninsula. The most famous wine, though, is a sweet fortified wine that also carries the name Setúbal, now a DOC. In 1907, the region was demarcated as Moscatel de Setúbal for the principal grape, Moscatel (Muscat). However, EU regulations state that to include the name of a varietal, a wine must be made at least 85 percent from that grape, and local customs allow as much as 30 percent of other grapes. Accordingly, since 1986 the DOC has been simply Setúbal.

Moscatel de Setúbal is made in the same manner as other fortified, naturally sweet wine, that is, fermentation is arrested with extra grape spirits before all natural sugars have a chance to ferment. The wine then has an extended maceration period with the Muscat skins, which gives a pronounced taste of fresh grapes to the wine. After as many as five months of maceration, the wine spends four to five years in large wooden casks.

By the end of that time, the wine is deep gold in color, smooth and rich, and intensely flavored. The lively acidity prevents Setúbal from being cloying. A glass of this ambrosial wine, full of spice, caramel, honey, walnut, and dried apricot flavors, is a dessert unto itself.

Near the Setubal Peninsula is the DOC of Bucelas, just east of Lisbon, Bucelas is one of the few Portuguese wine regions more famous for its whites than its reds. The cool climate and slate-filled soil are perfect for the Arinto grape. The resulting wines are a greenish-straw color, have a perfumed nose, and are very dry and clean.

Alentejo

Alentejo is a huge agricultural region, stretching from the Tagus River east to the border with Spain and encompassing one-third of Portugal's land mass. It is known as the country's breadbasket, covered as it is with grain farms. Portugal provides one half the world's cork, and Alentejo contains the majority of the country's cork forests.

After a period of disarray following the military-led uprisings of 1974 and 1975, Alentejo is again emerging as an important source of good table wines, with considerable help from the EU in the form of financial investment and technical advice. The climate is not conducive to growing quality grapes, with very limited rainfall (as low as 23 inches [59 cm] a year) and extreme temperatures that often soar to over 100°F (38°C) in summer. Careful vinification with modern technology such as temperature-controlled fermentation tanks compensates for nature's extremes. Red wines are made mostly from Aragonêz (local name for Tinta Roriz or Tempranillo), which lends elegance, Periquita with its blackberry and licorice aromas, and Trincadeira Preta which lends body and structure. After months in French oak barrels, the red wines emerge as complex, approachable, and long-lived, perfect accompaniments for the roasted meats and pungent cheeses of the local cuisine.

Seven villages within Alentejo have been granted DOC status, including Borba and Redondo. The small rural village of Evora, better known for the breeding farms that produce the proud animals for Spain's bull-fighting rings, is currently an IPR and under consideration as a DOC. There are also excellent wines coming out of other regions of Portugal, including Ribatejo, and Estremadura, as well as the small Terras do Sado south of Lisbon.

Madeira

The small island of Madeira (only 36 miles [58 km] long and 15 miles [24 km] wide) lies off the coast of Africa, a short plane ride from Lisbon. Its sparkling sunshine and white beaches make it a favorite vacation spot for European tourists. Claimed by Prince Henry of Portugal in 1420, the island was soon the site of vineyards. The soil is mineral-rich clay atop volcanic rock, sunshine and rainfall are abundant, and the terraced slopes of the southeastern facing hills were soon producing high-quality wine. With the help of British merchants, Madeira wines were soon shipped to the Continent and the New World. By 1768, Madeira was demarcated as an official wine region.

In the mid-1800s shippers began to fortify the wine with additional alcohol so it could better withstand the long sea voyages. It was further discovered that the heat in the ships' holds gave the wine additional smoothness and richness. Today modern equipment is used, but the winemaking process is essentially the same. After vinification, during which brandy is added to arrest fermentation, the wine is placed for three to four months in an *estufa*, a heated vat that emulates the sun and shipboard heat of yore and imparts comparable qualities, including the distinctive nutty flavor. (A small percentage is heated naturally by being put in wood barrels and stored for up to 20 years in hot attics.) After the aging and heating are complete, sweetening in the form of caramel will be added to various degrees, depending on the style of Madeira being made. The whole process is carefully regulated by Madeira's quality control agency, Insituto do Vinho da Madeira, or IVM.

Even though 85 percent of the island's vineyards are planted to the lesser red grape, Tinta Negra Mole, quality Madeira is made from four premium white grapes. In accordance with EU regulations, each style of Madeira contains at least 85 percent of the grape for which it is named. In ascending order of sweetness, the styles of Madeira are Sercial, Verdelho, Bual, and Malmsey.

> *Sercial:* The most delicate and lightest, with naturally high acidity, this dry, assertively flavored wine makes an excellent aperitif, especially good when matched with hors d'oeuvres of smoked fish or paté de foie gras.
> *Verdelho:* With higher sugar content and lower acidity than Sercial, Verdelho is made in an off-dry style. It, too, is very good as an aperitif.
> *Bual (Boal):* A heavier, richer wine, made in a sweet or semisweet style. The dark deep Bual with its intense raisin flavors can be served with caramel or coffee-flavored dessert. The Bual grape is the vinifera, Semillon.
> *Malmsey:* This is the sweetest and longest lived of the Madeiras. It is made from Malvasia grapes grown in the warmest, sunniest vineyards where they achieve maximum ripeness and sugar levels. Additional richness and concentration of flavors are acquired during several years in wooden casks. The rich flavors and high sugar content are never cloying because the acidity levels remain high. These extraordinary wines can retain their beautiful complex flavors for as long as 100 years.

SUMMARY

The progress made in the wine trade in both Spain and Portugal in the last half of the twentieth century, especially in the 24 years since both joined the European Union in 1986, is truly remarkable. A number of factors including: innovation in the vineyard, modernization of facilities, utilization of computers to streamline vinification, investing in research and teaching facilities, and cooperation between governments and private companies all worked together to improve the quality of the wine. The progress in the vineyard and the winery was matched by sophisticated marketing strategies and aggressive promotional programs that were aided by close cooperation between the government and businesspeople. All of these efforts were made possible by investment at the continental (EU), national, provincial, and local levels. All of these factors combined have helped move Spain's and Portugal's many wines into competitive and constantly improving positions within the worldwide marketplace.

SPANISH FOOD AND WINE PAIRING

appetizer
**gazpacho (a tomato-based raw
vegetable soup served chilled)**

Wine

Fresh white, light in body: Albariño from Rias Biaxas

second course
tortilla española (potato omelette)

Wine

Rosada: fruity, clean rosé made from the Garnarcha grape

main course
**valencian paella (casserole of rice, duck,
and green beans flavored with saffron)**

Wine

A red from Navarra, medium bodied,
very flavorful, and well structured

dessert
arroz con leche (rice pudding)

Wine

Small glass of oloroso Sherry, very rich and sweet

EXERCISES

1. Define the term *gran reserva* in Spanish wine law.

2. List some of the responsibilities of the two government agencies, Spain's INDO and Portugal's IVV.

3. What is the winemaking process that is used to make Cava? Describe how Cava differs from Champagne.

4. How has membership in the European Union affected the quality and marketing of wines produced in Portugal and Spain?

REVIEW QUESTIONS

1. What is the principal red grape of Rioja?

3. What is the most widely planted grape in Navarra?

4. What is the highest level of classification within Portugal's quality control laws?

5. Sherry is produced in what region of Spain?

6. Name the 11 vinho regional areas in Portugal.

7. Why is ruby Port still red while tawny Port is a golden color?

REFERENCES

Lord, T. (1988). *The New Wines of Spain*. San Francisco: The Wine Appreciation Guild. Spain, France, USA, Chile and Argentina. Madrid, Spain: Universidad Rey Juan Carlos Press.

Parode, N. (2008, November). *Bairrada: Home to the Baga grape*. Retrieved from http://www.intowine.com

Phillips, R. (2000). *A Short History of Wine*. New York: HarperCollins.

Voss, R. (2009, August). Portugal's changing center. *Wine Enthusiast*, 41–43.

{ GERMANY }

This chapter describes Germany's climate and geography and lists its major wine regions, while describing the styles of wine produced in each region. It also covers the German wine laws and their effectiveness, and explains how to decipher the information on a German wine label.

GERMANY:

1. Baden (p. 332)
2. Württemberg (p. 333)
3. Franken (p. 333)
4. Hessische Bergstrasse (p. 332)
5. Pfalz (p. 331)
6. Rheinhessen (p. 330)
7. Nahe (p. 332)

8. Rheingau (p. 327)
9. Mittelrhein (p. 332)
10. Ahr (p. 331)
11. Mosel-Saar-Ruwer (p. 323)
12. Saale-Unstrut (p. 333)
13. Sachsen (p. 333)

INTRODUCTION

In the United States, it seems that the least understood and most underappreciated category of wine is German whites. In the 1960s and early 1970s, when postwar production began to pick up in Europe, the bulk of German wine to reach these shores was made up of inferior, slightly sweet wines of the Liebfraumilch category. These heavily marketed brands, such as Blue Nun and Black Tower, dominated the U.S. market to such a degree that American consumers came to assume that all German wines are slightly sweet whites of lower quality. In actuality, most German whites are dry or barely off-dry. The whites, especially those based on the noble varietals, are wonderfully food-compatible and lovely sipping wines. Moreover, about one-third of Germany's total wine production is red. This represents a large increase over the past 10 years, primarily due to a surge in domestic demand. Germany is a far more versatile producer of wines than many Americans realize.

Another factor that has worked against the wider acceptance of German wines in this market is the indecipherability of their wine labels. German wine labels provide more explicit information than those of any other country. Unless one knows what to look for, however, it is intimidating to see all those words on a label, and the Gothic script that is commonly used does little to help.

The effort to learn about the varying styles of German wines, the evolution of Germany's wine laws (an ongoing process), and the philosophy behind the making of these versatile wines is well worth it. Germany is responsible for just under 5 percent of the world's total wine production, but its best wines are in the highest tiers of quality.

This meticulously tended vineyard is typical of many in Germany, with its rows closely spaced on a steep hillside. Notice how carefully the rows follow the slope of the land at the bottom of the photo, allowing maximum exposure to sunlight.
© Nigel Cattlin/Alamy

Winemaking is an ancient tradition in what is now Germany. There is credible evidence to suggest that viticulture was brought to the region by the Romans during the time of the expansion of the Roman Empire. In AD 570, the northern Italian poet Venantius Fortunatus mentioned steeply terraced vineyards along the Mosel River near the city of Trier (Robinson, 2006). Trier, the oldest city in Germany, was founded in AD 16 by the Roman emperor Augustus and archeological research near that city points to grape cultivation from that same era. Thus, grape growing and winemaking in Germany date from the first century.

Up until the time of Charlemagne, king of the Franks from 771 to 814, vineyards were concentrated on the west side of the Rhine (Rhein in German), in the region of Alsace and down the Rhine through the Palatinate (the Pfalz and Rheinhessen of today). Grape growing for wine extended along the Nahe River, a major tributary to the Rhine, and farther north along the banks of the Mosel and its two tributaries, the Saar and the Ruwer. The northernmost of these old Roman viticultural regions was the valley of the Ahr River.

Areas to the east of the Rhine, which were beyond the scope of Roman occupation, were not planted until later, as Christian monks moved into these districts to build their monasteries and spread the word of Christianity. In Franken, for instance, monks started planting vineyards in the eighth century, and Bavaria was widely planted to grape vines during the seventh century.

As in other parts of Europe during the Middle Ages, it was the Church and its monasteries and convents that owned many of the vineyards, and it was the monks, priests, and nuns who were responsible for keeping viticulture alive during that dark, unstable period (Figure 9.1). The members of religious orders maintained the tradition

FIGURE 9.1

The Cistercian monastery in the town of Eberbach on the Rhine has been producing wine for more than 850 years. Pictured here is the room holding the original wine presses. In this room the laymen worked (supervised by the monks), and here they were served their meals.

© clearlens/Shutterstock

of making fine wines and perfected winemaking methodology. They also provided the principal market for wine, both for consumption with their meal and for use in the sacraments. Some of Germany's most famous vineyards were planted and tended by religious orders during the High Middle Ages, and still bear the names that signify their religious origins.

As viticultural practices improved and acreage under vine increased, production in medieval Germany eventually exceeded demand. Wine could be exported. Part of the commerce in wine was controlled by royalty and the aristocracy, and certainly princes stepped in to collect their share of excise taxes and tariffs, including tolls along the rivers that provided the main method of transport of wine from grape-growing districts to the ports of trade farther north. As trade with northern German cities, England, the Low Countries, and Scandinavia expanded, the Church and aristocracy could not handle every facet of the growing business. Expansion in trade gave rise to the bourgeoisie, or middle class. The wine merchants traded German wine for heavier red wines from France, and to Scandinavia for fish and grain, and to England for grain and other foodstuffs.

The Thirty Years' War (1618–1648) dealt a severe blow to Germany's emerging wine trade. Many vineyards were torn out or allowed to deteriorate badly. However, by the late 1700s, winemaking and the concurrent trade were back on track in most regions. At this time governors, grape growers, and middle-class merchants worked together to create a system of regulations that set quality standards for wine and simplified wine naming. Strong emphasis was put on planting more of the noble grape varietals that were proven performers in the cool climate, especially Riesling. Authorities and peers also discouraged landowners from planting vineyards in locations that could not produce quality fruit (Figure 9.2). In the early nineteenth century, as the tensions between the German states and France, and among the German states themselves, began to dissolve, internal customs and tariffs slowly disappeared. At the same time, transportation improved, especially as the railroads expanded. These two factors

FIGURE 9.2

This historic village in the Mittelrhein, with its banked vineyards on steep slopes, old stone houses, historic cathedral, and commercial activity along the river, is typical of Germany's picturesque wine country.

RF/Binder Partners

Reading a German Wine Label

Designation, or Prädikat: the designation indicates level of ripeness of the grapes at harvest, and therefore, the style of the wine. There are six Prädikat categories in chronological order of picking and in descending order of ripeness.
Kabinett: The lowest level of ripeness. Wines at this level are slightly off-dry.
Spätlese: Grapes for this category are picked later ("spät" means "late"). The wines are off-dry with more body.
Auslese: "Selected" grapes are picked later, and have higher sugar levels. The wines are definitely off-dry and quite rich.
Beerenauslese: Individual bunches are picked after being partially infected with *Botrytis cinerea,* the "noble rot." These wines are rich, sweet dessert wines.
Eiswein: Eiswein, like Beerenauslese, are partially botrytized bunches of grapes picked after the first hard frost in which the grapes are frozen.
Trockenbeerenauslese: Literally translates as "selected dried berries." These grapes are picked once they are fully botrytized, that is, shriveled up by the fungus. Sugars are very concentrated, and the resulting wine is very sweet and rich in texture.

Region: Mosel-Saar-Ruwer is one of the 13 official wine regions.

Gutsabfüllung: Estate-bottled. This means the Weis family owns the portion of the Goldtröpfchen vineyard from which these grapes were harvested.

Quality Level: "Qualitätswein mit Prädikat" indicates this wine belongs to the highest level of quality.

Government Approval Number: All Prädikat wines and QbA wines must display an official approval number on their label, indicating the wine has met all standards for its level of quality.

Alcohol Content: The percentage of alcohol by volume.

Village: All grapes were grown within the borders of the town of Piesport.

VDP Logo: The initials stand for "Verbands Deutscher Prädikats-und-Qualitätsweingüter," Germany's most prestigious growers' association for Riesling.

Varietal: 85 percent must be the grape indicated.

St. Urbans-Hof

Winery Name: St. Urbans-Hof, named for the German saint of wine, is owned by the Weis family.

Vineyard: Goldtröpfchen is a famous single vineyard in the town of Piesport. 85 percent of the grapes must come from this vineyard. In Germany, there are over 2,500 individual vineyards that can be indicated on labels.

Vintage Date: By German law, 85 percent of the grapes must have been harvested in this year.

opened up the market for wine to such a degree that producers could not depend on selling their product locally. There was too much competition from the wines of other regions that were now available.

In the later nineteenth century the first designations of higher-quality wines showed up. At this time, another important development was the first attempts to produce dessert wines of specially selected or late harvest grapes. By 1830, a system of quality control laws had begun in order to describe and classify all styles and quality levels of wine. In that year, one region passed an impractical system defining 65 different levels of quality. Other states passed more workable ordinances defining quality levels with fewer tiers. Around this time several German states passed laws declaring that grapes within a vineyard were to be harvested at different times depending on their ripeness. Fortunately, a German scientist, Ferdinand Oechsle, had recently invented a method for measuring the sugar levels in grapes. The level of sugar is the clearest indication of the grapes' ripeness. Similar to the Brix method of measuring sugar discussed in Chapter 3, the **Oechsle** (UHK-sluh) system is still used today; by comparison, 1°Brix is equal to an Oechsle value of 4.08.

In 1892 the first national wine law was passed. It defined the borders of premier wine regions. It also spelled out which winemaking practices were to be controlled, such as chaptalization, the introduction of additional sugars during fermentation.

Through the nineteenth century the emphasis on quality in wine production continued. The governments of the states became involved with the wine business, through legislation to assist in exporting of wines and in the establishment of state-sponsored institutions for training and research in viticulture and winemaking. As German wines became more competitive in the international market, the owners of small plots of land, many of them peasant families or members of the bourgeoisie, lacked the resources to maintain high levels of quality through improved technology and investment in modern equipment. Several small neighboring landowners would team up into a **cooperative**, that is, a winery owned by a group of growers. This arrangement allowed pooling of resources, which resulted in an improvement in the quality of wine being produced, as well as distribution outside their local community. The cooperatives remain an important influence in German winemaking to this day.

Germany's progress toward production of high-quality wines and its participation in the international wine marketplace were dealt severe blows as the nineteenth century came to a close. Phylloxera destroyed vineyards throughout the region in the 1880s after being brought to Europe from North America. Another invader from North America, downy mildew was also a problem in this cool, damp climate, and no chemical yet existed to control it.

In the first half of the twentieth century, the German wine trade was set back by the two world wars, as was every aspect of Germany's economy and culture. The wars left vineyards decimated, labor supply limited as two generations of men were lost and foreign markets averse to German products. Fortunately, viticulture survived due to the dedicated efforts of private landowners and the increasing effectiveness of the winemaking cooperatives.

Between 1950 and 2000, the German wine trade made enormous strides forward. As the demand for the slightly sweet and very affordable Liebfraumilch increased in

European and North American markets during the 1960s and early 1970s, the temptation to produce more wine led to an increase in allowable yields per hectare, and increased use of fertilizer. Despite that weakening in quality control, Germany's best estates continued to produce some world-class wines. In the 1980s a more sophisticated base of wine consumers around the world turned away from semisweet whites and demanded dryer wines, particularly Chardonnay. Imports of German wine into the United States fell from almost 5,000,000 cases in 1980 to 1,800,000 cases in 2003. Now in the twenty-first century, German wine producers are putting more emphasis on high-quality wines. Americans are responding favorably to quality Rieslings from Germany. By the end of 2007, imports of German wines into the United States had increased to 2,100,000 cases (German Wine Institute, 2008). Although Great Britain imports more German wine in volume, in the *value* of wine imported, the United States is number one in the world. With that support, Germany is starting to reclaim its place as one of the world's greatest wine-producing countries.

WINE LAWS

Germany's quality control laws are among the strictest and most thorough. However, the country's efforts to ensure quality and consistency in wine production and to increase the marketability of its wines have created a system that is so complicated as to be counterproductive. As Germany's wine laws need to be streamlined and tightened, the labels need to be easier to read, and many groups, both private and governmental, will have to work more closely together so that their efforts are not redundant and confusing.

The original national Wine Law of 1892 defined boundaries of major regions and specified winemaking practices that were forbidden. It was amended in 1909. An important step forward for German viticulture was the Wine Law of 1930, in which many of the deficiencies of earlier laws were corrected. The definition of "quality wine" was refined, levels of quality were outlined, and certain winemaking practices that led to inferior wines were abolished. However, vineyard boundaries were often unclear, and quality levels were difficult to discern. Finally, in 1971, partly in response to pressures from the European Union and partly in response to market forces, the German government performed a major overhaul of its wine laws. The 1971 law greatly simplifies previous systems and is precise, definitive, and unambiguous. With only a few changes, this law has been the basis for producing and labeling German wines ever since.

Wine Categories

Under the Wine Law of 1971, all vineyards are delineated and registered, and the definition of a wine's quality level depends not on vineyard location, nor on yield per hectare, but on the level of ripeness of the grapes at harvest. This method of measuring quality may be precise in that the sugar at harvest is easily quantified, but it has also caused controversy because it ignores the concept of terroir, the idea that different vineyard sites can impart distinct character and superior quality to wine. Critics further object that the law could be construed as encouraging production of sweeter wines, although the international market is leaning toward dryer white wines.

The quality control laws continue to evolve (see the section "Revision to the Wine Laws" later in the chapter). Current German wine law divides its wine production into four main groups:

- **Tafelwein:** (TAH-fuh-vyn) Table wine or ordinary wine
- **Landwein:** (LAHNT-vyn) Regional wine
- **Qualitätswein bestimmter Anbaugebiet:** (kvah-lih-TAYTS-vine behr-SHTIHMT-tuhr ahn-BOW-geh-beet) Quality wine (often written as QbA)
- **Qualitätswein mit Prädikat:** (kvah-lih-TYATS-vine mitt PRAY-dee-kaht) Quality wine with designation (often written as QmP)

Tafelwein

As in other countries of the European Union, "table wine" signifies everyday wine, produced with very few, if any, standards or stipulations. This is wine to be consumed locally and is rarely exported. In Germany, the average person is more likely to drink beer on a daily basis than wine. Therefore, the demand for ordinary wine is very low. In some years as little as 2 percent of German wine production is in this category. Plain Tafelwein can have grapes grown outside Germany blended in. For Deutscher Tafelwein four large regions are defined.

- Mosel und Rhein
- Bayern
- Neckar
- Oberrhein

One of these geographic designations must show on the label.

Landwein

This designation, added in 1982 to parallel France's vin de pays designation, is rarely used. Wine at this level is assumed to be higher quality than Tafelwein as some guidelines govern its production. The regions defined for Landwein are smaller than, and fit within, the four Tafelwein regions. There are 21 Landwein regions, and the region must show on the label.

Qualitätswein bestimmter Anbaugebiet

This is the lower level of Germany's quality wine production and in most years encompasses the largest percentage of German production. The term means "quality wine from a specified geographic location." Standards of quality must be met. The grapes must be of authorized varieties and must reach a specified level of ripeness that allows natural varietal character to show (Figure 9.3). Moreover, for any grape varietal to be mentioned on the label, the wine must contain a minimum of 85 percent of that varietal. The same percentage must

FIGURE 9.3

This label from Maximillian von Othegraven is an example of a QbA label, that is, Qualitätswein bestimmter Anbaugebiet. The wine will reflect the terroir of the Mosel region, but does not indicate a style or level of ripeness.

Von Othegraven, Permission granted by Classical Wines

TABLE 9.1 German Land Designations

Division	Example	Definition
13 Anbaugebiete	Mosel-Saar-Ruwer	Specified wine regions
40 Bereiche	Saar	Smaller districts within a region
1,400 Villages	Ockfen	A specific village within the Bereich of Saar
163 Grosslagen	Scharzberg	A grouping, under one name, of several vineyards within one district or village
2,715 Einzellagen	Ockfener Bockstein	Individual small vineyard sites, each with its own name

also be true for any geographic designation of origin. The grapes must have been grown in one of the 13 approved regions or **Anbaugebiete** (AHN-bow-geh-beet). These 13 regions are subdivided into smaller geographic designations of first, a district **Bereich** (beh-RIKH), or village, and second, a group of vineyards, **Grosslage** (GROSS-lah-guh), or specific vineyard, **Einzellage** (I'n-tsuh-lah-guh) (Table 9.1). The name of the wine will sometimes incorporate the district (or village) and the vineyard site. However, most QbA labels indicate the Anbaugebiet only (Figure 9.4). Chaptalization, or the adding of natural sugars, is allowed at this level.

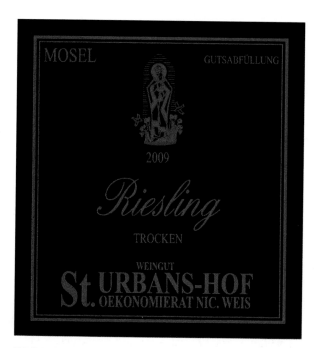

FIGURE 9.4

This is also a QbA label. Note, however, the term *Gutsabfüllung* on the St. Urbans-Hof label, which translates as "estate-bottled," signifying that the family that owns the St. Urbans-Hof winery also owns the vineyards in which the grapes for this wine were grown.

St. Urbans-Hof

Qualitätswein mit Prädikat

This is the highest category of classified wines in Germany. Translated as "quality wine with designation," the term signifies the geographic location where the grapes were grown and their level of ripeness at harvest time. The name of the wine, therefore, will have at least three words in it: the village, the vineyard (either Grosslage or Einzellage), and the **Prädikat** (preh-dih-KAHT), which shows the grapes' ripeness and hence the sweetness of the resulting wine (Figure 9.5). (No chaptalization of wines is allowed at the Prädikat level. The regulation on 85 percent minimum for grape varietal and geographic designation remains.) In 2007, in an effort to make German labels less cumbersome, the government allowed the term *Qualitätswein mit Prädikat* to be shortened to *Prädikatswein* on labels.

There are six categories of Prädikat, or special designations. In ascending order of ripeness these designations are:

1. **Kabinett:** From the word for "cabinet," the **Kabinett** (kah-bih-NEHT) category is the lightest and the driest of the Prädikat wines. Although there is often residual sugar at this level, it is often undetectable due to the racy acidity of the Riesling grape. Kabinett-level wines can be matched to a wide variety of foods and also make excellent aperitifs.

VON OTHEGRAVEN

1999
KANZEMER ALTENBERG
Riesling Auslese

UNGRAFTED VINE

Mosel · Saar · Ruwer

750 ml
alc. 10% vol

QUALITÄTSWEIN MIT PRÄDIKAT · PRODUCE OF GERMANY
GUTSABFÜLLUNG WEINGUT VON OTHEGRAVEN · 54441 KANZEM
A.P.NR 3 518 054 12 00 WWW.VON-OTHEGRAVEN.DE

V D P

FIGURE 9.5

This label from the von Othegraven estate is more specific both as to place of origin and to style. Like all Prädikat labels, it indicates the Bereich or town in which the grapes were grown (Kanzem), the single vineyard or Einzellage (Altenberg), and the Prädikat level (Auslese). The wine will be distinct in character, reflecting the terroir of the vineyard, and will be definitively off-dry in style.

Von Othegraven, Permission granted by Classical Wines

2. **Spätlese:** From the German word for "late," **Spätlese** (SHPAYT-lay-zuh) grapes are left on the vine longer and harvested when the sugar content is sufficiently high to make a slightly off-dry wine. Sugar is usually detectable in Spätlese wines, but the acidity is still fresh enough that the impression is not one of "sweetness." These wines are excellent with foods that are either very spicy (e.g., chili peppers, lemongrass), or tartly acidic (e.g., a lemon-based sauce), or have a lot of fruit (e.g., pork chops baked with apples).

3. **Auslese:** Meaning "selected," the grapes at the **Auslese** (OWS-lay-zuh) level are picked later still, when the sugar content has risen to a level that produces decidedly off-dry wine. Still nicely balanced with clean acidity to hold up the ripe fruit flavors and residual sugar, Auslese wines are nice as aperitifs. They can also be matched successfully to foods that also have a touch of sweetness, such as crabmeat, lobster, or pâté.

So far the designations are all for table wines, meant to be served during the meal. (*Note:* Do not confuse the English–American use of the term *table wine,* which merely signifies a nonsparkling, nonfortified, nonsweet wine meant to be served during meals, with the European Union's use of the term in its various wine laws. In those sets of wine laws, the term signifies a noncontrolled, lower-quality category of wine.)

The last three designations in Germany's Prädikat tier of wine production definitely fall into the category of dessert wines and are truly sweet.

4. **Beerenauslese:** Translated literally as "selected berries," the **Beerenauslese** (BAY-ruhn-OWS-lay-zuh) designation signifies grapes with high levels of sugar and some *Botrytis* (noble rot). Specific levels of sugar at harvest are spelled out in the laws for each region and each varietal. The resulting wines are gold in color, incredibly rich and ripe in flavor, with an impression of clover honey wrapping around the deep essence of the varietal. Risky to make and labor-intensive to produce, these wines are very expensive. In some drier years, noble rot does not occur and no Beerenauslese can be made at all.

5. **Eiswein:** **Eiswein** (ICE-vyn) is also richly sweet, but it is not fully botrytized. The sugars are concentrated when grapes freeze while still on the vine, sometimes into late December or even early in the new year. The grapes are picked while still frozen (Figure 9.8). When the grapes are pressed, ice crystals are

left behind and only the sweetest juice runs into the fermentation receptacle. Often the grapes show some *Botrytis* by the time they freeze. Eisweins have a higher acidity level than fully botrytized wines, even though the minimum sugar content must be at least as high as that for Beerenauslese. They reflect varietal flavors more clearly because the cloak of clover-honey and dried-apricot nuances imparted by the noble rot is not discernible.

6. **Trockenbeerenauslese:** **Trockenbeerenauslese** (TRAWK-uhn-bay-ruhn-OWS-lay-zuh), meaning "selected dried berries," are picked in late autumn or even early December. They are fully infected with *Botrytis*, and have shriveled on the vine as the fungus causes the skin to crack, allowing the water of the grape to evaporate (Figure 9.6). What is left is highly concentrated natural sugar. The wine that results is ambrosial—deep golden color, honeyed nose redolent of dried apricots and nuances of the varietal with rich, deep raisiny flavors. In some years no Trockenbeerenauslese (often abbreviated to TBA) can be produced due to a lack of the *Botrytis* fungus. Even in years when it is made, the quantities are always small (Figure 9.7). The price is very high, compensating the producer for the risk of losing the crop to rot or a killing frost, and for the difficulty of fermenting such a viscous juice.

FIGURE 9.6

Riesling grapes in the Schlossberg vineyard of the Rheingau region show the first signs of *Botrytis cinerea*, or noble rot.

© Cephas Picture Library/Alamy

FIGURE 9.7

From one of the most famous vineyards in the Rheingau, Berg Schlossberg in the town of Rüdesheim, this Trocken-beerenauslese is a lusciously sweet dessert wine. (For a picture of this vineyard see Figure 9.22.)

Georg Breuer, Permission granted by Classical Wines

FIGURE 9.8

These ice-encased grapes will be picked while still frozen. The ice will be separated from the grape at pressing, and the concentrated juice will become luscious Eiswein.
© WoodyStock/Alamy

Reading the Labels

Deciphering a German wine label is not as complicated as you may think, although with wine laws currently in flux there are some complicating factors. In general, however, the label of a Qualitätswein contains all the information the consumer could want in order to make a knowledgeable decision. Bear in mind the adage about wines getting better and more distinctive the smaller and more specific the geographic designation on the label. With German labels, this concept holds true as we move from Tafelwein up through Landwein to Qualitätswein bestimmter Anbaugebiet (often abbreviated to QbA), with each level being more specific and correspondingly higher quality. Within the QbA level, the adage continues to be true, as the geographic designation gets smaller and more specific.

Once we get to the Prädikat level, there is the added designation of quality, although here the quality is not based on the uniqueness of a specific vineyard or on a lower yield per hectare, as in some European countries. In Germany, that extra designation of quality is based on the level of ripeness of the grapes at harvest. In other words, the Prädikat label, like most European labels, tells you exactly where the grapes were grown, which gives you an idea of the character of the wine since the terroir of each Bereich and village is unique. A German Prädikat label, however, goes further: It also gives the consumer a solid idea of the style of the wine because the designation indicates where the wine falls on the stylistic spectrum from very dry to very sweet.

Revision to the Wine Laws

As stated earlier, there is considerable dissatisfaction with Germany's existing wine laws and how those laws are interpreted on labels. Many different voices are protesting the status quo. Producers, wine consumers, the importing and marketing companies that handle German wines in foreign markets, and government officials are all raising concerns about the effectiveness of the present situation in ensuring continuing quality and stylistic integrity, and in improving marketability. In this section, we summarize the controversy and the various movements within Germany's wine trade that are working to improve the system.

New Terms and Ratings

The traditional style for German white wines has been off-dry, that is, with a degree of unfermented, or residual, sugar to play off the natural fruit flavors. Because of the piercing acidity of the Riesling grape and its offspring, German whites can carry off a less-than-bone-dry style without being cloying. While staying true to their long heritage, German producers have embraced the latest technology. Temperature-controlled, stainless steel fermentation tanks allow a slow, cool fermentation within an inert container, promoting an aromatic and complex, yet clean and fresh, style. Precision-engineered centrifuges are now common, especially in the production of bulk, or medium-quality, wines.

Many producers now use stainless steel containers in which the wine can be chilled to 33°F (0.5°C) to kill the yeast, thus stopping fermentation and leaving the desired amount of residual sugar (Figure 9.9). However, in response to perceived market demand for dryer wines, many producers in recent years wanted to reduce or eliminate residual sugar (Figure 9.10). They wanted a mechanism whereby their labels could indicate to the buyer that the wine was not in the traditional off-dry styles, but was still a Qualitätswein. In 1982, the government approved an amendment to the Wine Law of 1971 authorizing the use of the labeling terms *Trocken* ("dry") and *Halbtrocken* ("half-dry," i.e., a semidry wine with no more than 0.6 ounce of residual sugar per quart). Many of Germany's very best wines are now made in these styles.

In 2000, further label terminology was approved and came into use in 2001: Classic and Selection. Classic wines are made from only traditional grape varietals and a wine must be 100 percent one varietal. Twenty-two grapes are approved for Classic wines, specific ones for each of the 13 regions. The name of the vineyard is omitted from Classic wines' labels. Selection wines are made from traditional grape varieties which meet the high quality standards prescribed for this level. Twenty-two varietals are approved for Selection wines. The vineyard name is listed on the label.

Germany has never had an official quality rating of its vineyards. The sites that have been noted for centuries for producing the highest-quality grapes were recognized in

FIGURE 9.9

These tall stainless steel tanks are typical of the highly mechanized, temperature-controlled fermentation tanks being used throughout Germany today.
© Frithjof Hirdes/Corbis

FIGURE 9.10

A vintner extracts a sample of his wine from a cask with a glass siphon called a wine thief. He will taste it to assure himself that it is evolving according to his exacting standards.
© Michael Pole/Corbis

the Wine Law of 1971 by being designated as individual Einzellagen. Lesser sites were incorporated into Grosslagen. Ratings were deemed unnecessary anyway since Germany's Prädikat designations are based not on vineyard location but on level of sugars in the grapes at harvest.

However, one group of producers has banded together to protest the traditional Prädikat designations, and to work toward official recognition of prime vineyards through a classification system. This group of vintners, the First Growth Committee, are all from high-quality estates in the Mosel, the Rheingau, the Pfalz, and Rheinhessen. They have persuaded the government to approve the use of the term **Erstes Gewächs** (first growth) to be used on the labels of a small group of selected vineyards. These producers make primarily dry-style wines, hoping that this practice would invite favorable comparisons to the dry wines of other European countries. By 2000, the process of selecting the rated vineyards had been completed only in the Rheingau, where 35 percent of the vineyards now carry the Erstes Gewächs designation. In late 2002, a group of producers published their own list of classified vineyards within all 13 Anbaugebiete. To complicate matters, the term used for classified vineyards differs from region to region. In the Mosel, the term is *Erstes Lagen*. The Rheingau retains the term *Erstes Gewäch*, while in other regions the term used is *Grosses Gewächs*. Some of the owners of these now-rated vineyards are declassifying their wines from QmP level to QbA to drop the Prädikat designations (based on sugar content) from the labels that might be misleading to consumers. It will take several years before the task of eliminating confusing terminology, and confirming uniform criteria for vineyard classification, are finalized under the auspices of the German government.

Trade Organizations

Many German vintners feel strongly that their obligation is to continue to make the highest-quality wines in the traditional style, while avoiding any measures that render the classification and labeling of German wines any more complicated than necessary. Many of these vintners have banded together to more effectively work toward their goals.

Charta Wines

A group of producers in the Rheingau who organized in 1984, **Charta** (KAR-tah) is dedicated to producing only the very highest-quality wines that are typical of their region (Figure 9.11). Charta promotes the wines from their estates as the best from the Rheingau. Charta wines must be 100 percent Riesling, are made

FIGURE 9.11

An example of a label from a Charta estate. There is no indication of Prädikat level of ripeness. Rather, it carries the winery's own designation for its high-quality Rieslings: Terra Montosa.

Georg Breuer, Permission granted by Classical Wines

in a dry style, which means these wines have to meet higher standards for minimum sugar content than is specified in national laws for Kabinett, Spätlese, and QbA wines. The back label of Charta wines shows twin Roman arches.

Verband Deutscher Prädikatsweingüter (VDP)

Originally a collaboration of Mosel producers, the VDP was founded in 1908 by the mayor of Trier, Freiherr von Bruchhausen. The group was dedicated to high-quality wines that "reflect the distinct character of their German origin" (http://www.VDP.de.). Later the Mosel group merged with similar associations from other regions, and in 1999 the Charta group merged with VDP. There are now 200 members from around Germany. The VDP is committed to the traditional style of German wines and to maintaining the Prädikat system. As stated by Nik Weis of St. Urbans-Hof in the Mosel, whose family has been active in VDP for generations, "The goal is to promote the German Estate Wineries, the quality of German wines, the traditions, and the best vineyards."

It may take another decade for all the various pieces to fall into place, as Germany's producers and government officials work to clarify standards, classifications, and labeling practices. In the meantime, Germany continues to produce a wide range of fine wines, many of them of the highest quality. Although German wine laws are currently being reassessed, the example on page 310 illustrates how to read a German wine label that conforms to all existing laws.

THE WINE REGIONS

Climate

Germany is one of the northernmost fine wine regions in the world. Its climate is heavily continental; the climate is influenced by weather patterns within the land formation, rather than by oceanic patterns. A region with little mitigating maritime influence will exhibit wide variation in average temperatures each year. To produce quality wines in such a volatile and difficult environment takes real dedication and skill. It is no accident that 80 percent of Germany's 252,000 acres (102,000 hectares) of vineyards are planted along steep riverbanks. The Rhine and its many tributaries provide a moderating influence on the climate, reflecting heat and light back onto the vines. The steepness of the slopes allows vines to capture as much sun as possible, while also providing some shelter from cool winds.

In most of Germany's vineyards, each individual vine is laboriously trellised onto its own stake rather than on the row-long trellises made of wire common elsewhere. This method is an advantage in steep vineyards this allows workers to reach any part of the vine without having to walk all the way around the row. It is estimated that it takes three times as many worker-hours to tend the vines on the steep terraced vineyards along Germany's rivers than is the case for flat rolling terrain (Figure 9.12).

Most of Germany's 78,000 grape growers (whose average holding is just 3.7 acres [1.5 hectares]) do not make their own wines, but sell their grapes to the 24,000 winemaking facilities. The hard work and close collaboration required to make wine in a northern region like Germany is well worth the effort, though, for the grapes acquire

FIGURE 9.12

The slope of the Doktor vineyard on the Mosel River near the town of Bernkastel is so precipitous that this worker needs a winch to help him back to the top, where he will again fill his basket with ripe grapes.

© Cephas Picture Library/Alamy

enough ripeness to develop aromatic bouquets and appealing fruit flavors, while retaining excellent acidity. Moreover, the stony soils on the hillsides provide an additional quality of unique minerality to the wines, especially the Rieslings.

Because of the volatility of its climate and the difficulty of working the steep vineyards, Germany produces a very small percentage of the world's wine (about 4.5 percent). Not surprisingly, Germany is by far the largest importer of wine in the European Union. However, despite large imports of French and Italian wines, after exporting a portion of its own annual production, only 2 percent of domestic production is surplus each year. Obviously, then, Germany is not a contributor to the "ocean" of excess wine in the contemporary world that has led to the instability of wine (and grape) prices in the international marketplace.

Grape Varietals

As explained in the chapter on viticulture, different varietals require different conditions to thrive. Early ripeners tend to ripen quickly on the vine. If given too much sun and warmth, they will become ripe and have to be picked before having fully evolved their flavors. The resulting wines will be "green," thin, and unpleasant. What early ripeners need is a long growing season and moderate temperatures. Germany—with its northern location, often overcast skies, and many rivers with their moderating influences—is perfect for these grapes. Most cool-climate varietals are white. Sixty-six percent of Germany's vineyards are planted to white grapes. Among the cool-climate grapes that thrive in Germany are the following:

Riesling

Riesling is the noblest and most important of Germany's white varietals. It accounts for 25 percent of acreage under vine. This increase in plantings of Riesling, and reduction in acreage of lesser white grapes, is a definite contributor to the rise in quality of German wines over the past decade or so. In Germany's northernmost vineyards Riesling is at its best, shedding extraneous fat and richness and allowing sleek simplicity and elegant style to shine through.

Müller-Thurgau

This clonal offspring of Riesling was developed in Switzerland by botanist Professor Hermann Müller in 1893 by crossing the noble Riesling with a grape indigenous to his country. The resulting wine, which combined the delicate flavors and crisp acidity of Riesling with the hardiness of the local varietal, was named for Professor Müller and his home district. The **Müller-Thurgau** (MEW-luhr TOOR-gow) is now planted in approximately 15 percent of German vineyards (down from 20 percent in just a few years). It is widely used in everyday blended wines, such as Liebfraumilch.

Silvaner

This workhorse of a grape is decreasing in importance. Useful as a blending grape, Silvaner contributes high acidity and a neutral background against which more distinguished varietals, such as Riesling, can show off their distinctive flavors and site-specific character. Presently barely 5 percent of total acreage is planted to Müller-Thurgau.

Pinot Noir

This noble red grape, called Spätburgunder in Germany, is on the rise, presently accounting for over 11.5 percent of vineyards. Many of Germany's Spätburgunders are too light in body and lacking in depth of flavor. Part of the problem, of course, is the cool climate in which the grapes struggle to reach adequate ripeness. The inadequacies could be somewhat alleviated, however, by lowering the allowable yield for this varietal (and other red grapes). Some producers, especially in the Rheingau, are making impressive red wines by voluntarily lowering their yields.

Other Grape Varietals

There are over 20 other grapes grown in Germany, from the truly obscure (e.g., Limberger, Gutedel) to the better known like Pinot Gris (Grauburgunder in German) and Pinot Blanc (Weissburgunder) (Figure 9.13A and B). (*Note:* The German word

FIGURE 9.13A AND B

These botanical cousins, the Pinot Gris (on the left) and Pinot Blanc (on the right), do well in Germany's cool climate, as do other members of the Pinot family.

allOver Photography/Alamy

Burgunder denotes a member of the Pinot family that is indigenous to Burgundy.) The older traditional grapes, many of which have long been associated with a particular region or district, are losing ground to the Pinot relatives. Even the ubiquitous Chardonnay, a Pinot cousin, was approved in 1991. It is not widely planted, however.

Two rare red grapes that have shown small increases in the past several years are the Dornfelder and the Portugieser. The origins of the latter grape are a mystery as no connection to any varietals grown in Portugal can be proven. The wines made from these two grapes have varied considerably in style and in quality. Surprisingly, Gewürztraminer, which produces such delicious wines across the border in Alsace, is not widely grown in Germany, accounting for less than 1 percent of vineyard area.

The Mosel

The Mosel River curves and twists like a huge shimmering ribbon as it winds among the rocky hills that stretch across Germany's southwestern midsection (Figure 9.14). Over the millennia, the river has gouged out gorges through these hills, leaving incredibly steep banks on each side. The banks of the Mosel and its two tributaries, the Saar and the Ruwer, are so steep, barren, and rocky that it is hard to believe anything can be cultivated there. However, the Romans were cultivating wine grapes here 16 centuries ago, and at one point only the highest, rockiest, and most inaccessible sections were left unplanted. Unfortunately there are more sections left bare today as fewer people can be found to undertake the backbreaking work of tending the terraced vineyards. There is an old saying in this region: "A true Moselaner has one leg shorter than the other." Working long hours in the sloping vineyards does not really lead to a shortening of the uphill leg, but it is incredibly hard work.

As the Mosel River has pursued its 150-mile route from France toward Koblenz where it feeds into the Rhine, it has deposited many layers of crushed rock in its winding path (Figure 9.15). These deposits have lent a distinct slatelike note to the wines

FIGURE 9.14

The beautiful Mosel River twists and turns among the steep, rocky hills it has gouged out over the many thousands of years that it has flowed through Germany's southwestern midsection.

© Martin Lehmann/ Shutterstock

FIGURE 9.15

The rock soils found throughout vineyards in the Mosel region soak up the sun's warmth during the day, and reflect it back onto the vines after the sun sets, thus helping with the ripening process.

© Nigel Cattlin/Alamy

FIGURE 9.16

The Devonian slate found in the soil of many vineyards in the Middle Mosel has a slightly bluish tint, and imparts a unique aroma reminiscent of petroleum to the Riesling wines from this region.

© Cephas Picture Library/Alamy

made from grapes grown in the 31,530 acres (12,760 hectares) of vineyards along the Mosel and its tributaries. This note of slate, called Schieferton, gives such a unique edge to the wines of the Mosel that the government of Prussia drew up an extensive map of the region in 1868 specifying the degree of Schieferton to be found in each vineyard. That carefully researched map has recently been reprinted as a continuing guide to the terroir of the Mosel's vineyards. The touch of slate gives the best Mosel Rieslings minerality that offsets the natural fresh green apple aromas and flavors (Figure 9.16). Racy acidity supports the fruit and slate, allowing these wines to exhibit an almost oxymoronic combination of delicacy and intensity.

The vineyards of the Mosel (formerly known as the Mosel-Saar-Ruwer) can be divided into five subregions: the Saar, Upper Mosel (between the village of Perl and the point where the Ruwer joins the Mosel), the Ruwer, the Middle Mosel (from the Ruwer to approximately the town of Zell), and the Lower Mosel (from Zell to Koblenz where the Mosel flows into the Rhine). These subregions correspond roughly to the six official Bereiche: Saar, Ruwertol, Obermosel, Moseltor, Bernkastel, and Zellwich. The six Bereiche are further divided into 19 Grosslagen and 525 Einzellagen (of which only about 60 vineyards are really noteworthy).

The westernmost vineyards are found along the Saar, which flows north into the Mosel River just six miles below the ancient city of Trier. Looking over the Saar in the village of Saarberg is a striking remnant of earlier times—a tall, fortified stone tower built in the thirteenth century as a lookout against invaders. Many of the estates along the Saar also date from that early period. The Grosslage Scharzberg groups together many of the vineyards along the Saar. The most famous of these vineyards

FIGURE 9.17

The famous Einzellage Scharzhofberg in the village of Wiltingen looks down on the stately manor house of the Egon Müller winery. The estate and portions of the vineyard have been in the Müller family since the late eighteenth century.

© Cephas Picture Library/Alamy

is the Scharzhofberg, an Einzellage near the village of Wiltingen (Figure 9.17). The historic village of Ockfen is also known for the quality of its Rieslings; its best-known Einzellage is the hilly Bockstein vineyard. Sitting on a steep hill facing south, with no other hills blocking it, Bockstein receives excellent sunlight. Its soil is hard, gravelly slate that forms a blue-gray dust on the fingers when touched. This is indicative of how easily the soil mineralizes, allowing the vines' roots to pick up mineral components.

The Upper Mosel region, roughly the area between the two tributaries, is similar in terrain and climate to the Saar region. Outside the city of Trier, the countryside is rural and picturesque. There are few private estates in this region. One large local cooperative does most of the cultivating and harvesting of grapes. The sparkling wine, or **Sekt** (ZEHKT) in German, from this region shows promise. The majority of the Sekt produced in Germany is by the Charmat (tank) method.

The vineyards of the Ruwer cover about a six-mile stretch, starting at the village of the same name and extending to the confluence with the Mosel River. The vineyards here are a little more sheltered than along the Saar. The soil is less gravelly and contains less slate, and there is a higher content of humus in the red soil. These two factors give Ruwer wines a little more ripeness and a more fully developed fruitiness than those from the Saar.

The subregion (and Bereich) of Bernkastel starts at the confluence of the Ruwer and Mosel and continues downstream almost to Zell. It is named for the town of Bernkastel, which lies in the middle of the region, on the banks of the Mosel (Figure 9.18). The surrounding steep hills with their red slate soil contain vineyards whose wines are among Germany's best. Of the Mosel's approximately 60 quality Einzellagen, over half

FIGURE 9.18

The beautiful and historic town of Bernkastel is located in the middle of the Bereich of the same name. Many of the Mosel's highest-quality vineyards are in the Bereich Bernkastel.

© www.germanwines.de, German Wine Institute

are in the Bereich Bernkastel. These exceptional vineyards are located in several villages along the river, starting with Treppchen in the village of Erden and progressing through Urzig where the Würzgarten vineyard is located and Wehlen with its pretty Sonnenuhr vineyard. The town of Bernkastel has two famous Einzellagen, Doktor and Graben (Figure 9.19). Moving farther downstream, the village of Brauneberg is well known for the Juffer Einzellage, and Piesport has the superb Goldtröpchen (Figure 9.20). Each of these vineyards imparts distinctive terroir. It is important to recognize that the best wines from this region are bottled by quality-conscious private estates. The labels from these producers will contain the word **Gutsabfüllung** (GOOTS-ab-few-lung) or "estate-bottled." There are also inferior wines from these villages made from grapes grown in less favorably located sections of the local vineyards and sold under a collective Grosslage designation.

At the town of Zell, one moves into the Lower Mosel subregion, which extends downriver to the town of Koblenz, where the Mosel meets the Rhine. The Lower Mosel has the highest percentage of Riesling in its vineyards of any section along the river. The river's slopes are particularly steep here, and there are virtually no sites that are smooth, flat, and easy to work (Figure 9.21). The wines from Bereich Zell are somewhat less delicate and refined than those from Bereich Bernkastel, but they can be very satisfying in their sturdy, true-to-varietal way. As one gets closer to Koblenz, the Rieslings show some of the more muscular character of Rhine wines.

Throughout the Mosel there is an impressive commitment to quality and noticeable pride in heritage. Many of the new owners and managers of the established private estates work hard to reach standards of excellence that surpass those set by national quality

FIGURE 9.19

The Einzellagen Doktor and Graben lie on hillsides above Bernkastel. Note the precipitous gradient of the vineyards, both of which are famous for the quality of their Rieslings.

© Cephas Picture Library/Alamy

FIGURE 9.20

The vineyards stretching up the hillside above the picturesque town of Piesport have perfect southern exposure, allowing the Riesling grapes to soak up the afternoon sun and ripen fully, while evolving unique mineral aromas and ripe fruit flavors.

© PHB.cz (Richard Semik)/ Shutterstock

control laws. Ernst Loosen of Weingut, Dr. Loosen near Bernkastel, Manfred Prüm of J.J. Prüm in Wehlen, Johannes Selbach of Selbach-Oster in the little village of Zeltingen just downriver from Wehlen, Wilhelm Haag of Fritz Haag near Brauneberg, and Nik Weis of St. Urbans-Hof on the Saar—innovative, adventurous vintners like these are dedicated to producing the best Rieslings possible from the Mosel, combining meticulous viticulture, time-honored tradition, modern technology, and creative promotions.

The Rheingau

Historically, the Rheingau is the most commercially successful wine region of Germany (Figure 9.22). Over the centuries, the Church and the landed nobility gave direction

FIGURE 9.21

Harvesting grapes in the Zeltinger Sonnenuhr vineyard. Across the Mosel lies the village of Wehlen.

© Cephas Picture Library/Alamy

FIGURE 9.22

A medieval castle stands in one of the Rhine's most famous vineyards, Berg Schlossberg, near the town of Rudesheim in the Rheingau.

© flonline digitale Bildgentur BmbH/Alamy

and structure to wine production, allowing the region to recover quite quickly from the natural devastations of the late nineteenth century and self-induced tragedies of the first half of the twentieth century. The Rheingau is relatively small at 7,630 acres (3,088 hectares) of vineyards. Ninety percent of those acres lie on the right bank of the Rhine, from the boundary with the Mittelrhein on the north, to the town of Wiesbaden in the south. The other 10 percent of Rheingau acreage is along the Main River that flows in from the east to meet the Rhine at the city of Mainz.

Except along the Main where the land is gentle and flat, the vineyards of the Rheingau are on steep sloping hills. The soil in the Rheingau is varied. Slate predominates. Downstream from Rudesheim, blue slate is prevalent whereas farther upstream, there is more of the reddish mineral-like slate found in the Lower Mosel. The climate of the Rheingau is conducive to growing ripe, fully developed, but nicely acidic grapes. The Rhine (which for most of its path runs north or northwest) takes a jog at Mainz and runs west–southwest for about 18 miles. This variation in topography gives the river's banks a southerly slope, making this area marginally warmer than locations further inland in the Rheinhessen. Annual rainfall of approximately 20 inches (51 cm) ensures that there is adequate water for the vines. Although winters are very cold (the river often freezes over) temperatures stay warm long enough into the fall to allow the Riesling grapes to fully develop their flavors. The Rheingau is overwhelmingly a white wine region, and the majority of the vineyards are planted to Riesling. (In 2009, the percentage of acreage planted to Riesling was 78.4 percent. The next most-planted grape here is the red Spätburgunder.)

In general, wines from the Rheingau are fuller, firmer, and more assertive than wines from the Mosel. Some writers describe Rheingau Rieslings as Germany's most "muscular" wines. There is little dispute that these are among the most elegant, distinctive, and long-lived Rieslings produced. When fully mature, a Rheingau Riesling from one of the better private estates can proudly stand with the best white wines in the world.

NIK WEIS OF ST. URBANS-HOF

Nik Weis, co-owner and General Manager of the St. Urbans-Hof estate in the small town of Leiwen on the Saar, is the third generation of his family to run the winery. Although still in his thirties, Nik has very clearly-defined opinions on viticulture, enology, and wine's place in world culture.

Nik's approach to vineyard management closely mirrors his family's longstanding concern for ecological balance. By limiting man's interference with the natural process of growing grapes, and using only gentle methods to help the grapes reach maturity, the Weis family concentrates its energy on producing wines that reflect the terroir of each vineyard.

St. Urbans-Hof owns sections of two of the Mosel's premier Einzellagen, Piesporter Goldtröpchen 5 acres (2 hectares) and Ockfener Bockstein 12 acres (5 hectares). The estate also owns over thirteen hectares of vineyards in three other villages. In total, the Weis family owns thirty-three hectares of vineyards, all of which are planted 100% to Riesling, which the family considers the traditional grape of Germany. St. Urban-Hof's Web site describes the Riesling as "the most fruity and flavorful of all white varietals."

Once the grapes are harvested and brought into the winery, Nik Weis and his cellar-master, Rudolf Hoffman, follow only traditional, time-honored methods of winemaking to allow the natural character of this noble grape to emerge. The grapes are carefully crushed and the must is allowed a short time to macerate with the skins to bring out flavors. After a gentle pressing of the skins and pulp, the must is moved to stainless steel tanks for a cool fermentation. When fermentation is complete, the wine is racked into large neutral barrels to rest and harmonize before being lightly filtered and bottled. Nik feels very strongly that when the noble Riesling is grown under the right conditions, is allowed to reflect the natural terroir of its vineyard, and is carefully handled in the winery, the result is the most food compatible of all wines. The bracing acidity of

Winemaker Nik Weis sits outside his family's winery in the village of Leiwen on the Saar River.
St. Urbans Hof

a Riesling, coupled with its plentiful fruit, assertive flavors and, often, a hint of residual sugar, make it the perfect foil for fatty meats, salty foods like anchovies or ham, or dishes in which there are natural fruits like Pork Chops braised with chopped Apples.

Flowing naturally from the Weis family's belief in traditional viticulture and winemaking, and their dedication to Germany's traditional style of Riesling-based wines, is their involvement for generations with the Verband Deutscher Prädikat Weinguten. The goal of the group is to promote the German Estate Wineries, a trade organization that works to heighten the quality of German wines, and to preserve the winemaking traditions of the country, and improve its best vineyards.

Nik is hopeful that the traditional system of grading Prädikat wines by the level of ripeness in the grapes will be continued. The touch of residual sugar in Rieslings is an integral part of their appeal, he feels.

As Nik has put it, "Sugar belongs in German Rieslings the way bubbles belong in Champagne".

There is only one Bereich in the Rheingau, Johannisberg, named for the town in the middle of the region. Sadly, this name has been misused by wine producers in several countries to try and attach legitimacy to their Riesling-based wines. The most famous Einzellage here is the historic estate Schloss Johannisberg (Figure 9.23). Other villages are Eltville with its Einzellage, Sonnenberg; Erbach with its incomparable

FIGURE 9.23

The legendary estate of Schloss Johannisberg is one of only four Einzellagen in the village of Johannisberg.
© PHB.cz (Richard Semik)/ Shutterstock

Macrobrunn vineyard; and Rudesheim with several Einzellagen, the most famous of which is Rosengarten. The village of Winkel is home to one of the Rheingau's most famous, and oldest, single estates, Schloss Vollrads.

Besides the two great estates of Schloss Johannisberg and Schloss Vollrads, other very reputable producers in the Rheingau include Georg Breuer in Rudesheim, headed by the energetic Bernard Breuer; the house of Dr. Robert Weil; and Langwerth von Simmern.

Rheinhessen

The topography of the Rheinhessen is very different from that of the Rheingau (or the Mosel). Instead of steep, rocky hills along river banks, the Rheinhessen is mostly flat, rolling agricultural land. The soil is more alluvial and loamy. Few of the small landowners plant only grapevines. This is the largest of Germany's 13 Anbaugebiete, encompassing more than 64,940 acres (26,000 hectares). In general, the region is protected from cold winds and excessive rain by the hills on its western border, which rise as high as 2,000 feet (610 meters) in altitude. However, within such a large region, there are different microclimates.

Overall, the best vineyard sites are located on the eastern edge in an area known locally as the Rheinterrasse, where the vineyards (many of them around the town of Niersteiner) are on eastern-facing slopes. The soil is full of a reddish slate that imparts a distinctive mineral-like intensity to the wines. Vineyards here are planted primarily to Riesling. There is some talk among property owners about creating a new official region out of the viticulturally more favorable Rheinterrasse.

Other parts of the Rheinhessen are not dedicated to Riesling, but rather to crossings like Müller-Thurgau or Scheurebe. The percentage of land dedicated to red varietals is also increasing. By 2009, 25 percent of acreage was occupied by red grapes, primarily Dornfelder and the prolific Portugieser. There are over 400 individual vineyards in the Rheinhessen, very few of them of any merit. Most of the grapes from small

FIGURE 9.24

Riesling vineyards surround the village of Deidesheim in the Pfalz. Conditions in this large region are so conducive to growing grapes that 90 percent of arable land is planted to vineyards.

© Cephas Picture Library/Alamy

vineyards are sold to cooperatives and made into pleasant, inexpensive still wines or increasingly, into decent, affordable Sekt (sparkling wine). One-third of all German exports come from the Rheinhessen. More than 50 percent of Liebfraumilch is made here.

The Pfalz

Formerly known as the Rheinpfalz, this is Germany's second largest wine region, with 58,060 acres (23,506 hectares) under vine (Figure 9.24). The Pfalz stretches along the left bank of the Rhine for about 50 miles (81 km). It lies on the eastern edge of the great Pfalz Forest and is well protected from the cold. Spring sets in early, and summers are long and warm. In July, the average temperature throughout the region exceeds the 64°F (18°C) considered the minimum for ripening grapes. The climate is very similar to that of the French wine region, Alsace, which lies just across the Vosges Mountains. So favorable are conditions that in parts of the southern Pfalz fully 93 percent of arable land is planted to grapevines. Of the region's 10,500 grape growers, about two-thirds deliver their grapes to cooperatives, producers' associations, or private cellars. For decades many of the bulk wines produced from these grapes were of mediocre quality, and in the 1970s and 1980s the reputation of the Pfalz was for inexpensive, pleasant, but unexciting wines. That is now changing.

Led by the 650 producers who estate-bottle their own wine, standards are rising fast. More acreage is being devoted to Riesling, and attention is being given to careful vinification methods. Because of the warmer temperatures, Pfalz Rieslings are generally fuller, riper, rounder, and higher in alcohol than Rieslings from other parts of Germany. Even with the fully evolved fruit flavors and higher sugar content at harvest, these wines retain lively acidity and an appealing elegance.

The best vineyard sites are in the north, including the famous Jesuitgarten in the village of Forst and Hohenmorgan in Deidesheim. Among the more important producers of high-quality wines are historic old houses like Basserman Jordan, which owns vineyard sites around Deidesheim, and Bürklin-Wolf, which dates from 1875 and owns prime vineyard sites in Forst, Deidesheim, and Wachenheim. With all the changes taking place and the emerging emphasis on quality, the Pfalz is one of the more exciting wine regions in the world.

Other Regions

Ahr

Fully 88 percent of the vineyards in this small region (only 1,300 total acres [526 hectares]) are planted to red grapes, most importantly to Spätburgunder (Pinot Noir). Due to rocky heat-reflective soils, and protection by hills from the northerly winds, conditions here allow ripening of red grapes. Most of the wine is made by the five co-operatives in the region, and cool fermentation and barrel aging are increasingly used. Local demand for these wines is so high that very few of them are exported. There is also a small amount of Riesling made.

Mittelrhein

This area north of the Rheingau has fairly cool temperatures and produces primarily Rieslings. These wines have high acidity and are mostly sold within the region.

Nahe

The Nahe River flows in a north–northeastern direction and feeds into the Rhine where that river takes its easterly jog. Although Müller-Thurgau is the most widely planted varietal, 25.7 percent of acreage is Riesling, most of it on the more desirable hillside vineyards rather than on the flatlands. There are good-quality, affordable Rieslings produced throughout the area, with some of the best coming from the section just north of the town of Bad Kreuznach.

Baden

The longest (250 miles/400 km) and most southerly of Germany's wine regions, Baden extends from the border with Franken in the north at the River Neckar all the way south to the border with Switzerland (Figure 9.25). The region effectively divides into two regions, with the section south of the town of Baden lying just across the Rhine from France's Alsace region and closely mirroring that region in its terrain. In the northern sections where granite is common in vineyard soils, especially around the historic and very beautiful old city of Heidelberg, some attractive and graceful Rieslings with excellent acidity are produced. Most of the harvest here is handled by cooperatives.

In southern Bereiche, where temperatures are warmer, alcoholic strength is higher than in other German wines. Müller-Thurgau is the predominate grape. It is often blended with Riesling and Silvaner into pleasant, light whites for local consumption or for sale to supermarkets. Increasing numbers of acres are now being planted to Spätburgunder, which can attain good ripeness at this southern latitude. As cooperatives and private owners continue to modernize their vineyards and their vinification methods, it is inevitable that more of Baden's whites, and her barrel-aged Pinot Noir–based reds, will find their way into export markets.

Hessische Bergstrasse

Hessische Bergstrasse starts at the River Neckar, just north of the Baden region. In essence, Hessische Bergstrasse is a continuation of the northern section of Baden and is very similar climatically and topographically. It is a very small

FIGURE 9.25

The vineyards of the Baden region, like this one above the town of Esslingen, are among Germany's southernmost. Their climate and soils are similar to those of France's Alsace region, which is located just to the west, across the Rhine River.
© Chad Ehlers/Getty Images

region with only 1,100 acres (454 hectares) under vine, 49 percent of which is planted to Riesling. Most of the wine produced is consumed locally.

Württemberg

Directly east of Baden's northern section lies Württemberg, whose 28,470 acres (11,522 hectares) of vines are planted along the sloping banks of the River Neckar and its tributaries. These vineyards are very steep, and most are terraced. The climate varies from north to south, but most of the region is under continental influences, especially in its easternmost Bereiche where the danger of fall and spring frosts are high. Most landowners have very small plots. Over 80 percent of the region's harvest is handled by cooperatives. Württemberg is Germany's largest producer of red wine, most of it very light in body, low in tannins, and undistinguished. The vast majority of this wine is sold locally. (Citizens of Württemberg have the highest per capita wine consumption in Germany.)

Franken

The Franken wine region is located east of Hessische Bergstrasse and north of Württemberg. Being so far east, and removed from the moderating influences of the Rhine, Franken's climate is essentially continental. It is one of the coldest wine regions in Europe. Winters can be severe. Most of the region's 14,900 acres (6,050 hectares) of vineyards are along the Main River. They are planted primarily to lesser white grapes. The wines of Franken are sold in a traditional flagon-shaped bottle. The most distinctive Silvaner wines are produced in this region.

Saale-Unstrut and Sachsen

The two wine regions in what was East Germany are just beginning to find their way into the modern world of winemaking. Both are small and very cold. Saale-Unstrut is the most northerly in Germany. Its 1,640 acres (663 hectares) are planted primarily to lesser white varietals, especially Müller-Thurgau. The chalky soil adds some body to the light and pleasant wines. Sachsen (Saxony in English), the smallest Anbaugebiete, is farther east, with the old city of Dresden, left in ruins by World War II air raids, at its center. The 1,000 acres (416 hectares) of vineyards located along the River Elbe are planted to various white varietals, mostly Müller-Thurgau and Weissburgunder (Pinot Blanc). As investment in replanting the vineyards and in upgrading the winemaking facilities continues, the wine business in these two regions is expected to grow and improve.

SUMMARY

It is somewhat ironic that one of the world's oldest and most traditional wine-producing countries is in a state of flux, holding on tenaciously to its heritage while looking to the future in its adjustments to the demands of a modern and international wine market. There is no doubt, however, that Germany will continue to produce extraordinary wines that complement a wide variety of cuisines, while the new, younger, highly educated and savvy generation of vintners, marketing executives, and government researchers move to increase international awareness, and acceptance, of these fine wines.

GERMAN WINE AND FOOD PAIRING

appetizer
rollsmops (pickled herring fillet rolled around gherkin)
Wine
Slightly off-dry Riesling Kabinett

main course
wild im rott wein (venison in red wine sauce)
spargel mit zerlassener butter
(asparagus with melted butter)
oven-roasted baby potatoes
Wine
A Spätburgunder (Pinot Noir) from the Rheingau region

cheese course
assorted German cheeses: würchwitzer spinnekase
(blue cheese from würzwitz) and allgäu emmanthaler
(hard cheese from the southern region)
Wine
Continue with the Spätburgunder

dessert course
schwarzwälder kirschtorte (black forest cherry pie)
Wine
Trockenbeerenauslese from the Rheingau

EXERCISES

1. Describe the differences between Einzellagen and Grosslagen.

2. What is the Oechsle system?

3. Is the Rheinhessen similar to the Rheingau in topography and soil content? If not, what are the differences?

4. Recently the terms *trocken* and *halbtrocken* were officially added to German wine law. Define the terms, and describe their significance to the future of the German wine trade, domestically and internationally.

REVIEW QUESTIONS

1. What is the smallest of the 13 Anbaugebiete?

2. List the six Prädikat designations at the QmP level in Germany's wine classification system. By what criterion is a specific wine assigned to one of these tiers?

3. Name the organization of winemakers in the Mosel that was formed in 1908. What is the stated purpose of this group?

4. What is the meaning of *Qualitätswein bestimmter Anbaugebiet*?

5. About one-third of Germany's wine production is red wine. What grapes are used for these wines?

REFERENCES

German Wine Institute. (2008) *Deutscher wein Statistik* Mainz, Germany: Author
Robinson, J. (Ed.). (2006). *The Oxford companion to wine* (3rd ed.). New York: Oxford University Press.

religious observance but as part of their daily cuisine. As for the wines from other countries in the region—Lebanon, Egypt, Turkey, Cyprus—it is unlikely that any of them (other than Château Musar) will attain a meaningful segment of the North American market in the near future, but they will undoubtedly become more visible here.

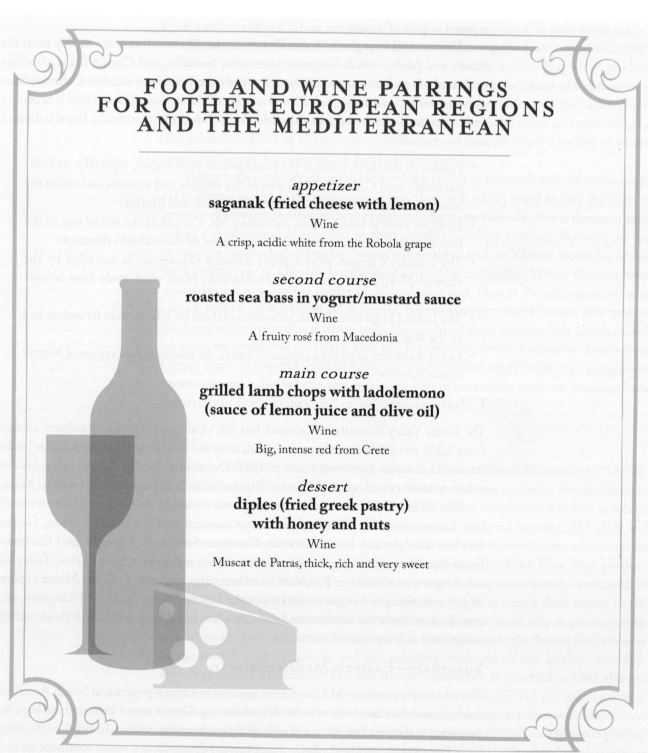

FOOD AND WINE PAIRINGS FOR OTHER EUROPEAN REGIONS AND THE MEDITERRANEAN

appetizer
saganak (fried cheese with lemon)
Wine
A crisp, acidic white from the Robola grape

second course
roasted sea bass in yogurt/mustard sauce
Wine
A fruity rosé from Macedonia

main course
grilled lamb chops with ladolemono (sauce of lemon juice and olive oil)
Wine
Big, intense red from Crete

dessert
diples (fried greek pastry) with honey and nuts
Wine
Muscat de Patras, thick, rich and very sweet

EXERCISES

1. Explain the significance of the terms *OPAP* and *OPE* in Greece's wine laws, being sure to list the differences between the two terms.

2. When were the French varietals first introduced into Israel's vineyards, and whose large gift made this planting possible?

3. There is one winery in Lebanon whose wines are well known and highly respected in the North American market. What is the name of that winery, and what style of wine does it produce?

REVIEW QUESTIONS

1. As a reaction to what scandal did the Austrian government tighten up the country's wine production laws?

2. What is Grüner Veltliner? Where was it originally developed?

3. For what two wines is Hungary most famous?

4. What is the most widely planted varietal in Switzerland?

5. What is Müller Thurgau? Where was it originally developed?

REFERENCES

Allen, L. (2003, November). Greece's enduring wine heritage. *Wine Spectator.*

Molesworth, J. (2005, December). Riesling. *Wine Spectator.*

Robinson, J. (Ed.). (2006). *The Oxford companion to wine* (3rd ed.). New York: Oxford University Press.

SECTION III

WINE REGIONS
OF NORTH AMERICA

THIS SECTION DISCUSSES WINE regions of North America in three chapters: California; The Pacific Northwest; and New York, Canada, and Other North American Regions. Domestic wines come in as many forms as their European counterparts and make up the majority of wine consumed in the United States. The wine regions of North America are covered in much the same way as the European wine regions in Section II, with sections on the areas' history as well as local grape-growing and winemaking techniques.

© 2012 Delmar Cengage Learning

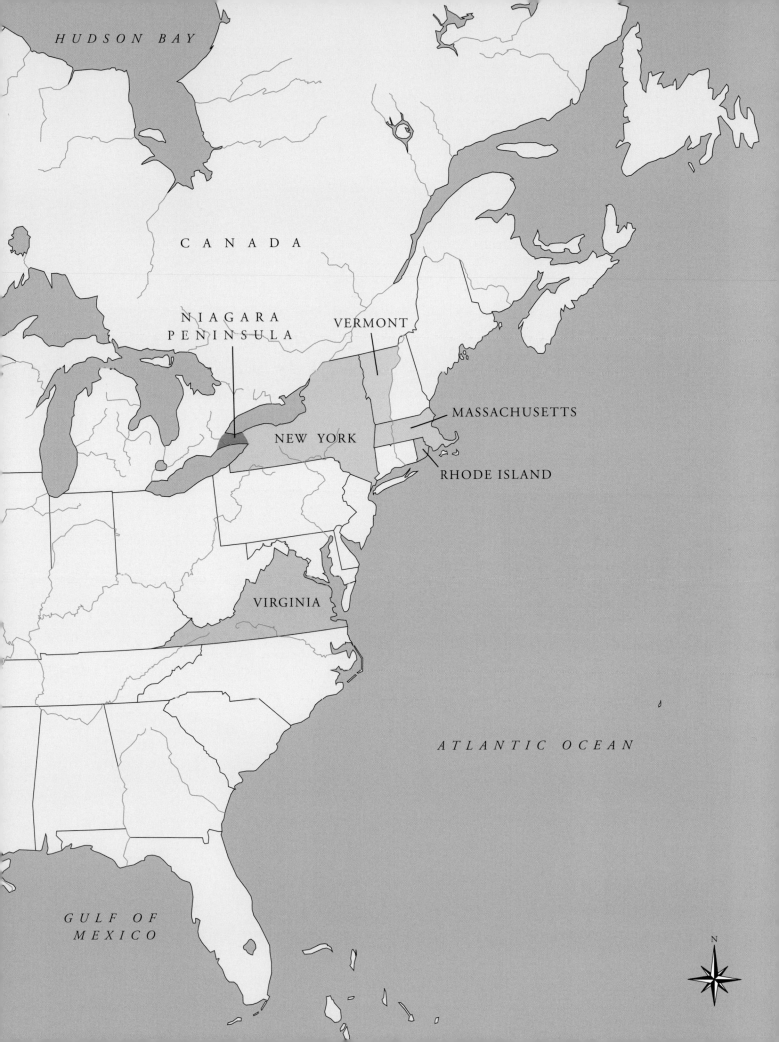

{ CALIFORNIA }

This chapter focuses on the history of winemaking in California and describes its various wine-growing regions and the types of wine that they produce. In addition, it discusses the importance of California in America's wine industry.

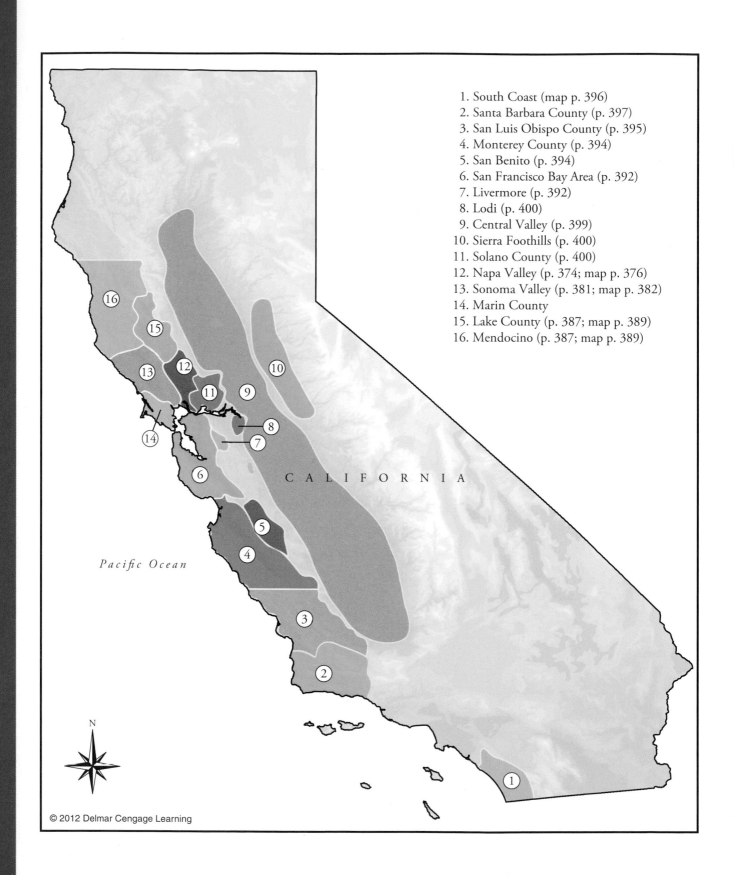

1. South Coast (map p. 396)
2. Santa Barbara County (p. 397)
3. San Luis Obispo County (p. 395)
4. Monterey County (p. 394)
5. San Benito (p. 394)
6. San Francisco Bay Area (p. 392)
7. Livermore (p. 392)
8. Lodi (p. 400)
9. Central Valley (p. 399)
10. Sierra Foothills (p. 400)
11. Solano County (p. 400)
12. Napa Valley (p. 374; map p. 376)
13. Sonoma Valley (p. 381; map p. 382)
14. Marin County
15. Lake County (p. 387; map p. 389)
16. Mendocino (p. 387; map p. 389)

CALIFORNIA

Pacific Ocean

N

© 2012 Delmar Cengage Learning

KEY TERMS

American Viticultural Area (AVA)

bench land

Bureau of Alcohol, Tobacco & Firearms (BATF)

California Wine Association (CWA)

degree days

heat summation

jug wines

Mission grape

mission period

Paris tasting

Serra, Junípero

Tax and Trade Bureau (TTB)

University of California at Davis (UC Davis)

Vallejo, Mariano G.

Wine Institute

INTRODUCTION

California is unquestionably the most important wine-producing region in North America (Figure 11.1). Containing 526,000 acres (212,000 hectares) of wine grape vineyards and more than 2,200 wineries, it is responsible for close to 90 percent of the wine that is produced in America (Wine Institute, 2008) as well as two-thirds of the wine that is sold nationwide. Extending more than 700 miles (1,100 km) north to south, California is known for both its mild Mediterranean climate as well as its beautiful landscape. Its temperate weather is characterized by wet winters followed by warm, dry summers. This cycle of wet and dry seasons makes it an ideal region to grow grapes as well as many other agricultural crops. Although vines require adequate water to grow, high humidity and rain during the summer when the fruit is on the vine can promote rot and mildew. The winter rains in California provide enough water, either by natural soil moisture or by irrigation, to mature the crop without relying on summer rain. Additionally, the summer weather also consistently provides enough warmth and sunlight to bring the grapes to their full ripeness. The Pacific Ocean has a large influence on California's climate with coastal regions being significantly cooler during the summer months than more inland regions.

California is important from the perspective of wine consumption as well. In addition to being the most populous state in the union, it also has one of the highest per capita consumption of wine. These two factors combined result in Californians drinking 18 percent of the wine that is consumed in the United States (Beverage Information Group, 2008). Because so much wine is both produced and consumed in the state, it plays a leading role in the U.S. wine market. Additionally, California is home to many of the businesses that support the wine industry such as grapevine nurseries, barrel makers, and cork suppliers.

FIGURE 11.1

Sonoma Valley vineyards.
© Pat Henderson

The development of winemaking in California reflects the melting pot of cultures that settlers brought with them to the state. European immigrants from different countries with diverse methods of viticulture and winemaking brought their knowledge and experience to the industry. Since the state did not have established winemaking traditions of its own, these Old World techniques flourished and were adapted in new ways that were best suited to the conditions in California. In addition there was a great deal of innovation and modernization applied to the winemaking methods immigrants brought with them. This blend of cultures began in the 1800s when the state was first being settled and continues to this day with large multinational wine companies investing in California.

CALIFORNIA WINE—HISTORICAL PERSPECTIVE

FIGURE 11.2

Franciscan friar, Father Junípero Serra, head of the California missions. During the mission period from 1769 to 1833, the friars introduced winemaking to California.

© *Northwind Pictures Archives*

Winemaking came to California with the Spanish missionaries, who were among the first Europeans to settle in California. Spain had occupied Mexico for more than 250 years when it expanded its territory, establishing 21 missions up the coast of California. The goals of the missions were threefold: to expand the territory of Spain and secure it for colonists, to convert the indigenous people of the region to Christianity, and to develop California's resources and send the proceeds back to Spain. The missionaries were led by a Franciscan friar, Father **Junípero Serra**, who established the first mission in San Diego in 1769 (Figure 11.2). Wine was essential to the new settlers who used it for sacramental purposes as well as for a beverage to be consumed with their meals. Soon after Father Serra arrived, he wrote in letters about the difficulty and cost of obtaining wine from Mexico, so the missionaries were very motivated to produce their own wine.

Although there were native grapevines growing throughout the state, they were unsuitable for winemaking, having smaller berries that were much less sweet than the European vinifera varieties. To alleviate this situation the friars imported vinifera cuttings to grow their own grapes to make wine. Although there is some academic dispute on exactly when and where the first vineyard was established, most historians believe it was in San Juan Capistrano in 1778 with the first vintage coming four years later in 1782 (Sullivan, 1998). Eventually grapes were planted at all but two of the missions, with the climates of the coastal missions of San Francisco and Santa Cruz being considered too cold and foggy to ripen grapes. The Los Angeles Mission with its temperate climate and fertile soil had the most extensive vineyards of the missions.

While the exact year of California's first vintage may be open to discussion, it is known that the first grapes grown for winemaking were the *vinifera* variety called **Mission grape**. Also called País or Criolla Chica in Latin America, Mission is a red grape that is a prolific producer and adapts to a number of growing conditions. The friars used it to make a variety of wine styles, including white, red, dessert, and brandy. Like Zinfandel, until recently its exact European heritage was unknown. In 2006 Spanish researchers, using DNA analysis determined that the Mission grape was descended from the Spanish variety Listán Prieto (Tapia et al., 2007). Mission produces a rather flavorless wine but this was probably of little consequence because the winemaking techniques were rudimentary even by the standards of the time. Grapes were trodden upon wooden platforms lined with animal skins with the juice collected in skin bags or wooden vats for fermentation and storage (Teiser & Harroun, 1983). In 1823 the last mission was established in the town of Sonoma, north of San Francisco Bay. Just 10 years later, in 1833, the now independent Mexican government ordered the secularization of the mission properties, and the missions and their lands went from church to government control. Although the winemaking methods of the mission may not have been advanced, their success inspired European immigrants who settled in the pueblos or towns that grew up around the missions.

Commercialization

By the time the **mission period** was coming to a close, private citizens were beginning grape-growing and winemaking operations in the state. The first large-scale commercial vintner was the appropriately named Jean-Luis Vignes (*vigne* is French for "vine") in Los Angeles. Called Don Luis by the Californians, he came from Bordeaux, and unlike the friars he had extensive knowledge of winemaking practices. He also looked beyond the Mission grape, importing more premium varieties from France. He eventually produced 1,000 barrels a year from his 100 acres (40 hectares) vineyard located along the Los Angeles River (Johnson, 1989).

In Northern California, Lieutenant **Mariano G. Vallejo** was sent to take over operations at the Sonoma Mission and pueblo after secularization. He quickly established a military barracks and began the process of laying out a town. He also restored the mission winery and its vineyard that had fallen into disrepair. His success in civic duties soon earned him the rank of general. Vallejo also was known for his skill in grape growing and winemaking as well as cattle ranching and other agricultural operations. He inspired many other early settlers to come to the North Coast and aided them by using his power as a government administrator to grant them tracks of land to develop. One notable settler was George C. Yount, the namesake of Yountville, who was the first person to plant grapes and make wine in the Napa Valley. Vallejo remained active in civic affairs even after California became a part of the United States, helping draft the state's constitution and serving as a senator in the first state legislature.

The success of Vignes and Vallejo as well as other early vintners was aided by California's expanding population. More and more settlers were arriving from the East Coast to take advantage of California's excellent climate for growing crops, and with the Gold Rush of 1849, there came an expanding base of consumers for their products. In 1856, a Hungarian immigrant named Agoston Haraszthy founded Buena Vista Winery in Sonoma. As a member of the state commission on viticulture, he traveled to Europe in 1861 and returned with thousands of cuttings of wine grape varieties and information on winemaking. His writings about the trip helped improve winemaking techniques as well as promote California wine. During the second half of the nineteenth century, commercial winemaking operations grew both in number and in size (Figure 11.3). With the completion of the transcontinental railroad in 1869, California wines became increasingly available on the East Coast.

The expansion of the industry was not without its ups and downs, and during this time grape growing and winemaking exhibited the classic boom and bust cycle that is common to many agricultural products. During boom times, increased demand for wine leads to high prices for grapes that eventually results in overplanting and excess production, ultimately lowering grape prices. When the price of grapes becomes too low, overall production stagnates or declines until the demand for wine increases, beginning the cycle over again. The boom and bust economic cycle was exacerbated by the destruction caused by the root louse phylloxera, discovered outside the town of Sonoma in 1873, and the economic depression of the late 1880s. Wine and grapes were often sold for less than it cost to produce them. Although these events were devastating, they did serve to weed out poor and inefficient producers and to replace the ubiquitous Mission grape with varieties that are more suited to winemaking. During this time some of California's most famous wineries were established: Charles Krug in 1861, Beringer in 1876, Inglenook in 1879, and Korbel in 1882 (Laube, 1999) (Figure 11.4). All these

FIGURE 11.3

The Vintage in California— At Work at the Wine-Presses. This well-known image illustrates how grapes were crushed and pressed in California during the middle of the nineteenth century. From the October 5, 1878, issue of *Harper's Weekly.*
© Corbis

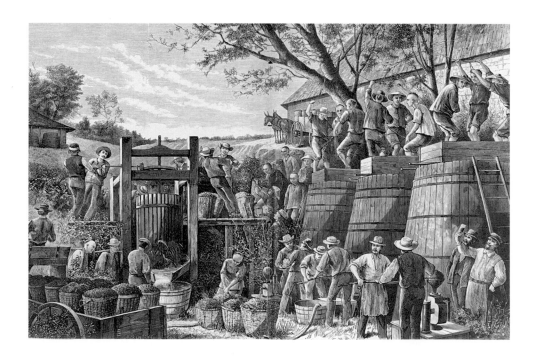

FIGURE 11.4

Unloading grapes at an early California winery. Grapes are brought to the top level of the winery and then crushed into fermentation tanks in the cellar below.

Wine Institute

wineries remain in operation today, albeit with different ownership than they had when they were founded in the nineteenth century.

To control production and to stabilize the wine market, some of the state's largest wineries joined together in 1894 to form the **California Wine Association (CWA)**. Eventually the CWA grew to include more than 52 wineries throughout the state, producing 80 percent of California's wine (Teiser & Harroun, 1983). As evidence of its size, the CWA's bottling plant in San Francisco lost more than 10 million gallons (37 million liters) of wine, enough to fill more than 4 million cases, in the 1906 earthquake. Later that year a large shipping and bottling plant was built on the shores of San Francisco Bay at Point Richmond, and for a time it was the world's largest winery. The CWA flourished, producing wine of good value, if of mediocre quality, until the onset of Prohibition in 1920.

Prohibition

The Eighteenth Amendment, also known as the Volstead Act, established national Prohibition in the United States and outlawed the manufacture and sale of alcoholic beverages from January 16, 1920, until December 5, 1933 (Figure 11.5). The antialcohol movement had been growing in the United States for more than 100 years and a number of individual states and communities passed their own "dry" laws during this time. During World War I, patriotic sentiment to preserve foodstuffs for the war effort rather than use them for alcohol production combined with the temperance movement to gain majority support for the Eighteenth Amendment. Although wine was not the primary target of Prohibition, the temperance movement was more concerned with whisky and other liquors, it was nevertheless included in the Volstead Act.

FIGURE 11.5

In New York during Prohibition, workers under police supervision dump contraband alcohol into the sewer.
Library of Congress

The enactment of Prohibition devastated the winemaking industry in California, closing all but the few wineries that were allowed to make wine for use in food flavoring or sacramental purposes. However, due to a clause in the Volstead Act that allowed the home production of up to 200 gallons (757 liters) of "non-intoxicating cider or fruit juice," which was interpreted to include homemade wine, the business of growing wine grapes in California actually flourished. Before Prohibition, the price of grapes grown in the Central Valley averaged $10 to $20 per ton; with the harvest of 1920, the best varieties were fetching up to $125 per ton (Teiser & Harroun, 1983). Growers who were accustomed to barely making a profit were producing as much as they could for shipping out to eastern markets for home winemakers. The red varieties that had thick skins and the most color were considered the most valuable because they could withstand the rail journey to the East Coast, and their deep color allowed home winemakers to stretch production by adding water and sugar to get more wine per pound of fruit. This meant that the classic wine varieties that replaced the Mission grape in the late 1800s were themselves replaced with varieties more suited for shipping. White wine grapes in particular were replaced with dark, thick-skinned grapes such as Petite Sirah and Alicante Bouschet, the latter variety being particularly prized because it is one of the few grapes that has dark red juice as soon as it is crushed or pressed, whereas most red grapes require skin contact after pressing to turn their juice red.

At the end of Prohibition in 1933, there was much anticipation by vintners that with its end would come a rapid resurgence of the wine industry. However, several factors prevented this from happening:

- During their long closure, wineries had fallen into disrepair, and there were few skilled winemakers available.
- Prohibition ended during the middle of the Depression, and there was little demand for wine and few resources available for rebuilding.
- People's tastes had changed and consumers had gotten used to poor quality homemade wine that was often sweetened or fortified with distilled alcohol to cover up the flaws.

In the first year after Prohibition there were 804 wineries in California; by 1940 one-third of them had failed. To help alleviate this situation, the **Wine Institute** was formed in 1934 as a trade organization to promote California wines and to lobby for regulations that were more favorable for wineries. Another organization that was instrumental in improving the quality of wine after Prohibition was the **University of California at Davis (UC Davis)**. A pilot winery was built on campus, and an academic program was established to train students as winemakers and grape growers (Figure 11.6). One of its most significant early accomplishments was categorizing the various grape-growing regions of the state by their climates and determining which varieties grew best in a given region. Unlike Europe, there was less of a tradition developed by years of trial and error to determine the proper growing regions for grape varieties. In a method called **heat summation**, or **degree days**, a vineyard is classified by the summation of its average temperature above 50°F (10°C) over the course of the growing season. For example, if the mean temperature for the day was 70°F, then the heat summation for that day would be 20°F (70 − 50 = 20). The heat

FIGURE 11.6

The Mondavi Institute for Wine and Food Science at the University of California Davis campus. It houses the Department of Viticulture and Enology, which was first established by mandate of the state legislature in 1880.
© Pat Henderson

summation for a region is the sum of all the heat summations for each day of the growing season. In this system Region I is the coolest with 2,500 degrees summation or less, and then the regions have 500-degree increments to Region V, which is warmest with a summation of greater than 4,000 degrees. At best, this is a very rough estimate of a vineyard's terroir and the grape varieties to which it is suited. However, even though the recommendations were not always followed, it proved to be useful in establishing what varieties might be suited for a given region.

Through the work of these and other organizations, the quality of California wine improved, and consequently, sales increased. The wines produced during this time were generally inexpensive and of good, if not great, quality. Few people thought the wines matched the quality of imported wines. This trend continued until the 1960s.

The Wine Revolution

The late 1960s began a period of great expansion in the California wine business. From 1971 to 1980, the per capita consumption of wine in the United States doubled from 1.2 to 2.4 gallons (4.5 to 9 liters) per year, and the number of wineries in the state went from 227 to 470 (Lapsley, 1996). This coincided with an influx of new wineries that were established in California's coastal valleys (Figure 11.7). Many of them were started by wine enthusiasts who wanted to make wines like those they had tasted from Europe. Winemakers invested more effort in obtaining better grapes, and improved their methods of production such as using stainless steel tanks and French oak barrels. Sales of wine increased dramatically during this time, particularly for the premium end of the market. At the same time as consumers were buying more, their tastes were also changing. In 1968 table wines (dry wines) outsold dessert wines for the first time since before Prohibition. A few years later in 1976 white wines outsold red for the first time.

This was also a watershed year in terms of the reputation of Californian wines. In May of 1976 Steven Spurrier, a Parisian wine merchant, held an event where wines from some of California's best vintners were matched in a blind tasting against some of France's best producers. The judges were all French and included some of the country's best-known wine experts. To the surprise of nearly all of those present, the red wine that won the competition was the 1973 Stag's Leap Wine Cellars Napa Valley Cabernet Sauvignon and the wining white wine was the 1973 Chateau Montelena Chardonnay that was produced from a blend of Sonoma and Napa fruit. California wines not only took the top honors for both red and white, but also received 5 of the top 10 places overall (Taber, 2005). The only

FIGURE 11.7

Rodney Strong Winery in Sonoma County, built in 1970, was one of the many new wineries that were started during the wine boom of the 1960s and 1970s.

Wine Institute

AMERICAN VITICULTURAL AREAS

For a wine to be labeled California the grapes that go into producing the wine must be grown entirely within the boundaries of the state. However, within the state there is a broad diversity of growing conditions that make its many regions suitable for producing a variety of grapes and wines. One method of identifying these grape growing regions, or appellations, is by political boundaries where the county of origin is used to describe the source of the grape. To be labeled Monterey County Chardonnay, a minimum of 75 percent of the grapes used to produce the wine must be grown in California's Monterey County. Using the county of origin is not always adequate to describe a grape-growing area because political boundaries do not always follow the border between different grape-growing climates or terroirs.

To better identify unique growing regions, in 1980 the **Bureau of Alcohol, Tobacco & Firearms (BATF)** allowed for the creation of **American Viticultural Areas (AVAs)**. Vintners and growers could petition the BATF to form an AVA in a specific geographic area with a common climate, soil type, and history of winemaking. In 2002 the BATF was reorganized and wine is now regulated by the Alcohol and Tobacco Tax and Trade Bureau, or as it is more commonly known, the **Tax and Trade Bureau (TTB)**. The first AVA established was Augusta, Missouri, in 1980. As of September 2010, there were a total of 198 AVAs in the United States, 111 of which are located in California. A complete list of AVAs can be found in Appendix B.

The largest AVA in the United States is the newly established Upper Mississippi River Valley, which covers over 19 million acres (7.7 million hectares) in Illinois, Iowa, Minnesota, Wisconsin; the smallest AVA is Cole Ranch in Northern California with only 150 acres (60 hectares). Occasionally AVAs are initiated by growers or wineries to include the vineyards at their own estates and little else. In these situations often the only wine that is bottled and labeled with the AVA is what the particular winery produces.

Appellations can overlap political boundaries such as state and county lines as well as other AVAs. The Carneros district, for example, extends over the southern portion of both the Napa Valley and the Sonoma Valley appellations. A single vineyard in the Sonoma County portion of the Carneros district may also be part of the Sonoma Valley, Sonoma Coast, and the North Coast AVAs. To be labeled with an AVA, at least 85 percent of the grapes used to make a wine must be from that region. If wines are blended from several areas of the state that do not have a common political boundary or AVA, they are labeled as California. If the grapes are grown, produced as wine, and then bottled all on winery property they can be labeled "Estate Bottled." Frequently, wineries will acquire grapes from outside the appellation that the winery resides in. In this case, the winery can bottle the wine as an AVA designate but cannot call it Estate Bottled even if it owns the vineyard. To be labeled with both an Estate and an AVA designation the winery and the vineyard must reside in the same AVA.

Unlike the French system of Appellation d'Origine Contrôlée, AVAs govern only the geographic origin of the grapes and do not dictate what varieties can be grown or winemaking techniques within the area. Furthermore, the TTB goes out of its way to state that the government sanction of the boundaries of an AVA makes no endorsement of quality of the grapes and wine that it produces. While having an AVA on the label does not make any official statement about the quality of a wine in the bottle, wines that are made from grape varieties that the appellation is renowned for do benefit from its reputation.

One complaint against the American system of viticultural areas is that to avoid litigation the government has been too free in allowing the establishment of new AVAs in areas that do not have a history of grape growing or a common terroir. Another criticism of the system is that large AVAs often include a number of climates and soil types that make many different types of grapes and wine. When the output of an AVA is too diverse, consumers have trouble knowing what to expect from the wine it produces. For example, in the Central Coast AVA, which has over 5.4 million acres (2.2 million hectares) of land with nearly 100,000 acres (40,000 hectares) of vineyards, the climate ranges from very cool, where Chardonnay would be appropriate, to warm, where Zinfandel would do better. By simply labeling a wine "Central Coast" the consumer does not know which area, warm or cool, the grapes for the wine were grown in and whether he or she should purchase a Chardonnay or Zinfandel. Conversely, if the consumer sees a Chardonnay from the Edna Valley AVA, which is much smaller and has a cool climate, his or her choice would be clearer. It is also important to remember that differences in vineyard and winemaking practices at various wineries can eclipse the similarities of the wines that they make from grapes grown in the same viticultural area.

reporter present at the tasting, George Taber, documented the event with an article in *Time* magazine. Known as the **Paris tasting**, it helped dispel the notion to wine consumers at home and abroad that California made second-class wines.

Throughout the 1980s and 1990s the California wine industry continued to evolve and improve its product. Although the growth in America's per capita wine consumption slowed and stabilized during this period, the market for premium wines continued to be strong. As the wine industry matured so did its consumers, and their tastes became more sophisticated. Wine producers referred to this phenomenon as "drinking less but drinking better" and it allowed the fine wine market to grow as sales of inexpensive **jug wines** sold in large bottles slowed. During this time established wineries grew in size, and some consolidated, forming large companies with several brands of wine.

The industry's successes continued to inspire individuals to enter the business and start small boutique wineries that specialized in a particular wine. Because of the increase in the value of land in wine growing regions, this required considerably more investment than it did at the beginning of the wine revolution in the 1960s. The high cost of vineyard land in Napa and Sonoma Counties helped spur development of premium wineries in other areas of the state such as Santa Barbara and Lake Counties.

Today at the beginning of the second decade of the new millennium, the cycle of boom and bust that has always been a part of the California wine industry continues. Increased sales of premium wine in the late 1990s encouraged wineries to plant new vineyards and vintners to increase the amount of wine they produced. This new production came on line at the same time as there was decreased demand due to a sluggish economy. This in turn led to prices being lowered on many grape varieties grown throughout the state. Many premium wineries, not wanting to lower their price too much, sold off their excess production in bulk to other wineries that would blend the wine from multiple sources and then bottle it under their own name. The wine produced was less expensive and often of very good quality, which continues to spur consumer interest in wine.

Another factor affecting the economic cycles of the California wine industry is globalization. U.S. consumers are becoming more familiar with wines from the Southern Hemisphere and Europe that compete directly with wines from California. These imported wines are often produced specifically for export to the United States and are frequently brought in by multinational companies that have winery holdings both in California and overseas. This global competition puts extra pressure on California winemakers to make a high-quality product and keep their prices affordable.

WINE REGIONS OF CALIFORNIA

California's large size and varied topography give it a wide range of growing conditions that are suitable for many different grape varieties and styles of wine. Grapes can be grown in most of the state except the northwest coast, which is too wet, and areas that are too high in elevation and therefore too cold. With irrigation even the desert areas in the southeastern part of the state can support vineyards and are the home of much of California's table and raisin grape production. Most of the grapes that are used for

Reading a United States Wine Label

As the wine industry has advanced in recent decades, wine labels have become much more elaborate. While in the 1960s wine was usually bottled with relatively plain labels with a minimum of information, today they are designed to be more eye-catching with multiple colors, embossing, gold leaf, and distinctive shapes. This is to try to get potential customers to notice the wine on the shelf; also, expensive labels are used to try to convey an impression of quality for the wine in the bottle. The importance of packaging to wineries is evidenced by the industry saying, "you sell your first bottle of wine to a customer with the outside of the bottle, and the second bottle of wine to the customer with what is inside." In addition to their importance in selling wine, labels must also provide information to the consumer. Some of the information on wine labels is provided by the winery to describe what the wine tastes like and how it was made. The federal government also mandates what information must be placed on a bottle of wine to accurately describe what the wine is, including standards of composition that must be met before certain claims can be made on the label. In recent years the amount of information required by law has expanded to include warnings about health and whether there are sulfites present in the wine.

The next three pages outline the basic requirements for wine labels in the United Sates. Different countries have different standards and terms that they use to describe their wines. Information on the labels of imported wines is outlined in their respective chapters of this book.

Front Label

Winery Name: Most names are acceptable as long as they are not offensive or misleading.

Vintage Date: 85 percent of the grapes used to make the wine must be harvested in the year listed as the vintage. If an AVA is listed as the appellation, then a minimum of 95 percent of the grapes must be from the vintage stated. If a vintage date is used, the appellation must be stated as well.

Appellation: The district the grapes were grown in. If listed as a political region such as county or state, at least 75 percent must be from the region listed. Some states have laws requiring that for a state to be listed appellation, 100 percent of the grapes must be grown in that state.

Alcohol Content: The percentage of alcohol by volume must be listed; if it is 7 to 14 percent, the label may also state "Table Wine" or "Light Wine."

F. Korbel & Bros.

Variety: The varietal of the grapes used to make the wine. The variety listed must be at least 75 percent of the grapes used to make the wine. Some states have higher percentage requirements and *Vitis labrusca* varieties like Concord need to have only 51 percent. If a varietal is designated on the label, an appellation must also be listed.

Reading a United States Wine Label
Back Label

Wine Notes: Not required, but many wineries add them to describe how the wine is made and what it tastes like.

Web Address: Also not required but an excellent source of more information about the wine.

Production Statement: "Vinted and Bottled by" or "Blended and Bottled by" are used for wines when less than 75 percent of the wine was fermented at the winery where it was bottled.

Sulfite Declaration: If the wine contains more than 10 PPM sulfur dioxide, "Contains Sulfites" must be included on the label.

Government Warning: Required on all beverages that contain more than 0.5 percent alcohol.

UPC Code: Not required by law but present on almost all wines sold at retail.

Winery Identification: The name of the winery and the city it is located in must be listed on the label.

Country of Origin: Required on all imported wines and used on U.S. wines that may be exported. Wines from outside of the United States must be labeled "Imported by" instead of "Bottled by."

KENWOOD.

Sauvignon Blanc continues to be Kenwood's most popular wine. This refreshing wine is superb as an apéritif and excellent with seafood, pasta and poultry dishes.

www.kenwoodvineyards.com

VINTED & BOTTLED BY KENWOOD VINEYARDS, KENWOOD, SONOMA COUNTY, CA

CONTAINS SULFITES
GOVERNMENT WARNING: (1) ACCORDING TO THE SURGEON GENERAL, WOMEN SHOULD NOT DRINK ALCOHOLIC BEVERAGES DURING PREGNANCY BECAUSE OF THE RISK OF BIRTH DEFECTS. (2) CONSUMPTION OF ALCOHOLIC BEVERAGES IMPAIRS YOUR ABILITY TO DRIVE A CAR OR OPERATE MACHINERY, AND MAY CAUSE HEALTH PROBLEMS.

PRODUCT OF USA

0 10986 00602 6

F. Korbel & Bros.

Other Terms Found on Wine Labels

Estate Bottled: For an estate designation, at least 95 percent of the grapes used to make the wine must be grown on the winery's own vineyards. Additionally, when the term "Estate Bottled" is used, both the vineyard and the winery must reside in the same appellation listed on the bottle.

European Names: It is permissible to use European place names such as Burgundy, Chablis, and Champagne as generic terms to describe domestic wines. However, they must clearly state the place of origin such as "California Chablis." See the section *What's in a Name?* on page 75.

Proprietary Names: Wineries are allowed to give their products a proprietary name. This is frequently done instead of varietal naming when the wine is a blend of several types of grapes with no one variety being more than 75 percent.

Reserve: Like the term "Old Vine," this has no legal definition. Although most wineries use "Reserve" for only a small amount of their best wines, some larger wineries use it on all their products to improve the wines' image to consumers.

Vintage Date: Since an AVA is listed as the appellation, 95 percent of the grapes must be harvested in the year listed as the vintage.

Vineyard Designation: If a vineyard is stated on the label, 95 percent of the grapes used to make the wine must be harvested from that vineyard.

Appellation: If an American Viticultural Area (AVA) is listed as the appellation of origin on the wine, a minimum of 85 percent of the grapes used to make the wine must be from that appellation.

Alcohol: If more than 14 percent, the term "Table Wine" cannot be used, and the percent of alcohol by volume must be stated.

HIRSCH VINEYARD
2009
SONOMA COAST PINOT NOIR

B. Kosuge Wines

ALC. 14.5% BY VOL.

B. Kosuge Wines

Production Statement: "Produced & Bottled By" means a minimum of 75 percent of the wine was fermented at the winery where it was bottled.

Volume: Every wine bottle must state the amount of wine it contains in metric units. In most cases the volume in ml is molded into the glass at the base of the bottle.

PRODUCED AND BOTTLED BY
B. KOSUGE WINES, SANTA ROSA, CA

www.bkosugewines.com

750ml | CONTAINS SULFITES

GOVERNMENT WARNING: (1) ACCORDING TO THE SURGEON GENERAL, WOMEN SHOULD NOT DRINK ALCOHOLIC BEVERAGES DURING PREGNANCY BECAUSE OF THE RISK OF BIRTH DEFECTS. (2) CONSUMPTION OF ALCOHOLIC BEVERAGES IMPAIRS YOUR ABILITY TO DRIVE A CAR OR OPERATE MACHINERY, AND MAY CAUSE HEALTH PROBLEMS.

B. Kosuge Wines

premium wine production are grown in the state's coastal valleys. Here the Pacific Ocean has a moderating effect on the climate, keeping it cooler than vineyards that are located more inland. During the summer months, warm daytime temperatures in the interior of the state create rising air that draws cool breezes from the Pacific Ocean into the coastal valleys. These breezes often carry a layer of fog with them that arrives in the late afternoon or evening and is burned off by the sun the following morning. This cooler climate allows the grapes to retain more of their varietal character and natural acidity, making the wines they produce more intensely flavored. Inland, in the Central Valley region, the weather is warmer, and soils are more fertile, vineyards here yield more tons per acre, and the grapes that are grown here are often used for less expensive wines. The Central Valley covers a large area, is the home to most of the state's agricultural output, and has the majority of California vineyard acreage.

Napa Valley

The Napa Valley lies in the temperate zone between Northern California's cool coast and warm interior. Beginning in the town of Napa, just north of San Pablo Bay (the northern section of San Francisco Bay), it runs in a gentle arc for 35 miles (56 km) to the northwest until reaching the slopes of Mount St. Helena (Figure 11.8). The appellation covers the vast majority of the land in the county and includes most of the watershed for the Napa River as well as part of Pope Valley to the east. It ranges in elevation from near sea level on the southern end of the valley floor, to 2,700 feet (820 meters) along the ridges of the mountains. Grape growing is by far the dominant agriculture in the Napa Valley with more than 45,000 acres (18,200 hectares) being planted to wine grapes.

FIGURE 11.8

Fall vineyards near Calistoga in the Napa Valley. Mount St. Helena dominates the northern end of the valley and marks the borders of Napa, Sonoma, and Lake Counties.

Roy Tennant/FreeLargePhotos .com

Historically the valley has been producing wine since the 1830s, and by the 1880s it had built a reputation for producing fine wine. However, Prohibition decimated its wine industry and it recovered very slowly after repeal. Napa Valley regained its reputation for producing great wines only when it became the epicenter for the wine boom of the 1960s and 1970s. During this period, there was a great deal of investment coming into the valley, and the number of wineries grew from less than 30 in 1965 to nearly 400 today. The Napa Valley is the most widely recognized of California's AVAs and is considered by many to be its premiere wine-producing region. This opinion is reflected in the fact that Napa Valley grapes and wines routinely command the highest prices in the state.

As the reputation of Napa Valley wine grew, more vintners came to the valley to establish vineyards and wineries. Some were wine enthusiasts who had been successful in another field of work and came to the valley to indulge in their passion for winemaking. Others were from large multinational corporations looking to diversify their business and take advantage of America's growing taste for wine. As the wineries grew in size and number, tourists began to flock to the area. This growth in tourism was aided by Napa's proximity to the San Francisco Bay Area. Visitors to San Francisco, as well as local wine enthusiasts, could visit the Napa Valley on an easy day trip from the city. In the 1970s, tourism became the county's largest employer after grape and wine production. By 2006, there were nearly 5 million visitors a year coming to the Napa Valley for wine tasting (Purdue University Tourism and Hospitality Research Center, 2006), causing traffic jams on the roads as well as crowding in the tasting rooms. To deal with these crowds, wineries routinely charge for sampling the wines in their tasting rooms, a practice that is less common in most other California wine regions.

As more of the area developed, there was greater concern that prime vineyard land was being replaced by subdivisions and that unmitigated growth was affecting the quality of life in the valley. In 1968, the first in a series of slow growth regulations was established in the form of an agricultural preserve. It was very controversial at the time because many growers and wineries did not want any constraints on how they could use or develop their property. Although land use regulations make it very difficult to start or expand wineries in the Napa Valley, they have controlled urban sprawl and preserved the valley's rural character. Today Napa has the smallest population of the 10 San Francisco Bay Area counties and in spite of all of the vineyard development, only 9 percent of the county's land is planted to grapes.

Regions of the Napa Valley

The Napa Valley is a large AVA with a wide variety of soil types and climates. The climate of the southern end of the valley is dominated by the cooling influences of San Pablo Bay. Here, particularly during the summer months, in the late afternoon cool breezes will blow in from the bay lowering the temperatures during the warmest part of the day. Cool climate varieties such as Pinot Noir and Chardonnay do best in this area of the valley. As you move up the valley toward the town of Calistoga, the bay has less of an influence and the climate becomes progressively warmer, making the area more suited to grapes that prefer warmer temperatures, such as Cabernet Sauvignon.

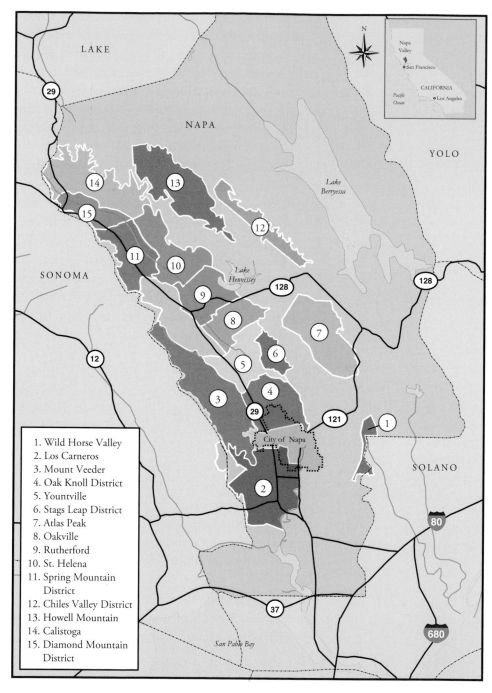

1. Wild Horse Valley
2. Los Carneros
3. Mount Veeder
4. Oak Knoll District
5. Yountville
6. Stags Leap District
7. Atlas Peak
8. Oakville
9. Rutherford
10. St. Helena
11. Spring Mountain District
12. Chiles Valley District
13. Howell Mountain
14. Calistoga
15. Diamond Mountain District

Elevation also affects the temperature. In much of the world, higher elevations are associated with cooler temperatures, but in coastal valleys like Napa the maritime influence on the environment makes the relationship between elevation and temperature more complicated. Since the fog often stays low as it moves up the valley in the evening, vineyards located above the fog layer will not benefit from its cooling effects (Figure 11.9). It is not unusual for hillside vineyards to have lower temperatures than the valley floor during the day and warmer conditions at night. These hillside vineyards typically experience more rainfall in the winter, and additionally are at lower risk of spring frost because cool night air will drain down from the hills and settle on the valley floor.

FIGURE 11.9

In California's coastal appellations, hillside vineyards are often above the morning fog layer that covers the vineyards located on the valley floor. This gives hillside vineyards more sun and elevated temperatures early in the day, resulting in a warmer terroir in spite of their higher elevation.

© Pat Henderson

In addition to the variation in climate, there is also a complex array of different types of soils found throughout the valley. Like much of California, the Napa Valley is very seismically active, and the numerous fault lines that are found in the appellation contribute to the diversity of its soils. The volcanic origin of the mountains is evidenced by the presence of hot springs and geysers found in the northern part of the valley. On the valley floor, the soils are a mix of sedimentary layers of old seabeds with the material that has washed down from the surrounding hills. Here the soils range from being heavy with clay that retains water to light with lots of sand and gravel that provides good drainage. Alluvial soils that are a mix of silt, sand, and gravel are found on the lands that flank the Napa River and its tributaries. Some of the best soil is considered to be the **bench land** that lies above the floodplain of the Napa River. In the middle of the valley, the "Rutherford Bench" is particularly known for producing fine Cabernet Sauvignon. The surrounding hillsides are often made up of thinner, rocky soils that are composed of sedimentary layers uplifted by geological faults or are derived from volcanic activity. These hillside vineyards are typically low in vigor, and if managed properly produce some of the most intensely flavored wines.

Sonoma Valley, Sonoma Mountain, and Bennett Valley AVAs

Established in 1982, Sonoma Valley is the county's oldest AVA. It reaches from the shores of San Pablo Bay on the south, 23 miles (37 km) to the northwest, and the small city of Santa Rosa. The appellation is framed by the Mayacamas range and Napa County to the east and to the west by Sonoma Mountain; it includes the entire Sonoma section of the Los Carneros AVA and the historic small town of Sonoma. Although there are many vineyards on the valley floor, the appellation also includes the mountainous terrain on either side of the valley. Fog and cool ocean breezes can come into the valley from the south, where there is a small gap at the southern end of Sonoma Mountain, or from the north through Santa Rosa. This makes the midsection of the valley around the small town of Glen Ellen slightly warmer than its upper and lower sections. The Sonoma Valley is perhaps best known for its Zinfandel, but its diverse conditions allow for the production of a number of grape varieties. On the southern end, the cooler climate is ideal for Pinot Noir and Chardonnay, and in the midsections of the valley, Sauvignon Blanc and Merlot (Figure 11.12). Cabernet Sauvignon is well suited to hillside vineyards that are above the fog layer.

Within the borders of the Sonoma Valley AVA are the smaller regions of the Sonoma Mountain and Bennett Valley AVAs. The Sonoma Mountain AVA is above the valley floor on the slopes of Sonoma Mountain from 400 to 1,200 feet (120 to 360 m). The soils are primarily of volcanic nature and are very well drained. Many of the vineyards have an eastern exposure that allows them to receive the full morning sun, which warms the vines quickly, and the afternoon sun on an oblique angle to moderate the temperature during the warmest part of the day. The appellation is home to the Jack London Vineyard, known for its Cabernet Sauvignon; it was the home of the famous author during his lifetime (Figure 11.13). The Bennett Valley region lays on the western edge of the Sonoma Valley between Sonoma Mountain to the south

FIGURE 11.12

A Sauvignon Blanc vineyard in the Carneros appellation located in the southern Sonoma Valley.

© Pat Henderson

FIGURE 11.13

The Jack London Vineyard on Sonoma Mountain; the ranch was owned by the author during his lifetime and is best known for its Cabernet Sauvignon. Before London's time, the ranch was also home to a large stone winery built by Kohler and Frohling, one of California's largest nineteenth-century producers.

© Pat Henderson

and Bennett peak to the north. The ocean breezes often pass through the valley on summer afternoons keeping the temperature moderate and making it well adapted for Sauvignon Blanc and Merlot.

Russian River, Chalk Hill, and Sonoma Green Valley AVAs

Named for the Russian fur trappers who settled on Sonoma County's coast in the early 1800s, the Russian River enters the county from Mendocino County to the north and continues south until it is just above Santa Rosa. Here the river turns to the west, traveling through a gap in the coastal range of mountains to the Pacific Ocean. The Russian River AVA covers much of the lower drainage of the Russian River and begins 6 miles (9.7 km) inland near the town of Guerneville, continuing up the river to the town of Healdsburg. The gap that is the pathway for the river also is a corridor for cool ocean air that travels into the interior of the county from the coast. Particularly during the summer months, vineyards located in the Russian River Valley are covered with a cooling layer of fog brought inland by sea breezes in the late afternoon. The fog persists throughout the night and burns off from the heat of the day the following morning.

The closer to the coast that a vineyard is located, the earlier in the afternoon it receives fog and the later it will last in the morning. These conditions make the western portion of the Russian River AVA one of the coolest in the North Coast counties and excellent for producing grapes such as Pinot Noir, Chardonnay, and Pinot Gris. Inland the climate becomes slightly warmer, and varieties such as Sauvignon Blanc and Zinfandel do well. Within the Russian River AVA are two subappellations, Chalk Hill to the east and Sonoma Green Valley to the west. The Chalk Hill AVA is bordered by Knights Valley to the east and Alexander Valley to the north. The soils are primarily of volcanic origin and Chardonnay is the most widely planted variety. On the western side of the Russian River AVA is the Sonoma Green Valley AVA, so named to avoid confusion with the Green Valley AVA in California's Solano County. It is a very cool region and has a number of exceptional Pinot Noir vineyards.

Dry Creek Valley and Rockpile AVAs

The Dry Creek Valley AVA lies between the Russian River AVA to the south and the Alexander Valley AVA to the northeast. The Dry Creek Valley begins in the town of Healdsburg and follows the path of Dry Creek, a tributary of the Russian River, 15 miles (24 km) to the northwest to Lake Sonoma at the head of the valley. The valley is somewhat narrow, being about 2 miles (3.2 km) across at its widest point. The Dry Creek Valley AVA includes much of the mountainous areas that border the valley itself. In the Dry Creek region cool winds from the coast are diverted by mountains, and the area is somewhat warmer than the Russian River AVA. Grapes were first planted in the 1860s and the potential for viticulture was quickly recognized. However, the region suffered after Prohibition and prunes became the dominant crop until the 1970s. In the lowlands along the banks of Dry Creek the soils are more alluvial in nature, and in the bench land above the flood plain the soils are more volcanic in origin. The appellation is best known for its Zinfandel and Cabernet Sauvignon; however, Chardonnay and Sauvignon Blanc are also widely planted and do well on the fertile soils of the valley floor.

The Rockpile AVA begins above Lake Sonoma in the western section of the Dry Creek AVA and extends to the Mendocino County border. Established in 2002 it is the county's newest appellation and is about one-fifth the size of the Dry Creek appellation. The area is very rugged, and the grapes grow predominantly in hillside vineyards. Even though the AVA is very young, it has already gained a reputation for producing quality Zinfandel.

Alexander Valley and Knights Valley AVAs

The Alexander Valley AVA is named for Cyrus Alexander, an early settler who received a land grant from General Vallejo. It is a wide valley created by the upper section of the Russian River as it passes through northern Sonoma County. It extends from just north of the town of Healdsburg 20 miles (32 km) north to the Mendocino County line. It is bordered by the Dry Creek Valley to the west and the prominent mountain Geyser Peak to the east, whose slopes are home to a large geothermal power plant. Being farther inland, it is a little warmer than the Dry Creek Valley and typically has deep, fertile, sandy loam soils. These conditions can make the grapevines very vigorous and growers must manage their vineyards to control excess growth. The appellation is perhaps best known for its Cabernet Sauvignon, but there are also extensive plantings of Sauvignon Blanc and Chardonnay. In the Geyserville area located in the middle of the valley, Zinfandel does particularly well.

The Knights Valley AVA is positioned between Alexander Valley to the west and the upper Napa Valley to the east. It has a warm climate that is similar to the Alexander Valley, and it is well known for its Cabernet Sauvignon as well as Sauvignon Blanc. The appellation's location on the eastern edge of Sonoma County is removed from urban areas, making it one of the least urbanized grape-growing regions in the county. Although it is located in Sonoma County, some think of the appellation as an extension of Napa Valley. One reason for this could be that the largest grower in the Knights Valley is Beringer Vineyards of St. Helena.

Other Sonoma County Appellations

The two largest appellations in Sonoma County are the Northern Sonoma and Sonoma Coast AVAs, at 349,837 acres (141,574 hectares) and 516,409 acres (208,983 hectares), respectively. While they are the largest AVAs, they are seldom used by wine producers and were primarily created by individual wineries that wanted to estate bottle grapes made from their widely scattered vineyards. The Northern Sonoma AVA covers the northern half of Sonoma County and includes all the territory of the Alexander Valley, Dry Creek Valley, Russian River Valley, Chalk Hill, Rockpile, and Knights Valley appellations. This large and diverse area covers a multitude of climates and soil types that are suitable to a wide selection of grape varieties. The Sonoma Coast appellation is even larger but has a more uniform cool climate. It extends along the western half of the county from San Pablo Bay on the south to Mendocino County in the north.

Lake and Mendocino Counties

The counties of Lake and Mendocino are part of the North Coast AVA and lie directly to the north of Napa and Sonoma Counties. As in Napa and Sonoma, the majority of the vineyards are located in the valleys between the mountains of the coast range. With the exception of Anderson Valley, the vineyards of Mendocino and Lake Counties are farther inland, and the mountains that separate them from the ocean are more rugged and higher in elevation. These factors result in less of a coastal influence than in Napa and Sonoma and, consequently, a generally warmer climate. This warmer climate, along with lower land costs, makes the grapes less expensive than those of Napa and Sonoma. In addition to the wineries in the area producing wines under a Lake or Mendocino appellation, wineries from other nearby regions look to the area as an economical source of quality grapes for their own brands.

Like Napa and Sonoma, there is a long history of agriculture with the production of hops, tree fruits, and nuts all being an important part of the local economy. Similar to what happened in Napa and Sonoma, these crops are giving way to grapes because of their greater market value. The counties maintain much of their rural character and to this day are less developed, with a smaller population than Napa and Sonoma. These qualities make Lake and Mendocino wine counties popular with tourists looking to avoid the crowds and high prices of their more famous neighbors to the south. Since the grape growing in Lake and Mendocino Counties is dispersed, the AVAs of the region are spread out as well. Many of the 15 AVAs located within these counties do not overlap or have contiguous borders.

Regions of Lake County

Lake County is named for Clear Lake, a large natural body of water situated in the middle of the county. Originally part of Napa County, it was split off in the 1860s.

Located inland and at a higher overall elevation than other North Coast counties there is little marine influence on the climate. These conditions make the days very warm; however, the altitude helps keep the nights cool. Much of the soil is of volcanic origin, produced from eruptions of the now dormant volcano Mt. Konocti that rises on the southern shores of the lake. The county has a long history of viticulture but was better known for its pears until the 1970s when large vineyards of Sauvignon Blanc and Chardonnay were planted in the rich valley soil that borders Clear Lake. In recent years vineyard development has accelerated due to growers moving in from Napa and Sonoma, where land costs have become prohibitively expensive. Many of the new vineyards are located in the hills that border the lake.

The Clear Lake AVA covers the land that surrounds the lake and includes most of the county's vineyards. The vineyards on the valley floor are best known for their Sauvignon Blanc with the hillside vineyards having more of a reputation for red varieties. There are two smaller subappellations located in the hills above the lake, the High Valley AVA to the north and the Red Hills AVA to the south. Here the warm climate and well-drained soils produce Cabernet Sauvignon of good quality and value (Figure 11.14). Lake County also has two small appellations—the Guenoc and Benmore Valleys. The Guenoc Valley AVA is located near the Napa County line and

FIGURE 11.14

An expansive vineyard located in the Red Hills appellation of Lake County.
© Pat Henderson

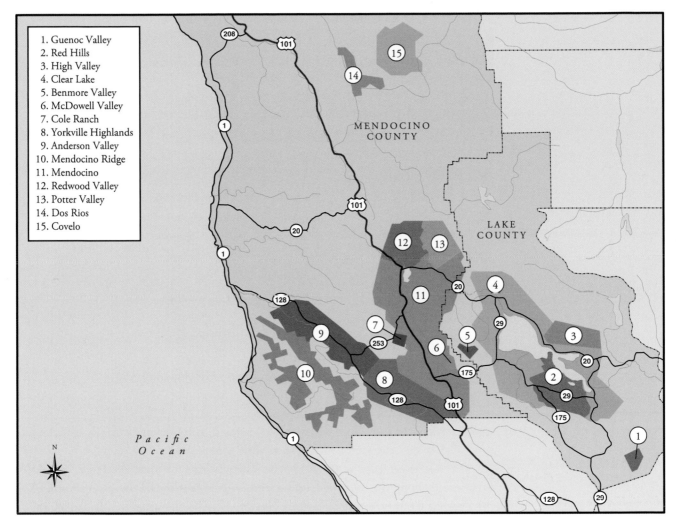

Legend:
1. Guenoc Valley
2. Red Hills
3. High Valley
4. Clear Lake
5. Benmore Valley
6. McDowell Valley
7. Cole Ranch
8. Yorkville Highlands
9. Anderson Valley
10. Mendocino Ridge
11. Mendocino
12. Redwood Valley
13. Potter Valley
14. Dos Rios
15. Covelo

THE APPELLATIONS OF LAKE AND MENDOCINO COUNTIES

© 2012 Delmar Cengage Learning

is used by only one winery. The Benmore Valley AVA lies in the hills on the western edge of Lake County near its border with Mendocino. The high elevation makes the region very cool, and Chardonnay is the predominate grape grown.

Regions of Mendocino County

Mendocino County is situated between Lake County to the east and the Pacific Ocean to the west. A large portion of the grape growing areas of the county was registered as the Mendocino AVA in 1984 (Table 11.3). The northern half of Mendocino County is heavily forested and better known for redwood trees than grapes, with the viticulture predominately taking place in the southern portion of the county. Organic viticulture is popular in the county, with one-quarter of the vineyards certified organic. Of Mendocino County's 10 AVAs, the Anderson Valley AVA is the coolest. Starting just 10 miles (16 km) from the coast, it is a long narrow valley that travels for 20 miles (32 km) inland along the route of the Navarro River and Highway 128 to the town of Booneville. The appellation grows slightly warmer as one moves inland or higher in elevation. The appellation has a number of small wineries that specialize in cool climate

TABLE 11.3 Appellations of Lake and Mendocino Counties

Appellation	Best-Known Varieties
Lake County	
Benmore Valley	Chardonnay
Clear Lake	Sauvignon Blanc, Chardonnay
Guenoc Valley	Not known for any one variety
High Valley	Cabernet Sauvignon, Zinfandel
Red Hills	Cabernet Sauvignon, Merlot
Mendocino County	
Anderson Valley	Chardonnay, Pinot Noir, Riesling, Gewürztraminer
Cole Ranch	Not known for any one variety
Covelo	Not known for any one variety
Dos Rios	Not known for any one variety
McDowell Valley	Syrah, Zinfandel
Mendocino	Produces a number of varieties
Mendocino Ridge	Zinfandel
Potter Valley	Sauvignon Blanc, Chardonnay
Redwood Valley	Red varietals
Yorkville Highlands	Cabernet Sauvignon, Sauvignon Blanc

varieties such as Pinot Noir, Chardonnay, Riesling, and Gewürztraminer. The Anderson Valley is also known for its sparkling wine production.

On the eastern edge of the Anderson Valley begins the Yorkville Highlands AVA. It continues along the route of Highway 128 until it reaches Alexander Valley AVA at the Sonoma County border. Because it is warmer and higher than the Anderson Valley, Sauvignon Blanc and Cabernet Sauvignon do well here. In the southwestern corner of Mendocino County is the Mendocino Ridge AVA, which covers the large area between the Anderson Valley and the Sonoma County line. What makes this appellation unique is that it is noncontiguous, only including the land above 1,200 feet (366 m) in elevation. By limiting the definition to the land above the fog line, the vineyards have a more uniform terroir despite the fact they are widely dispersed.

The majority of Mendocino County's grapes are grown in the valleys that flank the Russian River as it travels southward through Mendocino County. North of the county seat of Ukiah are two AVAs, both with extensive planting of grapes. The Redwood Valley AVA is slightly larger and situated to the west, and the Potter Valley on the east follows the east fork of the Russian River and is at a slightly higher elevation. Being more distant from the coast, they are warm regions that do not benefit much from the cooling effects of the ocean.

Traveling south along the river from the Redwood Valley there are two widely planted grape-growing regions that have not yet been granted AVA status. First is the Ukiah Valley that encircles the county seat. Here the valley broadens with the river plain and the weather becomes cooler. Below the Ukiah Valley is the Sanel Valley, which surrounds the town of Hopland. As of mid-2010, the AVA status of the Sanel

SOME OF THE
APPELLATIONS
OF THE NORTH
CENTRAL
COAST REGION

© 2012 Delmar Cengage
Learning

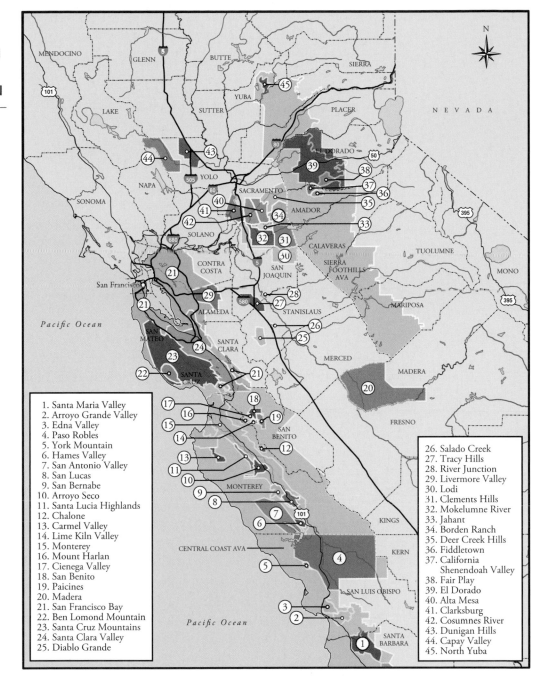

1. Santa Maria Valley
2. Arroyo Grande Valley
3. Edna Valley
4. Paso Robles
5. York Mountain
6. Hames Valley
7. San Antonio Valley
8. San Lucas
9. San Bernabe
10. Arroyo Seco
11. Santa Lucia Highlands
12. Chalone
13. Carmel Valley
14. Lime Kiln Valley
15. Monterey
16. Mount Harlan
17. Cienega Valley
18. San Benito
19. Paicines
20. Madera
21. San Francisco Bay
22. Ben Lomond Mountain
23. Santa Cruz Mountains
24. Santa Clara Valley
25. Diablo Grande

26. Salado Creek
27. Tracy Hills
28. River Junction
29. Livermore Valley
30. Lodi
31. Clements Hills
32. Mokelumne River
33. Jahant
34. Borden Ranch
35. Deer Creek Hills
36. Fiddletown
37. California
    Shenendoah Valley
38. Fair Play
39. El Dorado
40. Alta Mesa
41. Clarksburg
42. Cosumnes River
43. Dunigan Hills
44. Capay Valley
45. North Yuba

Valley was still pending. The Mendocino AVA is a large AVA that includes most of the county's vineyards. Mendocino County also has four small AVAs, the Cole Ranch, McDowell Valley, Dos Rios, and Covelo AVAs, all created for and used by individual wineries and growers.

The Central Coast

This huge viticultural area extends from the east side of San Francisco Bay, all the way to Santa Barbara in Southern California. It includes the grape-growing regions of

Alameda, Contra Costa, Monterey, San Benito, San Francisco, San Luis Obispo, San Mateo, Santa Barbara, Santa Clara, and Santa Cruz Counties. At nearly 5½ million acres (2.22 million hectares), the Central Coast is by far the largest AVA in California. Its size makes for such a great degree of variation in terroirs that the designation means little except to distinguish the cooler Central Coast vineyards from those located in the warmer regions of California's interior. Its climate ranges from being very warm in the inland valleys such as Paso Robles to very cool near the coast like the Edna Valley. Overall, it has slightly milder winters in the southern portion of the appellation than the north. Much like the large North Coast AVA, it is divided into a number of subappellations to help differentiate its varied growing conditions (Table 11.4). Wines from the Central Coast are frequently bottled using the county of origin as designation instead of using an AVA classification. The winemaking history of the district dates back to the time of the missions that stretched in a chain along the California coast, and the region has seen much new development in recent decades.

San Francisco Bay Area and Santa Cruz County

Although the San Francisco Bay AVA is technically part of the Central Coast AVA, few people associate it with the more prolific areas of the appellation to the south. While the southern and central portions of the Central Coast appellation had little vineyard and winery development between the time of the missions and the 1960s, the San Francisco Bay area has been home to vineyards and wineries since the early 1800s. In the time since World War II, the majority of the vineyards in the Bay Area have been replaced by subdivisions. The Santa Clara Valley in particular had a reputation for being one of the finest grape-growing areas in the state in the 1880s. Today, despite the fact the Santa Clara Valley has its own AVA, the region has little agriculture and is better known as the Silicon Valley. There are still some vineyards located in the southern end of the appellation near the town of Gilroy, but the historic grape-growing areas in the north of the appellation have been displaced by subdivisions and the high-tech industry. The Livermore Valley AVA located east of the bay also has a long history of winemaking and still has many vineyards, but this area is also threatened by urban development. Contra Costa County to the north of the Livermore Valley is another grape-growing region that has been decimated by housing and development. Prior to Prohibition there were more than 25 wineries and 6,000 acres (2,400 hectares) of grapes (Brook, 1999); now only a few remain.

The Santa Cruz Mountains AVA is located in the hills of the coastal range in Santa Cruz, San Mateo, and Santa Clara Counties. The appellation was one of the first in California, being formed in 1982, and is defined by the land that is above 400 feet (122 m) in elevation. When the Central Coast AVA was approved in 1985, the Santa Cruz Mountains AVA was excluded so the appellations were contiguous but do not overlap. The terrain is rugged and the soil can be very stony, resulting in low vigor and yields. The vineyards and wineries are generally small and dispersed throughout the area, with many vintners acquiring grapes from outside the appellation to supplement their production. Although it is not nearly as developed as the appellations north of San Francisco Bay, it too has a long history that was renewed during the wine revolution in

TABLE 11.4 Appellations of the Central Coast

The Central Coast AVA includes Alameda, Contra Costa, Monterey, San Benito, San Francisco, San Luis Obispo, San Mateo, Santa Barbara, Santa Clara, and Santa Cruz Counties

The San Francisco Bay Area AVA includes Alameda, Contra Costa, San Francisco, San Mateo, and Santa Clara Counties

Subappellation by County	Best-Known Varieties
Alameda County	
Livermore Valley	Chardonnay, Cabernet Sauvignon, Mourvèdre
Monterey County	
Arroyo Seco	Chardonnay
Carmel Valley	Cabernet Sauvignon
Chalone	Pinot Noir, Chardonnay
Hames Valley	Cabernet Sauvignon, Merlot
Monterey	Chardonnay is best known of many varieties
San Bernabe	Produces a number of varieties
San Lucas	Chardonnay, Cabernet Sauvignon, Merlot
Santa Lucia Highlands	Pinot Noir, Chardonnay
San Antonio Valley	Bordeaux and Rhône varieties
San Benito County	
Cienega Valley	Produces a number of varieties
Lime Kiln Valley	Produces a number of varieties
Mt. Harlan	Pinot Noir
Paicines	Produces a number of varieties
San Benito	Produces a number of varieties
San Luis Obispo County	
Arroyo Grande Valley	Chardonnay
Edna Valley	Chardonnay, Pinot Noir
Paso Robles	Syrah, Zinfandel
York Mountain	Zinfandel
Santa Barbara County	
Happy Canyon of Santa Barbara	Cabernet Sauvignon, Syrah
Santa Maria Valley	Chardonnay, Pinot Noir
Santa Rita Hills	Pinot Noir
Santa Ynez Valley	Chardonnay, Sauvignon Blanc, Syrah
Santa Clara County	
Pacheco Pass	Not known for any one variety
Santa Clara Valley	Chardonnay, Cabernet Sauvignon
San Ysidro District	Chardonnay
Santa Cruz County	
Ben Lomond Mountain	Not known for any one variety
Santa Cruz Mountains	Chardonnay, Pinot Noir, Cabernet Sauvignon

the 1960s and 1970s. Many wine enthusiasts with an independent viewpoint who were looking to start their ventures away from the more established regions of Napa and Sonoma were drawn to the isolation of the Santa Cruz Mountains. One of the innovators of this region was Randall Grahm who founded Bonny Doon Vineyard in 1983. It was one of the first wineries in California to become known for Rhône varietals like Syrah Grenache and was an early adopter of screwcaps on premium wines.

Monterey and San Benito Counties

While the San Francisco Bay area to the north had some degree of viticulture and winemaking from the time the region was settled to the present day, Monterey and San Benito Counties had little viticultural activity from the end of the mission period until the 1960s when a few vineyards were planted. Although there were few vineyards in the region, there was a great deal of agriculture. In Monterey County, the Salinas Valley in particular has ideal soils and climate for vegetable crops, but most growers considered it too cool and windy for wine grapes. In the 1970s wineries from outside the county, looking to expand their production, established large vineyard operations, and production rapidly grew (Figure 11.15). During the rapid development, varieties such as Cabernet Sauvignon were planted that were ill suited to Monterey's cool weather, and the results were far from perfect. The cool conditions gave the Cabernet Sauvignon that was produced a distinctly vegetative or "bell pepper" aroma that Monterey became known for. The unpopular flavors of the wines from Monterey slowed development, and vineyard acreage decreased in the early 1980s. In the 1990s high costs of vineyard land elsewhere in the state led vintners and growers to reconsider Monterey County, this time with a better understanding of what the marketplace desired and the appellation's terroir. Cool weather varieties like Chardonnay and Pinot Noir were planted in the northern part of the county, which was closer to the ocean and much cooler, and

FIGURE 11.15

A Chardonnay vineyard in the Salinas Valley of Monterey County.
© David Gubernick/AgStock1 Images/Corbis

warm weather varieties such as Merlot and Zinfandel were planted inland where it was warmer.

Today there are more than 40,000 acres (16,200 hectares) of grapes in Monterey County. The great majority of the vineyards are located in the large Monterey AVA that runs from Monterey Bay down Salinas Valley to the county border. Two-thirds of the grapevines in the appellation are white wine varieties and most of the crop goes to large wineries, many located outside of the appellation, that use it as a source of inexpensive, high quality, cool-climate grapes for their California or "Coastal" blends. While the county's vineyards and wineries are predominately large operations, Monterey is also home to a number of small producers and subappellations.

Moving down the Salinas Valley from the coast are the Santa Lucia Highlands, Arroyo Seco, San Bernabe, San Lucas, and Hames Valley AVAs, all located within the Monterey AVA. Generally, they have well-drained soils, and the appellations grow warmer the farther they are from the bay. The Santa Lucia Highlands on the western slopes of the valley is the closest to the coast; it is the coolest and has recently gained an excellent reputation for Chardonnay and Pinot Noir. The San Bernabe AVA, created in 2004, is like several other appellations in the state, it is home to only one vineyard and was created to benefit a single winery. However, unlike the others it is a very large vineyard with more than 5,000 acres (2,000 hectares) planted. Positioned just east of the Santa Lucia Highlands is the Carmel Valley AVA. It is much narrower than the Salinas Valley and protected by mountains from the maritime influences of the Pacific, making the appellation warmer and better suited to red varieties. Just to the west of the southern end of the Salinas Valley lies the San Antonio Valley AVA. The newest of the Monterey County appellations, it is a little warmer and has a climate more similar to Paso Robles to the south than it does to its neighbors in the Salinas Valley. The San Antonio Valley has been producing grapes since the late 1700s and is best suited to Syrah and Cabernet Sauvignon.

To the east of Monterey County is San Benito County. Smaller in both size and population, its vineyard development paralleled that in Monterey County. Like Monterey, the region has a mix of large vineyards and wineries as well as smaller producers. Additionally, in the north of the county on the valley floor, the climate is similar to that of the Monterey AVA, though to the south in the mountains of the Gavilan range this comparison ends and the climate becomes warmer. Similar to that found in the Burgundy region, the soil here has a great deal of limestone, which is rare in California. This drew vintners to the area for Chardonnay and Pinot Noir. In this part of the county the San Benito AVA resides which has the subappellations of the Cienega Valley, Lime Kiln Valley, and Paicines. Nearby are the Mt. Harlan and Chalone AVAs, which are used only by the wineries that reside in them. The majority of the Chalone AVA is in Monterey County; however, since the climate is more similar to the other AVAs of San Benito, it is included here.

San Luis Obispo County

San Luis Obispo County is located directly south of Monterey County. Much like Monterey, it has a long history of grape growing, dating back to the time of the missions, that was reborn during the wine boom, and the county has a dichotomy of large

*© 2012 Delmar Cengage
Learning*

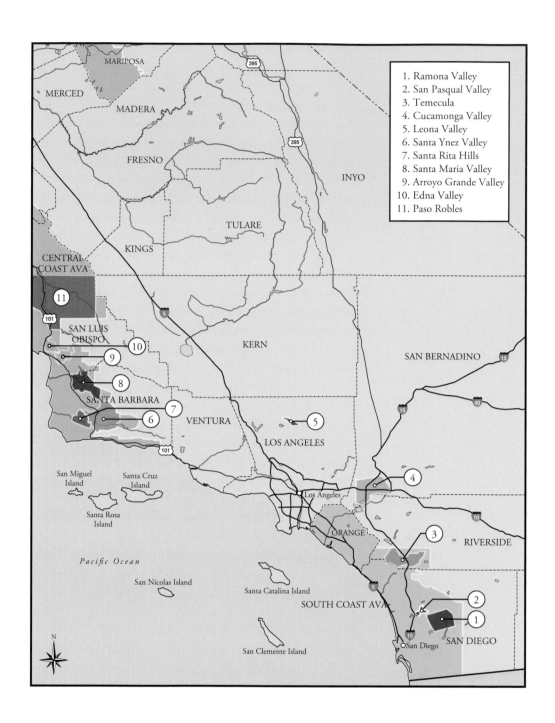

1. Ramona Valley
2. San Pasqual Valley
3. Temecula
4. Cucamonga Valley
5. Leona Valley
6. Santa Ynez Valley
7. Santa Rita Hills
8. Santa Maria Valley
9. Arroyo Grande Valley
10. Edna Valley
11. Paso Robles

and small producers. The largest AVA in the county is the Paso Robles appellation with more than 609,000 acres (246,000 hectares). Its northern border is the Monterey County line and the western edge of the AVA begins about 10 miles (16 km) in from the coast in the mountains of the southern portion of the Santa Lucia range. The appellation has experienced rapid growth in the last 20 years and currently has more than 26,000 acres (10,500 hectares) planted to wine grapes. Here the coastal mountains block much of the cooling influence from the coast, and the region is generally warmer than Monterey AVA to the north.

The Paso Robles AVA has two distinctly different terroirs located on either side of the Salinas River. To the west, the terrain is hilly, and soils that are composed of ancient seabeds and limestone are common. It is slightly cooler here than on the eastern side, with more rainfall in the winter. Just south of the town of Paso Robles there is a break in the mountains called the Templeton Gap that creates a path for ocean breezes, and vineyards in this area have cooler weather conditions than other parts of the appellation.

The western Paso Robles AVA is home to numerous small vineyards and wineries. To the east of the Salinas River the land becomes a broad plane characterized by sandy loam soils. The conditions are drier and warmer than they are in Paso Robles' western portion and the elevation ranges from 600 to 1,000 feet (182 to 300 m). The elevation helps keep the nighttime temperatures cool during the summer months, and frequently temperatures swing 45°F (25°C) between day and night. The open terrain in this part of the appellation allows for plantings that are more expansive, and larger vineyards and wineries are more common. Similarly to Monterey County, wineries from outside the area have invested in vineyard land to augment their production. The region is best known for reds such as Cabernet Sauvignon, Syrah, and Zinfandel, but there is also a considerable amount of Chardonnay planted.

South of the Paso Robles appellation the mountains diminish and the weather has a greater maritime influence. Here lies the Edna Valley AVA, which is much smaller and considerably cooler than Paso Robles. Most of the vineyards are planted on the valley floor where the soils are composed primarily of sedimentary material derived from ancient seabeds. The appellation is best known for Chardonnay and Pinot Noir. Edna Valley's southern location in the state makes for an early spring budbreak. This, combined with the cool summers, results in a long growing season. There are two other appellations in the county worth mentioning, York Mountain and Arroyo Grande. York Mountain is located in the mountains on the western edge of the Paso Robles AVA. It is slightly cooler than the land to the east and is the site of the first commercial vineyards in the region in the 1880s. The Arroyo Grande AVA is just south of the Edna Valley AVA and has a similar terroir.

Santa Barbara County

Santa Barbara County is the last of California's major viticultural regions before reaching the vast urban areas of Los Angeles. Its history goes back to some of the earliest vineyards in California when the friars of the mission period planted grapes there in the 1780s. However, there was almost no further vineyard development until the 1970s. The climate here is comparable to that in the southern portion of San Luis Obispo County where winters are mild and have limited rainfall. Spring comes early to the appellation and budbreak occurs about a month before the cooler grape growing regions of California's North Coast. The summers are cool and often foggy which gives the grapes high natural acidity but also creates a risk of botrytis. The county boasts 17,000 acres (6,900 hectares) of vineyards and more than 90 wineries (Figure 11.16); Chardonnay is the most popular variety followed by Pinot Noir. The proximity to the Los Angeles urban area brings in many visitors to Santa Barbara's

FIGURE 11.16

Late summer vineyards in the Santa Ynez Valley appellation of Santa Barbara County. The vines have been netted to protect the ripening grapes from being eaten by birds.

© Pat Henderson

wine county. Additionally, the appellation was featured prominently in the 2004 motion picture *Sideways* that brought notoriety to the region as well as its most popular red variety, Pinot Noir.

The two largest AVAs in the county are the Santa Maria Valley and the Santa Ynez Valley. The Santa Maria Valley AVA begins about 10 miles (16 km) inland on Santa Barbara County's border with San Luis Obispo County just east of the town of Santa Maria and runs for 15 miles (24 km) in a southeasterly direction. It is slightly cooler than the Santa Ynez Valley to the south, and Chardonnay and Pinot Noir are popular varieties. The Chardonnay from Santa Maria has a reputation for crisp acidity and tropical flavors. To the south is the Santa Ynez AVA and here, unlike most of the California coast, the mountains and valleys run in an east–west direction. Overall the appellation is a little warmer than the Santa Maria region but the vineyards near the coast are cooler than those that are more inland. Popular grapes include Chardonnay, Sauvignon Blanc, Riesling, as well as some Syrah. In the eastern portion of the Santa Ynez Valley lies the Happy Canyon of Santa Barbara AVA. Established in the fall of the 2009, it has approximately 500 acres (200 hectares) of vines and is best known for Cabernet Sauvignon and Sauvignon Blanc.

Two smaller and better-known growing regions in the county are the Sta. Rita Hills AVA and the Los Alamos Valley. The Sta. Rita Hills AVA is carved out of the western section of the Santa Ynez Valley AVA; it is a cool area widely planted to Pinot Noir. Lying between the Sta. Rita Hills and the Santa Maria AVA is Los Alamos Valley. Although it has more acres of wine grapes than Santa Ynez Valley, it does not currently have its own AVA. One reason for this is Los Alamos Valley has many large vineyards that produce grapes for big wineries that blend the wines they make with that from other appellations. Since wines made from Los Alamos Valley grapes are rarely kept separate, there is less of an incentive to give the region its own AVA.

Central Valley

California's great Central Valley extends for 450 miles (720 km) throughout the middle of the state. It drains the waters of the Sacramento River to the north and the San Joaquin River to the south through the Delta region into San Francisco Bay. Growing a diverse array of crops, its combination of fertile soils, warm weather, and irrigation make it the nation's most prolific agricultural area. It is also the state's most productive region for grapes, producing 75 percent of the wine grape harvest and 99 percent of the state's table grape and raisin production (California Department of Food and Agriculture, 2009). There are many large vineyards and the conditions allow for much higher croploads than the state's grape-growing regions near the coast. These vineyards generally produce a wine that has a more neutral flavor than coastal vineyards. The quality is also reflected by the price, with Central Valley grapes selling at an average of $400 per ton while Napa Valley grapes bring in more than $3,300 per ton. All the state's largest wineries are located in the Central Valley. Their huge outdoor stainless steel tanks give them a very different appearance than the small wineries of the coast (Figure 11.17).

The majority of the Central Valley's 235,000 acres (95,000 hectares) of wine grapes lie in its southern half, which reaches from the capital city of Sacramento down to Bakersfield. The Central Valley, despite its importance to the wine industry, does not have its own AVA, and the wines produced here are usually labeled "California." Although the climate makes the region better suited for warm weather grapes, there are large

FIGURE 11.17

An outdoor tank farm at Heck Cellars in the southern San Joaquin Valley. Large Central Valley wineries such as these produce the majority of the wine made in California.

Photo Courtesy Mark Stupich

plantings of cool climate varieties such as Chardonnay. During the 1980s, as consumers became more familiar with varietal names for their wine, growers began planting Chardonnay because it was popular with wine drinkers. Even though it does better in cool regions, it was worth more than white wine varieties traditional to the Central Valley such as French Colombard and Chenin Blanc, which were at the time usually bottled in jugs and labeled as "white table wine." This new category of inexpensive wines that were varietal labeled and bottled 25.4-oz (750 ml) packages, were called fighting varietals.

The entire valley is warm, but the area just south of Sacramento where the Sacramento and San Joaquin Rivers join does receive some cooling influences from San Francisco Bay. This area, which is known as the Delta region, contains the Central Valley's two most prominent AVAs of Clarksburg and Lodi. The quality of the grapes grown in these AVAs is considered superior to those grown farther south; consequently, they command higher prices. The Lodi appellation in particular has a long history of grape growing and winemaking but was little known outside of the area until recently. In the last decade, a number of producers have started bottling wines using the Lodi appellation, and no less than seven new subappellations have been established within the Lodi AVA since 2006. Grapes are also grown to the west of the Delta in Yolo and Solano Counties. These two counties span the area between the Clarksburg AVA and the North Coast appellation. This area is also slightly cooler than the southern Central Valley and includes several AVAs and a handful of wineries.

Other Grape-Growing Regions of California

The regions discussed so far contain the vast majority of commercial viticulture in the state of California. However, there are two additional appellations with smaller wine industries; they are the Sierra Foothills and Temecula. The Sierra Foothills AVA runs along the western flank of the Sierra Nevada mountain range above the Central Valley. It is a large appellation covering more than 170 miles (274 km) from Yuba County in the north to Mariposa County in the south. Being in the hills, the terrain is generally rugged with volcanic soils, and the climate of a particular vineyard varies depending on the elevation and exposure. Grape growing has been going on in the area since it was first settled during the time of the Gold Rush, and there were a number of vineyards and wineries prior to Prohibition. Despite its long history and size, it only has about 6,300 acres (2,500 hectares) planted to grapes. The great majority of its vineyards are planted with red varieties and it is most well known for its Zinfandel, some of which grows on quite old vines. The appellation can have very warm afternoons during the summer months, but the elevation aids in keeping the nights relatively cool. It also contains the subappellations of Fiddletown, El Dorado, North Yuba, and California Shenandoah Valley.

Like the Sierra Foothills, the Temecula AVA in Southern California also has a long history of winemaking, going back to the time of the missions and currently has about 25 wineries. It is a coastal valley that is situated in the southwestern corner of Riverside County about 20 miles (32 km) from the ocean. The coastal influences keep the valley cool in spite of its southern location just 70 miles (113 km) from the Mexican border. Its mild growing conditions make it well suited for white grapes, and it is predominately planted to Chardonnay and Sauvignon Blanc. In 2001, the district had over 2,500 acres (1,000 hectares) of wine grapes; however, in recent years vineyard acreage has fallen dramatically due to severe problems with Pierce's disease, which is fatal to grapevines. Pierce's disease is caused by a bacterial infection and is spread from vine to vine by insects. Pierce's disease has always been present in the state, and there have been several serious outbreaks over the years. The outbreak in Temecula was spread by the recently introduced insect pest from the southeastern United States, the glassy-winged sharpshooter. Currently the state is investing a great deal of resources to control the pest and prevent it from expanding its range in California.

FIGURE 11.18

Valley of the Moon Winery in Sonoma Valley. The winery, first established in the 1860s, has recently modernized its winemaking operations.
© Pat Henderson

Summary

California's history and climate have made it the natural center of wine production in the United States. Its diversity of growing conditions allow for the creation of a wide range of wines from the inexpensive everyday table wines produced in the Central Valley to the unique high end wines of the North Coast (Figure 11.18). In recent decades, the increasing popularity of wine has resulted in the growth of new winemaking regions outside California as well as the resurgence of the industry in areas where it has historic roots. In 2010, all 50 states had bonded wineries and there were 87 AVAs outside California registered with the federal government. Despite the growth of these new wine regions, California remains the nation's most important wine producer, setting trends in winemaking much as it does for many other consumer items.

CALIFORNIA FOOD AND WINE PAIRING

appetizer

fresh raw oysters on the half shell

wine

A dry Carneros blanc de noir sparkling wine

first course

**breast of rosemary chicken on a bed
of angel-hair pasta with an herb butter sauce**

wine

A Santa Maria Valley Pinot Noir

main course

**grilled London broil steak with garlic
mashed potatoes and grilled asparagus**

wine

A big-bodied Napa Valley Cabernet Sauvignon

dessert

fresh apricot tart with almond crust

wine

An Anderson Valley Late-Harvest Gewürztraminer

EXERCISES

1. How did Prohibition affect the wine industry in California?

2. How did Prohibition affect the tastes of wine drinkers in the United States?

3. What was the "Paris tasting" and what role did it have in building the reputation of California wine?

4. Describe the importance of California in the U.S. wine industry.

5. Discuss winemaking in California during the mission period.

REVIEW QUESTIONS

1. What effect does a vineyard's proximity to the coast have on its terroir?
   A. It makes it warmer.
   B. It makes it cooler.
   C. It makes it dryer.
   D. It has little or no effect.

2. When the Taxation and Trade Bureau (TTB) authorizes a new American Viticultural Appellation (AVA) it _____.
   A. States that the region grows superior wine grapes
   B. Limits the varieties of grapes that can be grown
   C. Specifies the types of winemaking practices that are allowed
   D. Specifies only the districts' boundaries and makes no statements of quality

3. Seventy-five percent of California's wine grapes are grown in _____.
   A. The Central Valley
   B. Napa County
   C. The Central Coast AVA
   D. The North Coast AVA

(Continues)

(Continued)

4. The vineyards of Mendocino County are best known for _____.
   A. The high price that their grapes command
   B. Organic viticulture
   C. Their late-harvest Zinfandel
   D. Their sparkling wines

5. California's coastal grape growing regions are characterized by _____.
   A. Wet winters and mild dry summers
   B. Dry winters and wet summers
   C. Freezing cold winters and scorching summers
   D. Mild winters that keep the vines from going dormant

REFERENCES

Beverage Information Group. (2008). *Adams wine handbook*. Norwalk, CT: Author.

Brook, S. (1999). *The wines of California*. New York: Faber and Faber.

California Department of Food and Agriculture. (2009). *Grape crush report 2008 crop*. Sacramento: State of California.

Johnson, H. (1989). *Vintage: The story of wine*. New York: Simon & Schuster.

Lapsley, J. T. (1996). *Bottled poetry*. Berkeley: University of California Press.

Laube, J. (1999). *California wine*. New York: Wine Spectator Press.

Purdue University Tourism and Hospitality Research Center. (2006). *Napa County visitor profile executive report*. West Lafayette, IN: Purdue University.

Sullivan, C. L. (1998). *A companion to California wine*. Berkeley: University of California Press.

Taber, G. M. (2005). *Judgment of Paris*. New York: Scribner.

Tapia, A. M., Cabezas, J. A., Cabello, F., Lacombe, T., Martínez-Zapater, J. M., Hinrichsen, P., and Cerveral, M. T. (2007). Determining the Spanish origin of representative ancient American grapevine varieties. *American Journal of Enology and Viticulture, 58*(2), 242–251.

Teiser, R., & Harroun, C. (1983). *Winemaking in California*. New York: McGraw-Hill.

Wine Institute. (2008). *A signature California industry, California wine*. San Francisco: Author.

{ THE PACIFIC NORTHWEST }

This chapter explains how

the wine industry developed in Washington and Oregon, and discusses how their respective climates and geography have affected the varieties of grapes that are grown and the styles of wine that they produce.

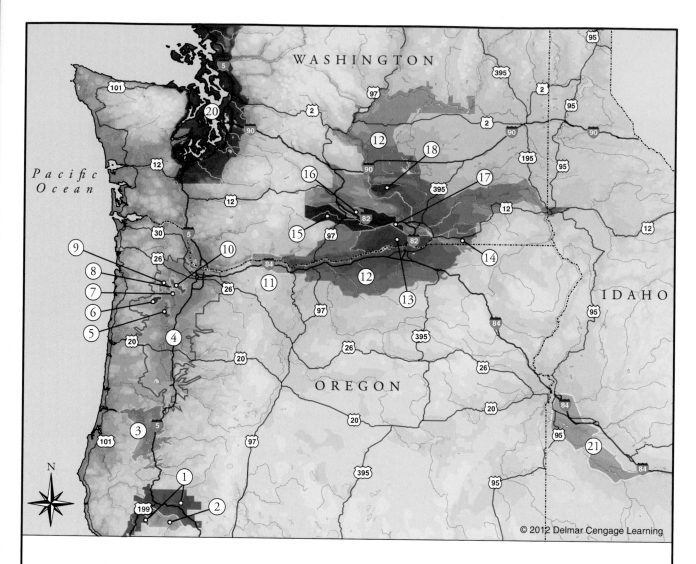

© 2012 Delmar Cengage Learning

OREGON:
1. Rogue Valley (p. 425)
2. Applegate Valley (p. 425)
3. Umpqua Valley (p. 425)
4. Willamette Valley (p. 423)
5. Eola-Amity Hills (p. 424)
6. McMinnville (p. 424)
7. Dundee Hills (p. 424)
8. Ribbon Ridge
9. Yarnhill-Carlton District
10. Chehalem Mountains
11. Columbia Gorge
12. Columbia Valley

WASHINGTON:
11. Columbia Valley (p. 416)
12. Columbia Gorge (p. 418)
13. Horse Haven Hills (p. 417)
14. Walla Walla Valley (p. 418)
15. Yakima Valley (p. 416)
16. Rattlesnake Hills (p. 417)
17. Red Mountain (p. 417)
18. Wahluke Slope
19. Columbia Valley
20. Puget Sound (p. 419)

IDAHO:
21. Snake River Valley (p. 426)

KEY TERMS

Concord

dry-farmed

Isabella

own-rooted

rain shadow

Stimson Lane
Vineyards & Estates

INTRODUCTION

The Pacific Northwest is one of the nation's most important wine-producing regions. Oregon and Washington's wine-growing regions range from 400 to 600 miles (650 to 960 km) north of California's Napa and Sonoma appellations. This places them at approximately the same latitude as the Bordeaux and Burgundy regions of France. Oregon and Washington combined account for about 4 percent of the U.S. wine production but have 16 percent of the nation's wineries. With comparable geography, history, and culture, the two states are similar in many respects. However, in spite of these similarities the wine industries of the two states have developed differently, giving each its own unique identity. Washington's vineyards are predominately in the dryer eastern part of the state, and several large producers make up the majority of the production (Figure 12.1). Oregon's vineyards, by contrast, are located primarily in the state's western half and small wineries and vineyards predominate (Figure 12.2). Washington and Oregon have three American Viticultural Areas (AVAs), the Walla Walla, Columbia Valley, and Columbia Gorge, which cross the boundary between the two states. The majority of the vineyard land in the Walla Walla and Columbia Valley AVAs lies on the Washington side of the border, while the vineyards of the Columbia Gorge appellation are more evenly distributed.

WASHINGTON STATE

After California, Washington State is the nation's second largest producer of premium table wine, making nearly five times as much wine as Oregon does. New York State produces slightly more wine than Washington, but much of its production is from non–*Vitis vinifera* grape varieties. In recent decades there has been dramatic change

FIGURE 12.1

An expansive vineyard located in Eastern Washington's Columbia Valley appellation.
Washington Wine Commission

FIGURE 12.11

Open-top stainless steel fermentation tanks at an Oregon winery. With open-top tanks, punching down the cap into the fermenting must is the most common method of extracting flavor and color from the skins.

Oregon Wine Board, Patrick Prothe Photography

OREGON STATE

Set in between California and Washington, Oregon is the country's fourth largest wine producer (Figure 12.11). While the size of Oregon's wine business is overwhelmed by its neighbors, its reputation for producing fine wine, in particular Pinot Noir, is not. Pinot Noir makes up over half of the vineyard acreage and is the state's most important variety. Like Washington State, the industry has had tremendous expansion in recent years. Despite the growth, the majority of producers remain very small, with most making less than 5,000 cases per year. This is evidenced by the fact that Oregon has 395 wineries, almost as many as Washington does, yet bottles only one-fifth as much wine (USDA, 2009b). The limited production of the wineries also contributes to the fact Oregon wines usually command higher prices than those of Washington State.

OREGON STATE WINE— HISTORICAL PERSPECTIVE

In the mid-1800s, settlers were attracted to Oregon's rich agricultural land and many came to settle the area by crossing the Oregon Trail. One of them, Henderson Luelling, was a horticulturist and planted Oregon's first grapevines in the Willamette Valley in 1847. Luelling, working with his son-in-law, William Meek, produced wine and in 1859 they won a medal at the California State Fair for their wine produced from the American grape variety Isabella (Hall, 2001). By the 1850s, viticulture was also being developed in southern Oregon in the Rogue River Valley. Here Peter Britt grew grapes and established a winery named Valley View Vineyard. The winery and vineyards were reestablished in early 1972 and continue to produce wine today. In the 1880s, two brothers named Edward and John Von Pessls came up from California to the Umpqua Valley region of southern Oregon. They planted cuttings they had brought with them of Zinfandel and other *vinifera* varieties obtained in the Napa Valley. To the north in the Willamette Valley, Earnest Reuter was making wine out of white *vinifera* grapes. Like his predecessor Henderson Luelling, he won praise outside Oregon with a gold medal at the 1904 world's fair in St. Louis.

Despite the fact that these early vintners enjoyed some successes, viticulture in Oregon never developed to the extent it did to the south in California. Although the coastal river valleys in southern Oregon have a climate similar to California's North Coast AVA, most of the state's agriculture takes place farther north in the Willamette

Valley, which growers considered too damp and cool for production of wine grapes. What little industry existed was wiped out by Prohibition in 1920. After its repeal, the industry did not benefit from protectionist laws that Washington State had, and it could not compete with the more established vineyards in California, which enjoyed a more consistent climate. After Prohibition a handful of small wineries did exist; however, most produced fruit wines from berries and other crops that were grown on their own farms. The great majority of these wines were consumed close to home and rarely left the state. In 1938, 5 years after the repeal of Prohibition, there were 28 bonded wineries in Oregon; just 20 years later in 1958, nearly all were closed.

The Beginning of an Industry

The lack of post-Prohibition development lasted until the 1960s, when a new generation of winemakers began to attempt to make table wine from traditional wine varieties. Two of the early producers were expatriates from California. In southern Oregon, Richard Sommer began Hill Crest Vineyard outside the town of Roseburg. He had been trained at the University of California–Davis where he was warned that Oregon would be too wet and chilly to successfully grow *vinifera* grapes. In the Willamette Valley, Charles Coury began growing Alsatian varieties such as Pinot Blanc, as well as some Pinot Noir, on Wine Hill where Ernest Reuter had grown grapes in the 1880s. Perhaps the most significant year of the decade for Oregon winemaking was 1966, when David Lett of the Eyrie Vineyard Winery planted the first Pinot Noir vines in the Dundee Hills region of the Willamette Valley. Having spent time in France, Lett was convinced that the climate of Oregon more closely approximated that of Burgundy than California's did. After the vines were mature, he used traditional Burgundian production methods to make his wines. At the end of the decade, the wine industry in the state was still very small with only five bonded wineries producing wine.

Over the next two decades, Pinot Noir would become Oregon's most notable wine and raise the reputation of winemaking in the state. The wineries that were established in the 1960s and 1970s were small and often built by an owner/winemaker in contrast to the large, capital-intensive wineries that were being built in California and Washington. Pinot Noir is a difficult grape to grow and its delicate flavors can be lost during processing at the winery. The variety seemed well suited to Oregon's capricious weather and the handmade, labor-intensive techniques used at its small wineries (Figure 12.12). Oregon winemakers were also among the first in the country to pay close attention to the aspects of clone selection with Pinot Noir production. As described in Chapter 2, Pinot Noir has a number of different clones that growers can select from when planting their vineyards. In 1975, Oregon State University in Corvallis began working closely with growers to import Burgundy Pinot Noir clones best suited for table wine production and make them available to the public.

The quality of Oregon Pinot Noir gained worldwide attention in 1979 when David Lett entered a 1975 Pinot Noir from Eyrie Vineyard into an international Pinot Noir competition in Paris where it placed 10th, ahead of many of Burgundy's best producers. These results sent shock waves around the wine world in much the same way as the Paris tasting of 1976 did for California winemakers. During this time Oregon

FIGURE 12.12

Chardonnay grapes being loaded into a tank press for whole cluster pressing. Whole cluster pressing is gentler than pressing fruit that has been crushed and destemmed before pressing.

Oregon Wine Board, Patrick Prothe Photography

also formed some of the strictest labeling and composition laws in the United States. In 1977, the Oregon Liquor Control Commission enacted rules that state:

- A wine labeled Estate must be grown within 5 miles (8 km) of the winery.
- The composition of a wine must be at least 90 percent of the varietal listed on the label.
- Generic terms of European appellations such as *Champagne* and *Burgundy* cannot be used.

The 90 percent minimum of a grape variety is considerably higher than the 75 percent required in California and Washington. By 1980 there were 34 wineries and 1,100 acres (445 hectares) of wine grapes in the state.

During the last two decades, the growing popularity of Oregon wine attracted new investment, and a few larger showcase wineries were built. During the 15 years from 1992 to 2007, the number of wineries in Oregon grew from 78 to 370 and it ranked fourth in production after New York State. Despite its successes, Oregon's wine industry has retained its modest character. Small independent producers are common, and the largest winery bottles only 125,000 cases a year. Oregon also has gained a reputation for white wines, most notably Pinot Gris and Chardonnay; however, Pinot Noir remains Oregon's most popular grape, representing 58 percent of the planted acres and half of the state's wine production (USDA, 2009b). First identified in 1990, phylloxera has been found in some vineyards. However, it has spread slowly and remained somewhat isolated. Consequently, half of the state's vines still grow on their own roots, although most new plantings are grown on rootstocks.

Wine Regions of Oregon

Oregon has 16 AVAs. Twelve are located west of the Cascade Mountains, 3 are in Eastern Oregon, and 1 spans the region between the east and the west along the Columbia River Gorge. Of the 12 western appellations, half were recently established—in 2005 and 2006. The western appellations have more of a maritime influence on their climate, and all have boundaries entirely within the state. East of the mountains, the 3 appellations are the Columbia River, Walla Walla Valley, and Snake River Valley. The first 2 are shared with Washington State to the north and the Snake River Valley is shared with Idaho to the east. All have drier climates than the western appellations. The Columbia Gorge AVA also spans the border with Washington; on its western edge the terroir is more similar to the Willamette Valley, and on its eastern side it is more like the Columbia Valley (Table 12.2).

Willamette Valley

The Willamette Valley appellation lies in the northwestern part of the state and is Oregon's most prolific region for agriculture. It is Oregon's largest and oldest AVA, established in 1984, and it contains the majority of the state's vineyards and wineries producing nearly 75 percent of the grapes harvested in the state. The boundaries of the appellation are approximately formed by the watershed of the Willamette River and extend from south of the city of Eugene to Portland, 125 miles (200 km) to the north. The climate is generally cooler and wetter than Napa and Sonoma but with a similar pattern of wet winters followed by dryer summers. This weather makes it an excellent region for the cool-climate varieties Chardonnay and Pinot Gris as well as Oregon's most popular variety, Pinot Noir (Figure 12.13).

Oregon is known for its rainfall, and it can be a major headache for vintners. The summers are usually dry, but storms often linger into the late spring, affecting bloom, or can come early in the fall during harvest. These conditions mean that mildew and bunch rot are always a concern, and there is not always enough warm weather for the grapes to ripen fully. The early fall rains are always a risk in the Willamette Valley, meaning that in some vintages the grapes never attain full maturity. For this reason the wines of the Willamette Valley experience more variation from year to year than those of California

TABLE 12.2 Appellations of Oregon State

Appellation	Best-Known Varieties
Willamette Valley	Pinot Noir, Pinot Gris, Chardonnay
Chehalem Mountains*	Pinot Noir, Pinot Gris, Chardonnay
Eola Amity Hills*	Pinot Noir, Pinot Gris, Chardonnay
Yamhill-Carlton*	Pinot Noir, Pinot Gris, Chardonnay
Dundee Hills*	Pinot Noir, Pinot Gris, Chardonnay
Ribbon Ridge*	Pinot Noir, Pinot Gris, Chardonnay
McMinnville*	Pinot Noir, Pinot Gris, Chardonnay
Southern Oregon	Produces a number of varieties
Umpqua Valley	Riesling, Syrah
Red Hill Douglas County	Not known for any one variety
Rogue Valley	Cabernet Sauvignon, Merlot, Syrah
Applegate Valley	Cabernet Sauvignon, Riesling
Columbia Valley (OR and WA)	Cabernet Sauvignon, Merlot, Syrah
Columbia Gorge (OR and WA)	Produces a number of varieties
Walla Walla Valley (OR and WA)	Cabernet Sauvignon, Merlot, Chardonnay, Syrah
Snake River Valley (OR and ID)	Riesling, Chardonnay

*AVA borders are within the Willamette Valley AVA.

FIGURE 12.13

Bins of Pinot Noir grapes ready for transport to the winery for crushing.

Oregon Wine Board, Patrick Prothe Photography

and Washington typically do. Oregon vintners are always quick to point out, however, that these conditions are similar to those of Pinot Noir's home in Burgundy. One advantage of Oregon's climate is that hard freezes that cause winterkill are much rarer than they are in Washington.

Although there are vineyards and wineries located throughout the appellation, many are concentrated just to the southwest of Portland. If there is an epicenter of Oregon wine country it lies here in Yamhill County, particularly between the small towns of Newberg and McMinnville. Yamhill County alone has one-third of the state's vineyards and grows 44 percent of Oregon's Pinot Noir. To those who have visited California's Sonoma and Napa Valleys, the area seems familiar in many respects. Like the wine country of the North Coast in California, the area is home to a number of vineyards and wineries. Here, however, there is less development and the wineries are less crowded and more rustic in nature. The smaller wineries are often one- or two-person operations and one is as likely to find the winemaker or owner pouring wine to visitors. This area has more than 150 wineries including some of the state's most well-known producers. The concentration of wineries and vineyards located within an easy drive to Portland, the state's largest city, has created a thriving trade in wine tourism. This success causes frequent traffic jams on weekends during the harvest season on the highway 99W, the region's major thoroughfare.

Appellations within Willamette Valley

Many of the best vineyards in the Willamette Valley are planted in the small ranges of hills that are laced throughout the countryside. Two of the most famous ranges are the Dundee and Eola Hills. Their sloping hillsides provide good drainage for both water and cold air during the winter and spring. If the vineyards are oriented to the south, they have better exposure to the sun, which is an advantage whenever growing grapes in a cool region. The extensive vineyard development in the northwestern section of the Willamette Valley has given birth to a half-dozen recently created smaller appellations. Just southeast of the Portland metropolitan area are the Chehalem Mountain, Ribbon Ridge, and Dundee Hills AVAs. Farther west are the Yamhill-Carlton and McMinnville AVAs. Just to the south of McMinnville on a small isolated range of hills lies the Eola Hills appellation. All of these regions feature gently rolling slopes that have a diversity of soil types made up of marine sediment, basalt, and red soil (Figure 12.14) that is high in iron.

At the southern end of the Willamette Valley, the vineyards are less concentrated and the soils have more clay content. This region has about 11 percent of the appellation's vineyards and about 50 wineries. Although the wine industry in southern Willamette Valley has fewer vineyards and wineries, it is home to the state's largest winery, King Estate.

FIGURE 12.14

In the hills west of Dundee, Oregon, the soil is being prepared for planting a new vineyard. The freshly tilled earth exhibits the red soil that the region is renowned for.

© Pat Henderson

Umpqua, Rogue, and Applegate Valleys

Established in 1984, the Umpqua Valley is centered on the town of Roseburg and was carved out by the Umpqua River and its tributaries. Located south of the Willamette Valley, it is a smaller appellation, only about a quarter the size of its neighbor to the north covering an area 70 × 35 miles (112 × 56 km). It lies about the same distance inland as the Willamette Valley, but because the coastal mountains are higher in this part of the state, the climate of the region experiences less of a moderating influence from the Pacific Ocean than the Willamette Valley does. This fact, coupled with its more southerly location, allows the Umpqua to have a warmer, drier climate than the Willamette Valley. This dryer terroir means that there is less concern of early rains affecting the harvest, and warmer grape varieties such as Cabernet Sauvignon, Merlot, and Syrah do well in the Umpqua Valley (Figure 12.15). Within the Umpqua Valley AVA is the smaller appellation of Red Hills Douglas County, formed in 2005.

The Rogue Valley appellation encompasses the valley formed by the Rogue River as it travels along Interstate 5 just north of the California border. Here in southern Oregon, agriculture is less common than it is in the Willamette Valley, and the timber and forest product industries are more prominent. The Rogue Valley sits at a higher elevation than the rest of Oregon's appellations, with most of its vineyards lying between 1,000 and 2,000 feet (300 and 600 m). It has a diversity of terroirs, with the areas to the west having a more coastal climate that is cooler and has more rainfall than those areas that are farther inland. The diversity of growing conditions allows for many different types of grapes and wines to be produced, and the appellation does not have a reputation for any one variety in particular. It was established in 1991 and in the year 2001 the subappellation of the Applegate Valley was formed within the borders of the Rogue Valley AVA.

In 2004, the Southern Oregon AVA was created, containing all of the Umpqua Valley, Rogue Valley, and Applegate Valley AVAs. Together these appellations grow roughly 15 percent of Oregon's wine grapes. Although this large AVA has a diversity of weather patterns, the entire region is generally much warmer and drier than the Willamette

FIGURE 12.15

A vineyard scene in southern Oregon's Rogue River Valley. Here the climate is warmer than the Willamette Valley to the north and the region has a better reputation for varieties such as Syrah and Cabernet Sauvignon rather than Pinot Noir.

© Pat Henderson

Valley. The Southern Oregon AVA has most of the state's Cabernet Sauvignon, Merlot, and Syrah, varieties that do not always ripen in the Willamette Valley.

Appellations of Eastern Oregon

These three appellations lie in the eastern half of the state along the borders with Washington and Idaho. The appellations together have about 1,600 acres (650 hectares) of vineyards, roughly 8 percent of Oregon's total acreage. The majority of both the Columbia Valley and the Walla Walla Valley appellations are in Washington State, and have much more in common with the growing conditions in Eastern Washington than with the appellations in western Oregon. The majority of the Snake River appellation resides within Idaho. Although it can be confusing for consumers and producers alike to have AVAs cross over state boundaries, it makes perfect sense considering an AVA should encompass a similar terroir regardless of the political boundaries it crosses.

IDAHO

Idaho has a small wine industry, ranked 17th in production by state, with the vast majority of its 2,000 acres (800 Hectares) of vineyards located in the Snake River Valley AVA that it shares with Oregon. The climate of the region is dry and slightly colder than Washington's Columbia River Valley, and cool-climate varieties such as Riesling and Chardonnay do best. Its vineyards are generally at a higher elevation than those in the Columbia Valley, making for cool nights that help preserve acidity in the grapes. The largest winery in the state is Ste. Chapelle which produces more than half of Idaho's wine. Like its neighbors to the west, it has undergone significant growth in recent years, with *vinifera* acreage doubling in the last 10 years.

Summary

Although the wines of the Pacific Northwest are often eclipsed by the volume of wine made in California, they represent a significant and growing segment of American wine production. With Washington State wines, consumers have come to expect high-quality Cabernet Sauvignon and Merlot as well as Chardonnay and Riesling presented at affordable prices. With Oregon wines, customers look for distinctive examples of Pinot Noir and Pinot Gris from small wineries with limited production. The wineries of the Northwest also enjoy a great deal of support in their home states and are becoming better known throughout the rest of the country. With both states, there is still plenty of opportunity for expansion in production, given increased demand from the marketplace.

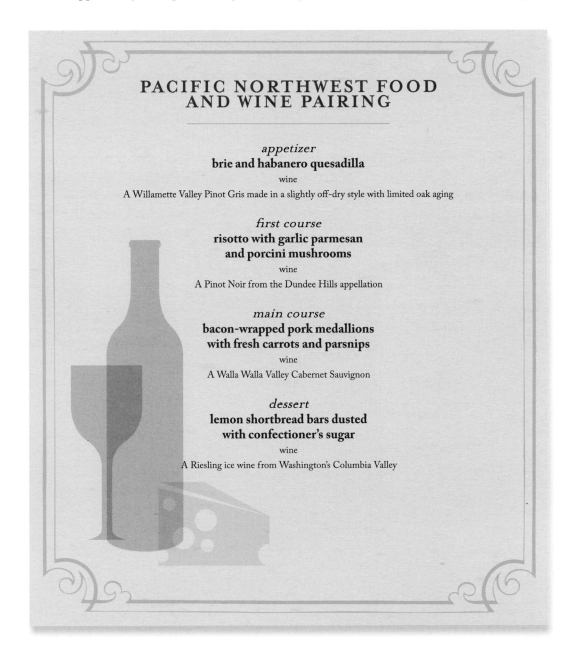

PACIFIC NORTHWEST FOOD AND WINE PAIRING

appetizer
brie and habanero quesadilla
wine
A Willamette Valley Pinot Gris made in a slightly off-dry style with limited oak aging

first course
risotto with garlic parmesan and porcini mushrooms
wine
A Pinot Noir from the Dundee Hills appellation

main course
bacon-wrapped pork medallions with fresh carrots and parsnips
wine
A Walla Walla Valley Cabernet Sauvignon

dessert
lemon shortbread bars dusted with confectioner's sugar
wine
A Riesling ice wine from Washington's Columbia Valley

EXERCISES

1. Who introduced Pinot Noir to Oregon and when was it first planted?

2. How do the size of Oregon and Washington wineries compare to one another?

3. How does the climate of Columbia Valley compare to the climate of the Willamette Valley, and how do the differences affect the varieties of grapes that are grown there?

4. What effect did the tax on out-of-state wines have on the development of Washington's wine industry?

5. Besides *vinifera* wine grapes, what other fruits have been used for wine production in the Pacific Northwest?

REVIEW QUESTIONS

1. What is the most significant threat to vineyards in Eastern Washington?
   A. Phylloxera
   B. Winterkill
   C. Drought
   D. Urban development

2. What is the most widely planted grape variety in Washington State?
   A. Syrah
   B. Chardonnay
   C. Cabernet Sauvignon
   D. Riesling

3. What are the three appellations that span the border between Washington and Oregon? _____, _____, and _____.

(Continues)

(Continued)

4. Which variety established Oregon's reputation for producing fine table wines?
   A. Pinot Noir
   B. Pinot Gris
   C. Isabella
   D. Chardonnay

5. Oregon state is ranked _____ in the nation for wine production.
   A. Second
   B. Third
   C. Fourth
   D. Fifth

REFERENCES

Hall, L. S. (2001). *Wines of the Pacific Northwest.* London: Octopus.

Irvine, R., & Clore, W. J. (1998). *The wine project: Washington State's winemaking history.* Vashon, WA: Sketch.

U.S. Department of Agriculture, National Agricultural Statistics Service. (2007a). *Vineyard acreage report 2006.* Olympia, WA: Author.

U.S. Department of Agriculture, National Agricultural Statistics Service. (2007b). *Washington winery report 2006.* Olympia, WA: Author.

U.S. Department of Agriculture, National Agricultural Statistics Service. (2009a). *Grape release.* Olympia, WA: Author.

U.S. Department of Agriculture, National Agricultural Statistics Service. (2009b). *2008 Oregon vineyard and winery report.* Portland, OR: Author.

{ NEW YORK, CANADA, AND OTHER NORTH AMERICAN REGIONS }

This chapter traces the history of wine production in New York State, as well as that state's effect on the development of the American wine industry. It also identifies New York's major wine regions, their respective climatic conditions, and the styles of wines produced. Next, the chapter describes the unique climatic and geological characteristics of Canada's major wine regions and the styles of wines produced in each, as well as Canada's role in the international wine market. Finally, the chapter outlines the history of wine production in the eastern, southwestern, and mountain regions of the United States; describes the types of wines made in these states; and discusses the role of these states in the American wine industry.

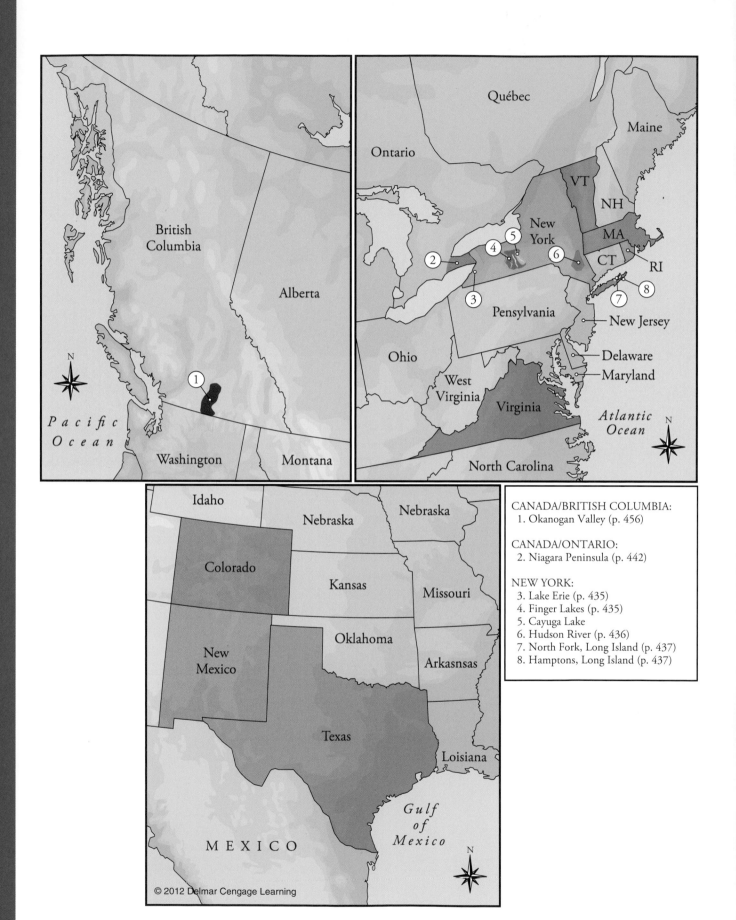

CANADA/BRITISH COLUMBIA:
1. Okanogan Valley (p. 456)

CANADA/ONTARIO:
2. Niagara Peninsula (p. 442)

NEW YORK:
3. Lake Erie (p. 435)
4. Finger Lakes (p. 435)
5. Cayuga Lake
6. Hudson River (p. 436)
7. North Fork, Long Island (p. 437)
8. Hamptons, Long Island (p. 437)

© 2012 Delmar Cengage Learning

KEY TERMS

Chambourcin

cross

designated viticultural area (DVA)

Frontenac

hybrid

Maréchal Foch

Seyval Blanc

Vidal Blanc

Vintners Quality Alliance (VQA)

Vitis labrusca

Vitis riparia

INTRODUCTION

There are currently federally bonded wineries in all 50 states of the United States, as well as in four provinces of Canada. These regional wines, from areas outside America's Pacific West Coast, are of increasing importance in the North American wine industry. This chapter looks closely at the wine regions of New York State, Canada, and the eastern, southwestern, and mountain regions of the United States.

NEW YORK STATE

One could say that the American wine business got its start in New York State. The country's first commercial winery, Jacques Brothers, was established in 1839 in New York's Hudson River Valley. In 1885 the winery was renamed Brotherhood winery, and in 2005 it was recognized as America's longest continually operating winery. However, grape growing and winemaking had a foothold in New York well before the Jacques brothers began their winery. Dutch colonists settled in the region before the *Mayflower* brought English settlers to the Massachusetts Bay Colony. The Dutch were followed by French Huguenots who, in 1677, began making wine near the town of New Pfalz. New York today is a vibrant wine region, producing 11.87 million cases of fine wine per year. There are currently 212 wineries in the state (compared to only 19 as recently as 1976), and over 35,000 acres (12,230 hectares) planted to wine grapes. However, the history of wine production in this state has had a spotted and difficult history, with several major setbacks.

NEW YORK STATE WINE— HISTORICAL PERSPECTIVE

The first wines made in New York by French immigrants in the late seventeenth century were made with local indigenous grapes of the botanical family *Vitis lambrusca* found growing wild. The results were less than impressive, so the French settlers imported *Vitis vinifera* vines from Europe. These transplanted varietals failed due to the extreme cold of winters, and later, to phylloxera, the local root louse that killed *vinifera* vines by attacking the roots and sapping the plant's energy. (Vines of the *labrusca* family were immune to the phylloxera due to genetic mutations over the many generations the two species had coexisted.) After the failed efforts with *vinifera* grapes, small production of wine continued using the Northeast's native *labrusca* grapes. The different varieties of indigenous *labrusca* grapevines were also bred to one another to form new varieties called **crosses.**

During the early and mid-1800s, grape growers were producing wines from a number of American grape varieties including Catawba, Isabella, Concord, and Alexander. It is from one of these, Alexander, that the first commercial winery made its wines. By the late nineteenth century, botanists had succeeded in crossing *vinifera* with *labrusca* vines forming a **hybrid.** These so-called French-American hybrids include **Maréchal Foch** (MAH-ray-shahl FOHSH), **Seyval Blanc** (say-vahl BLAHN), and **Vidal Blanc** (vee-dahl

BLAHN). Native varietals from farther south on the North American continent, like the *Vitis aestivalis,* and the **Vitis riparia,** a vigorous species found growing in damp sections along rivers and streams from Canada to the Gulf of Mexico) were also used for breeding new grape varieties. From this careful, controlled breeding emerged many new varietals suitable to wine production. Both French-American hybrids and crosses of American varietals were widely planted along the Hudson River and around the Finger Lakes, by new waves of French, German, and Swiss immigrants. Farther west, along the shores of Lake Erie, many acres were planted starting after the Civil War, including large plantings of Concord grapes, which went into grape juice and jelly. Commercial winemaking took off across New York, and a large wine industry emerged, centered on the town of Hammondsport in the Finger Lakes.

Prohibition dealt a severe blow to the nascent wine industry of New York. Many of its wineries discontinued producing wine, turning instead to growing fruit grapes, or simply went out of business. When Prohibition was repealed in 1933, wine production reemerged, but maintained its emphasis on the native and hybrid grapes, producing heavy, slightly sweet wine, with a bouquet often described as "foxy" for its resemblance to the scent of animal fur. Most growers sold their harvested grapes to the two or three large companies that controlled the state's wine industry. A specialized section of the New York wine trade concentrated on the production of sweet kosher wines from the Concord grape. In the late 1930s some pioneers, such as Frenchman Charles Fournier from the Champagne region, began to plant *vinifera* vines in the Finger Lakes district. But it was not until the arrival in New York in the 1950s of Dr. Konstantin Frank, a Ukrainian vintner and expert in *vinifera* grapes, that modern wine production got a start in New York. He did extensive research and identified areas where cool climate *vinifera* varietals like Riesling and Chardonnay could thrive.

Another boost to New York's wine industry was the Farm Winery Act of 1976, which was passed due to the growing interest in fine wine that was becoming evident across the United States. The act reduced fees for commercial wineries, increased tax benefits for small wineries, and allowed direct sales to consumers and restaurants. These critical changes made it economically feasible to own and operate a small winery (defined in the act as one that produces less than 50,000 gallons [190,000 liters] per year). The result was a considerable increase in the number of small and medium-sized wineries in New York. Today most of New York's wineries are of this size, the type of "boutique" winery at which the emphasis is on quality and innovation.

WINE REGIONS OF NEW YORK

The growing season in this large state varies from 180 days in northern, inland areas to up to 230 days in more moderate sections. The microclimates are strongly influenced by contiguous bodies of water. In upstate New York, many lakes were formed during the Ice Age as melting glaciers cut deep formations that gradually filled with water, and became Lake Erie (one of the Great Lakes) and the Finger Lakes and the Hudson River. The glaciers also left rich soil behind. Closer to the Atlantic, it is the ocean that has a moderating influence on climate. Here the soils are sandier and the terroir is very different from what one finds upstate. Among all the various growing conditions throughout New York, 4 regions have evolved as premier wine-producing areas. There are now a total of 10 AVAs within these four areas.

Finger Lakes

Named for the lakes' resemblance to a hand's fingers, this region, although not New York's largest geographically, is the state's most productive, producing 90 percent of New York wine (Figure 13.1). There are 63 bonded wineries around the lakes, and 10,000 acres (4,050 hectares) of vineyards. The Finger Lakes AVA was established in 1982. There are 11 lakes in total. The important lakes for wine production are Canadaigua, Seneca, Keuka, and Cayuga. These are among the deepest lakes in North America, and all are large enough to have moderating influences on the climate. Cayuga was granted its own AVA in 1988 when local vintners were able to prove that its lower elevation and deeper depth provided mesoclimates suitable for the recently planted *vinifera* varietals.

The vineyards of the Finger Lakes are planted to a variety of grapes, native American varieties and French-American hybrids as well as *vinifera*. George Fournier first introduced *vinifera* vines here in the 1930s, and later hired Konstantin Frank as a consulting viticulturist. As Dr. Frank had predicted, Riesling does extremely well here. As one vintner put it, "You can't find a bad Riesling here," but its plantings are still small—just over 600 acres (202 hectares) (Levine, 2009). Also planted is Chardonnay, often made into lively fresh sparkling wine by producers such as Glenora Winery. However, *vinifera* is still in the minority around the Finger Lakes, most of whose wines are still made from native grapes such as Concord, Niagara, and Catawba. Concord is the most widely planted red varietal, and is made into a soft, fruity wine. There have been promising reds made from the Bordelais varietal Cabernet Franc.

Lake Erie

Lake Erie provides more climate-moderating influences than the other Great Lakes due to the fact that it is lower in altitude and is downwind from Arctic air masses that prevail over Lakes Superior and Huron. Moreover, the huge Allegheny Plateau,

FIGURE 13.1

The sloping hillside vineyards in New York's Finger Lakes allow the ripening grapes to absorb sunlight, while the warmth reflecting back off the lake's waters further enhances the grapes' ripening process.

Photo by Randall Tagg Photography, provided by the New York Wine & Grape Foundation

3 miles (4.8 km) wide, acts to further trap the warmer air that radiates off the lake, thus increasing protection of the vineyards. The growing season averages about 185 days, from late April to early October. Precipitation is about 30 to 40 inches (76 to 102 cm) a year, and is evenly spread out over the year, allowing for adequate sunlight during the growing season. The Lake Erie AVA, established in 1983, extends into three states, New York, Pennsylvania, and Ohio, with a total of 42,000 acres (17,000 hectares), with 2,200 of those acres (890 hectares) in New York, the largest amount of acreage in the state planted to grape vines. However, the majority of those grapes are destined for juice or jelly, or are eaten as table grapes. There only eight wineries in the AVA, producing dry table wines, sparkling wines, and a few select dessert wines, mostly from French–American hybrids such as Seyval Blanc.

Hudson River Valley

Besides its distinction as America's oldest wine region, where wine has been produced continually for over 300 years, the Hudson River Valley, just a short drive from New York City, is also one of North America's loveliest wine regions. The valley, with its historic small villages full of charming houses, antique shops, and cafes, provides views of stately green hills sloping toward the river. Many of the hills are covered with vineyards that are sheltered by the ridges and rock cliffs of the Catskill Mountains to the west. The Hudson River with its steep palisaded valley acts as a conduit for maritime air and weather patterns coming off the Atlantic (Figure 13.2). The mesoclimate here is, therefore, milder than is the case farther upstate. This allows several *vinifera* varietals to thrive, primarily Riesling, Chardonnay, and Cabernet Franc, in addition to the hybrids that the region has grown since before Prohibition. The Hudson River Valley was officially recognized as an AVA in 1982. The emphasis now is strongly on delicately styled, *vinifera*-based table wines. There are currently 19 commercial wineries in the Hudson River Valley.

FIGURE 13.2

The Palisades, the 550-foot high cliffs along the western bank of the Hudson River, act as a natural funnel, pulling the moderating ocean air upriver, thus helping to ripen the grapes in vineyards along the river.

Photo by Randall Tagg Photography, provided by the New York Wine & Grape Foundation

Long Island

This is the newest wine region in New York. It is also the most exciting and the most promising. The wine country is at the extreme easternmost section of the island, where the surrounding waters of Long Island Sound to the north, Peconic Bay to the south, and the Atlantic Ocean to the east provide a mild enough climate for *vinifera* varietals such as Merlot, Chardonnay, and Cabernet Franc to thrive. The growing season averages between 204 and 233 days, perfect for varietals that need long hang-time to fully evolve their flavors. The soil, for centuries planted primarily to vegetables, especially the lowly potato, is rich in minerals and drains well. The region has 3,000 acres (1,200 hectares) planted to wine grapes, spread among three AVAs. The Long Island AVA was defined and approved only in 2001, preceded by the original growing areas of the Hamptons (approved 1985) and the North Fork AVA (1986). Due to a thriving tourism business (New York City is only 85 miles [137 km] away) and to considerable foreign investment (mostly by Europeans who recognize this as promising grape-growing region), Long Island is the fastest growing wine region in the eastern United States, producing some truly impressive wines. There are now 29 wineries in the North Fork, and 3 in the Hamptons. Among the leading producers are Wölffer Estate, founded by a wealthy German businessman, Lenz Winery, and Pindar. In 1989, the Long Island Wine Council was founded with the objective of promoting Long Island as a producer of world-class wines and a desirable travel and tourism destination.

New York has played an extremely important role historically in the evolution of the wine industry of the United States. Now, led by exciting developments on Long Island's North Fork, and by increasing emphasis upstate on *vinifera* varietals, especially Riesling, New York seems poised to claim its place again as one of this country's finest regions for wine production.

OTHER WINE REGIONS IN THE EASTERN UNITED STATES

Besides New York, other northeastern states producing promising wines are Connecticut, Rhode Island, and the south-central coast of Massachusetts. Portions of these three states are included in the regional AVA, southeastern New England. The boundaries of the AVA extend from south of Boston down along the Rhode Island and Connecticut coasts to north of New London. The boundaries never extend more than 15 miles (24 km) inland, ensuring a truly coastal climate. The ocean moderates temperature extremes, so that the average temperature in January is 30°F (−1°C) and 70°F (21°C) in July. Overall the climate is perfect for cold-hardy *vinifera* varietals like Chardonnay, Pinot Noir, and Riesling, as well as certain French hybrids such as Vidal Blanc. Among the area's leading producers are Sakonnet Vineyards of Rhode Island which makes a delightful rosé and lovely Gewürztraminer, and Westport Rivers of Massachusetts, whose sparkling wine, made from Chardonnay and Pinot Noir, is delicious (Figures 13.3 and 13.4).

It should be noted that wine production in the northeastern United States is not limited to New York and the three southern New England states mentioned here. Due to

FIGURE 13.6

A vineyard located outside of Grand Junction Colorado on. The high desert climate of Colorado's western slope is reminiscent to that of Eastern Washington.

© Pat Henderson

and British Columbia. Since these two provinces are literally a continent apart, the wines they make are very different. Ontario's vineyards lie mostly on the Niagara Peninsula, north of New York State. The climate here is very similar to that of New York's Finger Lakes. The specialty is ice wine, as well as German-style Rieslings. British Columbia is on Canada's West Coast, and its terroir closely resembles that of Washington State's Columbia Valley. Like the Columbia Valley, British Columbia is building a reputation for muscular reds, especially Merlot and Cabernet Franc. Its dry *vinifera*-based whites, like Chardonnay, can also be very good.

FIGURE 13.7

Chardonnay grapes can ripen in the northern sections of North America if temperatures are moderate and sunshine is plentiful.

Photo by Randall Tagg Photography, provided by the New York Wine & Grape Foundation

Canadian Wine—Historical Perspective

Winemaking in Canada can be traced to the early 1800s, when a German immigrant named Johann Schiller, recently retired from a military career, planted a small vineyard to native *labrusca* vines along a river west of Toronto. By 1890, there were 41 wineries throughout Canada. However, commercial winemaking did not have much time to develop, as Prohibition began in Canada in 1916, four years earlier than in the United States. The Great Experiment lasted only a few years in Canada, and upon its repeal in 1927, the provinces began granting licenses to new wineries. By the end of that first year after Repeal, 57 licenses to make wine were granted in the province of Ontario alone. In the ensuing decades, most wine made in Canada was of the slightly sweet, highly alcoholic style, and were made from *labrusca* grapes.

Canada's modern wine industry was born in 1975 when the small winery, Inniskillen near Niagara Falls, was granted the first commercial license. At this time the taste in wines across North America was switching away from sweet and fortified wines to dry, balanced table wines. As the demand for this style of wine increased, so did the determination of Canadian vintners to make better, more sophisticated wines. As the number of commercial (albeit small) wineries increased, the Canadian government saw the need to instigate some control over the production of wine and the use of the names of the grape-growing regions. In 1988, a countrywide appellation system, **Vintners Quality Alliance (VQA),** was introduced, originally in Ontario, and shortly thereafter in British Columbia. The VQA seal on a bottle's label signifies that the wine has been tested and meets a series of standards set by a board of local vintners, grape growers, and wine experts. The VQA also controls the use of appellations or **designated viticultural areas (DVAs).** The law stipulates that wines carrying the seal are made at least 85 percent from locally grown grapes, with the other 15 percent being grapes that were grown within the province in which the DVA is located. Only *vinifera* grapes are allowed. Furthermore, if a varietal name is given to the wine, 85 percent of the wine must be made from that varietal.

Wine Regions of Canada

Wine is produced in four Canadian provinces: Nova Scotia, Quebec, British Columbia, and Ontario. However, only British Columbia and Ontario have adopted VQA standards. Moreover, the small amounts of wine made in the other two provinces are not commercially significant, and are sold primarily to tourists.

British Columbia

British Columbia currently has 9,100 acres (3,680 hectares) planted to grapevines, with lots of room for expansion, as the province has more land area than France and Germany combined. Most of that acreage is devoted to *vinifera* grapes, due to the fact that in the late 1980s the provincial government offered a financial incentive to growers, encouraging them to tear out *labrusca* and hybrid vines and replace them with *vinifera*.

Reading a Canadian Wine Label

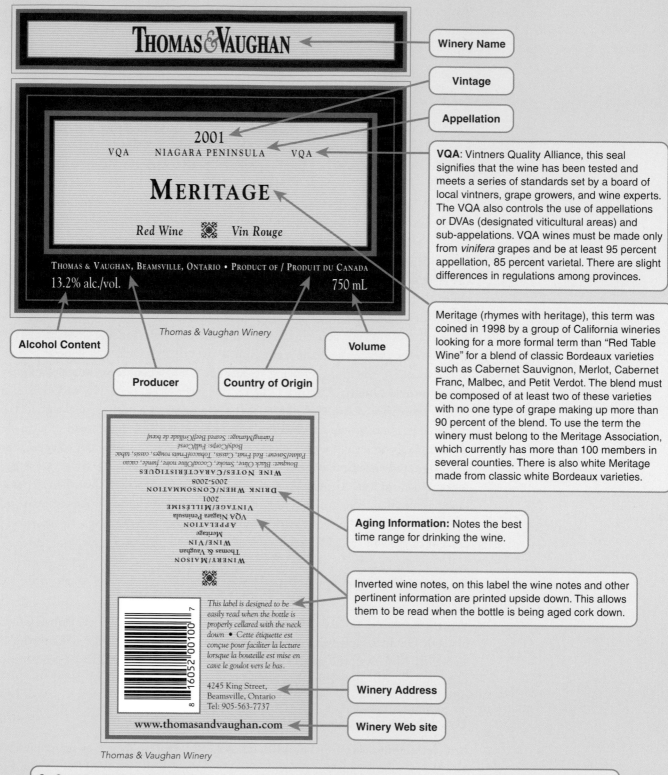

Winery Name

Vintage

Appellation

2001
VQA   NIAGARA PENINSULA   VQA

MERITAGE

Red Wine   ✦   Vin Rouge

THOMAS & VAUGHAN, BEAMSVILLE, ONTARIO • PRODUCT OF / PRODUIT DU CANADA

13.2% alc./vol.   750 mL

Thomas & Vaughan Winery

Alcohol Content

Producer

Country of Origin

Volume

VQA: Vintners Quality Alliance, this seal signifies that the wine has been tested and meets a series of standards set by a board of local vintners, grape growers, and wine experts. The VQA also controls the use of appellations or DVAs (designated viticultural areas) and sub-appelations. VQA wines must be made only from *vinifera* grapes and be at least 95 percent appellation, 85 percent varietal. There are slight differences in regulations among provinces.

Meritage (rhymes with heritage), this term was coined in 1998 by a group of California wineries looking for a more formal term than "Red Table Wine" for a blend of classic Bordeaux varieties such as Cabernet Sauvignon, Merlot, Cabernet Franc, Malbec, and Petit Verdot. The blend must be composed of at least two of these varieties with no one type of grape making up more than 90 percent of the blend. To use the term the winery must belong to the Meritage Association, which currently has more than 100 members in several counties. There is also white Meritage made from classic white Bordeaux varieties.

Aging Information: Notes the best time range for drinking the wine.

Inverted wine notes, on this label the wine notes and other pertinent information are printed upside down. This allows them to be read when the bottle is being aged cork down.

Winery Address

Winery Web site

Thomas & Vaughan Winery

On Canadian labels all information must be printed in both French and English on the front label, reflecting the country's bilingual status. On the back label having both French and English is optional. By treaty with the European Union, generic use of European names like "Chablis" is not allowed. Many Canadian wines are blends of both domestic and imported wines. These wines cannot be bottled under the VQA standards and have the statement "Cellared in Canada."

The most widely planted varietals are Merlot, Chardonnay, Cabernet Franc, Pinot Gris, Cabernet Sauvignon, Cabernet Sauvignon, and Riesling. The wine industry is spread among four distinct regions: the Okanagan Valley, Similkameen Valley, Vancouver Island, and the Fraser Valley.

Most of British Columbia's wine comes from the Okanagan Valley, which extends for 100 miles (161 km) in the south-central part of the province. The valley receives minimal rainfall (the southernmost section is Canada's only desert region). Summers are hot, with July and August temperatures often reaching over 100°F (38°C). The northern latitude means days are long. Irrigation is necessary in such a hot, sunlit region, and several large nearby lakes provide plenty of water for the vineyards. Long sunny days, carefully controlled water content and very cool nights, along with loamy-sandy soil, make for a grape-growers dream. Vintners are able to bring their crops to perfect ripeness, with acidity still intact. Although British Columbia is known for crisp, clean whites like Alsace-style Pinot Gris and vibrant Sauvignon Blanc, impressive progress has also been made with reds. The province also makes sparkling wines from white *vinifera* varietals, and is a reliable producer of Canada's most famous wine: ice wine.

Although British Columbia's wines are now sold in several European countries and a dozen U.S. states, most of its production is still sold within the province. Owners of many of the province's 140 wineries are working closely with the provincial government to create international market demand for their products.

Ontario

Being far inland, Ontario has a totally continental climate. Arctic air ensures a short growing season and very cold winters. Without the moderating influences of the two Great Lakes that are contiguous with its borders, Ontario and Erie, the province would be too cold for any viticulture. Fortunately, the deep lakes warm the region enough to make the growing of certain cold-hardy varieties possible. Most of Ontario's vineyards are clustered along the Niagara Peninsula where a huge escarpment, once the towering rocky shore of an Ice Age lake, provides additional protection from icy winds. The glaciers that carved out that ancient lake deposited a variety of deep, well-drained soils, also conducive to successful viticulture.

Ontario is Canada's largest producer of wine, accounting for about 75 percent of the country's wine. There are currently 15,000 acres (6,070 hectares) under vine. The VQA board in Ontario has approved three DVAs: the Niagara Peninsula, Lake Erie North Shore, and Pelée Island. Although some table wines are made from *vinifera* grapes, for instance, Chablis-style Chardonnays and some off-dry Rieslings, many vineyards in all three DVAs are still planted to hybrids, predominately Vidal Blanc and Maréchal Foch.

Despite the DVAs' progress with table wines, the undisputed star in Ontario is ice wine, made from grapes (usually Vidal Blanc) that have been allowed to continue ripening on the vine until frozen by a sudden deep frost. The frozen water of the grape is separated out before fermentation. The result is a richly honeyed but cleanly balanced dessert wine of incredible complexity, with lovely nuances of ripe peaches or apricots.

So serious are the Canadians about protecting the integrity of their ice wine that the VQAs of both Ontario and British Columbia have joined in an international agreement with Germany and Austria, pledging to use only the traditional, risky and labor-intensive method of making ice wine from naturally frozen grapes. Producers vow never to take the shortcut of picking ripe grapes and placing them in large industrial freezers. A consumer can know, when buying a Canadian ice wine, that the product he or she receives will be a delicious example of the genuine product for which Canada is famous.

SUMMARY

Producers of regional wines in North America are at a critical crossroads. Many wineries in lesser-known regions like New York State and New England, or the American South and Southwest, or in Canada's British Columbia and Ontario, have achieved success in selling their wines locally, usually within a tourism-oriented economy, to which many wineries contribute through tasting rooms, B&B's, and special functions. At this time, as grape growing and winemaking in these areas continue to improve, the question is whether regional wines will move beyond being tourist curiosities and be able to find acceptance in the international wine market.

Success will depend on a variety of factors. Finding the right varietal for the region is crucial, first being sure that the grape can thrive under the natural conditions of the region, and, secondly, that adequate demand for that varietal exists. For instance, many experts feel the demand for Riesling is increasing in North America and that the Finger Lakes of New York should concentrate on that varietal, as it has proven to thrive in that mesoclimate. Similarly, the very hot and sunny parts of Texas may need to abandon efforts with certain *vinifera* grapes to concentrate on truly "hot-climate" varietals, such as Spain's Tempranillo or Tuscany's Sangiovese. Niche marketing is also important, that is, creating a quality product that is unique to one's region. Successful examples include ice wine from the Niagara Peninsula, Gruet's sparkling wine from New Mexico, and Sakonnet's Rhode Island Red. Aggressive promotional efforts done in conjunction with other winery owners and quasi-governmental agencies, such as the Finger Lakes Wine Alliance, Vermont's Grape and Wine Council, or the British Columbia Wine Institute, could greatly heighten consumer awareness of regional wines. Over the next few decades, it appears that more of North America's regional wines will complete the processes of viticultural winnowing and strategic marketing, and then move on to take their rightful places in the international business of wine.

NORTH AMERICAN FOOD AND WINE PAIRING

first course
breast New England clam chowder
wine

A Nonvintage Brut Sparkling Wine from New Mexico

second course
broiled Maine lobster in herb sauce
wine

A dry Gewürztraminer from Rhode Island

main course
grilled tenderloin of beef
wine

A full-bodied Reserve Cabernet Franc from Virginia

dessert
apple pie with vanilla ice cream
wine

Ice Wine from Niagara Peninsula of Ontario Canada

1. What are the factors that influence the climate of New York's Finger Lakes region making it suitable for *vinifera* grapevines?

2. What role did the development of French-American hybrid varieties play in the development of wine industry in the Eastern United States?

3. What changes were mandated by the Winery Farm Act of 1976, and how did those changes affect the New York wine industry?

4. How does the terroir of the Okanagan Valley differ from that of the Niagara Peninsula, and how does it affect grape growing?

REVIEW QUESTIONS

1. What is the term used in Canada to indicate an officially approved viticultural area?
   A. VQA
   B. DVA
   C. AVA
   D. ROP

2. In what state was America's first commercial winery located?
   A. New Mexico
   B. Virginia
   C. New York
   D. Colorado

3. Ontario is acquiring a reputation for making excellent wines of what category:
   A. Dry crisp whites
   B. Sparkling wines
   C. Sweet dessert wines
   D. Big tannic reds

(Continues)

(Continued)

4. The state that has the largest AVA located entirely within the border of a single state is?
   A. California
   B. Missouri
   C. Colorado
   D. Texas

REFERENCES

Chittim, C. (2005, October). New Mexico winemaking: A colorful history. *Wines & Vines, 86*(10), 38.

Levine, D. (2009, May/June). A New York State of wine. *Arrive,* 42–47.

MacNeil, K. (2001). *The wine bible.* New York: Workman.

SECTION IV
WINE REGIONS OF THE SOUTHERN HEMISPHERE

THIS SECTION CONSISTS OF three chapters discussing the major wine-producing countries of the Southern Hemisphere. This is one of the fastest growing and most innovative regions of winemaking in the world today. The chapters cover Australia and New Zealand, Chile and Argentina, and South Africa, exploring their winemaking history and grape-growing and wine production methods.

{ AUSTRALIA AND NEW ZEALAND }

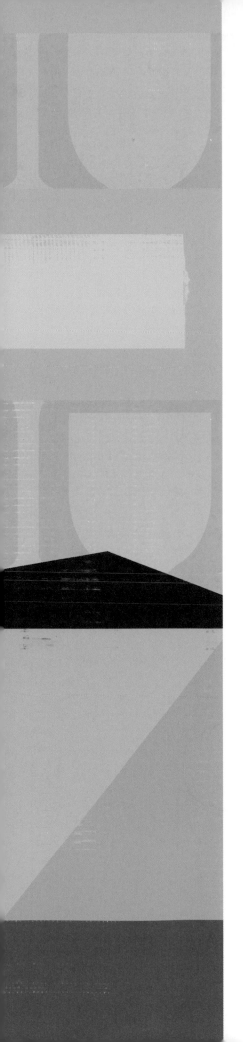

This chapter outlines the

history of winemaking in Australia and New Zealand and describes the climatic conditions of their grape-growing regions and the types of wine that they produce. It also discusses the importance of wines of Australia and New Zealand in the global wine market.

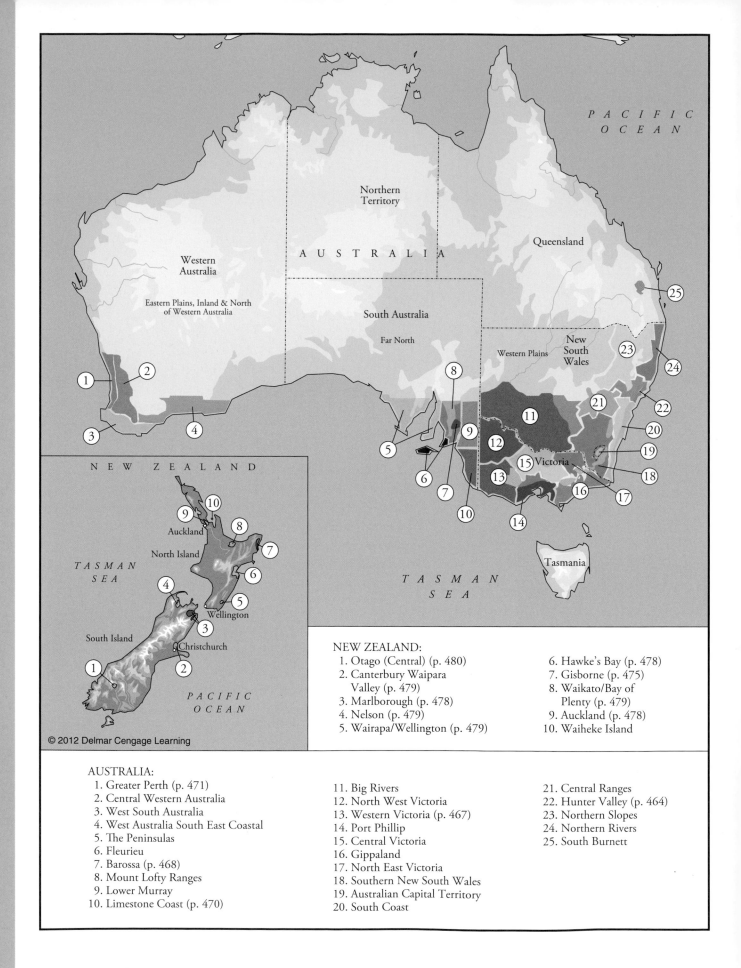

NEW ZEALAND:
1. Otago (Central) (p. 480)
2. Canterbury Waipara Valley (p. 479)
3. Marlborough (p. 478)
4. Nelson (p. 479)
5. Wairapa/Wellington (p. 479)
6. Hawke's Bay (p. 478)
7. Gisborne (p. 475)
8. Waikato/Bay of Plenty (p. 479)
9. Auckland (p. 478)
10. Waiheke Island

AUSTRALIA:
1. Greater Perth (p. 471)
2. Central Western Australia
3. West South Australia
4. West Australia South East Coastal
5. The Peninsulas
6. Fleurieu
7. Barossa (p. 468)
8. Mount Lofty Ranges
9. Lower Murray
10. Limestone Coast (p. 470)
11. Big Rivers
12. North West Victoria
13. Western Victoria (p. 467)
14. Port Phillip
15. Central Victoria
16. Gippaland
17. North East Victoria
18. Southern New South Wales
19. Australian Capital Territory
20. South Coast
21. Central Ranges
22. Hunter Valley (p. 464)
23. Northern Slopes
24. Northern Rivers
25. South Burnett

© 2012 Delmar Cengage Learning

KEY TERMS

Australian Wine and Brandy Corporation (AWBC)

cellar door

Geographic Indications (GIs)

Rhine Riesling

Shiraz

Wine Institute of New Zealand

INTRODUCTION

Australia and New Zealand are considered by many wine consumers to be the preeminent wine-producing regions of the Southern Hemisphere. The two nations have much in common: Both are located at the western edge of the South Pacific, isolated by water, and share a similar heritage. However, their viticulture and winemaking practices are different and both are uniquely suited to their terroirs and the types of wine that they produce. Being in the Southern Hemisphere, the seasons are opposite those in the United States and Europe, with harvest occurring in the months from February to April. This allows them to get young wines, particularly whites, from a given vintage to the market six months earlier than those made in the Northern Hemisphere. Australia and New Zealand enjoy a temperate climate that is well suited to grape growing, and in contrast to the United States, the climate becomes progressively cooler as one goes south.

Australia is such a large island it is considered a continent, and it generally has warmer and dryer weather (Figure 14.1). By comparison, New Zealand, located to the southeast of Australia, is much smaller and has a cooler climate (Figure 14.2). The export market is important to both countries with Australia exporting 63 percent (Australian Wine and Brandy Corporation, 2010) of the wine it produces, and New Zealand exporting 55 percent (New Zealand Winegrowers, 2009). While export sales have supported a great deal of growth, fluctuations in currency exchange rates and the global wine market have created volatility in the wine industries of both countries.

AUSTRALIA

Australia is a large country with a landmass nearly as large as the continental United States, but with a population of 22 million, has only 7 percent of the population of

FIGURE 14.1

Vineyards in Australia's Barossa Valley.

Wine Australia, © AWBC/ Matt Turner

FIGURE 14.2

Fall vineyards in Hawke's Bay region of New Zealand.
© Cephas Picture Library/Alamy

the United States. The vineyards, along with the population, are concentrated in southeastern Australia. The nation has a long history of viticulture and winemaking, but like much of the rest of the New World, Australia has undergone significant growth in the last 30 years. Since domestic consumption has been stable in recent decades, most of this growth has been fueled by exports, with Great Britain and the United States being the biggest markets. Today Australia is the world's sixth largest producer and home to nearly 2,000 wineries producing 137 million cases of wine a year, making its industry about 60 percent the size of that of the United States. The majority of these wineries have been established in the last 20 years and are very small, with limited production of high-end wines. However, these wineries make only a small fraction of Australia's wine. The five largest companies account for about 56 percent of the country's wine production (Table 14.1). These producers are all parent companies that own a number of wine brands that are familiar to the public and are multinational corporations with winery and vineyard holdings around the world.

The Australian wine industry has long had a reputation of being technologically innovative (Figure 14.3). The large multinational companies that are responsible for the majority of the wine production also have funded

FIGURE 14.3

Rotary fermentation tanks in a large Australian winery. As described in Chapter 3, rotary fermentation tanks extract flavor and color from grape skins during red wine fermentation by revolving to mix the cap (skins) and juice together.
© Charles O'Rear/Corbis

TABLE 14.1 Wine Brands of Major Australian Producers

Parent Company	Brands
Constellation Wines Australia	Amberley Estate, Bud Naked, Banrock Station, Barossa Valley Estate, Bay of Fires, Berri Estates, Brookland Valley, Chateau Reynella, Emu Wines, Goundrey, Hardys, Houghton, Kellys Revenge, Knife & Fork, Leasingham, Moondah Brook, Omni, Redman, Renmano, Stanley Wines, Starvedog Lane, Stonehaven, Tintara, Yarra Burn
Foster's Group	Abel's Tempest, Annie's Lane, Baileys of Glenrowan, Black Opal, Cellar No. 8, Coldstream Hills, Del Diablo Loco, Devil's Lair, Fifth Leg, Greg Norman Estates, Heemskerk, Ingoldby, Jamiesons Run, Killawarra, Leo Buring, Lindeman's, Metala, Mildara, Penfolds, Pepperjack, Robertson's Well, Rosemount Estate, Rothbury Estate, Saltram, Seaview, Secret Stone, Seppelt, Squealing Pig, St Huberts, T'Gallant, The Little Penguin, Tollana, Wolf Blass, Wynns Coonawarra Estate, Yellowglen
Casella Wines	Mallee Point, Yellow Tail, Yellow Tail Reserve, Yendah
Orlando Wines (Pernod Ricard Pacific)	Carrington, Gramps, Jacaranda Ridge, Jacobs Creek, Lawson's, Morris, Poets Corner, Richmond Grove, Russet Ridge, Saint Range, Trilogy, Wyndham Estate
De Bortoli Wines	3 Tales, Cosa Dolce, DB, Deen Vat Series, Emeri, Gulf Station, Hunter Valley, Jean Pierre, Melba, Noble One, PHI, Premium Fortified, Riorret, Rococo, Sacred Hill, Sero, Trevi, Windy Peak, Yarra Valley Estate Grown, Yarra Valley Reserve

much of the innovation. Being far removed from the traditions of the Old World, many wineries have developed methods of grape growing and winemaking that are suited to their terroir and the tastes of Australian customers. As Australia's export market developed, consumers overseas also found a taste for these wines. The demand of the export market fueled phenomenal growth; however, in recent years supply has outpaced demand leading to lower prices. Although it is difficult to generalize about the wine styles of a country as large and diverse as Australia, their exports have a reputation for being full-bodied and fruity wines that are easy to drink and reasonably priced.

AUSTRALIAN WINE— HISTORICAL PERSPECTIVE

In 1770, Captain James Cook reached Botany Bay on the southeastern coast of Australia and sailed northward to Cape York, claiming the coast for Great Britain. In 1788, a group of soldiers, settlers, and convicts arrived to form a penal colony at Port Jackson. The settlement was located where Sydney, in the state of New South Wales, now stands. The colony was very isolated and needed to become self-sufficient as quickly as possible. Grapes were planted along with other food crops, but they did not do well in the humid climate of Sydney Harbor. By 1791 Arthur Phillip, the governor of the settlement, had established a small 3-acre (1.2 hectares) vineyard 12 miles (19.3 km) inland at the Parramatta River. Here the weather was dryer than Sydney Harbor, and the vines were more successful.

One of the first commercial grape growers in Australia was John Macarthur. Macarthur arrived in Sydney in 1790 and perhaps is more famously known for being the first person to import Merino sheep to Australia, which would become the mainstay of the nation's wool industry and Australia's first major agricultural export. In 1805, he was granted 2,000 acres (810 hectares) of grazing land outside Sydney (Johnson, 1989). Ten years later in 1815, he began an 18-month journey through Europe with his two sons, James and William, to learn the craft of winemaking and to obtain grape cuttings to bring back to Australia. By 1820, he had established a 20-acre (8 hectare) vineyard outside Sydney, and within the decade they were producing more than 20,000 gallons (75,600 liters) of wine a year. His sons remained active in developing the Australian wine industry after their father's death in 1834.

Another early settler and vintner, Gregory Blaxland, is perhaps better known to Australians for being the first pioneer to cross the Blue Mountain range east of Sydney in 1813. He established a vineyard in 1818 on the 450 acres (182 hectares) he purchased in the Parramatta Valley. Here he experimented with a number of different grape varieties as well as other crops and was the first person to send wine from Australia back to Britain in 1822. The wines were fortified with brandy to protect them from spoilage on the long trip across the equator. In London his wines were awarded a silver medal in 1823 and a gold in 1828. His success raised the attention of others in Britain as well as in Australia.

Perhaps the best known of Australia's pioneering winemakers was James Busby; born in Edinburgh in 1801, he immigrated to Australia in 1824. Convinced that the wine industry in his future home had potential, Busby traveled to France to study grape growing and winemaking. When he arrived in Australia he received a grant of 2,000 acres (810 hectares) in the Hunter River Valley north of Sydney and established vineyards in what was eventually to become one of Australia's most important wine regions (Evans, 1973). He named his estate Kirkton after his Scottish birthplace. Several years later, he traveled to Europe to obtain more information on winemaking and cuttings of more than 500 varieties of grapes. When he returned to Australia, Busby donated the majority of cuttings to the government for the purpose of establishing an experimental garden at Sydney, and the remaining cuttings were planted at Kirkton. In addition to importing the grapevines, Busby also promoted the industry by writing a number of books about winemaking and grape growing in Australia, as well as on his travels through the wine regions of Europe. His association with the Australian wine industry ended in 1833 when he immigrated to New Zealand. Although he had departed the country, his books on winemaking and his work importing grape varieties were to influence the development of winemaking in Australia for years to come.

By the 1830s, Great Britain had colonized the entire continent and settlements were established in many locations. Vineyard development was progressing rapidly in the Hunter Valley, and vines were also planted in what are now Victoria, South Australia, and Western Australia (Figure 14.4). In addition to new arrivals from Great Britain, Australia also became a destination for immigrants from other countries in Europe. Throughout the 1830s and 1840s, settlers arrived from many countries and

were responsible for spreading agriculture across the continent. Many of the colonists from countries such as Germany, Italy, and France had knowledge of wine production that they had gained in their homelands. These settlers helped expand the Australian wine industry, planting vineyards in desirable locations and bringing in new techniques. It was during this time that many of Australia's best viticultural regions were first established. Two of the country's most famous wineries, Lindemans and Penfolds, were founded in the 1840s.

The discovery of gold in eastern Australia in 1852 had a significant effect on the country's fledgling wine business. Initially it slowed development because there was a shortage of labor as vineyard workers left to find their fortune in the mines. However, the gold rush that followed the strike brought in many new immigrants and the population doubled to just over 1 million between 1850 and 1860. After the gold played out in the mines, these newcomers provided a source of labor as well as a market for Australia's wineries. Over the second half of the nineteenth century, the wine business slowly expanded as new vineyard land was developed. The pace of expansion was slowed by international and domestic tariffs that discouraged the shipping of wine out of its home state. The temperance movement was also active at the time but was unable to pass nationwide prohibition laws as it had in the United States. As duties on exported wines were relaxed, international trade increased, and by 1900 approximately 500,000 gallons (1.9 million liters) of wine were exported to Great Britain (Walsh, 1979). In 1901, the federation of the states lowered trade barriers within Australia and dramatically increased domestic consumption.

In 1877, phylloxera was discovered in the Geelong area of the state of Victoria. While it destroyed nearly all the vineyards of the Geelong and Bendigo regions, the

Bottles of Yellow Tail Shiraz being loaded into cases on a bottling line. Yellow Tail is the most popular imported brand of wine in America. After it was introduced in 2001, sales in the US quickly grew to nearly eight million cases per year. However because the product was both very popular and inexpensive, its success lowered the perceived value of other Australian wines in the US Market.

W. J. Deutsch & Sons, Ltd.

infestation was slow to spread elsewhere. Consequently, most of Australia was saved from the devastation that was experienced in California and Europe. Today phylloxera is absent from the states of South Australia, Western Australia, Tasmania, and most of New South Wales, and there are very strict quarantines in place to prevent it from spreading to new areas.

In the period between 1900 and the Second World War, the industry continued to grow but also experienced setbacks from droughts, economic depression, and regional outbreaks of phylloxera, thus exhibiting the boom and bust cycle of development that is common to the wine business. The Second World War severely cut exports, but when it was over a new wave of immigrants came to the country, providing a new market for wine. The situation in the 20 years following the war was similar to that in the United States; there was slow growth, but it was limited by lack of consumer interest and wines of unexceptional quality. This began to change in the 1960s when interest in wine began to grow and producers improved their product. It was not until 1968 that table wines outsold dessert wines in Australia, and by the mid-1970s, still only 2 percent of production was exported.

During the 1980s and 1990s, production increased and Australia began to reach its potential for both quality and quantity of wine. Domestic consumption expanded during this time but not nearly at a rate to absorb the added production. There was, however, a rapidly growing market for Australian wines overseas. The modernization of the industry in the 1970s and 1980s allowed exporters to make a high-quality product, and favorable exchange rates allowed them to keep their prices low. At the turn of the millennium the growth accelerated and from 1999 to 2007 exports grew by 300 percent making Australia the world's fourth largest exporter of wine (Foley, 2009). This growth has been primarily driven by the low end of the market and by 2008 wines that sell for less than four Australian dollars per bottle made up 85 percent of exports. One of these less expensive wine brands, Yellow Tail, grew to be the most popular imported wine in America. After it was introduced in 2001, U.S. sales quickly grew to nearly 8 million cases per year. However, because the product was both very popular and inexpensive, its success lowered the perceived value of other Australian wines in the U.S. Market.

New vineyard plantings came into production at the same time the exchange rate for the Australian dollar became less favorable, making Australian wines more expensive in their export markets. This occurred at the beginning of the worldwide recession, which further lowered demand. The combination of events has resulted in an oversupply of grapes and wine being sold at unsustainably low prices. Recent drought conditions have lowered yields, but some growers are taking vineyard land out of production because it is not profitable.

WINE REGIONS OF AUSTRALIA

Although Australia is a very large country, most of the continent is unsuitable for viticulture. The northern part of the country has a subtropical climate that is too warm for growing wine grapes, and the interior is too hot and dry. There are many areas where the soil and the climate are appropriate, but there is inadequate water available for irrigation. Grape-growing regions are concentrated in the areas with a temperate climate located in the valleys along the country's southeastern coast between Sydney and Adelaide. The moderate climate of this area is one of the reasons it is also where the majority of Australia's population lives. There are also viticultural districts along the coast of Western Australia near Perth, as well as on the island of Tasmania to the south.

The wines of Australia are labeled by the state they were grown in or by appellation of origin in a system called **Geographic Indications (GIs)**. This method of classification subdivides the territory of each state into a series of zones, regions, and subregions (Table 14.2). States are divided into zones in a manner so that all of the land of the state is covered. Zones can be subdivided into regions, and regions can be further broken down into subregions. For an area to be classified as a region, it must have at least five independently owned growers each holding vineyards that are at least 12.4 acres (5 hectares) in size. These definitions are set by the **Australian Wine and Brandy Corporation (AWBC)**. The AWBC is a governmental organization that is responsible for both the regulation and promotion of the Australian wine industry.

This system of GIs is similar to the AVA system of viticultural areas used in the United States. Neither system of classification attempts to make any statement about a wine's quality, nor do they dictate which varieties can be grown in the region or what production methods can be used. Both GIs and AVAs only refer to the geographic origin of the grapes used to make the wine. As of 2009, there were 64 regions and 12 subregions of viticulture in Australia. There is also one all-encompassing appellation called South Eastern Australia that includes all of the grape-growing regions of the states of Victoria, New South Wales, South Australia, and Queensland. This appellation is primarily used by large wineries producing inexpensive wines blended from many parts of the country.

For a wine to be labeled as from a particular region, at least 85 percent of the grapes used to make the wine must be from that region. Additionally, 85 percent is also the standard for designating particular varietal or vintage on the label. As in California, it is illegal to add sugar to raise the °Brix of musts before fermentation but permissible

TABLE 14.2 Australian Geographic Indications (Wine Regions)

Australian State or Zone	Region	Sub-region
South Eastern Australia, includes the states of NSW, Vic, Tas, and part of SA & Qld		
South Australia		
Adelaide (Super Zone, includes Mount Lofty Ranges, Fleurieu and Barossa)		
Barossa	Barossa Valley	
	Eden Valley	High Eden Springton
Far North	Southern Flinders Ranges	
Fleurieu	Currency Creek Kangaroo Island Langhorne Creek McLaren Vale Southern Fleurieu	Clarendon

(Continues)

TABLE 14.2 Australian Geographic Indications (Wine Regions) *(Continued)*

Australian State or Zone	Region	Sub-region
Limestone Coast	Bordertown Coonawarra Mt. Benson Padthaway Penola Wrattonbully Robe	
Lower Murray	Riverland	
Mount Lofty Ranges	Adelaide Hills	Gumeracha Lenswood Piccadilly Valley
	Adelaide Plains	
	Clare Valley	Auburn Clare Hill River Polish Hill River Sevenhill Watervale
The Peninsulas		
New South Wales		
Big Rivers	Lachlan Valley Murray Darling (shared with Vic) Perricoota Riverina Swan Hill (shared with Vic)	
Central Ranges	Cowra Mudgee Orange	
Hunter Valley	Hunter	Allandale Belford Broke Fordwich Dalwood Pokolbin Rothbury
Northern Rivers	Hastings River	
Northern Slopes	New England Australia	
South Coast	Shoalhaven Coast Southern Highlands Sydney	
Southern New South Wales	Canberra District Gundagai Hilltops Tumbarumba	
Western Plains		
Western Australia		
Central Western Australia		
Eastern Plains, Inland and North of Western Australia		

(Continues)

TABLE 14.2 Australian Geographic Indications (Wine Regions) *(Continued)*

Australian State or Zone	Region	Sub-region
Greater Perth	Peel Perth Hills Swan District	 Swan Valley
South West Australia	Blackwood Valley Geographe	
	Great Southern	Albany Denmark Frankland River Mount Barker Porongurup
	Manjimup Margaret River Pemberton Warren Valley	
West Australian South East Coastal	Esperance	
Queensland		
Queensland	Granite Belt South Burnett	
Victoria		
Central Victoria	Bendigo Central Victorian Mountain Country	
	Goulburn Valley	Nagambie Lakes
	Heathcote Strathbogie Ranges Upper Goulburn	
Gippsland		
North East Victoria	Alpine Valleys	Kiewa River Valley Ovens Valley
	Beechworth Glenrowan	
	King Valley	Myrrhee Whitlands
	Rutherglen	
North West Victoria	Murray Darling (shared with NSW) Swan Hill (shared with NSW)	
Port Phillip	Geelong Macedon Ranges Mornington Peninsula Sunbury Yarra Valley	
Western Victoria	Grampians Henty Pyrenees	Great Western
Tasmania (has no regions or subregions)		
Northern Territory (has no regions or subregions)		
Australian Capital Territory (has no regions or subregions)		

to add acid to lower the pH. This is not surprising given the similarities in the climate of California and Australia; grapes almost always reach full sugar maturity at harvest but frequently have low acid.

New South Wales

As was previously stated, the first vineyards in Australia were planted in New South Wales. The state has 16 different wine regions and produces about one-third of Australia's wine. The wine industry of the state is centered about 90 miles (145 km) north of Sydney in the Hunter Valley in the foothills of the Brokenback range. The wine industry in this region produces a number of red varieties, with Cabernet Sauvignon and Shiraz being the most prominent. The **Shiraz** grape, which is also called Hermitage in Australia, is known as Syrah to much of the rest of the world. The name Hermitage comes from an appellation in the northern Rhône region of France where Syrah is grown. In Australia, the name Hermitage can be used as a synonym for Syrah but the wines cannot be exported to the EU. This is similar to the use of European place-names as generic terms for American wine as discussed in Chapter 3. Indigenous to the northern Rhône Valley of France, Shiraz is the most planted wine grape in Australia. Its popularity diminished in the 1960s and 1970s as the growers in New South Wales concentrated on Cabernet Sauvignon, but in recent years there has been a renewed interest in the variety. The weather in the Hunter Valley is always a concern for growers, hot and humid in the summertime with a perennial risk of fall rains. Additionally, much of the appellations soil is heavy in clay and drains poorly. Despite these difficulties, the Hunter Valley is one of Australia's best-known wine regions and produces a number of fine wines (Figure 14.5).

The principal white wines of the region are Chardonnay and Semillon. While Chardonnay is more widely planted, the region is probably better known for its

FIGURE 14.5

Early morning fog in the Hunter Valley region of New South Wales. Hunter Valley lies about 90 miles (145 km) north of Sydney and is the best-known appellation in New South Wales.

Wine Australia, © AWBC/ Matt Turner

Semillon. Until recently, the Semillon from Hunter Valley was sometimes referred to as Hunter Valley Riesling. Historically, the predominant white wine produced in the region was Semillon, with Chardonnay not becoming popular until the 1960s and 1970s. During that time, the introduction of new technologies and techniques, such as cold fermentation and gentle pressing, resulted in more flavorful white wines. In 1973, one of the area's wineries, Tyrrell, began producing an award-winning Chardonnay called Vat 47. Because of the Hunter Valley's close proximity to Sydney, tourism has played an important role in the development of the area's wine business. Fledgling wineries were supported by sightseers coming up from the city to see the wine country and purchase wine at the winery's "cellar door." **Cellar door**, being the Australian term for a retail tasting room located at the winery. Vintners also put special effort into designing attractive buildings and landscaping to aid in drawing in tourists.

West of the Hunter Valley, on the opposite side of the Great Dividing Range of mountains, Mudgee is best known for its Chardonnay and Cabernet Sauvignon. Surrounded on three sides by mountain ranges, its elevation varies from 1,600 to 3,000 feet (500 to 1,000 meters). The higher elevation gives the region a mild climate with cool nights. Settled in the mid-1800s, the early wine industry was shaped by German emigrants. Mudgee's vineyards grew extensively in the 1970s when many smaller wineries were established. Today many of the grapes it grows are shipped to Hunter Valley wineries for processing. About 200 miles (320 km) farther inland, is the Riverina region; this large district has a number of expansive vineyards that grow more grapes than the rest of the appellations in New South Wales combined. Most of these grapes are used by large wineries producing inexpensive blends for export; however, there are some small production lots of high-end dessert wines that are bottled from the region as well. The border between New South Wales and Victoria to the south follows the Murray River for much of its length. The Murray is Australia's largest river and is the source of irrigation for vineyards as well as other crops on both sides of the border.

Victoria

The wine industry of Victoria was begun by Swiss immigrants in the middle of the nineteenth century. By 1900, vineyards had spread across the entire state, and Victoria was producing the majority of Australia's wine. Unfortunately, as in Europe and California, the phylloxera epidemic wiped out a huge number of vineyards. In the last decades of the twentieth century it was one of the fastest growing wine regions, with a more than 10-fold increase in production from 1965 to 2000. Since then the vineyard acreage has stabilized and today Victoria grows about one-fifth of Australia's wine grapes. There are more than 800 wineries located throughout the state in 6 different wine zones and 20 wine regions. There are several large wineries, particularly in the Murray Darling Region in northwestern Victoria, but most are small producers making limited amounts of high-end wine. Among the most famous areas are the Goulburn Valley in the north central part of the state, Yarra Valley just to the east of Melbourne, and Western Victoria where the Grampians and Pyrenees regions lie. The far southwest section of the state produces some fine Rieslings, while the northeast produces complex Muscats and Tokays. Two other regions, the small Mornington Peninsula and the much larger Gippsland, are on the southeastern edge of the state. Their

Victoria

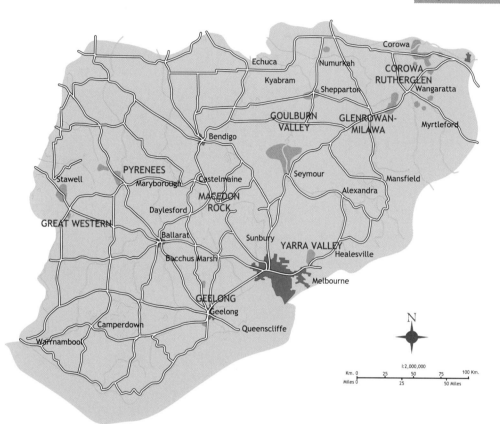

Vineyard Areas

Map courtesy of Kobrand Corporation (www.kobrandwine.com)

location on the southern tip of the continent gives them a cool climate, and Chardonnay and Pinot Noir do well here.

The Goulburn Valley is in the north-central section of Victoria near the border with New South Wales. The valley is formed by the Goulburn River, a tributary of the Murray River to the north. The region is best known for its Cabernet Sauvignon and Shiraz, as well as the white Rhône variety Marsanne. The Goulburn Valley is home to Tahbilk winery established in 1860; it is one of the most historic wineries in Australia. The Yarra Valley region, which lies about an hour's drive east of the city of Melbourne, also has a long history of winemaking dating back to the mid-nineteenth century. However, by the 1920s, economic depression and competition from wineries in other states had closed all the area's wineries. Beginning in the 1960s, a new generation of wineries were founded and since then the area has grown significantly (Figure 14.6). The Yarra Valley is particularly well known for its Pinot Noir, Chardonnay, and Cabernet Sauvignon.

FIGURE 14.6

A large vineyard in the Yarra Valley region of Victoria.
Wine Australia, © AWBC/Matt Turner

Western Victoria is home to the Grampians region; previously known as the Great Western region. It is less populated than areas to the east, and is famous for its natural beauty, national parks, and rich history of winemaking. One of the best-known wines produced in the region is a méthode champenoise sparkling wine called Great Western. Named after a town on the Western Highway, it is made at the Great Western Estate winery established in the 1860s by Joseph Best and now owned by Seppelts. The winery has an extensive network of wine storage caves, or "drives," that were dug in the 1860s by ex-miners after the gold rush. Area wineries also produce red wines such as Pinot Noir, Cabernet Sauvignon, and Shiraz–Cabernet blends as well as a uniquely Australian product, sparkling Shiraz. Blends combining Cabernet with Merlot or Shiraz are particularly common in Australia. It should be noted that Australian wines are required to list the major component first; that is, a Shiraz–Cabernet contains more Shiraz than Cabernet.

Southwest of Grampians bordered by the Southern Ocean on the south and South Australia to the west is the Henty region. Its costal location on the southern edge of the Australia's mainland makes its one of the coolest appellations on the continent and cool climate varieties such as Pinot Noir and Chardonnay.

South Australia

The state of South Australia lies between Victoria and Western Australia and contains 7 wine zones and 17 regions. The state has more land in vineyards than any other in Australia and produces more than 46 percent of the nation's wine. While Victoria to the east is known for having primarily small wineries, South Australia by contrast is dominated by large producers. It is not uncommon for these big wineries to bring in grapes and juice from the large vineyards over the border in New South Wales and Victoria for fermentation and bottling. In addition to these big wineries, South Australia is also home to some of the country's preeminent grape-growing regions, making some of Australia's most expensive and sought after wines.

The vineyards of South Australia lie primarily in its southeastern corner. The appellations of the Barossa Valley, Adelaide Hills, McLaren Vale, and Clare Valley are clustered around the city of Adelaide. The area is also home to Roseworthy Agricultural College. Now part of the University of Adelaide, it is Australia's premiere institution for the study of viticulture and enology (Figure 14.7). The Coonawarra and Padthaway regions are located 200 miles (320 km) to the southeast of Adelaide near the border with Victoria. Riverland is a large growing region directly north of Coonawarra on the Murray River near the border with New South Wales and Victoria. It is much farther inland than the other appellations, and here the vineyards are quite large and have higher yields, producing inexpensive wines. As previously mentioned, phylloxera has never come to the state and consequently most vines are own-rooted.

The Barossa Valley is about 40 miles (65 km) to the northwest of the city of Adelaide and is one of Australia's oldest and most famous grape-growing regions. First

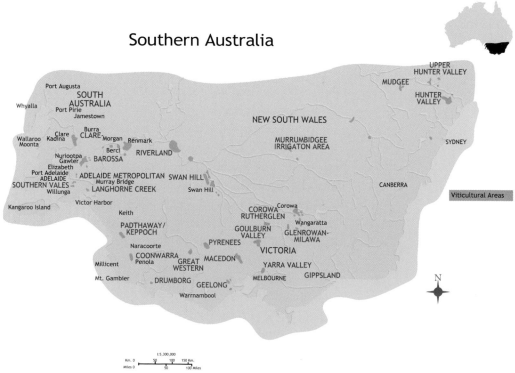

Map courtesy of Kobrand Corporation (www.kobrandwine.com)

FIGURE 14.7

A professor examines vines at the Australian Wine Research Institute at the University of Adelaide in Adelaide, Australia. Nets are used to protect the ripe grapes from birds.
© Charles O'Rear/Corbis

developed in the 1840s by German immigrants, the Barossa Valley is home to the headquarters of many of Australia's largest producers. The vineyards spread throughout the lower part of the region, following the path of the North Para River. The climate has warm summers and cool winters, and red grapes make up about two-thirds of the vineyards with Shiraz and Cabernet Sauvignon being the two most popular varieties. For whites, Semillon and Chardonnay are the most common varieties. One of the most historic wineries is Seppeltsfield, owned by the same company that produces Great Western sparkling wine in neighboring Victoria. The best-known Shiraz in the Barossa Valley is the Grange from Penfolds Winery (Figure 14.8). It has been made since 1951, and was called Grange Hermitage prior to 1990 vintage when it shortened its name to simply Grange to comply with European import requirements. Made from dry-farmed old vines of Shiraz, it is aged in new American oak and occasionally has a small amount of Cabernet Sauvignon blended in for complexity. Grange is perhaps the most highly regarded of all of Australia's wines, and its intense flavors allow it to age for as long as several decades.

Directly to the east of the Barossa Valley is the Eden Valley region, where the topography gradually climbs into the Barossa range of mountains and the elevation reaches 1,500 to 2,000 feet (450 to 600 meters). The soil is less fertile here than in

FIGURE 14.8

Penfolds Winery in the Barossa Valley region of South Australia. The winery is home to Penfolds Grange, a Syrah that is one of Australia's most famous wines.
© Charles O'Rear/Corbis

the valley below, and the climate is cooler. The cool conditions make the region ideal for white grape varieties such as Chardonnay and **Rhine Riesling**. Rhine Riesling, sometimes shortened to just Rhine, is an Australian name for the varietal Riesling, also known as White Riesling. To the south of the Barossa and Eden Valleys is the Adelaide Hills district, a series of gentle rolling hills about 9 miles (15 km) to the west of the city of Adelaide. Here the climate is even cooler than the Eden Valley, and spring frost can be a problem in low-lying areas. Varieties such as Pinot Noir and Sauvignon Blanc are planted along with the Chardonnay and Shiraz. To the south of the Adelaide Hills is the McLaren Vale region. The elevation is lower here, starting at the coast and increasing to 1,100 feet (350 meters) on the east. The appellation has a number of small wineries that produce a variety of red and white wines. The Clare Valley lies 75 miles (125 km) to the north of Adelaide. Being farther inland, it receives less of a moderating influence from the ocean and is warmer than the vineyard lands that surround Adelaide. Cabernet Sauvignon and Shiraz are popular, as well as Chardonnay and Riesling.

At the southeastern corner of South Australia lies the Limestone Coast Zone home to the Coonawarra and Padthaway regions. Coonawarra, about 220 miles (350 km) southeast from Adelaide, is regarded as one of the best regions for red wines in Australia. It lies between Naracoonte and Millicent and is the southernmost region in South Australia. The location results in much cooler temperatures and is the only region in Australia where severe frosts during the springtime are common. Coonawarra is particularly known for its soil, terra rossa, a vivid red topsoil that is found in thin bands that overlay soft limestone (Figure 14.9). The most widely planted grape is Cabernet Sauvignon, which makes up more than 50 percent of the grapes that are crushed. Cabernets from Coonawarra are renowned for their deep color and spicy fruit flavors. Other grape varieties produced in the region include Shiraz, Chardonnay, Merlot, Riesling, and Pinot Noir.

The Padthaway region, just to the north of Coonawarra, began to come into prominence in the 1990s. The climate in Padthaway is slightly warmer than Coonawarra, and although spring frost is less of a threat here, in 1988 it succeeded in wiping out almost Padthaway's entire crop for the year. The soil in Padthaway is primarily a sandy soil similar to that found in the Barossa Valley. However, some of Coonawarra's terra rossa can be found in isolated areas. The primary grape varieties are Shiraz, Chardonnay, Cabernet Sauvignon, Riesling, Merlot, and Pinot Noir.

Western Australia

Far from the urban centers and major grape-growing regions to the east, there is a small but growing wine industry in the state of Western Australia. Western

FIGURE 14.9

An excavation showing a soil profile of the root zone of a Shiraz vine grown in South Australia's Coonawarra region, illustrating the terra rossa for which the appellation is famous.
© Charles O'Rear/Corbis

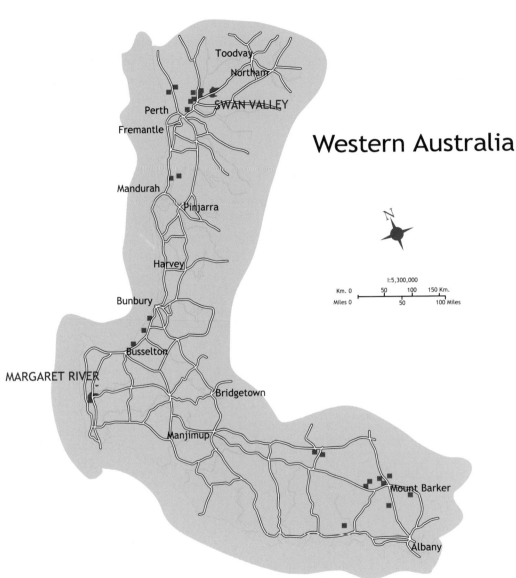

Western Australia

Map courtesy of Kobrand Corporation (www.kobrandwine.com)

Australia is home to nine wine regions and produces approximately 8 percent of Australia's vineyard land. Located on the continent's southwestern corner it is isolated by desert from the rest of Australia's viticultural areas. The state has some of the oldest grape-growing regions in the country, as well as some of the newest. Grapevines were first planted outside Perth as early as 1829 in what is now the Swan District region and the appellation is home to Olive Farm, the state's longest operating winery. The region is one of the warmest in Australia, and summertime temperatures can reach over 110°F (43°C). The Swan District and neighboring Perth Hills produce a number of red and white wines, but are best known for their whites, particularly Chenin Blanc.

On the southwestern corner of the continent, 250 miles (402 km) to the south of Perth, there is another group of viticultural districts that include the Margaret River, Pemberton, and Great Southern. This part of the state has a much shorter history of winemaking than the region around Perth does and did not begin to develop until the 1970s. During the 1980s, there was much growth and foreign investment, but today most of the wineries are small operations, and the area is still not home to any of Australia's largest producers. The area is best known for its red wines, such as Cabernet Sauvignon, Shiraz, and Pinot Noir, that are grown in the Margaret River region and Mount Barker (a subregion of the Great Southern district). White wines are also produced, and the Pemberton region is famous for its Chardonnay and Sauvignon Blanc. These regions experience a cooling influence from their proximity to the Indian Ocean and have a much more temperate climate than the vineyards around Perth.

Tasmania

Tasmania is a large island south of the state of Victoria. Although the first commercial vineyard was planted in 1823 (Halliday, 2007), winemaking had all but disappeared by the 1860s. The industry was not reestablished until the 1950s, when the Lalla Vineyard was planted on the Tamar River and Moorilla Estate was established in the Derwent Valley, north of the capital city of Hobart. These areas together with the Pipers Brook region, northeast of the Tamar River, and a small area on the east coast near the resort of Bichens continue to be the principal grape-growing regions. It is Australia's coolest area for grape growing and produces less than 1 percent of its wine. Today, there are about 90 wineries on record, but only a few are of notable size. Two of the largest are Piper's Brook Vineyard, established in 1974, and Tamar Ridge established in 1994.

In Tasmania, red and white grapes are grown in roughly equal portions, and because of the climate, early ripening varieties are preferred. Chardonnay is the most common white wine grape and Pinot Noir makes up 90 percent of the red plantings, both of which are well suited to cool weather. Sauvignon Blanc also shows great promise, producing intensely grassy wines that are similar in style to the Sauvignon Blancs of New Zealand. Other varieties are Semillon, Merlot, and Gewürztraminer. This is the one area of Australia where little Shiraz is produced.

New Zealand

New Zealand lies 1,300 miles (2,100 km) off the eastern coast of Australia across the Tasman Sea at roughly the same latitude as Tasmania. Its southerly location and maritime weather pattern gives the country a moderate but cool climate. Grapes have been grown in New Zealand nearly as long as they have been in Australia, but there was little development until the 1970s. This was due to a number of factors including antialcohol regulations, more difficult growing conditions, and poor winemaking practices. Today, for the most part, these issues have been dealt with and New Zealand is gaining a reputation for superior wines (Figure 14.10). In recent years there has been phenomenal growth with vineyard acreage doubling between 2003 and 2009. Yet in

FIGURE 14.10

A winter view of a young vineyard in the Central Otago region on New Zealand's South Island. The region is one of the southernmost grape-growing areas in the world and the most inland of New Zealand's appellations.
© Shutterstock/Neil Annenberg

spite of this expansion, New Zealand produces only about 15 percent as much wine grapes as Australia does. Although it makes less wine than Australia, New Zealand wines fetch a higher price in the international wine market, selling for almost twice as much per liter as Australian wines do.

New Zealand—Historical Perspective

The first *vinifera* vines were planted near Kerikeri on New Zealand's North Island by Samuel Marsden in 1819. Seventeen years later the famous Australian vintner James Busby settled nearby in Waitangi, planted grapes, and made New Zealand's first wine in 1836. Although New Zealand's commercial wine industry dates back to 1863, it was very slow to develop. Winemaking was widespread across the North Island but at a very small scale, and very little was exported. After phylloxera and powdery mildew arrived at the end of the nineteenth century, New Zealand growers imported native American grape varieties. Unlike grape growers in other countries, New Zealand's growers did not bother to use them as rootstock, instead using them to produce wine grapes directly, along with French–American hybrids. It was also allowable at the time to add both sugar and water to make up for underripe grapes and to increase yield. These vines and cellar practices produced wines of poor quality that were often fortified with alcohol to cover up their inadequateness. In 1960, the most widely planted grape variety in New Zealand was the American variety Isabella and only 12 percent of the wine that was produced was table wine (Halliday, 2000). Hardy and tolerant to cold and damp conditions, Isabella was also popular in the early vineyards of Oregon and Washington.

In addition to inadequate vineyard and winemaking practices, New Zealand also had tariffs and legal restrictions that inhibited growth. While nationwide prohibition was narrowly defeated in 1919, there were a number of laws enacted that were designed to discourage the consumption of wine and alcohol products. Wine could not be sold by the bottle in shops until 1955, restaurants could not sell wine until 1960, and supermarkets could not sell wine until 1990. Most of what little wine was consumed during the first 70 years of the twentieth century was imported, usually from Australia (Robinson, 1999).

This less than ideal situation began to change in the 1970s when the wine industry started to put a greater emphasis on quality. Increasing local interest in fine wines gave producers incentive to change their ways and concentrate on producing a better product. Vineyards were replanted with superior-tasting classic *vinifera* wine grapes, and winemakers improved their techniques as well. The **Wine Institute of New Zealand** was formed in 1975 to promote the industry, and the government also acted to help improve the quality of wine rather than solely trying to control its sale. In 1982, regulations were passed that limited the amount of water that could be added to wine, and in the mid-1980s, during a time of grape surpluses, the government helped subsidize growers to pull out unpopular varieties. From 1973 to 1983, wine production grew more than 350 percent, and a healthy export market developed. The rapid growth continued through the 1980s and 1990s, and at times there were periods when supply outpaced demand. Today New Zealand's wines are popular throughout the world and often command high prices. It is also known for producing some of the world's most intensely flavored Sauvignon Blanc.

New Zealand's climate makes it particularly well suited to early ripening varieties that are more flavorful when grown in cool growing conditions such as Chardonnay, Sauvignon Blanc, and Pinot Noir. These three varieties now account for 70 percent of New Zealand's vineyard acreage. The cool conditions and occasional summer rains can cause problems for growers in terms of mold and mildew, particularly with Sauvignon Blanc. Sauvignon Blanc's thin-skinned grape berries are sensitive to rot, and the variety can develop a thick canopy of leaves that inhibits air circulation around the clusters. The lack of air circulation, combined with Sauvignon Blanc's tightly bunched clusters, keeps damp berries from drying out. To deal with this problem, viticulturists in New Zealand have developed a number of innovative trellising systems to open up the canopy and control vine vigor. Opening up the canopy of leaves and exposing the fruit to fresh air and light not only reduces mold and mildew growth but also improves flavor and aids in ripening. These trellising systems have become popular in a number of wine regions around the world. New Zealand is not only innovative in its viticultural practices; it also embraced new techniques in packaging the finished wines. Many New Zealand wineries were early proponents of using Stelvin-type screw caps to seal bottles, particularly on their Sauvignon Blanc.

WINE REGIONS OF NEW ZEALAND

The two major islands of New Zealand form a long north–south chain, and no part of the country is more than 90 miles (145 km) from the coast. For this reason, the weather all over the country is dominated by the influence of the ocean. There is still a great deal of variation in growing conditions, however, due to the varied terrain and long length of the country. New Zealand is more than 900 miles (1,500 km) long, stretching from 35° south to 47° south in latitude. This compares roughly in distance and latitude as from Los Angeles to Portland, Oregon, in the Northern Hemisphere. Chardonnay vines grown in the cooler southern regions are picked six to eight weeks after the beginning of harvest in the north. On the South Island, the vineyards of the Otago region are the southernmost vineyards in the world. New Zealand's grape-growing appellations are divided into 10 growing regions, 6 on the North Island and 4 on the South Island (Table 14.3). The 3 largest regions, Marlborough, Hawke's Bay, and Gisborne, account for just over 90 percent of production (New Zealand Winegrowers, 2010). Historically, vineyards had been concentrated on the North Island, but in recent decades extensive planting has resulted in the South Island having more vineyard acreage.

Gisborne

The Gisborne region lies on the eastern edge of the North Island and produces about 8 percent of New Zealand's wine. It is a cool region that is best known for growing white varieties, which make up 90 percent of the vineyards. There is ample rainfall throughout the growing season, which increases the likelihood of rot and can cause problems during harvest. The vineyards are primarily grown on the deep, alluvial soils that exist along the river plains. Abundant water and fertile soils allow for higher yield, and the grapes grown in Gisborne are usually crushed by larger wineries to make value-oriented wine. In recent years, smaller wineries have been moving into Gisborne and concentrating on producing a higher-quality product. Chardonnay is the most popular grape, accounting for over half of the region's production and Pinot Gris is popular as well.

TABLE 14.3 Wine Regions of New Zealand

Appellation	Best-Known Varieties
Auckland/Northern	Chardonnay, Merlot
Canterbury	Pinot Noir, Chardonnay, Riesling
Central Otago	Pinot Noir
Gisborne	Chardonnay
Hawke's Bay	Chardonnay, Merlot, Cabernet Sauvignon
Marlborough	Sauvignon Blanc, Pinot Noir, Chardonnay
Nelson	Sauvignon Blanc, Pinot Noir, Chardonnay
Waikato/Bay of Plenty	Produces a number of varieties
Waipara	Pinot Noir, Riesling

Reading a New Zealand Wine Label
Domestic (New Zealand)

Front Label

Winery Name: Most names are acceptable as long as they are not offensive or misleading.

Variety: The varietal of the grapes used to make the wine. The variety listed must be at least 75 percent of the grapes used to make the wine. For wine labeled for export, the requirement is 85 percent.

Appellation or geographical indication: The district the grapes were grown in. Eighty-five percent of the grapes used to produce the wine must be grown in the region listed.

Vintage Date: 85 percent of the grapes used to make the wine must be grown the year listed as the vintage.

CR

CRAGGY RANGE
SINGLE VINEYARD
Sauvignon Blanc
MARTINBOROUGH
NEW ZEALAND
2 0 0 9

TE MUNA ROAD
VINEYARD

Craggy Range Vineyards Ltd.

Single Vineyard: Designates that the grapes were grown in the Te Muna Road Vineyard in Martinborough.

Wine labels for Australia and New Zealand contain much of the same information that is found on United States wine labels. This label of Craggy Range Sauvignon Blanc is produced for the domestic New Zealand market and has several items, such as the allergen statement and servings per bottle, that are not required for export. Since this wine is not destined for the United States, the government health warning is also absent. If the wine were to be exported, it would have to be labeled with the label information required by the destination country.

Reading a New Zealand Wine Label
Domestic (New Zealand)

Back Label

Wine Notes: Not required but many wineries add them to describe how the wine is made and what it tastes like. They must not be misleading.

Alcohol Content and Container Volume: The percentage of alcohol by volume must be listed. If it is under 15 percent the label may also state "Table Wine." The volume of wine must also be listed in metric units.

Allergen Statement: Since 2002 both Australia and New Zealand have required that potential allergens, such as egg or milk products, be listed when they have been used (typically for fining) in the production of a wine.

Sulfite Declaration: If the wine contains any added sulfur dioxide it must be listed on the label. Here sulfur dioxide is referred to as "preservative 220."

Servings per Bottle: The number of "standard drinks" or servings must be listed. A standard drink is equal to the amount of the wine that contains 10 grams of alcohol.

TE MUNA ROAD VINEYARD

Craggy Range is a family owned winery specialising in the production of expressive Single Vineyard wines. Our Martinborough vineyard is located at Te Muna, which means 'secret place'. This wine is sourced exclusively from several parcels of vines growing on a stony, limestone influenced soil adjacent to the Huangarua River. The wine has rich ripe flavours of limes, peaches and apples alongside the characteristic herbaceous components and a unique dry grainy texture on the palate. As with all our Sauvignon Blanc wines intervention in the cellar is minimal out of care and respect for characters of the vineyard. Enjoy within three years of vintage, lightly chilled, wherever there is sun, surf or seafood.

SAUVIGNON BLANC
MARTINBOROUGH 2009

Alc 13.5% by vol 750ml
This wine was fined with traditional fining agents based on milk and fish products.
Contains preservative 220
Contains approx. 8 standard drinks

9 421004 550352

PRODUCED AND BOTTLED BY CRAGGY RANGE VINEYARDS LIMITED,
WAIMARAMA RD, HAVELOCK NORTH, N.Z. WWW.CRAGGYRANGE.COM
WINE OF NEW ZEALAND

Craggy Range Vineyards Ltd.

Production Statement: The name and address of the winery that produced the wine.

Country of Origin: Required on all New Zealand wines.

Hawke's Bay

Hawke's Bay is on the southeastern coast of the North Island just below the Gisborne region. It is the second largest region in terms of production, growing nearly one-quarter of New Zealand's grapes. It has a long history of winemaking, with the first commercial vineyards being established in the 1890s. It has less rainfall and humidity than Gisborne and more sunny weather during the growing season. There is a great variety of soil types and terrain, making Hawke's Bay ideal for a number of grape varieties. As in the Gisborne, Chardonnay is the most widely planted grape; however, Hawke's Bay's warmer climate and added sunshine also allows red varieties such as Cabernet Sauvignon and Pinot Noir to do well. Sauvignon Blanc is also widely planted and makes a wine that has less of the varietal's grassy/herbaceous character than the grapes produced in the Marlborough region to the south. Hawke's Bay is widely considered one of New Zealand's best wine regions and is home to more than 70 wineries.

Marlborough

The Marlborough region lies on the northeastern edge of New Zealand's South Island where the Wairau River empties into Cloudy Bay. Viticulture did not begin in the region until 1973 when the large winery Montana established vineyards there. Since then, the Marlborough appellation has grown to hold 55 percent of New Zealand's vineyards and produce 68 percent of the country's wine (New Zealand Winegrowers, 2010). Internationally Marlborough is New Zealand's most well-known appellation. The region is cooler than the grape-growing areas on the North Island, but it is also dryer with abundant sunshine during the growing season. These conditions combine for a long growing season that allows the flavors of cool climate varieties to fully mature. Marlborough has the reputation for producing some of the most strongly flavored Sauvignon Blancs in the world, with strong notes of grass and gooseberries (Figure 14.11). The soil is alluvial and is very rocky in areas, which provides the vineyards with adequate drainage. Its most popular variety is Sauvignon Blanc and it accounts for three-quarters of production followed by Pinot Noir and Chardonnay. The region is now home to more than 130 wineries and in addition to table wine, there is a growing production of méthode champenoise sparkling wines.

Other New Zealand Wine Regions

The remaining wine regions of New Zealand contain only 24 percent of the country's vineyard land. These areas are growing rapidly, however, with many smaller premium wineries being established. This is evidenced by the fact that although these minor regions have one-quarter of the vineyards, they contain nearly two-thirds of New Zealand's 643 wineries (New Zealand Winegrowers, 2010).

On the North Island the appellations are:

- **Auckland/Northland**: Two small regions that run from the city of Auckland to the tip of the North Island. The area is warm and can be rainy during the growing season with a variety of soil types. Principal varieties are Chardonnay, Cabernet Sauvignon, and Merlot.

FIGURE 14.11

A Sauvignon Blanc vineyard in the Marlborough region of New Zealand. This appellation produces some of the most intensely flavored Sauvignon Blancs in the world.

© Shutterstock/Neale Cousland

- **Waikato/Bay of Plenty**: An area to the north and east of the Hawke's Bay appellation. It has only a handful of wineries and about 350 acres (142 hectares) of grapes. It has one of New Zealand's warmer climates, with soils that are generally heavy clay loam. Principal varieties are Chardonnay and Cabernet Sauvignon.
- **Wairarapa/Martinborough**: On the southern tip of the North Island just across the water from the Marlborough region. With a similar climate to Marlborough, it has a number of small producers that are well known for their Sauvignon Blanc, Pinot Noir, and Chardonnay wines. The region is also home to New Zealand's capital city of Wellington.

On the South Island the appellations include:

- **Nelson**: On the northern tip of the South Island east of the Marlborough region. It has a varied topography with a number of mesoclimates and soil types. Principal varieties are Sauvignon Blanc, Chardonnay, and Pinot Noir.
- **Canterbury/Waipara**: On the eastern side of the South Island. Vineyards are located both around the city of Christchurch and about an hour north in the Waipara subregion. Canterbury has a cool, dry climate with alluvial soils. Waipara has chalky loam soils and is slightly warmer, although spring and fall

frosts are a threat in both areas. Principal varieties are Pinot Noir, Riesling, Chardonnay, and Sauvignon Blanc.

- **Otago (also called Central Otago):** The coolest and most southern of New Zealand's wine regions. Being located more inland than most of New Zealand's grape-growing regions, the appellation has less of a maritime influence. Most of the vineyards are planted on hillsides for better sun exposure and frost protection. Pinot Noir is by far the most popular variety with 75 percent of the plantings.

SUMMARY

Australia and New Zealand are often grouped together in the minds of American consumers, but their diversity in terroir allows them to produce a number of varieties of wine in a wide range of styles. Australia is better known for its Shiraz, Cabernet Sauvignon, and Chardonnay that have full body and ripe flavors, whereas New Zealand is recognized for its Sauvignon Blancs and Pinot Noirs that have firm structure, good acid, and intense varietal character. Both Australia and New Zealand have a growing wine industry and a reputation for quality and value on the worldwide market. The two countries also have strong domestic markets but are dependent on exports to sell more than half of the wine that they make. The growth of the export market was aided by a relatively low cost of production when compared to the United States and Europe, as well as a favorable exchange rate. Recently in both countries, the rapid growth has resulted in an oversupply of wine and falling prices. The United Kingdom and the United States are the two biggest customers for New Zealand and Australian wines, and New Zealand and Australia also export a significant amount of wine to each other. Exporting wine in bulk containers for bottling overseas is also becoming more popular.

Australian and New Zealand wines have had an influence on the American wine industry. In recent years the introduction of their wines into the U.S. market has pressured domestic producers to keep their prices reasonable and, in some cases, to emulate the popular styles of New Zealand Sauvignon Blanc and Australian Shiraz.

AUSTRALIA AND NEW ZEALAND FOOD AND WINE PAIRING

appetizer
shrimp and orange wedge salad with avocado and cilantro, topped with creamy avocado dressing

wine

An intensely flavored and tart New Zealand Sauvignon Blanc from the Marlborough region

first course
seared salmon with a mushroom wine sauce

wine

A New Zealand Pinot Noir from the Otago region on the South Island

main course
herb-crusted lamb chops with roasted red potatoes and garlic

wine

Full-bodied Shiraz from the Coonawarra region of South Australia

cheese plate
assortment of cheeses havarti, gouda, edam, and fontina

wine

A Semillon from the Hunter River Valley in Australia

EXERCISES

1. What are the risks and benefits to the New Zealand and Australian wine industry by having a large percentage of their production exported?

2. What types of varieties are suited to New Zealand's climate?

3. In what areas of the Australian continent are vineyards concentrated and what factors make them suitable for wine grapes?

4. How does a nation's exchange rate affect the demand for its exported wine?

5. What were some of the reasons that viticulture and winemaking developed more slowly in New Zealand than in Australia?

REVIEW QUESTIONS

1. Which of the following is by far New Zealand's most productive region?
   A. Hawke's Bay
   B. Waikato
   C. Marlborough
   D. Gisborne

2. For both Australia and New Zealand the vineyards are cooler in _____.
   A. The northern portion of the country
   B. The inland regions that are away from the sea
   C. The remote regions away from urban development
   D. The southern portion of the country

3. The Australian method used to demark viticultural regions is called _____.
   A. Appellation of origin
   B. Australian Viticultural Area, or AVA
   C. Geographic Indications, or GIs
   D. Vintners District

(Continues)

(Continued)

4. Vineyard development in Australia is limited by _____.
   A. Availability of water
   B. Lack of undeveloped land
   C. Environmental regulations restricting further development
   D. Availability of labor

5. Which of the following New Zealand appellations has a climate that has the least influence from the ocean?
   A. Hawke's Bay
   B. Otago
   C. Wairarapa
   D. Waipara

REFERENCES

Australian Wine and Brandy Corporation. (2010). *Australian wine sector at a glance, 2009,* Adelaide, South Australia: Author.

Evans, L. (1973). *Australia and New Zealand complete book of wine.* Dee Why West, NSW Australia: Paul Hamlyn Pty. Ltd.

Foley, M. (2009, July 4). For Australian winemakers, more turns out to be less. *The New York Times.* p. 81.

Halliday, J. (2000). *Wine atlas of Australia and New Zealand.* London: HarperCollins.

Halliday, J. (2007). *Wine atlas of Australia.* Los Angeles: University of California Press.

Johnson, H. (1989). *Vintage: The story of wine.* New York: Simon & Schuster.

New Zealand Winegrowers. (2009). *Annual report.* Auckland, New Zealand: Author.

New Zealand Winegrowers. (2010). *Statistical annual 2009.* Auckland, New Zealand: Author.

Robinson, J. (1999). *The Oxford companion to wine.* New York: Oxford University Press.

Walsh, G. (1979). The wine industry of Australia 1788–1979. *Wine Talk.* Canberra: Australian National University.

{CHILE AND ARGENTINA}

This chapter discusses the

two most prominent wine-producing countries in South America—Chile and Argentina—focusing on their similarities and differences. It also covers the history of winemaking in each country, as well as their climates and viticultural regions. The chapter concludes with a discussion of the importance of Chilean and Argentine exports in the international wine market.

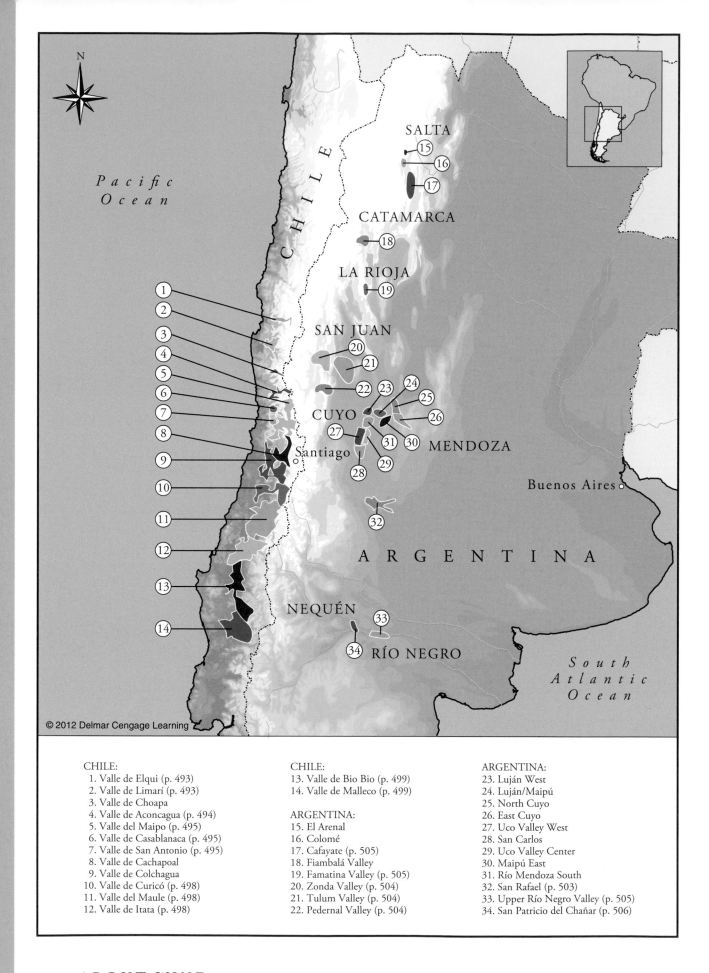

CHILE:
1. Valle de Elqui (p. 493)
2. Valle de Limarí (p. 493)
3. Valle de Choapa
4. Valle de Aconcagua (p. 494)
5. Valle del Maipo (p. 495)
6. Valle de Casablanaca (p. 495)
7. Valle de San Antonio (p. 495)
8. Valle de Cachapoal
9. Valle de Colchagua
10. Valle de Curicó (p. 498)
11. Valle del Maule (p. 498)
12. Valle de Itata (p. 498)

CHILE:
13. Valle de Bio Bio (p. 499)
14. Valle de Malleco (p. 499)

ARGENTINA:
15. El Arenal
16. Colomé
17. Cafayate (p. 505)
18. Fiambalá Valley
19. Famatina Valley (p. 505)
20. Zonda Valley (p. 504)
21. Tulum Valley (p. 504)
22. Pedernal Valley (p. 504)

ARGENTINA:
23. Luján West
24. Luján/Maipú
25. North Cuyo
26. East Cuyo
27. Uco Valley West
28. San Carlos
29. Uco Valley Center
30. Maipú East
31. Río Mendoza South
32. San Rafael (p. 503)
33. Upper Río Negro Valley (p. 505)
34. San Patricio del Chañar (p. 506)

KEY TERMS

alembic still

Carmenère

Côt

Criolla Chica

Criolla Grande

Malbec

País

Pisco

Torrontés

INTRODUCTION

Chile and Argentina are located in the "southern cone" at the base of the South American continent. This places them squarely in the middle of the Southern Hemisphere's temperate zone, and gives them the proper climate for growing grapes. Both countries have a long history of winemaking going back to when the first vines were brought to the region more than 450 years ago during the Spanish colonial period (Figure 15.1). Although Chile and Argentina have a common border, the Andes Mountain range that lies between them separates them both physically and culturally (Figure 15.2). This partition has allowed each country to develop its own unique style of winemaking. For most of the twentieth century their winemaking was targeted toward their large domestic markets, making inexpensive table wines that did not live up to the region's potential. In recent years the local consumption of wine has been declining and there has been great effort invested in improving vineyards and winemaking techniques to make wines that can compete on the world export market.

CHILE

Chile is the world's 10th largest producer of wine, bottling about one-third as much as the United States. Possessing the proper terroir to produce fine wines, it has grown dramatically in the last two decades to meet the demand brought on by the forces of

FIGURE 15.1

Vineyards in Chile's Aconcagua Valley region, the northernmost grape-growing region used for the production of table wines.
© Pat Henderson

FIGURE 15.2

Vineyards in Argentina's Mendoza region with the Andes Mountains in the background. The Mendoza region is the largest grape-growing region in Argentina, with three-quarters of the country's vineyard acreage.

Wines of Argentina (Garcia Betancourt)

globalization and the increasing world market for wine. The acreage of vineyard land in Chile expanded by more than 40 percent in the years from 1997 to 2002, primarily with new plantings of classic French varieties such as Cabernet Sauvignon, Merlot, and Chardonnay. In more recent years, the phenomenal growth has slowed somewhat but new plantings continue. These grapes from new vineyards have been going to more modernized wineries, producing wines targeted specifically for the export market in Europe and North America (Figure 15.3). The wine boom taking place in Chile today is reminiscent in many ways of those that previously took place in California and Australia. The economical cost of land and labor allows Chilean vintners to keep their prices low, and inexpensive wines are their primary export. As the industry is maturing, reserve style wines are becoming more common as Chile attempts to move into the high-end wine market as it has done in the $10-and-under category.

CHILEAN WINE—HISTORICAL PERSPECTIVE

The European *vinifera* grapevine was brought to Chile by the Spanish conquistadors, who also introduced it to the rest of Latin America. As was the case in California, wine was important to the Spanish colonizers as both a beverage and for sacramental

FIGURE 15.3

New stainless steel tanks being installed at Errázuriz Winery. In the last 20 years, many of Chile's established wine producers have modernized and expanded to keep pace with the growing export market.

© Pat Henderson

purposes, and it was much easier to produce it locally than to try to import wine from Spain. During the 1540s, former conquistador Francisco de Aguirre established the first Chilean vineyard in La Serena; shortly thereafter, Diego de Oro planted grapes outside Santiago. The most popular grape variety that was cultivated during this period was **País** (pa-EES). Called Mission in California and **Criolla Chica** (KREE-oh-yah chee-ka) in Argentina, País is a red grape that produces well under a variety of growing conditions; however, it makes a rather flavorless wine. Although its origins are in Spain where it is called Listán Prieto (Tapia et al., 2007), varieties like País are often referred to as "native" grapes because they were imported as seeds and then bred in the New World instead of being brought in as cuttings. País and other native varieties continue to be widely planted in Chile, and as late as 1997, País made up one-quarter of the grape harvest. These grapes are primarily used to make wines for domestic consumption and are being rapidly replanted with more familiar European grape varieties.

Over the next 300 years, winemaking in Chile developed very slowly in spite of the excellent growing conditions. Two main factors contributed to this slow progress. The first was that it was difficult to expand vineyards beyond the area around Santiago into outlying areas due to the frequent raids and attacks against the colonialists by indigenous people of the region. The second was the lack of a market due to the small domestic population and the difficulties in exporting wine. One of the early efforts in exporting wine to Peru in 1578 was met with failure when Sir Francis Drake, the English explorer and privateer, captured 1,700 wineskins en route to Peru. During the sixteenth and seventeenth centuries, vineyard land expanded and Chile began exporting inexpensive wine and brandy. Although Spain originally encouraged the export of wine as a revenue source, Spanish winemakers became upset when Chilean exports became a threat to their business. During the 1600s, the planting of new vineyards was banned for a period, later in 1774 the Spanish king forbade the export of any wine from Chile to other Spanish colonies. These laws were difficult to enforce, and in 1822 Chile won its independence, ushering in a new era for the country and its winemaking.

In 1830, the young country established an agricultural station called Quinta Normal in Santiago, with the goals of teaching students and performing research on how to improve grape growing and wine production. Italian and French grape varieties were established at Quinta Normal, and French trained enologists came to aid in the work (Ureta & Pszczólkowski, 1995). In 1851, Don Sylvestre Ochagavia imported classic French varieties for his vineyard, the first major commercial planting of traditional *vinifera* grapevines in Chile. The vines did very well, and his success inspired many others. In the second half of the nineteenth century, there was rapid expansion of vineyards planted to European varieties as well as improvement in winemaking techniques; this began the modern era of winemaking in Chile. During the period from 1850 to 1890, some of Chile's most famous wineries were established (Figure 15.4). Errázuriz, Concha y Toro, Cousiño Macul, and Santa Rita, among others, were all founded during this period and remain active today (Mathäss, 1997).

Production continued to expand primarily for the export market. In the 1880s, while phylloxera decimated the vineyards of Europe, wine from Chile was used to fill the demand. The root louse was never introduced to Chile, and today it is one of the few grape-growing regions where vines can be grown on their own roots. By the 1930s, European demand had slowed and Chile enacted prohibitionist laws that forbade the planting of new vineyards in an effort to restrict the production of wine. Soon after this World War II began, making shipping more difficult and isolating Chile from its European markets. After the war, the export market continued to decline, and the restrictive laws remained, which held production steady until they were repealed in the 1970s. During this time there was little advancement in wine quality, and nearly all the wine made was consumed domestically. When growers could expand their vineyards again, production soared at the same time per capita consumption was shrinking. This resulted in

FIGURE 15.4

Picking Cabernet Sauvignon in the Rapel Valley subregion of Chile's Central Valley.

Matt Wilson/Wines of Chile

overproduction, exacerbated by the fact that the wines being made were not of a quality that could compete on the global market.

At the beginning of the 1980s, Chile was plagued by overproduction and poor-quality wines. The winemakers of Chile dealt with the situation by concentrating on improving their product through modernization and increasing their emphasis on the export market once again. This course of action was successful because Chile possessed the necessary conditions for it to prosper, a good terroir for growing wine grapes and a low cost of labor, allowing the wines to be attractively priced on the world market. During this time, Chile began to attract international investment. Some of the world's most famous wineries including Torres from Spain, Lafite-Rothschild from France, and Kendall-Jackson from the United States, all began operations in Chile. The development of the Chilean industry was also aided by winemakers from around the globe who came to take advantage of the opportunities and brought with them their experience and expertise. During the 1990s, the value of Chilean wine exports grew from $30 million to $600 million (Sparks Companies Inc., 2002). The number of wineries that exported also rose; however, both the export and domestic markets remain dominated by a few large wineries.

Although the overall quality of Chilean wine has greatly improved, there are two distinct types of wine. One inexpensive and ordinary, made primarily for the domestic market, and a superior one made from classic European varietals, used mainly for the export market. Today wines from Chile have gained a reputation throughout Europe and North America for both quality and value.

On February 27, 2010, Chile was struck by a massive earthquake in the central part of the country about 200 miles (320 km) south of Santiago. Registering 8.8 on the Richter scale the earthquake killed more than 500 people and caused billions of dollars' worth of damage. The epicenter was near the major wine region of the Maule Valley and impacted a number of wineries and vineyards. In addition to the damage to winery buildings, wine tanks ruptured and stacks of barrels collapsed (Figure 15.5) resulting

FIGURE 15.5

Wineries in Chile's Central Valley region were heavily damaged by the severe earthquake that took place in February 2010.

© STRINGER/CHILE/Reuters/ Corbis

in the loss of an estimated 33 million gallons (125 million liters) of wine, or about 13 percent of the volume produced in 2009 (Moffett, 2010). The quake occurred just before the beginning of harvest and the loss of infrastructure severely affected production during the vintage. Chile is a country that is used to earthquakes, and fortunately strict building codes prevented the damage from being even worse. As Chile and its wine industry work to rebuild, other wine regions that are prone to earthquakes, such as California, are learning from their efforts.

WINE REGIONS OF CHILE

Chile exists along the narrow strip of land between the Pacific Ocean and the Andes mountain range and is more than 2,800 miles (4,500 km) long but averages only about 115 miles (180 km) wide. Running north to south it has a great range of climates, from some of the world's driest deserts in the north of the country, to cool rain forests in the south. In the middle of the country lies a temperate zone with a Mediterranean climate that is ideal for the production of wine grapes. Most of the vineyards producing grapes for table wine are located in an area that begins about 100 miles (160 km) north of the capital Santiago, and runs for 400 miles (640 km) south. This area is also home to the majority of the nation's population as well. The wide variety of soils and microclimates in Chile's viticultural zone provide a number of terroirs that are suitable for many different varieties of both wine and table grapes. The more northern regions are generally much dryer than those to the south are, yet have a mild climate. The southern vineyard regions are typically cooler and have more rainfall. The Pacific Ocean influences a vineyard's terroir, depending on how far inland the vineyard site is located. The coastal winds that bring this maritime influence inland are affected by the height of the mountains that lie between the vineyard and the ocean.

Chile's method of organizing grape-growing appellations is called Denominación de Origen (Denomination of Origin), or DO (the Spanish system of Appellations goes by the same name, see Chapter 8). This system divides Chile's wine country into five major grape-growing regions. From north to south, they are the Atacama, Coquimbo, Aconcagua, Valle Central (Central Valley), and the Región del Sur (Southern Region). These major regions are separated by a number of river valleys that run from east to west, which drain the runoff from the Andean mountain range. These river valleys form 15 subregions that are further broken up into a number of zones and areas. This is similar to the Australian system of appellations except that in the Chilean method of organization; zones represent the smallest geographic area instead of the largest (Table 15.1). Chilean law states that for a wine to be listed with a specific geographical area it must be made using at least 75 percent of grapes grown in that area. The 75 percent requirement also applies to the vintage and variety listed on the label. However, wine made for export follows the European standard of 85 percent for variety, region, and year.

Atacama and Coquimbo Regions

The two northernmost regions, Atacama and Coquimbo (ko-KIM-bo), are hot and dry and are considered too warm for the production of grapes for fine table wine. This

TABLE 15.1 The Grape-Growing Regions of Chile from North to South

Region	Subregion	Zone
Atacama	Valle de (Valley of) Copiapó	
	Valle del Huasco	
Coquimbo	Valle del Elqui	
	Valle del Limarí	
	Valle del Choapa	
Aconcagua	Valle de Aconcagua	
	Valle de Casablanca	
	San Antonio	Leyda
Valle Central (Central Valley)	Valle del Maipo	
	Valle del Rapel	Valle de Cachapoal
		Valle de Colchagua
	Valle de Curicó	Valle del Teno
		Valle del Lontué
	Valle del Maule	Valle del Claro
		Valle del Loncomilla
		Valle del Tutuvén
Valle del Sur	Valle del Itata	
	Valle del Bío-Bío	
	Malleco	

being said, there are many vineyards in these areas that have a history of winemaking and viticulture that goes back to the sixteenth century (Figure 15.6). Although there are several wineries in the Elqui (EL-kee) Valley and Limarí (lee-ma-REE) Valley of the Coquimbo region, most of the vineyards produce table grapes, much of which is exported to the Northern Hemisphere. The region also produces grapes that are used for the production of Pisco, a type of brandy.

FIGURE 15.6

Vineyards in the northern grape-growing Elqui Valley region of Chile. The grapes produced in this desert region are primarily used for the production of Pisco.
© Urosr/Shutterstock

PISCO

Pisco (PEE-skoh) is considered by many to be the national drink of Chile. It is a light-colored brandy and is enjoyed either by itself or mixed in a cocktail such as a Pisco Sour or Pisco and Cola. It is very popular in Chile and little known outside of South America. Of the more than 5 million cases a year that are produced, less than 25,000 cases are exported (Duijker, 1999). Pisco is also made in Peru but uses different grape varieties and has a different flavor than Chilean Pisco. The production of Pisco is strictly regulated by the government with laws that were first established in 1931 and revised in 1985. The grapes that are grown for Pisco can only come from the Atacama and the Coquimbo wine regions, and the fermentation and distillation must also take place in these appellations as well. There are 13 varieties of grapes that are allowed to be used for Pisco, the most common being various clones of Muscat and the varieties Pedro Jiménez and Torontel (called Torrontés in Argentina). The high percentage of Muscat in the base wine that is used for distillation gives the resulting brandy a distinct floral/fruity character.

The winemaking for Pisco is basic. The grapes are crushed and then given a small amount of skin contact before pressing to give the juice more flavor. After the juice has been fermented into wine it has about 13 percent alcohol. It is then distilled into brandy at 60 percent alcohol in copper **alembic stills** (uh-lem-bik). Alembic stills, also called pot stills, are batch process stills that are also used for the production of Cognac in France (Figure 15.7). Traditionally the Pisco was then aged in casks of raulí wood, which is a type of South American beech. Today most producers use stainless steel or concrete vats for the majority of their production, saving the use of raulí

FIGURE 15.7

A pot still used for the production of Pisco. This is similar to the type of still that is used for the production of Cognac in France.

© Gary Cook/Alamy

casks for their reserve lots. After aging, the Pisco is graded, blended, and bottled at 30 to 40 percent alcohol.

Aconcagua Region

The Aconcagua (ah-kohn-KAH-gwa) Region is the northernmost of Chile's true wine grape-growing regions; it is made up of three subregions, the Aconcagua, Casablanca, and San Antonio Valleys. Together the three valleys produce fewer than 5 percent of Chile's wine grapes. The Aconcagua River valley lies about 60 miles (100 km) north of Santiago, just to the west of Mount Aconcagua, the Western Hemisphere's tallest mountain at an elevation of almost 23,000 feet (7,000 meters). The region has alluvial soils and a warm climate with a long growing season. It is best known for growing red

FIGURE 15.8

grapes such as Cabernet Sauvignon. The first wine grapes were established here by Maximiano Errázuriz in 1870, and today the Errázuriz Winery remains active in the region and is one of Chile's largest producers (Figure 15.8).

The Casablanca Valley lies along the coast about 50 miles (80 km) west of Santiago. Viticulture is relatively new to the area; the first vineyards were established in 1982. Another of Chile's major wineries, Concha y Toro, was one of the first wineries to use grapes from Casablanca, and its success inspired many others to start vineyards here (Figure 15.9). Although the appellation is very young, it has had rapid growth in new vineyards and now has three times as much acreage as the Aconcagua and San Antonio Valleys combined. Because it is near the ocean, there is a strong maritime influence, and the climate is very cool. Morning fog is common during the growing season, and in springtime there is always a risk of frost. This cool weather makes the Casablanca Valley ideal for growing white wine grapes, particularly Sauvignon Blanc and Chardonnay, as well as cool-weather reds such as Pinot Noir. The San Antonio Valley is a relatively new region with limited plantings and lies directly south of the Casablanca Valley and has a similar terroir as its neighbor to the north.

Valle Central (Central Valley) Region

The Central Valley is Chile's largest viticultural region and grows 80 percent of Chile's grapes. It is made up of four subregions. From north to south, they are the Maipo (MY-po), Rapel (ra-PEL), Curicó (kur-ee-KOH), and the Maule (MOW-lay). In the Central Valley, the rainfall gradually increases as you move south. The Maipo River Valley

A Chilean Label Used for Export to the United States

Like the United States, the term Reserva (reserve), does not indicate any government sanctioned designation. However, when the term Reserva, Gran Reserva, or Reserva Especial are used the wine must have its appellation listed.

Winery Name: Most names are acceptable as long as they are not offensive or misleading.

Wine Name: To help designate this wine as a special bottling, the winery has given the name Etiqueta Negra (Black Label).

Variety: For export, when more than one grape variety is listed the total % of the varieties listed on the label must equal 100%. If there is only one variety listed on the label the wine must be at least 75% that variety for domestic (Chilean) use and 85% for export.

Appellation: When listed, 75% of the grapes used to produce the wine must be from that appellation. For export the standard is 85%.

Vintage Date: Like variety and appellation the standard for domestic sales is 75% for exported wines it is 85%.

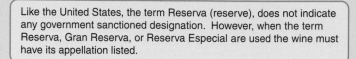

VSPT Wine Group

Wines Notes: Not required but many wineries add them to describe how the wine is made and what it tastes like. They must not be misleading.

Production Statement: The name of the winery that produced the wine.

Sulfite Declaration: If the wine contains more than 10 PPM Sulfur Dioxide "Contains Sulfites" must be listed on the label to be sold in the United States.

Government Warning: Required on all beverages that contain more than 0.5% Alcohol sold in the United States.

Country of Origin: Required on all imported wines.

Web Address: Not required but an excellent source of more information about the wine.

Volume: Every wine bottle must state the amount of wine it contains in metric units. In most cases the volume in ml is molded in to the glass at the base of the bottle.

Alcohol Content: The % of alcohol by volume in the wine must be listed.

FIGURE 15.9

The stainless steel aging cellar at Viña Mar winery in Chile's Casablanca Valley.
© Pat Henderson

is just south of Santiago, and its proximity to the capital has given prominence to the region from the very beginning. More than three-quarters of the Maipo River Valley's vineyards are devoted to red varieties and it is known for producing superior Cabernet Sauvignon. The Maipo was also one of the first viticultural areas in Chile established in the sixteenth century, and it was the first area to grow classic European varietals in the nineteenth century. The Maipo is a diverse region with a number of soil types and a wide range of elevation and rainfall. The growth of Santiago has put pressure from

FIGURE 15.10

While it is only a small portion of the production today, some producers are establishing organic vineyards to offer a new product to their export markets.
© Pat Henderson

FIGURE 15.11

A ripe cluster of Carmenère ready for harvest. Once popular in the Bordeaux region of France, now the variety is seldom produced outside Chile.

Matt Wilson/Wines of Chile

urbanization on many of the vineyards close to the city, and newer plantings are being set up farther into the countryside. Just south of the Maipo region is the Rapel Valley, formed by the Cachapoal and the Tinguiririca Rivers. The elevation of the coastal range of mountains in this part of the country is low, and they do not block cooling ocean breezes. This gives the area a maritime climate in spite of its somewhat inland location. Like Casablanca, the Rapel Valley has experienced considerable growth in recent years, primarily in red grapes. The Carmenère that is grown in the Rapel Valley is considered one of the best that is produced in Chile.

Carmenère (KAH-meh-NEHR) is a red grape that is similar in appearance to Merlot and is rarely cultivated outside Chile (Figure 15.11). Also known as Grand Vidure, prior to the outbreak of phylloxera it was popular in the Bordeaux region of France, but due to Carmenère's low yield, when the vineyards were replanted it was widely replaced with other varieties. Merlot and Carmenère were often confused, and during the 1990s most of what was thought of as Merlot in Chile was determined to be misidentified Carmenère. It produces a full-bodied, deeply colored wine that is becoming popular as a varietal wine that is unique to Chile.

The Curicó subregion is centered on the town of Curicó, 120 miles (200 km) south of Santiago. This is the widest part of the Central Valley and the terrain is made up of plateaus with small hills. This broad expanse allows vineyard operations to spread out and many of them are quite large (Figure 15.12). The soils are fairly uniform and generally made up of clay loam and decomposed volcanic material that drains well. The region has slightly less area in vineyards than the Rapel region to the north. Red and white varieties are grown here in roughly equal proportions with Cabernet Sauvignon and Sauvignon Blanc being the most popular varieties. The Maule River valley lies just to the south of the Curicó subregion and is the southernmost appellation in the Central Valley. The Maule has the greatest acreage of any area in Chile, more than 77,000 acres (31,000 hectares) planted to wine grapes. Cabernet and Merlot are the most widely planted varieties and there is significant acreage of Chardonnay and Sauvignon Blanc as well. There is still a great deal of the País variety planted in the Maule River Valley that is grown for the domestic wine market.

Región del Sur (Southern Region)

The Southern Region is made up of the Itata (ee-TAH-ta), Bío-Bío (BEE-o BEE-o), and the Malleco (mah-YAY-ko) River valleys. Being at the southern end of Chile's viticultural regions, they are generally cooler and wetter than the appellations to the north. The Itata River valley has been growing grapes since the time of the Spanish colonization and accounts for about 9 percent of Chile's wine grapes. It still has large areas of País and other less desirable wine grapes; however, lately there have been efforts to

FIGURE 15.12

A large vineyard in Chile's Valle Central (Central Valley), this is the most productive wine grape–growing region in the country.

Eugenio Hughes

replant them with better varieties. To the south of Itata is the Bío-Bío River Valley, it is cooler than the Itata region and grows about one-third as many grapes. Spring frost can be a problem and cool climate varieties such as Pinot Noir, Chardonnay, and Gewürztraminer do best here. This subregion is also very wet. Some areas receive more than 45 inches (115 cm) of rainfall per year. The southernmost of Chile's wine regions is the Malleco Valley, it has limited vineyard acreage and is primarily planted to Pinot Noir and Chardonnay.

ARGENTINA

Argentina has over a half-million acres (200,000 hectares) in grapes, nearly twice as much as Chile. By comparison, Argentina's wine industry is about two-thirds that of the United States. Investment in vineyards and wineries in Argentina has come more slowly than it did in Chile, being hindered by the unstable economic situation that has beleaguered the country. Recently, despite the economic meltdown that occurred in 2001, the situation in Argentina is beginning to improve. Like Chile in the 1990s, investors are beginning to be drawn to the country to take advantage of the low cost of vineyard land and labor. Although older plantings of more traditional Argentine varieties are still common, acreage is expanding in the classic European varieties, and wineries are being updated (Figure 15.13). However, this modernization is coming slowly and 80 percent of the country's output is inexpensive wine destined for the domestic market.

ARGENTINE WINE—HISTORICAL PERSPECTIVE

The first grapevines of European origin were introduced to Argentina from Chile in 1556. They were planted in the colonial settlement of Salta, in the north of the country. The early settlers discovered that some of the best locations for growing vines were in the foothills of the Andes. Vineyards were soon established to the south of

FIGURE 15.13

Salta around the town of Mendoza. Here the native varieties such as **Criolla Grande** (KREE-oh-yah gran-DAY) were widely planted. Criolla Grande is a "native" grape variety descended from *vinifera* seeds brought from Europe. It is similar to the País grape of Chile that is called Criolla Chica in Argentina. The production of wine grew slowly for the next 250 years, and the wine that was made was split between the small domestic market and the limited export trade. After independence from Spain in 1816 all this began to change. A new wave of emigration from the winemaking countries of Europe brought in new residents, forming a healthy domestic market for wine as well as expertise on how to make it. Many of the new residents came from Italy and Spain, giving more Spanish and Italian influence on the varieties of grapes grown and wines produced in Argentina.

In 1853, Argentina established a school of agriculture in the Mendoza region. The director of the school was French-born Miguel Pouget, who trained his students in modern French winemaking techniques and imported classic French wine grape varieties to Argentina for the first time. Many irrigation projects were completed during this time, which allowed the expansion of vineyards and many other forms of agriculture. The industry continued to grow and have a strong export market until the 1920s, when it experienced setbacks. The worldwide depression of the late 1920s, affected the demand for both the domestic and export markets. Additionally phylloxera was introduced during this time. Argentine growers, familiar with what phylloxera had done to the vineyards of Europe decades earlier, responded quickly with the widespread use of grafting and rootstocks. Unfortunately, this also had the effect of spreading viruses and other diseases. Phylloxera still exists in Argentina today, but because it is not widespread it causes little damage. Many of the older vineyards are grown on their own roots but most new plantings are grafted to resistant rootstock to avoid any potential problems with the pest.

Since the 1920s, Argentina has experienced severe economic and political instability, which has adversely affected the development of the wine industry. There was little foreign investment and modernization, and so the quality of the wine suffered. In spite of this, the national wine consumption remained strong, and a great deal of mediocre wine was produced for the domestic market. This situation began to change in 1970 when the per capita wine consumption began to decline from a high of over 23 gallons (90 liters) per year to less than half that amount today. Still Argentina consumes about four times as much wine per capita than the United States. Because of the declining domestic consumption, during the 1980s there was a severe overproduction problem and 36 percent of Argentina's vineyards, primarily the lower quality varietals, were taken out of production (Lapsley, 2001). Although vineyard acreage has declined, Argentina remains the fifth largest producer of wine after France, Italy, Spain, and the United States (Australian Wine and Brandy Corporation, 2008).

Today Argentina has realized that its wine future lies with the overseas market. Moreover, much like Chile, Argentina possesses the proper environment for growing grapes and a low cost of land and labor. This situation has spurred new development and has attracted international investors despite the unstable economic situation and exports have doubled in the last decade. One advantage Argentina has over Chile is that there is much more land available for planting. Currently Argentina depends on exports less than Chile does, with Argentina exporting 20 percent of its wine as compared to Chile's 50 percent. However, since Argentina produces more wine than Chile, when measured by total volume Argentina exports about 85 percent as much wine as its neighbor to the west. However, given the proper resources and development, Argentina has the potential to surpass Chile's export wine production. The United Sates and Canada account for almost half of Argentina's wine exports followed by the United Kingdom and Brazil.

FIGURE 15.14

Red grapes harvested and ready for transportation to the winery.

Wines of Argentina (Carlos Calise)

Much of Argentina's viticultural regions lie on the eastern slopes of the Andes mountain range. Being in the rain shadow of the mountains, the climate is generally dryer and warmer than what is found in the vineyards of Chile. To deal with the dry conditions, most vineyards are irrigated with runoff from the mountains. Additionally, the vineyards are generally planted at a higher elevation, which helps to keep the vineyards cool. Argentina also has more of a continental climate and less maritime influence than Chile does. Without the moderating influence of the Pacific Ocean, Argentina's vineyards experience more difficulties with spring frosts, hail, and heat waves than the vineyards in Chile typically do. However, being dryer, mildew and rot tend to be less of a problem. Chile also receives more of its rainfall in the winter, while Argentina can have precipitation during the summer but most vineyards depend on irrigation to support vines during the growing season. Argentina is a large country and there is a great deal of suitable land for viticulture (Table 15.2). The majority of the vineyard acreage is concentrated in the northwest of the country, but grapes are grown from the northern border with Bolivia to as far south as the border of the Patagonia region, two-thirds of the length of the country.

FIGURE 15.15

Vineyard with the Andes Mountains in the background; Mendoza grape growers depend on the irrigation water provided by the runoff of melting snow in the Andes.

Wines of Argentina (Carlos Calise)

Mendoza and San Juan Regions

The Provence of Mendoza is the largest wine region in Argentina at 58,000 square miles (150,000 sq km) and has about 75 percent of the country's vines. The appellation is centered on the city of Mendoza, which is only about 150 miles (240 km) east of Santiago, but it is more than 600 miles (950 km) west of Buenos Aires. Its proximity to Chile's wine country has encouraged a great deal of interaction between winemakers of both countries. The soil is generally sandy and the climate is desertlike, but because of irrigation there is a great deal of agriculture in the region (Figure 15.15). Being a dry climate in the rain shadow of a mountain range gives it a terroir similar to that found in eastern Washington State. The elevation ranges from 1,500 to 4,600 feet (450 to 1,400 m), and this altitude helps keep the vineyards cool, which preserves the grapes' natural flavor and acidity. Mendoza is considered one of Argentina's best appellations for quality, and there are more than 1,000 wineries in the district.

TABLE 15.2 The Grape-Growing Regions of Argentina

Cuyo	La Rioja	Famatina	
	Mendoza	Agrelo	
		Barrancas	
		Las Compuertas	
		Lujan de Cuyo	
		Lunlunta	
		Maipu	
		Perdriel	
		San Martin	
		San Rafael	
		Uco Valley	La Consulta
			San Carlos
			Tunuyan
			Tupungato
			Vista Flores
		Ugarteche	
		Vistalba	
	San Juan	Pedernal Valley	
		Tulum Valley	
		Zonda Valley	
North-West	Catamarca	Fiambala	
	Jujuy		
	Salta	Cafayate [Calchaquies] Valley	
		Molinos	
Patagonia	Neuquen		
	Rio Negro		

Due to Mendoza's size and variety of growing conditions, it has been broken into several subregions including the Agrelo, Luján de Cuyo, San Rafael, and Tupungato.

The Mendoza region has many vineyards of both classic European cultivars as well as lesser varieties such as Criolla Grande, but it is best known for two other varieties, **Malbec** (MAHL-behk) and Torrontés. Malbec is a grape that is native to the Bordeaux region of France, where it is called **Côt** (KOH). Considered to be a lesser grape in its home region, Malbec flourishes in its adopted home of Argentina, making full-bodied wine that is inky in color with a strong fruity character. Malbec can be prone to rot and it does well in Mendoza's dry climate. **Torrontés** (tohr-rohn-TEHS) is a "native" white grape variety that was first grown in South America. It is distinct from the Spanish grape variety that has the same name. It produces light-bodied, crisp wines that have a fragrant aroma similar to Muscat or Gewürztraminer. There are three varieties of Torrontés: Torrontés Riojano, which is the most common cultivar, Torrontés Sanjuanino,

FIGURE 15.16

The San Juan region lies just to the north of Mendoza and is Argentina's second most productive grape-growing region.

Wines of Argentina (Garcia Betancourt)

and Torrontés Mendocino. Recent DNA analysis suggests that all three cultivars are descended from Muscat of Alexandria with Torrontés Riojano, Torrontés Sanjuanino being crosses between Muscat of Alexandria and Criolla Chica (Agüero, Rodríguez, Martínez, Dangl, & Meredith, 2003). Torrontés is considered by many in Argentina to be the country's best white wine; however, Chardonnay commands higher prices and is more frequently exported.

The San Juan Provence lies on the northern border of Mendoza and is Argentina's second largest grape appellation, producing nearly 20 percent of the country's grapes. Its growing conditions are similar to Mendoza in many respects, but being farther north and closer to the equator, its climate is warmer. San Juan Provence is best known for making average-quality wines for domestic consumption as well as producing table grapes for the fresh fruit market (Figure 15.16). The San Juan region contains about 250 wineries, and the warm climate is ideal for making sweet fortified wines and brandy. The three principle wine appellations of the province are the Pedernal, Tulum, and the Zonda Valleys. The Zonda Valley is named for the warm, dry wind that descends the eastern slopes of the Andes that is called La Zonda. Although the strong breeze can damage grapevines, its drying affect helps prevent mildew and rot. Collectively, the Mendoza and the San Juan regions are referred to as the Cuyo (KOO-yo) region.

La Rioja and Salta Regions

The La Rioja (la ree-OH-hah) region lies between the San Juan region on the south and the Salta region to the north. The climate is warm and dry, but the wines are generally of better quality than those in the San Juan region. Recently there has been much planting of new vineyards, particularly to white varieties such as Torrontés and Chardonnay as well as Malbec. Vineyards are somewhat scattered, and the area produces much less fruit

FIGURE 15.17

Vineyards in Argentina's Salta region. Here the vineyards lie at a higher altitude than those in the Mendoza and San Juan regions to the south. This high elevation helps keep the vineyards cool in spite of their warm latitude.

Wines of Argentina (Garcia Betancourt)

than the regions of Mendoza and San Juan which are located to the south. The most internationally recognized wine region in the La Rioja region is the Famatina Valley.

The Salta (sal-TAH) is a small appellation in the far north of the country. It is located at a latitude of about 25 degrees south, roughly equivalent to the latitude of Miami in the Northern Hemisphere (Figure 15.17). The Salta region is about 600 miles (960 km) north of Mendoza. At low elevations the climate is subtropical, but higher in the mountains grapes for table wine can be grown. The area's vineyards are planted at elevations that range from 3,000 to 9,800 feet (1,700 to 5,500 m), making them some of the highest vineyards in the world. This high altitude makes the terroir very cool, and the Torrontés grape does quite well here, with the chilly climate preserving its fruity character. Cafayate is the largest viticultural region in Salta. Nearby are the small appellations of Jujuy and Tucumán, which have similar growing conditions to those found in the Salta.

Rio Negro and Neuquén Regions

Located in the far south of Argentina's wine country, the Rio Negro (ree-OH NAY-grow) and Neuquén (new-KEN) have limited plantings but great promise for superior wines. They are both cool regions that have long growing seasons with plenty of sunny

{ SOUTH AFRICA }

This chapter presents the

wine regions of South Africa, their climates, and the types of wine that they create. Additionally, it discusses the history of winemaking in the country and the dramatic changes that have taken place since the end of apartheid, along with the emerging role of wines in the global market.

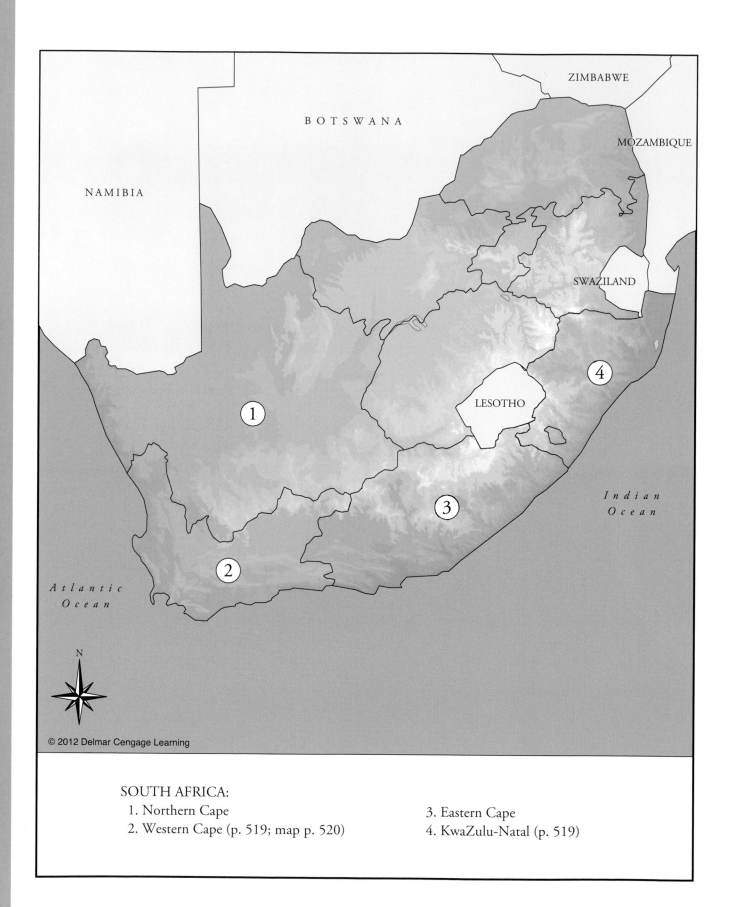

SOUTH AFRICA:
  1. Northern Cape
  2. Western Cape (p. 519; map p. 520)
  3. Eastern Cape
  4. KwaZulu-Natal (p. 519)

© 2012 Delmar Cengage Learning

INTRODUCTION

The country of South Africa possesses all of the attributes necessary for a wine-producing nation: a long history of grape growing and winemaking, a temperate Mediterranean-like climate along its southwestern edge, as well as many historical ties with wine-consuming nations in Europe. However, its potential was not realized until recently because of international boycotts in response to South Africa's policy of apartheid. The embargo hindered the modernization of the wine industry that was taking place in the rest of the world and cut it off from the export market that was desperately needed. With the demise of the apartheid regime and lifting of international sanctions in the early 1990s, there began a period of many far-reaching changes in the wine industry as well as the rest of the country. In the time since then there has been a massive redevelopment in vineyards and wineries with a new focus on making better wines and expanding sales to other countries. These efforts have been successful and today South Africa is ranked seventh in the world for production of wine and ninth in the world for exports.

SOUTH AFRICAN WINE— HISTORICAL PERSPECTIVE

South Africa is unusual in that it is able to trace the origins of its wine industry back to day one. Such precise information is thanks to Jan van Riebeeck, the first governor of the Dutch settlement at the Cape, who was meticulous in keeping a diary during his tenure. The region known today as the Western Cape is where the majority of South Africa's present-day vineyards are still grown. So much so that the terms *Cape* and *South Africa* are almost interchangeable when talking about the country's wines.

The Cape was a logical place to start wine growing in South Africa for two reasons. First, it has a Mediterranean climate; the cool, wet winters and warm, dry summers provide ideal conditions for producing quality wine grapes. Second, the Cape of Good Hope was also conveniently located halfway between Holland and the Dutch East Indies, a route plied by the Dutch East India Company in its profitable spice business. The suitable location, as well as the verdant growth noted by those who had landed there, encouraged the Company to start a settlement in what is today Cape Town at the foot of Table Mountain (Figure 16.1). This stopover would be used as a repair station for the Company's ships and as a place for growing crops to provide provisions for the ships' crews.

Jan van Riebeeck, previously a ship's surgeon, was chosen to head the expedition and establish the settlement at Cape Town. Commander van Riebeeck and the other members of the expedition arrived in Table Bay on April 6, 1652. At van Riebeeck's request, the first batch of vine cuttings arrived in 1654 but none survived. A second delivery provided results that were more positive. The vines were planted alongside the vegetables in the company gardens, a plot today located in the heart of Cape Town. On Sunday, February 2, 1659, van Riebeeck recorded in his diary: "Today, God be praised, wine pressed for the first time from the Cape grapes" (Leipoldt, 2004). The variety he quarantine of vine material. This helped prevent the introduction of new grapevine pests and diseases but proved a hindrance to growers wishing to bring in new clones or varieties. In 2002 KWV converted from a grower-owned cooperative to a publicly traded company.

If the South African wine industry was held back by the focus on cooperatives and quantity rather than quality, the situation was made even worse with the establishment of trade sanctions against apartheid. First beginning in the 1960s, the boycotts increasingly had an effect on the country's economy as more and more nations signed on. During this period, South African wine was banned and its citizens unwelcome in many countries. Throughout this repressive regime, South African producers had to look to the local market for sales, and their knowledge of winemaking trends was restricted, as travel opportunities were limited. The result was a wine industry that was isolated from the rest of the world and one that focused on making inexpensive wine of average quality for a small domestic market.

In the early 1990s international pressure helped bring political reform to the government with a relaxation of apartheid laws and release of political prisoners like Nelson Mandela. Once democracy was established, with the first democratic elections held in 1994, momentum for South Africa's reentry into the international arena grew rapidly and South African wines were officially welcomed back into the international fold when Nelson Mandela, the country's first democratically elected president, endorsed them and toasted his 1993 Nobel Peace Prize with Cape wine (Figure 16.3).

The surge of interest in South African wine was perhaps most immediately measured through the growth in exports. In 1991, 5.7 million gallons (23 million liters) of South African wine left the country. By 2008 that annual figure had risen to 108.5 million gallons (411 million liters) (South African Wine Industry Information & Systems [SAWIS], 2009). While the United Kingdom remains the most important market in terms of number of cases sold, the United States is gaining ground and now fills sixth

FIGURE 16.3

Nelson Mandela, South Africa's first democratically elected president, and his African National Congress colleagues toast his 1993 Nobel Peace Prize award with South African wine. International acceptance and soaring exports followed this endorsement.

© Walter Dhladhla/Getty Images

place (SAWIS, 2009). Behind these figures lay many reasons for this remarkable growth that go beyond the demise of apartheid and lifting of sanctions. The growth was also fueled by the growth in the international wine market, a favorable exchange rate, and the advances made in South African grape-growing and winemaking practices. Additionally, South Africa's historical links with European countries came into play. Many South Africans have family ties in the United Kingdom, Holland, Germany, and other countries, which provides a ready market for the wines and encourages the growth in tourism.

Thanks to the international interest and increased sales, South Africa has seen an explosion of privately owned wineries whose proprietors are focused on producing quality wines that are unique and speak of their South African origin. These small producers try to differentiate themselves from the large commercial brands made at grower cooperative wineries. In South Africa, privately owned wineries are usually referred to as **private cellars** and grower cooperatives are called **producer cellars.** There have also been big shifts in grape varieties planted and opening up of regions where wine grapes had not been grown before. Prior to 1992, the quota system restricted where vines could be grown, the authorities then focusing more on higher yields rather than higher quality. When it was dropped, new wineries were established increasing in number from 141 in 1991 to 504 in 2008 (SAWIS, 2009). The vast majority of this new growth has been in the Western Cape Geographical Unit, or as it is more commonly known, "the Cape." This scenically beautiful region has reliable weather during the growing season, good soils, and many mesoclimates that are suitable for a wide variety of wine styles. Many foreigners, including some high-profile winemakers from Europe and the United States, have also recognized the Cape's wine potential and have begun to do business in the region bringing with them their expertise as well as their capital.

Despite this rush of new wineries, 79 percent of the annual crush is still produced by South Africa's 58 cooperatives (SAWIS, 2009). As noted previously, cooperatives (producer cellars) are wineries owned jointly by the grape-grower members, who lower their expenses by pooling their winemaking and marketing costs. Here the crop is vinified at one cellar and while small quantities of the wine may be bottled under that cellar's own label, the majority is usually sold in bulk to larger wine merchants for blending and bottling.

The increased demand for wine also increased wine grape vineyard acreage from 207,560 acres (84,000 hectares) in 1994 to 247,000 acres (100,200 hectares) in 2004 (SAWIS, 2005). Since then the amount of new vineyard land being established has leveled off. Vineyard expansion appears limited compared with countries such as Australia or Chile because many vines were uprooted either because they were lesser varieties, such as Palomino, Kanaan, or Cape Riesling (an obscure variety not related to Riesling that is called Crouchen in France), or because they were planted under the wrong conditions. Replanting on better sites and with internationally recognized grapes such as Cabernet Sauvignon, Chardonnay, Sauvignon Blanc, and Shiraz (Syrah is generally called Shiraz in South Africa) as well as with other Bordeaux and Rhône varieties, has brought the country into line with international markets. Such changes also had the effect of shifting the imbalance between white and red varieties from 84.1 percent in favor of whites in 1991 to a more equitable 54 percent by 2004 (SAWIS, 2005). However, only in the districts of Paarl and Stellenbosch do red varieties outnumber whites.

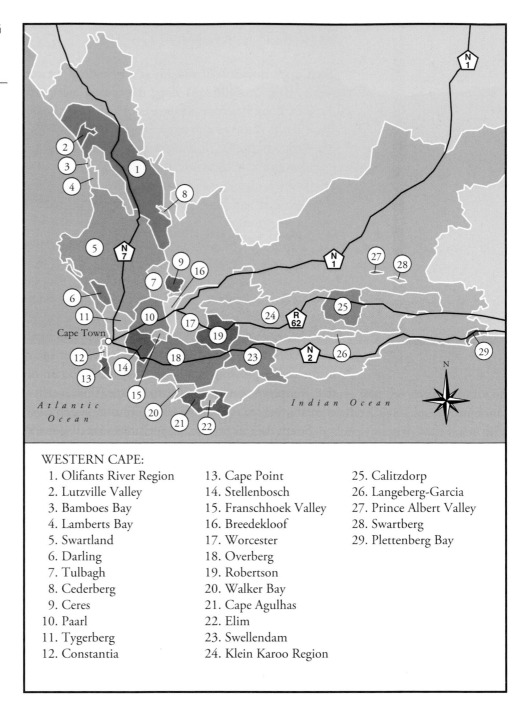

WESTERN CAPE:

1. Olifants River Region
2. Lutzville Valley
3. Bamboes Bay
4. Lamberts Bay
5. Swartland
6. Darling
7. Tulbagh
8. Cederberg
9. Ceres
10. Paarl
11. Tygerberg
12. Constantia
13. Cape Point
14. Stellenbosch
15. Franschhoek Valley
16. Breedekloof
17. Worcester
18. Overberg
19. Robertson
20. Walker Bay
21. Cape Agulhas
22. Elim
23. Swellendam
24. Klein Karoo Region
25. Calitzdorp
26. Langeberg-Garcia
27. Prince Albert Valley
28. Swartberg
29. Plettenberg Bay

estate wine has to be grown, made, and bottled on a single production unit (farm with vineyards and cellar) registered for this purpose. Likewise, single vineyard wines have to come from a registered unit, limited to a maximum of 14.5 acres (6 hectares) and from one grape variety only. Where applicable, these will be indicated on the label, the Wine of Origin designation being indicated by the letters *WO* as well as the words *Wine of Origin*. Recent legislation has opened the way for wines made from more than one official origin to state the various sources on the label. Claims for vintage or variety, whether locally or for export, require a wine to contain a minimum of 85 percent for both.

Reading a South African Wine Label

Front Label

"Kumkani"– Brand Name: English, Afrikaans, and African names are all used on South African wines. Provided they are not already a registered trademark, most names are acceptable.

"Lanner Hill"– Single Vineyard: Single vineyards have to be registered, not more than 14.5 acres (6 hectares), and from one grape variety only.

KUMKANI

LANNER HILL
SAUVIGNON BLANC

2005

The fruit for this wine was harvested at optimum ripeness from dry land vineyards on David Tullie's farm Lanner Hill on the crest of the Darling hills. The vineyard is situated 7km from the Atlantic Ocean and this cool growing climate is reflected in the distinct varietal character of the wine.

WINE OF SOUTH AFRICA

© Kumkani, Stellenbosch, South Africa

Wine Notes: Not obligatory, but the information in this case must be factual and be approved by the Wine & Spirit Board.

Sauvignon Blanc Grape Variety: A single varietal wine must contain a minimum of 85 percent of that grape. Only certain grape varieties are permitted under the Wine of Origin Scheme.

Vintage: The year in which the grapes were harvested. A minimum of 85 percent of the contents must come from the year declared on the label.

Wine of South Africa: Country of origin. Here not a compulsory item, as it appears without the other compulsory information.

Certification Sticker: Certification confirms all the legal requirements under the Wine of Origin Scheme have been met and the wine has been approved by the Wine and Spirit Board. The numbers enable the wine to be tracked right back to the vineyard. This is the small rectangular white label with numbers on it, stuck on the neck of the bottle.

Reading a South African Wine Label

European Export Back Label

Wine Notes: Explanations of the meaning of foreign names helps the consumer have a better understanding of why the wine was given this particular name.

Wine of Origin: Appellation, the demarcated area, in this case a ward Groenekloof, where the wine was grown.

Product of South Africa*: Compulsory Country of Origin. Words with the same meaning may be substituted.

Contains Sulfites*: Compulsory; must be indicated on all wine filled/bottled or sold after November 25, 2005. The spelling must be in the language stipulated by the destination market. Only required if the total sulfur level is more than 10 milligrams per liter.

KUMKANI
SINGLE VINEYARD

LANNER HILL SAUVIGNON BLANC

Derived from the Xhosa word meaning King – Kumkani is a leader amongst South African wines. A wine with stature & pedigree, it epitomizes the quality inherent in the rich diversity of the ancient soils, unique climates and winemaking heritage of South Africa.

The grapes for the Single Vineyard range of wines are grown in partnership with private, family owned farms – each wine reflecting a specific terroir.

This expressive, classic Sauvignon blanc reflects its cool climate origins. Ripe gooseberry flavours, flinty and full-bodied with a crisp lingering finish.

WINE OF ORIGIN GROENEKLOOF
WINE OF SOUTH AFRICA
CONTAINS SULPHITES, ENTHÄLT SULFITE
INNEHÅLLER SULFITER

Alc 14.5% A581 750ml

IMPORTED BY: OMNIA WINES, MOORBRIDGE COURT, MOORBRIDGE ROAD, MAIDENHEAD, SL6 8LT, UK

BARCODE NO: 6004786007684

© Kumkani, Stellenbosch, South Africa

ALC–14.5% by Vol*: Compulsory; in the United States, the given figure may differ by not more than 1.5 percent if the alcohol is less than 14 percent, over 14 percent a difference of 1 percent is permitted; in the EU a difference of 0.5 percent is permitted; and locally, in South Africa, the alcohol level on the label may vary by 1 percent in the actual wine.

Produced and Bottled: Omnia Wines, Stellenbosch, South Africa*, Winery identification. Either the A number or name and address is required for the local market. At present these may be replaced by the importer's details on wine for export, but from 2007 onward, the same rules that apply to South Africa will apply to exports.

A581: The A code numbers enable identification of the producer of the wine, if this information isn't provided on the label. The list of A numbers is held by the Liquor Products Division of the Department of Agriculture.

Compulsory items as indicated by an asterisk above have to appear "within the same field of vision on one or more labels of a container," that is, either front or back labels, or, if it's a wrap-around label, on one end of that label.

Reading a South African Wine Label
United States Export Back Label

KUMKANI

SINGLE VINEYARD

2005 LANNER HILL SAUVIGNON BLANC
WINE OF ORIGIN GROENEKLOOF

Derived from of the Xhosa word meaning King – Kumkani is a leader amongst South African wines. A wine with stature & pedigree, it epitomises the quality inherent in the rich diversity of the ancient soils, unique climates and winemaking heritage of South Africa.

The grapes for the Single Vineyard range of wines are grown in partnership with private, family owned farms – each wine reflecting a specific terroir.

This expressive, classic Sauvignon blanc reflects its cool climate origins. Ripe gooseberry flavours, flinty and full-bodied with a crisp lingering finish.

PRODUCT OF SOUTH AFRICA
CONTAINS SULFITES
ALC 14.5% BY VOL A581 750ML
Produced and bottled by Omnia Wines,
Stellenbosch, South Africa.

GOVERNMENT WARNING: (1) ACCORDING TO THE SURGEON GENERAL, WOMEN SHOULD NOT DRINK ALCOHOLIC BEVERAGES DURING PREGNANCY BECAUSE OF THE RISK OF BIRTH DEFECTS. (2) CONSUMPTION OF ALCOHOLIC BEVERAGES IMPAIRS YOUR ABILITY TO DRIVE A CAR OR OPERATE MACHINERY, AND MAY CAUSE HEALTH PROBLEMS.
IMPORTED BY: SOUTHERN STARZ, INC., HUNTINGTON BEACH, CA
www.southernstarz.com

BARCODE NO: 00000000000C0

Government Warning: A requirement for wines exported to the U.S. market.

© Kumkani, Stellenbosch, South Africa, Omnia Wines

Olifants River Region

This area is home to the most northern vineyards in the Western Cape. Inland, it is hot and dry, but with irrigation water readily available from the Olifants River, high yields are easily achievable. This led to the region to be associated with poor-quality, bulk wines. With the opening up of export markets, better-quality varieties have been planted; vines have also moved up from the fertile valley floors to mountain slopes. Viticultural practices have been upgraded, resulting in farmers being compensated based on overall fruit quality rather than simply on sugar levels. These improvements have encouraged lower yields and better-quality grapes. The climate is conducive to organic viticulture and several farmers are now taking this approach. In the cellars, winemakers have learned to craft consumer-friendly, early-drinking wines. Chenin Blanc and Colombard still hold sway but there are also considerable plantings of Shiraz, Cabernet Sauvignon, Merlot, Chardonnay, and Sauvignon Blanc.

There are some areas with cooler terroirs within the region, notably the newly established ward of Bamboes Bay fronts directly on to the Atlantic. The vineyards, lying virtually on the beach, are cooled by sea breezes brought up from the coast. To the south and about 50 miles (80 km) inland, the vineyards in the Cederberg Ward lies at an altitude of 3,614 feet (1,100 m) up in the Cederberg Mountains. Both of these diverse spots have the ability to produce superior Sauvignon Blanc.

CHENIN BLANC AND PINOTAGE

Of the many wine varieties growing in the Cape's vineyards, Chenin Blanc and Pinotage are of particular significance to South African winemakers. Chenin Blanc, which is also called Steen in South Africa, for many decades has been the most planted variety in the country. Even today, it heads the list, accounting for nearly 19 percent of vineyard area, although this is a dramatic decrease from its 31.2 percent share back in the early 1990s (SAWIS, 2005). Wine producers' appreciation of Chenin Blanc originally stemmed from the grape's excellent yields and versatility, it can be turned into anything from a quality sparkling wine to a fortified **jerepigo** (very sweet, unfermented grape juice fortified with grape spirit), and everything in between. Chenin Blanc is also used for the production of brandy.

Brandy has always been an important grape-based product and, as with table wine, the quality has been improving over recent years. Today about 8 percent of the wine that is made in South Africa is distilled in the traditional method that is used in Cognac. Such wine will be batch distilled twice in a pot still before undergoing a minimum of three years' aging in small oak casks. South Africa also boasts the world's largest potstill distillery; the KWV's Worcester premises house 120 potstills under one roof. Interest in brandy is not exclusive to the large spirits companies; there are also around 20 smaller privately owned cellars that produce pure potstill brandy.

Brandy aside, Chenin Blanc devotees' main focus is to elevate the grape to the same noble status and quality it enjoys in the Loire. Decent, everyday drinking wines with good fruit and fresh acid balance have always been produced, but they tend to mature quickly and lose their fruity appeal before the following harvest. Through the founding of the Chenin Blanc Association in 1999, the members intended to identify the best vineyards, some of them very old by South African standards, and ensure they were retained. The Association also categorized Chenin Blanc into six different styles from fresh and fruity, to rich and wooded, with the goal of giving the variety better focus and improving its image in consumers' eyes.

The same can be said about South Africa's own variety, **Pinotage** (pee-no-TAHJ) (Figure 16.5). In 1924, Professor Abraham Perold bred this red vari-

FIGURE 16.5

Pinotage, a cross between Pinot Noir and Cinsault, was first grown in South Africa in 1924. It is popular in its home country but is little known outside South Africa.
© Shutterstock/Senai Aksoy

ety, a cross between Pinot Noir and Cinsault, a red grape from the Rhône region of France. At that time Cinsault was also known as Hermitage in South Africa, hence the name Pinotage. Some 35 years later, this unlikely crossing provided the champion red wine at the Cape Wine show and in 1961 the first Pinotage appeared on the market. Like Chenin Blanc, it is a very versatile performer, slipping as easily into the role of sparkling wine made in the traditional méthode champenoise, as it does into fortified dessert wines. Naturally, it held some novelty value for foreign consumers when South Africa reentered the global market in the 1990s. To build on this interest the Pinotage Association was formed, its agenda being to research, improve wine quality, and promote Pinotage.

The enthusiasm with which Pinotage was planted, especially after lifting of sanctions, failed to take into account that it is a niche variety relatively unknown outside South Africa. Whereas demand for international varieties such as Cabernet Sauvignon and Shiraz is still increasing, Pinotage has yet to find a comfortable level of production; since 2001, its vineyard share has been decreasing. Although South Africa remains the variety's most important proponent, small amounts are also grown in other counties.

Klein Karoo (Little Karoo) Region

This region, the farthest east from Cape Town, is also the driest. Generally speaking, it is a semidesert, ideal for ostrich breeding, for which the region is renowned, but making irrigation essential for growing vines and limiting their spread. Apart from limited water, birds of the smaller flying kind, are the main problem the farmers of Klein Karoo. The grapes ripen when there is little other food available for the birds and the damage they can cause has led some farmers to net their vines (an example is Figure 14.7 on page 469). Nevertheless, a wide range of grape varieties are grown here, many on an experimental basis.

Where the region has made its mark is with fortified wines, Port styles in particular. These are wines made in the same way as Portuguese Port but South Africa's trade agreement with the European Union means the word *Port* was phased out on export markets in 2007 and will be locally by 2014. The town of Calitzdorp is affectionately known as the Port capital of South Africa (though excellent examples are also made in Stellenbosch and Paarl). The area has climatic similarities with Portugal's Douro Valley, and most of the wineries make one or more Port-style wines, which are described as Cape Ruby, Cape Vintage, and Cape Tawny, with the Portuguese terms plus the Cape identifying origin on the label.

As in other regions, there are exceptions to the general climate rule. The ward of Tradouw sits at the top of the pass that bears the same name, looking straight out to the Indian Ocean, some 28 miles (45 km) to the south. The vines thus enjoy an unhindered and beneficial cooling influence, allowing for the production of elegant Bordeaux-style blends and Chardonnay. Other cooler localities are also being explored.

Breede River Valley

An inland region, where the two main districts, Worcester and Robertson, track the Breede River (Wide River) along its course from the Witzenberg Mountains down to the Indian Ocean. Summer is a long, hot season with occasional flash downpours. Afternoon breezes coming up the Breede River from the sea temper the heat; this, together with the limestone soils, helps maintain good acid levels in the grapes. With its low average annual rainfall of around 10.6 inches (27 cm), irrigation is also essential

now produce excellent results. In this densely planted area, lesser common varieties like Viognier, Grenache, Mourvèdre, Barbera, Nebbiolo, Sangiovese, Tempranillo, and even Zinfandel are finding a foothold.

Paarl

The district of Paarl (PARL), which is Afrikaans for *Pearl,* borders on Stellenbosch to the north and, although part of the Coastal Region, is landlocked and generally warm. It has almost as many vineyard acres as Stellenbosch, with almost 17 percent of the nation's vineyards. It is home to some of South Africa's largest wineries as well as many of its smallest. Running roughly southeast to northwest, mountains are again a defining feature in this district (Figure 16.8). At the southern end, the Franschhoek Peaks tower above the long, narrow Franschhoek Valley, one of the earliest and best-known wards. The Berg River, which begins in these mountains, runs along the valley floor, through the town of Paarl itself, and eventually out into the Atlantic Ocean; en route it provides water for irrigation to those vineyards planted along its banks. In Franschhoek, the vineyards on the valley floor include some century-old Semillon vines. Away from the river, higher up on the mountain slopes, new vineyards are being put in where it is cooler and the vines grow less vigorously.

Depending on slope and aspect, anything from fine sparkling wine to robust reds can perform well here. There are even spots where Pinot Noir can produce enjoyable, if not great, wines. If summer temperatures reaching well into the 90s °F (30s °C) make this seem unlikely, the southeasterly wind again comes to the rescue as it pours over the mountain pass above the town, beneficially cooling the higher vineyards. Traditionally, white varieties have dominated plantings in an area where vines have always had strong competition from fruit orchards. Today reds make up 57 percent of the plantings in this picturesque valley, which is renowned for having some of the best restaurants in

FIGURE 16.8

The Paarl District lies more inland and to the north of Stellenbosch; it has nearly as much vineyard land in production as Stellenbosch, and a number of wineries both large and small.

© Schalke fotografie/ Melissa Schalke/Shutterstock

the wine country. Farther north, on the north face of Simonsberg Peak, is the Ward of Simonsberg-Paarl. The gentle slopes are well exposed and characterized by deep soils, ideal for the red varieties planted on the lower ground, the whites planted higher up to catch any cool breeze.

Around the town of Paarl and to the north there is little relief from the summer heat and rainfall decreases. Here the wines of the Ward of Wellington reflect their warm conditions and are mainly reds. Shiraz, along with its fellow Rhône varieties Mourvèdre and Grenache, Cabernet Sauvignon, Merlot, and Pinotage, are popular as both varietal wines and blends. Whites, able to hold their own in a richer style, also do well, Viognier, Chardonnay, and Chenin Blanc among them. In fact, Chenin Blanc remains widely planted in Wellington, primarily for making Sherry, which is still produced by the large wineries of KWV and Monis. Both wineries maintain soleras, although these are much smaller than even a decade ago.

Tulbagh

The Tulbagh District is located just over the northwestern boundary of Paarl. It is framed by peaks that tower above the Breede River, which flows out on its southeastern corner en route to Worcester and Robertson. This district is very warm in summer, but snow is a common occurrence on the higher peaks in winter. Soils here feature many large boulders among the river sand. Over the past decade, Tulbagh has seen a great deal of new investment with private wineries starting up all over the valley. White varieties still account for most of the vines, but the potential for quality reds is already evident.

Swartland

Swartland, the "blackland," is named for the indigenous dark, bushlike renoster-veld vegetation that dots the tops of the sweeping hills characterizing this district (Figure 16.9). As part of the major grain growing area of the Western Cape, golden wheat stretching to the horizon is the Swartland's very visible trademark with vines clustered close to the hilltops. The soils here are red and very deep, with good water retention properties. Because of this, in the past there was little irrigation used. Today it is an option installed by most new vineyards. Individual farm dams, replenished by the winter rains, are the main source of water for irrigation. This warm sunny area produces big-bodied red wines. Cabernet Sauvignon is the dominant red variety, but the Swartland is fast getting a reputation for being prime Shiraz country, with other Rhône varieties, such as Grenache, Mourvèdre, and Viognier as complexing partners.

Darling

A recently established district at the southern end of the Swartland, closer to the Atlantic Ocean, Darling has primarily the same soil types and weather conditions as the Swartland district that surrounds it. However, on its western edge, it is near to the Atlantic coastline, making it cooler. Wineries around Swartland and Darling used to be composed mainly of cooperatives. Today, as there is in the rest of the Cape's wine regions, many new privately owned wineries are being started.

FIGURE 16.9

Vines growing in the red soils of Swartland. This warm region is best known for its red varieties, such as Cabernet Sauvignon and Shiraz, which are usually made in a rich, ripe style. The region also produces much of South Africa's wheat.

© Danie Nel/Shutterstock

Tygerberg

The district of Tygerberg is not generally as well known as the ward of Durbanville that lies within it. This ward borders the outer reaches of Cape Town's northern suburbs where its vineyards are always under pressure from property developers. The Tygerberg Hills provide vines with both exposure and shelter, as do the cooling effects of the breezes and mists from the nearby Atlantic on summer afternoons. With unhindered exposure to False Bay, some distance away to the southeast, Durbanville receives some beneficial cooling effect from the famous Cape Doctor. Over the past 8 to 10 years, Sauvignon Blanc has grown in stature and quality and is by far the most planted white variety.

Constantia

Constantia has the same threat from urbanization as Durbanville. Fortunately, the mountain slopes Simon van der Stel recognized 320 years ago as being ideal for growing great wine continue to have outstanding vineyards. Although the taxes for such prime real estate do place a burden on the farmers. Until recently there were just a few wineries, three of them forming part of van der Stel's original land grant. Now a few more are opening up, their vineyards scaling even greater heights along the mountain chain. All are privately owned, small, and quality driven. Modern-day Constantia's forte is white varieties in general, Sauvignon Blanc in particular, but also Semillon and Riesling; for the reds, Merlot is showing promise on the lower, warmer slopes. Here the Klein Constantia Estate (Figure 16.10) has recreated the famed eighteenth-century Constantia dessert wine that it calls Vin de Constance.

Overberg, Walker Bay, and Cape Agulhas

These three districts, following the coast east from Cape Town, cover some of the Cape's newest wine territory, developed from virgin ground since the repeal of the

FIGURE 16.10

The barrel cellar of Klein Constantia. The winery has recreated the famed eighteenth-century Constantia dessert wine under the name of Vin de Constance.

Klein Constantia

quota system in 1992. Their importance exceeds the limited area under vine, around 3,374 acres (1,400 hectares) between the three districts (SAWIS, 2004). In these districts, the summer wind moderates temperatures but also blows in a cloud cover that carries with it the likelihood of rain. With rot an ever-present threat, meticulous viticultural practices are vital. All three are near the sea, so it might appear strange that none fall into the Coastal Region. This is one of the idiosyncrasies of the Wine of Origin Scheme, possibly because the majority of vineyards have been developed since the WO Scheme was implemented.

The Overberg is best known for its one ward, Elgin, internationally recognized for its apple orchards. As the fruit market fortunes have fluctuated, vines have gained a small foothold. Early results have proved so promising, that more vineyards are being established by some of the Cape's most highly regarded winegrowers. As in other cool areas, Sauvignon Blanc is the focus of attention, but other cool-climate varieties such as Gewürztraminer, Riesling, and Pinot Noir along with Cabernet Sauvignon, Merlot, Shiraz, and Chardonnay are all sharing in Elgin's newfound popularity. The whole area lies on a plateau, roughly 990 to 2,950 feet (300 to 900 m) above sea level, and the soils feature the shale, granite, and sandstone that are found in many other areas.

Walker Bay, to the south and east of Overberg, has a more temperate climate, but still is exposed to the unwanted rain that the southeasterly summer wind can bring. Here the Burgundy varieties Pinot Noir and Chardonnay do very well. Today, the six or so small cellars in the valley (not yet a ward, but this is under consideration) all produce respectable to very good examples of Pinot Noir. Shiraz is popular as it is elsewhere along with Merlot and Cabernet Sauvignon. Sauvignon Blanc, Chardonnay, and Chenin Blanc are leading white varieties.

Cape Agulhas is a new district at the southernmost point in Africa. Vines were first established here as recently as the end of the 1990s but since then the growth in new vineyard land has been steady. Sauvignon Blanc and Shiraz are again the favored varieties. The area around Cape Agulhas is very exposed and flat; the vines are thus at risk from wind, which can break the young shoots. As with is two neighbors rot from the cool, sometimes damp, summer conditions is also a threat. At present, most grapes are vinified outside the district.

FIGURE 16.11

Autumn vineyards in the picturesque ward of Constantia, just south of Cape Town.

Klein Constantia

SUMMARY

Since democratization and the dropping of sanctions, South Africa has adapted to the global requirements of the international wine market remarkably quickly. With a weak currency, exports soared; the return of a stronger Rand affected many companies. This spurred them to greater efficiency, with the result that exports continue to be strong foreign currency earners for the country. Today efforts are being made to develop the domestic market for wine to complement the export trade. Nevertheless, even after 16 years, the industry continues to evolve. New areas and varieties are still being explored and more than half of the vineyards were planted since the early 1990s. Better plant material and yet more quality varieties are required to allow South Africa to show its potential through its many and diverse mesoclimates. The young generation of viticulturists, winemakers, marketers, and researchers, who have not known the restrictive practices of the previous era, are well traveled and able to help the country realize this potential in the future.

SOUTH AFRICAN FOOD
AND WINE PAIRING

appetizer
smoked rainbow trout with capers and crème fraîche on toast points
wine
A dry Méthode Cap Classique sparkling wine from the Robertson District

first course
pasta primavera prepared with fresh vegetables
wine
A Pinotage from the Paarl District

main course
**sautéed ostrich filet
with peppercorns and garlic**
wine
A full-bodied Cabernet Sauvignon from the Elgin Ward

dessert
**flourless dark chocolate torte
with raspberry sauce**
wine
A Port-style red dessert wine from the Klein Karoo region

EXERCISES

1. What are some of the main changes in the South African wine industry since the dismantling of the apartheid regime?

2. Why can such a range of grape varieties be grown across the Cape vineyards?

3. Outline the conditions that limit production in South Africa.

4. What were the conditions that led to the establishment of the KWV?

REVIEW QUESTIONS

1. Pinotage is a cross between Pinot Noir and _____.
   A. Syrah
   B. Concord
   C. Cinsault
   D. Grenache

2. Which immigrants were instrumental in bringing winemaking to South Africa?
   A. Portuguese and British
   B. Spanish and Italian
   C. Germans and Americans
   D. Dutch and French

3. South Africa's system of appellations is called _____.
   A. Wine of Origin (WO) Scheme
   B. South Africa Viticultural Area (SAVA)
   C. South African Appellation of Origen (SAAO)
   D. African Viticultural Area (AVA)

4. The vast majority of South Africa's vineyards are located in the region known as the _____.
   A. Breede River Valley
   B. Paarl
   C. Orange River
   D. Western Cape

References

Hughes, D., Hands, P., & Kench, J. (1988). *The complete book of South African wine* (2nd ed.). Cape Town: C. Struik.

Leipoldt, C. L. (2004). *Food & Wine.* Stonewall: Cape Town.

South African Wine Industry Information & Systems (SAWIS). (2004). *Vines in the Wine of Origin areas.* Paarl, South Africa: Author.

South African Wine Industry Information & Systems (SAWIS). (2005). *South African wine industry statistics No. 29.* Paarl, South Africa: Author.

South African Wine Industry Information & Systems (SAWIS). (2009). *South African wine industry statistics No. 33.* Paarl, South Africa: Author.

SECTION V

THE BUSINESS OF WINE

THIS SECTION COVERS THE
business of wine within the food services.
The three chapters focus on marketing and
distributing wine, developing and managing
a wine list, and selling and serving wine.

THE MARKETING AND DISTRIBUTION OF WINE

This chapter explains the

various laws and industry standards that govern the selling and transporting of wine. In addition, it focuses on the three-tiered system of distribution used throughout the United States, as well as the various wholesale sales strategies used to market wine in this complex business world. Finally, the chapter discusses the alternative methods of selling wine.

KEY TERMS

differentiating characteristic

distributor (wholesaler)

FOB price

futures

laid-in cost (LIC)

margin on sell

markup

off-premise license

on-premise license

post off

supplier

three-tiered system of distribution

trade tastings

INTRODUCTION

The business of selling and serving wine in the United States is very complicated, with different laws governing the many different methods of shipping, selling, serving, and storing alcoholic beverages in the various states. The development of the wine industry in this country has a complex history, with several major historical events, some the result of Mother Nature's quirks and some caused by humans, disrupting the growth and improvement of the industry. If one is to become an effective buyer within the hospitality industry, he or she must have a solid grasp of how the various states control the distribution of alcoholic beverages, how the pricing is calculated by distributors, and how the laws within his or her state regulate the shipping of wines. Moreover, hospitality professionals must be familiar with the laws in the state where they do business that govern the serving of beverages in that state. This chapter gives an overview of the historic aspects of the wine industry, and also covers the basics of the current distribution system in major states. A new development in the modern wine industry is the international brand. Due to the fact that many of these brands are served as featured wines by the glass in American restaurants, it is important that hospitality professionals become familiar with these prevalent brands, how they have evolved, and how to best incorporate them into their wine program.

DISTRIBUTION OF WINE

History of the Wine Business

As we saw in Chapter 1, the production of wine in this country has had a rocky history. Wine has been made in America going back to the nineteenth century, the golden age of wine. It was during this time that several European countries were producing superb wines, thanks primarily to the advance of modern chemistry and microbiology. At this time, the French established their system to classify by quality level their finest wines. The wine industry expanded at this time as transportation methods greatly improved, thus allowing wines to be safely shipped to other markets around the world. In the late nineteenth century, the United States, especially California, began to sell wines to the eastern parts of this country, and to European countries. Just as wine showed real promise of becoming an important industry in this country, a major setback hit both in Europe and the United States in the mid-1800s in the form of the root louse, phylloxera. Indigenous to the eastern United States, the louse somehow found its way to southern French vineyards, most likely aboard a ship bringing American root cuttings to Europe, and from there the louse spread to vineyards throughout Europe, killing vineyards in many wine-producing countries. Ironically the vineyards of California, which had originally been immune to phylloxera due to longtime exposure to the louse, also became infected as the louse mutated and developed the ability to infect our native varietals.

The phylloxera problem was solved in the late 1800s and early twentieth century through the replanting of vineyards onto native American rootstock. However, the American wine industry suffered another serious setback, this one human-made. In

3-Tiered System of Distribution

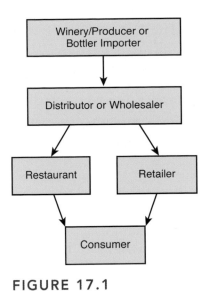

FIGURE 17.1

This chart outlines the three-tiered distribution system that still exists in many states. Wines (and other alcohol) must be sent from the producer to a licensed wholesaler who then sells it to a retailer or restaurant. From there it can be sold to a consumer.

© 2012 Delmar Cengage Learning

1920, the Volstead Act was enacted, prohibiting the sales or production of any alcoholic beverage (see Chapter 1). In 1933, Prohibition was eliminated allowing wine (and other alcoholic beverages) to be produced and legally sold in this country. After repeal each state was allowed to enact its own laws governing all aspects of the wine business.

State Laws on Selling and Transporting Wine

The fact that the federal government left it entirely to the individual states to decide on and create all state laws relevant to alcohol means that our country has a mélange of distribution systems, ranging from systems in which the state is the sole distributor of alcohol (these are called "control states"), to states that are free enterprise systems in which private companies operate at each level. These are called "open" or "competitive" states. There are also some states that are structured as "partial control states."

The majority of states are open states, and all of them have some form of **three-tiered system of distribution** (Figure 17.1) for alcoholic beverages, in which there are three separate businesses involved, each with a separate license and a separate function. In most states, alcohol must go from the producer, also called a **supplier** (i.e., winery or importer) to a **distributor** (also known as *wholesaler*) to a retailer or restaurant before it can be purchased by the consumer. In other words, one entity produces the wine, usually a winery; in the case of wine produced in another country, the importing company functions as the producer. The producer sells the wine to a wholesaler in a specific state. This company is licensed to sell the wine only in that one state. Moreover, the wholesaler can sell the wine only to businesses that are licensed by that state to sell to consumers. The wholesaler takes possession of the wine and stores it in a suitable warehouse, usually temperature-controlled. The wholesale company has a team of salespeople, usually trained in wines, that visit retailers and restaurants and bars to acquaint their buyers with the wine. The salespeople can of course sell only to licensed businesses. There are two types of licenses granted by the state to these businesses. **On-premise licenses** allow the licensee to sell alcoholic beverages to consumers, but the beverage can then be consumed only on the premises of the business. Such businesses are restaurants, pubs, bars, clubs, hotels, and so on. The other type of license is termed an **off-premise license**, which allows the licensee to sell alcohol to a consumer who can then consume the beverage only off the licensee's premises. These businesses are retailers, such as liquor stores and wine shops. The vast majority of wines purchased by restaurant operations (and by retailers) are selected and purchased from the offerings of the local wholesalers. When an operation is looking to add labels to expand the list, it turns to its local wholesaler representatives for guidance and recommendations about which products to offer.

The three-tiered system affects both the general consumer and hospitality professionals who are seeking to purchase wine. One noticeable effect is that each tier adds cost to the product. Each tier must make a profit, and these additional costs affect the final price of the product. The typical **markup** for the wholesaler is about 30 to 40 percent and for the retailer from 25 to 50 percent, depending on the product and the retailer. Many independent retailers may use a higher markup than chain operations because chain operations tend to sell a higher volume of wine. Restaurants are able to purchase wine at wholesale prices, which are typically 30 percent below retail cost. For example, a wine that is in a store for $15 would cost a restaurant about $10. The restaurant, in turn, would sell that wine for anywhere between $25 and $30.

Some states do allow *direct shipping* from producer to consumer, thus eliminating three of the "tiers" by bypassing the wholesaler and the retailer. In recent years there has been considerable action by wineries and importers as well as consumers to eliminate the three-tiered system, or at least to reduce the control the wholesalers and large retailers have over the distribution of wines. As of 2010, 37 states allowed at least some form of limited direct shipping. The laws governing liquor sales and shipping put in place after repeal do serve important goals, like making it more difficult for minors to obtain alcohol and ensuring an important source of revenues for the states. However, the three-tiered system can make it more difficult for restaurateurs to source and purchase wines, and force purchasers to do business with specific wholesalers. The legalities of buying and selling wine remains in flux, with new laws being established and new cases being brought before the courts; however, the three-tiered system pervades the industry as of now. (For more on U.S. wine laws, see Appendix A.)

Wholesale Sales Strategies

Wholesalers, as we saw earlier, procure the wine from producers, and distribute it to restaurateurs and retailers. There are several wholesalers in every market, each offering many wines to their customers. When adding wines to their lists, restaurateurs turn to the representatives of wholesalers in their area. However, with thousands of wines to pick from, it is difficult to know where to start so buyers turn to the sales representatives of their wholesalers for guidance. Accordingly, the wholesalers have developed many tactics to assist the buyers, and keep their attention focused primarily on the products within their company's portfolio.

First, the sales reps regularly visit their accounts (i.e., the stores and restaurants that buy from them). This way they can keep these customers abreast of what is developing among their offerings. They also offer the buyers and their staff a chance to taste current offerings, while they give relevant information on each wine. This type of support from the sales reps is invaluable to the restaurant management as it makes decisions about the wine list. A strong, trusting relationship between seller and buyer is mutually beneficial. The sales rep, by maintaining an advisory role rather than purely sales, earns the respect of the buyer and is likely to improve the amount of business he or she earns from that account. By maintaining good rapport with account reps, a restaurateur will obtain better pricing and improve access to products with small production or strict allocation.

Another tactic used by distributors is periodic discounts for certain wines. These are termed post offs. A **post off** is a discount applied to a specific wine or line of wines for a specific period of time. This benefits the wholesale company, which sells a large quantity of that wine during the period, and it benefits the restaurant, which receives a lower price on the wine. For this reason, wines on post off are often purchased to be sold as wines by the glass.

FIGURE 17.2

A walk-around tasting. These events are held by wholesalers so that members of the trade can sample their suppliers' wines.
© Chuck Pefley/Alamy

Another very effective tactic used by wholesalers is providing additional opportunity, above and beyond visits from sales reps, for their customers to taste wines in their portfolio. In many states wholesalers are able to host wine tastings for those in the industry. These are called **trade tastings** because they are open only to people active in the wine trade as retailers or restaurateurs. These events can have different formats. A walk-around tasting is quite informal, with tables set up with displays of the wine, and small samples of each wine poured, usually by a rep of the winery or of the local purveyor (Figure 17.2).

A sit-down tasting is a more formal, seminar-style setup, with a training lecture offered by a panel of experts. These events can be very informative and also offer valuable networking possibilities, and an opportunity to taste and learn about new wines on the market. An important point to be made here is that one must keep the palate fresh and the mind clear. The easiest way to do this is to be sure and spit out the wine after tasting. When tasting wine professionally, one is doing so for the purpose of analysis and evaluation, not enjoyment. It is important that participants pace themselves, drink plenty of water, eat some available food, and do not swallow the wine. This way attendees and hosts all achieve their goals of spreading knowledge about these wines.

Profitability in the Wine Industry

There is no secret about the fact that each tier of the distribution system needs to operate at a profit. Measuring profitability within the wine business is quite straightforward. There are several basic formulas that clearly show whether a particular pricing decision will be effective. We describe these formulas as we trace a hypothetical situation in which a winery in California is shipping its latest wine to a distributor on the East Coast.

FOB Price

FOB price is the price charged by the producer of the wine (or his or her importer) to wholesalers. (*FOB* stands for "free on board" and refers to the fact that this price is quoted from the specific point at which the customer takes possession of the goods.) The FOB is based on the cost of producing the wine plus approximately a 30 percent markup. When setting an FOB price, the producer is also concerned with hitting a specific price point at retail. The winery's marketing department will do a rough calculation on this for each state where the wine is sold before quoting an FOB price to the distributors. In our example, the winery partners decide to go with an FOB of $40.00 per case.

When this FOB price is quoted to the sales manager at the winery's Massachusetts distributor, she does a basic calculation before deciding to order any of the wine. She needs to know if the wine will produce an acceptable profit for her company.

Laid-in Cost (LIC)

Laid-in Cost (LIC) is the basis the wholesaler uses to decide the price she will use to sell the wine to retailers and restaurants. The calculation of LIC on domestic wines is shown as follows. Imported wines will have the additional expenses of federal excise tax, customs fees, brokers fees, and added insurance.

$$LIC = FOB + Freight\ costs + State\ taxes$$

Freight from the West Coast to destinations in the East will break down to about $1.00 per case depending on the quantity ordered. (Usually orders from wholesalers are in containers of 900 to 1,200 cases. The larger the order, the smaller the amount per case because you are spreading the shipping cost over more cases.)

Each state charges a different excise tax per case. In Massachusetts it is $3.50. So for Massachusetts a case of wine with an FOB of $40.00 will have LIC of $44.50; that is, $40 + $1.00 + $3.50 = $44.50.

Now that the sales manager has discerned what her LIC is, she is ready to settle on the price her company will quote to its customers; in other words, she is ready to set up the wholesale price.

Wholesale Price and Margin on Sell

The wholesale company takes its LIC and adds approximately 30 to 40 percent to get its wholesale price. A distributor always strives to set a price that is fair and appropriate for the product. This way the wine is more likely to sell through quickly. But far more important than the markup is the **margin on sell**. This is how a wholesaler really decides what price to quote. Margin is calculated in two steps:

$$Wholesale\ price - LIC = Gross\ profit$$

$$\frac{Gross\ profit}{LIC} = Margin\ on\ sell$$

> **Producer: FOB price** = Cost of production + markup of 30%
>
> **Distributor:** Wholesale price = LIC + markup of 30 to 40%
>
> **Retailer: Final price to consumer** = Wholesale cost + 30 to 50% markup

To continue with our example: The wholesaler takes the LIC of $44.50 and decides to aim for a wholesale price of $64.00, but first calculates his margin:

$$\begin{array}{r} \$64 \\ -\ 44.50 \\ \hline \$19.50 \end{array}$$

$$\frac{\$19.50}{\$44.50} = 43.8\%$$

Most distributors aim to make an average margin on sell of about 35 percent, so a margin of almost 44 percent is very nice indeed! Accordingly, our sales manager would probably place a very generous order for this new wine. She is confident that since this wine will retail in the fighting varietal category, it will sell well.

The sales manager did her job well. She knows how the retailers in her state do their pricing. After buying a case of the new wine, the retailer must price it appropriately if he wants it to sell through. In different states, retailers will do different markups. In Massachusetts most retailers employ a 50 percent markup. To calculate this, take the case price, divide by 12 (in standard-sized bottles, that is (750 ml); there are 12 bottles in each case) to get the bottle cost, then multiply by 1.5.

$$\frac{\$64.00}{12} = \$5.33$$

$$\$5.33 \times 1.5 = \$7.99$$

In our hypothetical example, we saw how the companies at each level calculated their profitability. The markup at each step was acceptable, and the ultimate person involved—the consumer—paid a fair price (Figure 17.3).

STRATEGIC MARKETING

In the complex world of the modern wine business, the selling of products is becoming more competitive and more sophisticated, thus requiring more strategic planning. There are still small boutique wineries in most wine regions of the world, including Europe, the United States, South America, South Africa, and Australia. However, an increasing percentage of the world's wine is sold by large corporate suppliers and their large wholesale associates. In any business, large corporations need to develop sophisticated marketing strategies for their sales efforts in order to stay ahead of the competition. A marketing strategy is a process that ideally allows an organization to concentrate its limited resources on an opportunity that most effectively allows it to increase sales and achieve a sustainable competitive advantage. Every wine has uniqueness, that is, a specific selling point that makes it appealing to the consumer. This is its **differentiating characteristic** that sets it apart from competing wines, and is part of what draws a buyer to that bottle. The purpose of a marketing strategy is to define a product's differentiating characteristic and then proceed to make the buying public aware of that unique characteristic. Most marketing professionals agree with the concept that there are three basic strategies incorporated into effective marketing plans:

- *Cost leadership:* The firm will deliver the same benefits as competitors but at a lower price.
- *Differentiation advantage:* A firm delivers benefits that exceed those of competing products.
- *Focus strategy:* This is the most intense strategy, and addresses a specific segment of the market.

Within the wine industry the most frequently utilized marketing strategy is that of cost leadership. Small boutique wineries in many regions of the world continue to depend on the age-old strategy of producing wines that are superior in quality to wines produced by competing wineries in the same, or a close, region. Such wines are unique in the level of their quality, their limited numbers, and their regional identity. In other words, they have a distinct inherent differentiating advantage. Wines of this level of quality often have a demand that exceeds their supply, and therefore are expensive. However, the majority of wines sold in the United States are brands that are able to deliver the same benefits as those of competing products but at a lower price. Brands employ the first marketing strategy previously mentioned: cost leadership. Brand wines are often defined by the price at which they are sold, with the lowest-priced brands being termed "super value" or "jug" (less than $3 a bottle). Next is "popular premium" or "basic" ($3 to $7); "fighting varietal" ($7 to $10); "classics" ($10 to $14); "premium" ($15 to $25); and finally "ultra-premium" ($25 and up). It should be noted that the exact price points and names given to these market segments varies quite a bit depending on who is defining them. The wine industry, which for centuries offered unique local products but is now highly competitive and international in nature, has become dependent on branding.

It is fair to say that brands now control the U.S. wine market. In any industry a brand is a symbol that is designed to represent something else, something that might not be inherent to the product. That symbol is meant to package all the characteristics, inferences, or associations that might be affiliated, however vaguely, with the product's category. In a roundabout way, branding helps differentiate a product from the competition by clearly defining its differentiating characteristic. The origin of the word *brand* is found in that same purpose: The "brand" was the scar burned into the hide of a steer so that there would be no doubt as to which ranch owned the animal.

In today's business world branding is a much more complicated concept than in the old American west. A brand needs personality, a truly identifiable personality. This helps humanize the product so that the prospective buyer's defenses are down and he or she feels an emotional link. Therefore, the first step in creating a brand is for the firm to become familiar with its market, and be certain who is likely to buy the product. Once that research has been done, the marketing company can start creating its new brand. Step one is the name. It is the foundation of the brand. It must have proper, positive connotations. The name must be pronounceable even for those whose native language is not that of the country that produces the product.

Once the brand has been created, the marketing people must work to incorporate differentiation into the newly branded wine. They need to differentiate their product from comparably priced wines by playing up something unique, such as region of origin ("grapes grown in California's Lake County"), age of the winery and heritage of the family ("fifth-generation winemaker"), or unusual food combinations ("perfect with spicy cuisine"). As the brand's identity is being established, the marketing team must convey a consistent message through all aspects of communication and promotion. Everything must give a similar image of the wine—print advertising, back labels, and point-of-sale material such as table tents, case cards, and shelf talkers. In the modern market for wines there is one more method of communicating a wine's differentiating characteristic to its potential buyers: the Internet. Americans are becoming more and more dependent on the Internet for news and for communicating and for decision making. Young people are particularly receptive to online marketing, and the importance of this group to wine marketers is increasing. The new generation of wine consumers, those between 21 and 34 years of age, are responsible for 46 percent of the increase in wine consumption in this country between 2003 and 2008 (Phillips, 2009). The most effective way to reach large groups of these enthusiastic consumers is online. Every winery, from Classified Growth Bordeaux to new affordable brands, needs to have a Web site. Also important is a regular voice on social networks like Twitter, Netlog, and Facebook where consumers can find the most up-to-date information about a specific wine. To be successful today, all marketers must incorporate the Internet into brand promotion and sales efforts.

Also critically important is the message conveyed to buyers, both on- and off-premise, by their sales reps. Therefore, supplier personnel must be very careful and very thorough in teaching the sales force at all their distributors how to discuss their wine, especially how to describe what differentiates it from competing brands. As the wine industry becomes ever more international in nature, effective brand creation and ongoing strategic marketing will become even more crucial to success in this increasingly competitive business.

Strategic Marketing Examples

It is important to understand the very different marketing efforts needed to sell the wines of an established winery versus the strategies needed to build a successful new brand. When one considers the complicating factors of the import market, the game becomes even more complex. The following two success stories illustrate these differences, and give a clearer idea on the wide variety of strategies marketing professionals can employ within the world of wine. First is the story of a remarkably successful brand created in California, Two Buck Chuck. Then is a condensed look at one of the most distinguished and respected wines from Spain, Vega Sicilia, and its very successful efforts to penetrate the ultra-premium market in the United States.

Charles Shaw Wines, Success at the "Super Value" Tier

Charles Shaw is one of the best-known and fastest growing wine brands in the United States. Producing the varieties Cabernet Sauvignon, Merlot, and Chardonnay among others, it is sold exclusively at the Trader Joes supermarket chain for as low as $1.99 per bottle. Trader Joes has more than 300 store locations nationwide with about half of the stores located in California. The low price of the Charles Shaw brand gave it instant notoriety and also is the source of the nickname that it is better known by, Two Buck Chuck. Charles Shaw is made by the Bronco Wine Company of Ceres California, which is the fourth largest producer in America bottling more than 20 million cases of wine a year under more than 50 different brand names (*Wine Business Monthly*, 2010). Bronco's CEO, Fred Franzia, is a controversial figure in the California wine industry who often pokes fun at the pretentious nature of wineries in Napa and Sonoma that produce more expensive wines.

Charles Shaw was the owner of a small Napa Valley winery in the 1970s that fell on hard times and he sold his brand name to Bronco. In 2002, Franzia reintroduced the label but this time it was released as a low-priced California appellation wine rather than a more expensive Napa Valley product. It immediately gained attention because

FIGURE 17.4

Since it was introduced in 2002 Charles Shaw, or as it is better known, Two Buck Chuck, has been one of the fastest growing wine brands in the United States.

Photo by Pat Henderson. Used with permission from Bronco Wine Company.

of its acceptable quality and economical price. The low price was possible for several reasons. Bronco owns extensive vineyard holdings in California's Central Valley that are capable of producing high yields at low cost and they also buy bulk wine and grapes from other wineries that have a surplus. Their wine producing facilities are centered on large outdoor tank farms designed for efficient production. Their large volume of production allows them to buy packaging material such as bottles and corks at discount. Another important cost-cutting factor is that they also distribute their own wines in California, eliminating the cost of the middleman in the state. Charles Shaw sells for $1.99 in California, however in other states the added cost of transportation and distribution raises the price to as much as $3.49.

When Charles Shaw was first released in 2002, it was during an economic downturn that caused a number of wineries to have surplus wine that they placed on the bulk market and also stimulated consumers' interest in "super value" wines. While few customers thought that it was the best wine available, most thought it was much better than the jug and wine-in-a-box offerings that had a similar cost per glass. Charles Shaw wines have also won some awards, but since there are multiple blends for each variety in a year, some critics complain that there is inconsistency from batch to batch.

Much like Bronco's CEO Fred Franzia, Charles Shaw holds a controversial place in the American wine market. Some complain of Bronco's business practices, and that Charles Shaw cannibalizes sales of more expensive wines in the $6 to $10 range and forces other producers to lower their prices and lower quality to remain competitive. Others begrudgingly admit the wine represents a good value for the price and has introduced many consumers to the idea that wine can be a part of the everyday diet and does not need to be saved only for special occasions. Whatever their feelings about the brand, few deny that "Two Buck Chuck" has been one of the most successful wine labels released in the last decade.

Vega Sicilia, a Successful Ultra-Premium Import

As was mentioned earlier in this chapter, small quality wineries in many regions continue to depend on the age-old strategy of producing wines that are superior in quality to wines produced by competing wineries in the same region. Such wines are unique due to their excellent quality, their limited numbers, and their strong regional identity. They have the advantage of a distinct, easily identifiable, and very impressive differentiating characteristic. However, even these prestigious wineries have to be cautious and well prepared when attempting to open a market where their wines, and even their region, are not well known. A good example of this type of strategic marketing is Vega Sicilia, a well-aged estate located in Ribero del Duero, Spain. This small winery has been producing wine since the mid-1880s. At the time the winery was purchased in 1982 by the Alvarez family, it was already known throughout Spain and was also popular in other European markets. However, the wines were practically unknown in the United States, even though interest in fine European wines was growing quickly.

comparing these notes at various points in the wine's life will provide a window into the changes that have taken place. This is the best way to begin to understand how wine develops with age, and should be undertaken whenever possible.

Buying Futures

Some wine producers will offer their wine as futures. Buying **futures** means that the wine is purchased before it is actually released to the market. This manner of purchasing is done for several reasons, but primarily for collectors to ensure they have access to the wines that they desire for their cellars. The customer can secure the quantities of the desired wines before the general public has a chance to buy the inventory. The wine is purchased and paid for before the buyer can possess it. Sometimes, the wine is not delivered to the customer for several years because it may be bought while it is still in barrel. The practice of selling wine as futures helps the winery in several ways. First, requiring the buyer to pay for futures allows a steady cash flow that helps pay for ongoing winery functions during down periods. Additionally, the practice helps ensure that the wine gets sold, instead of having excess inventory sitting in storage waiting for a buyer. This practice is most common in Bordeaux, although many other markets have recognized the benefits of selling wine as futures, and have begun to follow Bordeaux's lead. For highly allocated wines with limited productions, futures may be the only way to access the wines because little is available on the open market after the futures are purchased. For wines that are produced in high volumes and are not difficult to access, buying on futures is usually not recommended because they will be readily available in the market upon release.

Buying from Auctions and Private Cellars

The primary way for restaurants to acquire older wines is to purchase them at public auction (Figure 17.6). The auction market has taken off in the past 25 years. The large auction houses that specialize in wines obtain fine wines from the cellars of private collectors, estate sales, and the wineries' own stocks. The wines are then offered in a carefully organized event to the highest bidder. These auctions have high profiles and often attract serious collectors from around the world. Most of the established auction houses also provide online bidding for members. Bidding is highly competitive, and the large number of bidders and the small supply of the most desirable wines often leads to very high prices that might even exceed current value for some batches of wine. Auctions offer access to rare caches of wines that are otherwise not available. However, restaurateurs (and committed private collectors) should be prepared for bidding to rise, and must set a personal budget for their purchases.

FIGURE 17.6

Wine auctions are becoming more numerous in the United States, as they offer an excellent opportunity for restaurateurs and private collectors to acquire rare and/or older wines. At this fundraising event in California, the successful bidder celebrates his acquisition of a bottle of very fine California Cabernet Sauvignon.

© AP Photo/Eric Risberg

SUMMARY

The wine industry in the United States is very complex, with each of the 50 states having its own set of laws for the production, shipping, sale, and consumption of alcoholic beverages. To add to that complexity, the industry is at a place of flux. Many of the existing laws and industry standards are currently being questioned. Some critical state laws, such as those forbidding direct shipments from wineries to consumers, have been found to be unconstitutional by the highest judicial authority, the Supreme Court of the United States. The three-tiered chain of distribution that has been in existence since the repeal of Prohibition is being threatened on many levels, with retailers, restaurateurs, and consumers objecting to the added expense of the system, as well as the difficulty of finding certain products in different states. Another growing threat to the traditional methods of selling wine in this country is the increasing use of the Internet, especially among younger people. Additionally, the domestic wine business is seeing increasing competition from countries abroad, particularly in the creation of successful brands. It is inherent upon the modern American wine industry to be flexible, forward thinking, and strategic in its planning if it is to maintain a strong position in the contemporary international world of wine.

EXERCISES

1. Describe the three-tiered system of distribution, touching on ways in which this system can affect restaurant operators creating a wine list.

2. What is the first step in creating a brand? How will this first step help ensure that the brand will appeal to the demographic for which it is intended?

3. List some of the tactics used by wholesalers to assist their customers in choosing wines for their list.

4. What is meant by the term *differentiating characteristic*?

REVIEW QUESTIONS

1. Which of the following wine professionals is not directly involved in sales and marketing?
   A. Sales representative
   B. Retailer
   C. Viticulturist
   D. Distributor
   E. Importer

2. An off-premise establishment is one that:
   A. Sells wine at a steep discount
   B. A wine shop that is owned by the state
   C. Sells wine that is consumed away from the shop
   D. Can sell wine and beer, but not hard alcohol

3. Which of the following is not part of the laid-in cost of a case of wine?
   A. The cost of shipping
   B. The FOB price of the wine
   C. Overhead costs
   D. State taxes

(Continues)

(Continued)

4. Which of the following is not a part of the three-tiered distribution system?
   A. The retailer
   B. The supplier
   C. The distributor
   D. The shipping company

References

Cannavan, T. (2009). Vega Sicilia's estates. Retrieved April 2009 from http://www.wine-pages.com/organise/vega-sicilia.htm+Stevenson+%E2%80%9CWine-pages%E2%80%9D+Vega+Sicilia&cd=1&hl=en&ct=clnk&gl=us

Phillips, C. (2009). *Millennial wave hits wine*. Retrieved May 3, 2009 from http://www.millennialmarketing.com/2009/05/millennialwavehitswine/

Sesser, S. (2010, February 20). Spanish Greatness With a Long Wait. *The Wall Street Journal*, pW9

Wine Business Monthly (2010, February). The WBM 30 Profiles. *Wine Business Monthly, 17* (2), 36–59.

{DEVELOPING
AND MANAGING
A WINE LIST}

This chapter identifies the

key considerations to keep in mind when designing a wine program for a restaurant. It also covers how to choose the proper wines for the list and set their prices as well as how to put into practice a successful wine by the glass program.

greater selection of wines by the glass without running the risk of spoilage than a small bistro with a more limited clientele would be able to offer.

The wines offered by the glass are usually typical examples of their variety or style. For example, when most guests order a glass of Chardonnay, they expect one that has a fair amount of oak in the profile. If an operation offered only a crisp, lean, and steely Chablis, which is made from Chardonnay, as its house Chardonnay, this would not meet the expectations of most guests who order the wine. Although there are plenty of fans of Chablis, it is a distinctly different style of Chardonnay than many Americans tend to expect.

Choosing Wines to Sell by the Glass

The selection of house wines is the driving force in many restaurants' wine programs and can make a marked difference in both the guest experience and the overall profitability of the program. Careful selection can ensure happy guests and a profitable program. When selecting wines to pour by the glass, there are a few key points to remember: availability, pour size, price point, and style.

Availability

One strategy employed by many operations is to carefully select a house wine, and then to stick with it for an extended length of time. A wine that is chosen to be a long-term offering by the glass should be produced in sufficient quantities to be available for as long as it is needed. It would be disappointing to have strong sales of a certain wine by the glass, and then to find when the manager attempts to reorder it is no longer available. Obviously, only a limited amount of each wine is made every year, but many value wines are produced in large enough volumes that they are seldom out of stock between vintages.

An alternative way to approach selecting house wines is to frequently change the available selections. This method has advantages because it keeps the list fluid and the guests' interest in the wine program high. This strategy involves regularly choosing new offerings that meet the requirements of the wine program but still offer the guests variety and value. Historically, changing the list was a difficult process to undertake requiring a trip to the printing company, and consequently was not done very often. In the last 20 years as personal computers and printers have become nearly ubiquitous, the process of updating and changing wine selections has never been easier. Most restaurants now print their own wine lists in house, and this allows the operator to adjust the selections and update the list as needed. Frequent changes also allow the operator to take advantage of special pricing because a wine that is discounted can be added to the house wine selections.

Because of the added cost of presenting and serving the wine, combined with proprietors' desire to make a profit, the price of a wine sold at a restaurant is almost always greater than the same wine sold at a retail off-premise store. For example if a customer sees a wine on sale for $7.99 a bottle in the grocery store, and then later that night sees the exact same wine selling for $8.00 a glass, she would think that restaurant's wines were overpriced. To avoid this perception wine buyers can seek out wines that are less common so the customer is unlikely to come across them in a wine shop. Another solution is that some producers bottle a restaurant only wine that is not available for off-premise sales.

Pour Size

The standard pour size for wines served by the glass is 5 oz (150 ml). Since the standard size for a wine bottle is 750 ml it holds about 25 oz, this means that each bottle contains five glasses of wine. If the operation were to offer a smaller, 4-oz (118-ml) pour there are six glasses per bottle and if the restaurant offers a larger, 6-oz (177-ml) pour there are four glasses per bottle. The size of the house pour can depend on many factors, but the 5-oz pour is the most common. If the wine is used for a catering event, it may possibly be poured in a smaller size and be offered at a lower price to the guests. If the operation offers a larger 6-oz pour its prices may seem high when compared to other restaurants offering the same wine. The pour size chosen will affect the pricing of the wines and this should be taken into account when deciding on the appropriate pour.

Guests who purchase wine by the glass seek a certain perception of value. If a 5-oz pour is served in a 15-oz glass, it does not seem like a value to the guest, even if the amount of wine is the standard pour. Most guests are seeking perceived value, and a glass that is only one-third full does not "feel" like a value. However, if a glass is filled to near the brim although it may be perceived as a better value, the customer will not be able to swirl the contents of the glass and fully enjoy the wine's aroma (Figure 18.3). Some establishments serve wines by the glass in a "mini carafe." A mini carafe holds 4 to 6 oz of wine and allows patrons to feel like they are getting their money's worth without overfilling the glass. A restaurant must find the balance between its glass size and its pour size in order to present the perception of value to the customer.

FIGURE 18.3

Each of these three glasses contains the standard 5-oz (150 ml) pour of wine, although the perception of value changes based on the glass size. The largest glass on the right may best accentuate the wine's aromatics, while the small glass on the left appears fullest and therefore may appeal to consumers who seek value.

New England Culinary Institute Photographer: Paul O. Boisvert

Cost per Bottle	Estimated Markup
$8 and under	Three times cost
$8 to $15	Two and a half times cost
$15 to $20	Two times cost
$20 to $40	One and a half times cost
$40 and up	Cost plus $20

FIGURE 18.4

An example of estimated markups.

© 2012 Delmar Cengage Learning

Price Point

Wines chosen to be poured by the glass often fall into the lower priced "value" end of the spectrum. Guests who want to purchase a glass of wine generally expect it to be affordable and reasonably priced, and when chosen appropriately, the house wines can offer a good quality-to-price ratio for the guest. By choosing appropriately priced bottles, an operation can ensure profitability with sales of these wines (Figure 18.4). A general rule of thumb would be to look for wines that cost the restaurant $10 or less per bottle for sale as a house wine. Bottles in this price range allow the operator to price each glass in the $4 to $8 range, which is where most house wines are priced. Wines that cost more per bottle will need to be priced higher per glass or they may limit potential profitability for the restaurant.

Wine programs typically run a cost percentage between 28 and 35 percent. The **cost percentage** is the ratio of money spent to money earned for the operation. Having a cost percentage of 30 percent means that 30 percent of the money earned from a wine sale was spent on purchasing the wine. It is very common for house wines to have a lower cost percentage than reserve bottles, but the overall average usually falls within this range. For a bottle that has a cost of $10, with five glasses per bottle, the cost per glass is $2. If the operation sells each glass of wine for $6, then the cost percentage per glass is 33 percent ($2/$6 = 0.33). If the operation decided to sell that same glass for $8 instead, then its cost percentage would be 25 percent ($2/$8 = 0.25).

Deciding on an appropriate pricing strategy for wines sold by the glass involves determining the operation's ideal cost of goods as well as the general sensitivity of the customers to prices. Although it can be difficult to decide on an appropriate pricing strategy, careful analysis of the customers, the competition, and the restaurant concept can help an operator determine the most effective range of prices.

Style

Wine ordered at the table is almost always consumed with food. This being said, it is not uncommon for the wine to arrive several minutes before the appetizer or first entree arrives. For this reason wines for the by the glass lists should be well balanced and versatile so they can be enjoyed alone as well as an accompaniment to food. The wines should also have the style and characteristics to complement the menu as much as possible. Wines that are high in alcohol or have a heavy oak profile are not very versatile with food and do not make the best selections for house wines. Some people prefer Zinfandels with very ripe flavors and high alcohol, and this style should be available for these guests, but the house Zinfandel should have a lower level of alcohol to ensure that it works well with the menu.

Which Wines to Feature by the Glass

No matter what the type of restaurant, clientele, or location, several styles of wine and varietals should be available as house wines. These are the wines that customers ask for by name and expect to be available. For white wines, these include Chardonnay, Pinot Gris (Pinot Grigio), and Sauvignon Blanc (Fumé Blanc). Most guests who are interested in a glass of white wine will expect at least a couple of these varieties to be offered. For reds, the most popular wines include Cabernet Sauvignon, Pinot Noir, Merlot, Zinfandel, and Syrah (Shiraz). It is clearly in an operator's best interest to offer good examples of these wines by the glass to please the guests, but the available offerings should not stop there. If the customer base includes many newcomers to the world of wine, a White Zinfandel may be good to have on the list. Likewise, if the patrons are a little more sophisticated, a dry Riesling would be a good choice. In addition to these classic varietals, offering wines from unusual grapes or regions, such as an Argentinean Malbec, exposes the guests to a unique experience and helps generate interest in the wine program.

It is entirely possible to develop a comprehensive program of house wines that meets the expectations of the average guest and exceeds the expectations of many others. It would seem very unusual to a guest if Chardonnay were not available by the glass, even though you may stock a perfectly acceptable wine that would compare in profile to a Chardonnay. A comprehensive wine program would include the Chardonnay that the guest expects but also provide an appropriate alternative that the guest could also enjoy such as Pinot Blanc. The challenge faced by industry professionals is to meet the guests' expectations by providing them the wines they seek, while also educating them about similar wines with which they are less familiar.

The wines poured as the restaurant's house wines should be consistent, quality examples of the varietal or region being offered. Despite the fact that these wines usually are among the most affordable selections on the list, care should be taken to ensure that satisfactory wines are presented. If the operator chooses to pour a wine simply because it is cheap, chances are good that the guest will not enjoy it and will not purchase any more in the future. Wines should be selected that offer a great price-to-quality relationship for both the operator and the customer.

Whenever a new bottle of a wine being offered by the glass is opened, if it has a natural cork, it is a good idea for the bar manager to perform a quick taste test to make sure it is a sound bottle. This important step is overlooked in many establishments because of the extra time and effort it takes. However, it will save the server the embarrassment of being told that the glass they have just served has cork taint, especially if they have just served two other tables a glass of wine from the same bottle. The subject of cork taint is more fully explored in the next chapter.

Responding to Industry Trends

American taste preferences change from year to year and even from month to month. This greatly affects the products that Americans are interested in buying and should directly affect the wines that a restaurant offers to the guests. As buying patterns change, the savvy operator is monitoring industry trends and regularly adapting the list, phasing out those wines that are becoming less fashionable and adding those wines that are gaining in popularity.

A clear example of changing tastes would be the popularity of California Merlot during the mid to late 1980s. The demand and interest in these wines (and Merlots in general) experienced a huge surge in popularity during this time and restaurant wine lists reflected this demand. Then in 2004 the movie *Sideways* was released, where Pinot Noir was touted and Merlot was knocked, and consumer-purchasing trends swung like a pendulum. In the months following the release of *Sideways*, sales of Pinot Noir jumped 15 percent. The fickle nature of the American consumer can seem exasperating to restaurant operators, but it need not be. Simply because a popular movie bashes Merlot and lauds Pinot Noir, everyone does not stop drinking Merlot altogether. However, a wine list that does not contain many Pinot Noirs in the wake of a movie like *Sideways* is certainly missing an opportunity. A simple adjustment would be to add a couple more Pinot labels and perhaps reduce the size of the Merlot section according to guest preferences.

Preserving Open Bottles of Wine

Because the heart and soul of most restaurant wine programs is the by the glass offerings, a critical factor to consider is preserving the opened bottles of wine. Once a bottle of wine is opened, it begins a steady, often rapid decline due to the action of oxygen (oxidation), which can cause the wine to develop a stale or Sherry-like character. Because restaurants have to open a whole bottle of wine to sell a single glass, some system must be in place to ensure that the remaining portion of wine in the bottle remains in good quality until the next glass is sold. In some cases, the whole bottle is sold relatively quickly, and this is not of major concern. Wines sold less frequently, however, are likely to deteriorate before the entire bottle is sold.

Despite the relatively good markup on wines sold by the glass, wasting the unsold portions of the bottle after selling a glass will quickly erode a restaurant's profit margins. The full revenue from selling wines by the glass can only be realized if an operation sells the entire bottle. If half the bottle is wasted due to spoilage, the product cost percentage doubles. The operator can ensure that the entire bottle of wine remains saleable by employing some form of preservation for the open bottles of house wine. Some of the most common systems of preservation are discussed in this section.

Inert Gas

Perhaps the simplest and most affordable method of preserving open bottles of wine is using one of the canisters of inert gas available on the market. **Inert gas** (or nonreactive gas) is a gas that unlike the oxygen that is present in air does not interact with the substances that it contacts. These canisters are relatively affordable, often costing less than $10 and capable of preserving up to several dozen bottles of wine, depending on the canister size and the amount of wine left in the bottle. These canisters usually contain a blend of inert gases (such as nitrogen and carbon dioxide) which form a "blanket" over the wine and displace the oxygen in the bottle. The layer of gas prevents the oxygen from directly contacting the wine, and helps protect the wine from the oxidation that would otherwise occur. When used properly, these gas canisters are capable of preserving opened bottles of wine for several days (Figure 18.5). When using this technique, operators should taste their opened wines on a regular basis to ensure that the wines are holding up sufficiently before they are sold to guests.

FIGURE 18.5

Canisters of inert gas can be used to preserve open bottles of wine and help prevent oxidation. To use, simply insert the plastic tube into the bottle and spray several short bursts inside. Quickly reinsert the cork and the wine is then protected by a blanket of inert gas and will be less susceptible to damage from oxygen.

New England Culinary Institute. Photographer: Paul O. Boisvert

The benefits of this system are obvious: The gas is inexpensive to purchase and easy to use with very little training or time invested. Obviously, it is more effective than using no system at all and if the opened bottles of wine are gassed at the end of the day they will be protected until the next day's service period. For house wines that sell frequently, this is usually all that is needed with the rapid level of turnover. For high-volume wines, the gas system works fine and it is an easy and affordable way for an operation to preserve their open wines. These canisters are also popular with wine drinkers who are dining at home who wish to save unfinished bottle for a few days.

Cabinet Systems

Establishments that are serious about their wine programs may choose to invest in some form of cabinet system for preserving their open bottles of wine. Cabinet systems consist of an inert gas system coupled with a dispenser spigot and tubing to pour the wine. The cabinet and tubing provide a pressurized blanket of gas in the opened bottles and ensure minimal chance of oxidation to the open wines. These systems have advantages and drawbacks that need to be considered before an establishment commits to purchasing one. Depending on the size, the initial investment can be quite pricey, but these systems can help ensure longer term preservation and are therefore more useful with wines served by the glass that don't sell as frequently. Restaurants that invest in these systems are able to open and offer some more expensive bottles by the glass, without having to worry about the shelf life. This can further expand the options for guests by allowing the restaurant to provide some premium wines, usually only available by the bottle, as a glass offering.

There are several different producers of these cabinet style systems, most notably Cruvinet (Figure 18.6). Another advantage of these systems is that a large, polished cabinet system displayed in the dining room or bar area sends a clear message to the guests: we are serious about our wine program. The cabinet systems also give the operator peace of mind because these systems can preserve an opened bottle of wine for a week or more. If an operation does not sell the entire bottle of wine within that time, that bottle should probably not be offered by the glass.

The drawbacks to these systems are less obvious, although they should be considered before investing in one. They tend to be quite costly depending on the model, features, and the size of the unit. Even the basic models cost at least a thousand dollars, and the largest ones can run much more. Aside from the initial investment, these systems can have additional costs tied to upkeep. Because they rely on the presence of

FIGURE 18.6

A Cruvinet wine-dispensing cabinet. These types of cabinets use inert gas to protect the wine in the bottle as it is served over time from a spigot. They can be useful in protecting expensive wines that are sold by the glass.

Coutesy Cruvinet Winebar Company

an inert gas to protect the wine, there is the expenditure of periodically refilling the tank with gas.

Another concern is that in some models, a small amount of wine is trapped in the tubing between the preservative gas and the serving spigot. This wine is not covered by the blanket of gas and is therefore prone to oxidation. This can result in having to "bleed," or pour off, this wine from the line before reaching the preserved wine in the bottle. The amount of wine poured off may not be much, but if the wine being stored in the cabinet cost $100 per bottle, the value of an ounce is about $4. Many operators may choose to preserve only their higher-priced wines in the cabinet system and use a less expensive method to protect their house pours. Because of their expense, they are only common in operations of a certain size and scale.

Vacuum Systems

Various vacuum systems are available, including a simple version for the home and industrial models useful for restaurant settings. A vacuum system consists of a simple rubber stopper with sealed holes in the top and a separate pump that is held on the top of the stopper and pumped several times to remove air from the bottle. The pump works by removing most of the air from the headspace and creating a vacuum seal that minimizes both the presence of oxygen and its destructive effects on the wine. With some of the smaller home systems, a simple hand pump removes most of the air from the bottle (Figure 18.7). These types of vacuum systems are used primarily for short-term storage in the home.

Commercial versions of these vacuum pump systems are available, and they are more efficient at removing more oxygen from the bottle. One such system consists of a wall-mounted electric pump and a set of rubber stoppers. A stopper is placed into the top of an opened bottle of wine, and the bottle is held up to the electric pump. In a matter of seconds, the pump removes the air from the bottle and creates a vacuum seal capable of preserving the wine. This system is simple and quick to use. The initial investment can still be significant, although the upkeep costs really include only the cost of replacing the rubber stoppers as they wear out. It is easy to add additional wines by the glass, as well, because the operator simply has to have extra stoppers to seal the bottles. One disadvantage to vacuum systems is that they can remove any residual

FIGURE 18.7

This hand-operated vacuum can be used to protect un-finished bottles of wine for short periods of time.

© Pat Henderson

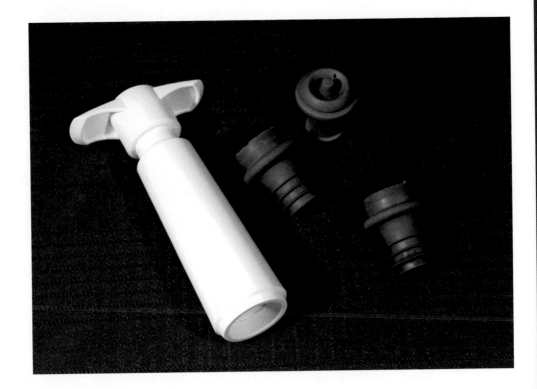

carbon dioxide (CO_2) gas that is still in the wine. Young whites that have not been aged in oak will often have a little bit of CO_2 left over from fermentation that gives the wine a crisp or fresh quality and using a vacuum system will diminish this. For this reason, these types of systems do not work with sparkling wine. Because sparkling wines provide their own inert gas (from their high concentration of CO_2) all they require for short-term storage is a special stopper that is designed to hold in the pressure.

If a restaurant operator is serious about recognizing the profits that can come from its wine program then the operator should be sure to employ some form of preservation system for open bottles of wine. Over the long term, the benefits and potential profits far outweigh the initial investment in a preservation system. Restaurateurs who elect to use no preservation system are risking dumping a portion of their profits down the drain in the form of spoiled wine.

Filling Out the Wine List

After the house wines or by the glass offerings have been decided, it is time to select the wines that will make up the remainder of the list. The key to selecting appropriate wines is to choose those that complement both the style of food offered and the expectations of the clientele that will be purchasing the wine. Having dozens of great French wines does very little for guests choosing wine in an Italian restaurant. Similarly, having many high-priced wines in a popularly priced restaurant might not be the best way to stock a wine list.

When deciding on how many labels and bottles are appropriate for the operation, one of the key things to consider is how much room is available to commit to storing wine. If the answer is very little, then creating a large inventory of wine is not a good idea. If, on the other hand, the operation has reserved a fair amount of space to be used for wine storage, the wine inventory can grow accordingly. Wines that are poured by the glass generally are sold and replaced frequently, so a large amount of storage is less of an issue. Many reserve wines sold by the bottle will remain in inventory for a considerable length of time, and these wines will demand sufficient storage space.

PRICING THE WINE LIST

Perhaps no other aspect of restaurant wine sales is as challenging to management as deciding on an appropriate pricing strategy. There are many different pricing strategies and viewpoints on what is considered an appropriate markup on wine. The markup is the difference between the bottle cost and the selling price. A wine that costs the restaurant $10, and is sold for $30, has a markup of $20. This wine also has a cost percentage of 33 percent ($10/$30 = 0.33). The factors that affect the markup and cost percentage include the restaurant concept and service style, the menu prices for food, the selections offered on the list, and the prices charged by the competition.

On one side of the pricing debate are the proponents of high markups who justify their exorbitant pricing by citing the extremely low profits achieved by most restaurant operations. They also cite the difficulties with purchasing and storing many bottles of fine wine, many of which will be held in storage as "overhead" for months (or years) before they are eventually purchased by a guest. Add to this the hidden costs involved with the service and sale of products to guests and it is tempting to side with the proponents of high markups. This practice is sure to upset the majority of guests, many of whom are very aware of the retail prices of the wines on the list. If a wine costs the restaurateur $12.50 a bottle wholesale, the same bottle would sell for about $20 retail in a wine shop. Consequently, if guests know that they can buy the same bottle of wine for $20 in a store that is offered at the restaurant for $60, they will be unlikely to purchase it no matter how good the food or service. This high markup mars the image of the restaurant and makes guests feel like they are being taken advantage of by high prices. It also ends up producing less revenue in the end as guests decide to purchase less wine because of the high prices.

The other pricing perspective focuses on maintaining fair pricing in an attempt to deliver value to the guests and increase sales with appealing prices. This method of pricing seeks to charge less of a markup in favor of moving a higher volume of wine. This approach takes less profit from an individual bottle but seeks to appeal to a greater number of guests with better prices. It is a classic example of higher volume with lower prices: If more people are able to afford a bottle of wine in the restaurant, more people will buy bottles of wine. Even though the operator may get less money for each bottle sold, over the long term the restaurant will sell more wine, therefore end up with higher wine sales.

In the modern era of wine, technology and a keen focus on quality have enabled producers to create better wines at better prices than at any point in history. This has allowed producers to bottle value brands from all over the world that deliver higher quality, even at the less expensive price points. Consumers can now select from a wide range of bottles priced in the $6 to $10 category at a wine shop, and they are quickly coming to expect a similar level of value in the restaurant setting. Fortunately, restaurant operators have access to the same value wines that consumers have, and this can translate to a wine list offering quality and value at every price point. It is better for a restaurant to set itself apart by having fair, even low, prices on wine than to be known for having high prices.

Sliding Scale Pricing

A **sliding scale** method of pricing takes advantage of the strengths of high markups and the benefits of lower pricing. A sliding scale is a pricing system that utilizes a variety of markups to balance profit for the operation with value for the consumer. In this situation, a restaurant might employ the highest markups on the lowest-priced wines and assign a lower markup on higher-priced wines.

Many operators have begun to focus on lowering their markups on higher-priced wines in a distinct effort to increase sales of those wines. This increases sales of wine and encourages guests to invest in bottles that are more expensive. A restaurant operator may assign a target cost percentage of 35 percent to the wine program. The operator would then assign the lowest tier of wines the highest markup, the middle tier an average markup, and the highest-priced wines the lowest markup. The wines that cost between $6 and $15 per bottle may have a target cost percentage of 25 percent. Wines that cost between $16 and $25 may have a target cost percentage of 35 percent, and those wines that cost above $26 may have a target cost percentage of 45 percent. The average of these three percentages is 35 percent. This method sets a fair price for both the operator and the guests. It also helps generate higher-end bottle sales because the highest-cost wines are marked up the least. The reality with this system is that since more wines are likely to be sold in the lower to middle price points, the overall cost percentage for the program could easily come in below the target of 35 percent.

For wines at the highest end of the price spectrum, an operator may simply assign a **fixed markup** to the cost of the bottle, instead of using the cost percentage method. The fixed markup method assigns a set amount of money to the cost of the bottle to determine the sales price. For example, for wines that cost $100 or more, the additional markup may be fixed at $30. This allows the operator to offer reasonably priced wines to the consumer and ensures that the operator is receiving a fair markup on its wines. This system is occasionally employed at all price points on wine lists, but is more common at the higher price points.

Incentives

Just as a perceptive operator will work to drive wine sales through the marketing of the wine program, restaurateurs who wish to increase the number of bottles of wine sold will create incentives to encourage guests to purchase bottles. One such incentive might be to offer 20 percent off all bottles of wine from the list on a given day of the week. Many restaurants now take this to another level, and offer half-priced bottles from the list on certain nights of the week. The operator is willing to drastically reduce its profits from selling the bottle in order to get people in the door, and it hopes to build customer loyalty every night of the week. These promotions can be done on slower days of the week, thereby increasing both the number of guests during these slower periods and wine sales overall. A promotion can even be tied to special menus, such as when running a special Italian dish, offering 10 percent off bottles of Italian wine. This type of selective marketing can be very effective at increasing both wine sales and guest traffic; however, incentives involving alcohol are prohibited by law in some areas.

One common mistake is to choose and price wines out of the range of affordability of the customers. If the average check per person is about $15, then having most selections priced above $50 will not encourage guests to purchase bottles of wine. By tailoring pricing to the clientele and service level, a wine list can be priced affordably and will be more effective at generating sales. A good rule of thumb is to price the bulk of your wines near the average check (excluding alcohol) for a party of two. This price bracket represents the "sweet spot" for wine sales. The sweet spot is the price range where the majority of the guests will find relative value and where the bulk of wines should be priced.

For example, if the typical check without alcohol for a party of two is around $30, then pricing the bulk of the wine list around that price point will help customers feel like they are getting value. Knowing that most guests will not purchase the cheapest bottles on the list and that the most expensive ones will be purchased in even smaller quantities allows the operator to put the bulk of the wine offerings into the most popular price brackets. Although there is no specific formula that can be followed for every operation, having a good idea of the clientele and their spending habits will help ensure proper pricing for the list. If the restaurant is a startup operation, trial and error will help find the best pricing methods. Regularly evaluating wine sales will help the operator find the right balance of price for the guest and profit for the operation.

To help understand this, imagine an example where the restaurant list will be set up with 100 selections (or labels) available. For an easy example, assume that 50 of these selections are red and 50 are white. Fifty of these wines would be in the sweet spot for the list, 40 would be just outside the sweet spot, and 10 selections would be in the extreme ends of the pricing. If the sweet spot for the list is in the $40 to $60 price range, then this would allow the operator to select 25 white and 25 red wines priced in this range. The operator would then source 20 white and 20 red wines that are outside of this range—perhaps 10 labels that are above $60 and 10 labels that are in the $25 to $40 range. The operator would then fill in the two extreme ends of the list by choosing five wines that are priced in the highest bracket and five wines that are at the value end of the spectrum.

An operator using this formula can easily choose wines that are appropriate for the setting and are priced to sell. This ensures that the bulk of the available wines are priced to appeal to diners, and it allows a wide enough range of pricing to allow the list to appeal to diners at both ends of the spectrum. As the operator assembles the wine list and analyzes the spending habits of the clientele, selections should be adjusted accordingly, tailoring the list to meet guest demand and to maintain proper profit levels. Using this system, the restaurant is able to assemble a complete wine list that covers the basic price points and appeals to a range of diners.

Providing Options

Part of the reason that guests dine out is that they like choices, and the wine list is no exception. By offering guests a broad selection of wines to choose from, we are able to appeal to many different taste preferences. However, the quest to offer options should not stop with representing different varietals and regions on the wine list; it should also include different pour sizes and possibly even different bottle sizes.

Bottle Formats

Another way to offer the guests choices is to offer wine in several different bottle sizes. One common bottle size is the **half bottle** (12.7 oz [375 ml]), which is half the volume of a traditional bottle (25.4 oz [750 ml]) and contains enough wine for about two glasses. Half bottles encourage guests who would not normally order a whole bottle of wine to order a bottle rather than a glass, and the reduced size can accommodate a couple who wishes to have a glass of wine with their meal but does not want to invest in (or consume) a full bottle. Some people may choose to try two different half bottles so they can enjoy one wine with the appetizers and another different wine with the main course. Because half bottles are usually priced at a little over half the cost of a full bottle, some diners may elect to try a more expensive wine at a lower cost. Half bottles are sometimes referred to as "splits"; however, in the case of sparkling wines a split refers to a quarter bottle (6.4 oz [187 ml]).

As previously mentioned, the traditional bottle size is 25.4 oz (750 ml), which contains enough wine for 4 to 5 glasses. This is the most common size of bottle and the one that our guests have come to expect. A **magnum** (50.7 oz [1.5 liters]) is a good choice for parties of four or more because it contains the same volume of wine as two regular size bottles. These are the smallest bottles in the large format category. **Large format** bottles are those that are larger than the traditional 750 ml bottles. Magnums contain 8 to 10 glasses of wine, so they are best sold to larger parties who would otherwise order two bottles of the same wine. Offering magnums demonstrates a diverse and complete wine list and can appeal to larger parties looking to purchase wine.

Even larger bottle sizes are also available, although they are somewhat rarer, especially in most restaurant settings (Figure 18.8). Very large bottles tend to be impractical in most restaurant settings, because of both the challenges of storing them and of serving them at a table. These bottles can be unwieldy for servers to handle

FIGURE 18.8

These large bottles are great for drawing attention to a restaurant's wine program when put out for display. Large format bottles can also be appealing to larger parties looking to purchase several bottles of one wine.

New England Culinary Institute. Photographer: Paul O. Boisvert

FIGURE 18.9

The three most common bottle shapes, from left to right: Burgundy, Bordeaux, and Hock. The Burgundy bottle with sloped neck is usually used for traditional Burgundian varieties such as Pinot Noir and Chardonnay. The Bordeaux bottle, also called Claret, has more prominent shoulders and is used for traditional Bordeaux varieties such as Cabernet Sauvignon. Finally, the tall and slender Hock bottle is traditionally used for varietals native to Germany and Alsace such as Riesling and Gewürztraminer.

© Pat Henderson

tableside, so special considerations should be taken into account when serving large format wines. (See the section "Tableside Wine Service" in chapter 19 for more detail.) Because large format bottles command high prices and tend to sell infrequently, they usually make up only a small portion of the wine list.

In addition to the wine bottles shown in Figure 18.8, there are also less common large format bottle sizes. The various sizes have names that differ slightly depending on whether the bottle is a Claret shape (Figure 18.9), usually used for red wines, or whether it is used for sparkling wine (Table 18.1).

Offering Samples and Flights

Most restaurant operations will offer guests samples of wine, but the methods for delivering this service vary. Some operations will simply offer a 0.5-oz to 1-oz (15 to 30 ml) taste of a specific wine that the guest has questions about, at no charge. This is very easy if the wine is one of the by the glass offerings. The idea is that the guest is going to purchase a glass of wine but wants to try it before buying it. It could be argued that this is not the best practice financially because every ounce that is given away is going to increase the operation's beverage cost. However, the amount of wine being offered is usually quite small and the ultimate outcome for the restaurant is positive. Guests who are offered a sample of a wine have an increased likelihood of purchasing a glass, whether it is the wine they sampled or another, and they will feel good about their experience.

TABLE 18.1 Standard Bottle Sizes

Number of Standard-Sized Bottles	Volume	Name for Bordeaux-Shaped Bottle	Name for Sparkling Wine Bottle
½	375 ml	Half bottle or "tenth"	Same
1	750 ml	Bottle or "fifth"	Same
2	1.5 L	Magnum	Same
4	3 L	Double magnum	Jéroboam
6	4.5 L	Jéroboam	Rehoboam
8	6 L	Impériale	Methuselah
12	9 L	Usually used for sparkling wine	Salmanazar
16	12 L	Usually used for sparkling wine	Balthazar
20	15 L	Usually used for sparkling wine	Nebuchadnezzar

One way to address the guests' desire to sample wine is to offer various pour sizes for all house wines. If guests are allowed to order a 1-, 3-, or 5-oz (30-, 60-, or 150-ml) glass, they can select the amount of each wine that they would like. The management simply prices the wines by the ounce; this allows the guests to sample the wines that they desire and allows the operation to generate sales from every ounce of wine that is poured.

A **wine flight** is a selection of wines offered together as a package. The general goal of offering a flight of wines is to allow guests to compare the wines and discern differences among them. A flight might include three Merlots from three countries, encouraging a comparative tasting of the same grape from three distinct climates or regions. A typical white wine flight might consist of three Chardonnays, one produced with no oak influence, one produced with a little oak, and one that employs lots of oak in the profile. By serving these three wines together, guests can analyze the effect that oak has on the wine and decide which one they like best. The experience is enjoyable and informative, allowing guests to formulate their own opinions as they experience and learn about the differences between the wines.

In general, flights are offered in smaller portion sizes than regular wines by the glass. This is practical since serving a guest three full glasses of wine at once would be irresponsible and could easily result in the guest becoming intoxicated. Additionally, by the time the guest has finished one glass of white wine, the other two glasses may be too warm to be fully enjoyed (obviously this is less of a concern with red wines). Usually the pour size for a flight of wines is 2 to 3 oz (60 to 90 ml) of each wine. This is enough to allow a good taste of each, but the total amount is little more than a full glass of wine. Pouring in this amount also allows guests to follow up by ordering an additional glass of the wine they enjoyed the most.

Organizing the List

Even though they may not always ask, many guests appreciate assistance when selecting wine for their meal. Staff members can offer this guidance, but the structure and layout of the list can also help guests to find the wine they are looking for. The way in which a wine list is structured reflects the goals of the operation and directly affects the manner in which guests find wines that they are interested in purchasing. There are many different ways to configure wine list, depending on the style of restaurant and the objectives of the proprietor. Some of the most common methods for wine list layout will be discussed in this section. In most cases, there is no best single method to use and the wine list layout may include several different aspects of the styles listed as follows.

By Region of Origin

Wine lists that are organized strictly by region would include a separate section for each of the major world wine regions represented on the list (Figure 18.10). This type of list would include a section for French wines, another section for Italian wines, and so forth. Each section would be further divided, such as Bordeaux, Burgundy, Rhône Valley, and Champagne for France. The benefits to this type of layout include the ability of guests to find wines quickly and conveniently from regions that they prefer. For

FIGURE 18.12

By grouping various wines according to their style and body, the guests can choose a wine that suits their preferences. This list groups together "light, crisp white wines" from various countries.

© 2012 Delmar Cengage Learning

Wine List Organized by Style

White Wines

Light-Bodied, Crisp Whites		Prices
Bordeaux, France	Château Haut Rian *Sauvignon Blanc*	$26
Marlborough, New Zealand	Brancott *Sauvignon Blanc*	$40
Friuli, Italy	Anselmi *Pinot Grigio*	$22

Medium-Bodied Whites		
Willamette Valley, Oregon	King Estate *Pinot Gris*	$30
Clare Valley, Australia	Peter Lehmann *Semillion*	$38
Napa Valley, California	Ferari Carano *Fumé Blanc*	$50

Full-Bodied, Rich Whites		
Sonoma, California	Sonoma Cutrer *Chardonnay*	$36
Mosel, Germany	JJ Prum *Riesling* Auslese	$74
Wachau, Austria	Hiedler *Gruner Veltliner*	$55

Red Wines

Light-Bodied, Fruity Reds		
Burgundy, France	Louis Jadot Beaujolais *Gamay*	$25
Willamette Valley, Oregon	Adelsheim *Pinot Noir*	$48
Veneto, Italy	Bolla *Bardolino*	$20

Medium-Bodied Reds		
Rioja, Spain	Marques de Caceres *Tempranillo*	$30
Chianti, Italy	Rufina *Chianti Classico*	$52
McLaren Vale, Australia	d'Arenberg "Custodian" *Grenache*	$37

Full-Bodied, Rich Reds		
Napa Valley, California	Cakebread *Cabernet Sauvignon*	$84
Ribera del Duero, Spain	Casa L'Ermita *Tempranillo*	$38
Rhône Valley, France	Guigal *Châteauneuf-du-Pape*	$65

This also helps expose less experienced customers to new wines. For example, a guest looking for an Italian Pinot Grigio in the "Light-bodied, crisp whites" section might stumble across a New Zealand Sauvignon Blanc that he or she wasn't familiar with. As both wines are in the selected category, the guest may be encouraged to try a new wine and find that they like it.

By Price Point

Some wine lists are organized according to price point, with the lowest-priced wines being listed first and increasingly more expensive wines down the list. This method allows guests to easily access wines that they can afford, but it also encourages them to select their wines based on price. It also discourages them from browsing the entire list because the natural tendency is to identify the upper limit of the budget and to select a bottle from that point or below. This may seem like a minor issue, but if guests are made aware of the full breadth of selections on the list regardless of price, it may encourage them to return for the more expensive bottle in the future. Often wines are arranged by price within a larger group. For example, if the wine list were arranged by varietal, the Pinot Noirs would be listed in ascending price.

Using Wine Descriptions and Recommendations

One of the key factors when deciding on the layout and design of a wine list is whether to include tasting descriptions on the list. Obviously, if space is an issue because of a large number of wines on the list, descriptors may not be an option. However, if space is less of a concern, then the operator may choose to have some tasting notes or wine descriptors for each wine in order to help guide guests in their selection. Some people feel very strongly about whether or not to have wine descriptors on the list, but this is partly a decision based on the style of operation as well as the type of clientele that frequents the operation. For example, if the majority of the guests at the operation are new to the world of wine, then descriptors may be very effective at helping them make an appropriate selection. If the majority of the clientele are wine aficionados, however, then a large number of descriptions may not be necessary. It is not uncommon for wine novices to avoid asking their server the details about a wine because they do not want to appear unknowledgeable. By having informative details about the wines being offered, a guest can get the information they need in a more private manner.

If an operator elects to have descriptors on the menu, several things should be considered as they are written. The descriptors should give a basic overview of the style of wine and a general commentary on its aroma and flavor profile. Descriptions should not be too elaborate or creative because this may not help the guest in making a decision, but rather deter or confuse them. The aim is to briefly describe the profile of the wine and guide guests in making a selection that they will be happy with.

One way to market wines on the wine list is to include a section that lists staff favorites or house favorites. This section should include wines priced in the sweet spot of the list and those wines that are excellent examples of their style or varietal. These could be wines chosen by the staff during tastings or those that offer exceptional price-to-quality ratios. Drawing attention to these wines in a special section makes them stand out and draws the guests' attention to them. Moreover, if the staff is involved in helping select the wines for this section, they take some ownership of these wines and will be encouraged to sell them.

Putting It All Together

Perhaps the best method for laying out the wine list employs a combination of these methods, with the addition of some descriptions designed to guide the guests in selecting their wine. An excellent, comprehensive layout could include a regional heading with varietal subheadings. In the white wine section of the list, this may include a heading for France, with subheadings for the main varietals, including Chardonnay, Sauvignon Blanc, Muscadet, and so forth. This allows the guests to focus on both the region of origin as well as the primary grapes used, and helps to guide those guests who desire Chardonnay but do not know that white Burgundy wines are made from Chardonnay. Accompanying the Burgundy listings could be a description to help inform the guest of the style of Chardonnay and to give key profile descriptors.

Restaurants that focus on a certain style of cuisine should make extra efforts to have the wine list reflect its concept. Italian cuisine tends to work very well with Italian wines, and the regional connection between local food and wine should not be overlooked. In addition, if the restaurant is located in a wine-producing region patrons will most likely be looking to find a good selection of local wines. In both of these cases, however, even if wine from a particular region dominates the list, there still should be an offering of some wines from outside the region to provide guests with various options.

List Formats

Once the wines are selected and the pricing strategy decided, the actual format should be chosen. The most common method of presenting the wine list to the customer is in some form of booklet or menu holder. Menu holders often contain clear plastic sheets that display the typed list. The wine list is typed on sheets of paper and inserted into the menu presenter. This method has some key benefits—namely the ability to change and update the list at a moment's notice. Because the inventory of wine can change frequently, it is critical to be able to update the list regularly. Nothing is worse than a guest deciding on a wine after much deliberation, only to then be informed that it is out of stock.

Some restaurants present their wine list in a formal, bound-book style format. These lists have a nice look and feel to them, but the ability to change and update selections can be somewhat limited. There is even one restaurant in Washington, DC, that has eliminated the actual list altogether; it simply displays the bottles on a stand in the dining room and guests are encouraged to browse the table, looking at the labels and selecting a wine simply by seeing the bottles. More informal establishments with fewer wines on the list may simply devote a page of their food menu to a listing of their wine selections. Another method is to list the house wines and by the glass offerings on the food menu and have a separate wine list with a complete listing of all the wines that are available by the bottle. Regardless of the manner in which you present your wine list to the guest, it should meet both the objectives of the wine program and the desires of the guest. Being creative allows the guests to feel that the experience is special and allows the operator to respond to changing labels and inventory levels.

STORING AND AGING WINE

After the wines for the list are selected and purchased, they must be stored in a well-organized manner that allows easy access. Additionally wine, like any other perishable product at the restaurant, must be stored under the proper conditions to prevent it from spoiling. The wine storage area, or "cellar" as it is traditionally known, must provide conditions for ideal development as the wine ages as well as ensure the wine is in the optimum condition when it is ready to be opened.

Temperature and Humidity Control

Proper control of the cellar temperature and humidity is of the utmost importance to preserving a fine wine's character (and value) as it is stored or aged. The best range of temperatures to store wine is between 55° and 60°F (12.8° and 15.6°C). Wines stored outside these temperatures run the risk of less than ideal development, and if the temperature becomes too warm, they can spoil before being opened. High-volume wines that are popular with the customers should be stored in a manner where they can be easily retrieved. Likewise there should be enough inventory of the popular white wines, stored at a temperature where they are ready to serve, to meet the expected short-term demand.

High-end restaurants often have a custom-built cellar created to house their wine (Figure 18.13). These expansive (and expensive) cellars often employ a temperature control unit, similar to an air conditioner, which regulates the internal temperature and humidity of the cellar to keep it within the ideal range. Setting up the proper environmental conditions for wine storage may be costly, but it is relatively inexpensive compared to the money wasted when special bottles of wine spoil. These units can be installed in many different storage spaces, and some companies now specialize in the design of custom cellar spaces. Custom-designed cellars usually cost at least several thousand dollars, and in some restaurant settings, the investment is worth the return. In restaurants with these cellar spaces, the area can function as an event room and as a marketing tool for the restaurant's wine program. When the operation has invested tens or hundreds of thousands of dollars in wine inventory, proper storage conditions are a necessity.

Humidity control is also important when storing wine because the corks that provide the airtight seal on wine bottles can dry out without enough humidity. The ideal level of humidity is relatively high, usually in the 70 to 80 percent range. The drying of the corks can cause oxygen to enter the bottle and spoil the wine. This is particularly significant when the wines are being aged for a long period of time. Higher levels of humidity can cause mold to form on the bottle labels; although this is unsightly, in

FIGURE 18.13

This custom wine cellar is beautifully designed and includes a small wine tasting area. It employs a temperature and humidity control unit to ensure optimum conditions to store and age wine.

Royalty Free/Corbis

most cases it does not affect the integrity of the wine in the bottle. A thermometer and hygrometer (humidity-monitoring device) should be kept in the storage space to regularly monitor the cellar environment.

Passive Cellars

For establishments that are lucky enough to have a basement to store their wine, this space can function as a great space to store the collection. A **passive cellar** is a storage area that does not employ any type of temperature or humidity control system to maintain consistent levels (Figure 18.14). The success of these cellars relies on the ambient temperature and humidity readings staying within an acceptable range to ensure that the wine ages safely. These cellars may experience fluctuations in both temperatures and humidity, depending on the season and even the time of day. These fluctuations should be slight enough that it does not affect the development of the wine, but in extreme situations the longevity of the wine can be at risk. Passive cellars are beneficial because the owner does not need to purchase and maintain a temperature control unit, so the initial start-up expense is less. The drawbacks to passive cellars can be numerous, but temperature and humidity fluctuations are the biggest concern. Additionally if the

FIGURE 18.14

This passive cellar is in a cool basement that provides the ideal storage conditions without the use of a temperature control system.
© Pat Henderson

wine is stored in a remote basement, the wine will not be as readily available to servers and not serve as a visual enticement for sales.

Racking and Security

Within the room for wine storage, some type of racking is necessary (Figure 18.15). Although this does not need to be expensive, it is critical to allow easy access to the wines as they are ordered by the guests. The racking often corresponds to **bin numbers**, which are an easy reference point for locating specific wines. As a guest orders a certain wine, it can be found in the numbered bin. Neck tags that can be labeled with the producer and vintage are also readily available and reasonably priced, and they allow service staff to select the appropriate wines quickly and accurately. The bin numbers can also be displayed alongside the wine on the wine list. The advantage here is a guest who is unsure how to pronounce the name of a winery or variety can request the wine by its bin number.

A safety factor with wine storage that must be considered is securing the wine inventory away from employee theft and misuse. Theft can occur in many situations, whether from an unscrupulous bartender deliberately misstating inventory or from wayward servers taking a bottle as an after-shift perk. Misuse can occur when the new line cook grabs a bottle of a '06 Chablis Grand Cru instead of the box of Chablis that is used for cooking in the kitchen. Although it may sound far-fetched, stranger things have happened. Any wine storage should be able to be secured with a lock, and access to the wine should be limited to management and bar staff.

FIGURE 18.15

These labeled bins allow easy access to stored wines. This method of storage allows service staff to find bottles quickly and easily when they are ordered during service. The bin numbers are sometimes included on restaurant wine lists.

Royalty Free/Corbis

Older Wine and Restaurants

Clearly, very few restaurant operations have the space required to age wines for years, and the financial investment required for such aging can also be prohibitive. Furthermore, not every restaurant will have customers who expect offerings of older fine wines, and the demand for these products should be evaluated before making a large investment for the list. For a few fine dining establishments with customers who are willing to pay an extra price for well-aged wines, the returns may be worth the investment. When serving older wines tableside they present several challenges that are more fully described in the section on decanting in Chapter 19.

SUMMARY

Choosing wines for the list and deciding on appropriate pricing can be a daunting task. By starting with a good idea of the spending habits of the guests, the competition's prices, and the goals for the operation, management can create a complete and diverse list that offers potential profit for the restaurant and perceived value for the customers. There is no specific formula for creating a list; it can be highly individualized based on the specific operation. If management sets goals for the wine program before starting, they can make their decisions based on their desired outcomes. Regardless of the format and pricing, guests should feel that they are being offered value, while the operator focuses on selling more wine. After the wines for the list are selected and purchased, they must be stored in an area that will provide the proper environmental conditions to preserve their quality as well as allow convenient access for servers.

EXERCISES

1. List some of the key factors to consider before creating a restaurant wine list.

2. Identify several pricing methods for wines sold by the bottle. How is pricing by the bottle different from pricing wines sold by the glass?

3. How would a restaurateur decide which wines to put on a wine list and which wines might not be good on the list?

4. Describe the various methods that can be used to preserve open bottles of wine and their advantages and disadvantages.

5. What considerations should be taken into account when selecting wines for the by the glass list?

REVIEW QUESTIONS

1. Which of the following is not a method used to preserve partially full wine bottles?
   A. Vacuum system
   B. Decanter
   C. Inert gas
   D. Cabinet system

2. For wine being sold by the glass, how should the glass be filled?
   A. One-quarter full, so the customer can easily swirl the glass
   B. To the brim, so the customers know they are getting their money's worth
   C. A balance between glass size and pour size must be found that gives the perception of value
   D. Fill size is set to 5 oz per glass by law

3. A standard-sized wine bottle holds ____.
   A. 12.7 oz (375 ml)
   B. 25.4 oz (750 ml)
   C. 33.9 oz (1 L)
   D. 50.8 oz (1.5 L)

4. Which of the following is not a common method of organizing a wine list?
   A. By vintage
   B. By variety
   C. By region
   D. By wine style

5. The majority of the wines on a wine list should be priced per bottle at a point roughly equal to ___.
   A. The average total cost of entrées for a table of four
   B. Twice the cost of the least expensive bottle of wine on the list
   C. The cost of the most expensive food item on the menu
   D. The average check for a party of two not counting alcohol

{ SELLING AND
SERVING WINE }

This chapter outlines the

fundamentals of selling and serving wine in a restaurant setting. It first describes the basic steps an establishment can take to promote a wine program, and how the sommelier and wait staff can aid guests in the selection of a bottle of wine that they will enjoy. Next, it explains the procedure for proper tableside wine service, followed by a section on staff training and how it can be used to ensure that all of the objectives of the restaurant's wine program are being met. The chapter concludes with a segment on the principles of responsible hospitality.

INTRODUCTION

The selling and serving of wine in a restaurant setting is distinctly different from enjoying a bottle of wine at home or at a friend's house. When a guest chooses to purchase a glass or bottle of wine in a restaurant, she makes a conscious decision to do so for a variety of reasons. This process is greatly influenced by the management of the restaurant and the manner in which they present their wine program to the guests. The sale is further supported and executed by the service staff, and all pieces need to be in place to ensure a helpful and seamless delivery of product to the customers.

Proper execution of the sales and service of wine in the restaurant is no accident; to the contrary, it is the culmination of many hours of preparation and planning, staff training, and a sizable investment on the part of the operation. It is not difficult to start a concise and inclusive wine program in a restaurant setting; it simply takes a plan and dedication on the part of the management and service team. The first step is to commit to providing superior wine service to the guests, and then to formulate a plan of action.

WINE SERVICE AND THE ROLE OF THE SOMMELIER

Throughout history, the role of promoting wine sales and ensuring appropriate wine service has often been the job of the **sommelier**. Historically the sommelier was responsible for stocking and maintaining the provisions and ensuring that products being served were sound and had not spoiled (MacNeil, 2001). This role has changed considerably through the years, and the modern view of the sommelier focuses on supporting the guest in the restaurant wine experience. This can involve design and

FIGURE 19.1

Many factors contribute to a restaurant developing a successful wine program. The most important is having an attentive and knowledgeable serving staff.

© Andresr/Shutterstock

printing of the wine list, acquiring and maintaining inventory, and selling and serving the wine tableside, as well as suggesting appropriate wine and food pairings.

Today this role is occasionally undertaken by a full-time, well-trained staff member whose focus is solely on the wine program, but not every operation can afford this level of commitment. In the vast majority of operations, the duties of a sommelier may be divided between the manager, service staff, and bar manager. Several people may help access and purchase wine, maintain inventory, develop the wine list, and sell the wine tableside. All staff must be prepared to discuss wine with, and sell it to the guests in order to support the wine program. In an establishment that is part of a chain of restaurants, the role may be taken on by a corporate wine buyer in the home office who establishes the core list and buys the wines for all of the chain's outlets.

Once guests have chosen to purchase a wine, steps must be taken to ensure prompt delivery of the wines to the table, proper presentation of the chosen bottle, and ongoing support of the guest's experience. Restaurant staff can do several things to make certain that the guests receive maximum enjoyment from their wine selection. Servers and sommeliers have the most direct impact on this process, but everyone from the bartender to the dining room manager can play a positive role. The proper execution of wine service further reinforces an operation's dedication to the guest experience and can easily build strong customer loyalty.

PROMOTING SUCCESSFUL WINE SALES

Why would guests who visit a restaurant choose to spend twice or even three times as much money for a bottle of wine in our operation than they would spend for the very same bottle at a retail store? The answer to this question lies in the level of service provided and the ability to deliver added value to their purchase. The concept of added value relates to the fact that a guest may pay more for a product, but the execution and delivery of that product enables them to get more as well. Adding value to the guest experience takes different forms in each operation. For example, the chef has worked to prepare and to offer distinct, flavorful, and unique dishes that the guests cannot easily replicate in their own kitchens. Even if a chef gives out recipes, the techniques employed in the kitchen, the inviting décor, and the fine level of service is difficult to match in the home. For the wine drinker, added value is measured differently. Value is added for these customers by having appropriate, polished glassware; by having attentive, knowledgeable servers who will open and pour the wine; and by having a professional level of service supporting the sale of wine through to the end of a meal.

From the time they arrive until the time they leave, the guests should be supported in their enjoyment and appreciation of the meal and the wine by the service staff. The guests have the opportunity to be entertained and educated by the staff, and they are able to pair a delicious wine of their choice with the entrée of their choice, prepared by a skilled chef. Both the wine and the food can benefit from this pairing. If the service supports this potential, the guests will be truly impressed and will feel like the money was well spent; if any piece is not satisfactory, the guests are not likely to return. If they do choose to return, they are unlikely to want to make the same level of investment

Using wine displays as part of dining room decor presents challenges however. To start, the vast majority of dining rooms are much warmer than the ideal temperature for wine storage. Storing the bulk of the wine inventory in the dining room guarantees that it will be kept too warm unless a temperature control system is used. This not only risks the longevity and quality of the wine, but also means that most of the wine may be served too warm. Wine served too warm does not have the quality or character that is demonstrated when it is served at the proper temperature. Another challenge inherent in dining room wine racking is access by servers or sommeliers. If the wine is not easily accessible by the service staff, it can cause a myriad of problems. Delivery of wine to a table could be delayed because the server has to spend extra time trying to locate the bottle ordered. If the bottle is near another table, that table might be inconvenienced when the service staff works around them to retrieve the selected bottle.

Despite these concerns, visible wine racking serves the same purpose as a display bottle of wine or a table tent announcing a special wine: high visibility and suggestive selling. A well-designed and appealing wine racking system or a designated wine room is sure to help stimulate wine sales. Guests who are wine enthusiasts may particularly enjoy sitting in a special wine room because of its unique ambiance.

Wine Dinners

A special event that showcases wine is an excellent method of promoting a restaurant's wine program. For example, management may work with the chef to organize wine and food pairing events, such as a **wine dinner**. A wine dinner usually has a number of courses each paired with a particular wine that is chosen to complement the course and are presented on prix fixe (fixed price) basis. Weekly or monthly wine dinners bring in revenue and offer diners a unique event outside the ordinary offerings of the restaurant. Winery representatives such as winemakers or salespersons may be available to host the dinners and provide firsthand information about the wine. If the wine dinners are offered on slower nights, they can help generate sales on otherwise quiet evenings with little effect on regular seating and kitchen performance.

Bringing Their Own Bottle

Many restaurants allow guests to bring their own bottle of wine from home to enjoy with their meal. Some operations allow this because they do not have a license that allows them to sell liquor on their premises. Other restaurants that do offer a wine list may allow guests to bring their own wine but charge the guests a fee for doing so, called a **corkage fee**. Corkage fees usually range from $10 to $20 and help to compensate for the loss of a sale from the restaurant's own wine list as well as cover the costs associated with the server's efforts and providing glassware. If a customer brings in a bottle of wine to a fine dining restaurant, more often than not it is a unique bottle that may have special significance to the guest. It is also likely that the customer is a knowledgeable consumer of wine and the server should treat the patron's wine with the same respect that is given to the wines offered on the wine list.

However, this practice is not allowed by all states, and one should be sure to check with the state liquor board to be certain that it complies with state law before guests are allowed to bring their own bottles. Regardless of state law, some operations choose not to allow corkage, in an effort to sell their own inventory of wine.

TABLESIDE WINE SERVICE

The presentation of the wine to guests, from wine glasses to pouring, is important to the enjoyment of their meal and is perhaps the most important aspect of a restaurant's wine program.

Glasses First

The first consideration when preparing to serve wine to a table is the glassware that the wine will be served in. There are almost as many different types of wine glasses as there are types of wine. Any wine glass should be large enough to accommodate the amount of wine being poured without the glass being filled to the rim, to allow the aroma to develop within the bulb of the glass. In any size glass, the amount of wine should never be more than about two-thirds of the space in the glass; an ideal amount is more like half to one-third the volume of the glass. As guests swirl the wine in their glasses the surface area is increased and the aromatic components of the wine are released. Without releasing these volatile constituents, the wine will smell less pungent and will not show very much of its character.

An exception to this standard fill level would be with those glasses used for a restaurant's house wines served by the glass. In this case, perceived value to the guest is almost as important as the ability to appreciate the wine's aromas. Many times, wines offered by the glass arrive at the table in a small- to medium-sized glass that is filled almost to the rim. Although this makes the guest feel that they are getting a good value for the dollar, the ability to swirl the wine and fully appreciate the aroma is greatly diminished. As discussed in Chapter 18, the restaurant needs to find the balance between perceived value and full enjoyment of the wine. The perception of value is most important for wines being sold by the glass, when a wine is purchased by the bottle the consumers know exactly how much wine they are getting for their money. As previously mentioned, using a small carafe in this situation allows the server to pour the glass to the proper fill height and the guests to feel like they are getting their money's worth.

The size and shape of the bowl on the wine glass is as much a matter of preference as it is practicality. Although there are specific types of glasses for almost every type of wine, few restaurants actually have the money to invest in more than a couple styles of glass. It is widely accepted that most wines smell and taste best in the appropriate wine glass. For instance, there is a marked difference between a Pinot Noir that is tasted in a glass with a tall, narrow bowl and the same Pinot tasted in the bulbous glass actually designed for the varietal. In addition to glasses for table wine, the restaurant should also have a supply of sparkling wine flutes and smaller glasses for dessert and fortified wines if they are a part of the wine list.

In some cases, restaurants may simply have one multipurpose glass that is used for every situation. This is less than ideal, but it is a situation often encountered in more value-oriented establishments. Many operators are hesitant to invest in expensive have access to service linens that are used during the process of wine presentation. The linen should be clean and folded, draped over the server's arm as they approach the table. A white wine service should use a white linen and a red wine a red linen; having red wine spots staining a white linen is unsightly, and a red linen does not highlight the color of the white wine. The linen is used to wipe the neck of the bottle and to prevent wine from dripping onto the table or the guests as the server pours for the party.

Removing the Cork

After the guest has confirmed that the wine being presented is the proper wine, the server should proceed to open it for the guests. The process of opening should be consistent among staff members. Service staff should all be trained on the proper method of opening wine tableside, and they should be allowed to practice until they feel comfortable with the techniques. Servers should always open bottles of wine in front of the table; bottles should never be opened in the back station and then brought to the table already opened (Figure 19.9). This may make the guest suspicious about when the bottle was opened and why it was not presented to the table first. Additionally, if the server has mistakenly grabbed the wrong bottle, there is no chance for the guest to ask for the correct bottle because the wrong one has already been opened.

Using the knife on the wine key, the server should proceed to cut the foil on the lip of the bottle (Figure 19.10). There are several techniques used to cut the foil, depending on the style of service desired. Some wine opener sets come with a foil cutter, a crescent-shaped device with rollers inside, that is rotated around the neck of the bottle. The rollers make a clean cut on the foil and allow it to be easily removed, but they also require the server to carry one more piece of equipment. The blade on the wine key works fine and it is very effective at removing the foil. The server can cut either above or below the lip of the bottle. Cutting below the lip is preferred because it helps prevent pieces of the foil from falling into the guests' glass of wine and because securing the knife under the lip gives better control, allowing a clean cut of the foil.

Bottles of wine are sometimes sealed with a wax-based coating instead of the traditional foil capsule (Figure 19.11). This wax coating may take the form of a small disc of wax that simply covers the top of the cork, or it could be more elaborate and involve a significant area of wax at the top of the bottle. Either way, servers are often tempted to cut the wax and attempt to remove it; this usually ends up creating a waxy mess on the bottle and leaves chipped wax on the table. Instead, service staff should be trained to ignore the wax and simply insert the worm of their wine key into the wax as if it were not there. As the cork is removed from the bottle, the wax is removed as

FIGURE 19.9

The process of presenting the wine to the guest allows her to confirm that it is the correct bottle and vintage. The server should identify the vintner, varietal (or blend), and vintage as the bottle is presented to the guest.

New England Culinary Institute. Photographer: Paul O. Boisvert

FIGURE 19.10

Using the blade on the wine key, the foil should be cleanly cut below the lip of the bottle and removed to allow access to the cork.

New England Culinary Institute. Photographer: Paul O. Boisvert

FIGURE 19.11

Some producers use wax blends instead of foil to seal their bottles. This bottle has a handy pull-tab to allow removal of the wax top.

New England Culinary Institute. Photographer: Paul O. Boisvert

well. This process is usually less messy than trying to remove the wax. Servers should then use their service linen to wipe the remaining wax from around the lip of the bottle prior to pouring.

Once the foil or wax is removed, the spiral or "worm" of the corkscrew can be used to remove the cork. Placing the point of the worm in the center of the cork ensures that it will enter the cork in the middle and allow easier extraction of the cork (Figure 19.12). The worm is twisted into the cork until about half a turn remains (Figure 19.13). It is important to insert the worm far enough into the cork to guarantee proper purchase to extract the cork without breaking it in half. However, the worm should not go all the way through the bottom of the cork because it can dislodge pieces of cork that get into the wine. Particularly old or brittle corks can cause a film of floating cork that is unsightly and may be offensive to the guests. At the very least, this can convey a lack of experience or focus on the part of the server.

After the worm is used to safely remove the cork from the bottle, the cork should be removed from the worm and presented on the guest's right side, either on a small

FIGURE 19.15

The server should pour a small (1- to 2-oz [30 to 60 ml]) sample for the host to evaluate and check for off-aromas or flaws.
New England Culinary Institute. Photographer: Paul O. Boisvert

of assuming that the man at the table or the eldest member of the dining party will be testing the wine.

In a situation where a party has ordered both a white and a red wine, the server should be sure to bring two glasses for the host to use for tasting, so that the residue from the first wine does not interfere with the second wine. If a party orders a second bottle of the same wine, it is appropriate for the server to bring a new glass for the host to sample the fresh bottle. If the wine is the same as the first bottle, it is not necessary to replace the guests' glasses with new ones.

The host smells and tastes the wine sample to determine if the wine is sound or if it is flawed in some way. Some aroma flaws such as cork taint are readily apparent as soon as the bottle is opened, but others may develop in intensity as the wine is exposed to air in the glass. If the cork has not made an adequate seal, the bottle may leak or the wine may have been exposed to excess air through the cork. While a sound cork does allow a small degree of exposure to the air helping the wine to age, excess oxygen will cause the wine to take on a Sherry-like or oxidized character. Older wines will often have a slight degree of oxidized character even if they have had a sound cork. As discussed earlier, the most common flaw encountered is likely to be cork taint, which is caused by the cork itself.

Sending Back the Wine

In cases where the guest chooses to send the wine back, prior to removing the bottle from the table, the server should find out why the guest is dissatisfied with the wine. There are many reasons why a guest may choose to refuse the wine selection, and each one has a different solution. For example, a situation where the guest simply doesn't find the style enjoyable will need to be resolved very differently from one where a guest feels that a particular wine is flawed, although both cases should result in replacement of the bottle. If the guest is disappointed by the style of wine, a knowledgeable staff member should make a concerted attempt to help the guest choose a replacement more to his or her liking. This should be undertaken by a manager or sommelier preferably, or at least someone who has enough knowledge to properly guide the guest through the options available on the list. If the guest feels the wine is faulty, however, then the bar or service manager should evaluate the faulty bottle and offer a replacement bottle of the same wine immediately.

Resolving guest dissatisfaction with a selected bottle of wine should be taken seriously and addressed as promptly as any other issue that arises during the service period. Prompt and proper resolution of the complaint can be very effective at showing guests that we care and that every aspect of their experience matters. If the wine truly is flawed, it can be used to educate staff in the detection of flawed wine or it could be sent back to the distributor for credit, so there is no excuse for not taking back a bottle that guests find unsatisfactory. It should be noted, however, that it is in bad taste for guests to refuse a bottle simply because it is "not what they expected." If guests have a question about a style of wine, they should feel comfortable requesting information or guidance from the service staff. Guests can also be offered a small taste of a wine from the by the glass list to see if they would like to order a bottle of it. Opening several bottles of wine to try to find one that the guests like is not an efficient way to run a wine program.

In the case of an extremely rare or expensive bottle of wine that is sold "as is," returning the bottle may not be allowed by the operation. If a special bottle of wine is virtually irreplaceable, the guest may be expected to pay for it, regardless of the condition of the bottle once it is opened. Obviously, this is a relatively rare situation, but it may arise. With properly trained staff who work to help the guest make appropriate selections, however, the chances of a guest refusing a bottle of wine can be greatly lessened.

Pouring the Wine

After the guest has smelled and tasted the sample portion, they should indicate permission for the server to pour for the other guests at the table. Once the host has approved, the server should proceed to pour the wine for the guests, making sure to pour for ladies first, then the gentlemen, and ending with the host. A typical pouring may involve serving the ladies first in a clockwise direction, then circling back around the table in a counterclockwise pattern while pouring for the gentlemen, and ending with the host, leaving the bottle at this position on the table. The server should pour from the guests' right side unless otherwise restricted.

With larger-sized groups (6 to 10), the server should be sure to pour enough so each guest receives an appropriate amount, but not so much that the bottle is empty by the time the host is served. If the pour size is controlled properly, all guests can be served some wine without the immediate need for another bottle. A classic example of bad etiquette is to not have enough left for the host and then to ask if she would like to order another bottle. Not only does it show a lack of focus, it sends the message to the guests that they are being coerced into spending more money. With groups of a dozen or more, the server should suggest that an additional bottle might be needed when the wine is first ordered.

If the guests order two different bottles, the server should inquire from the host as to the order of preference of delivery. Whites are usually brought before reds, but if two whites or two reds are ordered, the server should prompt the guest for guidance on their preference of delivery. If a white and a red are both to be brought at the same time, be sure to have the host sample the white first so the palate is kept fresh to taste the red (see Chapter 4 for more information on the proper tasting order). It might be possible for another server to assist in the presentation of two bottles simultaneously, to be sure that the guests receive both bottles in a timely fashion. The server should have already asked each guest whether they will be having white or red wine, and so can set appropriate glassware.

A useful tool for service staff who frequently pour bottled wine tableside is a laminated Mylar disc that is rolled up to form a spout and inserted into the neck of the bottle. There are several different brand names associated with these products such as

FIGURE 19.16

This laminated disc is inserted into the neck of the bottle to enable drip-free pouring of the wine.

© Pat Henderson

Pour Discs (Figure 19.16), and they can be ordered with the operation's logo or name imprinted on the side. These discs are very effective at eliminating the drips from pouring wine from the bottle. Since the discs are inexpensive and disposable (although limited reuse is possible), it may also function as a souvenir that the guest is able to take home after the bottle is empty.

Part of the service of wine in the restaurant setting involves the service staff repouring wine for the guests as necessary. This can be a delicate issue with some guests; when in doubt, ask the host what should be done about refilling guests' glasses. Traditional protocol involves the server pouring wine for guests who have emptied their glasses, but no assumption should be made that every guest would like more wine. A simple and effective technique is to approach the guest with the bottle and, prior to pouring into the glass, pause for a second or two. This simple pause allows guests to see that the server is going to pour wine and enables them to decline if they do not want more wine. Some parties may desire to pour the wine themselves and may ask the server not to pour once the initial pouring is done. The wishes of the guests should be honored at all times.

Decanting the Wine

A guest may ask to have an older bottle of wine decanted. Decanting a wine involves separating the wine from the bottle sediment through careful pouring of the wine into a glass container. The process of **decanting** is relatively straightforward but can greatly affect the overall impression and enjoyment of the wine. The vessel used for this process is a type of glass carafe that is called a **decanter**. The decanter is then used to serve the wine after it has been separated from the sediment in the bottle. As described in Chapter 5, as wines age, their composition changes and they often precipitate sediment in the bottle. Although it is harmless, sediment is unsightly and does not taste good. To separate the wine from the gritty deposit it has accumulated during aging is relatively easy, but demands a couple of easily acquired tools and some time on the part of the server.

Service staff should have access to a decanter that can be used for this process. Although there are dozens of styles to choose from, the basic design involves a bulbous bottom and a fluted top (Figure 19.17). The purpose of the bulb is to maximize the surface area of the wine to achieve the optimum level of aeration and release the esters to enhance the aroma profile of the wine. In an ideal situation, a wine that is in need of decanting would have been stood up straight for at least a couple hours and preferably a couple of days to allow the sediment to settle to the bottom of the bottle. In most restaurant settings, the wines that are most in need of decanting have been stored lying down where the sediment has settled along one side of the bottle. Once the bottle is picked up, the sediment is distributed throughout the wine once again, and decanting

FIGURE 19.17

Various sizes and shapes of decanters are available on the market today. These are some of the most common shapes and are used to aerate the wine to increase aromatics.

© Bruce Shippee/Shutterstock

FIGURE 19.18

A candle is traditionally used as a light source for decanting. After the foil has been removed, the bottle is slowly poured into the decanter while the server looks at the flame, visible here as bright red heart-shaped spot, through the neck of the bottle. This allows the server to see any sediment as it reaches the neck and stop pouring before it enters the decanter.

© Pat Henderson

becomes more difficult. It is critical, therefore, that a server or sommelier who is retrieving an older bottle of wine for a guest handle the bottle as gently as possible to avoid stirring up the sediment.

The goal of decanting is to pour the clean wine off the top of this sediment and leave the gritty residue in the bottle. A server decanting tableside should remove the entire foil capsule from the bottle of wine to allow a full view of the neck. A light source should be available for the server; historically this has been a candle, although a small flashlight may be easier to use, depending on the context. The light source is placed on the table and the wine bottle is held above the light as the server pours the wine into the decanter (Figure 19.18). As the wine is poured, the server should watch carefully. As the sediment approaches the neck of the bottle, the server stops pouring so that the sediment does not enter the decanter. This process leaves the wine in the decanter free of sediment and usually results in an ounce or two of wine being left with the residue in the bottle.

Some restaurants may wish to use a decanting funnel; these often include a screen that nests inside the funnel to catch the larger particles of sediment before they enter the decanter (Figure 19.19). These funnels are usually not too expensive and are particularly handy at filtering bottles that may have had the sediment stirred up on the way to the table, and are generally a good investment in a service setting for this reason.

An alternate (although related) use of a decanter would be when a guest requests the wine be aerated. The process

FIGURE 19.19

A decanting funnel with sediment from red wine. Decanting funnels make the process of decanting easier and come with a screen that will catch the any course sediment that leaves the bottle.

© Pat Henderson

of aeration is similar to decanting, although sediment is not a concern. Most wines, regardless of age, will benefit from some exposure to air to allow the release of the aromatic esters. Some wines, particularly younger, more robust wines, will benefit from air exposure. These wines might be described as "tight" or "closed," indicating that they are not as aromatic as might be expected. This subdued nose may be because of the wine being recently bottled. To encourage these wines to release their aromatics and "open up," they should be aerated. Because sediment is not an issue, the use of a candle is not required, and the foil capsule can be cut as with traditional wine presentation. The server simply adds the extra step of pouring the wine into the decanter to oxygenate it prior to pouring for the guests. Although many wines would benefit from this simple process, most guests will not request it unless they have a specific knowledge of the procedure. Wines that are especially old or fragile to start with should not be overly aerated because they could easily lose character when exposed to excessive oxygen.

Large format bottles require an extra level of attention and service, both because they represent an extra level of investment on the part of the guest and because their sheer size can make them unwieldy tableside. Magnums are still manageable tableside in the usual manner, but any bottle larger than a magnum requires extra steps. Bottles that are the equivalent of four or more regular bottles may need to be handled by two service staff members, if only for safety. These size bottles are large and heavy and dropping one would guarantee not just a large mess but also a significant loss of product for the operation. Pouring for each guest from a huge bottle is dramatic but impractical. A better solution is to have service staff open the bottle in the usual way, and then pour a good amount into a decanter and use this to pour for the host and then the guests. As the decanter is emptied, it is refilled from the larger bottle until the bottle is finished.

Serving Sparkling Wine

The process of opening Champagne and other sparkling wines tableside follows the same protocol as still wines, although there are a couple of key differences. The bottle is presented to the host in the same manner as a bottle of still wine would be. However, when it is ready to be opened a wine key is not required. The foil covering with sparkling wines usually has a perforation that allows the server to remove the foil capsule without cutting. The blade of a wine key could be used if necessary, but is usually not needed. When the foil is removed, the wire cage that holds the cork in place is exposed (Figure 19.20A). On the cage is a wire tab that is untwisted to loosen the cage and allow access to the cork. When the cage is loosened, great care must be taken with the cork because there is significant pressure inside the bottle. You should never aim the neck of the bottle at your face or a guest because the cork is capable of causing injury if it flies out unexpectedly.

A service linen is typically placed over the exposed cork to allow the server to maintain a proper grip on the cork. The cork should be held firmly with one hand, while the base of the bottle gripped with the other hand is twisted gently. Using the broad base of the bottle to turn provides more leverage than twisting the cork. The cork may have a tendency to fly out of the bottle, and it should be carefully controlled. The server should gently ease the cork out of the bottle, taking care to avoid the all-too-common popping noise that is often heard. A gentle sigh is more appropriate and professional, and demonstrates skill and confidence on the part of the server. The wine is poured for the guests in much the same fashion as for still wines, except that the glasses should be partly filled and the foam should be allowed to settle slightly before each glass is topped off (Figure 19.20B).

FIGURE 19.20A

The cork used to seal a bottle of Champagne has a characteristic mushroom shape. The cork is held in place with a wire cage to ensure that the pressure in the bottle does not force the cork out of the neck.

© Pat Henderson

FIGURE 19.20B

A small amount of Champagne should be poured in the glass and then topped off once the bubbles subside to avoid overflow.

© www.germanwines.de, German Wine Institute

Staff Training

Every restaurant should work to include education as a key part of their wine program, this includes education for the customer as well as for the staff. If a well-trained server is able to pass on some wisdom to the guest, the guest experience is positively affected and the guests are encouraged to return for another visit. As the service staff continues to pass on their knowledge, they become more comfortable and confident tableside and are further encouraged to improve their knowledge. A basic staff training program can easily be set up to allow the staff to increase their knowledge and understanding of wine, and also to help ensure that wine-drinking guests are getting the best level of service possible.

Management must first decide on the timing and the method of delivering staff training. Perhaps the easiest way to begin the process is during a staff meal before service. Many restaurants have a "family meal" or staff meal before commencing service for the evening, and this is a logical and comfortable time to introduce wine training. Often this time is used for team development, menu tasting and education, and addressing comments and concerns from the chef. It is easy to introduce wine education in this setting because the staff is already focusing on the impending service and expects to embark on some type of training, whether about the specials, the new menu, or the chef's input. Wine training that begins in this format often expands to include additional training sessions and helps to spark an increased staff interest in wine outside of the context of service.

Getting the staff comfortable with the basics of wine is the first critical step and forms a solid foundation for ongoing training. Afterward, shorter training sessions can then focus on new labels that are added to the list, including a tasting of the wine and suggested menu pairings. Many wine producers or local distributors are willing to visit the establishment and help with (or lead) tastings and training events. Taking advantage of resources in this respect will help guarantee a solid and diverse training program. If you can spark a passion for wine in the service staff, it will be sure to carry over to their lives outside work and will inspire them to learn more. This will benefit the operation because staff who are passionate about wine can share that passion with their guests. Increased sales and satisfied customers are the results.

Training during Staff Meetings

One of the key benefits of training staff during staff meetings is that most of the service staff is present and can be addressed as a group. A specific wine might be chosen to be discussed because it is the featured wine of the evening or because it will work particularly well with the evening's special. Either way, the tasting should be organized and meaningful and allow the staff to share information and opinions openly without fear of judgment. Building this supportive and education-based culture around wine instruction is essential to a successful training program.

Staff training is not simply an investment from the staff but one that management makes as well. Some of the costs include the actual cost of wine used for staff tastings, which can easily total hundreds, if not thousands, of dollars over the course of a year. Although some distributors may be willing to donate bottles of wine for daily tastings, this is not always allowed by state liquor laws, so the management should research the state laws regarding the donation of wines to be used for tastings. There is also the cost of labor because staff members should be paid for the time they spend in training. However, considering that the additional wine sales generated by a strong, well-trained service staff could total thousands of dollars per month, the investment is well worth the cost.

When training staff, it is critical to start simple and to give them meaningful pieces of information that are useful tableside and that help them understand wine on many levels. Chances are good that servers will encounter some guests who know at least something about wine, if not quite a bit, so if their knowledge isn't up to speed it will be immediately noticed. The staff should have a good grasp of what wine is and how it is produced; they should also know the essential aspects of grape production and climatic factors that influence grape production. Then they should have the opportunity to taste wines that demonstrate the concepts being taught. Scientific data and confusing terms should be kept to a minimum in the beginning, with the information becoming increasingly technical as the staff demonstrates understanding.

As the staff gains an understanding of the basic principles of wine, they can then apply the material to the wines offered on the wine list. When the learning is tied to the wine list, it creates a point of reference for the staff and helps to make them more comfortable tableside. Staff training that is undertaken outside of the context of driving sales in the restaurant and providing proper tableside service is only partially successful and is missing the opportunity to positively affect the operation's bottom line and the guest experience.

Regardless of the method of training, some type of assessment should be employed to ensure that staff is understanding and retaining the information and is ultimately held accountable for the material. This may be a short written quiz that the staff needs to pass, or an oral exam that mirrors an exchange likely to occur with a guest tableside. The focus should be on developing staff knowledge and increasing the comfort level in talking and teaching about wine. Some distributors will offer incentives to the service team or management for increased sales of specific wines. These incentives can take many forms, including promotional bottles or wine related accessories such as wine keys. Once again however, some state liquor laws may not allow this.

Using Wine Selling Points

As the servers open a bottle of wine tableside, it can sometimes be uncomfortable for them as the table watches what they do and analyzes their every move. Some servers are comfortable with this role and enjoy being on the spot while others may get intimidated. It helps to give the service staff some tips on engaging the table as they open and pour wine for the guests so that they feel comfortable during this process. This can be as simple as asking the guests if they have ever tried the selected wine and perhaps sharing some insight about it.

Every wine has a unique selling point or differentiating characteristic that may make it appealing to the consumer. This is part of what draws a guest to a specific bottle, the aspects that intrigue and encourage experimentation with various products. It may be the specific region of origin, a story about the winemaker or the winery, or simply some information about the label design. The differentiating characteristic might be more geared toward the restaurant, about why the restaurant chose that bottle for the list, the server's personal experience with the bottle, or how previous guests have enjoyed the wine. The culture of wine is steeped in history, and most wine regions have very rich histories with interesting stories that can be used as selling points. This takes the focus off the server and directs it to the bottle, creating another point of connection between the guests and the wine. Knowing even a little history can make for interesting discussion and add further value to the guest experience. And best of all, it gives the guests something to take home besides a cork or an empty bottle.

SERVING RESPONSIBLY

Wine and other alcoholic drinks are a part of an enjoyable evening out for many people. Moreover, whether one is consuming or serving alcohol you should always keep in mind the consequences of excess consumption. Serving responsibly, also called **responsible hospitality**, is the concept of serving your guests alcohol in a way that meets their needs as customers as well as protects them and your restaurant from potential harm. The possibility for excess drinking may be more obvious in a sports bar on game night, however responsible hospitality is just as important at a fine dining restaurant with white-jacketed waiters and it should be practiced at all venues that serve alcohol.

A restaurant's alcohol license is a very valuable asset and it can be revoked if the establishment does not follow the law. Additionally restaurants have been sued for damages by the victims of drunk drivers who had too much to drink at their establishment. The liability is not only limited to the owners, servers can also be held accountable. Besides the monetary risk, servers also have a moral obligation to help prevent deaths and injuries from driving under the influence (DUI).

Following the Law

As is the case with other regulations that govern alcohol, the rules that servers must follow vary quite a bit from state to state and even between cities. Policies that control when and what kind alcohol can be served, as well as who is allowed to serve it, depend not only on the location of the restaurant, but also what type of license it has. Many states require that employees who serve alcohol receive formal training in responsible hospitality. In some states, serving staff must attend a full day class that is sponsored by the state before they are allowed to serve alcohol. In other areas either nothing is required, or a short in house or online training session is sufficient. Even if it is not mandated by the government, it is always a good idea to have new staff undergo some kind of instruction in responsible serving. This is very easy to accomplish since there are now many programs online that are available for little or no cost. Whatever the method of training, it will not be successful if what is learned is not consistently implemented by management.

The drinking age within the United States is 21, and serving to underage patrons can result in a restaurant getting their license to serve alcohol either suspended or revoked. Once again the liability is not just limited to the establishment's proprietors; servers can lose their job and be fined for selling alcohol to underage patrons. Some jurisdictions employ "decoys" to monitor compliance with drinking age laws. Decoys are enforcement agents who are just under 21 years old and visit bars and restaurants to see if they can be served, and if they are, often a citation is issued on the spot. For these reasons, training for wait staff should include how to tell if a patron may be underage. Additionally which forms of identification are acceptable and how to spot a fake ID should also be covered. If it appears that a guest might be underage, they should always be asked to produce an ID.

How to Serve Responsibly

Just as a server should be familiar with the wine list and the styles of wine that are offered, they should be aware of the relative strengths of alcoholic beverages and how they affect the body. The subject of alcohol and its physiological effects are covered in Chapter 5. This knowledge helps a server properly monitor the guests' consumption and pace how quickly they get their drinks and food so they are less likely to over-consume. Servers must walk a fine line between encouraging sales and discouraging overdrinking. If a table has had a lot to drink with dinner, you should not be doing a hard sell to get everyone to enjoy a glass or two of Port with dessert. If someone at the table is the designated driver, or is simply not drinking, support their decision and treat their request for a mineral water with the same respect that you would if it was a glass of your finest Champagne.

When someone starts to get drunk, they begin to get louder and more confident, a little more alcohol and they start to slur their words and become unsteady on their feet. Even if there are no outward signs of intoxication, reaction time and coordination slows down with drinking.

It can be very difficult to tell if customers are simply enjoying themselves and getting a little boisterous, or if they are a little bit drunk. If you suspect that someone has had too much alcohol to drive, offer to call them a cab. If you have established a good rapport over the course of the meal, it can come off as a friend who is looking after their best interests. The patron can also be discreetly reminded of the consequences such as, "You know the police have really been cracking down on DUIs in this area on Friday nights; would you like me to call you a cab?"

If a patron has obviously had too much to drink, it is the server's responsibility to cut off their alcohol. This is without a doubt one of the most difficult aspects of a server's job. If the occasion arises they should:

- Deal with the situation as early as possible; if you can prevent overconsumption in the first place it is much easier than dealing with a patron who is out of control.

- Be discrete; this will likely be an embarrassing situation for everyone involved.
- Inform the patron that the law requires that he or she does not serve someone who is intoxicated.
- Apologize for the situation and inform the patron that he or she would be welcome to come back on another night.
- Do your best to see that the patron has a safe way to get home.

If the patron becomes angry or demands service, a manager should be standing by to assist with the situation. While it is rare in most dining establishments, if someone is very unruly, aggressive, or refuses to leave, the police should be summoned.

The Responsibilities of a Server

As part of good business practices, restaurant managers should be well informed on all of the laws and regulations that apply to their enterprise. It is part of their role as supervisor to make sure that all employees are aware of alcohol regulations and how they apply to their duties. As for the wait staff, they fulfill three primary, and some-times contradictory, roles: (1) to be a good salesperson who is knowledgeable about wine and promotes sales; (2) to be a good host, keeping guests happy and helping keep them from potential harm; and (3) to be a bit of a police officer who makes sure no laws are broken and protects the restaurant from liability. Finding the proper balance between all of these responsibilities can be difficult and it is one of the reasons that many states require formal training in the subject. However, properly handling all of these tasks is the most important aspect of good wine service and the true mark of a professional.

SUMMARY

The business of wine sales and service relies on a commitment from the service staff and management of a restaurant operation. A properly designed and executed sales plan coupled with well-trained service staff is the cornerstone to successful restaurant wine sales. The operators need to decide on appropriate methods for encouraging wine sales during every stage of the dining experience and need to support those sales with a professional level of service. All members of the service staff should be comfortable recommending wines from the wine list, discussing wines, and opening wine tableside. A lack of attention on any aspect of the wine sales procedure may result in disappoint-ed guests and can deter them from returning to visit the establishment. Focused and professional wine service is necessary to maintain a solid and well-rounded restaurant operation.

EXERCISES

1. What are some methods that restaurant operators use to encourage wine sales in the restaurant setting?

2. What are the proper steps to follow when opening a bottle of wine tableside?

3. What are some factors to consider when purchasing glassware for the wine program?

4. How should a server deal with a patron who has had too much to drink?

5. How does serving from a bottle sealed with a screw cap differ from serving from a bottle sealed with a cork?

REVIEW QUESTIONS

1. What is the primary reason the host of the table tastes the wine before the other guests?
   A. To see if the bottle is "corked"
   B. To see if the wine will go with the food
   C. So it can be returned if the host does not like it
   D. Out of respect since the host is paying for the wine

2. When serving sparkling wine, why is a small amount poured in the glass before it is then topped?
   A. To keep from disturbing the sediment
   B. So that any off-aromas are allowed to dissipate before it is tasted
   C. To make sure there is enough wine to serve everyone at the table
   D. To allow the foam to settle before the glass is filled

(Continues)

3. When opening a bottle of wine the server should always
_____.

   A. Open the wine behind the bar and then bring it to the table

   B. Hold the bottle under the arm for more leverage when pulling the cork

   C. Show the bottle to the host and confirm it is the bottle ordered

   D. Place the cork in the apron after it is pulled so there is no danger of it staining the tablecloth

4. To best appreciate a wine's aroma, a wine glass should be filled
_____.

   A. One-third to one-half of the way full

   B. Almost to the brim

   C. To 1 oz (30 ml)

   D. It does not matter how much it is filled

5. Besides removing sediment, decanters can also be used to
_____.

   A. Chill the wine

   B. Disguise the identity of the house wine

   C. Aerate the wine

   D. Remove cork taint

REFERENCES

MacNeil, K. (2001). *The wine bible.* New York: Workman.

{ WINE LAW IN THE UNITED STATES }

INTRODUCTION

The business of wine and alcohol is more heavily regulated than any other legal product in the United States with the possible exception of cigarettes. Multiple agencies at the federal, state, and local level all regulate the production, distribution, and sale of wine. There are numerous laws at every level of government that control wine and there is little uniformity of these statutes between state and local districts. These conditions make for a confusing array of wine laws across the United States. The laws are designed with two principal aims: first to collect taxes, and second to control and limit consumption.

The taxation of alcohol is considered a "sin tax" like those that are levied on tobacco and gambling. A common justification for taxes on alcoholic products is that they help compensate the government for dealing with the consequences of excessive consumption. All wines sold in the United States are subject to a federal tax, and states also apply additional excise taxes to wines sold inside their boundaries. State excise taxes range from $0.11 per gallon in Louisiana to $2.50 a gallon in Alaska. These taxes are in addition to the federal tax of $1.07 per gallon for wine containing 14 percent or less alcohol and $1.57 per gallon for wine over 14 percent, as well as any sales taxes that may be applicable. Wineries that produce less than 100,000 cases a year can receive a partial tax credit with the total amount depending on their size to offset part of these costs. There are different tax levels for different types of alcoholic beverages; typically the greater the alcohol content of the product the higher the tax. Sparkling wine is taxed at a higher rate than still wine at $3.40 per gallon.

There are also many laws by all levels of government designed to control how wine is distributed and sold. These laws govern who can sell what categories of wine, where and in what types of locations it can be sold, and what hours or days of the week it can be made available to consumers.

HISTORICAL BACKGROUND

The origins of this complex multitude of laws that govern alcohol go back to the repeal of Prohibition in 1933. The era of Prohibition had profound effects on the country's demand for wine as well as what styles of wine became popular with consumers. Similarly, Prohibition's repeal had a direct effect on how wine was regulated by government agencies. As discussed in Chapter 11, the Eighteenth Amendment to the Constitution enacted nationwide Prohibition on the production, sale, or consumption of alcohol in 1920 and was repealed with the Twenty-first Amendment in 1933. One of the stipulations of the repeal amendment is that states were allowed to govern all aspects of alcohol within their borders. This resulted in each state forming a set of its own unique laws to govern wine. In turn, many states granted a great deal of authority to cities and counties to control alcohol under their own local jurisdiction. Since standards of what is acceptable regarding wine consumption vary greatly from one area to the next, and although their number is declining, there are still many counties in the South and Midwest which continue to ban the sale of alcohol.

The ability of a state to regulate and limit the sale of wines produced in other states directly contradicts another part of the Constitution, the Interstate Commerce Clause. The Interstate Commerce Clause generally prohibits states from having exclusionary tariffs or laws on products imported from other states. However, courts have decided that the Twenty-first Amendment supersedes the Interstate Commerce Clause and therefore the Interstate Commerce Clause does not cover wine and other alcoholic products. There are exceptions to this; in 1984, the Supreme Court decided that states cannot have lower taxes on wines made within their own borders than they levy on wines produced in other states (Lee, 2005). Additionally, in 2005 the Supreme Court decided that states could not prohibit the direct shipping of wine from out of state wineries to consumers, yet allow direct shipping from in-state wineries. There have been a number of cases regarding wine regulation brought before the courts at every level in the United States, and the laws governing wine continue to evolve. If one can make any generalization, it is that protectionist laws that are designed purely to be exclusionary to wines produced out of state are not allowed, whereas laws designed to limit or control consumption of all wines regardless of the state of origin are permissible.

Federal Wine Laws

The majority of federal laws that govern wine are usually concerned with either the collection of federal excise taxes or the regulation of wine labeling. The agency that oversees the enforcement of federal laws is the Alcohol and Tobacco Tax and Trade Bureau, or TTB, formerly known as the Bureau of Alcohol, Tobacco & Firearms (BATF). Wineries, distributors, and retailers must all keep detailed records that ensure any bottle of wine that is produced or shipped is accounted for and its taxes are paid. Wineries must report to the TTB monthly to account for the amount of wine they produce and ship. Before it is sold, wine is stored in a bonded warehouse, a warehouse where the tax on the wine has not yet been paid. Once it leaves the bonded warehouse to be shipped to a distributor, the winery is responsible for paying the federal tax.

The TTB is also responsible for regulating wine labels. The TTB stipulates what information must be printed on all wine labels for wine sold in the United States, as outlined in Chapter 11. Wineries must submit their labels to the TTB to be approved before they are allowed to be used for a bottle of wine. The TTB examines potential labels to ensure that they have all of the required text and the text is printed at the size specified by law. The TTB must also approve of all graphics and names on the label as well as any statements the winery makes about its product. Wineries must be able to document all claims made on the label, such as the variety or appellation of the wine, are true and the alcohol content printed on the label is accurate.

Federal wine laws regarding labeling are currently evolving and becoming more stringent. Recently enacted federal bioterrorism laws require that producers be able to trace any product used in wine, such as yeast, fining agents, and corks to its origin. To facilitate this most wines are now bottled with a lot number or time code discreetly placed on the bottle. All producers of food products will be required to have this level of traceability; wine is ahead of most other food products because wineries have always been required to keep accurate records to prove statements about a wine's variety and appellation. In the future, ingredient labeling may be required, particularly for allergens such as egg whites, which are sometimes used for fining red wines. Also under consideration is calorie content labeling in a manner that is similar to what is now required on packaged foods.

State Wine Laws

The state laws that govern wine and alcohol are so complex and vary so much from state to state it is difficult to make any sweeping statements that would apply to all states. This being said, state wine statutes generally fall under one of the following categories:

- Laws that govern the distribution of wine
- Laws that govern the retail sales of wine
- Laws that govern the state taxation of wine
- Laws that govern the shipping of wine by producers and consumers

State Distribution Laws

There are four entities that are involved in getting wine into consumers' hands.

- Suppliers (wineries or importers) that produce or import the wine
- Brokers, companies, and individuals who represent the winery and sell its product for a commission
- Distributors, companies that purchase large amounts of wine in cases from suppliers and store it their own warehouses while they sell and distribute it to retailers by the case or by the bottle
- Retailers, either on-premise (restaurants and bars) or off-premise (wine shops and grocery stores), who sell wine directly to consumers

Every state has different laws that govern the actions of all of these groups; some states prohibit some of them from operating. States can be divided into two categories based on the degree of direct management they have over distribution channels. Currently 32 states have a competitive model of distribution, where the private sector distributes and sells the wine. States that have the competitive model for distribution are also referred to as *licensure states*. These states include many of the large markets for wine consumption such as California, New York, and Florida. The 18 remaining states use the control model of distribution. Here, state agencies manage and control either distribution or sales and in some cases both operations. Major control states include Pennsylvania, New Hampshire, and Michigan. Because of the efficiencies inherent in private companies competing against each other, the competitive model usually offers consumers better prices and a wider selection of wine. The control model offers states a lucrative source of revenue from their stake in the profits generated by wine sales. Even in states where the control model is not popular, it is difficult to repeal because if the revenue from alcohol sales were lost, other taxes would have to be raised. Washington State is considering changing from a control to a competitive model and is attempting to find a method that would be revenue neutral through new alcohol taxes and licensing fees.

In many states, the three-tier system of distribution is required by law. In this system, producers are not allowed to sell directly to retailers; instead they must go through a middle distributor who buys the wine from the winery before it can be sold to the retailer. These laws exist to prevent wineries from having undue influence on retailers. Some states have franchise laws that do not allow wineries to have more than one distributor or to change to another distribution company if they are dissatisfied with the one that they are currently using. In a three-tier state, if a winery cannot find a distributor that wants to handle its product it will not be allowed to sell its wine even if there are wine shops or restaurants that wish to carry it. These laws are particularly difficult for small wineries with limited production where the small amount of sales possible in a particular state do not justify the amount of money and effort it takes to acquire a distributor.

State Laws Governing Wine Sales

As previously stated, state and local governments have great latitude in establishing laws regarding alcohol, including how, where, and when it can be sold. In some control states such as New Hampshire and Pennsylvania, wine can be purchased only through state-owned stores. By controlling the sales of all wine, the state is assured that no one underage buys wine and that it receives all of the state excise and sales tax; in addition the states receives profits from the sale as well. In an effort to limit consumption, some states such as New York do not allow wine to be sold in grocery stores. This requires consumers to travel to a wine shop to purchase their wine instead of simply buying it with their groceries. Repealing this law has been under consideration several times, but as of 2010 it has not passed the state legislature. Other laws govern when wine and alcohol can be sold, either by banning it after a certain hour of the night or by not allowing the sale of wine on Sunday through the use of so-called blue laws.

States also have Alcohol Beverage Control (ABC) agencies that monitor wine retailers and enforce the states' laws. These agencies are in charge of issuing liquor licenses that retailers need to sell wine and other alcohol products as well as monitoring them to ensure all regulations are being followed. These agencies also control who is allowed to serve wine. In some states, servers must be of legal age to drink alcohol before they are allowed to serve wine to patrons. In other states, it is illegal for an employee of a winery to pour their own brand of wine at a tasting; it must be poured by a third party.

State Laws Governing Shipping

Many states do not allow the shipping of wine into the state unless it passes through established distribution channels. This type of shipping usually occurs when a consumer orders wine directly from the winery via phone or the Internet. States generally do not like these types of purchases because the state taxes are often not paid on such a transaction and wine could potentially be sold to minors. Suppliers counter that they would be happy to pay state taxes if they were allowed to ship wine into the state and that an adult signature can be required upon delivery to prevent underage people from obtaining wine.

The prohibition on direct shipping may cover not only wine sales but also any shipping of wine across the states' borders. Some states ban any outside importation of wine by consumers even if they are carrying it over the states' borders themselves for personal consumption. Wine being sent by a private citizen as a gift or as a donation to a charity is also banned in these states. In several states, it is not only illegal, it is also considered a felony to direct ship wine from outside the state to consumers. These laws are actively supported by many distributors that have a vested interest in keeping things the way they are.

Anti–direct shipping laws are seldom enforced against private citizens returning from vacation with a bottle of wine or people who send a bottle of wine to a relative as a gift. These bans do, however, have an effect on wineries that are not allowed to ship wines directly to consumers. Small wineries in particular that do not have nationwide distribution are the most affected, while it is less of a burden to larger wineries whose product is available through distributors in every state. Different shipping companies such as UPS, FedEx, and DHL all have varying policies on which states they will ship wine to, and the U.S. Postal Service does not ship wine under any circumstances.

Other states, particularly those with a significant wine industry, have more liberal laws governing the direct shipping of wine. As of 2010, there were 37 states and the District of Columbia that allow limited direct shipping of wine as long as certain regulations are followed. Usually these regulations involve registering with the destination state, and agreeing to pay the tax they levy on wine.

SUMMARY OF STATE LAWS

Since the laws of the different states are very complex and constantly changing, the most up-to-date information can be obtained from the Internet.

For web links to the Wine Institute, TTB, and the state ABC Web sites listed in Table A.1, log into www.cengagebrain.com to access The CourseMate that accompanies this text.

TABLE A.1 Shipping Laws and Distribution Models Listed by State

For links to Web sites of the Alcoholic Beverage Control offices for each state, log into www.cengagebrain.com and access the CourseMate that accompanies this text.

State	Direct Shipping	Control Model
Alabama	Prohibited	Control
Alaska	Limited	Competitive
Arizona	Limited	Competitive
Arkansas	Prohibited	Competitive
California	Limited	Competitive
Colorado	Limited	Competitive
Connecticut	Limited	Competitive
Delaware	Prohibited	Competitive
District of Columbia	Limited	Competitive
Florida	Limited	Competitive
Georgia	Limited	Competitive
Hawaii*	Limited	Competitive
Idaho	Limited	Control
Illinois	Limited	Competitive
Indiana	Limited	Competitive
Iowa	Limited	Control
Kansas	Limited	Competitive
Kentucky	Prohibited	Competitive
Louisiana	Limited	Competitive
Maine	Limited	Control
Maryland**	Prohibited	Competitive
Massachusetts	Prohibited	Competitive
Michigan	Limited	Control
Minnesota	Limited	Competitive
Mississippi	Prohibited	Control
Missouri	Limited	Competitive
Montana	Prohibited	Control
Nebraska	Limited	Competitive
Nevada	Limited	Competitive
New Hampshire	Limited	Control
New Jersey	Prohibited	Competitive
New Mexico	Reciprocal	Competitive
New York	Limited	Competitive
North Carolina	Limited	Control
North Dakota	Limited	Competitive
Ohio	Limited	Control
Oklahoma	Prohibited	Competitive

State	Direct Shipping	Control Model
Oregon	Limited	Control
Pennsylvania	Prohibited	Control
Rhode Island	Limited	Competitive
South Carolina	Limited	Competitive
South Dakota	Prohibited	Competitive
Tennessee	Limited	Competitive
Texas	Limited	Competitive
Utah	Prohibited	Control
Vermont	Limited	Control
Virginia	Limited	Control
Washington	Limited	Control
West Virginia	Limited	Control
Wisconsin	Limited	Competitive
Wyoming	Limited	Control

*Hawaii has different ABC offices for the different islands.

**Two counties in Maryland have control model distribution.

REFERENCES

Lee, Wendell. (2005). *Background on Anti-Direct Shipment Laws*, San Francisco: Wine Institute.

{ AMERICAN VITICULTURAL AREAS }

AMERICAN VITICULTURAL AREAS BY STATE
(EXCLUDING CALIFORNIA)

State	AVA Name
Arizona	Sonoita
Arkansas	Altus
Arkansas	Arkansas Mountain
Arkansas	Ozark Mountain [AR, MO, OK]
Colorado	Grand Valley
Colorado	West Elks
Connecticut	Southeastern New England [CT, MA, RI]
Connecticut	Western Connecticut Highlands
Idaho	Snake River Valley
Illinois	Shawnee Hills
Illinois	Upper Mississippi River Valley [IA, MN, WI]
Indiana	Ohio River Valley [IN, KY, OH, WV]
Iowa	Upper Mississippi River Valley [MN, IL, WI]
Kentucky	Ohio River Valley [IN, KY, OH, WV]
Louisiana	Mississippi Delta [LA, MS, TN]
Maryland	Catoctin
Maryland	Cumberland Valley [MD, PA]
Maryland	Linganore
Massachusetts	Martha's Vineyard
Massachusetts	Southeastern New England [CT, MA, RI]
Michigan	Fennville
Michigan	Lake Michigan Shore
Michigan	Leelanau Peninsula
Michigan	Old Mission Peninsula
Minnesota	Alexandria Lakes
Minnesota	Upper Mississippi River Valley [IA, IL, WI]
Mississippi	Mississippi Delta [LA, MS, TN]
Missouri	Augusta
Missouri	Hermann
Missouri	Ozark Highlands
Missouri	Ozark Mountain [AR, MO, OK]
New Jersey	Central Delaware Valley [NJ, PA]
New Jersey	Outer Coastal Plain

State	AVA Name
New Jersey	Warren Hills
New Mexico	Mesilla Valley [NM, TX]
New Mexico	Middle Rio Grande Valley
New Mexico	Mimbres Valley
New York	Cayuga Lake
New York	Finger Lakes
New York	The Hamptons, Long Island
New York	Hudson River Region
New York	Lake Erie [NY, OH, PA]
New York	Long Island
New York	Niagara Escarpment
New York	North Fork of Long Island
New York	Seneca Lake
North Carolina	Haw River Valley
North Carolina	Swan Creek
North Carolina	Yadkin Valley
Ohio	Grand River Valley
Ohio	Isle St. George
Ohio	Kanawha River Valley [OH, WV]
Ohio	Lake Erie [NY, OH, PA]
Ohio	Loramie Creek
Ohio	Ohio River Valley [IN, KY, OH, WV]
Oklahoma	Ozark Mountain [AR, MO, OK]
Oregon	Applegate Valley
Oregon	Chehalem Mountains
Oregon	Columbia Gorge [OR, WA]
Oregon	Columbia Valley [OR, WA]
Oregon	Dundee Hills
Oregon	Eola Amity Hills
Oregon	McMinnville
Oregon	Red Hill Douglas County, Oregon
Oregon	Ribbon Ridge
Oregon	Rogue Valley
Oregon	Snake River Valley
Oregon	Southern Oregon
Oregon	Umpqua Valley
Oregon	Walla Walla Valley [OR, WA]
Oregon	Willamette Valley
Oregon	Yamhill-Carlton
Pennsylvania	Central Delaware Valley [NJ, PA]
Pennsylvania	Cumberland Valley [MD, PA]

State	AVA Name
Pennsylvania	Lake Erie [NY, OH, PA]
Pennsylvania	Lancaster Valley
Pennsylvania	Lehigh Valley
Rhode Island	Southeastern New England [CT, MA, RI]
Tennessee	Mississippi Delta [LA, MS, TN]
Texas	Bell Mountain
Texas	Escondido Valley
Texas	Fredericksburg in the Texas Hill Country
Texas	Mesilla Valley [NM, TX]
Texas	Texas Davis Mountains
Texas	Texas High Plains
Texas	Texas Hill Country
Texas	Texoma
Virginia	Monticello
Virginia	North Fork of Roanoke
Virginia	Northern Neck George Washington Birthplace
Virginia	Rocky Knob
Virginia	Shenandoah Valley [VA, WV]
Virginia	Virginia's Eastern Shore
Washington	Columbia Gorge [OR, WA]
Washington	Columbia Valley [OR, WA]
Washington	Horse Heaven Hills
Washington	Lake Chelan
Washington	Puget Sound
Washington	Rattlesnake Hills
Washington	Red Mountain
Washington	Snipes Mountain
Washington	Wahluke Slope
Washington	Walla Walla Valley [OR, WA]
Washington	Yakima Valley
West Virginia	Kanawha River Valley [OH, WV]
West Virginia	Ohio River Valley [IN, KY, OH, WV]
West Virginia	Shenandoah Valley [VA, WV]
Wisconsin	Lake Wisconsin
Wisconsin	Upper Mississippi River Valley [IA, MN, IL]

American Viticultural Appellations in California with County Information

California AVA	County
Alexander Valley	Sonoma
Alta Mesa	Sacramento
Anderson Valley	Mendocino
Arroyo Grande Valley	San Luis Obispo
Arroyo Seco	Monterey
Atlas Peak	Napa
Ben Lomond Mountain	Santa Cruz
Benmore Valley	Lake
Bennett Valley	Sonoma
Borden Ranch	Sacramento, San Joaquin
California Shenandoah Valley	Amador, El Dorado
Calistoga	Napa
Capay Valley	Yolo
Carmel Valley	Monterey
Central Coast	Alameda, Contra Costa, Monterey, San Benito, San Francisco, San Luis Obispo, San Mateo, Santa Barbara, Santa Clara, Santa Cruz
Chalk Hill	Sonoma
Chalone	Monterey, San Benito
Chiles Valley	Napa
Cienega Valley	San Benito
Clarksburg	Sacramento, Solano, Yolo
Clear Lake	Lake
Clement Hills	San Joaquin
Cole Ranch	Mendocino
Cosumnes River	Sacramento
Covelo	Mendocino
Cucamonga Valley	Riverside, San Bernardino
Diablo Grande	Stanislaus
Diamond Mountain District	Napa
Dos Rios	Mendocino
Dry Creek Valley	Sonoma
Dunnigan Hills	Yolo
Edna Valley	San Luis Obispo
El Dorado	El Dorado
Fair Play	El Dorado
Fiddletown	Amador

California AVA	County
Guenoc Valley	Lake
Hames Valley	Monterey
Happy Canyon of Santa Barbara	Santa Barbara
High Valley	Lake
Howell Mountain	Napa
Jahant	San Joaquin
Knights Valley	Sonoma
Leona Valley	Los Angeles
Lime Kiln Valley	San Benito
Livermore Valley	Alameda
Lodi	Sacramento, San Joaquin
Los Carneros	Napa, Sonoma
Madera	Fresno, Madera
Malibu-Newton Canyon	Los Angeles
McDowell Valley	Mendocino
Mendocino	Mendocino
Mendocino Ridge	Mendocino
Merritt Island	Yolo
Mokelumne River	San Joaquin
Monterey	Monterey
Mt. Harlan	San Benito
Mt. Veeder	Napa
Napa Valley	Napa
North Coast	Lake, Marin, Mendocino, Napa, Solano, Sonoma
North Yuba	Yuba
Northern Sonoma	Sonoma
Oak Knoll District	Napa
Oakville	Napa
Pacheco Pass	San Benito
Paicines	San Benito
Paso Robles	San Luis Obispo
Potter Valley	Mendocino
Ramona Valley	San Diego
Red Hills Lake County	Lake
Redwood Valley	Mendocino
River Junction	San Joaquin
Rockpile	Sonoma
Russian River Valley	Sonoma
Rutherford	Napa
Saddle Rock-Malibu	Los Angeles
Salado Creek	Stanislaus

California AVA	County
San Antonio Valley	Monterey
San Benito	San Benito
San Bernabe	Monterey
San Francisco Bay	San Benito, San Francisco, San Mateo, Santa Clara, Santa Cruz
San Lucas	Monterey
San Pasqual Valley	San Diego
San Ysidro District	Santa Clara
Santa Clara Valley	Santa Clara
Santa Cruz Mountains	San Mateo, Santa Clara, Santa Cruz
Santa Lucia Highlands	Monterey
Santa Maria Valley	San Luis Obispo, Santa Barbara
Santa Rita Hills	Santa Barbara
Santa Ynez Valley	Santa Barbara
Seiad Valley	Siskiyou
Sierra Foothills	Amador, Calaveras, El Dorado, Mariposa, Nevada, Placer, Tuolumne, Yuba
Sierra Pelona Valley	Los Angeles
Sloughhouse	Sacramento
Solano County Green Valley	Solano
Sonoma Coast	Sonoma
Sonoma County Green Valley	Sonoma
Sonoma Mountain	Sonoma
Sonoma Valley	Sonoma
South Coast	Riverside, San Diego
Spring Mountain District	Napa
St. Helena	Napa
Stags Leap District	Napa
Suisun Valley	Solano
Temecula Valley	Riverside
Tracy Hills	San Joaquin, Stanislaus
Trinity Lakes	Trinity
Wild Horse Valley	Napa, Solano
Willow Creek	Humboldt, Trinity
York Mountain	San Luis Obispo
Yorkville Highlands	Mendocino
Yountville	Napa

{ # FRENCH
CLASSIFICATIONS }

BORDEAUX: THE 1855 OFFICIAL CLASSIFICATION OF THE MÉDOC

Château	Commune
First Growths	
Château Lafite-Rothschild	Pauillac
Château Latour	Pauillac
Château Margaux	Margaux
Château Haut-Brion	Pessac (Graves)
Château Mouton-Rothschild	Pauillac (Reclassified in 1973)
Second Growths	
Château Rausan-Ségla	Margaux
Château Rauzan-Gassies	Margaux
Château Léoville-Las Cases	Saint-Julien
Château Léoville-Poyferré	Saint-Julien
Château Léoville-Barton	Saint-Julien
Château Durfort-Vivens	Margaux
Château Gruaud-Larose	Saint-Julien
Château Lascombes	Margaux
Château Brane-Cantenac	Cantenac-Margaux
Château Pichon-Longueville-Baron	Pauillac
Château Pichon-Longueville	Pauillac
Château Pichon-Longueville-Comtesse de Lalande	Pauillac
Château Ducru-Beaucaillou	Saint-Julien
Château Cos d'Estournel	Saint-Estèphe
Château Montrose	Saint-Estèphe
Third Growths	
Château Kirwan-Cantenac	Margaux
Château d'Issan-Cantenac	Margaux
Château Lagrange	Saint-Julien
Château Langoa-Barton	Saint-Julien
Château Giscours-Labarde	Margaux
Château Malescot-Saint-Exupéry	Margaux
Château Cantenac-Brown	Cantenac-Margaux
Château Boyd-Cantenac	Margaux
Château Palmer	Cantenac-Margaux

Château	Commune
Château La Lagune	Ludon
Château Desmirail	Margaux
Château Calon-Ségur	Saint-Estèphe
Château Ferrière	Margaux
Château Marquis d'Alesme-Becker	Margaux
Fourth Growths	
Château Saint-Pierre	Saint-Julien
Château Talbot	Saint-Julien
Château Branaire-Ducru	Saint-Julien
Château Duhart-Milon-Rothschild	Pauillac
Château Pouget	Cantenac-Margaux
Château La Tour-Carnet	Saint-Laurent
Château Lafon-Rochet	Saint-Estèphe
Château Beychevelle	Saint-Julien
Château Prieuré-Lichine	Cantenac-Margaux
Château Marquis-de-Terme	Margaux
Fifth Growths	
Château Pontet-Canet	Pauillac
Château Batailley	Pauillac
Château Haut-Batailley	Pauillac
Château Grand-Puy-Lacoste	Pauillac
Château Grand-Puy-Ducasse	Pauillac
Château Lynch-Bages	Pauillac
Château Lynch-Moussas	Pauillac
Château Dauzac-Labarde	Margaux
Château d'Armailhac	Pauillac
Château du Tertre	Margaux
Château Haut-Bages-Liberal	Pauillac
Château Pédesclaux	Pauillac
Château Belgrave	Saint-Laurent
Château de Camensac	Saint-Laurent
Château Cos-Labory	Saint-Estèphe
Château Clerc-Milon	Pauillac
Château Croizet-Bages	Pauillac
Château Cantemerle	Haut-Médoc

THE 1855 OFFICIAL CLASSIFICATION
OF SAUTERNES AND BARSAC

Château	Commune
Great First Growth (Grand Premier Cru)	
Château d'Yquem	Sauternes
First Growths	
Château La Tour-Blanche	Bommes
Château Lafaurie-Peyraguey	Bommes
Château Clos Haut-Peyraguey	Bommes
Château de Rayne-Vigneau	Bommes
Château Suduiraut	Preignac
Château Coutet	Barsac
Château Climens	Barsac
Château Guiraud	Sauternes
Château Rieussec	Fargues
Château Rabaud-Promis	Bommes
Château Sigalas-Rabaud	Bommes
Second Growths	
Château de Myrat	Barsac
Château Doisy-Daene	Barsac
Château Doisy-Dubroca	Barsac
Château Doisy-Vedrines	Barsac
Château D'Arche	Sauternes
Château Filhot	Sauternes
Château Broustet	Barsac
Château Nairac	Barsac
Château Caillou	Barsac
Château Suau	Barsac
Château de Malle	Preignac
Château Romer du Hayot	Fargues
Château Lamothe	Sauternes

The 1959 Official Classification of Graves

In 1959 the *INAO (Institut Nationale des Appellations d'Origine)* completed the classifications of Graves estates. There are two lists, one for producers of exceptional white wine, and one for producers of exceptional red wine. Some estates are on both lists.

Château	Commune
Classification of Red Wines of Graves	
Château Bouscaut	Cadaujac
Château Haut-Bailly	Léognan
Château Carbonnieux	Léognan
Domaine de Chevalier	Léognan
Château de Fieuzal	Léognan
Château Olivier	Léognan
Château Malartic-Lagravière	Léognan
Château La Tour-Martillac	Martillac
Château Smith-Haut-Lafitte	Martillac
Château Haut-Brion	Pessac
Château La Mission-Haut-Brion	Talence
Château Pape-Clément	Pessac
Château La Tour-Haut-Brion	Talence
Classification of White Wines of Graves	
Château Bouscaut	Cadaujac
Château Carbonnieux	Léognan
Domaine de Chevalier	Léognan
Château Malartic-Lagravière	Léognan
Château Olivier	Léognan
Château La Tour-Martillac	Martillac
Château Laville-Haut-Brion	Talence
Château Couhins-Lurton	Villenave d'Ornon

The Revised Official Classification of Saint-Émilion, 2006

When Saint-Émilion was first classified in 1954, the INAO and local vintners agreed that the law should be written to allow a possible revision of the classification every 10 years. The most recent reclassification of 2006 was contested in the courts by a number of the chateaux that had been demoted from grand cru classé. After a protracted legal battle, a law was passed in 2009 that established the rankings as follows.

First Great Classed Growths (Category A)	
Château Ausone	Château Cheval-Blanc

First Great Classed Growths (Category B)	
Château Angélus	Clos Fourtet
Château Beau-Séjour Bécot	Château La Gaffelière
Château Beauséjour (Duffau-Lagarrosse)	Château Magdelaine
Château Bélair-Monange	Château Pavie
Château Canon	Château Pavie-Macquin
Château Figeac	Château Troplong-Mondot
Château Trottevieille	

Great Classed Growths	
Château L'Arrosée	Château Les Grandes-Murailles
Château Balestard-La-Tonnelle	Château Guadet St-Julien
Château Bellefont-Belcier	Château Haut-Corbin
Château Bellevue	Château Haut Sarpe
Château Bergat	Clos des Jacobins
Château Berliquet	Château Laniote
Château Cadet-Bon	Château Larcis-Ducasse
Château Cadet-Piola	Château Larmande
Château Canon-la-Gaffelière	Château Laroque
Château Cap-de-Mourlin	Château Laroze
Château Chauvin	Château La Marzelle
Château La Clotte	Château Matras
Château Corbin	Château Monbousquet
Château Corbin-Michotte	Château Moulin-du-Cadet
Château La Couspaude	Clos de L'Oratoire
Château Couvent des Jacobins	Château Pavie-Decesse
Château Dassault	Château Petit-Faurie-de-Soutard
Château Destieux	Château Le Prieuré
Château La Dominique	Château Ripeau

Château Faurie-de-Souchard	Château St-Georges-Côte-Pavie
Château Fleur-Cardinale	Clos St-Martin
Château Fonplégade	Château La Serre
Château Fonroque	Château Soutard
Château Franc-Mayne	Château Tertre-Daugay
Château Grand-Corbin	Château La Tour-du-Pin
Château Grand-Corbin-Despagne	Château La Tour-du-Pin-Figeac (Moueix)
Château Grand-Mayne	Château La Tour Figeac
Château Grand-Pontet	Château Villemaurine
Château Yon-Figeac	

POMEROL (NOT CLASSIFIED)

Pomerol has never officially been rated. However, it is widely accepted that the following are the area's leading estates, with Château Pétrus in a special category of its own.

Château Pétrus	
Château Certan-de-May	Château la Conseillante
Château L'Évangile	Château La Fleur Pétrus
Château Lafleur	Château Latour à Pomerol
Château Petit Village	Château Trotanoy
Vieux Château Certan	Château Beauregard
Château Le Bon Pasteur	Château Certan Giraud
Château Clinet	Clos L'Église
Clos Rene	Château la Croix de Gay
Château L'Église Clinet	Château Gazin

{ WINE ORGANIZATIONS AND PUBLICATIONS }

Following are lists of some organizations and publications to further enhance your learning. Many other resources exist for researching wine, but these will help you get started.

For links to these organizations' Web sites, log in to www.cengagebrain.com and access the CourseMate that accompanies this text.

Organization
American Wine Society
Appellation America
Australian Wine & Brandy Corporation
Burgundy Wines
California State University Fresno Winery
Canadian Vintners Association
The German Wine Institute
National Restaurant Association Education Foundation
New Zealand Winegrowers
Professional Friends of Wine
Rhone Rangers
Society of Wine Educators
Sopexa (formerly Food & Wines From France)
The Oregon Wine Board
U.C. Davis Department of Viticulture and Enology
Washington Wine Commission
Wine & Spirits Wholesalers of America
Wine Institute
Wine Lovers Page
Wines From Spain
Wines of Argentina
Wines of Chile
Zinfandel Advocates and Producers (ZAP)

Publication
California Grapevine
Connoisseurs' Guide to California Wine
Decanter
Practical Winery & Vineyard
Quarterly Review of Wines
Vineyard & Winery Management Magazine
Wine Business Monthly
Wine Enthusiast
Wine Spectator
Wines & Vines

{ GLOSSARY }

A

aeration (air-AY-shun) The process of incorporating oxygen into a wine.

Aglianico (ah-LYAH-nee-koh) Widely planted red grape of southern Italy.

Airén (ahr-yehn) The most widely planted grape in Spain, accounting for about one-third of total acreage. Especially prevalent in the dry central parts of the country, the grape is used in the production of brandy. It is also increasingly vinified into nondescript, but fresh, dry white wines.

Albariño (ahl-bah-REE-n'yoh) A white grape grown in Galicia, Spain (also called Alvarinho, grown in the Vinho Verde region of Portugal). It produces complex, aromatic wines with bracing acidity.

alembic still A type of copper "pot" still used for making Cognac Brandy, as well as Pisco.

alluvial Soils created by the flooding along rivers and streams.

Alvarinho (ahl-vah-REEN-yoh) See *Albariño.*

amabile (ah-MAH-bee-lay) Italian. Off-dry or semisweet.

American Viticultural Area (AVA) A particular area of grape growing with specific boundaries sanctioned by the government.

amphora (AM-fuhr-uh) A jar with an oval body, narrow neck, and two handles used by the ancient Greeks to transport wine. Plural, *amphorae* or *amphoras.*

Anbaugebiet (AHN-bow-geh-beet) German. A wine region. There are 13 Anbaugebiete (plural) in Germany. A smaller, officially recognized wine-producing district within an Anbaugebiet is called a Bereich.

anthocyanins (an-tho-SIGH-uh-nins) The compounds responsible for the color of red wine.

appellation (ap-puh-LAY-shuhn) An area of origin of grapes.

Appellation d'Origin Contrôlée (AOC) (ah-pehl-lah-SYAWN daw-ree-JEEN kawn-traw-LAY) French. "Controlled Place of Origin." In the French system, the highest level of classification for wine regions. The designation applies to all wines made from grapes grown in that region if the wine is made according to all guidelines for that appellation, as outlined in the AOC laws.

astringency The drying or "puckery" tactile sensation that is produced by tannins in wine.

Auslese (OWS-lay-zuh) German. Selected. Describes grapes picked at a high level of ripeness, thus with considerable sugars.

Australian Wine and Brandy Corporation (AWBC) A governmental organization responsible for the regulation and promotion of the Australian wine industry.

autolysis (aw-TAHL-uh-sihss) The breakdown of yeast cells.

AVA See *American Viticultural Area.*

B

Bacchus (BAK-uhs) The Roman god of wine.

Beerenauslese (BAY-ruhn-OWSlay-zuh) German. Literally "selected berries," the term refers to grapes that are picked one-by-one depending on the level to which they have been affected by *botrytis.* The wine produced is one of the two levels of dessert wine within Germany's Prädikat system.

bench land A plateau that lies above the floor of a river valley.

Bereich (beh-RIKH) German. A smaller, officially recognized wine-producing district within an Anbaugebiet.

bin number A number assigned to a wine that describes its area of storage in a restaurant's cellar area; bin numbers are used to facilitate ordering and locating specific wines when they are ordered by guests.

Biodiversity and Wine Initiative   A project set up between environmental bodies and the South African wine industry with the aim of minimizing the loss of threatened natural habitat from the expansion of vineyards.

biodynamic   A form of organic agriculture that is holistic in its approach, and seeks to integrate the farm with the natural environment. It is based on the teachings of Rudolf Steiner and it incorporates the use of homeopathic compounds.

Black Association of the Wine and Spirit Industry (BAWSI)   A South African association founded in 2002 with the aim of helping its black South African members play a more meaningful role in the wine industry.

blanc de blancs (blahn duh blahn)   A Champagne made from white grapes only.

blanc de noirs (blahn duh nwahr)   A Champagne made from red grapes only.

Blauburgunder   Swiss name for the Pinot Noir grape.

blind tasting   A tasting where the identities of the wines being served are not known by the tasters.

bloom   The period of flowering when pollination takes place.

bodega (boh-DAY-gah)   Spanish. A winery.

boom and bust   An economic cycle characterized by periods of overproduction and underproduction, typical for many agricultural products.

Botrytis cinerea **(boh-TRI-tis sihn-EH-ee-uh)**   A type of mold that grows on grape clusters that can be used to make dessert wine. Also called noble rot.

bottle bouquet   The term used to describe the increasingly complex aromatics that develop in wines as they age.

Brettanomyces **(breht-tan-uh-MI-sees)**   A yeast that can grow in wines while they are being aged that will produce a distinctive "barn yard" smell, considered by some to be a type of spoilage.

brilliant   The appearance of a wine clear of any visual defects.

Brix   See *degrees Brix*.

brut (BROOT)   The term used to describe a dry Champagne; also used by sparkling wine producers in other countries.

Bureau of Alcohol, Tobacco & Firearms (BATF)   Now replaced by the Tax and Trade Bureau (TTB).

by the glass (BTG)   Wines that are sold on an individual glass basis (as opposed to selling an entire bottle). This manner of selling wine usually represents the bulk of wine sales in the restaurant setting.

C

California Wine Association (CWA)   A large cooperative winery that produced most of California's wine from 1894 to 1919.

canes   The shoots of a grapevine on which the buds form.

cap   The layer of skins that is formed on the surface of a fermenting container of red must.

Cape Doctor   Summer southeasterly wind that moderates temperatures and helps prevent disease in the vines.

Cape Floral Kingdom   A World Heritage site in the Western Cape that contains the greatest number of indigenous plants in the smallest area on earth.

capsule   The foil or laminate covering that covers the cork and top of a wine bottle.

carbonic maceration (kar-BAHN-ihk mas-uh-RAY-shuhn)   A form of fermentation in which the clusters of grapes are not crushed prior to fermentation. Widely used in Beaujolais, it results in wine that is softer and fruitier than would be the case if the whole batch had been crushed, and then fermented.

Carmenère (KAH-meh-NEHR)   A red grape that is similar in taste and appearance to Merlot, widely planted in Chile but rarely grown elsewhere.

Cava (KAH-vah)   Spanish sparkling wine made in the méthode champenoise. The term, from the Catalonian word for "cellar," was adopted in 1970.

cellar door   The term used for a winery tasting room in Australia and New Zealand.

Chambourcin (shahm-boor-SAN)   A recent French hybrid; a very vigorous and productive red grape, planted frequently in Virginia.

Champagne (sham-PAYN)   A sparkling wine from the Champagne region of France.

chaptalization (shap-tuh-luh-ZAY-shuhn)   Addition of sugar after fermentation. Named for Jean Chaptal of France. Forbidden in all Qualitätsweins of Germany and in all wines made in California.

Charmat process (shar-MAHT)   A method of sparkling wine production where the secondary fermentation takes place in tanks rather than in the bottle.

Charta (KAR-tah)   German. A group of wine producers in the Rheingau dedicated to producing wines of higher quality than specified by German wine law. Founded in 1984.

Chasselas (shas-suh-LAH)   One of Switzerland's major white grapes.

classico (KLA-sih-koh)   Italian. A geographic designation for the highest-quality zone within an Italian DOC region.

clone (KLOHN)   A grapevine that is genetically identical to the parent grapevine that it is propagated from, retaining the same attributes.

clos (KLOH)   French. A walled-in vineyard. The term is often found in the names of Burgundy's vineyards.

Colheita Selecionada (cuhl-YAY-tah SEP-see-a-nod-a)   A Portuguese term for a very high-quality wine, from excellent vintages and often from prime vineyards.

Concord (KAHN-kord)   A native American grape variety used for grape juice production and some winemaking.

cooper   A barrel maker.

cooperative   A winery jointly owned by grape farmer members who deliver their crop to a central cellar, either for sale in bulk, or to one or more merchants for blending into their branded wines.

cordons   The branches of a grapevine that the canes grow from.

cork taint   A musty smell that is the most common problem associated with natural corks. It occurs when the cork has been exposed, either in the forest or during processing and storage, to mold growth and the corks absorb a compound called 2,4,6-trichloroanisole, more often called trichloroanisole or TCA, from the mold. TCA is the most prominent of several compounds that are produced by mold and can be detected in the aroma of a wine in levels as low as several parts per trillion.

corkage fee (CORK-ihj)   A fee that a restaurant may charge guests who bring their own bottle of wine to enjoy with their meal.

Cortese (kohr-THE-zeh)   Italian. Important white grape of Piedmont.

cost percentage   The cost percentage is the percentage of the selling price that was spent to buy the product.

Côt (koh)   A red grape variety native to the Bordeaux region of France; popular in Argentina, where it is called Malbec.

crianza (kree-AHN-zah)   In Spain, the youngest classification for wood-aged wines.

Criolla Chica (KREE-oh-yah chee-ka)   A "native" red grape variety that was first produced from seed brought from Europe. Popular in Argentina, called Mission in California and País in Chile.

Criolla Grande (KREE-oh-yah gran-DAY)   A "native" red grape variety bread from seeds brought from Europe that is found in Argentina.

cross   See *hybrid*.

cru (KROO)   French. Literally "growth," often used to signify a rated, or high-quality vineyard.

cuvée (koo-VAY)   A blend of wine, a French word that translates literally to "tub full" or "vat full."

D

decanter   A glass carafe used to serve wine, often in conjunction with decanting and aeration.

decanting   The process of using a decanter to separate a wine from its sediment.

degree days   See *heat summation.*

degrees Brix (°Brix)   The percentage of sugar by weight of a liquid.

demi-sec (DEHM-ee-sehk)   French. Literally "half-dry," but used to describe a Champagne that is quite sweet.

Denominação de Origem Controlada (DOC) (deh-naw-mee-nah-THYON deh aw-REE-hen con-traw-LAH-tah)   Portuguese. Literally, controlled denomination of origin, meaning the wine is from one of Portugal's protected appellations, and has been produced in compliance with the regulations of that region.

Denominación de Origen (DO) (deh-naw-mee-nah-THYON deh aw-REE-hen)   Spanish. A controlled appellation with specific regulations, the enforcement of which is overseen by a local branch of the national INDO.

Denominazione di Origine Controllata (DOC) (deh-NAW-mee-nah-TSYAW-neh dee oh-REE-jee-neh kohn-troh-LAH-tah)   Italy's set of laws enacted in 1963 to regulate the production of wine, protect the defined wine zones, and guarantee authenticity and consistency of style.

Denominazione di Origine Controllata e Garantita (DOCG) (deh-NAW-mee-nah-TSYAW-neh dee oh-REE-jee-neh contraw-LAH-tah eh gah-rahn-TEE-tah)   The highest designation in Italy's DOC laws, given only to the country's most prestigious wine zones.

depth   The intensity of color of a wine.

descriptive analysis   The process of describing and identifying the different smells present in a wines aroma.

designated viticultural area (DVA)   In Canada, an officially approved appellation.

dessert wines   Wines made with appreciable sugar.

differentiating characteristic   A marketing term for the unique quality of a product that differentiates it from the competition.

Dionysus (di-uh-NI-suhs)   The Greek god of wine.

disgorging   The process of removing the yeast from the neck of the bottle in méthode champenoise production.

distributor   An operation that acts as a go-between for the wine producer and the wine retailer. This is the second tier of the three-tiered system of distribution.

dolce (DOHL-chay)   Italian. Sweet.

dosage (doh-SAHJ)   The addition of a small amount of wine, usually sweetened, after disgorging.

doux (DOO)   French. "Sweet"; used to designate the sweetest style of Champagne, which is rarely imported into the United States.

dry wine   A wine without perceptible sweetness.

dry-farmed   Growing grapevines without supplemental irrigation.

dull   The appearance of a wine that is turbid or cloudy.

E

Egri Bikavér (EH-grih BIH-kah-vahr)   Hungary's most famous red wine. The name derives from a legendary battle against the Turks in the early 1500s, during which the residents of the town of Eger, known as the Magyars, were fiercely defending their town. During the battle, the Magyars drank large quantities of red wine, and, legend has it, the Turks, upon seeing the red-stained beards of their opponents, withdrew because they believed the Magyars obtained their great strength and ferocity by drinking the blood of bulls.

Einzellage (IN-tsuh-lah-guh)   German. A single vineyard. There are 2,600 Einzellagen in Germany's wine regions.

Eiswein (ICE-vyn) German. Ice wine. Made from nonbotryitised but very ripe grapes that have been frozen by a sudden drop in temperature. The grapes are picked from the vine while still frozen. The frozen water crystals are discarded during the crush, leaving a high concentration of natural sugars. The resulting sweet wine must have minimally the same sugar content as a Beerenauslese.

enologist Someone who studies wine, from the term *enology*.

enology (ee-NAHL-uh-jee) The study of winemaking, also spelled oenology.

esters (EHS-tuhrs) Aromatic compounds created by acid and alcohol molecules binding together during the course of fermentation and bottle age.

ethanol Beverage alcohol that is produced by yeast, also called ethyl alcohol.

extended maceration (mas-uh-RAY-shun) Delaying the pressing of red must until several weeks after fermentation has stopped.

extra brut (BROOT) Champagne to which no dosage or additional sugar, is added before bottling.

extra dry A confusing term used in Champagne to indicate a wine that is slightly sweet.

F

fighting varietals Inexpensively priced varietal wines that were introduced in the early 1980s.

fining (FI-ning) The addition of a compound that affects the composition of a wine but does not stay in solution.

fino (FEE-noh) A light, dry style of Sherry.

fixed markup A method of pricing that assigns a standard markup value to all wines within a certain price point; used to offset the high prices that would result from assigning one markup strategy to wines at all price points.

flight A group of wines evaluated at the same time in a wine tasting.

flor yeast (FLAWR YEEST) A harmless, film-forming yeast that floats on the surface of Sherry while it ages in casks.

FOB price The price charged by the producer of the wine (or his or her importer) to wholesalers. The FOB is based on cost of producing the wine plus approximately a 30 percent markup. It is derived from the term *free on board,* which means the buyer is responsible for the costs of shipping.

fortified wine A wine fortified through the addition of extra alcohol, usually in the form of neutral, that is, colorless and flavorless, brandy. The best-known fortified wines are Sherry, Port, Madeira, and Marsala.

free run The first fraction of juice that is released during pressing; usually it is the highest-quality juice.

French paradox The paradox that although the French have higher saturated fat in their diets they have lower heart disease than Americans, suspected to be caused by the moderate consumption of red wine.

frizzante (freet-TSAHN-teh) Italian. Slightly sparkling wine, as opposed to a truly sparkling wine or spumante.

Frontenac (FRUN-teh-nak) A French–American hybrid developed at the University of Minnesota. This grape, grown in Vermont and other northern states, produces red and rosé wines.

fungicide A compound that is applied to a vineyard to control rot.

Furmint (FOOR-mint) White varietal indigenous to Hungary.

fusion cuisine The blending of the culinary traditions of two or more nations to create new dishes.

futures A method of purchasing wine before it is released to the market, allowing buyers to secure the wines that they desire.

G

Garnacha (gahr-NAH-chah) A widely planted *vinifera* grape used in many of Spain's red wines. In France, the grape is called Grenache.

Geographic Indications (GIs) A method of classification that subdivides the territory of each Australian state into a series of Zones, Regions, and Subregions.

grafting The process of taking a cutting, or scion, and affixing it to a rootstock to produce a single grapevine with the positive aspects of each.

gran reserva (grahn ray-SAYR-vah) Spanish. Wine from excellent vintage years and from fine vineyards that have received considerable aging before being released for sale. Gran Reservas, by law, have been aged in oak casks for a minimum of two years, and then aged further in bottle or tank for at least another three years.

Grosslage (GROSS-lah-guh) German. Literally "large site," the term describes a number of contiguous vineyards that have been grouped together under one popular name. About 150 Grosslagen were created by the German Wine Law of 1971. Some of these are so large (average size 1,500 acres [607 hectares]) as to be meaningless, geographically and viticulturally.

Grüner Veltliner (GROO-ner FELT-lih-ner) Austria's most important indigenous grape.

Gutsabfüllung (GOOTS-ab-few-lung) German. Estate-bottled. The wine so labeled must be made by the same entity that grew the grapes and made the wine. A more restrictive term than *Erzeugerabfüllung*.

H

half bottle This size bottle holds half of the volume of a standard bottle of wine (375 ml).

haute cuisine (OAT kwee-ZEEN) The literal translation is "high cooking," the traditional French method of fine dining that incorporates multiple courses of elaborately prepared dishes.

heat summation A method of using average daytime temperature to provide a rough estimate of a vineyard's terroir. Also called degree days.

heavy soil Soil with a high percentage of clay that has a high capacity for holding water.

herbicide A compound that is applied to a vineyard to control unwanted plant growth.

Hermitage (her-mee-TAHZJ) An Australian name for the grape variety Syrah, also known as Shiraz.

house wine A term commonly used to describe a restaurant's standard offerings by the glass. This term has taken on a negative connotation in recent years because it implies an entry-level, basic wine.

hue The shade of color of a wine.

Huguenots (HUE-ga-nots) French Protestants who fled their homeland after the revocation of the Edict of Nantes in 1688, many of whom traveled to South Africa and helped establish the Cape's wine industry.

hybrid A new grape variety produced by breeding two varieties from different botanical species, most commonly a varietal from an American species (e.g., *labrusca*) with a French varietal from *Vitis vinifera*. Also called a cross, although the latter term is usually used to refer to breeding within a species.

I

imbottigliato dal produttore all'origine (ihm-boh-tee-LYAH-toh dahl PRO-duc-tor-ee ahl' oh-REE-jee-neh) Italian. Estate-bottled. A term that can appear on an Italian label; equivalent to France's misen bouteilles au château or au domaine.

Indicazione Geografica Tipica (IGT) (en-dee-KAH-zee-oh-nee gee-oh-GRAF-fee-kah TIP-eh-kah) Italian regional wine that reflects the terroir of the geographic region that shows on the label; equivalent to France's vin de pays.

inert gas A gas that does not interact with the substances that it contacts.

Instituto da Vinha e Vinho (IVV) The government agency at the national level that oversees Portugal's systems of controlled appellations.

Instituto Nacional de Denominaciones de Origen (INDO) The government agency that oversees Spain's DO system; equivalent to France's INAO.

Integrated Production of Wine A scheme introduced in 1998 setting guidelines and minimum standards for environmentally friendly practices in South African vineyards, cellars, and packaging.

international varietals Also called classic varietals, they are grape varieties that are most familiar to and popular with wine drinkers around the world. They include Chardonnay, Sauvignon Blanc, Pinot Noir, Cabernet Sauvignon, Merlot, and Syrah.

Isabella A native American red grape variety that was popular in Washington State.

J

jerepigo A South African dessert wine consisting of very sweet, unfermented grape juice fortified with grape spirit.

jug wines Inexpensive table wines that are sold in large bottles.

K

Kabinett (kah-bih-NEHT) German. The driest Prädikat within the QmP rankings.

Kadarka (KAH-dahr-kah) Hungary's most characteristic red grape.

Ko-operatiewe Wijnbouwers Vereniging (KWV) A large cooperative winery in South Africa.

L

Laid-in cost (LIC) The laid-in cost of a case of wine or spirits is the actual cost to the distributor of buying that case and "laying it in" to the company's warehouse. It is the sum of the FOB cost, shipping charges, and state taxes.

Landwein (LAHNT-vyn) German. Regional wine, a step above Tafelwein in quality in Germany's quality control laws.

large format bottle Any size bottle that is larger than the standard 750 ml format.

late harvest wines Wines that are made from grapes picked at a much higher sugar level than those for table wines.

lees (LEEZ) The solids that settle at the bottom of a vessel of wine.

light soil Soil with a high percentage of sand that has a low capacity for holding water.

loam A type of soil that is a mixture of clay, silt, sand, and organic matter that is fertile and drains well.

M

macroclimate The broad weather conditions of a particular wine-growing region.

magnum The smallest of the large format bottles. It holds the same amount of wine as two standard bottles (1,500 ml or 1.5 liters).

Malbec (mahl-BEHK) A red grape variety popular in Argentina, native to the Bordeaux region of France, where it is called Côt.

malolactic bacteria (ma-loh-LAK-tihk) The bacteria that convert malic acid to lactic acid.

Manzanilla (MAHN-zah-NEE-yah) A light style of Sherry, aged in the coastal region of Sanlúcar de Barrameda, Spain.

marc (MAHR) Grape skins after they are pressed.

Maréchal Foch (MAH-ray-shahl FOHSH) A French hybrid named for France's famous World War I general, widely planted in Canada and New York.

margin on sell A measurement used by wholesalers to determine the profitability of a specific product. The gross profit on a wine divided by the laid-in cost of that wine gives the margin on sell.

markup The difference between the restaurant's cost and the selling price of a product.

mesoclimate   Local weather conditions that affect a vineyard or a portion of a vineyard, more commonly known as microclimate.

Méthode Cap Classique (MAY-tohd cap KLAH-seek)   South African term for sparkling wine made in the same method as Champagne, a term not permitted for generic use.

méthode champenoise (may-TOHD shahm-peh-NWAHZ)   The traditional method of producing sparkling wine by fermenting it in the bottle.

metodo classico (MEH-toh-doh CLAH-seecoh)   A term used to describe a sparkling wine made in the méthode champenoise.

metodo tradizionale (MEH-toh-doh trah-dee-tsyoh-NAH-lay)   A term used to describe a sparkling wine made in the méthode champenoise.

microclimate   Local weather conditions that affect a vineyard or a portion of a vineyard, less commonly used to refer to the climatic conditions around a single vine.

Mission grape   A *vinifera* red grape variety grown by the missions. See also *Criolla Chica*.

Mission period   From 1769 to 1833, when a series of missions were established along the coast of California by Spain and Mexico.

moelleux (mwah-LEUH)   French. A term used to describe sweet wines, often used for dessert wines in the Loire Valley.

Moscato (mow-SKAT-oh)   A white grape often used to make sparkling wines; Muscat.

mousseux (moo-SEUHR)   French. Sparkling; used to describe sparkling wines made outside Champagne.

mouthfeel   The texture or body of a wine felt in the mouth.

Müller-Thurgau (MEW-luhr TOOR-gow)   A lesser white grape indigenous variety developed in Switzerland in the late nineteenth century and now widely planted in Germany. The grape produces characterless, flabby wines, and is slowly being phased out.

Muscadel (mus-kuh-DEHL)   A grape variety and wine style. The grape variety, both white and red versions, is a synonym of Muscat à Petits Grains. The wine style is the unfermented very sweet juice of the grape variety, fortified with grape spirit—in other words, a jerepigo.

***Muscadinia rotundifolia* (MUHS-kuh-dihn roh-tuhn-dih-FOHL-ee-uh)**   A grapevine that is native to the eastern United States, also known as *Vitis rotundifolia*.

must   Unfermented grape juice, either before or after it has been separated from the skins and seeds.

N

Nebbiolo (neh-b'YOH-loh)   Italian. Principal red grape of Piedmont.

négociant (nay-goh-SYAHN)   The middleman in wine production who purchases grapes from vineyard owners, and then makes and markets the wine.

net price   The wholesale price of a wine minus any incentives or bonuses offered on that wine. In other words, the actual price a licensee will pay for that case of wine.

noble rot   Pourriture noble in French; *Botrytis cinerea* in Latin. A mold that attacks the skins of grapes while they are still on the vine, causing the skins to crack, thus allowing the watery juice of the grape to evaporate. This evaporation greatly elevates the concentration of sugar in the grapes, which can result in every sweet but balanced dessert wines.

nonvintage   A wine that is made from grapes harvested in two or more years. Champagne is often nonvintage (abbreviated N.V.).

O

Oechsle (UHK-sluh)   German. A measurement of the level of sugar in grapes as an indication of ripeness. Named for German scientist Ferdinand Oechsle.

off-premise license   A license to sell alcoholic beverages that is limited to sales that will be consumed off the premises (i.e., retail stores).

oidium   Also known as powdery mildew, a fungus that attacks the vine but can be controlled by dusting the vines with sulfur.

olfactory bulb   The organ above the sinus that receives signals from the olfactory epithelium before sending them on to the brain.

olfactory epithelium   The membranes in the nasal septum that detect volatile compounds that are inhaled.

oloroso (oh-loh-ROH-soh)   The heavier, richer, dessert style of Sherry, aged in casks without the protective flor yeast.

on-premise license   A license to sell alcoholic beverages that allows the beverage to be consumed on the premises of the licensee (i.e., restaurants, bars, clubs, etc.).

organic   A form of agriculture that prohibits the use of synthetic chemicals such as human-made insecticides and herbicides.

own-rooted   When grapevines grow on their own roots instead of using a rootstock.

P

País (pa-EES)   A "native" red grape variety that was first produced from seed brought from Europe. Popular in Chile, it is also called Mission or Criolla Chica.

Palomino (pah-loh-MEE-noh)   A white grape of the Jerez region of Spain, widely used in the production of Sherry.

Paris tasting   A tasting that took place in Paris in 1976 in which California wines took top honors.

passive cellar   A cellar that does not employ any mechanical method of temperature or humidity control.

Pedro Ximénez (PEH-droh hee-MEE-nihs)   A white grape widely planted in the southern parts of Spain, and often used for Sherry.

pesticide   A compound that is applied to a vineyard to control unwanted organisms.

phylloxera (fihl-LOX-er-uh)   Root-eating aphid native to North America that devastated the vineyards of Europe and California in the late nineteenth century.

Pierce's disease   A bacterial disease that can kill grapevines.

Pinotage (pee-noh-TAHJ)   South African red grape variety, a cross between Pinot Noir and Cinsaut (then known locally as Hermitage), bred by professor Abraham Perold in 1924.

Pisco   A lightly colored brandy that is very popular in Chile.

pomace (PAH-muss)   Grape skins after they are pressed.

Port   A fortified red wine with about 10 percent sugar and 20 percent alcohol from the Douro Valley in northern Portugal.

Port-style   A wine made in the style of Port, but produced outside the Port region of Portugal.

post off   A periodic discount offered by wholesalers on bottles and cases of wine, usually offered on wines sold by the glass in the restaurant operation.

Prädikat (preh-dih-KAHT)   In German and Austrian wine laws, the ripeness of grapes at harvest time and thus the sweetness of the resulting wine.

press fraction   The juice that is released in pressing after the free run, usually of a lower quality.

primary fermentation   The first alcoholic fermentation, utilizing sugar from the grape juice.

primary lees (LEEZ)   The lees that form in juice before fermentation.

private cellars   A South African term for wineries that are privately owned.

producer cellars   A South African term for wineries that are owned by grower cooperatives.

Prohibition   The period of time from 1920 to 1933 when the purchase or sale of alcohol was illegal in the United States.

propriétaire (proh-pree-ay-TEHR)   French. Indicates that the entity that made a wine also owns the vineyard where the grapes were grown.

pumping over   Irrigating the cap with juice during fermentation.

punching down   Breaking up the cap during red wine fermentation by pushing it down into the juice.

Q

Qualitätswein bestimmter Anbaugebiet (QbA) (kvah-lih-TAYTS-vine behr-SHTIHMT-tuhr ahn-BOW-geh-beet)   German. The third level of quality in Germany's wine laws, used to show that the grapes in a bottle were all grown within 1 of the 13 wine regions (Anbaugebiete). There are few regulations or standards at this level. The majority of wines exported from Germany are at the QbA level.

Qualitätswein mit Prädikat (QmP) (kvah-lih-TYATS-vine mitt PRAY-dee-kaht)   German. The highest level of quality in Germany's system of quality control laws. The term means literally "quality wine with designation." There are five Prädikats, or designations, based on the quality of the grapes used and their level of ripeness when picked.

quercetin (KWER-si-tin)   A compound found in wine that has positive health effects.

quinta (KEEN-tah)   A Portuguese name for a farm or vineyard, it also applies to an estate that produces wine.

R

racking   The process of transferring clean wine or juice off the lees that form in a tank or barrel.

rain shadow   The weather condition where Pacific storms lose their moisture on the west side of the Cascades, creating a dry climate in eastern Oregon and Washington.

raulí   A type of South American beech tree used for making wine casks but being phased out with modernization.

Recioto (reh-CHAW-toh)   Italian. The ripest grapes in a bunch, usually those on the upper sides, often further concentrated by being dried on special mats in ventilated rooms.

reserva (ray-ZEHR-vah)   A Spanish term used to indicate additional aging. The law specifies a total of three years of aging either in cask or in bottle for reserva wines. In Portugal the term signifies a wine from a very good vintage.

responsible hospitality   The practice of serving alcohol in a responsible manner to minimize the risk of patrons overindulging.

resveratrol (rez-VEHR-ah-trawl)   A compound found in wine that has positive health effects.

Rhine Riesling (RINE REEZ-ling)   An Australian name for the grape variety White Riesling.

riddling (RIHD-ling)   The process of moving the yeast to the neck of the bottle in méthode champenoise production.

riserva (ree-ZEHR-vah)   Indicates additional aging for Italian wines, usually partly in oak barrels.

Robola (roh-BOH-lah)   White grape indigenous to Greece grown mostly in the mountains.

rootstock   A grapevine that is resistant to soil pests that is used as a root system for grafting wine grape varieties.

rosé   A pink wine made in one of two methods. The first method is to use red grapes but allow only a very short maceration period so that minimal color is extracted from the skins. The second method is to add a small amount of white wine to a red wine after fermentation is complete.

ruby Port   The simplest, most straightforward style of Port (and the most affordable). Bottled after only two or three years in cask, it is deep ruby in color and has a vivid fruitiness.

S

Saccharomyces cerevisiae (sack-a-roe-MY-seas sair-a-VIS-e-eye)   The species of yeast that is most often used for winemaking. The name is derived from the Latin terms for sugar-fungus and grain, the latter referring to its most common use in bread making.

Sangiovese (san-joh-VAY-zeh) Principal red grape of Tuscany.

scion (SI-uhn) A cutting from a cane of a grapevine used to propagate another grapevine that is genetically identical to the parent.

sec (SEHK) French. Dry.

secco (SEH-koh) Italian. Dry.

sediment The gritty accumulation that appears in the bottle after considerable age—a combination of tannin, acid, and color molecules that have precipitated out of solution as they became larger.

Sekt (ZEHKT) German. A quality sparkling wine.

sensory evaluation The process of using the effect a wine makes on one's senses to review and describe a wine.

Serra, Junípero A Franciscan priest who founded the missions in California.

Seyval Blanc (say-vahl BLAHN) A French hybrid widely planted in Canada and parts of the eastern United States.

shatter The process of unfertilized flowers falling off the grape cluster.

Sherry A fortified wine native to Spain done in a wide variety styles that have an oxidized character.

Shiraz (shee-RAZ) An Australian name for the grape variety Syrah, also known as Hermitage.

sliding scale A method of pricing that applies various cost percentages to wines at different price points. This ensures that the guests are offered reasonable value at all levels of the wine list.

solera (soh-LEH-rah) A sequential system of aging wine in barrels. Used primarily in Jerez, a solera allows wine from various vintages to be aged in the same system, thus evening out quality differences between vintages.

sommelier (saw-muh-LYAY) The person responsible for organizing and sustaining a wine program in a restaurant setting.

sparkling wine Wine with bubbles or effervescence.

Spätlese (SHPAYT-lay-zuh) German. The second designation in the QmP level. *Spätlese* means "late," and these wines are picked later in the fall, after the Kabinett grapes. The exact ripeness, or must level, is explicitly spelled out in German wine law for each region and each varietal. Spätlese wines are not sweet, but off-dry.

spritz A slight degree of effervescence in a still wine.

spumante (spoo-MAHN-tay) Italian. Sparkling wine.

stemmer-crusher A machine used to separate grape berries from stems and break the berries open to release the juice.

still wine A wine without effervescence.

Stimson Lane Vineyards & Estates The parent company of Chateau Ste. Michelle Winery, the largest in the state of Washington.

sulfur dioxide A compound that is used as a preservative in wine.

superiore (soo-payr-YOH-reh) Italian. Designation for wine of better quality, with higher alcohol content and/or additional aging.

supplier In the alcoholic beverage industry, the person or company that supplies the product to a wholesaler (i.e., winery, importer, or marketing company).

sur lie (soor LEE) Aging your wine on the yeast lees after fermentation.

sustainable viticulture Growing grapes in a manner in which the vineyard practices do not degrade the fertility of land or the surrounding environment.

T

table tent A small tabletop display that can be used to advertise specials or specific wines.

table wine A still wine that is also dry and with moderate alcohol content.

Tafelwein (TAH-fuh-vyn) Table wine, the lowest level of quality for German wines. A very small percentage of Germany's wines fall into this category.

tannin buildup In red wines, repeated sips of the same wine will taste increasingly astringent.

tannins   Polyphenolic compounds that contribute bitterness and astringency to wine and play an important role in a wine's flavor, texture, and aging qualities. They are primarily derived from grape skins, but seeds, stems, and oak barrels can also contribute to a wine's tannins.

tartrates   Potassium bitartrate, a naturally occurring compound in wine that forms crystals on the sides of containers, such as bottles or barrels that wine is stored in.

tawny Port   A wine aged much longer in wooden casks than a ruby, and which thus has lost its reddish color and taken on a golden-brown, or tawny, hue. Most tawny Ports are bottled with an indication of age on the label.

Tax and Trade Bureau (TTB)   The U.S. government agency that regulates alcoholic products.

Tempranillo (tem-prah-NEE-yoh)   The most important grape of Spain, the backbone of many of its greatest red wines.

terroir (tehr-WAHR)   A French term used to describe the unique character a wine exhibits due to the specific physical characteristics (i.e., terrain, soil composition, drainage, precipitation, prevailing winds, average temperatures, etc.) of the location where the grapes were grown.

tête de cuvée (TEHT duh koo-VAY)   French. Literally "top batch," used in Champagne to designate the deluxe bottling of a producer.

texture   The tactile sensations that are produced when wine is tasted. See also *mouthfeel*.

three-tiered system of distribution   The method of distribution of alcohol in the United States mandating that products are transferred from a producer to a wholesaler to a retailer or restaurant operation.

3 V's (vintner, varietal, and vintage)   The vintner is the producer of the wine (who made it); the varietal is the grape that is used to make the wine; the vintage is the year that the grapes were harvested.

threshold   The level at which a taster can detect a given flavor compound.

tirage (tee-RAHZH)   The process of aging a bottle of sparkling wine on its fermentation lees.

Tocai Friulano   A white grape widely planted in northeast Italy.

Tokaji Aszú (toh-kah-YEE AHS-oo)   Hungary's famous dessert wine, made from botrytized grapes from the Tokaj-Hegyalja region.

Torrontés (tohr-rohn-TEHS)   A white grape variety with a fruity flavor, native to the Rioja region of Spain. It is also the name of similar "native" white variety found in Argentina.

trade tasting   An event sponsored by a winery or wholesaler to allow industry professionals to taste wines that are recently released.

trellis   A support for grapevines.

trichloroanisole (TCA) (TRY-claw-row-AN-ee-sol)   A chemical compound that results from the interaction of chlorine and wood products, most commonly corks.

Trockenbeerenauslese (TRAWK-uhn-bay-ruhn-OWS-lay-zuh)   German. Literally "selected dried berries," this is the fifth designation within the QmP level of quality. The grapes are picked late in the fall, when they are fully botrytized, and thus shriveled (dried). The resulting wines are very rich and sweet, yet retain enough acidity to be balanced. Very rare, risky, and labor-intensive, and thus expensive.

twist top   Also known as a screw cap. A twist top closure is a metal top that is used to seal a bottle instead of a traditional cork.

U

ullage (UHL-ihj)   The head space between the wine and the container it is stored in. For example, in a wine bottle, the space between the wine and the end of the cork.

University of California at Davis   A University of California campus with research and degree programs in viticulture and enology.

V

Vallejo, Mariano G. A general and rancher who helped settle the Napa and Sonoma Valleys.

véraison (vay-ray-ZON) The beginning of ripening of a grape berry.

vertical flight A group of the same type of wine from consecutive vintages.

Vidal Blanc (vee-dahl BLAHN) A French hybrid, the basis for many of Canada's famous late-harvest dessert wines, as well as many ice wines.

vin de pays (van duh pay-YEE) "Country wine," the second level of classification in French wine laws.

vin de table (van duh TAH-bl) The lowest level of classification in French wine laws.

vin délimité de qualité supérieure (VDQS) (van deh-lee-mee-TAY duh kah-lee-TAY soo-pehr-YUR) In French law, the classification of wine regions just below Appellation d'Origin Côntrolée.

vin doux naturel (van doo nah-tew-REHL) Indicates a naturally sweet wine made by arresting fermentation early on through the addition of alcohol to kill the yeast, leaving high levels of unfermented sugar.

vino da tavola (VEE-noh dah TAH-voh-lah) Italian. Table wine; the lowest designation in Italy's DOC laws.

vintage (VIHN-tihj) The year in which the grapes for a wine were harvested.

Vintners Quality Alliance (VQA) Canada's quality control agency.

viticulture (VIHT-ih-kuhl-cher) Grape growing.

Vitis labrusca (VEE-tihs luh-BRUSH-kuh) Species of the *Vitis* genus that is indigenous to North America, especially in the northeastern regions.

Vitis riparia (VEE-tihs rih-PEHR-ee-uh) A very hardy species of the *Vitis* genus, prevalent in the Eastern United States, usually in damp areas along streams. Often used to breed rootstocks.

Vitis vinifera (VEE-tihs vihn-IHF-uh-ruh) The species of grape that is most commonly used for producing wine.

Viura (vee-OO-rah) The dominant white grape of Spain, particularly in Rioja. Also called Macabeo.

volatile A compound that can evaporate and become airborne.

Volstead Act The Eighteenth Amendment implementing the prohibition of the sale or consumption of alcoholic beverages.

W

wholesaler See *distributor*.

Wine Aroma Wheel A method of identifying and categorizing aromas found in wine.

wine dinner A dinner where individual courses of food are paired with different wines that complement the dishes.

wine flight A series of wines that are poured in smaller portions and served together or with accompanying courses.

Wine Institute A trade organization for California wineries.

Wine Institute of New Zealand A trade organization of grape growers and winemakers that promotes New Zealand Wine.

wine key Also called a corkscrew. This is the tool that is used to open wine bottles. The key components of a wine key are the worm, the knife blade, and the lever.

Wine of Origin (WO) Scheme The method used to demarcate South Africa's wine regions, first implemented in 1973, which divided the winelands into three levels of decreasing size: regions, districts, and wards.

winterkill Damage or death of grapevines caused by severe cold during their dormant period.

C

Cabernet Franc
  California, 380
  Canada, 445
  France, 162, 171, 172, 215, 216t
  Hungary, 345
  Italy, 257, 258t, 263
  New York, 436, 437
  overview, 38–39
  Washington State, 414t
Cabernet Sauvignon
  aging, 70
  Australia, 464, 465, 466, 467, 469
  blends, 38–39, 42–43
  California, 375, 377, 378t, 380, 381,
    383t, 386, 390t, 393t, 394, 395
  Canada, 445
  Chile, 488, 495, 498
  climate, effect of, 26
  extended maceration, 62
  flavor profile, 113t
  France, 162, 171, 219
  Hungary, 345
  Italy, 234–235, 251, 254, 257, 263
  New Zealand, 475t, 478
  Oregon, 423t, 425
  overview of, 39
  soil and site, effect on, 25
  South Africa, 523, 526, 527, 529, 531
  Spain, 286
  Texas, 440
  Washington State, 410, 414t, 416, 417
Cabinet systems, preserving open bottles,
  565–566
Cahors, 223
Cake, pressing skins, 63–64
California
  American Viticultural Areas,
    627t–629t
  Barbera, 38
  Cabernet Sauvignon, 39
  Central Coast, 391–400
  Central Valley, 399–400
  Chenin Blanc, 40, 41
  Gewürztraminer, 41
  Grenache, 41–42
  history of wine, 14, 362–370
  Lake and Mendocino Counties,
    387–391, 389, 390t
  maps of, 360, 376, 382, 389, 391, 396
  Merlot, 42–43
  Napa Valley, 374–381, 376, 378t
  organic viticulture, 36–37
  overview of, 361–362
  Petite Sirah, 44
  Pinot Noir, 45
  regions, overview, 370, 374
  Sangiovese, 46
  Santa Cruz County, 391–394, 393t
  Sauvignon Blanc, 47

  Sierra Foothills, 400–401
  Sonoma Valley, 381–387, 382, 383t
  Temecula, 400–401
  Zinfandel, 48–49
California Wine Association (CWA), 365
Calistoga, 378t, 379–380
Campania, 264, 265t
Canada
  British Columbia, 443, 445
  history of wine, 443
  Ontario, 445–446
  overview, 441–442
Cane-pruned vines, dormancy, 37, 38
Cannonau, 265t
Cannonau di Sardegna, 265t, 267
Canterbury, 475t, 479–480
Cap Classique, 527
Cape Agulhas, 530–532
Cape Doctor, 527, 530
Cape Floral Kingdom, 518
Cap management, 61–62, 67
Carbonic maceration, 62
Carignan, 219
Cariñena, 288
Carmel Valley, 393t
Carmenère, 498
Carmignano, 246t, 253–254
Casablanca Valley, 495
Casella Wines, 457t
Caspian Sea, 6
Castelão Frances, 294
Castilla y León, 282–283
Cataluña, 286–288
Catawba, 435
Catholic Church, history of wine
  California, 362–363
  Champagne, 205
  Chile, 488–489
  France, 155–156, 177
  Germany, 308
  overview, 11–12
  Spain and Portugal, 276
Cava, 287
Cayuga, 435
cellar door, 465
Cellars, restaurant wine list, 578–582
Cencibel, 289
Central Coast, California
  Monterey, 394–395
  overview, 391–392
  San Benito, 394–395
  San Francisco Bay, 391–394, 393t
  San Luis Obispo, 395–397, 396
  Santa Barbara, 397–399
Central Otago, 475t, 480
Central Valley, 399–400
Chablis
  appellation, 182–184, 183
  France, 176, 179t
  map of, 181

Chablis Grand, 176
Chalk Hill, 383t, 385–386
Chalone, 393t
Chambolle-Musigny, 186
Chambourcin, 439
Champagne
  development of, 13
  fermentation of, 74–78, 75, 77
  France, 155
  Gruet, 441
  history of, 8, 205–206
  opening, 608–609
  producers and styles, 207–209
  South Africa, 526
  viticulture in, 206–207
Chardonnay
  Argentina, 504, 506
  Australia, 464–465, 466, 469, 472
  California, 375, 378t, 379, 380, 383t,
    384, 385, 386, 390t, 393t, 394, 395,
    397, 398, 400, 401
  Canada, 445
  Chile, 488, 495, 499
  fermentation, 68
  finishing process, 71–73, 72
  flavor profile, 112t
  France, 175, 179t, 182–184, 183, 185,
    206, 209
  Hungary, 345
  Italy, 239–240t, 263
  New York, 434, 435, 436, 437
  New Zealand, 474, 475t, 478
  Oregon, 422, 423t
  overview, 40
  South Africa, 523, 526, 527, 529, 531
  Spain, 286
  sparkling wines, 74–78, 75, 77
  Texas, 440
  Washington State, 410, 414t, 416
Charlemagne, 12, 153–154
Charles Krug winery, 364
Charles Shaw, 548–549
Charmat, Eugéne, 77
Charmat method, 77, 325
Charta wines, 319–320
Charvet, Paul, 411
Chasange-Montrachet, 189
Chasselas, 342
Château d'Yquem, 170
Château-Grillet, 199
Château Haut-Brion, 169
Châteauneuf-du-Pape, 41–42, 155–156,
  196, 202, 203–204
Chateau Ste. Michelle, 412, 417, 419
Chehalem Mountains, 423t
Chenin Blanc
  Australia, 471
  California, 400
  France, 215, 216t, 217
  overview, 40, 41

Property of the SAAC